Business Law and Ethics Exam Review

Frank J. Cavico
Bahaudin G. Mujtaba
Nicholas-Michel Polito

ILEAD Academy, LLC
Davie, Florida. United States of America
www.ileadacademy.com

Frank J. Cavico and Bahaudin G. Mujtaba, 2021. *Business Law and Ethics Exam Review*

ISBN-10: 936237-19-9
ISBN-13: 978-1-936237-19-7

Subject Code:
BUS010000: Business & Economics-Business Law
LAW000000: Law-General
LAW022000: Law-Corporate

ILEAD Academy, LLC
Davie, Florida. United States of America
www.ileadacademy.com

Preface

This book is an exam review book. As such, the book provides a succinct review of fundamental principles of business law, business ethics, and tax law subject matters in the form of a comprehensive and extensive test bank of over 2000 questions. The book is designed for college level business law and/or business ethics courses as well as tax law courses. The book commences with an overall introduction of its purposes and supplies an overview of the material presented and the types of questions asked. The book encompasses not only the traditional business law subjects, such as contracts, which area is covered heavily, torts, and business organizations, but also government regulation of business subject matters, such as securities law and anti-trust, which typically form the basis of upper-level college business law courses. The book also covers important accounting subject matters, such as the liability of accountants and basic tax law. The field of business ethics is addressed too, and ethics is treated first as a branch of philosophy and then in the sense of applied business ethics. The book also includes coverage of subject matters related to and usually taught with business ethics, that is, the social responsibility and sustainability (that is, environmental responsibility) of business.

The questions used for testing purposes are in the form of True and False and Multiple Choice (MC) types of questions. The MC questions are not fact-pattern based; rather, they are basic ones dealing with the knowledge and understanding of fundamental principles. After each question, the correct answer is furnished; and then explanations are provided after each question as to why the correct answer is the correct one and the others are incorrect. The authors in their choice of questions as well as the explanations and illustration thereof seek to stress the "real-world" applications of these subject matters. Moreover, the knowledge and understanding of essential doctrines, principles, and rules are tested by a variety of questions with different wording and approaches to be as certain as possible of student mastery of the materials.

The book, however, is not intended as a substitute for a traditional business law, government of regulation of business, or tax law text, let alone a course; rather, this book is intended as a supplement, review, and exam-testing work. This book is primarily based on textbooks by the authors, as delineated in the bibliography, as well as the authors' years of exam preparation; thus, this book can be viewed as a testing "companion" for any standard, college-level, business law, business ethics, government regulation of business, and tax law text. This book, as noted, is designed for college students; however, law students taking law school exams and ultimately Bar exams as well as accounting students taking business law and tax law classes at the undergraduate and graduate level and ultimately the CPA exam will find the book very useful too, principally as an initial tool to be sure they are cognizant of the basic principles explained, illustrated, and tested herein; and if so, then the law and accounting students can "graduate" to the much more difficult, typically fact-pattern-based and reasoning-required, types of MC questions (which actually is the authors' next project), which the student will confront at the law school, graduate accounting and tax, and professional level.

The authors thus trust that their modest and "basic" academic undertaking will be a valuable guide, review, and testing modality to help ensure the students' academic, business, and professional success. The authors thank you for your consideration.

Sincerely,

Frank, Bahaudin, and Nicholas

Table of Contents

1 - Law and the Legal System

This book is an exam review book aimed at college students, especially business students, taking courses in business law and business ethics. The book has a great number of college level True-and-False and Multiple-Choice questions, together with explanations as to the correct and incorrect answer(s), on a wide variety of subject matters covered in such business law and ethics courses. The book also includes with each subject matter section a brief introduction explaining to the student reader the most important doctrines, concepts, and rules that the student must be cognizant of to master the material and to do well on exams. The book has over 25 subject matter sections, which encompass the following: traditional business law subjects, such as contracts, torts, products liability, and corporations; government regulation of business subjects, such as anti-trust, securities, and discrimination law; business ethics subjects, such as ethics as a branch of philosophy, applied business ethics, as well as social responsibility and sustainability. The book also includes certain specialized subject matters, such as the liability of accountants and tax law.

A theme of the book is to inculcate to the student readers the importance today of the values of legality, morality, social responsibility, and sustainability when making business and management decisions. These values, as the student will soon see, are not merely "academic" for class exam-taking purposes, but rather are real-world values that are indispensable today to becoming a leader in business and the professions, achieving personal and business and professional success, and being able to sustain that success. The first subject matter section sets the foundation for the book by examining some basic definitions and concepts about the law and the legal system and the nature of legal reasoning.

Introduction to Legal Reasoning

First and foremost, the student must be aware that the United States is a federal system; and as such there is the national government, called the "federal government," as well as constituent government entities, called "states." Consequently, there will be federal law as well as state (and local) law for the student to be concerned with in any business endeavor. The student must know the basic sources of the law, to wit: constitutions, statutes, case law (called the "common law"), and rules and regulations of administrative agencies. Other sources of the law are international treaties and executive pronouncements or orders. Law is divided into two main categories: public law, which affects the people as a whole, for example, constitutional and criminal law; and private law, which "just" affects the rights of individual people, for example, contract and tort law. Law is further divided into criminal law, which deals with wrongs that are committed against society as well as the victim; and civil law, which deals with the disputes between individual people, such a breach of contract or tort lawsuits. Regarding the common law or case law the student must be cognizant of the system of precedents and *stare decisis*, which are at the heart of Anglo-American law. The student also must know the fundamentals of the legislative process, that is, how Congress and the state legislatures make law, including the power of the courts to engage in statutory interpretation. Accordingly, the student must know the structure of the federal as well as state court systems as well as the powers of the different levels of courts. Another very important area for the student to know is the jurisdiction of the various courts and how jurisdiction is obtained to hear and decide cases. Moreover, such critical concepts as the distinction between *in personam* and *in rem* jurisdiction as well as the presence of state Long Arm statutes to acquire jurisdiction must be learned. Furthermore, the student must be aware of the distinction between courts of law and courts of equity as well as the remedies that are available to an aggrieved party by each court. Finally, the student must comprehend certain basic aspects of civil procedure, to wit: how a lawsuit commences with the filing of a complaint and an answer, the steps in a lawsuit, the nature of pre-trial discovery, the various motions to the judge that can be made, the process of selecting a jury, the functions of the judge and jury, the standard of proof in civil as compared to criminal cases, the verdict as opposed to a judgment, and the right to appeal the decision, the power of an appellate court, and the scope of review on appeal.

True and False Questions with Answers and Explanations

1. The doctrine of *stare decisis* holds that similar cases should be decided in the same way as prior cases with the same or similar facts.
(True: The doctrine is an old common law one still valid that gives predictability and stability to the law.)

2. The principal work of a court is to issue advisory opinions on hypothetical cases.
(False: Job of a court is to try real cases and issue judgments.)

3. The principal role of a jury is to ascertain the applicable law which will govern a case.
(False: Role of a jury is to decide the facts; the judge decides the law).

4. The major functions of an appeals court are fact-finding and the retrial of cases.
(False: Main function of an appeals court is to determine if a lower court made an error in the law.)

5. A complaint officially notifies a defendant that he or she is being sued.
(True: Complaint is also called a petition in some states.)

6. Discovery findings are generally admissible at trial as evidence.
(True: Depositions and interrogatories would be examples.)

7. Common law exists only at the federal level.
(False: Common law exists at the state level.)

8. The Plain Meaning rule of statutory construction holds that a court should apply the terms of a statute according to their plain and accepted meaning.
(True: Thus, the court should not overly interpret the statute and consequently not usurp the legislative role by "legislating from the bench.")

9. If there is a direct precedent lacking on which a court can base a decision a court is allowed to examine past cases with similar facts to the case at issue.
(True: Such is the nature of precedent in the common law which gives the law a sense of stability and predictability.)

10. For a court to render a legally binding decision it must have jurisdiction of the subject matter of the lawsuit and jurisdiction over the parties before the court.
(True: Otherwise the decision has no legal effect.)

11. A state court system typically has a supreme court, courts of appeal, and courts of original jurisdiction where cases are first brought.

(True: The courts of original jurisdiction are typically called circuit courts on the state level and district courts on the federal level. Also, on the state level courts of original jurisdiction include county courts.)

12. Courts of appeal typically retry cases if the facts were in dispute at the lower court.
(False: Courts of appeal rarely retry cases; their main purpose is to determine if the lower court made a mistake in the law.)

13. Federal cases usually originate in the U.S. Claims Court.
(False: Federal cases usually originate in the federal District Courts.)

14. Judges for the federal court are appointed by Congress on long-term contracts.
(False: The President appoints judges to the federal courts who serve for life subject to appointment and who must be confirmed by the Senate.)

15. Diversity of citizenship is one means to secure original jurisdiction by the federal district courts.
(True: And diversity exists even though no federal question is involved, though there is a monetary requirement for the dispute in question.)

16. When the U.S. Supreme Court chooses to hear an appeal from a state supreme court the Supreme Court can reverse a decision when the Court determines that the state supreme court made an error regarding state law.
(False: The Supreme Court can reverse if an error in federal law was made, not state law.)

17. The "common law" is termed as such because it is strictly consistent among all the states in the U.S.
(False: Key word is "strictly," though there are fundamental principles in common there are many variations among the states.)

18. The doctrine of *Stare Decisis* makes the law less predictable.
(False: Just the opposite as stare decisis means in Latin "let the decision stand"; that is, cases with the same or similar facts should be decided by the law in prior cases which are legal precedents.)

19. When there is a case with no prior legal precedent the judge must appoint a mediator to try to find an amicable solution to the dispute.
(False: Arbitration and mediation are always favored by the law, but they are not mandatory, though in some states mediation is required for medical malpractice cases. Even if there is no precedent the judge must still try and decide the case, typically referring to the mores and standards of behavior in the community; and when the judge does decide his or her decision will emerge as a precedent.)

20. Typically, a judge can grant either equitable as well as legal remedies.
(True: This is a basic legal principle; however, before a judge can grant an equitable remedy there must be evidence that the legal remedy was insufficient to do justice, for example, an injunction to stop a continuing trespass where the damages to property are minimal, such as one "cutting across" another's lawn as a short-cut.)

21. A statutory law promulgated by a state legislative body supersedes (is superior to) a case decided by a state court judge.
(True: Members of legislative bodies are thought to be "closer to the people," since they are elected by the people on a regular basis, whereas in most states judges are appointed by the

governor. The supremacy of the legislative branch over the judicial branch means that if legislators do not like the way judges are deciding cases they "simply" can pass a law to the contrary.)

22. For a court to have valid authority to decide a case it generally must have jurisdiction of the persons involved as well as the subject matter of the dispute.
(True: This is a fundamental legal principle A court that lacks jurisdiction issues a void judgment.)

23. A state Long Arm statute allows a state court to acquire jurisdiction of title to real property disputes against out-of-state residents.
(False: Long Arm statutes enable a court to decide certain personal claims against out-of-state residents, but not title to real property disputes as they must be decided in the state - actually the county in the state - where the property is locates.)

24. Typically, state appeals courts try cases and obtain evidence *de novo*, that is, anew, by impaneling another jury.
(False: The main function of appeals courts is to determine if the lower court judge made an error of law or allowed prejudice to unduly sway a jury. Appeals courts to not retry cases and impanel new juries. When the appeals court reverses a lower court ruling the case is then heard again at the lower court, that is, the court of original jurisdiction, level.)

25. In the U.S. all the federal courts were created in Article III of the Constitution.
(False: The Supreme Court was created in the Constitution but the federal courts of appeal, district courts, and specialized courts were created by Congress.)

26. Appellate courts review the records of cases from lower courts to determine if a lower court judge made an error in law.
(True: This is the main function of appellate courts. Appellate courts can also overrule a lower court decision if there was evidence of prejudice that unduly influenced the jury.)

27. Justices to the U.S. Supreme Court are appointed by the Attorney General.
(False: Supreme Court justices are appointed by the President subject to confirmation by the Senate. The Attorney General does appoint Administrative Law Judges (ALJs) to the administrative courts of federal agencies, such as the Federal Trade Commission.)

28. Federal courts have exclusive jurisdiction over cases dealing with patents, copyrights, and trade secrets.
(False: Although the federal courts have exclusive jurisdiction over patents and copyrights state courts also have jurisdiction over trade secrets, which primarily are based on state law, the common law and/or the Uniform Trade Secret Act.)

29. The Supreme Court has the power to review a decision from a state supreme court decision on U.S. constitutional grounds.
(True: Yet the Supreme Court taking of the case is not automatic, but rather discretionary pursuant to the filing by a party of a writ of certiorari to the court.)

30. The preponderance of the evidence standard means that in a civil case the plaintiff must convince the jury that based on all the evidence presented it is more likely than not that the plaintiff's allegations are true.

(True: At times, the expression "50% plus 1% of the evidence" equals a preponderance of the evidence, as opposed to a "clear and convincing" standard, which is phrased as "75% of the evidence."

31. A Long Arm Statute will give a court in one state the power to obtain jurisdiction over a non-resident person due to activities committed within the state.
(True: Examples are when the non-resident caused an auto accident in the state or sold defective products in the state, as such activities meet the requirements of "minimum contacts" with the state to satisfy the Due Process clause of the 14th Amendment.)

32. A federal district court can take jurisdiction of a case based on diversity of citizenship, that is, the parties are from different states, but only if there is a question arising out of a federal statute that needs to be resolved.
(False: For diversity jurisdiction a federal question is not necessary; however, diversity of citizenship jurisdiction requires that the amount in controversy be $75,000 or more.)

33. Venue in a civil case is typically where the defendant resides.
(True: In a criminal case it is where the crime occurred. Venue should not be confused with jurisdiction, which is the power of a court to hear and try a case, whereas venue is the most appropriate geographic location to try the case within the court's jurisdiction.)

34. Typically, courts of appeal conduct new trials in which evidence is submitted and witnesses are examined.
(False: Courts of appeal review transcripts of cases from lower courts to determine if a lower court judge made an error at law.)

35. A trial court judge and jury are in a better position to evaluate the testimony of witnesses since they can observe directly conduct, demeanor, gestures, and non-verbal behavior during the trial.
(True: That is why appellate courts usually defer to the trial court's findings of fact and just review transcripts of the lower court proceeding.)

36. An appellate court can challenge a lower court's finding of fact only when the finding is clearly erroneous.
(True: Examples would be when there is no evidence to support a finding of fact or the evidence is contrary to the factual findings.)

37. Federal court judges are elected by the people.
(False: Federal court judges are appointed by the President subject to confirmation by the Senate.)

38. The Supreme Court must issue a writ of *certiorari* and hear a case if there are constitutional issues presented or there is a conflict between courts of appeal.
(False: The writ of certiorari is discretionary, though if the constitutional issue is important or the subject matter that is causing the inconsistent decisions in the courts of appeal are important the Supreme Court will usually take the case.)

39. A default judgment is a notice from a bankruptcy court that one now owes money to another party.
(False: A default judgment is a judgment issued by a court against a defendant who has failed to appear in a court to answer or to defend against a plaintiff's claim.)

40. Improper venue is a valid reason for a court to grant a motion to dismiss a case against a defendant.
(True: Other examples are improper delivery of the complaint or summons or the plaintiff's failure to state a claim for which relief could be granted.)

41. In a motion for summary judgment a judge may consider evidence outside the pleadings.
(True: Examples would be sworn statements, that is, affidavits, by parties or witnesses or other documents relating to the case.)

42. Interrogatories, that is, written questions where answers are prepared and then signed under oath, are directed at witnesses to a lawsuit.
(False: Interrogatories are directed only at the parties to a lawsuit, whereas depositions, that is, sworn testimony consisting of answers to questions asked by attorneys and recorded, can be directed at the parties to a lawsuit and witnesses.)

43. During *voir dire* only the judge is allowed to ask questions of potential jurors to see if they are biased, have any conflicts-of-interest, or have any connection to the case, including knowing prospective witnesses as well as the parties.
(False: In most states, it is the attorneys for the parties to the case that ask the questions to the jurors, though the judge may do all or part of the questioning.).

44. A motion for a directed verdict will be granted by a judge on the grounds that the plaintiff has presented insufficient evidence to support the plaintiff's claim and thus to justify granting the plaintiff's requested remedy.
(True: Such a motion is rare, however, since the judge, in essence, will be taking the case away from the jury.)

45. The "greater weight of the evidence" means the more persuasive and convincing force or effect of the evidence presented as a whole.
(True: This is a basic proposition.)

46. The common law is afforded predictability, consistency, and stability by the use and system of precedents as well as the doctrine of *stare decisis*.
(True: These are fundamental concepts. Stare decisis means "let the decision stand" and thus when a case is to be decided a judge will look for governing precedents, that is, prior cases with the same or similar facts. Attorneys can research these cases too and thus provide guidance to their clients on how a judge may rule.)

47. Courts must never depart from precedents or else the common law legal system would collapse.
(False: Courts typically do follow precedents, but circumstances may change and thus a new precedent may be issued. For example, for many, many years hospitals had charitable immunity on grounds of public policy because they were new institutions and not financially viable and thus one lawsuit could literally wipe them out. Today, however, hospitals are "big business" with insurance, and thus the precedent changed and now hospitals can be sued for negligence and other legal wrongs.)

48. The common law consists of cases that are decided by judges on a case-by-case basis.
(True: And the decisions by the judges stand as precedents to be applied in future cases with the same or similar facts as per the doctrine of stare decisis.)

49. Long Arm statutes are federal statutes that are used to decide lawsuits where the parties are citizens or residents of different states.
(False: Long Arm statutes are state statutes that are used for a party to gain jurisdiction over an out-of-state defendant who committed some legal wrong in the state.)

50. The clearest and most definitive source of international public law would be a treaty.
(True: This is a basic proposition. Treaties are also called "conventions," as the Convention against Bribery by the Organization of Economic Cooperation and Development).

51. The pleading which notifies the plaintiff of the defendant's responses to the plaintiff's allegations in the plaintiff's Complaint is called an Answer.
(True: The complaint and the answer form the pleadings. If a defendant does not answer the complaint within the time period set forth under state or federal procedural law the defendant risks having a Default Judgment entered against him or her.)

52. Case or common law consists of laws passed by the federal (that is, national) Congress in the U.S. and not by the states.
(False: Case or common law consists of judge-made decision going back in Anglo-English laws to "Old English" days. Case law rulings, though forming precedents, can be overruled by contrary legislative laws since the legislative body is the body "closest to the people" since legislators are elected whereas most judges are appointed.)

53. Punitive damages can be awarded in federal court cases with the amount to be determined solely by the jury with no limits.
(False: In federal courts there is a $300,000 maximum limit on punitive damages.)

Multiple Choice Questions with Answers and Explanations

1. Which of the following is FALSE about the doctrine of *Stare Decisis*?
   a. It is an example of administrative agencies excessive authority due to general delegations from Congress.
   b. It allows a court to follow precedents, that is, previous court decisions.
   c. It makes it easier to predict the result in a particular case.
   d. It makes the law more uniform and consistent.
   e. It is a fundamental doctrine of Anglo-American common law.

(The correct answer is a. Stare decisis has nothing to with grants of power by Congress or other legislative bodies to administrative agencies. All other answers are hallmarks of Stare Decisis going back to English kings Alfred the Great, William the Conqueror, and Henry I and Henry II.)

2. The elements that must be present for a lawsuit to be heard in a U.S. federal court are:
   a. The court must have jurisdiction over the person.
   b. The court must have jurisdiction over the subject matter of the lawsuit.
   c. The plaintiff must have Standing to Sue.
   d. The plaintiff's lawsuit must be an actual Case or Controversy.
   e. All of the above.

(The correct answer is e. These are fundamental principles. The latter two are derived from the Constitution. Standing to Sue means that the plaintiff has suffered some type of actual harm and is not litigating in the abstract; and Case or Controversy means that there is an actual dispute and not a hypothetical one.)

3. Which of the following is NOT an equitable remedy under the common law?
   a. Injunction
   b. Money Damages
   c. Rescission
   d. Specific Performance

(The correct answer is b. Money damages under the common law were called a "legal" remedy. Equitable remedies were available under the common law when money damages would be inadequate to redress a legal wrong. Note that rescission can be granted by a court, for example, to cancel a contract induced by fraud, or done by the parties in the case of a mutual rescission of a contract.)

4. Pursuant to the typical court procedure in a civil case lawsuit, the "pleadings" typically consist of:
   a. The complaint and the answer.
   b. A plea to a judge for leniency at sentencing time.
   c. Giving depositions
   d. Answering interrogatories.

(The correct answer is a. Depositions, which are answers to questions given orally under oath, and answering interrogatories, which are written questions the parties to a lawsuit ask each other and answer in writing, are part of the Discovery phrase of a civil lawsuit. Answer b. is a criminal law procedure.)

5. Which of the following is a FALSE statement?
   a. The law in the United States has been influenced mainly by the French Napoleonic Code.
   b. One principal purpose of the law is to protect persons and their property from improper interference from others.
   c. Those rules that must be obeyed and followed by people or otherwise be subject to legal sanctions can be construed as "law."
   d. Law serves both to maintain the *status quo* and to facilitate orderly change.

(The correct answer is a. The law in the U.S. is based on the common law of England, that is, judge-made decisions. The French Napoleonic Code consists mainly of detailed statutory rules and has greatly influenced European and Latin American countries.)

6. Each of the following is a function of law EXCEPT:
   a. Helping to shape moral views and standard
   b. Helping to maintain the status quo
   c. Allowing personal retaliation by victims against their aggressors
   d. Helping to facilitate orderly change.

(The correct answer is c. Self-defense against an aggressor is legal, as well as initiating prosecution and suing the aggressor civilly for assault and battery; but personal retribution is neither a purpose of, nor condoned by, the law.)

7. Common law pursuant to the Anglo-American legal system characteristically consists of:
   a. Laws that all nations have in common.
   b. Laws that affect everyone, except wealthy people and politicians
   c. Opinions that have been issued by judges when deciding previous cases
   d. Laws with which most people are familiar.

(The correct answer is c. U.S. law is based on English law, which predominant is the common law, that is, rulings and opinions by judges in prior cases which stand as precedents to be followed common to or throughout the realm of England, thereby providing stability and predictability to the law.)

8. Which of the following is a TRUE statement?
   a. Most states require mediation of civil disputes in which the amount in controversy is over $75,000.
   b. There is a single court system shared by all the states and the federal government in the United States.
   c. State appellate courts when they review trial court decisions usually listen to new testimony from witnesses or view new evidence related to the case.
   d. States typically have an intermediate appellate court between the trial court level and the state supreme court.

(The correct answer is d. At the trial court level in states there are courts of original jurisdiction, usually called district courts, as well as county courts, the latter for real estate disputes and minor civil and criminal matters. State appellate courts do not retry cases; they determine if the lower court judge interpreted the pertinent law correctly or if there was some error, procedural or substantive, in the lower court proceeding. If there was a problem with the lower court ruling or trial, the appellate court will remand the case back to the lower court for a new trial.)

9. Which of the following is a FALSE statement?
   a. The United States Supreme Court was created by the U.S. Constitution.
   b. The United States District Court is the general jurisdiction trail court in the federal system.
   c. Supreme Court decisions form legal precedents.
   d. The minimum amount in controversy for a federal court to hear a case involving a federal question is $75,000.

(The correct answer is d. The $75,000 amount is a requirement for federal diversity cases, that is, for a federal district court to have jurisdiction over a case that has parties who are citizens or residents of different states. There is no monetary requirement for a federal question case, that is, a case arising out the Constitution, federal statutes, or federal administrative rules and regulations.)

10. Which of the following is a FALSE statement?
   a. The requirement of a minimum amount in controversy for federal jurisdiction applies to diversity of citizenship cases.
   b. The legal requirement of "standing" requires that a plaintiff have a direct stake in the outcome of a case that is filed.
   c. *In rem* jurisdiction can never be grounds to obtain jurisdiction of a lawsuit.
   d. A forum-selection clause in a contract allows parties to a contract to agree on the court that will have jurisdiction over a particular case.

(The correct answer is c. In rem jurisdiction is a case whereby a party is seeking to assert some right in property owned by another. Jurisdiction can be obtained merely by the filing of a notice of the lawsuit in a publication that circulates in the county where the property is located. An example of an in rem action would be a mortgage foreclosure. Whereas with in personam jurisdiction, a party is attempting to assert a personal right against another person, for example, a breach of contract lawsuit to recover money damages, and as such the plaintiff bringing the lawsuit must obtain personal jurisdiction over the defendant, by serving him or her with a summons and copy of the complaint or petition. "Standing" is a Constitutional requirement stemming from the jurisdiction of the Supreme Court and federal courts to "cases and controversies," that is, actual, concrete and factual disputes, and not hypothetical and theoretical ones. Forum-selection clauses in contracts determine where a case will be heard; and choice-of-law clauses determine which state's law will apply to a case that has contact with more than one state.)

11. Which of the following is a FALSE statement?
    a. A state court can use a Long-Arm statute to obtain *in personam* jurisdiction over non-residents.
    b. A court can issue a summons ordering a defendant named in a complaint to appear in court.
    c. Interrogatories are written statements given by witness after a trial.
    d. Small Claims courts have limited jurisdiction.

(The correct answer is c. Interrogatories are written questions to parties which they answer under oath and which are submitted prior to trail during the discovery phase of a lawsuit. The other responses are basic civil procedural principles. The jurisdiction of Small Claims courts is typically constrained by monetary limits, usually $5000; and these courts have more informal and expedited procedures.)

12. Which of the following is a TRUE statement?
    a. The trier of fact in a jury trial is the judge.
    b. In most trials, the defendant bears the burden of proof.
    c. *Voir dire* is the process by which the judge informs the jury about what law to apply when they decide the case.
    d. An appellate court reviews the record of the trial court.

(The correct answer is d. Appellate courts do not retry cases; they "merely" ascertain based on the record, that is, transcripts and evidence submitted, if the trial court judge made a mistake in interpreting or applying the law or in admitting certain evidence or if there was some other procedural or substantive error in the trial. The trier of fact is the jury; yet the parties may waive their right to a jury trial and have the judge decide the facts of the case along with the law. It is the plaintiff, the party bringing a civil lawsuit, or the government if the case is a criminal one, that has the burden of proof on all elements to the cause of action or crime asserted. Voir dire is part of the jury selection process whereby a judge and the attorneys ask the prospective jurors questions in order to determine if they have any biases or conflicts-of-interest regarding the upcoming trial.)

13. Which of the following is a TRUE statement?
    a. The decision of a jury is typically known as the verdict.
    b. An appellate court usually reverses a lower court decision if the appellate court believes there is a slight error in the factual record.
    c. State supreme court decisions are immediately appealable to the federal courts.
    d. State courts are usually subject to detailed oversight by the federal judiciary.

(The correct answer is a. After the jury enunciates a verdict in a civil case if the verdict is for the plaintiff the judge will then issue a judgment typically ordering the defendant to pay a sum of money, which the jury awarded as damages, plus interest at the "judgment rate," which is the rate set by state statute, typically about 8-9%. Appellate courts, as noted, typically do not reverse decisions based on the factual record, unless perhaps there is evidence of an abuse of discretion or an arbitrary or capricious ruling by the lower court judge. A state supreme court decision will only be appealable to the federal courts if there is a federal question or a constitutional issue involved. The federal judiciary is not involved with supervising state courts.)

14. A party to a lawsuit may file a motion to dismiss:
    a. if the court lacks jurisdiction.
    b. if the complaint does not state a claim for which relief can be granted.
    c. if the amount in controversy is under $10,000
    d. Either a and b.

(The correct answer is d. Both are grounds for filing a motion to dismiss, and note that the court can lack jurisdiction over the person of the defendant and/or the subject matter of the lawsuit.)

15. A party loses a lawsuit and files an appeal. The appellate court is MOST LIKELY to review the trial court's:
    a. interpretation of the law.
    b. consideration of the creditability of the witnesses.
    c. findings of fact.
    d. evaluation of the conduct of the witnesses.

(The correct answer is a. The main function of an appellate court, as noted, is to make sure the judge ruled correctly on the law's interpretation and/or application. The credibility of the witnesses, including their conduct while testifying, is for the jury, the typical finder-of-fact in a trial. Unless there is an obvious problem with the factual record from the lower court, for example, no evidence to support a jury verdict, the appellate court will take the factual record from the lower court as it finds the record.)

16. The United States has a common law legal system. Common law systems are based primarily on?
    a. administrative rules and regulations.
    b. case law.
    c. detailed codified law in statutes.
    d. executive orders.

(The correct answer is b. Anglo-American law is based primarily on case law, called the common law from old English days, though day there are many statutes as well as administrative rules and regulations. Civil law countries have detailed codified statutory law in statutes, whereas in the U.S. the statutes are more general, thereby relying on the courts to interpret the statutes on a case-by-case basis.)

17. In a trial in a U.S. state court, a judge TYPICALLY:
    a. very actively participates in a trial.
    b. does not actively participate in a trial.
    c. is expected to question witnesses in a trial.
    d. is influenced by politics.

(The correct answer is b. Rarely do judges participate in trial aside from maintaining the order and dignity of the court room and trial as well as ruling on motions and objections to evidence and also instructing the jury as to the pertinent law before deliberations. Judges must be neutral and unbiased and thus unaffected by politics.)

18. The doctrine of *stare decisis* requires the court to find cases that, compared to the case before it, have:
    a. entirely different facts.
    b. no facts, only conclusions of law.
    c. precisely identical facts.
    d. the same or similar facts.

(The correct answer is d. Stare decisis, therefore, is the heart of a common law system, since the prior cases with the same or similar facts are precedents which legal rulings therein as a general rule must be applied in deciding the current case at bar. Stare decisis and precedents, therefore, provide predictability, uniformity, and stability to the legal system.)

19. In a given case, most courts today may grant:
    a. equitable remedies only.
    b. legal remedies only.
    c. equitable or legal remedies, but not both.
    d. equitable remedies, legal remedies, or both.

(The correct answer is d. In the "olden days" in England there were separate courts – Courts of Law, wherein the judges provided the legal remedies, mainly money damages, as well as Courts of Equity, originally called Courts of Chancery, named after the King's "executive" secretary, the Chancellor, wherein the judges provided equitable relief, for example, decrees of injunction or specific performance. Today, the two types of courts and thus remedies have been merged and a judge today can grant either legal or equitable relief; however, to grant the latter there must be a showing that the legal relief, usually in the form of damages, is not adequate to right the asserted wrong, for example, in the case of a continuing trespass where there is no or very little damage to the property.)

20. In a breach of contract lawsuit if the losing party appeals the case, the United States Supreme Court is:

a. required to hear the case again.
b. required to hear the case if the case was heard in a federal court.
c. required to hear the case if the case was heard in a state court.
d. not required to hear the case.

(The correct answer is d. Breach of contract cases are typically tried in state court; however, if there is diversity of citizenship, that is, the parties are from different states, and the amount in controversy is $75,000 or more, a federal district court will have jurisdiction; but the federal court will apply one of the state's laws depending on the application of the Conflicts-of-Laws doctrine. Moreover, the Supreme Court is not obligated to hear the case as its jurisdiction in such a matter is purely discretionary, very likely not to be exercised unless there is also some important federal question or constitutional issue involved.)

21. In a trial for negligence in a state court if the losing party wants to appeal the lower court decision, he or she will proceed to:

a. the state appellate court.
b. the nearest federal district court.
c. the nearest federal court of appeals.
d. the United States Supreme Court.

(The correct answer is a. Unless there is diversity of citizenship, as noted, the state appeals court will hear the appeal of the lower court decision.)

22. After a jury determines a verdict against a defendant, the defendant can make a motion to the judge for:

a. a directed verdict.
b. a judgment on the pleadings.
c. a new trial or for a judgment notwithstanding the verdict.
d. summary judgment.

(The correct answer is c. Since there is already a verdict the proper motion is for a new trial or for a judgment notwithstanding the verdict due perhaps to there being no evidence to support the jury verdict, improper conduct by jurors, such as bias or conflicts-of-interest during jury deliberations. A judgment on the pleadings, which is also called a summary judgment, is a motion for a judge to rule as a matter of law on a case since the pleadings indicate the facts are not in dispute.)

23. France has a civil law legal system. Civil law systems are principally based on

a. administrative rules and regulations.
b. case law.
c. detailed statutory codified law.
d. executive pronouncements.

(The correct answer is c. Civil law legal systems stem from the French Napoleonic Code, wherein the law is principally in the form of detailed statutes called codes. Most European countries, but not England, of course, have civil law legal systems as do most Latin American countries.)

24. Common law is called the "common law" mainly because:
    a. It was the law that applied to everyday people but not the aristocracy.
    b. It was intended to be applied uniformly throughout the realm and therefore be common among the courts of the various jurisdictions in England.
    c. It was the law which applied to everyday situations in the towns and villages
    d. Its name comes from the town commons which often surrounded the courthouse.

(The correct answer is b. The fact that the common law was to be applied uniformly by means of the system of precedents and the doctrine of stare decisis, which means "let the decision stand," gave not only uniformity but predictability and stability to the law and government.)

25. Which of the following is NOT true regarding common law?
    a. The common law of the United States originally came from England.
    b. Judges must strictly follow precedent in all cases.
    c. A drawback of common law is that legal decisions may be followed by judges after they have become outdated or no longer relevant.
    d. Common law is called common law because judges in England were intended to apply laws similarly is all jurisdictions in the country, thereby making the law common to all.

(The correct answer is b. Judges should and are expected to follow the rulings in prior cases that have the same or similar facts, that is, precedents, due to the doctrine of stare decisis. However, if the policy rationales behind an earlier decision change a court can deviate from precedent. For example, when hospitals were first being established, they were granted charitable immunity status from lawsuits since one lawsuit could financially cripple a hospital. Yet years later as hospitals became big, powerful, and financially secure institutions, as well as entities which could obtain insurance, the precedents were changed and today, of course, hospitals can be sued for negligence as well as other legal wrongs.)

26. The term for jurisdiction based on the location of a piece of property is:
    a. Long Arm jurisdiction.
    b. In *personam* jurisdiction.
    c. In *rem* jurisdiction.
    d. Subject matter jurisdiction.

(The correct answer is c. In an in rem action a plaintiff is proceeding against a piece of property, for example, to obtain title to real estate. Service is established by the publication of the notice of the lawsuit in a newspaper that regularly circulates in the locale where the property is located. Whereas in personam jurisdiction means that a plaintiff is suing a person, typically for money damages, and in such a case jurisdiction over the person must be obtained by the service of a summons and copy of the complaint against the defendant. Subject matter jurisdiction means simply that court has jurisdiction over the matter in dispute, for example, a probate court have jurisdiction over a will contest, and a county court in the county where land is located having jurisdiction over a title dispute lawsuit regarding the land.)

27. A law passed by a state to give its courts the jurisdiction over persons and businesses located in other states in known as:
    a. Diversity of citizenship statute
    b. Venue statute.
    c. Long Arm statute.
    d. In *personam* statute.

(The correct answer is c. A Long Arm statute is a state legislative pronouncement that enables citizens of the state to obtain personal jurisdiction over out-of-state defendants who have had sufficient contracts with the state, for example, by doing business in the state or by being involved in an auto accident in the state. Personal jurisdiction is obtained by serving the Secretary of State in the non-resident's state. Jurisdiction is the power of a court to hear a case; however, there may be many courts within that area where the court has jurisdiction; and as such venue is the proper physical location of the court where the case will be heard, for example, in a court located where an auto accident occurred, where a contract was formed, or where the real property is located.)

28. The first step in a lawsuit is when the plaintiff files a:
    a. Notice of lawsuit.
    b. Intent to sue.
    c. Complaint.
    d. Summons.

(The correct answer is c. In some states the complaint is called the petition. The summons is the personal service of the complaint which gives notice of the lawsuit by the plaintiff and which must be responded to by the defendant in an answer, wherein the defendant admits or denies the allegations in the complaint; and if the defendant does not answer there will be a default judgment issued against the defendant.)

29. Which of the following is TRUE?
    a. Juries issue verdicts and judges enter judgments.
    b. Juries can either issue judgments or verdicts.
    c. The trial judge cannot change or overturn a jury's verdict once it has been issued.
    d. If a case is appealed, the jury will return to hear the case again.

(The correct answer is a. As noted, a judge is allowed to change or overturn a jury verdict pursuant to a motion for a new trial or a motion for a judgment notwithstanding the verdict. Appeals courts do not impanel juries; rather, appeals courts examine the record of the case, facts and laws, to see if the lower court judge made any mistake in the interpretation or application of the law, or if there was sufficient factual evidence to support a jury verdict, or if the judge made any procedural mistakes, for example, admitting evidence that legally should have been excluded. If an appeals court overturns a lower court case a new jury will be impaneled to hear the case, or perhaps just part of it, for example, a damage award.)

30. The common law consists of:
    a. Laws which all civilized nations have in common.
    b. Laws which affect everyone, including poor people.
    c. Rulings and opinions which have been issued by judges when deciding previous cases.
    d. Laws which most people are or should be aware of.

(The correct answer is c. As noted, these prior decisions form precedents which should be followed when deciding new cases with the same or similar facts as per the doctrine of Stare Decisis.)

31. The concept that case decisions become a basis for decisions in later similar cases is known as:
    a. Chancery law.
    b. Universal law
    c. Common law.
    d. Statutory law.

(The correct answer is c. Chancery deals with courts in Old English days that could grant equitable remedies, such as an injunction, when legal remedies by the law courts, such as monetary damages,

were inadequate to right a wrong. Statutory law, of course, is legislative law enacted by federal or state legislatures.)

32. The distinguishing feature of a common law system is:
    a. Requiring guilt to be proven by clear and convincing evidence
    b. Using judicial panels to decide all cases.
    c. Having similar procedures for civil and criminal cases
    d. Following precedents in making decisions.

(The correct answer is d. Guilt must be established by the criminal law standard of "proof beyond a reasonable doubt." "Clear and convincing" evidence is the usual standard for a civil law case of fraud or deceit, whereas a "preponderance of the evidence" is the general standard for civil law cases. Cases under the common law are typically decided by juries. Moreover, there are constitutional protections guaranteeing the right to a jury trial, which right goes back to the Magna Charta of 1215. However, the right to a jury trial can be waived and thus a judge can hear the case deciding the facts as well as the law.)

33. "*Stare decisis*" is the doctrine of:
    a. Separation of powers so that decisions are not made by a single branch of government.
    b. Following precedents so that legal rulings in earlier similar cases are followed in later cases.
    c. Constitutional principles being applied when making any legal decisions.
    d. Ethical principles being applied to be sure that legal decisions are just and moral

(The correct answer is b. Separation of powers is of course the division of the federal government into three distinct branches – legislative, executive, and judicial. Court decisions must comply with the Constitution and presumably moral, ethical, and just too.)

34. Which of the following kinds of jurisdiction would be required for a court to hear a case?
    a. Subject matter and in *personam* and in *rem.*
    b. Subject matter or in *personam* or in *rem.*
    c. Subject matter and either in *personam* or in *rem.*
    d. In *rem* and either subject matter or in *personam.*

(The correct answer is c. Courts must have jurisdiction over the subject matter of the lawsuit and either jurisdiction over the person of the defendant if there is a personal obligation or debt involved or jurisdiction over the "rem" or basis of the lawsuit, which usually is a dispute involving land or real estate.)

35. The concept of in *personam* jurisdiction is that:
    a. A court has the power to enforce a judgment against a particular person.
    b. A party has a personal stake in the outcome of a particular case.
    c. Special requirements must be met in non-corporate cases involving natural individuals.
    d. The case has been filed at the correct location within the state.

(The correct answer is a. Compare to in rem jurisdiction where a court has the power to enforce a judgment against a thing or piece of property. The requirement that a party has a personal stake in the case is to meet the "standing" requirement for lawsuits, as courts do not pass judgment in the abstract or theoretically or hypothetically.)

36. Which of the following is TRUE about Venue?
    a. It is an alternative to meeting jurisdiction requirements.
    b. Its requirements must be met in addition to meeting jurisdiction requirements.
    c. In most cases, venue selection is up to the defendant.
    d. It allows a party to select the court most likely to decide a case in its favor.

(The correct answer is b. Once it is determined that a court has jurisdiction over a case venue determines where in that court's jurisdictional territory the case will be heard. A request for a change of venue is made by a defendant; but venue is decided by a judge based on matters of convenience as well as to be sure a defendant gets a fair trial.)

37. Questions in writing served by one party on the other prior to trial are called:
   a. Interrogatories.
   b. Depositions.
   c. Pleadings.
   d. Document Productions.

(The correct answer is a. The answers to interrogatories are given under oath and become part of the pre-trial discovery of a case along with depositions, which are oral answers to questions under oath with the attorneys present. The pleadings are the complaint, which commences the lawsuit by the plaintiff, and the answer, which is the defendant's response to either affirm or deny the allegations made in the complaint as well as to assert any affirmative defenses.)

38. When an appellate court receives a case appealed to it, it usually will:
   a. Retry the case with a new jury.
   b. Retry the case with the original jury.
   c. Retry the case with the appellate court judge acting as the jury.
   d. Review the record of the trial court to see if there were any errors of law made by the judge.

(The correct answer is d. Appellate courts to do retry cases under any circumstances; rather, if the decision of the lower court judge is overturned, for example, by the lower court judge incorrectly applying the law or admitting improper evidence, the appeals court will order a new trial at the lower court level.)

39. Which of the following statements is FALSE?
   a. Common law is a term for law that is common throughout the world in all major legal systems.
   b. Money damages are the usual remedy at law today in common law legal systems.
   c. Equitable remedies include injunctions and decrees of specific performance.
   d. Generally, a state court can exercise jurisdiction over anyone physically within the boundaries of the state.

(The correct answer is a. Common law, emanating from Old English days, means the law is primarily based on judge made decisions which form precedents, which should be followed in subsequent cases with the same or similar facts. Note that if money damages are not a sufficient remedy to "right a wrong," then a party can seek an equitable remedy from a judge.)

40. Civil law can mean:
   a. The law dealing with legal wrongs committed by one private party against another private party
   b. The law of many Latin American and European countries, based on detailed statutes, and originally based on the Napoleonic Code
   c. The law that requires people to be moral to one another
   d. A and B

(The correct answer is d. People should act morally; yet no one is going to be sued for acting immorally UNLESS some law is also broken in the process.)

41. The statutory process of legislative lawmaking is constrained by:
   a. Subject matter limitations imposed by constitutions
   b. Procedural requirements

c. A requirement that statutes be reasonably definite and not vague
d. All of the above.

(The correct answer is d. An example of subject matter limitations would be that the U.S. Congress can also legislate within the scope of its express or enumerated powers set forth in Article I of the Constitution, for example, the power to make laws regarding bankruptcy and immigration. The 5th and 14th Amendments to the Constitution require that statutes be reasonably definite and not vague.)

42. In the context of the legislative process, "police power" best means:
   a. The power of a state legislature to enact laws that benefit and protect the health, welfare, and safety of the citizens and residents of the state
   b. The enumerated powers that the states gave to the federal government
   c. The authority of the police to engage in a warrantless search in an emergency.
   d. The "plain meaning" rule for statutory interpretation.

(The correct answer is a. As noted, Congress can legislate only within the confines of its enumerated powers; whereas states have a much more broad "police power" on which to base legislation. "Plain meaning" means that if the wording of a statute is clear and precise, no interpretation of that wording is permissible, and thus the courts will not interpret the statute and give it its plain meaning.)

43. The judicial power of the courts in the U.S. encompasses:
   a. Adjudication, that is, the application of legal principles and rules to factual disputes in arrive at a reasoned legal decision
   b. Judicial review, that is, the power to evaluate statutes and actions of the other two branches of government to make sure they are constitutional
   c. Statutory interpretation, that is, the power of the courts to construe and clarify legislation to ascertain the statute's precise meaning.
   d. All of the above.

(The correct answer is d. These are all fundamental legal principles. Note that the courts' power of judicial review is not explicitly in the federal Constitution; rather, the Supreme Court in the famous Marbury v. Madison case arrogated to itself this very important power.)

44. Typically, state court systems have:
   a. A Supreme Court at the top of the state system
   b. Courts of Appeal, usually called District Courts of Appeal, which have appellate jurisdiction
   c. Courts of original jurisdiction which try cases, usually called Circuit Courts
   d. All of the above.

(The correct answer is d. These are very basic legal principles. There are also county courts below state courts of original jurisdiction to try small civil matters, land and real estate disputes, as well as misdemeanors.)

45. Which of the following is/are TRUE statements?
   a. Jurisdiction is the power of the courts to try cases and to decide certain types of controversies.
   b. Original jurisdiction is the power a court possesses to hear and decide a case when it first enters the court system.
   c. Appellate jurisdiction is the power a court possesses review a judgment of a lower court.
   d. All of the above.

(The correct answer is d. These are all very basic legal principles.)

46. Which of the following is a FALSE statement?

a. An action in *personam* is one in which the plaintiff is seeking to hold the defendant liable on a personal obligation.
b. In an action in *personam* the court need only have jurisdiction over the subject matter of the controversy.
c. An action in *rem* is one in which the plaintiff is seeking to enforce a right against certain property owned by the defendant.
d. Long Arm statutes allow a lawsuit to be instituted against an out-of-state defendant in the plaintiff's home state if the defendant does business in the state or has sufficient contacts with the state.

(The correct answer is b. In personam jurisdiction requires a court also obtaining personal jurisdiction over the defendant, usually by the sheriff serving the defendant with a summons and a copy of the complaint. Examples would be lawsuits for breach of contract and for the tort of negligence.)

2 - Alternative Dispute Resolution

Introduction

Arbitration and mediation are known as alternative dispute resolution procedures. The student must know the distinction between the two, how they differ from the traditional judicial method of resolving disputes, and the advantages and disadvantages of each compared to each other and a traditional lawsuit in court. Specifically, regarding mediation, the student must know what mediation is, how mediation arises, what the mediator does, and the confidentiality of the process. Specifically, regarding arbitration, the student must know what arbitration is, how it arises, what the arbitrator does, and the confidentiality of the process. Most importantly, the student must be aware of how an arbitration hearing differs from a traditional jury trial. Also, very important for the student to know is that arbitration awards are enforceable in court. Moreover, also extremely important for the student to know is that it is very difficult for a court to overturn an arbitration award on appeal, though there are some important exceptions that the student must be cognizant of too Finally, the student must have an awareness of online dispute resolution services and procedures.

True and False Questions with Answers and Explanations

1. Usually a mediator makes a legal decision that binds the parties to a dispute.
(False: Arbitrators can make binding decisions; whereas mediators are conciliators and facilitators who suggest solutions to dispute.)

2. Mediation is a method of alternative dispute resolution.
(True: Arbitration is another method. Mediators attempt to bring the parties together, for example, by pointing out the strengths and weaknesses of their positions, in an attempt to reach a mutually agreeable and amicable compromise-type solution to their dispute.)

3. An arbitration clause in a contract will usually require that the parties first submit the dispute to a neutral mediator to try to reach a compromise solution.
(False: Arbitration clauses require usually that the parties must submit their dispute to binding arbitration by a third-party; mediation is a separate form of alternative dispute resolution.)

4. If a party to a contract with a binding arbitration clause is dissatisfied with the decision of an arbitrator, the party can always appeal the case into the traditional court system.
(False: It is very difficult to appeal the decision of an arbitrator. A showing of bad faith, fraud, and/or prejudice usually is required. An allegation that the arbitrator made a mistake as to the applicable law is insufficient.)

5. Arbitrators cannot render legally binding decisions; they can only make recommendations since arbitrators are not real judges.
(False: Arbitrators selected by the parties are not only empowered to render legally binding decisions in cases, but also it is very difficult to appeal an arbitrator's decision. Mediators, however, only make recommendations to the parties in an attempt to reach a settlement of a dispute.)

6. U.S. law mandates that all legal disputes and controversies be adjudicated and settled in traditional courts before a jury.
(False: Arbitration and mediation are alternative ways to settle legal disputes that avoid traditional jury trials.)

7. In an arbitration proceeding the arbitrator must get detailed instructions from a traditional court judge before resolving a dispute.
(False: The arbitrator decides the law as well as the facts of the case. Moreover, if the arbitrator "got the law wrong" there is no usually no appeal to a traditional court unless there is evidence of bad faith or prejudice.)

8. Arbitration is the process where the disputing parties with the help of a third-party conciliator try to devise a mutually agreeable solution to their dispute.
(False: That is mediation; whereas arbitration is the process where a third-party arbitrator makes a binding decision in a dispute.)

9. The use of alternative dispute resolution (ADR) is decreasing rapidly in comparison to traditional litigation.
(False: ADR is growing rapidly since it is supported by the courts and since many employers have ADR clauses in their employment contracts, thereby compelling employees to use ADR as opposed to the traditional court system. However, there is some controversy today as to whether ADR is appropriate in sexual discrimination and harassment cases, especially when combined with mandatory confidentiality agreements, and consequently there are some legislative proposals to ban ADR in such employment disputes.)

10. Arbitration is rarely used in international trade disputes.
(False: Moreover, the Supreme Court generally upholds arbitration clauses in international contracts, assuming the host country's arbitration procedure is a fair one with basic due process rights. As such, Choice of Law and Choice of Forum clauses in contracts are of the utmost importance as they will determine where the ADR occurs and what law the arbitrator will use to decide the dispute.)

Multiple Choice Questions with Answers and Explanations

1. Regarding alternative dispute resolution mechanisms, which if the following is a FALSE statement?
    a. Mediation is a process by which a neutral, third-party acts as a conciliator and assists the parties to a dispute to reach a compromise solution.
    b. Arbitration is a process whereby the parties to a controversy submit their dispute to a neutral third-party, who is not a traditional judge, for a final and binding decision.
    c. An arbitrator's decision generally cannot be appealed to the traditional court system if one of the parties is dissatisfied with the determination and thinks the arbitrator got the facts and the law wrong.
    d. An arbitration clause in a contract between an employer and an employee is as a general rule not enforceable against the employee since it would be unfair to the employee to prevent him or her from going to a traditional court to sue the employer.

    (The correct answer is d. Arbitration is favored by the law; and consequently, arbitration clauses in employment contracts are generally legal and enforceable. However, if the employment issue

in dispute involves Title VII of the Civil Rights Act the EEOC can sue the employer for discrimination or harassment in a traditional court regardless of the arbitration clause.)

2. When can a court set aside an arbitration award?
    a. When a judge would have made a different decision.
    b. When the award violates public policy.
    c. When there is evidence of bad faith.
    d. Answers b. and c.

(The correct answer is d. Arbitration awards are very difficult to overturn on an appeal to the traditional court system. Even if a judge would have made a different decision based on the facts presented, and even if the judge feels the arbitrator interpreted the applicable law incorrectly, a judge cannot overturn the award. There are some exceptions, however, including when an award violates the public policy of a jurisdiction ("public policy" means actions that advance the protection and the promotion of the health, safety, and welfare of the people in that jurisdiction) as well as when an award is in bad faith, for example, the arbitration hearing was not fair or the arbitrator was biased or prejudiced or had a conflict-of-interest.)

3. The alternative dispute resolution procedure whereby a neutral third-party assist the disputing parties to come to an amicable resolution of their dispute is called:
    a. Arbitration
    b. Mediation
    c. Informal action
    d. Mentoring

(The correct answer is b. The key difference between arbitration and mediation is that in the former the arbitrator makes a binding decision on the parties, whereas in mediation the mediator does not make any decision; rather, the mediator assists the parties to try to get them to come to an amicable resolution to their dispute, for example, by making settlement recommendations. Mentorship occurs when one person helps, advises, guides, and coaches another on how to do better, especially in business settings. Informal action is typically found in administrative law where agencies can make policy by informally acting, for example, by issuing guidelines, as opposed to making law and policy by means of rulemaking and/or adjudication.)

4. A method of avoiding litigation for a breach of contract is/are:
    a. Mediation
    b. Arbitration
    c. Rescission
    d. Answers a. and b.

(The correct answer is d. Mediation and arbitration are called alternative dispute resolution procedures because they can be used instead of traditional litigation in a court. Rescission is the cancelling of a contract by a court of equity, thereby requiring a trial, on the grounds of fraud, mistake, duress, undue influence, or forgery.)

5. What is FALSE about arbitration?
    a. The arbitrator can make a legally binding decision.
    b. Generally, the rules of evidence are not followed as strictly as they would be in a traditional court trial.
    c. There will be a traditional jury in an arbitration proceeding due to the 7th Amendment's guarantee of jury trials.
    d. The right and duty to arbitrate arises from a contractual agreement between the parties.

(The correct answer is c. The 7th Amendment guarantees the right to a jury in lawsuits at common law and not arbitration hearings, which the parties by contract have voluntarily agreed to use to

resolve their dispute instead of a traditional lawsuit in court. The rules of evidence, moreover, are not as strictly followed, especially the Hearsay Rule. The arbitrator can make a legally binding decision, which is, in addition, very difficult to appeal successfully to the traditional courts.)

6. What is FALSE about mediation?
   a. Typically, it is conducted in a confidential manner.
   b. It is mandatory in all breach of contract disputes where the damages asserted are more than $75,000.
   c. The mediator does not make a binding decision.
   d. The mediator must be mutual, impartial, and fair.
   (The correct answer is b. Mediation as a general rule is based on a voluntary agreement between the disputing parties. There are some exceptions, however, for example, in medical malpractice lawsuits in some states which by statute require mediation. The mediator is a facilitator and conciliator only; he or she does not make a binding decision. In most states, mediation is a confidential process; however, in some states confidentiality can be waived with the consent of the parties and the mediator. The $75,000 figure is the amount of money that must be in controversy for a federal court to take jurisdiction of a "diversity" case, that is, a lawsuit between litigants of different states.)

7. What is FALSE about arbitration?
   a. The Federal Arbitration Act of 1925 makes arbitrator's decisions enforceable in federal court.
   b. It is less expensive and less time-consuming than the traditional judicial manner of resolving disputes.
   c. It is usually a confidential process.
   d. A traditional judge has wide authority to overturn an arbitration award on appeal
   (The correct answer is d. The authority of a court to overturn an arbitration award is very limited, for example, if there is evidence of fraud, corruption, bribery, bias, or conflict-of-interest, or if the arbitrator exceeded his or her authority in the arbitration agreement, for example, by deciding an issue that was not subject to arbitration. State laws in addition to the federal law make arbitration awards enforceable. Also, state statutory laws as well as the common law make arbitration a confidential process.)

3 - Business Ethics, Corporate Social Responsibility, and Sustainability

Introduction

Today, typically, business students are required to take in addition to the standard business law course a course in business ethics; moreover, an ethics course usually includes a discussion of social responsibility, focusing on corporate social responsibility (CSR) when applied to business, as well as "sustainability," that is, environmental responsibility. These subject matters can be deemed to be "values" because they possess worth to the business person today. Accordingly, the student must know, and be able to differentiate among, these seminal values. Legality, of course, is based on the law, morality is based on ethics, which is a branch of philosophy, and social responsibility and sustainability are based on current definitions and conceptions of these terms. Regarding ethics, the student must be aware of exactly what it is, that is, the branch of philosophy wherein there are ethical theories and principles that are used to reason to moral conclusions as to what is moral or immoral, good or bad, right or wrong, and just or unjust.

Yet, the student also must be aware that morality and ethics are separate values from the law; thus, there is no legal liability for acting immorally unless some law is also violated in the process. Nonetheless, the discerning student should be cognizant of the fact that today there is an expectation that business will act not "merely" legally but also in a moral manner. However, the student must be aware that there are several ethical theories, that some are conflicting, and consequently that it is difficult at times to determine exactly what or who is "good" or "bad." Nevertheless, the student must know at a minimum the four major ethical theories in Western Civilization (which obviously is not the only civilization, but the one in which ethics courses in the U.S. are premised philosophically). These theories are as follows: Ethical Egoism, wherein morality is based on self-interest; Ethical Relativism, wherein morality is based on societal beliefs and mores; Utilitarianism, wherein morality is based on the predominant good consequences produced by an action; and Kantian ethics, wherein morality is based on the application of a formal test, called the Categorical Imperative, to the action itself. The student must also be aware that Utilitarianism, based on the writings of the English philosophers and social reformers, Jeremy Bentham and John Stuart Mill, and Kantian ethics, based on the writings of the German philosopher and university professor, Immanuel Kant, are the two major, "modern" (relatively speaking, of course) ethical theories in Western Civilization; yet they are diametrically opposed in principle since the Utilitarians focus on the consequences of an action in determining morality thereby regarding the action itself as neutral; whereas Kant said to disregard the consequences of an action in determining its morality, and rather apply to the action itself the formal test, which he called the Categorical Imperative, and which he posited as the supreme, true, objective, and universal ethical principle. In addition, the student must realize that the afore mentioned four ethical theories are secular-based theories that consist of reasoning from principles to arrive at a logical moral conclusion. One certainly can have religious-based ethics (which some might say is preferable for a variety of reasons), but since most required college ethics courses are not based on, and may not even include, religious-based ethical theories, the authors herein will be practical and just deal with secular-based ethics.

As emphasized, in addition to acting legally and morally there is an expectation today that a business also will be a socially responsible and sustainable one. As such, the student must be aware of and know the definitions of these concepts. Traditionally, social responsibility, also known as Corporate Social Responsibility (CSR) when applied to business, means that a business is involved in charitable causes and philanthropy, and civic-minded efforts as well as engaged in the community as a "good corporate citizen." Sustainability is a more modern variant of social responsibility, which at times is considered as the newer part of the value of social responsibility, but at times construed as separate value. In either case, sustainability today means that a business is environmentally responsible; that is, the business is doing more than "merely" obeying the law, but is also "going green" by engaging in environmental protection and conservation efforts as well as the production of "green" energy by means of solar and wind techniques. A major theme is this exam review book, as the astute student will discern, is that a business student and soon-to-be a business manager, leader, or owner must think and act above-and-beyond the law to ensure that the business acts in a legal, moral, socially responsible, and sustainable manner; and, most importantly, it is critical for the student to be aware of that it is in the student's and business person's long-term self-interest to do so.

True and False Questions with Answers and Explanations

1. Business ethics is the study of how companies can become very profitable without necessarily breaking the law.
(False: Business ethics is the field of ethics applied to business to determine business actions which are moral or immoral, regardless of the degree of profitability or legality.)

2. A criticism of the Utilitarian ethical theory is that it can ethically justify actions that cause pain and suffering to a minority of people.
(True: "The ends justify the means" pursuant to Utilitarianism, and thus if an action produces the "greater good" it is moral even if it causes some pain and suffering.)

3. Cost-benefit analysis is a key component to Kantian ethics.
(False: Kant focuses on the action itself and not its consequences in the form of any cost-benefit analysis.)

4. Kant emphasized the consequences of putting an action into effect in ascertaining its morality.
(False: Kant focused on the form of an action and not its consequences in determining its morality.)

5. Stakeholder analysis in business means that a business leader should look beyond the shareholders and thus examine the effects of corporate actions on other groups, such as employees, local community, and society as a whole.
(True: Stakeholder analysis is also called "constituent group" analysis, and thus is similar to the ethical theory of Utilitarianism, though the later is an ethical theory which makes moral conclusions.)

6. Codes of Ethics adopted by companies must apply equally to executives and managers as well as employees.
(True: Otherwise, they will be regarded as mere "window dressing" or just another set of more punitive rules imposed on the employees.)

7. A business leader today must keep abreast of changing societal expectations of what constitutes "socially responsible" and "sustainable" behavior by business.
(True: Legality is based on the law; morality is based on ethics; but what is socially responsible and sustainable conduct is based on what societal expectations for business are.)

8. The Kantian approach to ethical reasoning maintains that one should not commit an immoral action regardless if there are positive consequences for some people.

(True: This is the essence of Kant's Categorical Imperative ethical principle; that is, if an action is immoral, for example, by demeaning and disrespecting a person, the action is immoral regardless of any good consequences produced, for example, an exploitative "sweat-shop" that produces good products for the consumer and makes money for several stakeholders, but exploits the employees.)

9. The pursuit by people of their own economic interest to obtain money and power is a key feature to the Utilitarian ethical theory.
(False: This is the key feature of the doctrine of Ethical Egoism, which is based on one pursuing one's own self-interest, though taking a long-term approach in so doing. Utilitarianism takes more of a stakeholder approach in determining morality, as per its cardinal principle, to wit: "An action is moral if it produces the greatest amount of good for the greatest number of people.")

10. Unethical behaviors are endemic to business since business profits and morality are always mutually exclusive.
(False: There are many examples of business people and companies that are very successful economically and who have conducted themselves in a consistent moral manner, for example, H. Wayne Huizenga, the entrepreneur, and only one, to have founded three Fortune 500 companies, Waste Management, Blockbuster Video, and Auto Nation, as well as Extended Stay America.)

11. In most states in the U.S. corporation law requires companies to have code of ethics with clear moral rules stated and sanctions for violations.
(False: Codes of ethics are certainly advisable for companies, assuming they are not mere "window-dressing," but they are not legally mandatory.)

12. "Sustainability" for business today is conceived in terms of a business being environmentally responsible.
(True: And being responsible by going "beyond" the law to conserve energy, for example, "green offices" and "green buildings," as well as protecting the environment, for example, by eliminating plastic bags in supermarkets and plastic straws in restaurants and bars.)

13. In a completely free-market economy regulatory agencies like the Federal Trade Commission would be unnecessary since all business people and companies would see that it is in their long-term self-interest to act morally and ethically.
(False: Alas, some people cannot clearly see where their own self-interest lies; and others act immorally regardless due to short-term thinking, greed, and/or overweening ambition. As such, regulatory agencies are necessary to make determinations of illegality and "police" unethical business conduct, such as monopolizing commerce and engaging in deceptive trade practices.)

14. When an employee "blows the whistle" and reports wrongdoing at his or her company the employee will typically be protected by a state Whistleblower Protection Act since the employee is acting in a moral and ethical manner to protect the public good.
(False: The employee's moral and ethical motivations are irrelevant legally; to be protected by any whistleblowing statute the employee must report actual legal wrongdoing to an appropriate government agency first and not the media.)

15. In many countries and cultures, the payment of bribes to government officials is an accepted way of doing business.
(True: Moreover, if such "bribes" are considered to be morally appropriate in that country or culture then pursuant to the doctrine of Ethical Relativism bribery would be deemed moral.)

16. A fundamental notion of Kant's Categorical Imperative is that a person should only act on those principles that he or she as a rational person would prescribe as moral laws to be obeyed by all.
(True: This is the Universal Law test of the Categorical Imperative. Examples would be precepts against cheating, stealing, and lying. Of course, some people do not act in accord with this principle, and they do cheat, steal, and lie; but as a result they then will be criticized as acting immorally. Moreover, Kant condemns such people as "parasites" on an otherwise moral universe where the vast majority of the people do not cheat, steal, or lie.)

17. The law provides very clear and precise moral guidelines to business people.
(False: The law is the law, and thus the law provides legal guidelines, and at times these guidelines are not that precise, for example, the line between illegal insider trading and legally trading on inside information, or the line between an illegal bribe and a legal "good will" gift to a foreign government official.)

18. Utilitarianism is the principal branch of deontological ethics.
(False: Deontology is duty-based ethics, and thus the ethical theories of the German philosopher Immanuel Kant are the principal theories of deontological ethics. Utilitarianism is consequences-based ethics, focusing on the consequences of an action in determining morality.)

19. Virtue Ethics, as exemplified by Plato and Aristotle, focuses on the classical Greek notion of developing and exhibiting good moral character instead of following rules.
(True: This is a basic proposition. One can develop one's good character by finding people of good character and learning from and imitating them.)

20. The behavior of top management is a very important factor in the company developing a moral character and exhibiting ethical conduct.
(True: As oft said, "a fish rots from the head," and thus immoral conduct by top managers will likely be followed by the employees and any company code of ethics or conduct will be perceived by the employees as mere "window dressing" to be ignored or violated.)

21. A Utilitarian believes that the form of an action is the primary way to determine its morality and that the consequences of putting the action into effect are secondary or even irrelevant.
(False: Focusing on the form of the action is the heart of Kantian ethics, which disregards consequences, whether good or bad, in determining morality. Examining the consequences is the Utilitarian approach to determining morality, as predominant good consequences equal a moral act, and the obverse.)

22. The overall trend today is to assume that business leaders have some responsibility to ensure that their organizations are "sustainable" ones.
(True: And "sustainability" is thought of in terms of being environmentally responsible; that is, not merely obeying environmental laws but not wasting energy and water and trying to conserve natural resources for future generations.)

23. Conservative economist Milton Friedman is known for the famous saying that the "social responsibility" of business is to make money!
(True: Of course, he meant legal profit maximization.)

24. The long-term promotion of self-interest is an appropriate argument for a company to be a socially responsible one.

(True: Of course, one must assume the company is being socially responsible in a smart, prudent, and perhaps "strategic" way, that is, for its socially responsible actions to be tied to its brand, mission, image, products, and/or services.)

25. Standards of what is "moral" or "ethical" are very consistent from country to country and society to society.
(False: Many moral standards are country/society-based, as per the ethical theory of Ethical Relativism whereby what a society believes is moral is moral for that society; that is, morality is relative to societal beliefs, customs, and mores.)

26. Government intervention in an otherwise "free" and capitalistic economy may be morally justified in the instances of "market failure," such as the occurrence of monopolizing conduct.
(True: Utilitarianism and the benefit of the "greater good" of society would ethically support such intervention. Other examples would be restraints of trade, such as price-fixing, and insider trading.)

27. Ethics is the theoretical study of morality, whereas morals are views as to what is right or wrong.
(True: Ethics, a branch of philosophy, is the intellectual framework, the thought-systems, the theories and the principles therein that one uses to reason to moral conclusions as to right or wrong or good or bad or moral or immoral. As such, the terms ethics and morality from a philosophical standpoint are not synonymous, but different, though in everyday parlance people use the terms interchangeably.)

28. Plato would likely object to the hierarchy of authority found today in the typical large business corporation.
(False: Plato's conception of a "just state" is a hierarchical, stratified, class-based, and authoritative entity, which parallels in some degree a large business corporation.)

29. Aristotle' Ethics of Virtue is primarily concerned with the inculcation and development of virtuous traits and the cultivation of moral character.
(True: As such, Aristotle's ethics differs from an ethics created by the rational establishment of ethical theories and the derivation of moral rules by reasoning from the theories.)

30. One defense of Ethical Egoism is that the public good and the general welfare will benefit by people seeking to fulfill their selfish desires and to attain their personal goals.
(True: This is the classic defense from the British economist, Adam Smith, but he also notes that people must be rational, prudent, and "enlightened" egoists. Of course, one problem may be that this defense of Egoism seems to partake of certain aspects of the Utilitarian ethical theory.)

31. For Machiavelli, ethics, morality, and virtue are merely instrumental values.
(True: As a follower of the Sophists of ancient Greece, who were relativists, Machiavelli believed there was no intrinsic truth or value to ethics, morality, and virtue; however, these concepts had instrumental value as they might be relative to and thus a means to one's success in achieving power, fame, and glory.)

32. Machiavelli regards conventional "badness" or "vice" as a tactic to be used continually and regularly if one has the power to do so.
(False: Machiavelli advises that if it is absolutely necessary and expedient to do a traditional "bad," vice-like, evil, or immoral act to achieve or to maintain power, then do it, and do it well and carefully to achieve one's objective; but then stop doing it, or one may like doing "bad" to much, which will cause problems later on, Machiavelli counsels.)

33. One benefit to a sincere Ethical Emotist is that one is morally infallible.
(True: Since pursuant to the ethical theory of Ethical Emotism morality is based on one's feelings or emotional reaction to a situation, so long as one honestly reports one emotional reaction and then "translates" it into a moral opinion a person is always right. Moreover, one can change one's moral opinion if one has a differing moral reaction. As such, this theory is a very personal and subjective one.)

34. Cultural relativism is a prescriptive ethical theory that sets forth moral norms.
(False: It is Ethical Relativism that is the prescriptive ethical theory that sets forth moral norms or precepts based on what a society believes is moral. Whereas cultural relativism is merely a descriptive sociological theory that describes different peoples and cultures and their beliefs, customs, and mores. There is neither an ethical nor a moral component to it.)

35. If one is an Ethical Relativist one can rightfully and properly criticize the moral beliefs and practices of one's own society.
(False: Since pursuant to Ethical Relativism what a society believes is moral is moral for that society an Ethical Relativist cannot logically criticize the morals of his or her own society; but if a person does so he or she is not an Ethical Relativist, but likely a follower of another ethical theory.)

36. Since making and accumulating money is materialistic and selfish money cannot be construed as a good thing in any Utilitarian analysis.
(False: Money has instrumental value as it can be a means to happiness and satisfaction, which "pleasures" certainly can be registered and counted in any Utilitarian calculus.)

37. It is possible under the Utilitarian ethical theory to ethically legitimize an action as moral even if it causes some pain, suffering, and unhappiness.
(True: As the old maxim says, "The ends justify the means"; and consequently if an action overall produces more good and pleasurable results than bad or painful results the action is moral. At the least, all affected by the action were counted, but the good outweighed the bad. Note that the German philosopher Immanuel Kant found this to be an illogical and immoral result; that is, how can one have an ethical theory that morally legitimizes pain, suffering, and unhappiness?)

38. Kant would condemn Utilitarianism as an immoral ethical theory since in his opinion "the ends do not justify the means."
(True: Kant is diametrically opposed to Utilitarianism. Instead of focusing on the consequences of an action to determine its morality Kant says to focus on the action itself; and then Kant says to apply to the action his supreme ethical principle, the Categorical Imperative, to determine if the action is moral or immoral, regardless of the consequences it produces.)

39. Natural rights exist, according to John Locke, only if they are specifically granted by the government to its citizens.
(False: Natural rights are derived from the Natural Law and come from human nature and people's status as human beings; and these rights are accorded to all people everywhere; they are not derived from or dependent upon any government or legal system. Prime examples of natural rights are the right to life, liberty, and property that one rightfully acquires in the state-of-nature.)

40. According to Machiavelli, morality is a relativistic concept and thus a traditionally "bad" act, such as lying, may become a "good" act if one must lie to gain or keep power.
(True: Machiavelli, as a follower of the Sophists of ancient Greece, did not believe there was any intrinsic, objective, real, truth or value to morality or ethics. Rather, morality and ethics had

"merely" instrumental and relative value. As such, if one must lie, by all means do so and do it well and efficaciously, and then the traditional bad "act" now becomes a "good" act.)

41. One problem for business today is not that business people are immoral or amoral but that they may be ethically insensitive and/or ignorant.
(True: Business people are trained to look at the practical and legal consequences of decision-making but not necessarily the moral aspects. They thus may not expand their scope of analysis to ask that even if good from a profitability standpoint as well as legal a decision might immoral, such as a legal, though exploitative, "sweat-shop" in a developing country with very little or no law protecting workers. Moreover, many business people as students or in corporate training have had exposure to laws and regulations governing business but not necessarily ethical theories and principles that are used to make moral determinations.)

42. Typically, business people find it easier to deal with the economic and financial, and even legal, ramifications to business decision-making than the moral consequences.
(True: Business people may lack the awareness of the moral consequences of actions beyond profitability and the law as well as lack the education and training in ethics which is necessary to make moral determinations.)

43. In the field of moral philosophy, ethics and morality are usually treated as synonymous terms and concepts.
(False: From a philosophical vantage-point morality or morals is the conclusion of what is right or wrong or good or bad, whereas ethics is the intellectual thought-systems encompassing ethical theories and principles that one uses to reason to moral conclusions. Morality thus is the "end" and ethics is the "means.")

44. Intrinsic values are deemed to be good and valuable because of their consequences and because they are a desired means to an end.
(False: Intrinsic values are good and valuable in-and-of-themselves. An example would be happiness; that is, it is quite simply good and valuable to be happy – period! A value which is good because it is a means to certain ends is called an "extrinsic" or "instrumental" value. An example would be money which has value since it is a means or "instrument" to buy things that will make a person happy. And thus, who says that "money can't buy happiness"!!!!)

45. Moral rules as well as exceptions to moral rules are established principally by means of reasoning from ethical theories and principles.
(True: It is a fundamental philosophic concept that one uses ethics to reason to morality, including establishing moral "rules" and exceptions thereto. Of course, one problem is that there are many ethical theories, and some clash, for example, in Western ethics the conflict between Utilitarianism and Kantian ethics, meaning that one may come up with two different moral conclusions based on the same set of facts since one is applying two different ethical theories.)

46. Most moral questions are clear and demonstrably correct answers that can be scientifically proven.
(False: The existence of many different ethical theories may lead one to differing moral conclusions; and there is no "Supreme Court of Ethics" to tell one which ethical theory or for that manner moral answer is the "correct" one. Thus, one should heed the advice of Aristotle to the "educated" person, and that is not to impose too much precision on a subject matter that defies it, namely ethics!)

47. Inductive reasoning involves reasoning from general principles and definitions.
(False: This is deductive reasoning. Inductive reasoning, for example by using Socrates' Socratic Method, involves obtaining answers to certain questions, for example, who is a "just" person and what is a "just" action, and then looking for the commonalities from the answers and next using these commonalities to form a basic definition, which then can be applied as a principle. That is, one proceeds from the "particulars" to the "general.")

48. The legal law relies primarily on coercion and force whereas morality and ethics rely primarily on persuasion, self-interest, and social sanctions.
(True: One cannot be sued for acting immorally, for example perhaps, nepotism in a small firm, unless one has violated some legal law. Yet business people who act legally but immorally risk bad publicity and consumer boycotts, for example for their perhaps legal but exploitative sweat-shops overseas. Moreover, an astute business person should realize that it is in his or her self-interest in the long-run to be perceived as, and rightfully so, not only a legal but also a moral business person.)

49. According to the Sophists, moral terms such as "justice" had no objective basis in truth or reality, as they were merely relative terms relative to the person using them.
(True: "Man is the measure of all things, seen and unseen," said the Sophists, thus underscoring their cardinal belief in the relativity and subjectivity of all things. However, even though morality, ethics, and justice did not possess any real, fixed, objective truth or value, these terms might have instrumental value as a means to an end, such as convincing some potential followers that one is a moral leader.)

50. The saying, "Justice is the will of the stronger" is likely to be one of Socrates aphorisms.
(False: Such a saying is from the Sophists, the philosophical opponents to Socrates in ancient Greece. To the Sophists, who were complete relativists when it came to the objective and intrinsic truth to anything the definition of justice they provided was for them a "real-world" and practical one. Socrates, however, believed there was a fixed, objective, real, and true definition of "justice" which he advised to look for using his Socratic Method.)

51. An ethics that appeals to one's feelings, conscience, or "heart" lacks any reasons for any moral conclusions as one simply reports his or her emotional reaction of approval or disapproval to a situation.
(True: This is the ethical theory of Ethical Emotions, wherein one may see reasons, but they will come after the moral conclusion which is emotion based. That is, the reasons are post hoc in that they come after the emotion-based moral conclusions. For example, one can feel good and happy about Robin Hood of Old English day and thus Robin is moral based on one's initial feelings; but then some reasons are supplied, for example, if he was stealing it was only from the rich, and he gave the money to the poor, and, really, was it actually stealing or rather merely a means-tested "transit" fee to guide people through Sherwood Forest!)

52. For Plato, the Form of the Good is the final expression and absolute source of morality and goodness.
(True: This is a fundamental Platonic concept. Plato compares it to the sun, which gives light, life, and growth to everything.)

53. Plato's philosophical theory of Organizational Ethics, including his conception of a Just State, is a very elitist formulation that reflects distrust for the masses of people and democracy.
(True: The Rulers, who are the intellectuals, are in charge; and the Auxiliaries, for example, the military, and the Producers, for example, the trades people, are governed by the Rulers, so as to achieve a harmonious and just and good state.)

54. For Aristotle, the highest good is the fulfillment of one's physical senses, though he would counsel moderation in seeking pleasures.
(False: Above is the philosophy of Epicurus, also known as Hedonism, but again even Epicurus would counsel moderation in pleasure-seeking so as not to "burn yourself out." For Aristotle, the greatest good is to develop one's intellect.)

55. Aristotle maintains in the Doctrine of the Mean that the virtuous or moral choice is a rationally determined mean between two extremes of deficiency or excess.
(True: As the old saying goes, "The middle-road is the safest," as well as for Aristotle the most moral. An example would be the virtue of courage, which is the desired and virtuous mean between being foolhardy or rash and being a coward.)

56. In a business context, Aristotle's Doctrine of the Mean would indicate that a corporation should only be concerned with legal profit maximization and not be concerned with social responsibility.
(False: A corporation heeding Aristotle's Mean principle would avoid the two extremes regarding social responsibility, that is, not being too socially responsible so as to harm the company, but not being socially irresponsible or non-responsive, which also might harm the company. The objective is the mean, that is, to be socially responsible in a prudent, moderate, smart, and strategic way, that is, with one's social responsibility efforts ideally tied to one's image, brand, products, and/or service, for example, Home Depot being involved with the charity Habitat for Humanity.)

57. A major problem with Aristotle's Ethics of Virtue is that it does not focus on the quality of an action to determine if the action is morally right or wrong.
(True: Aristotle is concerned in his Ethics of Virtue with the inculcation and development of moral character as opposed to rationally establishing ethical principles and moral rules. As such, one must presume that the virtuous person of good moral character will always do the moral act.)

58. A true Psychological Egoist cannot acknowledge the existence of a purely altruistic act.
(True: This is the logical result of this doctrine as everything and anything even remotely beneficial to another is always and only done to benefit oneself, even if indirectly or even if one merely feels good about it.)

59. An Ethical Egoist thinks mainly of what will benefit himself or herself.
(True: This is a fundamental proposition. However, the Ethical Egoists would advise to be prudent about maximizing your own self-interest, for example, by taking a long-term perspective and thus be willing to undergo some short-term effort, expense, and sacrifice, and also by treating people well, regardless of one's perhaps contrary inclinations, since it is "better to have friends than enemies.")

60. Public good and the general welfare are based on people fulfilling their selfish desires, according to one defense of the doctrine of Ethical Egoism.
(True: Actually, this is the classic defense of the doctrine by the economist, Adam Smith, who said that the "baker bakes bread not for benevolence but for money"; but the baker bakes well, and thus if everyone finds his or her niche in society and performs their job or function well, not only will they benefit but so will society as there will be more efficiencies and more goods and services. Of course, one may discern that this defense of Egoism "borrows" some of the major tenets of the Utilitarian ethical theory.)

61. When people's desires and objectives conflict, the doctrine of Ethical Egoism contains an arbitrating mechanism to settle differences in a fair and balanced manner.

(False. A major problems with Ethical Egoism is that there is no arbitrating mechanism so decide the issue when egos conflict, for example, who gets the job or the promotion. Now, one would hope that rational people would see that it is in their own long-term self-interest to devise legitimate standards for positions or promotions, but the problem is that when "pushed to the edges" the question as to whose ego will be satisfied will come down to who is the most powerful, as per the Sophists who said "Might makes right.")

62. The Sophists believed that ethical principles and moral rules are universal, objective, impersonal, and external.
(False: This is a Socratic belief; but for the Sophists, just the opposite! The Sophists were total relativists who believed there was no real, objective truth to anything. All was individual, personal, subjective, internal, and instrumental.)

63. Machiavelli had a positive and laudatory view of people and human nature.
(False: The vast majority of people are weak, stupid, ignorant, and thus, as the astute aspiring Prince ought to be aware, easily led as well as misled.)

64. Machiavelli's political philosophy logically stems from the teachings of the Sophists of ancient Greece.
(True: Machiavelli, like the Sophists, was a relativist; as such there are no universal moral standards; and consequently something resembling traditional virtue, such as being honest and truthful, might be "bad" if it hinders one from gaining power; and conversely something resembling traditional vice, such as lying and deception, might be "good" if it helps one to gain power.)

65. Machiavelli draws no distinction between morality in the public arena and the private sphere.
(False: In the private sphere, that is, when one is associating with one's family members and close friends, one can always be traditionally moral, for example, always tell the truth. However, when one enters the public arena, one must be prepared to jettison traditional morality and thus be prepared to do if absolutely necessary and in an expeditious manner a traditional bad act, such as lying, which then becomes a "good" act because it is indispensable to one achieving or maintaining power.)

66. To be successful Machiavelli would advise a business leader to always adhere to traditional conceptions of morality and ethics.
(False: It is a "moral jungle" out there, says Machiavelli, and thus in order to be successful one must be prepared to do the occasional, necessary, and expedient traditionally "bad" act, such as bribery, which now has become in Machiavelli's relativistic universe a "good" act.)

67. Machiavelli regards conventional "badness" as a tactic to be used continually and regularly.
(False: One should act whenever possible in a traditionally good manner, advises Machiavelli, or at the least appear to be good; but if at some point it is necessary to do a traditionally bad act to gain or keep power, then by all means do it (and do it well but stop doing it when it is no longer necessary.)

68. One problem with Machiavelli's philosophy is that a person who aggressively seeks power and maintains power by "machiavellian" means may find himself or herself corrupted by the singular pursuit of power.
(True: As the old saying goes, "Power corrupts, and absolute power corrupts absolutely.")

69. Ethical Emotism is an ethical theory in which the right answers to moral questions can be debated and resolved in a logical, rational, and principled manner.

(False: An Ethical Emotist makes his or her moral judgments based on feelings, that is, his or her emotional reactions of approval or disapproval to certain events. An Ethical Emotist may supply reasons to bolster his or her emotion-based moral conclusion but the reasons will come after the emotions and attendant moral conclusion.)

70. One benefit to being an Ethical Emotist is that one is morally infallible.
(True: So long as one is being honest and reports one's true feelings and emotional reaction to a situation as moral or immoral one is infallible in one's moral conclusion.)

71. One convenient aspect of being an Ethical Emotist is that one can change one's opinion about a moral issue simply by having and expressing a different feeling or emotional reaction to the issue.
(True: Since pursuant to Ethical Emotism morality is emotion-based one can change one's moral opinion simply by having a differing emotional reaction. For example, one may strongly feel that the Chinese practice of "harvesting" executed prisoners' organs and selling them to wealthy Westerners is immoral; however, if one needs an organ transplant and cannot obtain one locally and one has the money then perhaps one's feelings about the matter, and thus one's moral opinion, may dramatically change.)

72. Morality is a societal-based phenomenon, according to the doctrine of Ethical Relativism.
(True: This is a fundamental proposition since, what a society believes is moral is moral for that society.)

73. An Ethical Relativist would deny that there are moral standards which are universally true for all people and at all times.
(True: Ethical Relativism, as per its title, is a relativistic ethical theory in which morality is based on societal-based mores and customs.)

74. One advantage to Ethical Relativism is that it is very easy to determine what constitutes a "society" for the purposes of the doctrine.
(False: Perhaps in a very homogeneous society, like Japan, it is easy to do so, but in most countries, especially ones like the U.S. which are very heterogeneous, it is a difficult challenge to define the contours of a "society," particularly when there are minority groups within a society, and minority groups within the minority groups.)

75. One advantage to Ethical Relativism is that different societal practices can be morally compared, evaluated, ranked, and ultimately judged right or wrong.
(False: This is a major drawback to the Ethical Relativism theory. Since each society has its own "true" moral standards and beliefs there is no arbitrating mechanism to determine which is better or correct. Very simply, ascertain the moral standards in the society, adopt, and conform, as per the old maxim, "When in Rome, do as the Romans.")

76. If one is an Ethical Relativist it is right and proper to criticize the moral practices and beliefs of other societies.
(False: Don't be a cultural and moral "imperialist"! What a society believes is true and right morally is true and right for that society, so simply adhere to "local" moral standards, and certainly do not criticize them.)

77. If one is an Ethical Relativist it is right and proper to criticize the moral practices and beliefs of one's own society.
(False: What a society believes is true morally is in fact true so one must conform to societal-based moral standards. Of course, if one IS criticizing one's own society's moral norms or for that matter

another society's moral norms, then perhaps one is not an Ethical Relativist but an adherent to another ethical theory.)

78. The doctrine of Legal Positivism would maintain that a businessperson should rely on the law as the basis for decision-making when confronted with a moral question.
(True: Pursuant to Legal Positivism the law is the source and standard for legal issues but also for moral questions. As such, what is legal is also moral. One can, of course, try to change the law, but if one is doing so on moral ground then perhaps one is not a Legal Positivist but a follower of another ethical philosopher.)

79. According to the Hobbesian view of Legal Positivism there is no such thing as a morally bad or unjust law.
(True: Since the law is the standard for morality and ethics there logically is no such thing as a morally "bad" law; rather, there is just a law-law. Of course, if one has problems with certain laws on moral grounds, such as slavery which was legal in the U.S. until the Civil War, then perhaps one is not a Legal Positivist.)

80. According to the English philosopher Jeremy Bentham, Utilitarianism is an objective, scientific, mathematical, and empirical ethical theory.
(True: "Accounting," "book-keeping," and "scientific" ethics, Bentham says, though there is very little guidance as to how one is to mathematically measure and weigh good v. bad consequences to see which prevails.)

81. According to the Utilitarians, some people's pleasure and pain count more than others since some people are more important, influential, and worthwhile.
(False: One positive aspect to the Utilitarian ethical theory is that everyone's pleasure and pain gets counted equally since people are all human beings who feel pleasure and pain. This is a very egalitarian ethical theory; consequently, there are no "special" or "privileged" people. Of course, when the "counting" is done, and if there are more good results than bad, the action is moral, but at least the minority of people who were pained got counted.)

82. The Utilitarians would counsel to take a long-term perspective as to the consequences of an action in determining its morality.
(True: Yet not so long as to guess or speculate as to consequences. Using "history as your guide" and "your common storehouse of knowledge" look for probable consequences of putting the action into effect or at the least look for the reasonably foreseeable consequences.)

83. Since money is too materialistic and mercenary to be a good, it cannot be used as a measurement in quantifying pleasure and pain.
(False: The Utilitarians have no problem with making money or using money in the Utilitarian calculus since money can buy things that can give you happiness, satisfaction, and pleasure.)

84. Utilitarianism fails the second test of Kant's Categorical Imperative – the Kingdom of Ends test – since people cannot be treated as a mere means even to justify the production of a greater good.
(True: And this "means" is why Kant condemned Utilitarianism as an immoral ethical theory. According to the Kingdom of Ends test a person must be treated as an "ends," that is, a worthwhile human being deserving of dignity and respect; and thus any action which treats a person as a tool, an instrument, or a means is demeaning and disrespectful and thus immoral, regardless of the amount of good created.)

85. One problem with Utilitarianism is that there is no principle to in the theory to determine how the greater good should be distributed.
(True: The theory just says that an action is moral if it "produces the greatest amount of good for the greatest number of people" but how this greater good should be distributed is a mystery.)

86. The Rule version of Utilitarianism requires that individual, unique, particular, and concrete actions be subject to the Utilitarian test.
(False: This is the Act version, which focuses on narrow and factual actions, whereas the rule version examines general and broad categories of actions. For example, determining the morality of "bribery in business" is a Rule Utilitarian approach, whereas determining the morality of a specific bribe to a specific foreign official in a specific country by a specific company is the Act Utilitarian approach.)

87. One major criticism of Utilitarianism is that if may sacrifice justice for the minority in an attempt to maximize the greater good.
(True: Everyone gets counted; everyone's pleasure and pain get registered; but when the counting is done if there are more good consequences than bad the action is immoral even if a minority of people were treated in an unjust fashion.)

88. Kant would condemn Utilitarianism as an immoral ethical theory since "the ends do not justify the means."
(True: If the means are immoral because they fail Kant's supreme ethical test, the Categorical Imperative, the action is immoral even if the "ends" are the greater good.)

89. The Agent-Receiver test in Kant's Categorical Imperative is in essence the Golden Rule of the Bible made secular by Kant as an ethical principle.
(True: "Do onto others as you would want them to do unto you," says the Bible. Similarly, pursuant to the Agent-Receiver test Kant would ask one to ask oneself if one would be willing to accept an action if one did not know whether one would be the agent/giver of the action or its receiver; and if not, the action is immoral.)

90. Emotion, according to Kant, is the source and ultimate basis for morality.
(False: Reason, says Kant, is the source and ultimate basis for morality.)

91. One is acting morally, according to Kant, when one seeks to maximize happiness for oneself.
(False: One is acting morally when one is doing one's duty and obeying the reason-based moral "law" as ascertained by the Categorical Imperative, Kant's supreme ethical principle.)

92. The Categorical Imperative, according to Kant, prescribes certain types of action as absolutely morally required, regardless of any particular end or desire.
(True: Have a strong moral character, a "good will," and do one's duty to obey the moral precepts based on the Categorical Imperative, regardless of any particular end or desire. That is, command oneself to do what one's reason tells one is the moral thing to do, and command oneself not to do what one's reason tells one is the immoral thing to do.)

93. Lying is immoral, according to Kant, since lying cannot be logically "legislated" into a universal moral "law" or precept.
(True: Lying, argues Kant, is immoral because it self-destructs when made into a universal principle because if the moral norm was that lying is moral everyone would lie, and no one would believe anyone, and thus lying would lose its efficaciousness. Lying is illogical and thus fails the first test of Kant's Categorical Imperative, the Universal Law test, and consequently lying is immoral.)

94. One problem with Kantian ethics is that two secondary moral rules can pass the supreme ethical principle – the Categorical Imperative – yet conflict.
(True: An example would be as follows: slavery is immoral and lying is immoral based on the Categorical Imperative. As such, what happens when one is forced to lie to protect an escaped slave, since there is a conflict between the two secondary moral rules? One suggestion would be to see if the greater good is accomplished by lying, which perforce takes out of Kantian ethics into Utilitarianism.)

95. Moral rules based on the Natural Law are those legislated by the United Nations.
(False: Natural law is an ethics-based phenomenon and not a legalistic one by the UN or any legislative body. Natural law, as per the philosopher John Locke, encompasses moral standards that exist in the State of Nature and which are discovered by the use of one's reason in order to understand the moral order of things.)

96. The failure to comply with the Natural Law carries civil and/or criminal sanctions.
(False: Natural law is not legalistic law and as such there are no legal ramifications. However, one can be condemned as acting immorally if one violates the ethical precepts of the Natural Law.)

97. According to the philosopher John Locke there is a natural right to own property.
(True: However, this property must be obtained by a person's labor and enterprise by developing the property from the State of Nature when everything was held in common.)

98. One advantage of Locke's Natural Rights theory of ethics is that it can provide very specific and precise rules to guide moral conduct.
(False: There may be agreement as to people having "self-evident" natural rights, such as the right to life, liberty, and the pursuit of happiness, but determining what these rights exactly are is a challenging endeavor.)

99. One problem with Rousseau's Social Contract theory of ethics is that it is very difficult to determine with any exactitude what constitutes the General Will of the people.
(True: Is the General Will a philosophic ideal to be determined by the leadership, or is it a democratic reflection of the will of the people, perhaps obtained by counting votes?)

100. According to Machiavelli, Fate or Fortune rules one-half of a person's actions, and thus a smart person should be prepared to adapt one's actions to the circumstances imposed by Fate or Fortune.
(True: Machiavelli said the Fate flows like a river which at times goes over its banks, so learn to bend with the contours of the river as well as to take precautions against flooding. Do what you can to protect yourself within reason; yet if one is doomed by Fate, then one is doomed.)

101. Kant maintained that since Fate rules all one's actions, one cannot be held morally accountable for bad conduct.
(False: Kant believes in Free Will and thus one can choose to obey the moral "law" as determined by the Categorical Imperative and command oneself to do what is moral and not do what is immoral. Hopefully, one is not unduly influenced by greed, over-arching ambition, or personal gain or pleasure, and thus one will do what one knows is the right thing to do and not do what one knows is the wrong thing to do.)

102. A Kantian resolves moral questions by finding out what most people believe is right.
(False: A Kantian resolves moral questions by applying Kant's supreme ethical principle, the Categorical Imperative, and then reasoning to the right moral answer.)

103. Self-control is a necessary trait of a moral person, according to the German philosopher, Immanuel Kant.
(True: One must have a "good will," that is, the strength of moral character and concomitant self-control to do what one's reason is the moral thing to do and not do what one's reason tells one is the immoral course of action.)

104. Pursuant to the doctrine of Ethical Egoism acting imprudently against one's self-interest is immoral.
(True: However, the Ethical Egoisms would say to take a long-term view of maximizing one's self-interest and thus be willing to underdo some short-term work, pain, expense, and sacrifice to achieve one's greater long-term good.)

105. Ignorance will always excuse a person from any responsibility for acting immorally.
(False: Ignorance may provide an excuse, but not if one as a reasonable person had a duty to know the facts. One cannot simply, as the old saying goes, "put your head in the sand," and then claim ignorance.)

106. The Principle of Last Resort can indicate when one has a moral obligation to act to rescue or help another.
(True: Last Resort, it must be emphasized, is an ethical principle which will tell one when he or she must act morally. There are five requirements to the principle: 1) a peril, that is, someone needs rescuing; 2) proximity, that is, the would-be rescuer is nearby; 3) capability, that is, as Kant said, "ought implies can," and thus the would-be rescuer is capable of bringing about the rescue; 4) last resort, that is, the would-be rescuer is the last realistic alternative to avoid the peril; and 5) the rescuing would not cause harm equal to or greater than the original peril. The classic example is drowning peril where the rescuer is a very good swimmer and the only person close-by and can pull off the rescue without drowning. Then there is a moral obligation to rescue, and not attempting to rescue would subject one to moral opprobrium (but not legal liability as Last Resort is an ethical principle). However, if a big shark appears see the fifth requirement as there will be no moral obligation to rescue, yet if one does rescue despite the danger and one safely returns with the drowning person then the rescuer is now a hero.)

107. If business fails to be socially responsible it thereby automatically immoral too.
(False: Morality is based on ethics; and as such one acts immorally by acting affirmatively in an immoral matter due to the violation of some superseding ethical principle. Also, one acts immorally if one has a moral duty to act and one does nothing. The lack of social responsibility by a business, that is, not being a "good" corporate citizen, not contributing to charities, and not getting involved in community and civic affairs, does not make one immoral (assuming no moral duty to "get involved"), but it does make one socially irresponsible or at the least socially non-responsive.)

108. One's role as a member of a profession may require a degree of altruistic behavior.
(True: Altruistic behavior is being very socially responsible with some real effort, sacrifice, and expense involved. An example would be attorneys who are required by their professional organizations, the state Bar Associations, to perform some pro bono legal services for the poor.)

109. All members of a profession are professionals but not all professionals are members of a profession.
(True: Professionals, such as plumbers and electricians, are professionals, that is, they have special skills, knowledge, and expertise that the public depend on. All members of a profession, such as doctors and lawyers, have this professional knowledge in their respective spheres, and there

certainly is the dependency factor. However, in addition, and most importantly, members of a profession are governed in addition to the law by the Codes of Ethics of the profession, which are rule-oriented, "policed," enforced, and have sanctions for violations, including disbarment from the profession.)

110. According to the economist Milton Friedman the only moral responsibility of the corporation is to make money.
(True: Of course, Friedman would add to make money legally! Yet as a result of this conservative view a corporation cannot be evaluated from an ethical or moral perspective, "merely" a legal one.)

111. If the board of directors take a Utilitarian approach to corporate decision-making they will only focus on maximizing the profits of the shareholders.
(False: A Utilitarian would advise the board to consider the consequences of corporate decision-making on all the stakeholders and constituent groups, including of course the shareholders, affected by corporate decisions.)

112. The function of a corporate ethics audit will be to see if the firm is acting morally.
(True: An ethical or moral audit is beyond an accounting audit or even a legal one. The objective is to ensure that the company is acting in a moral manner.)

113. A true corporate code of ethics need only restate minimum legal principles and rules in a "practices" section.
(False: A true code of ethics will have some aspects that go "beyond the law" to ensure moral conduct too, for example, by giving the employees some type of appeal rights in discharge situations even though none are required under the traditional "employment at-will doctrine." Another example would be a prohibition of any types of payments to foreign government officials even though the Foreign Corrupt Practices Act allows "facilitating and expediting" payments (that is, "grease" money or "tips") as well as payments that are related to the demonstration and explanation of a company's products and services, such as reimbursement for travel, hotels, meals, etc.).

114. An employee is only required morally to engage in "whistleblowing," that is, disclosure of wrongdoing by the employee's company and/or co-workers if the employee is protected by a federal or state Whistleblower Protection Act.
(False: Morality is different from legality, and as such if the employee is a Kantian and it is the employee's duty based on the Categorical Imperative to "blow the whistle," the employee morally must do so regardless of the consequences, including adverse ones to himself or herself, such as the loss of one's job if there is no legal protection.)

115. It would be moral under Kantian ethics for a multi-national corporation to abide by the laws as well as customs and mores where the company does business.
(False: Obeying local laws and customs to achieve morality is an Ethically Relativistic approach to morality, not a Kantian one. Kant would say that if the local laws and/or customs fail the Categorical Imperative, for example, by not providing adequate health and safety protections to workers, they are immoral because they do treat human beings with dignity and respect, even if they are legal and customary.)

116. In order to determine if paying a bribe is moral, a Utilitarian would ascertain the consequences on all the people and entities affected by the bribe, including the host country's society.
(True: The Utilitarians would take a broad stakeholder analytical approach to morality, whereas the Ethical Egoist would just look at the consequences to the company.)

117. A U.S. firm that closes a plant and relocates it overseas will always be committing an immoral act due to the job losses in the United States.
(False: The morality of such an action will depend on the ethical theory being used to evaluate its morality. For example, pursuant to Utilitarianism if there are more good consequences created by moving the plant overseas then the relocation might be moral. The job losses of the U.S. workers would be counted, of course, and their "pain" registered, but that "bad" may be outweighed by a greater good to the shareholders, the employees in the host country, etc. Of course, the Utilitarians would say to always try to minimize the pain of any afflicted stakeholder group, for example, for the U.S. employees who would lose their jobs to get a transfer option, severance packages, and help finding a new job.)

118. If moving a dangerous industry overseas results in more good than bad consequences, then the action is moral pursuant to Kantian ethics.
(False: This is a Utilitarian perspective. For Kant if the work is so dangerous that it is demeaning and disrespectful to the employees and treats them like disposable things or instruments or mere means then the action fails the Categorical Imperative and is immoral regardless of any legalities or greater good produced.)

119. If out-sourcing and off-shoring jobs are legal, then those actions are moral pursuant to the doctrine of Legal Positivism.
(True: Legal Positivism is an ethical doctrine that says what is legal is also moral, period!).

120. If pollution produces more good than bad consequences, then pollution may be moral pursuant to a Utilitarian ethical analysis, even if a local community stakeholder group is adversely affected.
(True: It is the greater good that determines morality under Utilitarianism, which means that there can be some bad consequences, such as to the local community, but if more good consequences are produced for the other stakeholders then the action, such as pollution, would be moral. The pain of the local community members would be registered and counted, of course, but then outweighed by the greater good. Such is the nature of Utilitarianism.)

121. Paying one's workers overseas the legal minimum wage of the host country will very likely mean that the employer is also acting morally pursuant to Kantian ethics.
(False: The employer would be acting morally pursuant to the doctrine of Legal Positivism, but very likely not Kantian ethics as the Kingdom of Ends test in the Categorical Imperative might require the U.S. employer to pay not "merely" the legal minimum but a "living wage" in order to treat its employees with dignity and respect.)

122. Mandatory, random, urine drug-testing will always be regarded as an immoral action pursuant to Utilitarianism because it is very likely that some employees will feel emotionally upset by this practice.
(False: Perhaps under the doctrine of Ethical Emotism the practice might be deemed immoral, but under Utilitarianism if there are more good consequences than bad produced by such testing the practice is moral even though it might upset some people.)

123. Pursuant to the employment at-will doctrine an employee can be discharged for an immoral yet legal reason.
(True: This is the traditional employment doctrine in the United States, though there are exceptions to it. Note, however, that an employee cannot be discharged for an illegal reason as that would convert the discharge into a legally "wrongful discharge.")

124. Kantian ethics demands that an employee not be discharged for an arbitrary or capricious or irrational reason, even if it is legal to do so.
(True: Kant's Categorical Imperative would indicate that such a discharge would be demeaning and disrespectful to the employee who is being treated as a mere thing, for example, a means to vent the employer's spite and anger when the employee's favorite sports team beats the employer's team.)

125. According to the Sophists moral standards are objective, impersonal, universal, and eternal.
(False: Just the opposite, actually the total and complete opposite, as the Sophists were total relativists who did not believe in the objective and universal truth to anything. Everything was personal and relative to you; otherwise it did not matter let alone exist. "Man is the measure of all things, seen and unseen," said the Sophists.)

126. The failure of a business to be socially responsible means that the business is immoral too.
(False: Morality or immorality is based on reasoning from ethical theories and principles; whereas social responsibility or the lack thereof is based on current definitions of the term, usually of a charitable and civic- and community-minded nature. As such, a business can be a moral one, but not be a socially responsible member of the community by not taking part in charitable and civic affairs.)

127. The "value" of morality is an instrumental one according to the Sophists but an intrinsic one according to Kant.
(True: Morality is not real or true but rather has value because it can be a tool, instrument, or means to obtain other things of value, such as money and power, according to the relativism of the Sophists. However, Kant believed that there was intrinsic truth and value to morality, which was "categorically" real and true, as per his Categorical Imperative ethical principle.)

128. Kant's supreme ethical principle, the Categorical Imperative, demands that all people be treated with dignity and respect even if the result is the loss of a very profitable business opportunity.
(True: Disregard consequences, said Kant; and do what is right, that is, obey the Categorical Imperative and thus treat all people with dignity and respect, regardless of any personal loss.)

129. Pursuant to the doctrine of Legal Nonfeasance wealthy, U.S., multi-national corporations have a moral duty to aid the world's poor.
(False: Legal Nonfeasance is a legal and not an ethical principle. Legal Nonfeasance means that as a general rule there is no legal duty to help anyone, aid anyone, or rescue anyone unless there is some type of legal duty to do so, for example, in the case of innkeepers and common carriers. Whether there is any type of ethics-based moral duty for such corporations to help the poor is another question.)

130. A Kantian ethical formalist believes that good results must be measured and weighed against bad results in determining the morality of an action.
(False: Results or consequences of an action are immaterial to Kant; rather, one must concentrate on the action itself and apply a formal test, the Categorical Imperative, to determine if an action is moral.)

131. Obeying legal laws to avoid punishment is Kant's highest stage of moral development.
(False: For a Legal Positivist, perhaps, but not for Kant who believed the highest stage of moral development was the recognition, acceptance, and application of his supreme ethical principle, the Categorical Imperative, to determine the morality, including to determine if the law itself is just and moral.)

132. The overall trend in business today is that business leaders have some responsibility for the moral behavior of their organizations above-and-beyond acting legally.
(True: In many developing countries there may be an absence of law, weak laws protecting workers and the environment, or laws which are not enforced due to corruption. Consequently, there are many worker and environment and consumer organizations that will examine companies to make sure they are not acting in an exploitative and immoral manner.)

133. Long-term self-interest is an example of a rational argument for supporting at least a prudent degree of social responsibility by business.
(True: Studies show that consumers prefer to buy from and people prefer to work for companies that are regarded as "socially responsible." As such, the smart and shrewd business will tie its social responsibility efforts to its mission, brand, values, products, and services, for example. Home Depot being involved with the charity Habitat for Humanity.)

134. Legal Positivists believe that the law must be subservient to eternal, universal, objective moral rules which are part of a larger philosophical ethical system.
(False: Legal Positivists abjure ethical theories and principles as determinants of morality, as there are too many ethical theories, conflicting ethical theories, and always circuitous ethical reason in a vain effort to determine what exactly is moral. Rather, say the Legal Positivist, use the law as the source of and standard for morality; and, accordingly, what is legal is moral, and the obverse.)

135. The philosophical study of business ethics is fundamentally distinct from the general study of ethics since business is all about making money and thus morality is a non-issue.
(False: Philosophy and ethics apply to all human endeavors, including business; and a business would be well-advised and well-served today to consider not merely the profit-making and legal aspects of its operations but also the moral implications.)

136. The view today is that a socially responsible company will always seek to make the maximum amount of money legally for the shareholders.
(False: Today, though the shareholders merit prime consideration, the socially responsible business will engage in "stakeholder" analysis and thus ascertain the effects of business decision-making on other stakeholders or constituent groups affected by its actions, including society as a whole and future generations.)

137. Kantian-based ethics is premised on acting so as to do the greatest amount of good for the greatest number of people.
(False: This is the basis of the Utilitarian ethical theory.)

138. A criticism of the Utilitarian ethical theory is that it focuses mainly on people and society as a whole as opposed to individuals and their rights.
(True: Accordingly, the Natural Law and Natural Rights theorists as well as Kantian ethics would criticize Utilitarians on these grounds.

139. The corporate social responsibility (CSR) approach to social problems will involve a less active role for business and business leaders and managers.
(False: A more active role will be the result; and today there is an expectation that business will be involved; however, that involvement should be in a prudent, smart, and strategic manner.)

140. Current thought in business is that business leaders should take the lead in solving all social problems.

(False: Government (with the power to tax) is supposed to be the primary entity to redress social problems and to provide for the "general welfare" as the Constitution says. Yet business has a role to play by being socially responsible and sustainable, that is, environmentally responsible.)

Multiple Choice Questions

1. A person who believes that moral decisions should be based on the production of the greatest amount of good for the greatest number of people is a follower of what ethical theory?
   a. Utilitarianism
   b. Ethical Relativism
   c. Kantian ethics
   d. Situational ethics
   (The correct answer is a. This is the core principle of the Utilitarian ethical theory. Ethical relativism is societal-based ethics; Kantian ethics bases morality on the form of an action and the application of a formal test and not the consequences of the action. "Situational ethics" is a more relativistic, egoistic, and Machiavellian way of defining ethics.)

2. Which of the following are NOT examples of arguments made against corporate social responsibility (CSR)?
   a. Losing focus of business' traditional primary purpose and diminishing short-term profit maximization
   b. Costs and effort of social, community, and civic involvement
   c. "Big business" has too much power in the community as it is
   d. All of the above.
   (Correct answer is d. All are arguments that have been made against corporate social responsibility. However, the main countervailing argument for CSR is that if done in a moderate, prudent, and strategic way (by tying social responsibility efforts to a business' image, brand, mission products/services) the company and all its stakeholders, including of the course the shareholders, will benefit in the long-run.)

3. Bribery, though commonly thought wrongful, arguably can be considered moral pursuant to:
   a. Utilitarian ethics if the overall greater good is achieved by paying the bribe even though there are certain negative consequences for some stakeholders (such as the competition and the host society).
   b. Ethical egoism from the vantage point of the company paying the bribe if they really need the contract with the foreign government and they have a policy of "letting the locals deal with the locals."
   c. Ethical relativism, if making the "gifts" (that is, "bribe" payments") to foreign government officials is considered to be an acceptable and appropriate practice and custom in the host county.
   d. All of the above.
   (The correct answer is d. These are all logical and reasoned conclusions based on the application of the three ethical theories)

4. All of the following are ethical theories EXCEPT:
   a. Utilitarianism
   b. Kant's Categorical Imperative
   c. SEC Rule 10b(5)
   d. Ethical Egoism

(The correct answer is c. SEC Rule 10(5) is a rule, that is, a law, emanating from a federal administrative agency pursuant to rulemaking proceedings which are quasi-legislative in nature.)

5. Pursuant to traditional philosophical analysis which of the following statements is/are true?
   a. Morals and morality are different from ethics.
   b. Intrinsic values are different from instrumental values.
   c. Cultural relativism is different from ethical relativism.
   d. All of the above

   (The correct answer is d. Morality is the conclusion of what is right or wrong or good or bad, whereas ethics is the philosophical thought-system or intellectual framework which one reasons to what is moral. An intrinsic value is one that is inherently good without the need for any justification or explanation, for example happiness or the appreciation of beauty; whereas instrumental values are good because they are tools or instruments to obtain something else of value, for example, being polite or having money, which one can use to buy things to make you happy! Cultural relativism is merely a descriptive theory which describes cultural mores, for example, some societies bury their dead and others cremate them, or, a more pleasant example, some countries in the Caribbean permit topless bathing while others do not; there is no moral component to it. However, ethical relativism is an ethical theory that sets forth moral precepts; it is prescriptive as well as descriptive. For example, in the Cayman Islands and the Bahamas it very likely would be considered immoral to bathe topless on the beach but in the Dutch and French Islands it would be considered morally permissible.)

6. Which of the following is FALSE about Socrates?
   a. He believed that there was universal, objective, and permanent truth to ethics and morality.
   b. He believed along with the Sophists that virtue comes from having money and the best reputation that money can buy.
   c. His Socratic Method contained an important element of inductive reasoning and argumentation.
   d. He equated virtue with knowledge.

(The correct answer is b. Socrates was a direct opponent of the relativism and disingenuous and specious argumentation and "sophistry" of the Sophists. "Goodness is real, and reality is good," said Socrates. He said that money comes from having virtue, that is, one should be a good and moral person and you will be successful too. All the other responses are hallmarks of Socrates' philosophy.)

7. Which statement is FALSE about the ancient Greek philosophers?
   a. Plato's conception of a Just State is an organizational ideal that evidences a distrust of democracy.
   b. Aristotle's Doctrine of the Mean advises one to be virtuous by selecting the virtuous "mean" between two vice extremes of deficiency and excess.
   c. Aristotle's Ethics of Virtue puts primary emphasis on developing and cultivating good moral traits of character.
   d. The Sophists believed that justice, ethics, and morality were universal, objective, permanent, and unchanging norms and standard

(The correct answer is d. The Sophists were total relativists. "Man is the measure of all things, seen and unseen," said the Sophists. That is, nothing is real intrinsically and certain concepts, such as religion, ethics, morality, and justice, have no intrinsic, universal, and objective value; rather, they merely have instrumental value, that is, they are tools for a smart and shrewd person to acquire power and money. All the other responses reflect fundamental principles of Aristotle and Plato.)

8. Which statement is FALSE about Ethical Egoism?
   a. The doctrine contains an arbitrating principle to justly decide cases of conflict wherein two egos collide in wanting the same thing.
   b. As a general rule, an ethical egoist would advise that it is better to treat people well and with respect than to abuse and belittle them.
   c. As a general rule, an ethical egoist would advise that one should be prepared to undergo some short-term pain and sacrifice in order to obtain greater long-term gain.
   d. Machiavellian "ethics" is an egoistic ethics for the person with a big ego and "princely" ambitions.

(The correct answer is a. One major problem with Ethical Egoism is that it does not contain any arbitrating principle to determine whose ego is satisfied, for example, who gets the job or promotion, when more than one person wants it. Hopefully, rational egoistic people can devise pertinent and legitimate standards for the job or promotion, yet that is not always the case; and consequently when egos collide one may end up a "might makes right" situation, or, as the Sophists said, "Justice is the will of the stronger." The other responses reflect the rational and prudent Ethical Egoism expounded by the English economist Adam Smith.)

9. According to Machiavelli:
   a. People are generally selfish, greedy, treacherous, cowardly, irrational, gullible, short-sighted, and stupid.
   b. Achieving power and success and ultimately fame and glory are the most important moral criteria for any person or enterprise.
   c. A "virtuous" action is anyone that can successfully achieve a desired end, even if the action has been traditionally designated as "bad" or "immoral."
   d. All of the above.

   (The correct answer is d. These are all hallmarks of Machiavellian "ethics." Machiavelli is a follower of the Sophists' relativistic philosophy and as such since there is no universal and intrinsic truth, justice, morality, or ethics, one can use a traditionally "bad" action, such as lying or deceit to achieve an end, such as acquiring money or power, and consequently since the "bad" action was an efficacious, one it can now be called a "good" one.)

10. President Abraham Lincoln very succinctly explained his rationale for his condemnation of and opposition to slavery, to wit: "As I would not be a slave, so I shall not be a master." Lincoln's reasoning *best* exemplifies what ethical theory?
    a. Legal Positivism of Thomas Hobbs
    b. Ethical Relativism of the Sophists
    c. The Categorical Imperative of Immanuel Kant
    d. Utilitarianism of Bentham and Mills.

    (The correct answer is c. This famous quote from Lincoln illustrates clearly Kant's supreme ethical principle, the Categorical Imperative, especially the third test, the Agent-Receiver test, which asks if one did not know what role one would have, that is, the giver of an action, for example, the slave owner, or the receiver of the action, for example, the slave, would one as a rational person be willing to accept the action; and if not, such as the case herein, the action is immoral.)

11. A major criticism that Kant would make of Utilitarianism is that:
    a. It is an egalitarian doctrine that registers the pleasure and pain of everyone affected by an action.
    b. It counts the pleasure and pain of animals since they feel pleasure and pain.

c. It is an immoral ethical doctrine because it can morally legitimize the suffering of a minority in an effort to achieve the greater good for society as a whole.
d. It is difficult to get an accurate definition of "society" in order to determine societal moral norms.

(The correct answer is c. The response in c is the major criticism made by Kant of the Utilitarian ethical theory. Said Kant, how can one have an ethical theory that morally legitimizes pain and suffering of anyone. For Kant one must focus on the action itself to determine morality since consequences are immaterial; whereas for the Utilitarians consequences are the key to morality since if there are more good consequences than bad produced by an action it is moral regardless of the presence of some pain and suffering. Answers a and b can be viewed as positive aspects of Utilitarianism; and answer d is a problem with the doctrine of Ethical Relativism.)

12. What does Kant mean by having a Good Will?
    a. Feeling good about an action so that it is moral pursuant to Ethical Emotism.
    b. Determining what the General Will of society is pursuant to Rousseau's Social Contract theory.
    c. Being nice, polite, and cheerful to people since being nice is an instrumental value.
    d. Having the moral strength of character to do what your reason tells you is the moral thing to do and not to do what you know is wrong.

    (The correct answer is d. Kant said that reasoning to what is right or wrong pursuant to his Categorical Imperative Principle is relatively easy to do. However, the hard part to being moral is to command yourself to do what your mind and reason tell you is the moral thing to do, and not do what your mind and reason tell you is immoral. Having a Good Will means one should do one's duty to oneself, command oneself, have the strength of character and obey the Categorical Imperative to do what is right regardless of the consequences.)

13. Which statement is NOT part of Kant's Categorical Imperative?
    a. When in Rome, do as the Romans would do.
    b. Treat people always with dignity and respect.
    c. Act only under those maxims that you would be willing to have as "universal laws."
    d. Act only if you would be willing to be the agent/giver or the receiver of the action.

    (The correct answer is a. The first response is reflective of the societal-based theory of Ethical Relativism whereby one just has to adhere to societal norms to be moral. The other responses are major components of Kant's supreme ethical principle, the Categorical Imperative.)

14. According to the Natural Law theory of John Locke:
    a. All people are equal and free by the Law of Nature.
    b. One important reason by people in the State of Nature band together and form governments is to protect property rights.
    c. The Natural Law is the only true standard of morality.
    d. All of the above.

    (The correct answer is d. These are all fundamental aspects of the Natural Rights theory.)

15. According to the Natural Rights theory of John Locke:
    a. All people possess in the State of Nature and thus by the Natural Law certain inalienable rights – the right to life, liberty, and property.
    b. Natural Rights supersede any legal, government, or political laws.
    c. Natural Rights supersede any social conventions and local customs.
    d. All of the above.

    (The correct answer is d. These are all fundamental aspects of the Natural Rights theory.)

16. Kant was a believer in:
    a. Fatalism
    b. Determinism
    c. Free Will
    d. Relativism
    (The correct answer is c. Kant is a believer in reason-based ethics pursuant to his Categorical Imperative ethical principle, as well as duty-based ethics, that is, doing one's duty to oneself as a moral person to do what one's reason tells one is the right thing to do and not to do what one's reason tells one is wrong. Consequently, without free will and the freedom and ability to choose the moral course of action Kantian ethics falls apart since one is fated or determined to act morally or immorally. With ethical relativism there is no reasoning component to ethics; rather, one must just be a good observer to ascertain the moral precepts and standards of a particular society, and then merely adhere to them to act morally.)

17. In the old American pre-Civil War South, slavery for many Southerners could be considered:
    a. Moral if one was a Legal Positivist.
    b. Moral if one as an Ethical Relativist
    c. Immoral if one was a Kantian.
    d. All of the above.
    (The correct answer is d. Since slavery was legal under Legal Positivism slavery is moral since the law was the source and standard for morality. If the prevailing thought in the South was that slavery was moral than pursuant to societal-based Ethical Relativism slavery was moral. Kant, of course, would condemn slavery as immoral pursuant to the Categorical Imperative since it is disrespect and demeaning to human beings as it treats them as mere things or property, which indeed it did in the pre-Civil War South in the U.S.)

18. The term "corporate social responsibility" is today BEST defined in the U.S. by:
    a. Federal statutory incorporation law.
    b. Securities and Exchange Commission (SEC) Rule 10b(5)
    c. Kant's ethical writings condemning the corporate form of business for being selfish, greedy and immoral
    d. Current definitions in business of the term which indicate that a company should be socially responsible and thus contribute to charities and civic organizations, but in a prudent and smart manner.
    (The correct answer is d. Social responsibility is not based on the law or ethics but rather on current definitions of the term, which today have a charitable and civic-minded focus.)

19. The BEST approach to social responsibility for business today would be to emulate:
    a. Robin Hood of "Merry Olde England" days (who stole from the rich to give to the poor, and who became a big hero)
    b. Marie Antoinette, Queen of France during the Revolution (who said, when told the poor had no bread to eat, said "Let them eat cake," and who, alas, was beheaded)
    c. Francis of Assisi, the son of a rich Italian merchant, who gave away everything to the poor, including the clothes he was wearing, and thus walked around Assisi naked (but who later became a Saint)
    d. Home Depot for focusing prudently and primarily on Habitat for Humanity in their charitable giving and community help efforts.
    (The correct answer is d. This is a "fun" question but nonetheless provides an excellent illustration of a company engaging in social responsibility in a good and smart and strategic way as its charitable giving is tied to the company's mission, brand, products, and services.)

20. Which is a FALSE statement about social responsibility?
    a. Social responsibility is a "real-world" concern for modern business managers; it is not merely an "academic" issue.
    b. Social responsibility and ethical egoism are not mutually exclusive and contradictory values.
    c. A challenge for business today is to ascertain the exact nature and proper degree of social responsibility.
    d. Social responsibility activities and contributions are mandated legally for large multinational global corporations by the World Bank and the United Nations.

    (The correct answer is b. Social responsibility is not mandated by the World Bank, the United Nations, or for that matter the U.S. government. It can be in the long-term self-interest of a company to be a socially responsible one and thus not antithetical to ethical egoism.)

21. Which of the following is a CORRECT statement regarding the definition of the term "social responsibility" in a business context?
    a. A socially responsible businessperson believes that the formal legal law is inferior to universal moral and ethical principles that can be determined by intuition.
    b. Social responsibility is the branch of philosophy that focuses on morally right and wrong behavior.
    c. Social responsibility is based on current societal views as to how and the extent a business should contribute to charities and civic organizations and be involved in helping the community as well as being environmentally responsible and sustainable.
    d. A business cannot adhere to social responsibility principles and the doctrine of ethical egoism since both are always mutually exclusive.

    (The correct answer is c. Social responsibility is a value separate from the law and legality as well as morality and ethics. However, one can well argue that pursuant to the doctrine of ethical egoism it is in a company's long-term self-interest to be socially responsible as well as environmentally responsible, that is, "sustainable," in a moderate, prudent, and strategic manner for the deservedly good reputation the company will achieve and the resulting good benefits to be derived therefrom by being known as a "socially responsible" firm.)

22. Which of the following is a CORRECT statement regarding the definition of corporate "social responsibility"?
    a. In the interests of preserving personal freedom, the law in the United States codifies in detail social responsibility rules.
    b. For a social responsibility analysis, the acceptable standard for moral behavior is compliance with the legal law.
    c. As a general rule there is no legal requirement for a company to be a socially responsible one and give to charities.
    d. Typically, a business can be sued by community action groups if it is not socially responsible since it is thereby acting immorally in the community.

    (The correct answer is c. Social responsibility is not as a general rule required by the law. Moreover, it is a separate value from morality, which is based on ethics, and consequently the fact that a company is not a charitable and community-minded one does not necessarily make it an immoral company, "merely" a socially non-responsible one.)

23. All of the following are basic social responsibility principles EXCEPT:
    a. The responsibility of business beyond shareholders to stakeholders

b. The responsibility of business to maximize profits in the short term in order to do the most good for the shareholders
c. Sustainability, that is, respect for and preservation of the environment
d. Becoming engaged and involved in civic and charitable activities.

(The correct answer is b. Social responsibility requires that the consequences of a business action on the stakeholders beyond the shareholders, including society as a whole, should be considered when contemplating a decision.)

24. The doctrine that holds that business has an obligation to generally do good charitable deeds for society and be engaged in the community is BEST described as:
    a. Moral minimum
    b. Maximizing profits
    c. Social responsibility
    d. Corporate legal status.

    (The correct answer is c. This is the basic and traditional definition of "social responsibility." Morality is based on ethics, which is a separate value from social responsibility, as is legality. Of course, to be socially responsible a business should be legal and moral too.)

25. Someone who argues that a manufacturer should take into account the interests of the community where it has its plants in decisions involving the plant is arguing MOST DIRECTLY for which value to be applied to business?
    a. Machiavellian ethics
    b. Corporate social responsibility
    c. Maximizing profits in the short-term
    d. Legal misfeasance

    (The correct answer is b. Corporate social responsibility means taking into account the interests of stakeholders, such as the community, beyond the shareholders, as well as taking a long-term view in maximizing profits. Legal misfeasance means that one is acting in violation of some law, civil or criminal.)

26. Which of the following is a CORRECT statement regarding the definition of corporate "social responsibility"?
    a. In the interests of preserving personal freedom, the law in the United States codifies in detail social responsibility rules.
    b. For a social responsibility analysis, the acceptable standard for moral behavior is compliance with the legal law.
    c. A minimum socially responsible standard for business is compliance with the law.
    d. By law in the U.S., an employer typically is required to provide to the mayor of a local community where the employer does business a clear set of social responsibility standards and rules based on the values of the local community.

    (The correct answer is c. In a broad sense social responsibility means: first, acting legally based on the law, which is the minimum standard; secondly, acting morally based on ethics; and then contributing to charities, being engaged in the community, and being "sustainable," that is, environmentally responsible. The standards of a community may have an influence on social responsibility efforts as well as form the basis for moral precepts pursuant to the doctrine of ethical egoism, but social responsibility is not legally required.)

27. A *conservative* interpretation and definition of corporate "social responsibility" would TYPICALLY reflect the view that:

a. Corporate social responsibility should be mandated and closely regulated by global organizations, such as the United Nations.
b. There is insufficient government regulation in the U.S. in place to deal with corporate socially responsible decision-making.
c. Social responsibility decisions in business should be decided by the Environmental Protection Agency according to agency "sustainability guidelines."
d. It could in the long-term, self-interest of business to "get involved" in the community in a prudent manner and then publicize its civic and charitable activities.

(The correct answer is d. Social responsibility done in a smart, shrewd, and strategic manner, which benefits the company and its stakeholders, including naturally the shareholders in the long-rum, should appeal to a person with a conservative mind-set. Social responsibility is not generally required by the law, and certainly a person of conservative political and/or economic beliefs would not want it to be legally dictated.)

28. Which of the following is a CORRECT statement regarding the definition of the term "social responsibility" in a business context?
    a. A socially responsible businessperson believes that the formal legal law is inferior to universal moral and ethical principles that can be determined by intuition.
    b. Social responsibility is the branch of philosophy that focuses on morally right and wrong behavior.
    c. Social responsibility is based on current societal views as to how and the extent the business should contribute to charities and civic organizations and be involved in helping the community.
    d. A business cannot adhere to social responsibility principles and the doctrine of ethical egoism since both are always mutually exclusive.

    (The correct answer is c. Social responsibility is a value distinct from the law and ethics; yet it is influenced by societal beliefs, for example, by including today environmental responsibility in the form of "sustainability" as a component. As emphasized, social responsibility is not mutually exclusive with ethical egoism since it certainly can be in a company's long-term self-interest to be regarded as, and deservedly so, as a socially responsible company.)

29. NOT being socially responsible MOST LIKELY subjects one and one's company to:
    a. Civil legal liability based on the principle of Last Resort.
    b. Criminal legal liability based on the principle of Nonfeasance.
    c. The revocation of its corporate charter, particularly in a liberal state.
    d. Criticism in the local community for not being a "good corporate citizen"

    (The correct answer is d. No one is going to prosecute or sue civilly a company for not be involved in the community or charities in a socially responsible way unless, of course, some law otherwise is violated. Moreover, the lack of social responsibility will not result in a corporate charter being revoked by the state. Consequently, the only negative result is that a company may be condemned for not being socially responsible and such condemnation could harm the company's reputation with its customers, clients, and even its own employees.)

30. Social responsibility can BEST be described as:
    a. Acting legally and morally
    b. Acting in a sustainable, that is, environmentally responsible manner.
    c. Taking an active part in one's community affairs and contributing to charities
    d. All of the above.

    (The correct answer is d. This is the best and broadest description of "social responsibility" that includes the values of legality based on the law, morality based on ethics, as well as the

traditional charitable and civic definition of social responsibility as well as its newer component of sustainability in an environmental protection and conservation sense.)

31. Social responsibility is BEST described as a company being:
    a. Saintly in the moral sense
    b. Helpful and engaged in a prudent and moderate manner in the community
    c. Lawful only
    d. Altruistic to all stakeholders.
    (The correct answer is b. Legality is a foundational element to social responsibility. However, a company need not be "saintly" nor even altruistic, that is, very, very socially responsible at some substantial cost and consequent harm to the owners/shareholders; rather, it is best that a company be socially responsible in a prudent and moderate manner.)

32. Corporate social responsibility (CSR) can BEST be thought of as:
    a. Business giving to charities
    b. Business getting involved in the community with civic events
    c. Business acting in an environmentally sustainable manner
    d. All of the above.
    (The correct answer is d. Again, this is the best and broadest conception of CSR encompassing the traditional definition of charitable and community-engagement as well as the newer component of sustainability. Note that a company should strive to be smart, shrewd, and strategic about its social responsibility activities and efforts and thus seek to tie them to the company's mission, brand, values, products, and services, as well as to get good publicity for these "good" CSR efforts and activities.)

33. The moral theory of ethical relativism can best be characterized by:
    a. The consultation of an outside source, such as an academic book or scholarly person, for moral guidance.
    b. The belief that the moral rules should be determined by persons who do not know whether they would be the giver or receiver of a proposed action.
    c. The belief that a person must decide what course of action is moral based on what a society believes is proper and right.
    d. Determining which course of action produces the greatest amount of good for the greatest number of people.
    (The correct answer is c. Answer b is a statement of Kantian ethics; and answer d is a statement of Utilitarian ethics.)

34. A MAJOR criticism of utilitarianism is:
    a. Moral and ethical rules are too rigid and fixed over time.
    b. Some persons would take actions which they believe to be moral, but which most persons in a society believe to be immoral.
    c. Decisions require the weighing and measurement of qualities and consequences which are not subject to precise determination and measurements.
    d. Decisions are not allowed to take into account a particular person's conscience.
    (The correct answer is c. Utilitarianism is supposed to be, as per its creators Bentham and Mills, a "bookkeeping" or accounting ethical theory; yet it is very challenging to determine the precise measurements of good vs. bad consequences when contemplating a decision. What most people in a society believe is moral is more akin to the theory of ethical relativism.)

35. Kantian duty-based approach to ethics is PRIMARILY based on the concept that one should:
    a. Achieve the greatest good for the most people.
    b. Avoid immoral behavior as determined by reason regardless of the consequences.
    c. Conform to society's moral standards.
    d. Place his or her employer's interests first.
    (The correct answer is b. Kant would say to use one's reason and apply the formal test of the Categorical Imperative to determine if an action is immoral, and if so to abjure it regardless of the consequences. Answer a is a statement of Utilitarianism; answer c is a statement of Ethical Relativism; and answer d is more reflective of Ethical Egoism.)

36. A PRINCIPAL argument against utilitarianism is that it:
    a. Gives profits priority over costs.
    b. Ignores the practical costs of a given set of circumstances.
    c. Justifies human costs that many persons may find morally unacceptable.
    d. Requires cost-benefit analyses of simple situations.
    (The correct answer is c. These are all arguments that can be asserted against Utilitarianism; however, the principal one is that the "ends justifies the means," that is, an action can be moral if the overall result is the production of predominant good consequences even though some bad consequences, pain, and suffering are also created. To paraphrase, Kant, how can one have an ethical theory that morally legitimizes pain, suffering, and unhappiness.)

37. The "Golden Rule," "Do unto others as you would have them do unto you," is most DIRECTLY reflected in which ethical theory?
    a. Ethical relativism.
    b. Utilitarianism.
    c. Ethical fundamentalism.
    d. Kantian ethics.
    (*The correct answer is d. Kant's Agent-Receiver test, which is the third part of his Categorical Imperative supreme ethical principle, is essentially the Golder Rule of the Bible made secular by Kant. Ethical fundamentalism is more reflective of pure religious ethics.)*

38. One MAJOR criticism of Ethical Relativism is that:
    a. Moral and ethical rules are too rigid and fixed over time.
    b. Some persons would take actions which they believe to be moral, but which most persons in a society believe to be immoral.
    c. Decisions require the measurement of qualities which are not subject to precise measurements.
    d. Decisions are not allowed to take into account the mores or customs in a society.
    (The correct answer is b. Since ethical relativism is societal based what a society believes is moral IS moral for that society and thus to be moral one must conform and adopt to the prevailing moral mores and customs, or one should get out of that society.)

39. Kantian ethics can BEST be described by:
    a. The consultation of an outside source, such as an academic book or scholarly person, for moral guidance.
    b. The belief that a person must decide what course of action is proper based on that person's own set of emotions or feelings.
    c. Determining which course of action produces the greatest amount of good for the greatest number of people.
    d. A set of universal moral rules based on reasoning which must be applied regardless of consequences.

(The correct answer is d. Kant says that the supreme, true, and objective ethical principle, the Categorical Imperative, will guide the rational person using his or her reason to determine what is moral or immoral regardless of the consequences. Basing morality on one's feelings or emotions is reflective of the theory of Ethical Emotism or Subjectivism.)

40. Socrates' famous statement: "Goodness is real, and reality is good" is BEST manifested in what ethical theory?
    a. Machiavellian ethics
    b. Kantian ethics
    c. Legal Positivism
    d. Ethical Emotism

    (The correct answer is b. Kant posits his supreme ethical principle the Categorical Imperative as the one true, real, universal, and objective test for morality. Machiavelli does not believe that there is any truth or objectivity to morality; rather, morality is relative to a person, especially a powerful and shrewd person, who can use "morality" as an instrument to achieve the ends of power, fame, and fortune.)

41. Which of the following is the MOST ACCURATE statement?
    a. Immanuel Kant would support the Golden Rule of religion ("Do unto others as you would have them do unto you").
    b. Ethical relativism has been widely adopted as an ethical theory because of its universal moral norms and strict guidelines.
    c. A corporation's board of directors is not allowed to take into consideration the effects of a corporate decision on the stakeholders beyond the shareholders as the duty of the board is to maximize profit for the shareholders.
    d. Social audits are now the legally mandated norm in the corporate governance arena.

    (The correct answer is a. Kant's agent/receiver test, which is part of his Categorical Imperative ethical principle, is essentially the Golden Rule of the Bible made secular by Kant. Ethical relativism is definitely not a universalist ethical theory as it is societal-based and different societies can have differing moral norms and precepts. Today, there are state "constituency" statutes that allow the board, but in most cases do not require the board, to take into consideration other stakeholders, such as the employees and the local community, when making corporate policy decisions. Social audits, that is, to determine if the firm is acting in a socially responsible manner, are not legally required as a general rule, though they certainly are advisable from an ethically egoistic standpoint.)

42. Someone who makes moral decisions ascertaining what a particular society believes is moral is applying which ethical theory?
    a. Ethical Relativism
    b. Utilitarianism
    c. Legal Positivism
    d. Kantian ethics

    (The correct answer is a. This is a basic statement of Ethical Relativism; that is, what a society believes is moral IS moral for that society. Legal positivism is an ethical theory but one that uses the law for the source and standard of morality, and as such "what is legal is moral," and the obverse.)

43. The ethical theory of Ethical Emotism can BEST be characterized by:
    a. The consultation of an outside source, such as an academic book or scholarly person, for moral guidance.
    b. The belief that persons who have a "veil of ignorance" about their place or station or role in society should determine the rules for that society.
    c. The belief that a person must decide what course of action is proper based on that person's own set of feelings and emotional reactions to an event.
    d. Determining which course of action produces the greatest amount of good for the greatest number of people.
    (The correct answer is c. According to ethical emotism if one feels "bad" about an action it is immoral, and the obverse, meaning, of course, that no reason is required, and also that one can be infallible morally so long as one is honestly reporting his or her emotions. The "Veil of Ignorance" is an ethical principle posited by the modern philosopher and political scientist, John Rawls, which is based on Kant's agent/receiver test in the Categorical Imperative. The goal is to establish a society that is just and fair to all regardless of what place, station, or role a person may have in a society.)

44. Someone who believes that moral decisions should be made so that the greatest amount of good in total results from the actions believes in what ethical theory?
    a. Ethical relativism
    b. Utilitarianism
    c. Legal Misfeasance
    d. Kantian ethics
    (The correct answer is b. This is the fundamental tenet of the Utilitarian ethical theory. Legal misfeasance means when one is acting one is acting wrongfully by violating some law, civil or criminal, for which one can be sanctioned by the state.)

45. A MAJOR criticism of Utilitarianism is that:
    a. It is an egalitarian doctrine.
    b. It has a stakeholder analytical component.
    c. Decisions require the measurement of quantities and qualities that are not subject to precise measurement.
    d. Decisions are allowed to try to advance the general welfare.
    (The correct answer is c. The Utilitarian ethical theory requires that the consequences of an action be predicted as to consequences that are probable or reasonably foreseeable and then these consequences must be measured, weighed, and quantified, which can be a very challenging task. All the other responses are positive aspects of the Utilitarian ethical theory.)

46. Which course of action would the AGGREGATIONIST view of Utilitarianism require to be taken:
    a. The one that conforms to societal mores and standards as to what is moral and good.
    b. The one that provides the greatest overall good, even if the benefit of that alternative only flows to a few people.
    c. The one that respects the dignity of all people regardless of consequences.
    d. The one that makes the greatest number of people feel better than they were previously.
    (The correct answer is b. The Aggregationist view of Utilitarianism differs markedly from the Distributionist version which places emphasis of the wider distribution of the good produced by an action even if there is more good produced, yet for fewer people, by an alternative action. The problem arises due to a conflict in the core principle of Utilitarianism, that is, the "greatest good" for the "greater number," meaning there is a conflict and thus two branches of Utilitarianism.)

47. Someone who believes that moral duties are based on universal rules, and that the actor must abide by the same rules being applied to others, believes in which ethical theory?
    a. Ethical Relativism
    b. Utilitarianism
    c. Ethical egoism
    d. Kantian ethics
    (The correct answer is d. This is a fundamental Kantian ethical principle, as indicated in the "universality" part of his supreme ethical principle, the Categorical Imperative.)

48. The "Golden Rule," "Do onto others as you would want them to do unto you," is MOST DIRECTLY reflected in what ethical theory?
    a. Ethical relativism
    b. Utilitarianism
    c. Aristotle's Doctrine of the Mean
    d. Kantian ethics
    (The correct answer is d. Kant took the Golden Rule of the Bible and made it secular in his agent/receiver test, which is part of the Categorical Imperative, his core ethical principle. The agent/receiver asks if one, as a rational person, would be willing to have an action done to oneself if one did not know if one would be the agent, that is, the giver of the action, or its receiver. Aristotle's Mean Doctrine says for one to choose the mean between the two extremes of excess and insufficiency, for example, courage is the mean between being rash and foolhardy and a coward. The mean, said Aristotle, is the correct course of action – practically, theoretically, and morally.)

49. Kantian ethics can BEST be characterized by:
    a. Taking a long-term view of what is best for yourself.
    b. The belief that a person must decide what course of action is proper based on that person's own set of beliefs and feelings.
    c. Determining which course of action produces the greatest amount of good for society.
    d. A set of universal moral rules based on reasoning that must be applied in all situations and characterized by logic, consistency, and rationality.
    (The correct answer is d. Reasoning is key for Kant as one will reason to the existence of the Categorical Imperative as the absolute, objective, and true test for morality. The other responses reflect in order ethical egoism, ethical emotism, and Utilitarianism.)

50. Deontology is another name for:
    a. Ethical relativism
    b. Utilitarianism
    c. Plato's conception of a "just" organization
    d. Kantian ethics.
    (The correct answer is d. "Deontology" means duty-based ethics, which is at the heart of Kantian ethics, as one's moral duty, as established by one's reason, is to obey the Categorical Imperative and as such to act morally and eschew acting immorally regardless of the consequences to oneself and others. Utilitarianism is known as a "teleological" or "consequentialist" ethical system because one determines morality by the consequences of an action and not the action itself, which is neutral for Utilitarians.)

51. Which of the following is NOT part of the beliefs of Kantian ethics?
    a. All like cases should be treated alike.
    b. Treating others as you want to be treated.

c. Choosing a course of action that produces the greatest good for society.
d. Abiding by the rules applied to others in making decisions.
(The correct answer is c. If an action fails the Kant's supreme ethical principle, the Categorical Imperative, the action is immoral regardless of the good consequences it produces and for whom. Kant says to disregard consequences in determining the morality of an action; rather, focus on the action itself and apply to it the formal test of the Categorical Imperative. The other responses all reflect parts of the Categorical Imperative.)

52. One CRITICISM of ethical relativism is that:
    a. It requires people to be culturally competent.
    b. There is no arbitrating mechanism in the doctrine to determine which society's moral precepts are true and right.
    c. Decisions require the measurement of quantities and qualities that are not subject to precise measurements.
    d. It really requires one to take several courses in philosophy and ethics to ascertain what is moral based on this ethical doctrine.
    (The correct answer is b. Being culturally competent should make one a very good ethical egoist as one can discern the mores, customs, and especially the moral precepts of the people of a particular society. However, which society's moral norms are the true and correct ones is not possible to ascertain by this theory since what is morally right for a society is morally right for that society. Measuring good vs. bad is a problem with the Utilitarian ethical theory.)

53. Someone who makes moral determinations based on furthering his or her own self-interest is applying which ethical theory?
    a. Ethical relativism
    b. Utilitarianism
    c. Ethical egoism
    d. Kantian ethics.
    (The correct answer is c. The key word is "ego," though the ethical egoists would say to take a long-term view of maximizing one's own self-interest as well as to as a general rule treat people well as that will inure to one's own benefit in the long-run too. The other responses are major and quite differing ethical theories.)

54. The statements, "Man is the measure of all things" and "Justice is the will of the stronger," can best be attributed to:
    a. Socrates
    b. The Sophists
    c. Aristotle
    d. The Natural Rights theorists.
    (The correct answer is b. These are statements attributed to the Sophists of ancient Greece who were travelling professors, consultants, and philosophers. They did not believe in the universal, objective, intrinsic truth to anything; they were total relativists; but they were also the first ethical egoists as everything was relative to you and to your success, money, fame, and power. As such, even though they did not believe in the intrinsic truth to morality and ethics, they actually taught these subjects because they believed that having such knowledge would be a good, useful, instrumental tool to your gaining a reputation a moral and ethical person, and thereby contributing to your success. The aforementioned statements reflect the Sophists' relativism and egoism and "real-world" objective of acquiring power. Their philosophical opponent in ancient Greece was Socrates, who did believe in the intrinsic, universal, and objective truth to morality and ethics; however, he did not know necessarily what they were!

However, by means of his method of Socratic reasoning, that is, reasoning from particulars to a general principle, he hoped to know the *true meaning to morality and ethics.)*

55. Abraham Lincoln's famous statement regarding slavery, "As I would not to be a slave, so I shall not be a master," indicated that his core ethical principles were based on:
    a. Sophism
    b. Kantian ethics
    c. Ethical Relativism
    d. Democratic-Socialism.
    (The correct answer is b. Lincoln's famous statement was a succinct and rational application of the agent/receiver test of the Categorical Imperative from Kantian ethics. Ethical relativism in the pre-Civil War South, at least for the planter class and perhaps for others, would ethically construe slavery as moral since that was the prevailing moral norm in the South at the time.)

56. Machiavellian "ethics" is basically premised on the views of:
    a. The Roman Catholic Church
    b. Socrates
    c. The Italian political scientist and philosopher, Niccolo Machiavelli
    d. The Italian parliament.
    (The correct answer is c. Machiavelli is a more modern-day, relatively speaking, follower of the Sophists. Since all was relative anyway and since there was no real intrinsic truth to morality or ethics, justice, or virtue, one could in order to obtain power and advance one's "princely" ego do a traditional "bad" act, such as lying or deceit, which if successful is now a "good" act since it helped one achieve power.)

57. Kant condemned Utilitarian ethics as an immoral ethical theory most strongly because:
    a. It is difficult to predict the consequences of an action.
    b. It is difficult to measure quantities of consequences.
    c. It is difficult to ascertain the qualities of consequences produced by an action.
    d. It can treat human beings as means or instruments in order to achieve a greater good.
    (The correct answer is d. All the afore mentioned responses are problems with the Utilitarian ethical theory, but for Kant the major criticism of Utilitarianism was that the "means can justify the ends," that is, an act that harms some people, tramples their rights, and causes pain and unhappiness, might nonetheless be a good act if it produces a greater good for a majority of people affected by the act. The classic example is a foreign "sweat-shop" where the workers are exploited and working under unsafe conditions, but nevertheless the manufacturing facility makes a good product which is sold to U.S. consumers and which causes pleasure to the consumers and certainly the shareholders as well as all the other affected stakeholders. Consequently, the pain of the exploited workers is outweighed by the pleasure to the other stakeholders. So, Kant would say that logically how can one have an ethical theory that morally legitimizes pain-and-suffering; and thus, contends Kant, Utilitarianism is an immoral ethical theory!)

58. Rights-based ethical theories:
    a. Are generally based on producing the greater amount of stakeholder happiness
    b. Determine the moral worth of an action regardless of their production of happiness
    c. Are largely based on the examination of the consequences of an action
    d. Classify corporate social responsibility among the positive rights that must be enforced by government regulatory agencies.
    (The correct answer is b. English philosopher, John Locke, is the major proponent of a rights-based theory of ethics. According to Locke, regardless of the law and consequences of actions

people as human beings have certain natural rights which derive from the natural law which comes ultimately from God. People had these rights, for example, to life, the pursuit of happiness, as well as to the property they found, worked and developed in the State of Nature when there was no government. The purpose of government is to protect legally these rights that people naturally have.)

59. Rights-based ethical theories:
    a. Are generally classified as modern versions of Utilitarianism
    b. Stem from the writings of the English philosopher John Locke.
    c. Are largely consequentialist in nature
    d. Classify corporate social responsibility among the positive rights that must be enforced by government.

    (The correct answer is b. See explanation above. Social responsibility is neither a natural right nor a legal mandate, though, harkening back to ethical egoism, it is a good idea for business.)

60. Which of the following is NOT an accurate statement about the Utilitarian ethical theory?
    a. It determines the moral worth of an action based on what a society believes is morally right
    b. It may allow the personal interests of individuals to be sacrificed in that the collective good be attained
    c. It is usually regarded as a consequentialist ethical theory
    d. It determines the moral worth of an action by whether the action achieves the greatest overall balance of satisfaction over dissatisfaction.

       (The correct answer is a. Answer a is a reflection of the theory of Ethical Relativism. The other responses are accurate statements reflecting the Utilitarian ethical theory.)

61. Which of the following statements is NOT accurate?
    a. One problem for business today is not that businesspeople are immoral or amoral, but that they may be ethically ignorant and/or unaware.
    b. Typically, it is easier for most business people to deal with economic and even legal issues than moral ones.
    c. In the field of moral philosophy, ethics and morality are usually treated as synonymous terms.
    d. Ethics is the theoretical study of morality, whereas morals are views as to what is right or wrong or good and bad.

    (The correct answer is c. Ethics is the branch of philosophy composed of ethical theories and principles that one uses to reason to moral conclusions. Accordingly, ethics consists of the intellectual theories, thought-systems, and theoretical framework that one uses in a logical manner to reason to moral conclusions and moral precepts. Most businesspeople are well-versed in the practical aspects of doing business and certainly are aware of the legal ramifications of business decision-making, but they may be ignorant of the moral ramifications as well as how to handle these moral issues ethically.)

62. Which of the following statements is CORRECT?
    a. Intrinsic values are deemed to be good because of their consequences and because they are a desired means to an end.
    b. Moral rules, as well as exceptions to moral rules, are established by means of ethical principles.
    c. There are no important differences between social conventions and moral rules.
    d. Most moral questions have clearly demonstrable correct answers that can be scientifically established.

(The correct answer is b. Ethical principles derive from ethical theories and are used to reason to moral rules. Ethics, however, since there are many ethical theories as well as the critical fact that the two "modern" ones, relatively speaking, in Western Civilization, Utilitarianism and Kantian ethics, are diametrically opposed, renders ethics and morality not quite "scientifically" precise. Intrinsic values, such as happiness and aesthetics, that is, the appreciation of beauty, especially in art, are good, true, and real without any explanation. Values that are deemed to be merely "instrumental" are good because of the good consequences they produce, for example, being nice and polite to people, even if you do not like them! Social conventions are established by a society for proper behavior in that society; but when they have a moral component they become a moral rule. For example, in some societies the social convention is to allow topless bathing; whereas in other societies topless bathing is regarded as immoral and as such in those societies, by means of the prescriptive ethical theory of ethical relativism, a moral precept against topless bathing has been established, which one should conform to in that society.)

63. Which of the following is NOT an accurate statement?
    a. According to the Sophists, moral terms such as "justice" had no basis or truth in any objective, fixed reality and thus were merely relative terms, relative to the person using them.
    b. The highest stage of moral development according to Lawrence Kohlberg is to obey the law and to uphold the current ruling legal order.
    c. For Plato, the Form of the Good is the final expression and absolute source of morality and goodness.
    d. Plato's theory of Organizational Ethics including his conception of the Just State is a very elitist notion that reflects distrust for the masses and democracy.

(The correct answer is b. For the modern philosopher Kohlberg the highest level of moral development is to be able to reason to moral conclusions based on ethical theories and principles regardless of the law. Merely obeying the law is important, of course, but it is a lesser stage of moral development. Kohlberg, moreover, has created a now famous and widely used test, called the Defining Issues Test, to determine a person's level of moral development or moral maturity.)

64. Which of the following is a CORRECT statement?
    a. Plato likely would object to the hierarchy of authority found today in the typical business corporation.
    b. For Aristotle, the highest good is the fulfillment of the physical senses, though he counsels moderation in seeking pleasures.
    c. Aristotle maintains in the Doctrine of the Mean that the virtuous or moral choice is a rationally determined mean between two extremes of deficiency or excess.
    d. An intelligent person resolves all moral issues by consulting on what most people feel is moral.

(The correct answer is c. As noted, the Doctrine of the Mean is a core ethical as well as practical principle for Aristotle. Seeking and fulfilling the pleasures of the physical senses is a reflection of the hedonistic philosophy, as exemplified by the philosopher Epicurus, who did advice to be moderate in your pleasure-seeking. Plato likely would approve of a hierarchical corporate structure since his conception of a Just State is a hierarchical and stratified one with distinct roles for the people on each level, with the educated and wise rulers, of course, being on top! Determining morality by searching out how people feel about a issue can be a very exhaustive, personal, subjective, variegated, conflicted and thus confusing undertaking.)

65. Which of the following is NOT accurate?
    a. One benefit to being a sincere ethical emotist is that one is morally infallible.
    b. One convenience to being an ethical emotist is that one can change one's mind about a moral issue simply by expressing a different feeling about an action.
    c. Morality is a societal-based phenomenon according to the doctrine of ethical relativism.
    d. Cultural relativism is a prescriptive ethical theory that sets forth moral norms.

    (The correct answer is d. Cultural relativism is merely a descriptive theory; it only describes the fact that there are different societies with different customs, practices, and conventions. There is no moral component to it. However, when one is making a moral conclusion based on a societal precept then one is now engaging in a prescriptive ethical theory, to wit, ethical relativism. For example, one can say that in the Caribbean there are some islands, Dutch and French, that have topless bathing; whereas other islands, English, for example, the Caymans Islands and the Bahamas, do not have it, and these statements are merely descriptive. However, when one adds that the people in Bahamian and Cayman society believe that topless bathing is immoral, then one is engaging in the prescriptive theory of ethical relativism.)

66. Which of the following is a CORRECT statement?
    a. One advantage to ethical relativism is that it is very easy to determine what a society is for the purposes of the doctrine.
    b. An ethical relativist would deny that there are moral standards that are universally true for all peoples in all societies for all times.
    c. One advantage to ethical relativism is that different societal practices can be morally compared, evaluated, ranked, and ultimately be judged right or wrong.
    d. If one is an ethical relativist, it is right and proper to criticize the moral practices and beliefs of one's own society.

    (The correct answer is b. Ethical relativism is, as emphasized, a relativistic ethical theory in which morality is societal-based, that is, what a society believes is moral is moral for that society. Therefore, one cannot criticize one's own society since the prevailing moral belief is the standard for morality. One thus should just conform and adopt. Of course, there are many societies and consequently there is a divergence of mora beliefs, with some beliefs contradictory, and there is no arbitrating mechanism in the theory to determine which societal belief is true and correct.)

67. Which of the following is a CORRECT statement?
    a. According to the Utilitarian ethical theory, a personal and subjective calculation of the good is required since some people are more important and worthwhile than others.
    b. Utilitarianism underscores the long-term consequences of an action in determining its morality.
    c. Even though some consequences will never be fully knowable, a Utilitarian would advise that one guess and speculate as to the consequences in order to determine the morality of an action.
    d. Since money is too materialistic a good, it cannot be used as a measurement in quantifying pleasure and pain.

    (The correct answer is b. Utilitarians say to take a long-term perspective in determining the consequences of an action; yet not so long as to engage in guessing and speculation; rather, using, in their terms, "history as your guide" and your "common storehouse of knowledge" look for the probable, likely, and reasonably foreseeable consequences that an action would produce. Utilitarianism is a very egalitarian ethical theory. A core principle is that "pleasure and pain are the sovereign masters of human beings," and as such people seek pleasure and avoid pain. There are no "privileged" people in the Utilitarian ethical concept since all feel

pleasure and pain equally as human beings. Money certainly can be calculated and counted for Utilitarians since money can be instrument to secure pleasure.)

68. Which of the following is NOT an accurate statement?
    a. One major criticism of Utilitarianism is that it may sacrifice justice and trample rights of the minority in an attempt to maximize the greater good for the majority.
    b. It is possible pursuant to Utilitarianism to ethically legitimize an action as moral even though it causes pain and exploitation.
    c. Kant would condemn Utilitarianism as an immoral ethical theory because he maintains that the "ends do not justify the means."
    d. Emotion, according to Kant, is the source and ultimate basis for morality.
    (The correct answer is d. Reason, said Kant, is the source and ultimate basis for morality; and as such a rational and logical person will reason to the existence of Kant's formal ethical test for morality, the Categorical Imperative, as the true, supreme, objective, and absolute test for morality. Based on the Categorical Imperative Kant condemned Utilitarianism as an immoral ethical theory since it could morally justify the pain and suffering of the few to promote the pleasure and happiness of the many.)

69. Which of the following is NOT a correct statement?
    a. A categorical imperative, according to Kant, prescribes certain types of actions as absolutely necessary from a moral vantage point regardless of any end or result or any particular desire.
    b. When Kant emphasizes the concept of "good will," he means to have fun and enjoy life because life is short and uncertain.
    c. Lying is immoral according to Kant because lying cannot logically be "legislated" into a universal moral law.
    d. Utilitarianism fails the second test of Kant's Categorical Imperative – the Kingdom of Ends test – because people cannot be treated as mere means even to justify the production of greater good.
    (The correct answer is b. Having a "good will," said Kant, means that one should have the moral character and moral strength to do what is morally right based on the Categorical Imperative ethical principle and not do what is morally wrong, regardless of the consequences, including to oneself. As per lying, Kant would say that on rational person would want to live in a society where lying is the permissible moral norm, and as such it cannot be made into a universal moral norm.)

70. Ethics is BEST described as:
    a. The study of ultimate reality.
    b. The theoretical study of morality.
    c. The constitutional analysis of equal protection and due process decisions
    d. None of the above.
    (The correct answer is b. Metaphysics is the study of ultimate reality, that is, what is really real; whereas ethics is the branch of philosophy consisting of ethical theories and principles that one uses to reason to morality. The law, of course, is separate from ethics and morality, though, of course, one hopes that the law is moral and just.)

71. Instrumental values can be BEST described as:
    a. Useless since they have no intrinsic worth.
    b. Useful because they can be used as a means to produce or achieve other values or things of worth.
    c. Useful only when they are legislated into law.
    d. None of the above.

(The correct answer is b. Even though a value, such as morality, may have no intrinsic worth, that is, not being absolutely real or true, it can, as per the Sophists, have instrumental value since it can be a tool or means to produce or lead to something else of value, for example, being perceived as a moral person or business. Legality is separate from morality and ethics. There are legal sanctions for non-compliance with the law, but no one is going to sue a person for acting immorally unless some law is otherwise violated. Yet, there may be non-legal adverse consequences for a person, or a business being perceived as immoral, for example, not having friends, associates, customers, clients, and employees.)

72. Ethical relativism is BEST described as what type of a theory?
    a. Legal since it is based solely on a society legislating laws.
    b. Prescriptive since it sets forth moral norms.
    c. Descriptive since it reports on different customs and practices.
    d. None of the above.

    (The correct answer is b. Ethical relativism is an ethical theory that is prescriptive since it sets forth moral norms based on societal beliefs. However, these societal moral norms may be legislated at some point into law. Cultural relativism is the merely descriptive theory which merely describes different societies and their customs and beliefs but without stating any moral norms or precepts.)

73. Ethical egoists TYPICALLY and prudently would say that the doctrine of ethical egoism:
    a. Has no limits if one has a "big ego" and a lot of power.
    b. Is constrained by taking a long-term approach.
    c. Is constrained because it is often in one's self-interest to take the interests of others into account.
    d. B and C.

    (The correct answer is d. The classical "modern" ethical egoist, the English philosopher and economist, Adam Smith, would argue that one to be a true and successful ethical egoist should take a long-term perspective in maximizing one's self-interest, and thus be willing to undergo some present pain, expense, and effort in order to maximize one's future greater good. Moreover, even if one has a big ego and a great deal of power Smith would also argue to treat people well, that is, make them part of your team, co-op them if necessary, and certainly do not insult, abuse, or bully them since to do so is immoral because such bad behavior will likely come back to hurt one in the long-term.)

74. The MAJOR problem with the doctrine of ethical egoism:
    a. Most people are shy and hesitant about seeking to fulfill their self-interest.
    b. Most people are usually more interested in the welfare of other people than themselves.
    c. The doctrine does not provide a mechanism to settle differences when egos clash.
    d. If each person satisfies his or her self-interest, the general welfare will be served.

    (The correct answer is c. Similar to ethical relativism when societal moral beliefs clash, there is no arbitrating mechanism in ethical egoism to decide whose ego should be satisfied, for example, who gets the position or promotion. As such, the doctrine can lead to a situation of "might makes right," that is, the person with the biggest ego and the most power will get what he or she wants. Adam Smith argued as per his

    "invisible hand" theory that if everyone seeks to fulfill their own self-interest society and the general welfare will be served because people will be doing what they want, and they will do it well and thus there will be more money, goods, services, and efficiencies. As Smith said, "the baler bakes bread for money not benevolence.)

75. The famous French adage, "The heart has its reasons that reason knows not," is MOST ACCURATELY reflected in what ethical theory?
   a. Kant's Categorical Imperative.
   b. Ethical Relativism.
   c. Ethical Emotism
   d. Legal Positivism.
   (The correct answer is c. This statement is a reflection of the ethical emotism theory whereby one's feelings, emotional reactions, and conscience determine morality, and neither reasoning from ethical principles, nor societal standards, nor the law.)

76. One ADVANTAGE of Ethical Emotism as an ethical theory is:
   a. The constancy and reliability of feelings as a moral guide.
   b. Moral infallibility in making moral judgments.
   c. The use of reason in resolving moral disputes.
   d. Moral objectivity and universality.
   (The correct answer is b. As long as one is reporting one's emotional reactions to an action correctly and honestly one is making a true and infallible moral conclusion, yet so is everyone else even if a differing emotion produces a different moral reaction. The result, of course, is subjectivity and moral conflict and complexity if not chaos.)

77. According to ethical relativism:
   a. There are no moral standards which are universally true.
   b. Morality is societal-based.
   c. Different societies have different views as to what is right and wrong.
   d. All are true.
   (The correct answer is d. These are all basic elements of the theory of ethical relativism, wherein one does not need to be a philosopher or ethics scholar to determine morality; rather, one just needs "sharp eyes and ears" on the ground to determine accurately what the moral norms of a society are, for example, making a nice culturally appropriate "gift" to a government official, and then to conform and adapt to them, and thus one will be acting morally, at least in that society where one is or one is doing business.)

78. A PROBLEM with the theory of ethical relativism is:
   a. Defining the appropriate "society."
   b. The inability to make comparative moral judgments between and among societies.
   c. The inability to criticize a society as immoral for its moral norms.
   d. All are problems.
   (The correct answer is d. These are all problems! One cannot criticize another society since its moral beliefs are true for that society. Moreover, one cannot even criticize one's own society. It is impossible to determine, furthermore, which society's moral beliefs are true and correct since what a society believes is moral is moral for that society.)

79. Pursuant to Legal Positivism:
   a. There is no such thing as a bad or unjust law.
   b. The law is the basis for morality.
   c. If one is acting legally, then one is acting morally.
   d. All are true.
   (The correct answer is d. Since pursuant to the doctrine of Legal Positivism, as created by the philosopher Thomas Hobbes, the law is the source and standard for morality, and thus what is legal is moral and what is illegal is moral. The result is that there is no such thing as an unjust or immoral law since the law is also the moral precept. For example, in the pre-Civil War South in

the U.S. slavery was legal, and as such pursuant to Legal Positivism was also moral. Of course, the law can be changed but there may be moral reasons to seek a change in the law, which means another theory may be intruding upon and superseding Legal Positivism.)

80. A PROBLEM with the Utilitarian ethical principle is that:
    a. It is difficult to foresee the long-term consequences of an action.
    b. It is difficult to weigh and measure the good v. bad consequences of an action.
    c. It is difficult to ascertain how the good should be distributed.
    d. All are problems.
    (The correct answer is d. These are all problems, yet the main problem, at least according to the German philosopher Immanuel Kant, is that the "ends can justify the means" with this theory; that is, if an action produces greater good consequences the action is moral even though it causes some pain, unhappiness, and dissatisfaction.)

81. One ADVANTAGE of the Utilitarian ethical principle is that:
    a. It is very egalitarian as all people and groups affected are counted.
    b. It has a broad stakeholder component that is similar to modern business constituent group analysis.
    c. It conforms to the way most people think about acting by focusing on the consequences of an action.
    d. All are advantages.
    (The correct answer is d. Most people, especially business people today, are well versed in stakeholder analysis, which forms a principal part of the Utilitarian ethical theory. Moreover, most people think in terms of ascertaining if an action will produce more good or bad consequences, yet they reflect just on themselves; but the Utilitarians say to broaden the scope of the analysis to consider other stakeholders affected by the action beyond oneself.)

82. According to Kant, morality is FUNDAMENTALLY based on:
    a. What society believes is moral.
    b. A determination of the greater good.
    c. Reason and rationality.
    d. What the law says is legal.
    (The correct answer is c. Reason and rationality are the fundamental components of Kant's ethical theory and his supreme ethical principle, the formal test of the Categorical Imperative, which supersedes consequences, societal beliefs, and the legal law.)

83. According to the Universal Law principle in Kant's Categorical Imperative, what is moral basically depends on:
    a. What the United Nations says is legal.
    b. What a country's legislature says is legal.
    c. What a society regards as moral law.
    d. What would happen, using one's reason, if all people followed a particular action?
    (The correct answer is d. By "universal law," Kant does not mean any legalistic type of law from any government entity; rather, he means that logically ask yourself what would happen if an action, for example, lying, stealing, or cheating, was made a universal moral law in a society? Would anyone who is rational want to live in such a society where it is moral to do these actions.)

84. By having a "good will," Kant FUNDAMENTALLY meant that one:
    a. Should use one's conscience and intuition to determine morality.
    b. Should have the strength and will-power to get power and position and to achieve one's goals.

c. Should have the strength of character to do what is morally right and not do what is morally wrong.
d. Should always be the first to buy a "round of drinks" for one's friends at Happy Hour.

(The correct answer is c. As emphasized, Kant means by "good will" to command yourself to do your moral duty, based on reasoning from the Categorical Imperative, do what is morally required and not to do what is immoral, regardless of any consequences, including to yourself.)

85. Social responsibility theories:
    a. Are generally classified as modern ethical versions of Utilitarianism
    b. Determine the moral worth of an action regardless of their consequences
    c. Are largely precise legalistic formulations
    d. Classify corporate social responsibility as typically the corporation engaging in community and civic affairs in a prudent manner.

    (The correct answer is d. Social responsibility is a value distinct from morality and ethics as well as the law. It is neither mandatory legally or required morally, but it is a very good and instrumental value for business today to engage in social responsibility actions in a prudent, smart, and strategic manner.)

4 - Constitutional Law

Introduction

The U.S. Constitution is the supreme law in the United States. The Constitution has two major purposes: first, to set up the government, which is a federal system composed of a national, called "federal" government, and constituent government entities called "states"; and second, to protect the people by means of the Bill of Rights from the very government that the Founding Fathers set up in the Constitution. The Constitution by means of the power granted to Congress by the Interstate Commerce Clause in Article I is also the source of the government's power to regulate business. The Constitution protects "persons," including corporations (for most protections in the Bill of Rights) against abuse of power by government – all levels and entities of government, including government as an employer. When government acts the term that is used to trigger constitutional protections is called "state action," though as noted any governmental action can be the trigger. Consequently, the student must be cognizant of the fact that the federal Constitution (with the exception of the 13th Amendment prohibition against slavery and involuntary servitude) does not apply to the private sector, and thus, though a common misconception, the federal constitution does not provide a private sector employee with rights that can be asserted against his or her private sector employer.

The student must comprehend seminal Constitutional concepts, to wit: federalism, the Separation of Powers, whereby power on the national level is divided between the legislative power of Congress in Article I to make law, the executive power in a President in Article II to enforce the law, and the judicial power in the Supreme Court (and the "lower" federal courts to be created by Congress) to ensure that laws comport with the Constitution; and the system of Checks and Balances, whereby the branches of government have certain checks and balances on the others, for example, Congress making law, the President signing or vetoing law, Congress being able to override a veto, and the Supreme Court to ensure that any law passed by Congress is constitutional. The student also must know that the powers not granted to the national government, mainly the enumerated powers given to Congress in Article I, are reserved to the states.

Regarding the powers of Congress in Article 1, the student must be aware of the afore mentioned power of Congress to regulate commerce among the states as well with foreign nations, the power to tax, as well as the "Necessary and Proper" clause, which gives Congress the power to make laws which are necessary and proper for carrying out its enumerated powers, thereby creating a source of "implied" powers for Congress. The President's power is found in Article II, the most important parts of which are the "Take Care" clause, which grants the President the executive power to "take care that the laws be faithfully executed," as well as the President being deemed the Commander-in-Chief. Article III sets forth the Supreme Court' original and appellate jurisdiction, and Article III also extends the federal judicial power to "inferior" federal courts as Congress deems necessary to establish, for example, the federal courts of appeals with appellate jurisdiction, the federal district courts with original jurisdiction, and specialized federal courts, such as bankruptcy courts. The student also must know that federal judicial power extends to "cases and controversies," that is, actual, concrete, and factual disputes where the litigants have adverse interests, and that federal jurisdiction applies to cases with "federal questions," that is, arising out of the Constitution or the laws of the U.S., as well as "diversity" cases, that is, cases between citizens of different states (noting that for the latter the amount in controversy must be at least $75,000).

As emphasized, critical to business and thus to business students is the Interstate Commerce Clause that is the source of the government's power to regulate business. The student must clearly understand that, as per Supreme Court interpretation, the power of Congress to regulate interstate commerce is very broad indeed, encompassing the power to regulate commercial and non-commercial activities, activities that directly or indirectly affect interstate commerce, including activities that are wholly intrastate. However, the student must know that there still is room for state regulation if there is no express federal prohibition and if there is no discrimination against interstate commerce and the state regulation does not unduly interfere with or burden interstate commerce. The student also must be aware of the Preemption doctrine, which arises when federal regulation of a subject matter is so extensive and pervasive that no state regulation is permitted since Congress has "preempted" the field.

The first ten amendments to the Constitution are collectively known as the Bill of Rights. The student should be familiar with these amendments and how they have been interpreted by the Supreme Court and the federal courts, especially as pertaining to business. The student also should be aware of the Due Process and Equal Protection clauses of the 5th and 14th amendments. Particularly important is the Due Process clause, going back to the Magna Charta of 1215 in England, whereby government cannot take away life, liberty, or property, for example, fining a business, without "due process" of law, meaning essentially notice of the proposed government action and a fair hearing. Also, very important to the student is the 1st Amendment right to freedom of speech, which right corporations possess too. The student, especially the business student, must be able to define and differentiate "political speech" from "commercial speech," that is, for the latter advertising and marketing. Concomitantly, the student must know the two differing tests that are used to regulate speech, that is, the "compelling interest" test for political speech and the "substantial interest" test for commercial speech. Moreover, for the latter, the student must comprehend the degree of protection afforded to the advertising and marketing of "vice" (though of course legal) products and services, and the critical distinction the courts make as to the targets of any advertising and marketing, that is, to adults as opposed to children. Regarding the 4th Amendment's prohibition against unreasonable searches and seizure, the student should be aware of the differing requirements for a warrant, that is, for a law enforcement warrant under the criminal law as opposed to an agency inspection pursuant to administrative law, which latter topic will be addressed more fully in the administrative law section to this book. Finally, the student must understand the government's power of Eminent Domain as well as the restrictions on this power imposed by the 5th Amendment to the Constitution.

True and False Questions with Answers and Explanations

1. The federal Constitution grants constitutional rights to private sector employees.
(False: The Constitution grants people rights which they can assert against government, including public sector employers. Note that a few states, such as California, grant some constitution rights, such as privacy, to private sector employees.)

2. The federal Constitution does not protect corporations since they are artificial legal business entities created pursuant to state law.
(False: Though an artificial legal entity a corporation nonetheless possesses most constitutional rights, such as First Amendment freedom of speech, but not all rights, such as the Fifth Amendment protection against self-incrimination.)

3. The statement in the Magna Carta (1215) that no person "shall be taken or imprisoned or disseized or outlawed or exiled or in any way destroyed…except by the lawful judgment of his peers and the law of the land" is the foundation for constitutional Due Process and trial by jury rights.
(True: The essence of Due Process is that when government seeks to deprive a person of "life, liberty, or property" he is she is entitled to notice and a fair hearing, which in certain circumstances includes the right to a trial by jury.)

4. The federal government in the United States possesses all the powers not specifically granted to the states in the Constitution.
(False: Just the opposite, as the federal government is only granted specific powers, called "enumerated powers," in the Constitution whereas all powers not given to the federal government are reserved to the states.)

5. Congress cannot regulate commerce solely within a state as the regulation of such commerce is a prerogative of the state, which existed before the federal government.
(False: Even solely intrastate commerce can be regulated by Congress if the commerce has an impact on interstate commerce which Congress can regulate pursuant to the Commerce Clause in the Constitution. A state by controlling activities within its borders nonetheless cannot substantially impair interstate commerce, or substantially hinder interstate commerce, or lock in its economy to commerce from other states. For example, a state can require interstate truckers to stop at a weigh station to determine the weight of the truck for road tax purposes, but a state cannot require a trucker to stop at the border to change the mud flaps on the truck since the state believes one type of mud flap to be superior to another as changing flaps at the border would substantially impede interstate commerce. Similarly, a state cannot prohibit the importation of materials into the state, even waste materials for landfills, as that would be tantamount to locking-in the state's economy.)

6. Certain Constitutional protections apply to corporations even though the corporation is a not a real person, but an artificial entity created pursuant to state law.
(True: For example, the corporations have First Amendment free speech rights as well as 14th Amendment due process protections, but not the 5th Amendment privilege against self-incrimination.)

7. The Bill of Rights in the U.S. Constitution confers absolute rights to the people which cannot be abridged or diminished by the courts.
(False: Constitutional rights are not absolute, as exemplified by the famous statement by Justice Holmes regarding the First Amendment free speech rights that "one cannot yell fire in a crowded theater." Another example would be the First Amendment right of freedom of religion which was not construed to allow the Mormons to practice polygamy.)

8. First Amendment rights to political speech do not include corporations since they typically are big, wealthy, and powerful and their political speech would unfairly dominate the political arena.
(False: Corporations not only are treated as natural persons for First Amendment free speech rights (both political as well as commercial speech) but the Supreme Court in the famous Citizens United case ruled that these rights extend to publicizing their positions on political issues and candidates but not directly giving money to candidates or campaigns.)

9. If there is a conflict between a federal law and a state law the federal law will supersede the state law, even a state constitutional law.
(True: Federal law is superior due to the Supremacy Clause in the Constitution.)

10. Commercial speech receives greater protection by the federal courts pursuant to the Constitution than political speech since marketing and advertising are essential aspects to a capitalistic system.
(False: Commercial speech, though protected as speech even with a monetary motive, is accorded less protection than political speech. The former can be regulated according to the Supreme Court if the government has a "substantial government interest" whereas the latter can only be regulated if the government can be the much more demanding "compelling interest" test.)

11. The Bill of Rights in the U. S. Constitution protects citizens from abuses and the trampling of their rights in both the public and private sectors.
(False: The Bill of Rights provides protections only against government abuse and contravention of rights, including federal, state, and local governments, government agencies, and government employers. There may be many rights that one can assert against, for example, a private sector employer, such as the Civil Rights Act, which is based on Congress' power to regulate interstate commerce, but at the federal level a private sector employer does not "owe" its employees any constitutional rights.)

12. The Bill of Rights protects only the interests of real, natural people, and not corporations since the corporate form of business did not exist when the Bill of Rights was promulgated.
(False: The Supreme Court has ruled that most of the protections of the Bill of Rights, such as the First Amendment free speech provisions, do apply to corporations even though the corporation is "only" an artificial legal person created by state law. An example of a right that the corporation would not have is the 5th Amendment privilege against self-incrimination.)

13. As a general rule government can regulate the context of speech but not the content.
(True: The courts grant government a great deal of latitude in regulating the context of speech, that is, where and when one or a group may exercise free speech rights, the need to obtain a permit, the posting of a bond, the need to supply bathroom facilities, and the requirement to stay within police lines and/or barricades. However, government cannot discriminate in the afore mentioned requirements depending on whether certain speech is "favored" or not.)

14. The 4th Amendment prohibits all searches unless government obtains a warrant supported by probable cause and signed by a judge.
(False: Under the 4th Amendment government agencies are allowed to conduct inspections with "blanket warrants" whereby the agency, for example, OHSA, inspects certain businesses in certain areas for health or safety violations. Probable cause of a violation is not required, as in a traditional police warrant, so long as the inspection is within the scope of the agency's regulatory authority.)

15. The Fourth Amendment protects only persons and not businesses.
(False: Businesses, including corporations, have 4th Amendment rights, though the standards for an administrative inspection of a business are less stringent than a traditional law enforcement search.)

16. In order to restrict commercial speech, that is, advertising and marketing, in a state the legislature only needs to show that the speech causes too much consumption of goods or services in the state.
(False: The test for restricting commercial speech is that the government must show that there is a "substantial government interest" involved, and it is very dubious that causing people to purchase a great deal of legal goods or services without any deception will be sufficient.)

17. The constitutional right to procedural Due Process typically requires that before the government can fine a person, he or she must be accorded notice and a fair hearing.
(True: This is a fundamental legal principle in the 14th and 5th Due Process clauses in the Constitution, which protections go back to the English Magna Charta in 1215.)

18. A federal legal system is one in which there is a division of power between a national government and constituent government entities.
(True: This is a basic proposition. The U.S. as per the Constitution is a federal system with a national, that is, federal, government and states, as is Mexico. Canada is also a federal system with a national government and provinces.)

19. The First Amendment to the U.S. Constitution sets up in Article I the Executive branch of government.
(False: The First Amendment, guaranteeing freedom of speech, religion, assembly, and petitioning the government for grievances, is the first amendment in the Bill of Rights. The Executive branch, moreover, is set up in Article II of the Constitution. The legislative branch, Congress, is created in Article I.)

20. It is likely that a private sector employee who wants to challenge his or her employer's policy of mandatory drug testing will be unsuccessful legally on federal constitutional grounds.
(True: The rights accorded in the Constitution, such as the right to privacy and the 4th Amendment prohibition against unreasonable search and seizure, apply only to government, including government employers, and not the private sector.)

21. The Exclusionary rule maintains that evidence obtained by means of an illegal search and seizure is not admissible in a court of law.
(True: This is a basic principle of the Fourth Amendment, though there are some exceptions.)

22. The individual states in the U.S. are allowed to regulate certain aspects of interstate commerce so long as the state law neither discriminates against interstate commerce nor unduly burdens or impedes interstate commerce.
(True: For example, differing state speed limits as well as weigh stations for trucks for road tax purposes would be permissible; but forcing a trucker to change mud flaps or forbidding certain types of fruits or vegetables to protect local farmers would be impermissible.)

23. The Constitution provides that both the states and federal government have joint jurisdiction over foreign commerce.
(False: The Constitution expressly grants to the federal Congress the exclusive right to regulate foreign commerce.)

24. The Supremacy Clause of the Constitution has been interpreted by the Supreme Court to mean that any state or local law that conflicts with the Constitution is unconstitutional and invalid.
(True: This principle even applies to state constitutional law.)

25. Pursuant to the Takings Clause of the 5th Amendment government can take private property for a public purpose or use but only with the consent of the property owner.
(False: Consent is not necessary. A "taking" can be forceful; but the government must provide just and fair compensation to the property owner whose property was seized for the "public good.")

26. Pursuant to the Commerce Clause in Article I as interpreted by the Supreme Court all state restrictions on interstate commerce are invalid.
(False: States can regulate certain aspects of interstate commerce so long as they do not unduly burden or impede interstate commerce or discriminate against interstate. States can neither "lock-in" their local economy nor "look-out" competition from other states, nor can states unduly hinder the "free flow" of interstate commerce.)

27. Small and medium-sized businesses really do not have to worry about government regulation by administrative agencies since they are focused on large and powerful corporations.
(False: All businesses must be concerned with regulatory law by administrative agencies. Moreover, even if a federal agency chooses not to exercise jurisdiction because the business or dispute is too small, there very likely will be a corresponding state agency that will have jurisdiction. These state regulatory agencies are at times colloquially called "baby" agencies, such as a "Baby FTC" which would parallel the Federal Trade Commission headquartered in Washington, D.C.)

28. A standard criticism of administrative agencies is that the enabling legislation that creates them and gives them legal authority to make rules and regulations is too narrowly drawn thereby substantially curtailing the agency's authority.
(False: Just the opposite, as the criticism is that legislative bodies give the agency too much power by giving them wide authority to make law with only the most general standards, for example, the Federal Communications Commission which is granted the power to regulate communications and grant licenses in the "public, interest, convenience, and necessity.)

29. Agencies can make rules and regulations and legally hold that the violations of these rules and regulations will be a crime as well as a civil wrong.
(False: Agencies cannot define and create crimes; only a legislative body can do that. However, a legislative body can convert the civil violation of an agency rule into a crime, for example, when Congress criminalized the Securities and Exchange Commission's Rule 10b-5 prohibition against insider trading into a crime (actually a serious crime, a felony, with possible imprisonment of up to 20 years as per the Sarbanes-Oxley Act of 2002).

30. The Separation of Powers doctrine established in the Constitution for the federal government also prohibits administrative agencies from exercising executive and legislative powers.
(False: As opposed to the federal government as set up in the Constitution, where there are three distinct branches of government, in an administrative agency one finds a combination of powers as agencies not only have the legislative power to make laws by rulemaking, the executive power to investigate and to enforce laws, and the judicial power to determine violations of its laws.)

31. As a general rule when a court on appeal reviews an agency decision it will not inquire as to the wisdom of the decision.
(True: So long as the agency "got the law right," possessed "substantial evidence" to support any factual findings and did not abuse its discretion or act in an arbitrary or capricious manner, a court will uphold the agency decision even though a judge might have made another perhaps wiser one.)

32. The heads or commissioners of agencies are appointed by the President for life-time terms.
(False: There are term limits, typically five years. Moreover, there are requirements that not all agency heads can be from the same political party, for example, at the National Labor Relations Board only three of the five members can be from the same political party.)

33. At an administrative law hearing the administrative law judge (ALJ) can only determine questions of fact since questions of law must be determined by the heads of the agency.
(False: The ALJ decides both the facts and the law of a case. Of course, appeal can be made to the heads of the agency as well as the traditional courts and the heads of the agency as well as judges can substitute their interpretation of the law for that of the ALJ.)

34. A court can overturn a factual finding by an Administrative Law Judge (ALJ) if that factual finding is not supported by "substantial evidence" in the record.

(True: This is a basic proposition of administrative law and procedure. "Substantial evidence" means relevant evidence that a reasonable person would accept as sufficient to support the factual conclusion.)

35. The "exhaustion" doctrine in administrative law requires generally that before a person can appeal an ALJ's decision into the traditional court system he or she must utilize all appeal procedures in the agency even if time-consuming and costly.
(True: The idea is that at a higher level in the agency there may be a reversal of the ALJ's decision, thus obviating a court appeal. There are exceptions to "exhaustion," however, for example, when the heads of the agency have publicly declared that they agree with the ALJ's decision against a party, thereby making in futile to appeal through the agency to its heads, and thus the litigant can go immediately from the ALJ level into the traditional court system.)

36. Congress creates administrative agencies and delegates to them to power to make laws in their respective subject matter areas since members of Congress usually lack the scientific and technical expertise to deal with many complex issues.
(True: The above is a major reason why the courts through the years have upheld not only the creation of specialized administrative agencies, like the Nuclear Regulatory Commission, but have granted them wide delegations of power.)

37. The U.S. Constitution protects private sector employees from abuses of power and invasions of privacy by their corporate and business employers.
(False: The U.S. Constitution protects people from interference and abridgement of their freedoms by government, including government employers at all levels – federal, state, and local, but not by abuses by private sector employers.)

38. Commercial speech is accorded the same level of First Amendment protection by the federal courts as political speech.
(False: Commercial speech, that is, advertising and marketing activities, is speech and thus is protected by the First Amendment, but there are different standards for the government to regulate or punish commercial from political speech. As such, political speech, that is, politics, campaigning, public affairs type speech, can only be repressed if the government has a "compelling government interest," for example, to stop a riot; whereas, commercial speech can be repressed and the government only has to meet the lesser standard of demonstrating a "substantial government interest" for punishing the speech, for example, ads geared to children for adult-type products, such as alcohol.)

39. Pursuant to the Takings Clause of the Fifth Amendment to the Constitution, the government can take property for public use without compensating the property owner.
(False: The 5th Amendment allows the "taking" but requires "just compensation" to be paid to the property owner, to be determined, if necessary, by a court.)

40. Businesses, as well as individuals, are protected from "unreasonable" searches and seizures by the Fourth Amendment to the U.S. Constitution.
(True: However, if search of a business is deemed to be an "administrative" one an agency, such as OHSA, can get a "blanket warrant" based on the need to check certain businesses in a designated area for health and/or safety violations. The traditional police "probable cause" standard for a criminal warrant would not be necessary in the preceding situation.)

41. Only individuals and not corporations are protected under the First Amendment "free speech" rights in the U.S. Constitution.

(False: Corporations are regarded as "persons" for most constitutional rights, including free speech rights. However, one exception is the 5th amendment right to self-incrimination which is limited only to corporate papers and documents. Also, the courts make a distinction between the "political speech" of a corporation, which is granted the highest degree of protection, and commercial speech, that is, advertising and marketing, which is granted a lesser degree of protection.)

42. A corporation is entitled to the 14th Amendment right to Due Process before government can impose a fine or sanction.
(True: A corporation is regarded as a person for Due Process rights, which right means notice of proposed government action, a fair hearing, a decision with adequate legal and factual reasons, and an opportunity to appeal the decision.)

43. Under the Commerce Clause in the U.S. Constitution, Congress can regulate every business and commercial enterprise in the United States.
(False: Congress's power to regulate commerce is broad as it has the power to regulate activities that are interstate commerce or affect directly or indirectly interstate commerce or impede interstate commerce; but Congress' power is not absolute and this if a business enterprise is strictly intra-state Congress does not have the power to regulate it.)

44. State laws that substantially interfere with interstate commerce violate the Commerce Clause in the Constitution.
(True: This is a basic proposition of constitutional law. For example, a state cannot require a trucker to change the mud flaps on the truck to the state's unique mud flap requirements upon entering the state as this would be a substantial interference.)

45. Because of the First Amendment to the Constitution a state cannot regulate or restrict advertising.
(False: Advertising is deemed by the Supreme Court to be "commercial speech," which is protected by the 1st Amendment. However, if a state has a "substantial government reason" for restricting and regulating the speech, such as advertisements for the sale of traditional "vice" products, such as tobacco and alcohol, or services, like gambling, though legal, but aimed or targeted at children.)

46. If they conflict, a federal statute will supersede a state law, including a state constitutional law.
(True: As per the Supremacy Clause of the Constitution all laws made pursuant thereto prevail over conflicting state law, including state constitutional law.)

47. Since the U.S. is a capitalistic country "commercial speech" receives the same degree of protection under the First Amendment as political speech.
(False: Commercial speech is speech and thus is protected by the First Amendment but the legal standard to regulate it (a "substantial" government interest) is a lesser standard to meet than for political speech (a "compelling" government interest.)

48. The federal Bill of Rights protects people from abuses of power in both the public and private sectors.
(False: The federal Bill of Rights only protects the people from abuses of power and transgression of their rights by government, including government employers, and not by private sector entities. Note, however, that the 13th Amendment which prohibits slavery and involuntary servitude applies to both public sector and private sector entities and parties.)

49. By means of their inherent sovereign "police power," the states have exclusive authority to regulate interstate commerce.

(False: The federal Congress by means of its enumerated powers in Article I has the power to regulate interstate commerce. However, states also can regulate interstate commerce so long as their regulations do not substantially interfere with or impede the free flow of interstate commerce. For example, a state law requiring all drivers in the state to be licensed in that state by that state would be unconstitutional as it would be a big burden on interstate commerce, travel, and traffic. But requiring interstate truckers to go through "weigh stations" or "agricultural inspections" at or near the border would be permissible for road tax and health reasons, respectively, and the burden on interstate commerce would not be substantial.)

50. The 5th Amendment would forbid the government seizing private property pursuant to Eminent Domain and turning the property over to a developer to improve it.
(False: Based on a significant Supreme Court case, called the Kelo case, government is allowed to seize private property, even if it is not blighted, to improve the area. The rationale is that a public purpose or use is served by the economic growth, which outweighs the private owners' property rights. Of course, the government as per the 5th Amendment, must pay the property owners just compensation for the seized property.)

Multiple Choice Questions with Answers and Explanations

1. The U.S. Constitution established the following branches of the national, that is, federal, government:
   a. Legislative, Executive, Judicial, and Administrative Agencies
   b. Legislative, Executive, Judicial, Administrative Agencies, and the Media
   c. Legislative, Executive, Judicial
   d. Legislative, Executive, Judicial, and the Church
   (The correct answer is c. This is basic political science. Administrative agencies are not in the Constitution but were created later by Congress to fulfill specialized functions, like the Nuclear Regulatory Commission and the Securities and Exchange Commission. Administrative agencies, it is important to note, have been delegated law-making powers by Congress and thus can promulgate laws in the forms of rules and regulations. Administrative agencies, therefore, are at times called the "4th branch of government," but not a branch designated in the Constitution. The media may be powerful and protected by the First Amendment, but the media is not part of government. The U.S. does not have a "state-media," nor a state-sponsored church for that matter.)

2. Under the U.S. constitutional system, fundamental constitutional doctrines that seek to prevent an abuse of power by the federal government are:
   a. The Separation of Powers doctrine
   b. The division of the federal government into three branches or divisions
   c. The system of "checks and balances"
   d. All of the above.
   (The correct answer is d. These are all very basic elements to the structure and function of the federal government in the Constitution, which were designed by the Founding Fathers to prevent too great a growth and centralization of government power and thereby to avoid the creation of an all-powerful central, and perhaps tyrannical, government. The three branches of government are the legislative, executive, and judicial, and their separated powers are, respectively, lawmaking, law enforcement, and adjudication. "Checks and balances" is a system whereby one branch of government has a "check" on another, for example, the President having the power to appoint

Supreme Court justices but the Senate having the power to confirm them. Another example would be Congress' power to make laws, which the President can either sign or veto, and if a veto the Congress can override the veto.)

3. Which of the following is a FALSE statement?
   a. Congress has the power in Article I of the Constitution to regulate interstate commerce.
   b. The power of Congress to regulate business pursuant to the interstate commerce clause in the Constitution is very broad.
   c. States cannot pass any law that regulates any aspect of interstate commerce since the federal Congress has sole and exclusive jurisdiction in this area.
   d. States may be able to pass laws that regulate certain aspects of interstate commerce for health and safety reasons if there is no direct conflict with federal law, no discrimination against commerce from other states, and no undue burdens placed on interstate commerce.

   (The correct answer is c. States can pass laws that regulate interstate commerce, such as having interstate truckers go through weigh stations for road tax purposes; but state regulations cannot unduly burden or impede interstate commerce, such as states having different mud flap requirements thereby requiring interstate truckers to stop in certain states to change mud flaps.)

4. Which of the following is a TRUE statement?
   a. Powers not given to the states by the U.S. Constitution are reserved for the federal government in Washington, D.C.
   b. The states in the United States are not permitted to have their own constitutions because doing so could conflict with the U.S., that is, federal constitution.
   c. The U.S. Congress has the power to create administrative agencies.
   d. The doctrine of *stare decisis* means that a law passed by a legislative body will stand until it is changed by a new legislature.

   (The correct answer is c. The Supreme Court has not only permitted Congress to transfer its sovereign law-making power to administrative agencies by means of the Delegation Doctrine, but also the Court has allowed very broad transfers of power to be made with only the most general guidance, for example, a grant to an administrative agency to regulate, including promulgating laws by making rules and regulations, in the "public interest, convenience, and necessity." Powers not expressed granted to the federal government, particularly the enumerated or express powers of Congress, are reserved to the states. Since the U.S. is a federal system states are allowed to have their own Constitutions as well as the three corresponding branches of government: yet no state constitutional provision or state law can conflict with the U.S. Constitution, which is the "supreme law of the land." Stare decisis is Latin for "let the decision stand," which is the foundation of the system of precedents under Anglo-American common law, and not statutory law.)

5. Which of the following is a FALSE statement?
   a. One of the major purposes of the U.S. Constitution is to limit the government's ability to interfere with individual rights.
   b. The concept of federalism means that the federal government holds the entire government power in a nation.
   c. Enumerated powers consist of express powers given to Congress.
   d. Federal statutes take precedence over state constitutions.

   (The correct answer is b. In a federal system, like the U.S. there is a division of power between the national government, called the "federal government" in the U.S., and constituent government entities, called "states" in the U.S., which have the power to legislate based on the traditional "police power" of a state to protect the health safety and welfare of its citizens and residents. Other countries also have a federal system of government, for example, Canada with

provinces, as well as Mexico with states, and Russia too. The purpose of the Bill of Rights, now including especially the 5th and 14th amendments is to protect the individual rights of the people from government abuse and infringement. Enumerated powers are those expressly granted to Congress in Article I of the Constitution; all other powers are reserved to the states. Since the Constitution and all laws made pursuant thereto are the "supreme law of the land," federal statutes take precedence over state law, including state constitutions.)

6. Which of the following is a TRUE statement?
   a. The judicial branch has the authority to examine acts of the legislative branch but not the executive.
   b. The legislative branch of the U.S. government cannot change laws that have been interpreted by Congress.
   c. The preemption doctrine holds that the U.S. Congress can override Supreme Court decisions by a 3/4s vote.
   d. The Supremacy Clause of the U.S. Constitution means that the Constitution and all laws passed pursuant to the Constitution are the supreme law of the land.

   (The correct answer is d. Answer d is the seminal legal principle in the U.S. By virtue of the famous Marbury v. Madison decision, the Supreme Court has the power of "judicial review," meaning the power to ensure that all laws and actions of the other branches of the federal government as well as the states comport to the Constitution. The legislative branch can always change laws enacted by a prior Congress, assuming the necessary votes are present, of course. Congress cannot override Supreme Court decisions by any percentage vote; rather, Congress, specifically, must vote to confirm Supreme Court justices by a majority vote. Preemption is a doctrine that holds when Congress or an administrative agency has so extensively and pervasively regulated a particular field, such as airline safety, no state legislation is permissible since Congress has "preempted" the field.)

7. Which of the following is a FALSE statement?
   a. Procedural due process prevents the government from taking a person's property if it would be unethical to do so.
   b. The Equal Protection Clause of the 14th Amendment requires that similarly situated persons be treated similarly by the government.
   c. Generally, regarding free speech rights, if a less restrictive means is available for the government to achieve its goals, the government must use the less restrictive alternative.
   d. Obscenity is not considered to be protected speech under the 1st Amendment.

   (The correct answer is a. Ethics, based on moral philosophy, is separate and distinct from the law. The government can take a person's property, and for that matter his or her life or liberty, but the government must comply with the Due Process clause of the 5th and 14th Amendments. As such, the government must provide notice of the proposed taking, a fair hearing, a decision with reasons, both factual and legal, as well as an appeal. The Equal Protection Clause requires similar treatment; however, government is allowed to discriminate, though the term "classify" is used, but if the discrimination is based on economic classifications, for example, out-of-state residents paying more for in-state fishing licenses or college tuition, the government just has to show a rational and reasonable justification. Yet if the discrimination is based on a "suspect" category, such as race or national origin, or if a fundamental right is involved, such as freedom of speech, there is a test called "strict scrutiny" whereby the government must show a "compelling" reason for its action. Obscenity is definitely not free speech protected by the 1st Amendment; however, determining exactly what is "obscene," as opposed to merely "indecent," had been a big challenge for the courts. A fundamental principle of 1st Amendment law is that any restrictions on free speech must be as narrowly drawn as possible so as to not prohibit "good speech," and as

such if there is another reasonable alternative in regulating speech that is narrower and less restrictive, it must be used by the government.)

8. Which of the following is a TRUE statement?
   a. Offensive speech is generally considered to be not protected by the 1st Amendment.
   b. Commercial speech generally is not protected by the Constitution since it merely involves marketing and advertising activities.
   c. The First Amendment protects only actual spoken or written speech but not symbolic speech or other expressions.
   d. A state can regulate an area affecting interstate commerce if the federal government has not preempted the field and the state regulation neither places an undue burden on interstate commerce nor discriminates against interstate commerce.

(The correct answer is d. Answer d is a basic statement of the law regarding the states' concurrent powers to regulate interstate commerce. Commercial speech is definitely protected by the 1st Amendment regardless of its economic rationales as opposed to political speech involving public affairs. Symbolic speech, such as flags and pictures, is protected as well as expressions, such as dancing. Speech can be offensive, for example, gross and insulting, and still be protected, and actually speech can be hateful, for example, racist speech, and still be protected.)

9. Which of the following is a TRUE statement?
   a. The "police power" of a state does *not* give the state any general authority to regulate business since that is the whole responsibility of Congress and federal administrative agencies.
   b. Garbage or waste that is transported across state lines can be construed as interstate commerce regardless of economic value.
   c. The Commerce Clause of the Constitution gives Congress the power to regulate commerce with foreign nations and Indian tribes only.
   d. Congress can only regulate activities that are actually interstate commerce, but not activities that affect interstate commerce.

(The correct answer is b. The Supreme Court has interpreted very broadly Congress' power to regulate commerce between or among the states, including garbage. Congress also has the power to regulate commerce with foreign countries and Indian tribes. For example, a state cannot "lock in" its economy or "lock out" business from other states, including the garbage and landfill business. Congress's power to regulate interstate commerce extends to activities that directly or indirectly affect interstate commerce, even if the activities are solely intrastate. States have the concurrent power to regulate certain aspects of interstate commerce that occur within the state, for example, weigh stations for interstate truckers for road tax purposed, but states cannot discriminate against interstate commerce or impede the free flow of interstate commerce.)

10. Which of the following is a TRUE statement?
    a. The federal government in the U.S. retains all powers not specifically delegated to the states.
    b. The federal government in the U.S. cannot regulate commerce within a state, even if the commerce concerns more than one state, since states existed before the federal government.
    c. When state regulations in the U.S. impinge on interstate commerce, commerce must yield to the state regulations, no matter how heavy the burden placed on interstate commerce, since states have the right to control activities within their border.
    d. Some constitutional protections in the U.S. apply to business entities such as corporations.

(The correct answer is d. Corporations have most of the protections of the Bill of Rights but not all, for example, corporations do not have the 5th Amendment privilege against self-incrimination. The Constitution reserves to the states all powers not expressly granted to the federal government. Moreover, states do not express or enumerated powers to legislate as does Congress; rather, state legislatures can enact laws based on the traditional "police power" of the state, that is, laws designed to protect, promote, and advance the health, welfare, and safety of the citizens and residents

of the state. States cannot regulate interstate commerce if do so places an undue burden of the free flow of interstate commerce. However, Congress can regulate even purely intrastate activities if they have a direct or indirect effect on interstate commerce.)

11. Which of the following is a TRUE statement?
    a. The Bill of Rights in the U.S. Constitution confers absolute rights, not subject to interpretation by the U.S. Supreme Court.
    b. Political speech that would otherwise be protected by the U.S. Constitution's First Amendment loses that protection if its source is a corporation since many corporations are big and powerful and could dominate the media.
    c. Commercial speech is not protected by the First Amendment since the motive is always about making money and not advancing good causes.
    d. Hateful speech is protected by the First Amendment.
    (The correct answer is d. Speech can be hateful, for example, racist or pro-Nazi speech. However, there is a developing body of law dealing with Hate Crimes which can be based on violent acts with a hate motive, of course, but which can also be based on a specific and clear hateful verbal threat with an imminent and immediate threat of violence to a person. The Supreme Court has the power to interpret the Bill of Rights as well as federal statutes. Corporations not only possess political speech, but they can now spend money on their own political ad campaigns for candidates, parties, or causes, though they are forbidden from directly contributing to a candidate or party. Commercial speech, that is, marketing and advertising, are also protected by the 1st Amendment, though the government can regulate and punish commercial speech if the government meets the "substantial interest" test.)

12. The U.S. Constitution takes precedence over:
    a. A state supreme court decision
    b. A provision in a state statute or state constitution
    c. A state constitution, statute, or supreme court decision
    d. None of the above.
    (The correct answer is c. The U.S. Constitution is the "Supreme Law of the Land" thus supersedes all state constitutions, laws, and court decisions. Moreover, since not only the Constitution is supreme, but all laws made pursuant to the Constitution are supreme too, meaning a federal will supersede a state constitution or state supreme court decision.)

13. Pursuant to the commercial speech doctrine under U.S. constitutional law:
    a. commercial speech is not constitutionally protected since the motive is for business to make money
    b. commercial speech is given the same degree of protection as political speech since it is speech
    c. commercial speech is not constitutionally protected since most commercials on television, especially around dinner-time, are loud, annoying, and gross
    d. commercial speech must be true and non-deceptive and involve a legal product or service to gain constitutional protection.
    (The correct answer is d. Commercial speech is granted 1st Amendment free speech protection even if the motive is monetary and even if the marketing and advertising campaigns are annoying, etc. However, to be protected the commercial speech must be true and not false, that is, not be a lie, as well as not deceptive, that is, not misleading by inducing a consumer to arrive at an erroneous decision. Moreover, even if true and not deceptive and of course involving a legal product or service, the government can still regulate and punish commercial speech if the government has a "substantial interest" to do so, for example, protecting children from adult-like (though legal) "vice" products and services. Recall that for the government to regulate and punish political speech the government must overcome the much more strict "compelling interest" test.)

14. Which of the following statements is NOT correct?
   a. Generally, a state court can exercise jurisdiction over a nonresident by showing that he or she had sufficient contacts with the state.
   b. A lawsuit involving a federal question can originate in a federal district court in the United States.
   c. The United States Supreme Court has automatic appellate jurisdiction over all cases decided in the state courts.
   d. An answer to a lawsuit can admit to allegations made in a complaint in a civil lawsuit.

(The correct answer is c. The Supreme Court does not have automatic appellate jurisdiction over state court cases, even cases decided by the supreme court of the state; rather, the U.S. Supreme Court has discretionary jurisdiction, that is, if a significant federal issue is presented the court can grant jurisdiction when a Writ of Certiorari is filed by one of the parties and accepted by the Supreme Court. The Due Process clause of the 14th Amendment requires that for a state to have jurisdiction of a non-resident defendant the defendant must have had sufficient contacts with or a nexus to the state, for example, driving in the state, contracting in the state, or otherwise doing business in the state. The other responses are basic procedural principles. Of course, an answer, which is a response to the filing of a complaint or petition by a plaintiff, typically denies most of the allegations in the complaint.)

15. Which of the following is a TRUE statement?
   a. A federal form of government is one in which sovereign power is vested entirely in a central governing authority.
   b. The federal government in the U.S. retains all powers not specifically delegated to the states.
   c. The state governments in the U.S. retain all powers not specifically delegated to the federal government.
   d. Congress cannot regulate commerce within a state, even if the commerce concerns more than one state, since the states existed before the federal government.

(The correct answer is c. A fundamental Constitutional principle is that all powers not expressly granted to the federal government are reserved to the states. A federal form of government consists of a division of sovereign power between a national government power, called the "federal" government in the U.S., and constituent government entities, called "states" in the U.S. though other countries have provinces. Congress can regulate purely intrastate commerce if the activity has an adverse effect, even if indirect, on the free flow of interstate commerce, for example, a state not allowing its products to be sold outside the state.)

16. Which of the following is a FALSE statement?
   a. The U.S. Constitution expressly states in Article I that Congress has the power to regulate interstate commerce.
   b. When state regulations in the U.S. impinge on interstate commerce, commerce must yield to the state regulations, no matter how heavy the burden placed on the commerce, since states possess sovereignty within their borders.
   c. When there is a direct conflict between a federal and state law in the U.S., the state law is rendered invalid.
   d. Some federal constitution protections in the U.S. apply to business entities such as corporations.

(The correct answer is b. States may possess sovereign power within their borders, but the Supremacy Clause of the Constitution is supreme, and thus Congress as per its enumerated or express power in Article I can regulate and prohibit state activities within their own borders that impede the free flow of interstate commerce. The other responses are basic constitutional principles. Corporations possess, for example, rights under the 1st, 4th, 5th double jeopardy, 14th due process, as well as other constitutional protections, but not the 5th Amendment privilege against self-incrimination.)

17. Which of the following is a FALSE statement?
    a. Federalism is recognized in the U.S. Constitution as the premise for the structure of government in the U.S. as well as the basis for the relations between the national government and the states.
    b. The 10th Amendment to the U.S. Constitution states that the powers not given to the national government or denied to the states are reserved to the states or the people.
    c. The doctrine of delegated powers means the powers that the Congress has which can be delegated, that is, transferred, to state legislative bodies so they can pass laws.
    d. If Congress has been deemed by the courts to "preempt" a field usually by the existence of pervasive and detailed federal regulation, no state regulation will be allowed.

    (The correct answer is c. The Delegation Doctrine means that Congress can create administrative agencies and delegate, that is, transfer, to them the power to make laws by rulemaking, which is quasi-legislative, and results in rules and regulations, and also by adjudication, which is quasi-judicial, and results in decisions by an Administrative Law Judge which are precedents. An example of preemption would laws pertaining to airline safety. The other responses are basic constitutional principles.)

18. Which of the following is a FALSE statement?
    a. The 5th and 14th Amendments protect persons from being deprived of life, liberty, and property by the government without Due Process of Law.
    b. A corporation is not protected by the 4th and 14th Amendments since a corporation is not a real person.
    c. Commercial speech dealing with marketing and advertising is protected by the 1st Amendment but not as fully as political speech.
    d. The government can regulate commercial speech if it has a substantial interest to do so and the regulations are narrowly tailored.

    (The correct answer is b. A corporation, though an artificial person created pursuant to state law, does possess most Constitutional rights, including those guaranteed by the 4th and 14th Amendments. The other responses are basic constitutional principles.)

19. Which of the following is a TRUE statement?
    a. The 4th Amendment protection against unreasonable searches and seizures by government does not apply to business searches, only people and their homes.
    b. The U.S. Constitution prohibits the government taking private property since to do so would be "communistic."
    c. There is no specific right to privacy in the U.S. Constitution.
    d. The U.S. Constitution protects private sector employees from abuse of their rights by their private sector employers.

    (The correct answer is c. There is a right to privacy granted by the Constitution, but it is not expressly specified; rather, it is implied from the other amendments, particularly the 4th and the 9th. Government has the eminent domain power to seize private property for public use but as per the 5th amendment government must pay just compensation for the seizure. The 4th Amendment's protections apply to businesses too, but the requirements for an administrative agency to obtain a warrant for a business inspection are much less stringent than for law enforcement to obtain a criminal law warrant which must be based on probable cause. The Constitution does not protect private sector employees, only government employees. There are, of course, many other laws that afford rights to private sector employees, for example, the Civil Rights Act and the National Labor Relations Act which are based on Congress' power to regulate interstate commerce.)

20. Which of the following is/are TRUE?
    a. Political speech is protected by the 1st Amendment.
    b. Commercial speech is protected by the 1st Amendment.
    c. Indecent speech is protected by the 1st Amendment.
    d. All of the above.

    (The correct answer is d. All these types of speech are protected, as opposed to obscene speech, which is not. However, the government has more leeway in regulating indecent speech, for example, the Federal Communications Commission curtailing the use of certain "curse words" on public radio stations during hours when young people might be listening. Of course, it is a challenge – legally and practically – to determine exactly the line between obscene and "merely" indecent speech.)

5 - Administrative Law

Introduction

Administrative law deals with the law of administrative agencies – federal, state, and local – at times called the "4th branch of government" due to their importance and formidable presence in our lives. Since there are a multitude of agencies the student should concentrate on the federal level and know how agencies are created, that is, by means of the delegation doctrine, and the key fact that agencies are given by Congress legislative, executive, and judicial powers. Moreover, the student must be aware that Congress has empowered agencies to make law with only the most general guidance. The key fact is that agencies make law! The student thus must know how agencies make law by means of adjudication, the judicial power, as well as by rulemaking, the legislative power. The student must be cognizant of the fact that the agency judicial proceeding, frequently before an Administrative Law Judge (ALJ), is not the equivalent of a traditional trial. Regarding rulemaking, the student also must know that there are two types of rulemaking – formal "on-the-record" rulemaking and "notice-and-comment" rulemaking – and be able to differentiate the two types.

Adjudication and rulemaking are known as "formal" agency actions, yet it is equally important for the student to know that agencies can act "informally" to make policy as well as the types of informal agency actions. Also important for the student to know is how agencies seek information, for example, by subpoenas and inspections, as well as the constitutional rights parties and business have when the agency seeks information. Critically important to know are the protections in the 4th and 5th amendments, as well as in the Due Process protections in the 5th and 14th amendments.

Due Process requires that an agency adjudication be a fair one; and as such the student must be aware of the basic elements to "fairness." Due process also affords a party aggrieved by an agency decision the right to an appeal to the traditional court system, and consequently the student must understand how decisions are appealed to the courts, the judicial "roadblocks," such as "standing," "ripeness," and "exhaustion," that can preclude or forestall appeal, and how a judge will evaluate an agency decision on appeal, specifically when the judge looks at agency legal determinations, factual determinations, and how the agency used its discretionary. Finally, the student must be aware of the Sovereign Immunity doctrine and how it has been waived, especially at the federal level in the Federal Torts Claims Act, and also by means of the "Constitutional Torts" doctrine.

True and False Questions with Answers and Explanations

1. Specialized government agencies have been created by legislatures to deal with problems that members of the legislatures lack the time and expertise to deal with.
(True: Most members of legislatures are lawyers and not scientists or doctors. Prime examples of specialized agencies would be the Nuclear Regulatory Commission and the Food and Drug Administration.)

2. Administrative agencies have the power to make law because of a delegation of power to the agencies from the executive branch of government.
(False: Delegation of law-making powers is done by the legislative branch.)

3. If there is a conflict between a statute passed by Congress and a regulation or rule promulgated by a federal administrative agency the agency regulation or rule supersedes the statute since the agency is composed of subject matter experts whereas members of Congress are mainly lawyers.
(False: A statute will always prevail over an administrative agency rule or regulation if there is a conflict since members of Congress are elected and thus "closer to the people.")

4. The Constitution mandates jury trials in all administrative agency proceedings.
(False: There are no juries at an administrative hearing as a general rule. The judge, known as an Administrative Law Judge (ALJ), decides the facts as well as the law. The ALJ's decision can be appealed through the agency to its heads and then to the traditional courts but there will not be any juries involved or separate fact-finding either, as the factual record determined at the ALJ hearing will be utilized in the appeals.)

5. If one cannot afford an attorney at administrative law hearings the law requires that the government will always provide legal counsel.
(False: Unless the administrative hearing results in a loss of liberty, for example, a parole revocation hearing, legal counsel is not provided by government as it would be in criminal law matters. Of course, one can be represented by an attorney at an administrative law hearing, if one can afford an attorney or seek the help of some type of legal aid organization.)

6. Rules and regulations promulgated by an administrative agency are considered to be laws.
(True: They have civil law ramifications, for example the imposition of monetary fines, not criminal consequences, unless Congress or a state legislature has converted the violation of an agency rule into a crime.)

7. The Constitution requires that at an administrative hearing before an Administrative Law Judge (ALJ) a person be provided with an attorney if he or she cannot afford one.
(False: The constitutional requirement of counsel for the indigent will only arise if the administrative hearing results in a criminal law type sanction, for example, a parole revocation hearing where if the parolee loses, he or she will be re-incarcerated. Legal aid societies funded by state Bar Associations and taxpayer and charitable funding may be a source of legal aid for the indigent who appear before an ALJ.).

8. A common criticism that is made against federal administrative agencies is that the Congressional law that creates the agency, called "enabling legislation," is too narrowly set forth, thereby giving the agencies too little authority.
(False: Just the opposite is true. The criticism is that the laws creating the agencies and the delegations of power granted too them are much too general and imprecise, consequently granting agencies too much power. For example, in the first administrative agency created on the federal level, the Interstate Commerce Commission, the agency was given the power to regulate the trucking industry and other aspects of interstate commerce in the "public interest, convenience, and necessity" but with no further guidelines from Congress. Another example would be the Federal Trade Commission which can regulate marketing and advertising and prohibit and punish "unfair and deceptive" ads, yet without these terms being defined by Congress. The idea is that the agency itself by means of rulemaking and adjudication should define these general grants of power in specific cases and regulations.)

9. Typically, Congress provides careful oversight of administrative agencies by promulgating precise guidelines for agency action.
(False: The initial grant of power to an agency is very broad and general; and usually Congress does not legislative more precise standards; however, Congress can provide oversight by means of hearings

by Standing Committees that have jurisdiction over certain agencies as well as Special Committee hearings. Also, Congress can indirectly control agencies by approving or disapproving their budgets.)

10. Generally, judicial review of an agency decision does not include an inquiry in the wisdom of the agency's decision.
(True: So long as the agency applied the law correctly, had "substantial evidence" from the record as a whole to support any factual determinations, and did not act in an arbitrary or capricious manner or abused its discretion a court will not overturn the agency decision even though a court believed it was not a wise one and the court would have issued a better one.)

11. The Constitutional doctrine of Separation of Powers prevents agencies from performing legislative, executive, and judicial functions.
(False: Separation of Powers exists at the federal as well as state level in the makeup of the government divided into three separate and distinct branches with "checks and balances" on one another. However, legislative, executive, and judicial powers are combined in an agency, which many people feel is too much of an "undemocratic" concentration of power in a government entity, though the courts have upheld these concentrations of power. So, for example, the federal Food and Drug Administration (FDA) can promulgate a rule saying how much meat must be in a frozen "meat" pizza, which is the legislative function. Next, the FDA can send out its inspectors to see if its rule is complied with, which is the executive function. Finally, if the agency feels there is a violation and seeks to enforce its rule with sanctions, which is again the executive function, the pizza company is entitled to basic Due Process, which will be a hearing before an FDA Administrative Law Judge, which is the judicial function. The ALJ's decision can always be appealed to the traditional courts, if one has the initiative, time and money, especially for specialized legal counsel.)

12. On the federal level Congress has delegated the power to administrative agencies to make the violations of its rules a crime.
(False: Agencies by virtue of the delegation doctrine are empowered to promulgate rules and regulations and impose civil fines and sanctions for their violation, but an agency cannot create or define a crime; rather, Congress can convert the violation of an agency rule, for example. SEC Rule 10b-5 prohibiting insider trading, into a crime.)

13. Congress can delegate to administrative agencies law-making powers but only with precise standards and guidelines as to how that power should be executed since the Constitution vests the power to make laws to Congress.
(False: Though many political scientists have found this to be regrettable from a democratic perspective, nonetheless the Supreme Court has permitted delegations of law-making power to administrative agencies with only the most general and vague guidance, for example, to make rules and regulations in an area based on the "public interest, convenience, and necessity.")

14. Administrative agencies are called the "4th branch of government" because they were added to the Constitution by amendment since they are so necessary to public health and safety today.
(False: Administrative agencies are neither in the original Constitution nor added to it by amendment. Nevertheless, they are called the "4th branch" because Congress with the Supreme Court's approval has granted very wide degrees of legislative, as well as judicial and executive, powers to agencies, who can make law in the form of rules and regulations, enforce laws as per the executive, and adjudicate violations of their laws. How to control such agencies with combined powers and functions is a daunting challenge today.)

15. Agencies can act "informally" to make policy.

(True: Formal methods to making policy are adjudication, formal rulemaking ("on-the-record" rulemaking), and notice-and-comment rulemaking. In these afore mentioned formal methods the agency makes law using its quasi-judicial power of adjudication and its quasi-legislative power of rulemaking, and as such when the agency makes law it also concomitantly makes policy. "Informal' agency actions consist of guidelines, advice, opinions, negotiations and settlements, press releases, and speeches, which do not have the force of law but do give an indication of what the agency's policy is on a certain matter.)

Multiple Choice Questions with Answers and Explanations

1. Administrative agencies can make law and policy by:
   a. Informal rulemaking.
   b. Adjudication.
   c. Formal rulemaking.
   d. All of the above.

   (The correct answer is d. These are all basic methods by which agencies make law and policy. Adjudication is the quasi-judicial aspect of an agency's function, and results in a decision after a hearing before an Administrative Law Judge. Rulemaking is the legislative function of administrative agencies. Formal rulemaking occurs is based on a formal record being established. Informal rulemaking, also known as "notice and comment" rulemaking, can be based on information not in the formal record. "Notice" means interested parties must be given notice of an agency's proposed rulemaking; and "comment" means these parties are allowed to submit oral and/or written, at the discretion of the agency, comments regarding the proposed rule. However, the heads of the agency can promulgate a rule by using information obtained not in "comment" process.)

2. Which of the following is FALSE regarding federal administrative agencies?
   a. Congress typically delegates to administrative agencies the power to make laws in the form of rules and regulations.
   b. Administrative agencies, such as the Occupational Health and Safety Administration, cannot conduct inspections since an inspection is a "search," which can only be conducted by the police or other law enforcement agency pursuant to a traditional criminal law search warrant.
   c. Administrative agencies typically can impose civil fines after a due process hearing in which a person or business is adjudicated to be in violation of an agency rule or regulation.
   d. The decisions of administrative agencies can generally be appealed to the traditional court system assuming that procedural requirements for an appeal are met.

   (The correct answer is b. Agencies are allowed to conduct inspections for which warrants are required. However, agencies can obtain "blanket-type" warrants that allow them to make inspections of certain businesses in certain geographic areas to ensure compliance with agency rules. Agencies do not need to demonstrate the traditional law enforcement showing of "probable cause" of a violation in order to obtain a warrant. The other three answers are all accurate and fundamental administrative law principles.)

3. Administrative agencies can make law by which of the following methods?
   a. Adjudication
   b. Formal rulemaking
   c. Notice-and-comment rulemaking
   d. All of the above.

   (The correct answer is d. Adjudication is the quasi-judicial function of agencies where a hearings officer, called especially on the federal level an Administrative Law Judge (ALJ), renders a

decision after a hearing, which decision can be appealed but does stand as a precedent. Formal rulemaking is the quasi-legislative function of administrative agencies whereby the heads of the agency, in essence, votes to pass rules and regulations. "Formal" means that there is a formal legislative-type hearing and, most importantly, the ultimate decision must be based only on the evidence brought forth at the hearing. Formal rulemaking thus is at times called "on-the-record" rulemaking. Notice-and-comment rulemaking is often called "informal" rulemaking since the decision-makers can base their ultimate decision on information not "on the record." However, there are notice provisions for proposed rulemaking and "interested" members of the public are allowed, at the discretion of the agency, to comment on the proposed rules.)

4. What is TRUE as a general rule about administrative agencies making and changing law and policy?
   a. An agency can change its existing law and policy.
   b. An agency can make inconsistent determinations.
   c. An agency can make erroneous decisions and give erroneous advice.
   d. All of the above.
   (The correct answer is d. All the foregoing responses are true as a general rule. Traditional judicial doctrines, like res judicata, that is, the "matter is decided," do not apply to agencies. However, there is an exception if a party reasonably relied on an agency determination or agency advice and as a result was substantially harmed or greatly inconvenienced when the agency changes its mind or gives "bad" advice. In such a situation because a court will step in to prevent injustice. Of course, the more inconsistency as well erroneous advice the agency imparts the greater the likelihood that the courts and legislative bodies will lose the respect for and trust of the agency.)

5. What is FALSE about agency adjudications?
   a. A jury will not be present at an agency adjudication and an administrative law judge will decide the facts as well as the law of a case.
   b. The traditional rules of evidence of a trial, such as the hearsay exception and the cross-examination of witnesses need not be as strictly followed in an agency adjudication.
   c. A party can utilize the services of an attorney, and the government will not provide one if the party before the agency is poor and destitute.
   d. A party is entitled to appeal the decision of the administrative law judge within the agency and then into the traditional court system.
   (The correct answer is c. Unless the agency matter is a criminal or criminal-related one, for example, the a parole revocation hearing where the person can end up in prison, the government will not provide an attorney, and if one is poor and destitute he or she will have to rely on legal aid and other pro bono services for legal representation.)

6. How can agencies obtain information?
   a. Informally requesting information
   b. Subpoenaing information
   c. Conducting inspections
   d. All of the above.
   (The correct answer is d. If an agency request for information is refused the agency can obtain a subpoena to require testimony and materials. However, the matter the agency wants the information for must be within the purview of the agency's jurisdiction, purpose, and function as well as be "reasonable," that is, not an over-broad "fishing expedition." Note that regarding inspections the agency must first obtain a search warrant, but an administrative law warrant is not the same as the traditional criminal law warrant, where a police officer would have to demonstrate "probable cause" to a judge; rather, agency warrants can be "blanket" type

warrants whereby an agency is going to conduct inspections to protect the public health and safety in certain areas for certain types of businesses, for example, that restaurants meet health codes.)

7. What Constitutional amendments protect people and businesses when agencies seek to collect information?
   a. The 4th Amendment prohibition against unreasonable searches and seizures.
   b. The 5th Amendment privilege against self-incrimination.
   c. The 5th and 14th Amendments Due Process clause.
   d. All of the above.

   (The correct answer is d. These are all fundamental constitutional protections against agency conduct. The 4th Amendment requires a warrant for an agency search or inspection, but as noted an "administrative warrant" will suffice. Note too that there are exceptions for warrantless administrative searches in emergency situations and for businesses that are "pervasively" regulated, such as gun stores. Regarding the 5th Amendment privilege against self-incrimination, note that it applies just to real, natural people and not artificial persons like a corporation. Yet it does protect a person from testifying if his or her testimony would provide a link in a criminal chain leading to conviction. The 5th, moreover, also protects a person's books and records. The Due Process clause of the 5th and 14th Amendments harken back to the Magna Charta of 1215 in England. Due Process means that when the government, including of course administrative agencies, is seeking to deprive a person, here including a corporation, of his or her life, liberty, or property, for example, the agency is seeking to fine a business, that person is entitled to Due Process of Law. Due Process, in essence, means that a person is entitled to adequate notice of what the government is intending to do, a fair hearing under the circumstances, a decision with reasons – factually and legally – for the decision, and the right to appeal the decision. The fairness of the hearing will depend on the situation, for example, a criminal case in which the government is attempting to deprive a person of his or her freedom will require a traditional criminal law trial; whereas if an agency "merely" seeks to fine a business the "fair" hearing will before an Administrative Law Judge (ALJ).)

8. On appeal, a judge can review an agency decision by an ALJ to see:
   a. if the decision is supported by "substantial evidence."
   b. if the decision is legally correct.
   c. if the decision is arbitrary and capricious.
   d. All of the above.

   (The correct answer is d. These are all basic aspects of a judge's review of an agency decision. Note first that when it comes to agency legal determinations the judge is not bound at all by the agency's interpretation of the law; and as such the judge can freely substitute his or her legal interpretation for that of the agency. However, regarding factual determinations, the judge is bound by the "substantial evidence" test, which holds that if there is in the record as a whole relevant, substantial evidence to support the agency's factual determination, the judge is bound by it even if he or she would have decided the factual issue differently. Finally, a judge always has the power to overturn an agency decision if it is arbitrary and capricious, which includes an abuse of discretion component, which means that the agency considered factors that it should not have or failed to consider factors that it should have done.)

9. What legal doctrines can forestall or preclude a party when appealing an agency decision into the court system?
   a. Exhaustion
   b. Standing
   c. Ripeness
   d. All of the above.

(The correct answer is d. "Exhaustion" means that a party is required to exhaust all avenues of appeal within the agency since he or she may prevail at a higher level, thereby obviating any judicial review. There are some exceptions to exhaustion, for example futility, as where the heads of the agency have already given a fixed opinion on the case, or if the appeal process would cause great harm or expense to a party. "Standing" is a Constitutional requirement stemming from the statement in the Constitution that the judicial power to extends to "cases and controversies," which has been interpreted to mean that a party cannot litigate theoretically or in the abstract; rather, to have standing a party must suffer an actual "injury in fact," either physically, economically, and/or aesthetically. "Ripeness" arises when the agency has made a law or enunciated a policy, but it has not yet been applied and enforced. Unless there is some great hardship a reviewing court may tell an appealing party to wait until the law or policy is applied to him or her, because it might not be, thereby again obviating any judicial review.)

10. What is TRUE about the sovereign immunity of government doctrine?
    a. It stems from the old English maxim that "The King can do no wrong."
    b. The federal government has partially waived its sovereign immunity in the Federal Tort Claims Act.
    c. The Constitutional Torts doctrine allows people to proceed legally in tort against government officials and officers at the federal, state, and local level who intentionally deprive people of their constitutional rights.
    d. All of the above.

    (The correct answer is d. The Federal Tort Claims Act will allow people injured through the negligence of federal employees to sue and recover against the government. Lawsuits for intentional torts, like assault and battery and false imprisonment, are also permitted, but only if the wrongdoers are federal law enforcement personnel. The Constitutional Torts doctrine is based on the Civil Rights Act of 1871 and allows lawsuits for money damages. This doctrine has been used as a major civil rights tool, especially in preventing local government officials from seeking to deprive minorities of their right to vote.).

6 - Torts

Introduction

The law of torts is based primarily on state common law. The two broad categories of tort law are the law of negligence and the law of intentional torts, which can be divided into two main categories – intentional torts against the person and intentional torts against property. The student must be cognizant of the fact that though tort law is civil law certain actions, for example, the intentional torts of assault and battery, can be both civil wrongs and criminal wrongs, though naturally with a different burden of proof for the later. Intentional torts to the person encompass assault, battery (and the student must be able to differentiate between the two), false imprisonment, intentional infliction of emotional distress (and the student must be able to distinguish this legal wrong from negligent infliction of emotional distress, particularly the "impact" requirement for the latter), invasion of privacy (and the student must know the four types of "invasion" recognized under the common law), and intentional interference with contractual or business relations. Fraud in the form of deceit, that is, intentional misrepresentation, is also an intentional tort, which will be covered in the Contract law section dealing with the genuineness of the agreement. Defamation is recognized as a "quasi-intentional" tort, and as such the student must know the distinction between libel and slander, the requirements for a lawsuit for defamation, particularly the publication requirement, as well as the defenses to defamation, especially that truth is an absolute defense, as well as the distinction between absolute privileges and qualified or conditional privileges, and especially how the latter can arise in the employment context. Regarding intentional torts to property, the student must know the definitions and basic elements of trespass to land (and how trespass differs from the legal wrong of nuisance), trespass to chattels, and conversion. Finally, the student must know the defenses to intentional torts, particularly self-defense.

As opposed to intentionally acting and causing harm, negligence law is based on acting in an unreasonable, careless, and/or imprudent manner. Of course, to be liable for acting carelessly one first must have a duty to act, and consequently the student must understand the important distinction the common law makes between not acting at all, called "non-feasance," as opposed to acting in an unreasonable manner, called "misfeasance." Moreover, the student must be aware of some of the major exceptions, common law as well as statutory, that create liability for not acting. For the tort of negligence, it is critical for the student to know the four required elements to the tort of negligence: duty, breach of duty, causation, and damages. Regarding breach of duty the student must know the doctrine of *res ipsa loquitur* ("the thing speaks for itself"), which favors plaintiffs; and regarding causation the student must know the distinction between factual causation and proximate causation, also called "legal" causation, which latter doctrine actually favors careless defendants. The student also should know of specialized negligence doctrines, such as negligent infliction of emotional distress with its "impact" requirement, as well as the doctrine of negligence *per se*, dealing with violations of statutory duties. The student must be aware of the types of damages that can be recovered for the tort of negligence, as well as the defenses to that tort, especially the distinctions among contributory negligence, comparative negligence, and assumption of the risk.

True and False Questions with Answers and Explanations

1. Pursuant to negligence law a careless person is legally responsible for all the harmful consequences of his or her careless actions even if remote due to public policy considerations.

(False: A careless person based on the doctrine of Proximate Cause is only responsible for the foreseeable harmful consequences of his or her careless action, and not the unforeseeable, remote, or strange consequences.)

2. Slanderous *per se* statements encompass statements that a person has committed a crime of moral turpitude.
(True: Also, that a person has engaged in improper or unethical conduct in his or her trade, business, or profession.)

3. Libel consists of statements which are defamatory and in written form.
(True: Slander consists of oral statements which are defamatory.)
4. Fraud can be based on the expression of an opinion or prediction by an expert.
(True: Otherwise, opinions and predictions are not actionable as fraud; as opposed to statements of material fact.)

5. Pursuant to negligence law causation-in-fact means that a defendant is legally liable for injuries or harm caused if to do so is the fair and ethical thing to do.
(False: Causation-in-fact which is a necessary element to a lawsuit for negligence means that the defendant's careless conduct must be a cause in fact, that is, an actual scientific cause of the plaintiff's injuries.)

6. The essence of the intentional tort of fraud is a knowing and purposeful misrepresentation of material fact designed to induce a person to rely on the misrepresentation.
(True: This type of fraud is known as deceit and must be distinguished from negligent misrepresentation or a good faith mistake.)

7. The tort of wrongful interference with a contract is based on a party knowingly and intentionally interfering with a contractual relationship between two parties.
(True: The tort is also applicable to interference with existing business relationships.)

8. The misappropriation of another person's name of likeness for commercial purposes is a form of an invasion of privacy tort.
(True: The misappropriation must be intentional; however, no evidence of hate, spite, or ill will is necessary.)

9. A merchant who detains a person for shoplifting may be liable for false imprisonment if the person detained is held in an unreasonable manner and/or for a reasonable amount of time.
(True: Merchants have some protection under the common law and statutes when it comes to detaining suspected shoplifters, but the detention must be reasonable in manner and time and the merchant must have had a reasonable suspicion of shoplifting.)

10. If a libelous communication is conditionally privileged and the privilege is not abused one cannot sue for defamation even if the libel is false.
(True: The conditional privilege will protect even false and defamatory statements assuming the privilege is not abused, for example, by communicating the statements beyond those who have a "need-to-know" or when there is evidence of malice.)

11. A key element to the tort of fraud is that the deceived party justifiably and reasonably relied on the misrepresentation.
(True: As per the old common law, how can one reasonably rely on a lie when one knew, or should have known, the truth.)

12. The reasonable and prudent person standard is used in intentional tort law to ascertain how a person should have reacted to the intentional tort of battery.
(False: The reasonable person standard is used for negligence law, that is, one must act as a reasonable person would have under the same or similar circumstances.)

13. Pursuant to the proximate cause element in negligence law a careless defendant is liable for all the harmful consequences of his or her careless act.
(False: The negligent defendant is liable only for the reasonably foreseeable consequences from his or her careless act, not the remote, unforeseen, or unusual consequences.)

14. Wrongful interference with an employment contract between an employer and employee usually will arise if a third-party seeks to recruit the employee to a new firm.
(False: Assuming there is no attempt to influence the employee to breach his or her current contract, no violation of any covenant not to compete, and there is no defamation asserted against the employer, third-parties, such as "head-hunters," can recruit employees for new positions. Such is the nature of our capitalist system.)

15. The use of a person's name or likeness without permission and for the benefit of the user is one form of the tort of invasion of privacy.
(True: This tort also is called misappropriation of use of one's name or likeness.)

16. Defaming a person's business, trade, occupation, or profession is known as defamation *per se*.
(True: Slander per se if the defamation is oral; and libel per se if written. Per se in either type of defamation means that damages are presumed.)

17. If a plaintiff in a negligence lawsuit is also guilty of negligence the plaintiff is barred from any recovery pursuant to the Comparative Negligence doctrine.
(False: The plaintiff can still sue and recover but the plaintiff's degree of negligence is apportioned and deducted from his or her monetary recovery.)

18. In order to commit an intentional tort a person usually must intend the consequences of his or her act or know with substantial certainty that certain consequences will occur.
(True: Intent is critical, but intent can be transferred, such as in the example of a person who intends to hit person A, but misses and hits B, who can sue the actor for the intentional tort of battery, which in addition to amounting to a civil wrong is a crime.)

19. The intentional tort of battery can only occur if the defendant causes serious physical harm to the victim.
(False: A battery can be based on an offensive touching as well as a harmful physical act, for example, for the former when one pats another in a sexual manner.)

20. One cannot recover damages for emotional distress negligently caused unless one suffers a severe physical injury.
(False: A severe physical injury is not required; however, most states will require some type of "impact," which can be slight, for example, when a car negligently driven just barely hits a person thus not causing any physical harm but an "impact" likely causing emotional distress. There are exceptions to the "impact" rule, however, for example, when a parent witnesses his or her child being negligently harmed the parent can sue for emotional distress damages even if not "impacted" at all.)

21. To be actionable as defamation an oral defamatory statement must be communicated to a third person but a written one need not be communicated.
(False: Whether oral/slander or written/libel defamatory statements must be communicated to a third person(s) in order to be legally actionable as per the "publication" requirement.)

22. A person's right to privacy based on the common law encompasses a person's exclusive use to his or her name and likeness.
(True: The common law tort of invasion of privacy includes not only intruding on a person's private sphere but also impermissibly using one's name or likeness, for example, in an advertising campaign.)

23. Persuading and inducing an employee to break his or her contract with the employer in order to hire the employee for one's firm would typically amount to the intentional tort of interference with contract.
(True: The conduct in question is not legitimate competitive behavior. One usually can hire employees away from their current employment but not by inducing them to breach their employment contracts, though perhaps one can unintentionally cause the breach.)

24. Slander *per se* can be predicated on statements that a person is incompetent in his or her professional, occupation, or trade.
(True: Slander per se, that is, in-and-of-itself without the need to prove special damages, which are assumed can also be based on statements that a person has committed in proprieties in his or her profession, occupation, or trade.)

25. The doctrine of *Res Ipsa Loquitur* will allow a jury to infer negligent conduct even though negligence on the part of the defendant has not been proven.
(True: Res Ipsa Loquitur, or "the-thing-speaks-for-itself, was devised to help a plaintiff when there is a difficulty of getting evidence, for example, when a patient wakes up after surgery with a sponge in him or her, or when a creature gets into a can of soda somehow; and the unusual nature of the harm and the fact that the defendants controlled the instrumentality that caused the harm indicate that someone must have been negligent. When a judge grants a Res Ipsa instruction it does not mean that the plaintiff automatically wins; rather, the burden of proof is switched, and the various defendants, for example, all the doctors and nurses in the operating room, or all the parties on the marketing chain, must convince the jury that they were not negligent; and then it is up to the jury to make the determination of whether negligence was present. Note, however, that the causation and damages elements to negligence still must be proven.)

26. The doctrine of Comparative Negligence will bar any recovery to a plaintiff when the evidence indicates that the plaintiff was also careless and his or her carelessness contributed to his or her injury.
(False: The doctrine of Contributory Negligence will bar any recovery, but that doctrine is mainly disfavored now, replaced by Comparative Negligence, whereby a jury is allowed to apportion fault, and thus to deduct from a plaintiff's recovery the percentage thereto attributed to the plaintiff's own fault.)

27. The Proximate Cause doctrine in negligence law deals with whether the harm caused to a plaintiff is sufficiently connected to the careless conduct of the defendant.
(True: The Proximate Cause doctrine benefits careless benefits. Pursuant to the doctrine a careless defendant is not responsible for all the harms factually caused to a plaintiff by the defendant's careless conduct, called "causation-in-fact. Rather, a careless defendant is not responsible for the unusual, remote, or unforeseeable harms caused by his or her carelessness in acting.)

28. One of the elements, that is, requirements, to a successful negligence lawsuit is that the defendant owed to the plaintiff a duty of care.
(True: This is a basic proposition; yet this issue can become complicated because the duty of care owed is owed only to foreseeable defendants, that is, people who are in the "danger zone" or risk being harmed if the duty of care is violated.)

29. The fact that an injury occurred of course indicates that someone must have been negligent.
(False: Negligence is not liability without fault. Injuries can occur, for example, due to Acts of God, for example, a strong wind blowing dust or a bee into a car and distracting the driver, or to accidents which are simply unavoidable even if the parties were without fault. However, if the occurrence of an injury is so unusual and the instrumentality that caused it is in control of the defendant then the doctrine of Res Ipsa Loquitur may be applicable and if so, the defendant may have to show that it was not negligent. The classic examples being a sponge left in a patient after surgery or a soda can that explodes or has a "creature" or object in it.)

30. The Proximate Causation doctrine in negligence law protects careless defendants.
(True: According to Proximate Causation even if an injury is factually caused by the careless conduct of a defendant, he or she is only responsible for the reasonably foreseeable harms caused and not remote, unusual, or strange harmful results.)

31. The doctrine of *Res Ipsa Loquitur* when granted by a judge will allow a jury to infer negligence even though negligence cannot be directly established.
(True: Res Ipsa Loquitur will arise if an injury is caused in an unusual manner and the instrumentality that caused it is in control of the defendant. As such, negligence on the part of the defendant will be inferred; however, the defendant is allowed to produce evidence that it was not negligent; and then the jury will weigh the inference and the rebutting evidence.)

32. The breach of duty standard in negligence law is governed by the "reasonable person" test.
(True: One has a duty when one acts to act as a reasonably prudent person would under the circumstances. One does not have to act perfectly just reasonably. However, if one acts below that standard in a careless, unreasonable, or imprudent manner one has breached the duty of due care, and assuming causation and damages, one will be liable for negligence.)

33. A retail merchant is always strictly liable when a customer falls and hurts himself or herself in the merchant's store since ordinarily a merchant will have "slip and fall" insurance.
(False: Strict Liability applies to sellers of defective products and people who engage in ultra-hazardous activities, like dam-building and crop-dusting. A retail merchant would only be liable if it was negligent, for example, not cleaning up the proverbial banana peel, which the merchant was informed of, in a prompt and careful manner. Insurance, of course, is highly advisable for obvious reasons, but it does not "translate" to automatic liability without fault.)

34. It is possible for an event to occur which causes harm to a person, yet no one involved being held legally liable therefor, because no one acted in an unreasonable or imprudent manner.
(True: Despite what the plaintiffs' lawyers say, there are "unavoidable accidents" as well as Acts of God which can cause injury without anyone being at fault, for example, when a car driver causes an accident because a gust of wind blew sand into his or her eyes or a bee flew into the vehicle. The duty under common law negligence is to act as a reasonable person would under the circumstances, and not be an insurer of perfect conduct.)

35. In a negligence lawsuit where the defendant claims that the plaintiff is at fault too and thus partially to blame for the plaintiff's own damages, this defense is called "imputed liability."

(False: The defense is called Comparative Negligence which allows a jury to find a plaintiff responsible to some degree for his or her own negligence, give that degree of fault a percentage, and then accordingly deduct from the damages awarded to the plaintiff that percentage attributed to the plaintiff's own fault. Whereas "imputed liability" is liability imputed to the employer when an employee commits a negligent act within the course and scope of employment, regardless if the employer was not directly negligent, as the liability is "vicarious," that is, indirect.)

36. Pursuant to negligence law a defendant can be held strictly liable for harm caused if it has good liability insurance.
(False: Negligence is based on fault, that is, acting in an unreasonable and imprudent manner; having or not having insurance is irrelevant to imposing liability. Strict liability, that is, liability without fault, for ultra-hazardous activities, such as dam building, and imploding buildings with explosives, as well as for products which are deemed defective pursuant to products liability law.)

37. Most states have a contributory negligence doctrine which means that if a plaintiff is even slightly at fault in causing an accident the plaintiff can recover nothing from the defendant.
(False: Contributory Negligence is now mainly a historical concept, replaced by the doctrine of Comparative Negligence, which allows a plaintiff, even if also at fault, to recover in negligence against a defendant for the plaintiff's injuries, but a jury will determine the percentage of fault attributed to the plaintiff and reduce his or her damages accordingly.)

38. Assumption of the risk is a complete defense to a negligence lawsuit.
(True: If one knowingly and voluntarily assumes a known risk and is injured one cannot sue for negligence, for example, being hit by a hockey puck or baseball at a game or using a product which clearly has a defect.)

39. An opinion, even if given by an expert, will be deemed to be mere "sales talk" or "puffing," and thus will not be characterized as fraud even if erroneous.
(False: Opinions as well as predictions that are provided by a person deemed to be an "expert" due to occupation, avocation, knowledge are treated by the law as "fact" and thus can form the basis for a lawsuit for fraud or deceit as well as for breach of warranty.)

40. The Proximate Causation doctrine of negligence law deals with whether a plaintiff's injuries are sufficiently connected to the careless conduct of the defendant to impose liability on the defendant.
(True: As such, if the harm caused to the plaintiff by the defendant's conduct is deemed to have occurred in such an unusual, remote, improbable, and/or unforeseeable manner the defendant, though careless, is not liable as a matter of policy. Note that proximate causation prevails even if the harm to the plaintiff was caused as a matter of fact through a chain of occurrences by the defendant.)

41. To establish a successful negligence cause of action the plaintiff must first establish that the defendant owed the plaintiff a duty of care.
(True: This is a fundamental proposition. The basic and general duty which is imposed by the law is that one must act in a situation as a reasonable and prudent person must act. There are, of course, specialized duties created by the common law and by statute.)

Multiple Choice Questions with Answers and Explanations

1. In ALL tort lawsuits, there must be:
   a. a legal duty owed to the plaintiff by the defendant.

b. the intent to harm by the actor.
c. the showing of a defect.
d. None of the above.
(*The correct answer is d. The legal duty, for example, in a negligence case, is owed by the defendant actor to the plaintiff to act as a reasonably prudent person. The intent to harm is only required for certain intentional torts, such as assault and battery, and not for the tort of negligence. The presence of a defect is part of the strict liability tort for products.)*

2. In a negligence lawsuit, the causation element would be satisfied by a showing of:
   a. an intentional action by the defendant that intended to and caused harm to the plaintiff.
   b. actual cause-in-fact and proximate cause of the injury.
   c. a purposeful malicious act by the defendant that causes harm to the plaintiff.
   d. None of the above.
   (The correct answer is b. Both cause-in-fact, that is, the careless act caused the plaintiff's harm regardless of the length and convolution of the causation-chain, as well as proximate cause, that is, the plaintiff's harm was a probable or reasonably foreseeable result of the defendant's careless act are required. Proximate cause, at times called "legal cause," serves a limitation on cause-in-fact to benefit careless people!)

3. Which of the following is FALSE regarding the tort of defamation?
   a. Libel is written defamation.
   b. Truth is an absolute defense to a defamation lawsuit.
   c. "Publication," that is, communication of the defamatory statement to a third-party, is a required element to a defamation lawsuit.
   d. In the case of a "slander per se," for example, a defamatory statement accusing a person of committing a serious crime of moral turpitude, damage to the plaintiff's reputation is *not* presumed since the defamation is merely oral.
   (The correct answer is d. Since damages are presumed in a case of slander per se due to the seriousness of the derogatory false statements. The other answers are true, accurate, and basic principles. However, note that for answer c there may not be "publication" due to an "intra-corporate" exception where the statements are transmitted internally within a company to people, such as HR personnel, who have a need-to-know.)

4. Which of the following are encompassed by the traditional common law tort of intentional invasion of privacy?
   a. An appropriation of a person's name or picture without his or her permission for commercial advantage.
   b. An intrusion by the defendant into the private life or private domain of the plaintiff.
   c. Public disclosure of private facts, that is, facts not in the public record, about a person, even if the facts are true.
   d. All of the above.
   (The correct answer is d. These are all true, accurate, and basic legal concepts. Note, though, that in answer b some courts will require that the intrusion be also "outrageous.")

5. Which of the following is FALSE about the tort of trespass?
   a. A person cannot be liable for trespass by intentionally throwing objects on another's land or causing third parties to come on the land since that person did not physically come on the land.
   b. A trespass can occur against personal property, called "chattels" under the common law.
   c. The intent required for a trespass is only the intent to do the act that constitutes the trespass.
   d. Regarding a trespass to land, actual injury to the land is not required; nominal damages can be given for the mere act of the trespass itself.

(The correct answer is a. A trespass to land can occur by throwing objects on the land or causing others to come on the land. The other answers are all true, accurate, and basic legal concepts. However, it is important to note that pursuant to answer c, mistake is not a defense, for example, coming on someone's land thinking it is one's own property or that there is an easement to cross the land.)

6. Which of the following are required elements to the common law tort of negligence?
   a. Duty and breach of duty
   b. Factual causation (also called cause-in-fact) and proximate (also called "legal") causation
   c. Damages
   d. All of the above.

   (The correct answer is d. These are the fundamental elements to a lawsuit for negligence. The duty, imposed by law, is to act as a reasonably prudent person would under the circumstances. A breach of duty, that is, conduct that falls below the afore mentioned standard, is usually determined by a jury. Note that both factual causation, that is, the defendant's carelessness was the cause of plaintiff's injuries regardless of the length and convoluted nature of the causation chain, and proximate causation, that is, it was reasonably foreseeable that the defendant's carelessness would cause the ultimate harm to the plaintiff, are required. Damages are broadly construed to include physical injury, harm to property, economic loss, pain-and-suffering or emotional distress, and punitive damages if the negligent conduct was gross or in wanton disregard of safety and care.)

7. Which of the following is a TRUE statement?
   a. A tort of battery occurs only if the victim suffers actual serious physical harm.
   b. One cannot recover damages for emotional distress absent a showing of serious personal and physical injury.
   c. An oral defamatory statement must be communicated to a third-party to be actionable but not a written one.
   d. An individual's right to privacy under the common law typically includes the exclusive use of his or her likeness.

   (The correct answer is d. Misappropriation of one's name or likeness is one of the four common law invasion of privacy torts. Actual physical harm is not a perquisite for a battery as this intentional tort can be based on contact that is "merely" offensive, for example, touching a person in an inappropriate sexual manner. Similarly, serious personal and physical injury are not necessarily prerequisites for recovering emotional distress damages. Although one needs an "impact" to recover for negligent infliction of emotional distress, the impact can be slight, for example, a car that comes very close to smashing into a person but then brakes and stops just in time and barely touches one. All defamatory statements, whether oral or written, must be communicated to third parties to be actionable.)

8. Which of the following is a TRUE statement?
   a. Legitimate competitive behavior can constitute wrongful interference with a contractual relationship if one's competitor cannot compete successfully.
   b. Unintentionally causing a party to break a contract with another will constitute wrongful interference with a contractual relationship.
   c. Slanderous *per se* statements include statements that a person has committed improprieties while engaging in a profession or trade.
   d. Under the doctrine of strict liability, a defendant is liable for the results of his or her acts only if he or she intended those results.

   (The correct answer is c. If slander is regarded as Per Se then damages to reputation are presumed. Maligning one in his or her trade or profession is one example of a slander Per Se; and another example would be accusing someone of a crime. Legitimate competitive behavior, although harming

a competitor economically, is not tortious. Convincing a key employee of a competitor to break his or her contract with the competitor to work for one's firm may rise to the level of intentional interference with contractual and business relations. However, unintentionally causing the breach of contract will not be tortious since the interference tort is an intentional one. Strict liability is not based on intent; rather, it is based on doing what the law regards as ultra-hazardous activities or manufacturing or selling products which the law deems to be "defective.")

9. Under the common law, a tort can MOST ACCURATELY be described as:
   a. Any violation of an ethical or moral duty.
   b. Another term for a crime or misdemeanor.
   c. Any action performed in breach of a prior agreement which allows the victim to recover damages.
   d. A civil wrong which allows the person injured or harmed to recover damages.

   (The correct answer is d. Torts are civil wrongs as opposed to criminal law wrongs, which can be either felonies or misdemeanors. Breaching agreements is part of contract law, which also is part of civil law, but a different type of wrong based on not fulfilling contract promises, and with more limited damages. Ethics is a branch of philosophy containing ethical theories which one uses to reason to moral duties and moral precepts. One, of course, hopes that the law is just, that is, moral and ethical.)

10. The tort of assault and the tort of battery:
   a. Are two names for the same tort.
   b. Are strict liability torts.
   c. Can occur independently or together.
   d. Require proof of each of the separate elements of negligence.

   (The correct answer is c. A battery is a harmful or offensive touching, whereas an assault is the reasonable apprehension of a battery, for example, when a person points a gun, even if unloaded, at another, but does not shoot. As such, they can occur together, as they usually do, or separately, especially considering that there is no requirement that one even be aware of the battery when it is committed, as in the "Sleeping Bandit" case who "steals" kisses from young ladies while they are sleeping.)

11. Which of the following statements is/are TRUE:
   a. One major problem with using negligence for product liability lawsuits is that the plaintiff must show that the defendant breached his or her duty of care by acting unreasonably.
   b. The failure of a landowner to warn a guest about a known but hidden or latent danger usually will lead to liability for negligence.
   c. Strict liability is a "no fault" system as opposed to negligence which is based on carelessly acting.
   d. All of the above.

   (The correct answer is d. These are all fundamental legal principles. Note that the doctrine of Res Ipsa Loquitur can help the plaintiff establish the breach of duty element. Landowners have various duties under negligence law to people who come upon the land, for example, business invitees, guests, and even trespassers. Business invitees who come onto the land for the benefit of the landowner are owed the greatest duties, for example, the landowner not only warning of damages but affirmatively inspecting the land to look for dangers and remedying them. Guests, including social guests and unsolicited sales people, come onto to land primarily for their own benefit. The landowner has a duty to warn guests of dangers that the landowner is aware of or should be aware of, but there is no affirmative duty to look for hazards. Trespassers under the common law are owed a duty not to be intentionally harmed, for example, by traps; however, some states have imposed a duty to warn even trespassers of hazards which are not obvious. Strict liability is a no-

fault system; however, there must be engagement in an ultra-hazardous activity, like crop dusting with chemicals, or making and/or selling a product which the law of products liability regards as "defective.") .

12. Which of the following is NOT one of the general categories of torts?
  a. Strict liability for ultra-hazardous activities.
  b. Criminal.
  c. Negligence.
  d. Intentional.

(The correct answer is b. Tort liability is civil liability for negligent torts, intentional torts, as well as for strict liability for ultra-hazardous activities. A tort is viewed as a "private" wrong committed by one party against another. The primary sanction for tort liability is the payment of money damages. Criminal liability is, of course, a separate body of law, premised on an offense being a public wrong, that is, committed against society as a whole ("Breaching the King's Peace," as the old English cases say) as well as against the victim. Criminal law has different procedures and burden of proof, and the primary sanction is imprisonment.)

13. Under Merchant's Protections statutes:
  a. Reasonable grounds for detainment are necessary only if the period of detainment is long.
  b. The length of detainment is not relevant as long as there are reasonable grounds for detainment.
  c. The investigation and the period of detainment must both be reasonable.
  d. Merchants do not have any moral responsibility to investigate possible investigations of the suspect because this is the job of law enforcement.

(The correct answer is c. These state statutes protect merchants from lawsuits, especially the intentional tort of false imprisonment. Generally, these statutes permit a merchant who has a reasonable suspicion of shoplifting to make a reasonable investigation of the suspect for a reasonable amount of time, and thereby to avoid liability.)

14. The following elements are required to be proven in a negligence case EXCEPT:
  a. The defendant owed a duty of due care to the plaintiff.
  b. The defendant was fully aware of the consequences of his or her actions when they were performed.
  c. The defendant breached the duty of care.
  d. The defendant's conduct was an actual cause in fact, as well as the proximate cause, of the injury to the plaintiff.

(The correct answer is b. The defendant need not be fully aware of the consequences of his or her careless act, merely that they were reasonably foreseeable consequences of acting in an unreasonable and careless manner.)

15. The doctrine which arises when a defendant violates an existing statutory duty intended to prevent the injury in question to persons of a class which includes the plaintiff is called:
  a. Negligence *per se*.
  b. *Res ipsa loquitur*.
  c. Proximate cause.
  d. Assumption of the risk

(The correct answer is a. An example of negligence Per Se is when an auto driver violates traffic control laws. Note that negligence Per Se just establishes the duty and breach of duty elements to a negligence lawsuit. The plaintiff thus still must prove causation and damages. Res Ipsa Loquitur is a doctrine that benefits plaintiffs by shifting the burden of proof and persuasion when an injury occurs in such an unusual manner that under ordinary circumstances someone had to be negligent, and also that the defendant had sole control of the instrumentality which caused the injury. An example would

be when a car under normal driving conditions swerves off the road and causes an injury, and the defendant was driving the car. Proximate cause is a doctrine that benefits careless defendants by holding them liable not for all the harmful consequences of their careless acts but only the reasonably foreseeable harmful consequences. Assumption of the risk is a defense to a negligence lawsuit when a person knowingly and voluntarily assumes a risk, for example, by attending a baseball game one risks getting hit by a ball.)

16. Persons who engage in abnormally dangerous or ultra-hazardous activities:
    a. Are liable only if all the elements of negligence are proven against them.
    b. Are liable only if they intended to cause a certain injury or harm.
    c. Are generally not liable for the injuries they cause because as matter of public policy no one would otherwise undertake these dangerous but often necessary activities.
    d. Are liable to persons they injure even if they are not at fault.
    (The correct answer is d. This liability is a form of strict liability, the rationale for which is that people and businesses who engage in such activities, like construction blasting and demolition, will have insurance to cover any harm or losses caused. Neither intent nor negligence are factors; and public policy will not exonerate such actors. Actually, public policy by means of strict liability is in essence compelling these people and businesses who engage in these very dangerous activities to get insurance.)

17. Which of the following is TRUE about punitive damages?
    a. They can be awarded in a negligence cause of action if the defendant acted in a grossly negligent manner.
    b. They are awarded only if consequential damages are also awarded.
    c. They are awarded where specific performance is not available.
    d. Their purpose is to give the non-breaching party to a contract the benefit-of-the-bargain.
    (The correct answer is a. Punitive damages generally are awarded for intentional torts with the purpose of punishing the wrongdoer and having the punitive award act as a deterrent to other potential wrongdoers. They are not awarded in negligence cases unless the defendant acted in a grossly negligent or reckless manner indifferent to the safety of others, for example, playing with a loaded gun or driving under the influence, both of which would be criminal violations too. The other responses deal with contract law remedies where punitive damages are very, very rare, perhaps arising in a bad faith case where an insurance company breaches a policy for no good reason to the detriment of a poor person.)

18. False imprisonment is MOST ACCURATELY defined as:
    a. A person being held in prison without bail when formal charges have not yet been filed.
    b. The intentional confinement or restraint of another without authority or justification and without that person's consent.
    c. The unethical holding in prison of one who was convicted of crime that the person really did not commit.
    d. A confinement caused when one accidentally causes another to be confined without that person's consent.
    (The correct answer is b. The first response is legitimate criminal law procedure. Holding a person unethically may be immoral, but presumably the incarcerated person had a fair trial, and also attempts can be made for a new trial if new evidence is found. Accidentally confining a person will give rise to a negligence lawsuit but not one for intentional tort.)

19. Which of the following is TRUE about intentional infliction of emotional distress?
    a. Recovery of damages is allowed any time there is some amount of mental distress.
    b. There must be some physical contact with the plaintiff.

c. The defendant's conduct must go beyond all possible bounds of decency and be regarded as atrocious, outrageous, and utterly intolerable in a civilized society.
d. The plaintiff must have witnessed severe physical injury to a relative or other very close or significant person in the plaintiff s life.

(The correct answer is c. Physical contact is not required for this intentional tort, just that the conduct be outrageous, such as telling a child that his or her parents have died in a car accident as a "joke," but also the emotional distress of anguish caused must be severe. Physical contact is required for a successful lawsuit for negligent infliction of emotional distress, as per the old common law "impact" rule; but the final response in most jurisdiction is an exception to the "impact" rule.)

20. The MOST ACCURATE statement of the test that is applied in determining if a defendant was the proximate cause of the plaintiff's injuries is:
a. Was it foreseeable to the plaintiff that the defendant would engage in this particular conduct?
b. Given this particular injury to the plaintiff, was it foreseeable that the defendant was the cause?
c. Was it reasonably foreseeable that the defendant's conduct could lead to this kind of injury?
d. Was the injury foreseeable to the plaintiff prior to the injury's occurrence?

(The correct answer is c. The doctrine of proximate causation, also called "legal" causation, benefits carelessly acting defendants, who pursuant to the doctrine are not liable for all the consequences of their careless acts, but rather just those consequences which are considered to be reasonably foreseeable, as ultimately determined by usually a jury. As such, the defendant is not liable for the consequences of an action, even if careless, if the harms caused are deemed to be strange, remote, unusually, or caused in a convoluted and attenuated manner.)

21. The doctrine in negligence law which shifts the burden of proof from the plaintiff to the defendant is called:
a. Negligence *per se*.
b. *Res ipsa loquitur*.
c. Comparative negligence
d. Directed verdict.

(The correct answer is b. Negligence per se deals with a presumption of negligence benefitting the plaintiff when the defendant violates a statutory based duty. Comparative negligence is a partial defense to negligence where if the plaintiff was also careless his or her carelessness will be allocated a percentage of causation for his or her own injuries, which will reduce the monetary judgment paid to the plaintiff by the defendant. A directed verdict is a procedural legal doctrine by means of which a judge in a civil after hearing all the evidence, which is one-sided and overwhelming, can take the case away from the jury and direct a verdict for a party.)

22. The legal doctrine that arises when one intends to cause injury to another certain person, but instead actually causes injury to another third person is MOST ACCURATELY called:
a. The Transferred Intent Doctrine
b. The Unavoidable Accident Doctrine
c. The Negligent Actor Doctrine
d. The Unforeseeable Consequence Doctrine.

(The correct answer is a. When one purposely intends to harm another, for example, by going to strike a person with one's fist, and the actor misses, but hits another person, the intent to commit the act, in this case a battery, is transferred from the intended target to the victim, who thereupon can sue for the intentional tort of batter. The other doctrines are all aspects of negligence law, where one does not intend to harm anyone, but one acts carelessly and unreasonably and does so. An unavoidable accident is one in which there is harm, but no one is negligent, which unfortunate consequence is at times called an Act of God, for which there is no liability. An example would be

when a big bee enters a car through an open window causing the driver to be startled and to lose control.)

23. The intentional tort of false imprisonment is MOST ACCURATELY defined as:
    a. Being held in jail without bail while waiting for an arraignment.
    b. The intentional confinement or restraint of another without authority or justification and without that person's consent.
    c. The holding in prison of a person convicted of a crime who is appealing the conviction.
    d. A confinement that is caused by accidentally confining another person without that person's consent.
    (The correct answer is b. Note that false imprisonment is also a crime, and if the person is moved, called under the common law, asportation, the crime is now the more serious one of kidnapping. The first and third response are legitimate aspects of criminal law procedure; and accidentally confining one may be grounds for a negligence lawsuit but not an intentional tort.)

24. A non-public person in a tort defamation lawsuit must demonstrate all of the following elements EXCEPT:
    a. There was an untrue statement made that maligned the plaintiff's character or reputation.
    b. The statement contained a factual assertion and was not a mere opinion.
    c. The statement was communicated by the defendant to at least one person other than the plaintiff.
    d. The defendant definitely knew that the statement was false.
    (The correct answer is d. That is why the tort of defamation is called at times a "quasi-intentional" tort since the intent requires is the intent to publish and not the intent to defame. As such, there is no requirement that the defendant knew, let alone knew definitely, that the defamatory statement was false. The other responses are basic elements of the defamation cause of action. Note that if a "public figure" is suing the media for defamation he or she must prove that the defendant media acted with "malice," that is, they knew or should have known that the defamatory statement was false.)

7 - Products Liability

Introduction

Products liability law is a broad area of the law that encompasses several subject matters, to wit: breach of contract, fraud/deceit, negligence, strict liability, breach of warranty under the Uniform Commercial Code, and statutory consumer protection law. This section of the book will focus on the doctrine of strict liability, whereas the other subject matters as they relate to products and otherwise are covered in other sections. Strict liability law is based on common law tort; it is judge-made law with the precedential decision being made by the California Supreme Court in 1963. All states now adhere to the basic common law strict liability principles, though some limitations have been made by state statutes.

The fundamental principle emanating strict liability law for products is that for liability a product must be "defective" and "unreasonably dangerous to the consumer," though in most states if a product is deemed "defective" the law will presume that it is unreasonably dangerous to the consumer. Consequently, it is essential that the student know the three ways that a product can be a defective product, to wit: defective due to it being flawed or a run-a-way product (that is not meeting the manufacturer's own standards for that type of product); defective because it lacks a warning or the warning is inadequate, as well as defective because it is defectively designed. Moreover, regarding the latter the student must know the aspects of the design defect test for strict liability, to wit: the state-of-the-art when the product was made (and note not at trial), the possible safety modifications and improvements that could have been made, yet with the constraints of practicality of use and economic feasibility to making any safety alterations.

Most importantly, the student must understand that this liability is "strict," that is, without fault and thus there is no need to demonstrate negligence. In addition, as opposed to warranty law, this liability cannot be disclaimed and the notice and privity requirements of warranty law do not affect strict liability, meaning in the latter case that anyone injured by a defective product can sue and not just the buyer of the product. Furthermore, the student must be cognizant of the fact that anyone on the marketing chain who deals in that type of product – from manufacturer, to wholesaler/distributor, to retailer – can be fully liable to the injured consumer; so for example, a retailer can be held strictly liable for a product designed and made by a manufacturer which comes to the retailer in a sealed box which the retailer cannot open. In such a case, the retailer can always sue up-the-chain to the manufacturer (but "good luck with that" if it is in China!). The student now can discern some of the key rationales behind strict liability law, that is, to keep manufacturers current with the state-of-the-art, that is, the level of science, engineering, and technology, to advance safety, and to force entities on the marketing chain to obtain products liability insurance so an injured consumer can recover for his or her injuries. Finally, the student must comprehend that strict liability, though "strict," is not absolute liability since, first, the product must be defective; and secondly, there are defenses, such as misuse or abuse of a product, disregarding instructions, and assumption of the risk.

True and False Questions with Answers and Explanations

1. Retailers of products cannot be held strictly liable for design defects in a product made by the manufacturer.

(False: Anyone on the marketing chain in the business of making, distributing, selling the product is liable, even if it comes to the retail merchant in a sealed box or container, which is why entities on the marketing chain should obtain products liability insurance.)

2. There is no duty by the seller of a product to warn of risks of harm that are obvious to a reasonable person.
(True: For example, there is no duty to warn that a knife is sharp and can cut and that one can fall off a bicycle. Yet, manufacturers and merchants "err on the side of caution" and thus in many instances "over-warn" even if the warnings seem silly.)

3. Under the design defect test for strict liability whether any feasible safety modifications could have been made to a product is measured by the state-of-the art of science and technology on the date of the products liability lawsuit.
(False: The time frame is the date when the product was made, not possibly many years later when the civil trial occurs).

4. In a strict liability law suit the injured consumer must show that the manufacturer was negligent in making a flawed product.
(False: Strict liability is not the same as negligence; thus, evidence of fault or negligence is not required. The plaintiff just needs to show that the product is flawed, that is, the product does not conform to the manufacturer's own standards for that type of product.)

5. Products liability law is based on the socialist premise that money must be taken from wealthy and unscrupulous business people and given to the deserving poor and needy.
(False: Products liability law is based on risk-spreading, risk -sharing, insurance, and promotion of safety rationales, as well as compensating victims of defective products)

6. Strict liability is based on the fundamental premise that if a product is defective and causes harm not only the manufacturer but also any seller of the product is liable without any evidence of individual fault.
(True: If the product is defective because it is flawed any seller on the marketing chair is liable and there is no need to prove fault in how the product became flawed.)

7. Retailers are not strictly liable for defective products made by a manufacturer since it would not be fair and ethical to hold a retailer liable for the manufacturer's ineptitude.
(False: Retailers of that type of product are liable, even if the product comes to the retailer in a sealed package; consequently, the retailer should have insurance; and also the retailer who has to pay a victim can sue the manufacturer to recoup its losses.)

8. A manufacturer can be strictly liable for a design defect in a product even if the manufacturer was not negligent in the creation of the design of the product.
(True: Strict liability is liability without fault, that is, without proof of negligent conduct; and thus the manufacturer can be liable under the design defect test of strict liability which is a separate cause of action.)

9. The doctrine of strict liability applies only to products which are ultrahazardous or extremely dangerous.
(False: Strict liability applies to products which are defective because they are flawed, lack an adequate warning, or contain a design defect.)

10. In order to recover pursuant to strict liability for a product that is defective because it is flawed the injured party must prove that the manufacturer was negligent in creating the flaw in the product.
(False: The injured party need only prove that the product did not meet the manufacturer's own standards for that type of product. Strict liability is a separate type of lawsuit from negligence.)

11. A Statute of Repose may prohibit liability under products liability law for products that are a certain number of years old.
(True: These statutes and the time-periods, typically 20 years, are based on state law.)

12. Products liability law does not include strict liability as the latter is only for ultrahazardous as to construction blasting and not merely manufacturing and selling products.
(False: The doctrine of strict liability does apply to the manufacturer and selling of products that are deemed to be legally "defective" because flawed, lacking an adequate warning, or defectively designed.)

13. The duty of care of the manufacturer of a product encompasses providing a clear and conspicuous warning of all potential misuses of the product.
(False: Only warnings of reasonably foreseeable product misuses are required.)

14. Strict liability for defective products does not apply to the seller of a product that receives the product in a sealed container from the manufacturer and sells it without change or modification.
(False: The retailer is still liable and presumably has products liability insurance. Also, the retailer can always sue "up the chain" against the wholesaler and manufacturer.)

15. The doctrine of strict liability in tort does not require that the product be defective, merely that it caused harm to the consumer.
(False: The product must be deemed to be legally defective because it is flawed, lacks an adequate warning, or is defectively designed.)

16. Defenses to a product liability law suit include abuse or misuse of the product.
(True: Defenses also include not following instructions for use.)

17. Pursuant to the doctrine of strict liability a defendant is liable for harms only if the defendant intended the harmful results.
(False: Intent is not an issue for strict liability; neither is negligence. That is, defective product that results in harm will trigger liability even if the manufacturer was careful in making that product line. Similarly, if strict liability is based on ultra-hazardous activities, such as demolishing building with explosives, the "blaster" is liable for any harm even if the blasting was done otherwise carefully.)

18. Under the doctrine of strict liability, a retailer cannot be held strictly liable for a product that was defectively designed by the manufacturer which comes to the retailer in a sealed package or container and which is not opened or altered by the retailer.
(False: The retailer in most states is liable and thus should obtain products liability insurance. Also, the retailer can always sue up-the-chain to the manufacturer, presuming of course the manufacturer is not bankrupt or in China!)

19. In order to avoid being held strictly liable for a defective product based on a failure to warn, a manufacturer must warn the consumer of any risks of product use.
(False: The duty to warn does not extend to warning of risks that a reasonable and rational person should be aware of, for example, that a knife and scissors are sharp, and that one can fall from a bicycle. However, manufacturers now tend to "err on the side of caution" and warn of many risks that

one would think that a reasonable person would be aware of, for example, that one can fall from a loft bed as well as the "classic" McDonald's hot, actually very hot, coffee case that coffee is in fact hot.)

20. To determine if a product is defectively designed a jury would look at the state and level of science, engineering, and technology at the time of trial to ascertain if any safety improvements and modifications could have and should have been made to the product.
(False: The timeframe to look at the state-of-the art is when the product was made, not at trial, since in civil cases in large cities many years can pass before a products liability lawsuit is heard.)

21. Strict liability for products means that a manufacturer must exercise the highest degree of care in making a product or otherwise be liable for any harms caused by the product.
(False: Strict liability of products is based on a product being defective by either being flawed, lacking an adequate warning, or being defectively designed. Being careful, even very careful, in manufacturing the product would preclude a lawsuit for negligence but not for strict liability since "strict" essentially means liability without fault, i.e., without negligence.)

22. A bystander injured by a defective product cannot sue the manufacturer under the strict liability theory because the bystander did not buy the product from the manufacturer.
(False: The lack of a contractual relationship, called "privity" under the old common law, has been abolished for strict liability suits, and thus the injured bystander can sue.)

23. A manufacturer will be held strictly liable for a product that causes harm if the manufacturer did not incorporate the very latest safety features regardless of cost since one of the main purposes of strict liability is to promote safety.
(False: Yes, the promotion of safety is a rationale behind strict liability, but the manufacturer is only obligated to incorporate safety features at the time the product was made, and, moreover, this obligation is constrained by the cost of the safety features as well as the practicality of adding them to the product. For example, adding ejector seats with parachutes to passenger aircraft is likely "do-able but how much would such a modification cost and realistically how practical would it be.)

24. The lack of an adequate warning will render a product defective under strict liability law.
(True: Also, if a product is flawed, that is, it does not meet the manufacturer's own specifications, or if it is defectively designed the product will be deemed defective.)

25. Pursuant to strict liability law, a manufacturer can be deemed liable for a product that causes harm even though the manufacturer was very careful in making the product.
(True: Strict liability is not negligence law, and as such exercising care, even the utmost care, is not a defense; rather, strict liability is based on a product being deemed "defective," even if carefully made because it lacked a proper warning or could have been made safer in design.)

26. The doctrine of Market Share Liability was created as a legal device to apportion liability across multiple manufacturers of the same product.
(True: This doctrine is used when an injured plaintiff cannot determine exactly which manufacturer made the product that caused harm; and as such damages are apportioned based on the share of that product market each manufacturer has.)

27. In a product liability action, the injured plaintiff must have purchased the product directly from the defendant.
(False: The old doctrine of "privity," meaning there must be a contractual relationship between the parties for a lawsuit to be instituted, has been abolished in product liability actions. Therefore, the injured consumer who bought the product from a retailer can sue the manufacturer who made the

product. Moreover, members of the purchaser's family, friends, and even bystanders who are injured by the product can sue any entity on the marketing chain.)

28. The courts consider the profitability of a product to the manufacturer as a criterion to determine if there was a failure to warn of a danger of using the product.
(False: Profitability is not a factor, as the test for warnings under strict liability is that a manufacturer must warn of risks of product use that a reasonable person would not be aware of.)

29. Assumption of the risk and misuse of a product are valid defenses against strict liability.
(True: As such, one should not use a clearly broken chain saw, or juggle with chain saws, or if so for the latter, do it very carefully!)

30. A supplier's or distributor's failure to warn about the dangers of a product can give rise to a strict liability claim for a defective product.
(True: Strict liability for defective products applies to all the parties on the marketing chain, including suppliers, regardless of fault, who thus have a duty to provide adequate warnings even if the manufacturer fails to do so. A supplier or for that matter a retailer who has to pay a strict liability judgement can always sue up-the-chain to get relief from the manufacturer.)

31. An improper design can render a product legally defective even though the product as manufactured is flawless.
(True: The fact that the product meets the manufacturer's specifications for that type of product is irrelevant under the design defect aspect of strict liability law, which holds that if the product at the time of its making could have been made more safe by virtue of the state-of-the-art at that time, considering economic feasibility and practicality of use, the product is defective due to design.)

32. Design defect liability under strict liability law can readily be disclaimed by a wholesaler, distributor, or retailer since none of these parties designed the product that caused harm.
(False: Strict liability is "strict" not only because it is, as opposed to negligence, without fault, but also because it cannot be disclaimed. Of course, any of the afore mentioned parties who has to pay a judgment can always sue the manufacturer, assuming they can get jurisdiction.)

33. A wholesaler may be legally liable under the Strict Liability doctrine for a product defectively designed by the manufacturer.
(True: Liability is strict, and thus without fault, and the wholesaler is liable even though it did not design the product and actually even if the wholesale did not touch it (perhaps by merely transferring commercial paper or documentation regarding the product). The wholesaler's remedies are to sue the manufacturer if forced to pay a judgment and, as always, to have products liability insurance.)

34. A product can be in good condition, that is, meeting the manufacturer's specifications and not flawed, and still be defective pursuant to the doctrine of Strict Liability.
(True: The product can be defective because it lacks an adequate warning or because it is defectively designed because it does not incorporate safety alternatives and modifications that could have been adopted based on the state-of-the-art when the product was made, given the constraints of practicality of use and economic feasibility.)

35. A product manufacturer is not liable pursuant to the "design defect" test of strict liability if it can prove its product was not flawed.
(False: A productive can be defective due to design, even if the product is not flawed, because the design did not incorporate feasible, economical, and practical safety modifications and alternatives when the product was manufactured.)

36. Pursuant to the doctrine of strict liability, a manufacturer may be liable for harm caused by its product even though the manufacturer exercised all possible care in making and selling the product.
(False: Strict liability means liability without fault and is a separate legal doctrine from negligence. For example, a product even if carefully made may not have certain state-of-the-art safety features which were possible practically and economically to incorporate when the product was made, and thus the produce would be defectively designed, making the manufacturer liable under the strict liability doctrine.)

37. If a consumer uses a product improperly the seller has no valid defense under the Strict Liability doctrine since the liability is without fault.
(False: Improper use of a product, as well as abusing a product or disregarding instructions, are all valid defenses. So, do not climb on a cracked ladder, continue to use a toaster that is emitting smoke, or juggle with chain saws!)

Multiple Choice Questions with Answers and Explanations

1. Which of the following statements is TRUE regarding evidence of a product defect?
   a. If the product does not meet the manufacturer's own production standards for that type of product it is a "flawed" product and the manufacturer is strictly liable therefor.
   b. A design defect is established by evidence that the manufacturer careless deviated from its own production standards.
   c. A retailer is not strictly liable for a defective product that came to the retailer from the manufacturer in a seal container which the retailer was not allowed to open.
   d. Strict liability can be disclaimed and excluded from a consumer transaction if the consumer buys the product AS IS or WITH ALL FAULTS.

   (The correct answer is a. A product can meet the manufacturer's own standards and still be defectively designed because it did not incorporate practical, economical, and feasible safety improvements that existed when the product was made. Retailers are strictly liable for products defectively designed by the manufacturer regardless of the product coming to the retailer in a sealed container. The retailer who pays a judgment to a consumer can sue the manufacturer to recoup its losses. Strict liability, unlike the UCC's implied warranty of merchantability, cannot be disclaimed by a "catch-all" disclaimer.)

2. Each of the following is generally recognized as a defense to a strict liability in tort products case EXCEPT:
   a. The defendant was neither negligent nor at fault.
   b. The plaintiff abused the product.
   c. The plaintiff did not follow instructions or otherwise misused the product.
   d. The plaintiff assumed the risk of using a product that was defective.

   (The correct answer is a. All others are defenses. Since strict liability for products is "strict," the lack of negligence or fault by a defendant is moot; rather, liability is based on a product being flawed, lacking an adequate warning or being defectively designed.)

3. A design defect under strict liability law occurs when:
   a. a product falls short of the manufacturer's own established standards.
   b. the product meets the manufacturer's own standards, but the standards failed to incorporate current safety modifications when the product was made.
   c. the manufacturer fails to provide adequate warnings of risks associated with product use.

d. All of the above.
(The correct answer is b. The safety improvements must be achievable based on the state-of-the-art when the product was made and could be incorporated in a practical and economically feasible manner. Answers a, which is called a "flaw" defect, as well as c, are other ways a product can be defective, though in the latter case the manufacturer need not warn of risks that a reasonable and rational person should be aware of.)

4. Which of the following can be said to be a product "defect" pursuant to the doctrine of strict liability?
   a. The lack of a warning or an adequate warning on a product.
   b. A flawed product, that is, one that does not meet the manufacturer's own standards for that product.
   c. A product that does not incorporate state-of-the-art safety modifications which are feasible practically and economically.
   d. All of the above.
   (The correct answer is d. These are the three ways that a product can be deemed to be defective pursuant to the strict liability doctrine as applied to products. Note too that strict liability is viewed as a tort law principle thereby allowing tort damages to the injured consumer.)

5. Which of the following is a FALSE statement?
   a. If only one product is flawed out of thousands of similar products that were made by a manufacturer, the one flawed product might not be the basis for a negligence lawsuit, but could be the basis for a products liability lawsuit based on the doctrine of strict liability.
   b. Failure to warn about the dangers of a product can make an otherwise safe product defective pursuant to strict liability law.
   c. A defect in a manufactured product can make the manufacturer liable for injuries caused by the product even if the manufacturer exercised due care in the manufacture of the product.
   d. In a products liability lawsuit based on strict liability, an injured plaintiff need only prove that the product caused him or her harm.
   (The correct answer is d. The injured plaintiff must prove that the product is "defective" since strict liability is not a doctrine of absolute liability. A product can be deemed to be defective because it is flawed, that is, despite due care, it does not meet the manufacturer's own standards for that type of product. A product can also be deemed "defective" if it lacks an adequate warning or is defectively designed.)

6. Which of the following is a TRUE statement?
   a. The doctrine of strict liability has eliminated the doctrine of negligence as a potential legal theory for an injured person to recover for harms caused by a product.
   b. A product can be deemed defective if it is defectively designed even though it meets the manufacturer's own standards for that type of product.
   c. The doctrine of strict tort liability applies to the sale and lease of products and services.
   d. Strict liability can be effectively disclaimed or excluded from the transaction by a bold, conspicuous, and clear disclaimer.
   (The correct answer is b. The design defect theory for finding a product to be defective is separate and distinct from the product "flaw" standard as well as from the inadequate warning standard. Negligence is still a viable theory for a consumer to sue a manufacturer or any entity on the marketing chain for product-caused injuries, yet, of course, the injured consumer must be able to prove the elements of negligence, which requires evidence of carelessness, which may be difficult to obtain from inside the manufacturer's facility. Strict liability applies just to products not services. Strict liability, unlike warranty law under the UCC, cannot be disclaimed.)

7. Which of the following is a TRUE statement?
    a. One of the major requirements for a suit based on strict liability is that the product must be legally "defective."
    b. The doctrine of strict liability applies only to abnormally dangerous activities, but not to products manufactured and sold to consumers since that would not be fair to careful manufacturers.
    c. To succeed in a products liability lawsuit based on strict liability, the plaintiff must be more than a mere injured bystander who was injured somehow by the product.
    d. A product manufacturer violates the doctrine of strict liability if it does not incorporate the very latest safety features, regardless of cost and practicality, since U.S. law places a very high regard on consumer safety.

    (The correct answer is a. The finding that a product is "defective" is essential to strict liability for products. Regardless of care, not only the manufacturer but also the wholesaler, distributor, and retailer can be liable; and as such to protect themselves they should obtain products liability insurance. There is also a strict liability doctrine that applies to people and businesses that engage in very hazardous activities, such as dam building. For the design defect aspect to defectiveness of a product the manufacturer is obligated to incorporate safety features that existed at the time the product was made and not at the trial which might be several years later. Moreover, a manufacturer is not obligated to incorporate these safety features if to do so would render the product impractical and useless, like a knife that cannot cut, or if it would be economically not feasible to do so, like putting tank armor around cars).

8. Which of the following is a FALSE statement?
    a. Under strict liability law, a manufacturer may be deemed liable even if it has exercised all possible care in the making of the product.
    b. Products liability law does not encompass strict liability torts.
    c. The doctrine of strict liability can apply to products without adequate warnings of risks of use.
    d. Strict liability can be imposed for defects in the design of products that increase the extent of injuries to consumers if an accident occurs.

    (The correct answer is b. Strict liability for defective products is the "heart" of products liability law! Strict liability is liability without fault and thus the exercise of due care is immaterial if the product is "defective." Moreover, strict liability is a tort, meaning tort damages, including recovery for pain-and-suffering, are remedies for the injured consumer. Inadequate warnings, such as not telling the consumer how very hot the coffee is, as well as design defects, for example, the lack of a safety guard on an electric saw, will make a product defective.)

9. A wholesaler or distributor who is a defendant in a product liability suit based on strict liability can avoid liability if:
    a. The plaintiff had not purchased the product causing the injury.
    b. The distributor exercised reasonable care in all ways with respect to the product causing the injury.
    c. This product had been used for many years by other users without injury.
    d. The defect which caused the injury occurred after the product left the wholesaler or distributor.

    (The correct answer is d. Wholesalers and distributors are generally strictly liable, regardless of fault or negligence, and thus the exercise of reasonable care is immaterial. However, for a negligence lawsuit the fact that the product has been used for many years without mishap may prove beneficial to a defendant, particularly regarding a lack of a warning assertion. The fact that the plaintiff has not purchased the product, called "privity" under the old common law, is immaterial in a products liability lawsuit, and thus bystanders who are injured can sue. Note, though, that privity still may be a problem with a breach of warranty lawsuit under the Uniform

Commercial Code. Finally, the fact that the defect in the product occurred afterwards is a viable defense.)

10. If a manufacturer produces a defective product, sells it to a wholesaler or distributor, who sells it to a retailer, who sells it to a consumer, who is injured, which entities in the marketing chain are potentially liable under the doctrine of strict liability?
   a. Only the manufacturer.
   b. Only the manufacturer and wholesaler and distributor.
   c. The manufacturer, wholesaler, distributor, and retailer.
   d. Only the party at fault.
   (The correct answer is c. All parties on the marketing chain are liable for defective products, regardless of faulty, and regardless if the product comes to them from the manufacturer in a sealed container which they do not touch. The wholesaler, distributor, and/or retailer who must pay a judgment to an injured consumer can always sue "up-the-chain" to the manufacturer, assuming that they can get jurisdiction and the manufacturer has some assets. Recall that one of the purposes of strict liability for products is to persuade entities on the marketing chain to purchase insurance, which cost they can add to the price of a product, so that the injured consumer has some entity and source of funds for a recovery.)

11. What is the significance of a "defect" in a products liability case based on strict liability?
   a. It is not required if there is clear evidence that a product harmed a person
   b. It is a required element in the proof of such a case.
   c. Its presence would eliminate liability for the defendant.
   d. The party who caused the defect is the only one who can be held liable.
   (The correct answer is b. Strict liability for products is not a principle of absolute liability; rather to hold a manufacturer, as well as a wholesaler, distributor, or retailer, strictly liable there must be evidence that a product was "defective" and the defect caused the injuries to the plaintiff.)

12. Which of the following is a TRUE statement?
   a. One of the requirements for a suit based on strict liability in the U.S. is a failure to exercise due care.
   b. The doctrine of strict liability applies only to abnormally dangerous activities, such as construction blasting with explosives, but not to products and goods manufactured and sold to consumers since manufacturing is not normally ultra-hazardous.
   c. To succeed in a products liability lawsuit based on common law negligence, the injured plaintiff must prove that there was a failure to exercise due care by the manufacturer or seller of the product.
   d. One essential requirement for a products liability lawsuit based on strict liability is clear and convincing evidence of a failure to exercise reasonable care.
   (The correct answer is c. Negligence is premised on a failure to act as a reasonable person under the circumstance, which failure the plaintiff must demonstrate by a "preponderance of evidence" to typically the jury. The "clear and convincing" evidentiary standard is used for intentional misrepresentation, fraud, deceit tort cases. Strict liability applies to both very dangerous activities as well as to products that are deemed "defective.")

13. Products Liability law can be based on:
   a. Negligence
   b. Warranty law
   c. Strict liability
   d. All of the Above.

(The correct answer is d. Note that product liability actions can also include breach of contract and the intentional tort of fraud/deceit.)

14. Pursuant to the doctrine of strict liability for product:
    a. A product can be deemed defective even if it is not flawed
    b. An inadequate warning will make a product defective
    c. Even if a manufacturer is not negligent in the manufacture of a product the product can still be deemed defective.
    d. All of the above.
    (The correct answer is d. These are all very basic strict liability principles for products. Negligence is a separate cause-of-action as is breach of warranty under the UCC.)

15. Which of the following is/are legal constraints on the defective design component of strict liability for products?
    a. State-of-the-art
    b. Practicality of use
    c. Economic feasibility
    d. All of the above.
    (The correct answer is d. These are all basic constraints on the design defect doctrine, which may require the manufacturer to incorporate safety features that were available when the product was made if it is practical and economically feasible to do so. Recall that under this design defect standard the product is not flawed; rather, it could have been made safer with modifications and improvements.)

8 - Criminal Law

Introduction

A crime is a legal wrong against the public as a whole; and as such it is different from private wrongs, such as breach of contract and tort. Consequently, the student must be aware of the basic fact that there are thus two bodies of law – civil and criminal, with different definitions, classifications, elements, procedures, defenses, and sanctions, which sanctions can include for crimes monetary fines and imprisonment, whereas for civil wrongs the main sanction is the payment of money damages. The student must be aware of the two fundamental requirements to establish criminal liability – the wrongful, overt act, called "*actus reus*," which has been defined as criminal, and that this wrongful act was performed with the requisite state-of-mind, called "*mens rea*." Also critical to the students understanding of criminal law are the fundamental classifications between felonies, serious crimes punishable by death or imprisonment for more than a year, and misdemeanors, lesser crimes punishable by fines and/or imprisonment for less than a year. Similarly, another major classification is between crimes against the person, such as murder, and crimes against property, especially the theft crimes, such as robbery, larceny, and burglary. The student also must know that an act, such as purposefully hitting another person, that is, a battery, can be a civil wrong as well as a crime. Most importantly, the student must be cognizant of the higher standard of proof in criminal cases, "proof beyond a reasonable doubt" that the state prosecutor must demonstrate, as opposed to the lesser standard in civil cases, that is, the "preponderance of the evidence" requirement that the plaintiff must show. The student also must be aware that there are a variety of defenses to criminal law behavior, such as insanity, self-defense, entrapment, and Statutes of Limitation.

Regarding the criminal law process and procedures, the student must have a basic awareness of the four main stages, to wit: the arrest, the plea, plea bargaining, and the trial. Although also covered in the Constitutional Law section the student must know the fundamental constitutional protections that a criminal defendant is entitled to, to wit: the 4th Amendment prohibition against unreasonable searches and seizures and the concomitant warrant requirement, established by a showing of "probable cause," as well as the critical Exclusionary Rule for evidence obtained illegally; the 5th Amendment's Privilege against Self-Incrimination and the Double Jeopardy clause; and the 6th Amendment's right to a jury trial, legal representation, including an attorney provided for by the government, and the right to confront witnesses in open court, as well as the seminal *Miranda* rule, whereby a person must be notified of his or her right to obtain counsel. For business students, in particular, a basic comprehension of "white-collar" crimes, such as bribery, mail and wire fraud, and embezzlement, as well as types of "organized crime," such as money laundering and "loan-sharking," is called for. In addition, the student should know of the important anti-organized crime statute, the Racketeer Influenced and Corrupt Organizations Act (RICO). Furthermore, the student must know the major types of "cyber" crimes, to wit: "cyber-stalking," "hacking," and "spamming." Finally, the student should have a basic awareness of the Federal Sentencing Guidelines and especially how they impact corporate criminal activity.

True and False Questions with Answers and Explanations

1. If a jury construes the evidence in a criminal case as reasonably indicating a guilty or not guilty verdict, then the jury's verdict must be not guilty.

(True. The "beyond a reasonable doubt" burden of proof in criminal cases means the jury must be convinced of the defendant's guilt, on all elements of the offense charged, beyond a reasonable doubt, that is, to a moral certainty.)

2. When a person commits a homicide but with premeditation or deliberation that person typically may be guilty of first degree murder.
(True: If there is no premeditation or deliberation, but there is malice aforethought, that is, acting in wanton disregard of the consequences to the victim, the crime typically will be second degree murder.)

3. The crime of voluntary manslaughter will arise if there is an intent to kill but no malice.
(True: An example would be a crime committed in the heat-of-passion, but lacking malice.)

4. The crime of involuntary manslaughter arises when a killing results from an act of negligence but there is no intent to kill.
(True: An example would be when a drunk driver causes the death of another person.)

5. The burden of proof in a criminal law case is a "clear and convincing" evidence.
(False: The "clear and convincing" standard is used for certain types of civil law cases, such as fraud; it is a higher standard than the usual "preponderance of the evidence" for civil cases; but lower than the "beyond a reasonable doubt" standard for criminal matters.)

6. If a juror has a reasonable doubt as to any element of the prosecution's case against the defendant, the juror must find for the defendant.
(True: A reasonable doubt would be a doubt that would cause a prudent and careful person to hesitate before acting.)

7. Hearsay evidence is generally not admissible as evidence in court.
(True: Hearsay is an oral or written statement which is made outside of court that is later offered in court by a witness who was not the person who made the statement in order to prove the truth of the matter in the statement.)

8. A misdemeanor is a crime punishable by a fine or by imprisonment of less than one year.
(True: Misdemeanors are lesser crimes than felonies; imprisonment for misdemeanors is typically in a local jail and not a prison.)

9. An act of omission can be a crime but only when a person has a legal duty to perform an action.
(True: For example, failing to file a tax return.)

10. To commit a crime a person must have committed a wrongful act or omission and have a wrongful mental state.
(True: One must do a wrongful/illegal act, for example, killing a person, with the intent to kill, which would be the crime of murder.)

11. Larceny is the theft and taking away of personal property by fraudulent means.
(True: Examples would be pick-pocketing or an employee taking away a company's supplies home without permission.)

12. The crime of bribery can only occur if the intended bribe-taker takes the money or something of value given.
(False: Even the offer to make a bribe is illegal, regardless of whether the person offered the bribe accepts it; and accepting the bribe is another crime.)

13. If a person makes a mistake about the law while committing an act he or she lacks the requisite mental state to commit a crime.
(False: A mistake in fact may negate the mental state, as when a person mistakenly walks off with another's luggage; but a mistake in law will not, as "ignorance of the law is no excuse.")

14. Deadly force can be used in self-defense if there is a reasonable belief that imminent death or grievous bodily harm will otherwise result.
(True: Yet assuming the defender has not provoked or initiated the attack).

15. Generally, deadly force can be used to defend a dwelling only if there is a violent unlawful entry and the person believes deadly force is necessary to prevent death or grievous bodily harm.
(True: Also, in some jurisdictions, deadly force can be used if a person believes it is necessary to prevent the commission of a felony in or to the dwelling, such as arson.)

16. The entrapment defense means that a police officer, typically an undercover agent, suggests that a crime be committed and then pressures or induces a person to commit it.
(True: Police can set traps for criminals but cannot push or pressure a person into committing a crime. A key factor is whether the person who committed the crime was predisposed to do it or was pressured or unduly influenced into doing it by the police.)

17. The Fourth Amendment allows general or "blanket" criminal law warrants to search houses in a neighborhood for drugs and other contraband if the neighborhood has a reputation for being a "high-crime" area.
(False: To compare, administrative agency warrants, for example for OHSA inspectors, can be based on general and neutral area inspections of businesses for health and safety violations; but criminal law warrants can only be issues on a showing of probable cause.)

18. Probable cause for a criminal law warrant means that a police officer must demonstrate to a judge that the officer has reasonable grounds that a search will reveal a specific illegality.
(True: That is, the police must convince the judge that the search (and seizure) is more likely justified than not.)

19. The Fifth Amendment prohibition against double jeopardy means that once a person is acquitted in a criminal case, he or she cannot be sued by the crime victim in civil court for money damages.
(False: Double jeopardy does not preclude civil suits. Moreover, the state prosecution for a crime will not prevent a federal prosecution for the same activity.)

20. Generally, the Sixth Amendment right-to-counsel means that a statement made by a person while being interrogated by the police but without his or her lawyer present is inadmissible.
(True: The exception would be if a person knowingly, voluntarily, and purposefully waives his or her right to counsel.)

21. The Exclusionary Rule means that any evidence obtained by police in violation of a person's Constitutional rights as well as any evidence otherwise illegally obtained will not be admissible in court.
(True: The rule is based on the old "fruit of the poisonous tree" concept that tainted evidence is inadmissible at trial. At times, however, a guilty defendant may "get off on a technicality.")

22. The Miranda Rule means that a person who is arrested must be informed by the police of certain Constitutional rights.

(True. The rule is based on the famous 1966 Supreme Court case of Miranda v. Arizona. These rights include the right to remain silent and the right to have an attorney. If the Miranda warnings are not given, statements made by the accused are inadmissible in court, though there are exceptions.)

23. Before an arrest warrant can be issued there must be a showing of probable cause that a person has committed a crime.
(True: Probable cause means there is a probability, or substantial likelihood that a person has committed or will commit a crime.)

24. In a criminal trial the entire burden of proof is on the state.
(True: As such, the defendant does not have to prove anything.)

25. A "not guilty" verdict in a criminal case means that the jury concluded that the defendant was innocent.
(False: The "not guilty" verdict only means that there was insufficient evidence presented at the trial for the government to meet its "beyond a reasonable doubt" evidentiary standard.)

26. A defendant in a criminal case is not required to prove anything or to present evidence.
(True: This is a basic right as the burden of proof is on the state to present evidence and to demonstrate guilt. Moreover, the fact that the defendant did not testify and remained silent and/or did not present any evidence cannot be commented on by the prosecution and that fact cannot be considered as evidence of guilt by the jury.)

27. A reasonable doubt as to the guilt of a defendant can arise from the evidence, a lack of evidence, or a conflict in the evidence introduced at trial.
(True: If there is any wavering, vacillation, or the evidence indicates that the defendant could be guilty or not guilty, a juror must find for the defendant. One must have an abiding conviction of guilt after weighing all the evidence.)

28. Expert witnesses are allowed to give their opinions.
(True: Yet, like other witnesses, a juror may believe or disbelieve all or any part of an expert's testimony.)

29. No witness is disqualified because of age.
(True: The critical consideration is not the witness' age; rather, the key fact is whether the witness understands what is true and what is not true as well as understands the nature of and duty to tell the truth.)

30. A witness can be discredited by a jury if the witness has spoken to an attorney before testifying.
(False: It is entirely proper for a lawyer to talk to a witness about what testimony the witness would give if called upon to testify.)

31. In order to convict a person of a crime a juror must be 100% sure that the defendant is guilty.
(False: The standard for the criminal law is "beyond a reasonable doubt," not 100% certainty of guilt; and thus if there is some evidence of guilt but countervailing evidence of lack of guilt and the

defendant could be either guilty or not guilty, the juror must find for the defendant as a reasonable doubt as to guilt arises.)

32. The Foreign Corrupt Practices Act (FCPA) treats as a civil and criminal wrong all bribes in business.
(False: There are exceptions and affirmative defenses in the act that will permit payments to foreign government officials, for example, "facilitating and expedition" payments and legitimate and reasonable payments related to the demonstration and explanation of a firm's products and/or services.)

33. The "facilitating and expedition" exception to the FCPA will legally authorize payments to high-level government officials who have discretionary authority to award contracts with their government.
(False: This exception applies to lower-level government officials with ministerial, that is, clear-like authority, over routine government actions, such as processing visas and customs paperwork.)

34. State Whistleblower Protection Acts make it a crime for an employer to retaliate against an employee who discloses illegal conduct at the company.
(False: For those states that do have such statutes they make retaliation by the employer against the whistle-blowing employee, who presumably follows the requirements of the particular state's statute in properly "blowing the whistle," a civil, and not a criminal, wrong.)

35. When doing business in a foreign country the Foreign Corrupt Practices Act (FCPA) may permit the payment of money in the form of "grease" payments to lower level government functionaries.
(True: This is the "facilitating and expediting" exception in the Act which permits relatively small sums of money or modest gifts, often called "tips" or "grease," to lower level government officials, that is, clerks with only ministerial authority, to obtain quick and smooth performance of routine government actions, such as getting the utilities turned on, licenses issued, and inspections done, that a firm is legally entitled to.)

36. If a defendant in a criminal case does not testify in his or her own behalf a juror is allowed to construe that fact as evidence of guilt.
(False: A defendant under the 5th amendment to the Constitution has the right not to testify; and no inferences as to guilt can be made from him or her not testifying. The burden of proof to demonstrate guilt "beyond a reasonable doubt" is on the state.)

Multiple Choice Questions with Answers and Explanations

1. To be convicted of a crime under U.S. laws, the prosecution typically must prove the case against the defendant:
   a. By a preponderance of the evidence.
   b. By clear and convincing evidence.
   c. Beyond a reasonable doubt.
   d. None of the Above.
   (The correct answer is c. Reasonable doubt is the typical criminal law standard in the U.S. If a jury has any doubt as to guilt and that doubt is a reasonable one the juror must find for the defendant. The preponderance of the evidence is the standard used in civil cases (colloquially phrased as "50% plus 1%" of the evidence). Clear and convincing is an intermediate standard between the two usually use for civil fraud/deceit cases (and which is colloquially phrased as 75% of the evidence.)

2. Which of the following is TRUE about the Foreign Corrupt Practices Act (FCPA)?
   a. As a general rule, bribing a government official to wrongfully obtain a contract with the foreign government is a legal wrong.
   b. Facilitating and expediting payments of small sums of money to lower level government officials to speed up routine government "paper-work" that a firm is entitled to have processed is legal.
   c. Legitimate and reasonable expenditures and payments and reimbursements of money to foreign government officials for travel, lodging, and meals that are related to a firm's demonstration and explanation of its products and services are legal.
   d. All of the above.

   (The correct answer is d. Answer "a" is the general rule; and "b" and "c" are two of the major exceptions to the FCPA.)

3. "Cyber" crimes today encompass:
   a. Identity theft
   b. "Cyber-stalking"
   c. "Hacking" and "spamming"
   d. All of the above.

   (The correct answer is d. These are all basic types of crimes "inspired" and made possible by today's technology. Identity theft is when a person steals another person's identity or identification or financial information in order to access online and steal a person's financial resources. "Cyber stalking" is the technological equivalent of "stalking," that is, following or harassing a person, but now done online on the Internet. "Hacking" is the breaking into a computer or computer system without authorization, usually for the purposes of theft of information, for example, trade secrets or other confidential and proprietary information. "Spamming" is the mass sending of unauthorized bulk emails.)

4. Which of the following is FALSE about criminal law and procedure?
   a. The level of proof that a plaintiff must demonstrate in order to prevail in a civil trial alleging the commission of the intentional tort of deceit is greater than in a criminal trial.
   b. The victim of a crime may also be able to bring a civil lawsuit against the perpetrator.
   c. After a criminal defendant has been found to be by a jury non-guilty, the victim can still bring a civil suit for money damages against the same defendant if the victim has not already done so.
   d. Procedural protections for a defendant in a criminal case are greater than those for a defendant in a civil case.

   (The correct answer is a. The level of proof in a criminal case – "proof beyond a reasonable doubt" - is the highest level of proof. The lowest level is in a civil case – "preponderance of the evidence"; however, for a civil case for intentional fraud or deceit there is an intermediate level of proof – "clear and convincing evidence." Since civil cases and civil law and procedure are separate and distinct from criminal cases and criminal law and procedure, with the former being private wrongs, such as breach of contract, whereas the latter are wrongs against the state, such as murder, called in Old English Days, "breaching the King's peace," one can pursue both civil and criminal remedies. Moreover, even if there is a not-guilty verdict in a criminal case the victim can still sue the defendant civilly since the burdens of proof are different, as noted. Finally, another important distinction between civil and criminal cases is the degree of Constitutional protections given to a criminal defendant, such as the Privilege against Self-Incrimination, and the right-to-counsel, including a pro bono Public Defender if the defendant cannot afford legal counsel.)

5. Which of the following does NOT come under the general category of Tort Law?
   a. Strict liability for products
   b. Negligence for careless acting
   c. Crimes
   d. Intentional interference with contract

   (The correct answer is c. Crimes are governed by criminal law and criminal procedure whereas the other responses are all aspects of tort law, which is governed by civil law and civil procedures.)

6. What is/are key factors when it comes to fining a corporation for criminal behavior pursuant to the Federal Sentencing Guidelines?
   a. Whether the executives, officers, and managers knew of and condoned the criminal conduct or were they purposefully ignorant
   b. Whether the executives, officers, and managers cooperated with and assisted the government in the investigation of the case and the bringing of criminal proceedings.
   c. Whether the company had an effective legal compliance program at the time of the wrongdoing, was it communicated to the employees whose conduct was monitored, and was it enforced by sanctions for violations.
   d. All of the above.

   (The correct answer is d. These are all significant factors. Also, note that the philosophy behind the Sentencing Guidelines is to set severe penalties but then to give companies a significant incentive in the form of substantial fine reduction for cooperation, self-reporting, and compliance programs.)

7. What is prohibited by the Racketeer Influenced and Corrupt Organizations Act (RICO)?
   a. Money laundering
   b. Loan sharking
   c. To use money from racketeering activity to buy an interest or to maintain an interest in a business.
   d. All of the above.

   (The correct answer is d. Note that "money laundering" is the storage and/or transmission of "dirty" money through legitimate businesses and banks, that "loan sharking" is the charging of interest on loans more than the permissible legal interest rates, and that "racketeering" is very broadly defined under RICO to include money laundering and loan sharking, and gambling, prostitution, narcotics, counterfeiting, as well as mail and wire fraud, embezzlement and bribery.)

8. What is FALSE about the 4th Amendment's prohibition against "unreasonable searches and seizures?
   a. Probable cause is based on a reasonable belief that a suspect has committed a crime.
   b. Police and law enforcement officials are allowed to make the determination as to whether probable cause for an arrest is present since they are trained professionals.
   c. Evidence obtained in violation of the 4th Amendment is illegal and thus banned from trial pursuant to the Exclusionary Rule.
   d. An exception to the Exclusionary Rule may arise if the police act without a warrant or an invalid warrant but in good faith and obtain evidence otherwise inadmissible.

   (The correct answer is b. The determination of probable cause must be made by a neutral judge or magistrate and not the police and law enforcement. The "good faith" exception could arise when the police make a mistake or rely on erroneous information from third parties.)

9. What is NOT a category of theft crime?
   a. Arson
   b. Larceny

c. Forgery
d. Burglary

(The correct answer is a. Arson is the purposeful and malicious burning of a home or business or public building, including one's own home or business. Arson is a very serious crime and a felony. Burglary is the taking of one's personal property from one's home or business by an unauthorized entry. Larceny is the intentional, wrongful, and fraudulent taking of one's personal property, including intangible property such as trade secrets. Note that larceny can be further divided into larceny by trick and larceny by false pretenses. Forgery is intentionally and fraudulently creating a fake document or altering a document with the intent to adversely affect the legal rights or liability of another person. Forgery also may include in some states the unauthorized use of another's credit card.)

10. What is/are FALSE about the criminal law process?
    a. Most criminal cases are disposed of by plea bargaining.
    b. There is a higher standard of proof than in civil law cases.
    c. The defendant does not have to testify in his or her own behalf, but the prosecution is permitted to point out to the jury the fact of the defendant not testifying.
    d. A mistake in fact may negate a person's state-of-mind necessary for a crime.

(The correct answer is c. Since the entire burden of proof is on the state the defendant has an absolute right not to testify, and, moreover, the prosecution is forbidden to comment to the jury that the defendant has not taken the stand in his or her self-defense. A mistake in fact may provide a viable defense, for example, when a person takes a bicycle mistakenly thinking it is his or her own, and thus the act is present, but the requisite mental state is not; but there may be civil liability for trespass to chattels for a temporary dispossession or conversion for a longer one.)

9 - Contracts

Introduction

Contracts are the essence of business and thus business law. When an agreement rises to the level of a contract a business person can rely with some certitude that the promises and performance in the contract will be fulfilled; otherwise, there will be a legal sanction in the form of a civil lawsuit for breach of contract or other redress. Contracts, then, are the "heart" of business. Thus, contract law is the major feature of this exam review book; and as such contract law is divided into the following principal categories: nature and types of contracts; mutual agreement in the form of an offer and an acceptance; consideration; legal capacity; legality; the genuineness of the agreement; the Statute of Frauds and the writing requirement; third-party rights and responsibilities under a contract; performance, discharge, and termination of contracts; and damages and remedies for a breach of contract. Furthermore, the student must know that whether a contract is formed is not governed by the subjective personal feelings of the parties, but rather by the Objective Theory of Contracts, which holds that contract formation as well as interpretation are based on an objective "reasonable person" standard.

Nature and Types of Contracts

In one sense learning the law is like learning a foreign language since one must learn key words, definitions, and concepts in order to later comprehend and communicate in that language. In this section the student will be exposed to the "language of the law," that is, certain critical definitions and distinctions that will be necessary to understand and apply later legal principles. As such, the student must know the definitions of and be able to differentiate between or among the following, to wit: a valid, void, voidable, and unenforceable contract; an executory vs. and executed contract, an express vs. an implied vs. a quasi-contract; a written vs. an oral contract vs. a contract under seal; and a bilateral or mutual contract vs. a unilateral contract.

True and False Questions with Answers and Explanations

1. A quasi-contract is a legal fiction created by a court to redress unjust enrichment of one party at the expense of another when there is no real contract.
(True: A court will "pretend" that a contract exists to prevent unjust enrichment; but the court sets the price of the contract.)

2. The Uniform Commercial Code (UCC) since it is statutorily based completely repeals all the old common law of contracts.
(False: The UCC just applies to contracts for the sale of goods, not all contracts and thus common law contract principles are applicable to contracts for real estate and service and employment contracts.)

3. An implied contract is premised all or in part on conduct that evidences an intention to form a contract as well as indicates the terms of the contract.
(True: Implied contracts are to be avoided, of course, due to potential ambiguity.)

4. Oral contracts are never enforceable since people are known to lie.

(False. Unless governed by the Statute of Frauds oral contracts are valid and enforceable though to be avoided to due lapses or differences in memory, witnesses leaving the jurisdiction, death of witnesses, or possible fraud.)

5. Express contracts are imposed by a judge to redress unjust enrichment if a person is taken advantage of in an unethical manner.
(False: The means of redress for unjust enrichment is called a quasi-contract.)

6. If a contract is voidable either one or both parties to the contract may be able to disaffirm it, that it, to set it aside without any adverse legal consequences.
(True: An example would be contract made by a minor, but which only the minor can disaffirm. Voidable contracts must be differentiated from void contracts, which are null-and-void from the beginning.)

7. If there are ambiguous terms in a contract a judge will construe them against the party to the contract with greater economic power as that is the just thing to do.
(False: The terms are construed against the party that drafted the contract and/or inserted the terms.)

8. To help explain the terms of a contract a court may allow evidence of prior dealings between the parties.
(True: This principle also applies to terms in a contract which are vague and ambiguous.)

9. Pursuant to the Objective Theory of contracts, a person's words and actions are deemed to mean whatever the person subjectively and personally thought them to mean.
(False: The standard under the Objective Theory is what a "reasonable person," as determined by a jury, would think the words and actions would mean.)

10. Pursuant to the Plain Meaning Rule, the meaning of a contract can be determined from the face of the document as well as signed and notarized affidavits from the parties.
(False: The Plain Meaning Rule requires that the meaning must be determined by reference to the face of the document. Also, the Parole Evidence Rule may prohibit modification to contracts by prior or contemporaneous writings even if notarized.)

11. The common law governs all types of contracts.
(False: Contracts for the sale of "goods," that is, tangible, physical, personal property, are governed by the Uniform Commercial Code, which modern statute makes some significant changes to the old common law of contracts.)

12. The Objective Theory of contracts maintains that the intent to enter into a contract is determined by objective facts as ascertained pursuant to the "reasonable person" standard.
(True: Therefore, the parties personal, subjective intent is not controlling; it is what a jury applying the reasonableness standard determines as intent is controlling. As such, if a party is joking or acts out of anger those subjective feelings are not dispositive as to whether there is a contract.)

13. In order to be valid a contract must be in writing, prepared by an attorney, and affixed with a seal.
(False: Oral contracts are as a general rule permissible though not advisable; attorneys are not required though obviously advisable; and a seal is no longer required.)

14. If a contract is deemed to be "voidable," either one or both of the parties can disaffirm, that is, set aside the contract.
(True: This is a basic principle. For example, if there is a mutual mistake either party can disaffirm, and if a contract is made by a minor with an adult only the minor can disaffirm.)

15. A quasi-contract since it is a legal fiction has no legal efficacy.
(False: Although a "pretend" contract created by a judge, the quasi-contract is a legal and legitimate device to prevent the unjust enrichment of one party by another.)

16. A choice-of-law provision in a contract will set forth the jurisdiction whose law will apply to the contract.
(True: There also can be choice-of-forum provisions in contracts whereby the jurisdiction that will hear any disputes will be set forth.)

Multiple Choice Questions with Answers and Explanations

1. The elements of a valid contract are:
   a. Mutual agreement and consideration
   b. Capacity and legality
   c. A writing if the Statute of Frauds applies
   d. All of the above.

(The correct answer is d. These are the fundamental elements of a valid contract. Note that an oral contract may be possible if the Statute of Frauds is not applicable to the transaction.)

2. Which of the following is a FALSE statement?
   a. A quasi-contract has legal validity even though it is not a real contract.
   b. An executed contract is one in which all the contract terms have been fully performed by both parties.
   c. The intention to enter into a contract is governed by the subjective personal feelings of the parties.
   d. In a unilateral contract, one party makes a promise and in return wants the performance of an act

(The correct answer is c. The intention to enter into a contract is governed by the objective theory of contracts, that is, would the hypothetical "reasonable person," as determined by a jury, believe that a contract was formed. Even though a quasi-contract is a legal fiction, that is, a "pretend" contract, it has validity when it is created by a judge to prevent the unjust enrichment of one person by another.)

3. Which if the following is a *false* statement?
   a. All promises are legally binding contracts.
   b. The common law principally governs the formation of contracts.
   c. Pursuant to the objective theory of contracts, the intention to enter into a contract is determined by objective facts that are interpreted by the "reasonably prudent person" standard.
   d. An express contract between businesses need not necessarily be in writing.

(The correct answer is a. For a promise to be legally binding under the common law it must be supported by consideration. An express contract between whomever can be oral if the Statute of Frauds does not apply to the transaction.)

4. Which of the following is a FALSE statement?
   a. Parties can form a contract without putting the terms in writing.
   b. An executed contract is one that has been fully performed by all the parties to the contract.

c. A voidable contract is a valid contract but one that can still be disaffirmed and set aside by at least one of the parties to it.
d. A quasi-contract has no legal efficacy since it is a "pretend" contract.
(The correct answer is d. Quasi-contracts, as noted, have legal validity. Also, as noted, contracts can be oral unless the Statute of Frauds applies.)

5. A contract whereby a contractor has finished the construction as per the contract and in the future the homeowner will pay the contractor as per a promise in the contract is what type of contract?
   a. executory on the contractor's part
   b. executory on the homeowner's part
   c. fully executed
   d. fully non-executed
   (The correct answer is b. The contractor has executed its contract performance but since the performance of the promise to pay is in the future the contract is executory as per the homeowner.)

6. The intent of the parties to enter into a contract is governed by what doctrine?
   a. the objective theory of contracts
   b. the subjective theory of contracts
   c. the doctrine of *Res Ipsa Loquitur*
   d. the principle of *Caveat Emptor* ("Let the buyer beware.")
   (The correct answer is a. The objective theory and thus the "reasonable person" standard controls the intent to enter into a contract. Res Ipsa Loquitur, that is, "the thing speaks for itself," is a principle of negligence law. Caveat Emptor may come into play when a seller is silent about problems with the subject matter of a contract and the aggrieved buyer wants to sue for fraud.)

7. What type of contract is formed when one person makes a promise to another in return for the other person's promise?
   a. unilateral contract
   b. bilateral contract
   c. voidable contract
   d. promissory estoppel
   (The correct answer is b. A bilateral contract is also called a mutual contract. Promissory estoppel is an exception to the consideration requirement for a valid contract.)

8. Which of the following is TRUE regarding contract validity?
   a. A quasi-contract is a void contract since it is a legal fiction.
   b. A voidable contract is a good contract but either one or both parties may be able to disaffirm and set aside the contract.
   c. A voidable contract is a legal nullity since one or both parties may have a "free way" out of the contract.
   d. An executed contract is one which written by an attorney and signed and sealed by the parties.
   (The correct answer is b. As opposed to a void contract, which is a legal nullity, a voidable contract is a good one until it is disaffirmed.)

9. Which of the following is TRUE regarding contracts?
   a. Implied-in-fact contracts are void since they are based on conduct and assumptions and inferences and not express words.
   b. A contract that is fully performed by both parties is called an executory contract.
   c. A contract that has been fully performed by one party but not the other is called an executed contract.

d. A unilateral contract as a general rule must be accepted by the full and complete performance of the requested act.

(The correct answer is d. A major problem with unilateral contracts and an ethical weakness to the common law is that in a unilateral contract situation where there is some performance but not complete performance the party making the promise, likely a promise to pay for the performance, may revoke his or her promise since the contract has not been fully performed and thus there is no technical "acceptance" of the unilateral offer. Some states provide redress by saying that the commencement of the requested performance is the acceptance; others suspend the promisor's right to revoke for a reasonable time to allow time for full performance; and others simply use the quasi-contract doctrine.)

10. Which of the following is NOT a correct statement?
    a. The common law of contracts governs all types of contracts in the United States.
    b. A contract is an agreement between two or more parties that can be enforced in a court of law.
    c. Pursuant to the objective theory of contracts, the intention to enter into a contract is determined by the "reasonable person" standard.
    d. A voidable contract is a good contract until either one or both parties set it aside by disaffirming it.

    (The correct answer is a. As will be seen there is a newer body of contract law, the Uniform Commercial Code, which is state-based statutory law, that governs contracts for the sale of "goods." The old common law of contracts applies to all other types of contracts as well as sales of goods disputes where the UCC does not have a pertinent rule.)

11. Which of the following is a TRUE statement?
    a. A void contract is a good contract if it is in writing as per the Statute of Frauds.
    b. A unilateral contract is accepted under the common law by the full performance of the requested act.
    c. An express contract must be in a formal writing prepared by an attorney.
    d. An executed contract is one in which at least one party has completely fulfilled his or her contractual promises.

    (The correct answer is b. A writing will not save a void, usually illegal, contract. An express contract can be oral, let alone prepared formally by an attorney. Words, oral or written, make an express contract, as opposed to an implied contract, which is based in whole or in part on conduct.)

10 - Mutual Agreement – The Offer and Acceptance

Introduction

The first step in the formation of a contract is the mutual agreement requirement, which is composed of an offer, made by an offeror, and an acceptance made by an offeree. The student first must know the requirements and essential components of a valid offer, and especially be able to distinguish "offer" language from mere preliminary negotiations type of language. Next the student must know how offers come to an end, notably revocation by the offeror including when a revocation is legally effective. The student also must know the difference between a firm offer under the common law as opposed to an option. When an offer is accepted by the offeree the first requirement of a valid contract, mutual agreement, is present. As such, the student must know what an acceptance is and when it is effective, especially regarding the latter the old but still good "Mailbox Rule."

The student also must know that the offeree can reject the offer; and also the student must know when a rejection is legally effective. Critically important in the common law is the "Mirror Image" rule and what happens when the offeree changes or adds to or subtracts from the offer in a purported acceptance. Similarly, the student must know what a counteroffer is and its legal effect and be able to distinguish a counteroffer from a mere inquiry. Two problem areas that the student should be cognizant of are when the offeror attempts to use silence as an acceptance and what may happen regarding the acceptance of unilateral offers when an offeror revokes a unilateral offer before complete performance by the offeree.

True and False Questions with Answers and Explanations

1. Generally, advertisements are considered by the law to be offers.
(False: Advertisements generally are invitations to make offers.)

2. The existence of an offer is the first step in the contract formation process.
(True: The offer begins the process followed by the acceptance, which forms the mutual agreement requirement.)

3. A person will never be held to a contract unless he or she manifests a clear and unambiguous intent to be bound.
(False: The standard for intent is the "reasonable person" standard pursuant to the Objective Theory of Contracts.)

4. Offers to the general public can be revoked by communicating the revocation in the same manner as the offer without proof of actual communication to an offeree.
(True: The rationale is that the offer is not made to any specific offeree.)

5. Under the common law of contracts if a contract leaves the price to be determined at a later date the law will not permit the parties to settle on a price term to that contract later.
(True: A definite price is an essential term to a common law contract, as opposed to a UCC contract for the sale of goods.)

6. Generally, the offeror cannot revoke his or her offer until the offeree has at least a reasonable amount of time to consider and accept it.
(False: An offer as a general rule can be revoked by the offeror any time up until acceptance).

7. As a general rule silence will not be construed as an acceptance.
(True: There are exceptions, but this is the general rule.)

8. An acceptance is effective on dispatch as a general rule presuming the means of acceptance is reasonable under the circumstances.
(True: The rule is called at times by its old common law name, the Mailbox Rule.)

9. Generally, in the case of the formation of a unilateral contract the offer is deemed to be accepted immediately upon the mere beginning of performance of the requested act.
(False: Unilateral contracts as a general rule can only be accepted by the full 100% performance of the requested act.)

10. Pursuant to the common law an acceptance must be a "mirror image" of the offer.
(True: Any changes in the purported acceptance render it a counteroffer and thus "kill" the original offer).

11. An acceptance under the common law may be effective even when it is never actually received by the offeror.
(True: This result can happen pursuant to the old Mailbox rule where an acceptance is effective on dispatch, which is why the offeror should say in the offer "acceptance only effective upon receipt.")

12. If the offer is silent as to the method by which the acceptance is to be communicated the offeree can accept by using any means reasonable under the circumstances.
(True: The circumstances might include the method the offer was communicated, the nature of the goods, or market conditions.)

13. As a general rule, advertisements are not considered to be offers but rather as mere invitations to make offers.
(True: There are exceptions, for example, when an advertisement contains specific terms requests a specific act, such as coming to the merchant's place of business on a particular day and time, and most importantly limits the quantities of goods involved.)

14. An offer for a reward, for example, to return a lost pet, is not an offer since it is not communicated to any specific individual.
(False: Reward offers are an exception based on public policy to the "communication" rule that offers must be communicated to specific persons.)

15. The offeree has the power pursuant to contract law principles to cancel his or her offer before it is accepted.
(False: It is the offeror that has the power to cancel or revoke his or her offer up to the time of acceptance, and the note the offeree who has the power to accept or reject the offer.)

16. If no time is specified in an offer as to its termination date the offer expires after 30 days or if the goods are perishable after 14 days.
(False: Offers without termination dates expire after the passage of a "reasonable" amount of time; and the fact that the goods are perishable as well as the fact that the market for the goods is a highly fluctuating one are factors that would impact on what is "reasonable.")

17. An offer is automatically terminated on the death of the offeror.
(True: As well as the bankruptcy of the offeror, so as not to burden the estate and heirs of the offeror.)

18. As a general rule a unilateral contract offer can be revoked at any time up to the full and complete performance of the requested act.
(True: Such is the traditional common law rule, which can be very unfair if 99% of the requested act is done and then the offer is legally revoked. Some states therefore state that the beginning of the act gives the performing party a reasonable amount of time to perform. Other states use the old contract remedy of quasi-contract to provide redress to the partially performing party.)

19. To ascertain whether an offer was a legitimate one or simply made as a joke or in anger the court will examine the subjective intent of the parties.
(False: The standard is an objective one, that is, typically a jury will use the objective "reasonable person" standard in deterring whether a statement should be construed as an offer or a mere joke or statement made in anger.)

20. To accept a unilateral contract offer most states require that the requested act be fully performed.
(True: This rule means that the offer for a unilateral contract can be revoked by the offeror before full performance, which situation can be very unfair to the partially performing party, though the quasi-contract doctrine might provide some relief.)

21. Pursuant to the Uniform Computer Information Transaction Act (UCITA) when an offer is in the form of an electronic message and the offer evokes an electronic message accepting the offer the acceptance is effective on receipt by the offeror.
(True: This is a major statutory change from the common law, where the traditional rule, at times called the "mailbox rule," held that an acceptance (assuming reasonable means thereof) was effective on dispatch, not receipt.)

22. For an agreement to form the basis of a valid contract there must be an offer and acceptance.
(True: This is the first step, assuming the agreement is genuine, followed by the requirements of consideration, capacity, legality, and a writing if required by the Statute of Frauds.)

23. A statement of an intention to enter into negotiations to form a contract generally will be considered an offer since the end-result could be a contract.
(False: Generally, statements indicating an intent to enter negotiations are not construed as offers, but merely preliminary negotiations, for example, the statement by a party that "I would like to get X price for certain goods.")

24. The intent of a party to communicate a serious and legitimate offer is determined primarily by the assumptions and beliefs of the party making the offer.
(False: Whether a true offer has been made is determined pursuant to the Objective Theory of contracts, that is, how a "reasonable person" (perhaps as determined by a jury) would construe the statement, and not the subjective beliefs of the parties.)

25. Pursuant to the common law an offer to be legitimate must contain terms that are precisely, exactly, and scientifically stated.
(False: An offer merely must be "reasonably definite" under the common law.)

26. If no time for acceptance is specified in an offer the offer will automatically expire in 30 calendar days.

(False: The offer will expire after the passage of "reasonable" period-of-time, which time period may hinge on the nature of the subject matter, for example, if perishable goods, or the goods are sold in a market which fluctuates greatly.)

27. The common law Mirror Image rule requires that the acceptance must correspond exactly to the terms of the offer.
(True: Otherwise the purported "acceptance" is treated as a rejection and a counteroffer. Note, however, that under the Uniform Commercial Code for contracts for the sale of goods there, may be additional terms in the acceptance and still be a contract and, moreover, if both parties are merchants these additional terms may become part of the contract.)

28. According to the common law Mirror Image rule the offeree must accept the offer in its entirely with no changes, modifications, additions, or subtractions or a contract will not be performed.
(True: Such a purported acceptance by the offeree will be construed as a rejection and a counteroffer.)

29. An advertisement by a merchant for the sale of certain goods will usually be construed as an offer to members of the consuming public.
(False: Advertisements as well as sales "flyers," circulars, displays, etc. are viewed as not offers but "invitations to offers," that is, offers to the general public to come in to the merchant's business and make an offer to the merchant. This common law rule protects merchants. However, if a merchant engages in "bait-and-switch" tactics by not having the advertised sale goods, i.e., the "bait," available and then attempting to switch the consumer to similar but higher-priced goods the merchant may violate the Federal Trade Commission rule prohibiting such tactics.)

30. An invitation by one person to another to begin to commence contract negotiations will usually be considered as offer type language.
(False: Such "invitation" to negotiate language will be construed usually as preliminary negotiations and not offer-like language, for example, "I would like to get" or "Would you give," as opposed to "I offer" or "I want" language. Yet, remember the Objective Theory of contracts and the "reasonable person" standard.)

31. As a general rule an offer needs to be communicated to the offeree to be valid.
(True: A major exception deals with reward offers; that is, a person can perform the requested act in the reward offer, such as returning a lost pet, and then see the offer, and still collect the reward though there was no prior communication of the offer.)

32. Pursuant to the common law the revocation of an offer by the offeror will only be legally effective when it is received by the offeree.
(True: Such a common law rule could create a big problem for the offeree if the means of acceptance is deemed to be reasonable and thus effective on dispatch, because the offeror may wrongly assume that his or her dispatch of the revocation is effective on actual dispatch, but in the meantime and before receipt the offeree has accepted.)

33. When the offeree asks a question to the offeror about the offer the offer is automatically rejected.
(False: A question can be a mere "inquiry" in which the offeree just wants more information about the offer and which will not be construed as a rejection. An example, would be an offer for the sale of a painting where the offeree asks: "Does the price include the frame"? Such a question, even if answered in the negative, will not "kill off" the offer.

Multiple Choice Questions with Answers and Explanations

1. The requirements for a valid offer in contract law is (are) the following:
   a. The manifestation of a definite intent to enter into a contract by the offeror and the communication of this intent to the offeree.
   b. Reasonable definitiveness as to the terms of the offer.
   c. Seriousness of the intent on the part of the offeror as determined by the "reasonable person," objective theory test.
   d. All of the above.

   (The correct answer is d. These are all fundamental and accurate contract law requirements. Note that for the first answer at times it is necessary to determine, using a reasonable person test, whether words indicate an intent to contract or are merely preliminary negotiations. Also, communication means that as a general rule an offer communicated to an offeree cannot be accepted by anyone else. Note that for answer b the basic terms under the common law are the identity of the parties and the subject matter, the consideration, and the price as well as the "signature of the party to be charged," that is, the party who is denying a contract. Note too that under the UCC the price term is not necessary as the UCC will apply a "reasonable price" at the time of delivery of the goods. Note, moreover, in answer c that an offer made as a joke or in anger by the offeror may nonetheless be construed as a legitimate offer since the subjective intent of the offeror is not controlling; rather, the "reasonable person" as determined by a jury would determine the validity of the offer. Finally, note that if the Statute of Frauds applies a writing may be required.)

2. Which of the following is a FALSE statement?
   a. Mutual agreement consists of an offer and an acceptance.
   b. Death of the offeror terminates the offer even if the offer could still be accepted and carried out by the estate of the offeror.
   c. A counteroffer is treated as a rejection of the offer as well as a new offer.
   d. Revocation refers to the offeree communicating to the offeror that the offeree does not want to accept the offer.

   (The correct answer is d. Offerors can revoke their offers whereas offerees can reject offers. Counteroffers equal a rejection and thus the original offer is dead and consequently the offeree cannot change his or her mind and try to accept the original offer. Note that the death of an offeror also kills off any offers the offeror made so his or her estate is not burdened. Contracts, however, are another matter which the estate may be liable for unless they are discharged, for example, by impossibility due to the death of the performing party in a personal services contract.)

3. Which of the following is a FALSE statement?
   a. An option is irrevocable during the option time period.
   b. An offer made in jest or as a joke where a reasonable person would conclude that it was made in jest or as a joke cannot result in a contract.
   c. The offeror is the party to decide whether to accept the offer and thus make a contract.
   d. A contract remains executory so long as any party to the contract has not fully performed.

   (The correct answer is c. Offerors make offers; and offerees accept or reject. An option is a "firm offer," that is, one with a promise to hold the offer open, in which the offeree has paid consideration to keep the offer open, which means it is not revocable for the time period stated. The objective theory of contracts means that a "reasonable person" would decide whether certain language is a joke or legitimate offer language that which can be accepted.)

4. Which of the following is a FALSE statement?
   a. An offer for a unilateral contract generally may be able to be revoked at any time prior to the performance of the requested act.
   b. Under the objective theory of contracts, the courts will look at the subjective intent of the parties to determine if a contract was formed.
   c. A contract may be oral and be enforceable.
   d. The doctrine of quasi-contract seeks to prevent unjust enrichment when no real contract actually exists.

(The correct answer is b. The objective theory is based on the "reasonable person" standard, as noted, and not the subjective intent of the parties.)

5. What is a FALSE statement regarding contract formation?
   a. An invitation to make an offer will always be construed as an offer to promote business transactions.
   b. An offer in order to be legally valid must be reasonably definite.
   c. The offer as a general rule must be communicated to the offeree.
   d. Revocation is the retraction or withdrawal of the offer by the offeror.

(The correct answer is a. Invitations to make offers, for example, merchants' advertisement, window displays, price circulars, etc., are not construed as offers as a general rule; rather, they are construed as the merchants making invitations to the public to come into the merchants' shops and make offers to purchase the merchants' goods. The rationale of this common law rule is to prevent merchants from being "over-accepted" if the merchant has limited quantities of an item. However, if an unscrupulous merchant is engaging in "bait-and-switch" tactics, for example, never having the advertised "sale" items in stock and then trying to persuade the consumer to buy other items, which of course are not on sale, an aggrieved consumer can contact the Federal Trade Commission or a state equivalent as such bait-and-switch tactics violate consumer law as deceptive sales practices. Offers need only be "reasonably definite" under the common law; however, more precision will be required as to a quantity term in an offer.)

6. Which of the following is a FALSE statement about contract formation?
   a. A counteroffer is merely a return offer by the offeree which continues the negotiations to form a contract.
   b. The Mirror Image rule requires that an acceptance must have the same terms as the offer.
   c. An inquiry will not be construed as a counteroffer.
   d. If the means of an acceptance is deemed to be "reasonable," the acceptance will be legally effective on its dispatch.

(The correct answer is a. Counteroffers by the offeree are construed as rejections which kill off offers; there is nothing left to accept. However, a mere inquiry, by which the offeree just wants more info about an offer, for example, does the offer to sell the painting include the frame, does not kill off the offer, which still can be accepted or rejected depending on the answer to the inquiry. The fact that a reasonable means of acceptance means that the acceptance is effective on dispatch is called the Mailbox Rule, which can create major problems for parties that contract through the mails. Today, of course, the mails have been superseded by electronic communication, thereby minimizing the at times adverse effects of the Mailbox Rule.)

7. Which of the following is a FALSE statement?
   a. Pursuant to the common law "mirror-image" rule, an offer must be accepted in its entirety without modification, changes, deletions, or conditions, or else no contract can be formed.
   b. An advertisement is generally treated as an invitation to the public to make an offer to a merchant.

c. An invitation to negotiate usually will be construed as constituting an offer to enter into a contract.
d. An offer as a general rule needs to be communicated to the offeree to be effective.
(The correct answer is c. Invitations to negotiate would most likely be construed as preliminary negotiations and not "offer" language. Any modification or change to an offer is a counteroffer and thus a rejection of by the offer by the offeree pursuant to the Mirror Image rule. Note that the Uniform Commercial Code makes some major changes to the old common law Mirror Image rule.)

8. Under the common law an offer comes to an end upon the following events EXCEPT:
   a. Death of the offeror
   b. Rejection by the offeree
   c. Counteroffer by the offeree
   d. The offeree seeking more information about the offer
   (The correct answer is d. These are basic propositions. The offeree seeking more info is called an "inquiry," which will not kill off the offer.)

9. Which of the following actions would terminate an offer under the common law?
   a. Revocation by the offeror
   b. Counteroffer by the offeree
   c. Rejection by the offeree
   d. All of the above.
   (The correct answer is d. Again, these are fundamental principles of the common law of contracts.)

10. In order for an offer to be valid under the common law, the following requirements as a general rule must be complied with EXCEPT:
    a. The offer must be reasonably definite as to its key terms
    b. The offer must be in writing and include a statement as to how long it will be held open
    c. The offer must be communicated to the offeree.
    d. The offer must manifest an intent to enter into a contract.
    (The correct answer is b. Offers and for that matter contracts can be oral. If an offer does not state a time period for which it is open the common law will imply a "reasonable time," which is influenced by the subject matter, for example, perishable goods or goods that greatly fluctuate in a market, or what the means of communication was in making the offer.)

11. Under the common law, the Mailbox Rule maintains that:
    a. An acceptance which is dispatched in a reasonable manner will be effective when it is sent even if the offeror does not receive it
    b. Offers and acceptances can no longer be communicated legally through the mails since E-contracting is easier and quicker.
    c. An offer that says "time is of the essence" is effective when sent in the mail.
    d. A revocation of an offer is effective when it is dispatched by the offeror.
    (The correct answer is a. What is reasonable mainly depends on the facts and circumstances of a case but important factors would be the type of communication the offeror used in making the offer, the subject matter of the offer, and the history of the parties dealings. "Time is of the essence" is a clause in a common law contract to be used when a party wants performance on an exact day, and if not there will be a breach of contract. Note that under the common law even if a contract has a performance date the date for performance will be that date and a reasonable time thereafter, which is why a "time is of the essence" clause is a very important part to a contract when a party absolutely needs and wants performance on an exact day. One can still use the mails

for contracting but there are risks when one combines the revocation, rejection, and acceptance rules, particularly when they are effective.)

12. Which of the following is a TRUE statement?
   a. One cannot really accept a reward offer if one does the requested act and then learns of the reward for it since there is no technical "communication" of the offer to an offeree.
   b. Pursuant to the common law an offer usually does not have to be communicated to the offeree in order to be effective.
   c. Under the common law in order to exercise an effective power of acceptance the offeree must accept the offeror's terms unconditionally and unequivocally.
   d. . The death of an offeror will not terminate the offer since the offeror's estate can still contract on the offeror's behalf.

(The correct answer is c. The correct answer once again is a restatement of the common law Mirror Image rule. Reward offers are an exception to the communication requirement for an offer based on grounds of public policy to encourage people to aid law enforcement and return lost items and pets.)

11 - Consideration

Introduction

Consideration is a key element to a contract because under the common law promises are not legally enforceable unless they are supported by consideration. Accordingly, determining if consideration is present is a fundamental aspect of contract law and analysis. The student thus must be cognizant of the principal test for ascertaining the presence of consideration, called the "Detriment to the Promisee" test, as well as the types of legal "detriment" that the promisee can undergo to make the promisor's promise enforceable. The student must also be aware that under the common law a court is just concerned with the "presence" of consideration and not the "adequacy" of consideration. Consequently, a court will not be "policing" contracts to see if the consideration given is fair and ethical. The student must comprehend the rule that consideration must be a "bargained for exchange" and how that rule applies to cases of "past consideration" and "moral consideration." The student, moreover, must be aware of examples of insufficient consideration, particularly when a party is already obligated to perform some duty by virtue of a pre-existing public duty or a pre-existing private contractual duty as well as the exceptions to these pre-existing duty rules. Finally, the student must know the exceptions to the consideration requirement, especially the doctrine of Promissory Estoppel.

True and False Questions with Answers and Explanations

1. Social promises are always enforceable in court because it is just to do so.
(False: A promise not supported by consideration is generally unenforceable).

2. Unequal bargaining power between the parties to a contract will render it unenforceable since a court will always weigh the value of the respective promises.
(False: Unequal bargaining power will not in-and-of-itself vitiate a contract. A court is concerned with the presence of consideration and not the adequacy of consideration; and thus as a general rule a court will not "police" contracts for fairness.)

3. Consideration requires that the act or promise to perform must have direct monetary or economic value.
(False: Consideration can be forbearance, for example, quitting smoking or promising the quit.)

4. Courts usually will examine the adequacy of the consideration in a contract to ensure that the exchange is an equal and fair one.
(False: Courts are concerned with the presence of consideration, not its adequacy, assuming no fraud, mistake, duress, and undue influence. Courts generally do not "police" contracts for fairness; and as such one can make all the "bad bargains" that one can!).

5. If only one party to a contract has the power to cancel the contract, but that party is required contractually to give two weeks-notice, there is no consideration because the party with the power to cancel has given an illusory or fake promise.

(False: The two-weeks-notice limitation is legal detriment and thus the promise is a real one and thus there is consideration.)

6. In a liquidated debt situation there is no legitimate dispute as to the existence of the amount of the debt.
(True: As opposed to an unliquidated debt where either is in dispute.)

7. Where there is a liquidated debt, a debtor putting a notice on the back of a check "payment in full" generally will discharge the debt if the check is endorsed by the creditor.
(False: The majority rule is that the creditor can still sue for the balance of the debt, though in some states the endorsement is effective. The notice would discharge the debt if it was unliquidated and thus in dispute.)

8. Forbearance as a general rule is considered to be legal detriment for the consideration requirement to a contract.
(True: Assuming, of course, that one has the legal right to give up or to promise to give something.)

9. The principal test to determine if consideration is present in a contract is called the "benefit to the promisor" test.
(False: The principal test is the "detriment to the promisee" test.)

10. The consideration element in contract law will make a promise legally enforceable in a court of law.
(True: Assuming, of course, the other requirements of a contract are present.)

11. A promise not supported by consideration is not enforceable by a lawsuit even though it is neither moral or ethical to break one's promise.
(True: Consideration is critical to the enforceability of promises. There is clearly a distinction between legality, based on the law, and morality, based on ethics, which is a branch of philosophy.)

12. A formal seal with an imprint in wax by a signet ring is required today as a contract formality in real estate contracts over $500,000 in value.
(False: In modern times the requirement of a seal has been abolished in all contracts.)

13. The Objective Theory of contracts maintains that an offer made in jest or out of anger may be the basis for a contract even if the person making the offer subjectively did not intend to make an offer.
(True: The Objective Theory is premised on a "reasonable person" test, not subjective or personal intentions.)

14. An offeror makes an offer to an offeree; a promisor makes a promise to a promisee.
(True: One cannot get more basic than this!).

15. A bilateral contract is formed when a promisor gives a promise in return for the performance of an act.
(False: A bilateral contract is based on the making of a promise for a return promise. A contract based on a promise being given for the performance of an act is called a unilateral contract.)

16. If the detriment performed by the promise causes the promisor's promise to pay the "bargained-for-exchange" requirement of consideration is fulfilled.
(False: Just the opposite, the promise must cause the detriment, not the opposite, which result might be unfair but legal due to consideration rules.)

17. The promise to perform a contract duty that one has pre-existing duty to perform by a prior contract is generally insufficient consideration.
(True: As such, a promise to pay a party more money for the performance of a pre-existing contract duty is not enforceable because not supported by consideration. There are exceptions, for example, when the performance unforeseeably has become much more difficult.)

18. If the parties to a contract agree to cancel or rescind their contract and enter into a new contract with similar terms but for more monetary payment the courts will not enforce the new agreement due to the pre-existing private duty rule.
(False: Mutual rescission will cancel the prior agreement and then the parties are free to negotiate a new agreement.)

19. A promise made regarding a beneficial performance to a party that has already occurred is enforceable on grounds of morality and ethics.
(False: Due to the bargained-for-exchange rule of consideration the promise is not enforceable regardless of moral and ethical concerns.)

20. The doctrine of Promissory Estoppel means that a promisor can legally refuse to fulfill a promise.
(False: Promissory estoppel is an exception to consideration; that is, the promisor's promise is enforceable even without technical legal consideration if the requirements of the doctrine are present.)

21. Promises to family members and friends create moral obligations enforceable by a court of law.
(False: Promises must be supported by consideration to be enforceable; moral obligations are insufficient.)

22. The rule that consideration must be a "bargained for exchange" means that the detriment, that is, the performance, can cause the promise to pay.
(False: Just the opposite; the promise must cause the detriment, which means that the promise to pay for a previously done performance is not enforceable regardless of a lack of fairness.)

23. Option contracts are irrevocable.
(True: It is the payment or promise of some type of consideration by the offeree to the offeror which supports the offeror's promise to keep the offer open for a period of time, as opposed to a "firm offer" which under the common law is revocable by the offeror regardless of any promise to hold it open. Yet note there is a Uniform Code exception for merchants called the Merchant's Firm Offer, which is irrevocable even without consideration if certain conditions are met.)

24. Legally sufficient detriment to fulfill the consideration requirement to a contract may consist of forbearance from a legal act.
(True: "Legal" is critical as one must have the legal right to do the activity one is promising not to do or not doing.)

25. The courts under the common law generally will evaluate the adequacy of consideration in a contract since a court is supposed to do "justice" and prevent people from making "bad bargains."
(False: Just the opposite as a court is merely concerned with the presence of consideration and not the adequacy, meaning courts will not "police" contracts for fairness and consequently one can make all the bad bargains one wants. Note, however, there is a limited exception under the Uniform Commercial Code for contracts that are deemed "unconscionable" by a court.)

26. An illusory promise is not enforceable by either party to the contract due to a lack of consideration.
(True: There is no legal detriment to an illusory promise, for example, an unrestricted cancellation clause whereby a party has a "free-way" out of the contract, and consequently there is no consideration.)

27. The promise to pay a debt which is barred by the Statute of Limitations will always require new consideration to revive the debt obligation.
(False: This is an exceptional situation based on public policy where the mere promise itself will revive the obligation and thus the promise to pay will be enforceable even without consideration, though a writing may be required in some states.)

28. All promises are construed as legally binding contacts since that is the ethical approach to take to making-promises.
(False: A promise not supported by consideration is not enforceable as a contract regardless of any ethical or moral concerns.)

29. A bilateral contract is created when one party makes a promise and wants, and gets, a return promise from the other party.
(True: This is a basic principle, as opposed to a unilateral contract situation where one party makes a promise and wants in return not another promise but the performance of an act.)

Multiple Choice Questions with Answers and Explanations

1. The consideration element to a contract under the common law can as a general rule be satisfied with:
   a. The promisee doing an act or refraining from doing an act in consideration of the promisor's promise.
   b. The promise making a return promise to do something or to refrain from doing something in consideration of the promisor's promise.
   c. Both a. and b.
   d. Neither a and b.
   (The correct answer is c. The first two responses form the essence of the consideration requirement under the common law and are known as "legal detriment" on the part of the promisee. Without legal detriment a person as a general rule may legally break his or her promise, though it may not be moral to do so. Also, when the promise refrains from doing an act or promises to refrain this is known in the law as "forbearance." However, to be valid as consideration the promisee must refrain from, or promise to refrain from, an action that he or she has the legal right to do. For example, a promise to quit doing illegal drugs would not be consideration but a promise to quit smoking would be construed as legal "detriment" despite the good health effect and thus would be consideration.)

2. What is an example of insufficient consideration?
   a. Performing a requested act that one has the legal right to perform
   b. Making a return promise to do an act that one can legally do
   c. Making a return promise not to do an act that one has the legal right to do
   d. Promising to perform an act that one has a public duty to do.
   (The correct answer is d. A pre-existing public duty, for example, of a police officer or fire-fighter to do their jobs, or a witness in court to tell the truth, will vitiate the legal detriment since the promise is already legally obligated to perform these actions. Not doing or promising not to do an act that one has a legal right to do is called "forbearance," which is detriment and thus which is consideration.)

3. Which of the following is TRUE about the consideration requirement for a valid contract?
   a. The common law is concerned with the presence of consideration, not the adequacy of consideration.
   b. Forbearance, that is, a promise not to do something, cannot be consideration.
   c. The promisor is the person to whom a promise is made.
   d. Modification of a common law contract does not require new consideration, only a written agreement between the parties.

   (The correct answer is a. Promisors make promises to promises. Judges just look for the presence of consideration and under the common law do not get concerned with the adequacy of consideration; that is, judges do not measure and weigh the worth of a promise for an act or return promise. Modification of a contract under the common law will require new consideration; but note that the rule is different under the Uniform Commercial Code, as will be seen.)

4. Which of the following constitutes legal consideration for a contract under the common law?
   a. a promise based on a moral obligation
   b. a promise to modify a contract with new performance
   c. a promise based on past consideration
   d. a promise based on a pre-existing public duty

   (The correct answer is b. New performance, that is, something different, even if minor, will be construed as detriment and thus be legal consideration.)

5. An example of valid consideration is:
   a. Past moral obligations
   b. The performance of public duties one is already obligated to perform
   c. The performance of private contractual duties that one is already obligated to perform
   d. None of the above.

   (The correct answer is d. These are all examples of insufficient consideration.)

6. The rule that consideration must be a "bargained for exchange" means that:
   a. The consideration in the contract must be fair and ethical.
   b. A past moral obligation can motivate a promise to pay.
   c. The promise of the promisor must cause the detriment to the promisee.
   d. The parties must engage in mediation before any lawsuits for breach of contract can be instituted.

   (The correct answer is c. One cannot have under the common law the act come first and then a promise by a promisor to pay for the act, perhaps due to moral or ethical feelings. The promise must cause the act. The common law just looks for the presence of consideration, not whether it is fair or ethical. Under the common law one can make all the "bad bargains" one wants to, assuming no fraud or deceit, of course. Mediation is not required for breach of contract disputes unless, of course, it is contractually required in a particular contract.)

7. Which of the following is a FALSE statement.
   a. The common law is concerned primarily with the presence of consideration and not the adequacy of consideration.
   b. A promise by a party to pay another for refraining from performing a legal act is generally enforceable under the common law.
   c. The pre-existing common law rule of contracts allows a party who is bound by a prior contract to perform a duty to use that same performance as new consideration.
   d. An offeror can revoke an option contract if the offeror feels that the consideration given for it is insufficient.

(The correct answer is c. Using the same performance that one is already required to do by a pre-existing public or private contractual duty is insufficient consideration. Forbearance, as noted, is detriment and thus consideration, assuming of course that one is refraining from or promising to refrain from doing an act one has a legal right to do. Option contracts, wherein the promise to keep the offer open is supported by consideration, are not revocable as an ordinary offer would be.)

12 - Capacity

Introduction

The legal requirement of capacity deals with "legal capacity," that is, those circumstances that would render a contract voidable by a party due to some type of condition, state, or infirmity of that party that renders him or her with no or diminished contractual capacity. Capacity does not mean that one has the intelligence, knowledge, maturity, and business sense to make "good" contracts. As emphasized in the prior section, the common law is concerned not with the adequacy of consideration but just the presence of consideration, meaning one can make all the "bad bargains" one can and not expect any help from the courts to overturn them.

Accordingly, the student must know who lacks contractual capacity. The main category, which has significant business implications, deals with "minors," that is, young people not over the state age for making contracts, which is typically 18 years of age. As such, the student must know the general rule that a contract by a minor is voidable at the option of the minor (but not the adult, usually a merchant) and, most importantly, that in most states the minor's only responsibility is to give back the consideration if the minor is able to do so regardless of any loss, damage, destruction, or depreciation to the consideration.

The student also must be aware of two major exceptions to this rule, first, when the minor lies about his or her age, and when the subject matter of the contract is/are "necessities." The student also must be cognizant of the doctrine of ratification, that is, when the minor, either expressly or impliedly, can ratify contracts made when he or she was a minor. Finally, the student should be aware that person can lack contractual capacity if he or she is under the influence of drugs or alcohol, the victim of "undue influence," or is insane.

True and False Questions with Answers and Explanations

1. A contract by a minor for the purchase of goods can be disaffirmed by the minor up until the age of majority and a reasonable time thereafter.
(True: Conversely, a minor after reaching majority can ratify the contract made while a minor either expressly or impliedly by continuing to use the goods for more than a reasonable time after reaching majority.)

2. A minor who misrepresents his or her age nevertheless can still disaffirm a contract and is not liable for any loss, damage, or depreciation to the goods sold.
(False: In most states the minor can disaffirm but the minor is responsible for any loss, damage, or depreciation.)

3. Minors are legally obligated to pay the contract price for goods that are deemed to be "necessities."
(False: The contract is valid but the minor needs only to pay a "reasonable" price as set by the court.)

4. Ratification of a contract by a minor must be done by a signed writing when the minor reaches the age of majority.
(False: Ratification can also be implied, for example, by the minor continuing to use the goods for more than a reasonable time after reaching the age of majority.)

5. As a general rule a minor can disaffirm a contract and is not responsible for any loss, damage, or depreciation to the goods.
(True: As such, it is very risky for a merchant to deal with a minor unless the minor certifies that he or she is at or over the age of majority or, preferably, the merchant gets an adult to co-sign the contract as a surety or guarantor.)

6. A minor cannot disaffirm a contract for automobile insurance due to public policy safety concerns.
(False: The minor can disaffirm the contract as well as the contract for the auto itself, unless the auto and the insurance are deemed to be "necessities.")

7. As a general rule a person who is intoxicated can disaffirm a contract made while intoxicated and need not make any restitution to the other contract party since it would not be fair to the intoxicated party.
(False: A party who is intoxicated can disaffirm but the majority rule is that the intoxicated person is liable for any loss, damage, or depreciation of the subject matter.)

8. A contract by a person who has been adjudged to be mentally incompetent is voidable by his or her guardian.
(False: Such contracts by people deemed legally to be mentally incompetent are void, not voidable. Whereas people who may be mentally incompetent but not deemed so after a legal proceeding can enter into voidable contracts.)

9. Minors who misrepresent, that is, lie, about their age can still set aside their contracts made while minors.
(True: Such contracts are still voidable by the minor; however, in most states because of the misrepresentation the minor may be responsible for any loss, damage, depreciation, or destruction of the goods, as opposed to a minor who does not lie about his or her age.)

10. A minor's right to disaffirm a contract is contingent in most states on the minor paying a "reasonable" price for the goods or services since to do otherwise would be unfair to the merchant.
(False: The general rule is that a minor can disaffirm a contract and not be responsible for any loss, damage, depreciation, or destruction to the goods as well as use of services. There are two main exceptions, however, for goods deemed "necessities" and when the minor misrepresents his or her age.)

11. A contract entered into by a person who is intoxicated is a void contract due to the person's inebriated state.
(False: A contract by an intoxicated person may be voidable depending on the degree of intoxication but in most states the intoxicated person is liable for any damage, loss, depreciation, or destruction of the goods as well as the use of any services.)

Multiple Choice Questions with Answers and Explanations

1. Which of the following is a TRUE statement?
   a. To disaffirm a contract, a minor must act before reaching the age of majority.
   b. The contract by a person adjudged insane after a legal proceeding is a voidable contract.
   c. A minor may be liable for a contract matter if the subject matter is a "necessity."

d. A person who is under the influence of drugs or alcohol can disaffirm a contract and not be liable for any loss or damage to the goods.

(The correct answer is c. Minors are liable for contracts for necessities, such as medical care; however, the judge will set the price of the contract, so the minor is not taken advantage of. Determining exactly what is a "necessity" is at times a challenging question, though some states use the "station-in-life" rule to look at the minor's lifestyle to ascertain what is a necessity to him or her. Minors have until the age of majority and a reasonable time thereafter to disaffirm and set aside contracts they made while minors. A contract by a person legally declared insane is a void one. The contract by a person who is under the influence of drugs or alcohol is a voidable one but he or she is liable for any loss or damage to the consideration.)

2. What is a FALSE statement about the contractual capacity requirement of a contract?
   a. Contract capacity means that one has the intellectual capacity and business "smarts" to enter into lucrative deals.
   b. Minors' contracts generally are voidable at the option of the minor.
   c. Disaffirmance is the legal right of a party without contractual capacity to set aside the contract.
   d. A minor is allowed to ratify, that is, to give assent to, a contract made when he or she was a minor.

   (The correct answer is a. Contractual capacity means legal contractual capacity not intellectual capacity. Ratification can be express by the minor when he or she turns 18 years of age or implied, for example, by the minor continuing to use the goods or services for more than a reasonable amount of time after turning 18 years of age.)

3. As a general rule the contract made by a minor:
   a. is void since public policy protects minors from being taken advantage of by unscrupulous adults.
   b. is voidable at the option of the minor or merchant contracting with the minor
   c. is voidable at the option of the minor
   d. must be in writing and co-signed by an adult to be enforceable

   (The correct answer is c. The contract with a minor SHOULD be co-signed by an adult who should sign as a surety, which topic will be covered in a later section. Minors contracts are voidable but just by the minor.)

4. Regarding contracts made by a minor which of the following is FALSE?
   a. A minor is permitted to set aside the contract even after reaching the age of majority but only for a reasonable time thereafter.
   b. An adult is not permitted to set aside a contract made with a minor.
   c. The minor is obligated to pay the agreed price on a contract for necessities.
   d. A minor who represents his or her age may still be allowed to disaffirm the contract but may be liable for loss, destruction, and/or depreciation to the subject matter.

   (The correct answer is c. In a contract for necessities, as noted, the judge determines the price. The general rule is that the minor is not responsible for loss or damage to the goods, but an important exception is when the minor lies about his or her age.)

5. When a minor continues to use goods purchased as a minor after the minor has reached the age of 18 years the minor may have committed an:
   a. Express ratification
   b. Implied ratification
   c. Quasi-contract
   d. Illegal act.

   (The correct answer is b. Note that the use of the goods after 18 years must be for more than a reasonable amount of time.)

6. Necessities for which a minor may be bound on a contract LIKELY would include all of the following EXCEPT:
   a. Education
   b. Medical care
   c. Warm winter clothes in a cold winter jurisdiction
   d. Transportation in the form of a car

   (The correct answer is d. Transportation generally is considered a "luxury" and not a necessity; yet if the minor needs the car or other form of transportation to get to work to support himself or herself or to help the minor's family then it may be considered a "necessity." Determining what is a necessity compared to a luxury is often difficult, and reference naturally must be made to state precedent case.)

13 - Legality

Introduction

Another requirement to a valid contract is legality; that is, the subject matter of the contract must be legal, the contract must have a legal purpose, and the contract must not be contrary to statute as well as not be against the "public policy" of the state (which policy is determined by legislative and judicial pronouncements.). Accordingly, the business student must know of the types of illegal contracts that one can find in a business setting, for example, usurious contracts, gambling contracts (though it must be pointed out that legal vs. illegal gambling is an ever-changing area of the law), contracts with exculpatory clauses, contracts by people and businesses without required licenses, and, most importantly, covenants-not-to-compete in the sale of a business and in employment contracts. Regarding unlicensed people and businesses, it is critical for the student to know the distinction between revenue-raising vs. regulatory licensing statutory schemes, as well as the "protected parties" exception to the latter.

Regarding covenants, which topic very likely will soon be more than a mere "academic" matter for the vast majority of students, the student must know the requirements that make a covenant-not-to-compete legal in the sale of a business as well as legal in an employment context; and regarding the latter the student must know that in most states for employment the employer must demonstrate a legitimate business reason for the covenant in order to sustain the covenant. Moreover, the student must know that in some states there are additional requirements for a legal covenant in the employment context as well as the fact that at least one state, California, as of this writing, has statutorily invalidated covenants-not-to-compete in an employment contract situation. Finally, the student must be aware of the doctrine of severability or divisibility when it comes to contracts that have legal and illegal parts.

True and False Questions with Answers and Explanations

1. Exculpatory clauses are generally favored and upheld by the courts on grounds of public policy.
(False: The opposite is the case; they are disfavored because it is public policy to hold people responsible for their own careless acts; but there are exceptions.)

2. An illegal contract always violates a criminal law statute.
(False: An illegal contract can also call for the commission of a tort or be against public policy.)

3. A covenant-not-to-compete standing alone and that is otherwise not part of a contract is illegal.
(True: Covenants must be ancillary to, and thus part of, a larger contract; otherwise they violate public policy.)

4. One cannot sue an unlicensed professional, such as a doctor or lawyer, for malpractice since any contract with the unlicensed professional would be illegal and void due to the lack of a license.
(False: The Protected Parties exception allows the aggrieved party to sue for malpractice despite the absence of a license).

5. A contract by an attorney who is not licensed in a state but who agrees to represent a "client" in that state is not enforceable by the attorney unless or she is successful in the representation and secures a money judgement or settlement for the "client."
(False: Such a contract is illegal and void regardless of the competency of the representation. Moreover, there is an exception for the benefit of the "client" who can sue the attorney for legal malpractice regardless of the underlying illegality of the contract. Finally, the unlicensed attorney may find himself or herself in serious legal difficulty for practicing law in a state without a license.)

6. As a general rule an exculpatory clause in a contract whereby one party attempts to free himself or herself from legal liability for that party's own negligence is unenforceable.
(True: Based on the public policy rationales that a party should be legally liable for his or her careless conduct; but there are some exceptions, for example, when the contract parties are very large and sophisticated business entities represented by attorneys and if the exculpatory language is very clear, specific, and specifically makes reference to "negligent" conduct.)

7. A contract that requires the commission of a tort is a voidable contract at the option of the aggrieved party.
(False: Such contracts are deemed illegal and void the same as contracts which call for the commission of any illegal act or whose subject matter is illegal.)

8. If a contract has an illegal subject matter the contract is illegal, void and the legal system will "leave the parties where it finds them."
(True: And the fact that some consideration has been transferred to a party is moot. The legal system will not help that party get his or her money or other consideration back.)

9. An agreement with a clause stating that a party would not be liable for fraud will be enforceable if the contract was knowingly agreed upon.
(False: Such a clause would be stricken from the contract as an Exculpatory clause. The aggrieved contract party thus could sue for fraudulent inducement to enter into the contract.)

10. Generally, the courts will not enforce a covenant-not-to-compete against an employee if it makes it difficult for the employee to find another good job.
(False: In most states the effect on the former employee is not taken into consideration if the covenant is reasonable as to time and place and the employer can demonstrate a legitimate business reason for the covenant, for example, protecting confidential information.)

11. In most states a court will enforce a covenant-not-to compete in an employment contract if it is reasonable in time and space/area and the employer can demonstrate that it has a legitimate business interest to protect.
(True: Note that some states have additional requirements, for example, New Jersey where the covenant cannot cause an "undue burden" to the employee, or Pennsylvania where the covenant cannot be "oppressive" to the employee. Note too that in California covenants-not-to-compete in employment contracts are illegal and null-and-void as per statute.)

12. Covenants-not-to-compete in the employment context are illegal by virtue of federal law as unconstitutionally hindering a person from making a living and advancing himself or herself economically.
(False: There is no federal law that bars such covenants in employment; however, one state, California, has made covenants-not-to-compete illegal in employment, though they are still valid in California in the sale of a business.)

Multiple Choice Questions with Answers and Explanations

1. What as a GENERAL RULE makes a covenant-not-to-compete legal in an employment contract?
   a. Reasonableness as to time and duration.
   b. Reasonableness as to area, place, and territory.
   c. The employer being able to demonstrate that the covenant was reasonably necessary to protect a legitimate business interest of the employer.
   d. All of the above.

   (The correct answer is d. These are all basic requirements in an employment context and reflect the majority rule in state law in the U.S. Note that for covenants in contracts for the sale of a business just the first two must be satisfied. Finally, note that the courts will accept a variety of employer interests that are deemed to be worthy of protection by a covenant, for example, the employee having customer and client relationships, thereby establishing good will, access to confidential information and trade secrets, such as customer and client lists, and when the employer has made an investment in the employee's education and training that the law regards as unique, specialized, valuable, substantial, and/or extraordinary, such as paying for a degree or the obtaining of a professional license.)

2. For a covenant-not-to-compete to be legal in the contract for a sale of a business, the covenant must be:
   a. Reasonable as to time/duration.
   b. Reasonable as to place/area.
   c. Not unduly impede the seller of the business if he or she wants to start a similar business.
   d. a. and b.

   (The correct answer is d. There are only two requirements that are necessary to have a valid covenant-not-to-compete in the sale of a business wherein the seller promises not to compete against the buyer in the same or similar type of business – reasonableness as to time and reasonableness as to place. Any burden or hindrance on the seller in commencing a new business is not a factor.)

3. Which of the following is a TRUE statement?
   a. Exculpatory clauses in contracts are typically upheld by the courts.
   b. A non-compete agreement in the contract for the sale of a business will not be found to violate public policy if it meets the tests of reasonableness as to time and place.
   c. All gambling agreements are illegal contracts since gambling is immoral.
   d. The age of majority for legally contracting in most states is 25.

   (The correct answer is b. Covenants in business will be upheld if just the two requirements are met, that is, reasonableness as to place, area, or trade territory, and reasonableness as to time or duration. The courts do not like exculpatory clauses because a contract party, typically a business, is attempting to free itself from liability for its own negligence; and thus the courts regularly strike them down however, in rare circumstances a court will enforce an exculpatory clause in an agreement if the parties are on comparable terms in size, power, money, legal representation, etc. Gambling may be immoral, depending on one's ethical views, but it is becoming increasing legal in more and more states, including online gambling. The age for contracting is, as noted, 18 years of age in most states.)

4. Which of the following is a FALSE statement?
   a. State licensing statutes require certain professionals and occupations to be licensed by the state in which they practice.
   b. Usury is the charging of excessive rates of interest.

c. An unlicensed professional can still be sued for malpractice by an aggrieved client even though the professional lacks a license.
d. Minors contracts are illegal and void at the option of the minor.

(The correct answer is d. As noted, minors contracts are voidable at the option of the minor. A contract by an unlicensed professional is illegal and void, but there is an exception called the "protected party" exception that allows a "client" of the unlicensed professional to sue him or her for breach of contract and malpractice. Of course, the unlicensed professional will be in big trouble under the state's criminal law for practicing law or medicine or any other profession without a required license. The typical state usury rates are interest of 18-25% per year depending on the size of the loan.)

5. Which is a TRUE statement regarding the legality of a contract?
   a. Covenants-not-to-compete are illegal in all states in employment contracts since they could prevent a person from earning a good living.
   b. The lack of a revenue-raising licensing statute will completely void a contract due to illegality.
   c. If a contract is deemed to be divisible and severable a court will separate the illegal part and enforce the rest of the contract.
   d. The courts typically will allow exculpatory clauses in contracts on grounds of "freedom of contract."

(The correct answer is c. Covenants-not-to-compete in business as well as employment are legal in most states if certain requirements are met. A handful of states, however, in an employment situation, would ask if the covenant is an "undue burden" on the employee, as in New Jersey, or "oppressive" towards the employee, as in Pennsylvania; and also note that California has banned covenants-not-to-compete in employment contracts but not contracts for the sale of a business. Finally, since covenant law is highly state dependent reference must be made to the pertinent state's law, which could be a problem if more than one state has a connection to the contract, for example, formation in one state and performance is in another. This "conflicts of law" problem could be solved if in the contract there is a "choice-of-law" clause which indicates which state's law will apply to the contract as well as a "choice-of-forum" clause which indicates in which state a contractual dispute will be litigated. Regulatory licensing schemes exist to protect the public from incompetent and/or unethical professionals, for example, licenses for doctors and lawyers. Revenue-raising licensing schemes exist "merely" to raise money, for example, a municipal occupational license. The lack of a license by a person or business will not invalidate the contract if there is no license, meaning a person can sue the unlicensed business for breach of contract AND vice versa too. However, the unlicensed person or business must comply with the licensing statute and obtain a license or be fined.)

6. In order to be valid in an employment context a covenant-not-to-compete generally must meet the following requirements EXCEPT:
   a. Be reasonable in time/duration and place/geography
   b. Protect a legitimate business interest of the employer
   c. Not be overbroad in the interests protected
   d. Be reasonable as to the amount given as consideration to the employee for signing the covenant.

(The correct answer is d. The promise by the employee in the covenant-not-to-compete must be supported by consideration, which is usually found in the mutual promises in the original employment contract, or in a modification thereof when the employee receives a promotion and/or raise; but recall that under the common law a court is just concerned with the presence of consideration and neither its adequacy or reasonableness.)

7. A clause in a contract whereby one party seeks to eliminate his or her liability for negligent or careless performance is called:
   a. Unconscionable
   b. Exculpatory
   c. Deceit
   d. Mitigation

(The correct answer is b. Typically, courts invalidate exculpatory clauses in contracts since the state's public policy is to make sure people and businesses are legally responsible for their legal wrongs, including negligence; but there are some rare exceptions in which a court will uphold an exculpatory clause in a contract. "Unconscionability" is a Uniform Commercial Code concept whereby if the contract is one for the sale of goods and the contract is so grossly unfair and so one-sided that it "shocks the conscience" of the court, a judge will not enforce the contract.)

8. A typical example of an illegal contract is:
a. A contract to commit a tort.
b. A contract against public policy.
c. A usurious contract.
d. All of the above.

(The correct answer is d. These are all basic categories. An example of a contract against public policy would be a contract to sell one's kidney.)

14 - Genuineness of the Agreement

Introduction

The mutual agreement necessary to form a contract must be "genuine," that is, it cannot be improperly obtained by means of mistake, fraud, duress, or undue influence. Otherwise, the contract is voidable and can be set aside by the victimized party, who can ask a judge for a decree of rescission to cancel the contract or interpose any of the afore mentioned doctrines as a defense if sued for breach of contract. Regarding mistake, it is critical for the student to know the distinction between a mutual mistake and a unilateral mistake as the rules of law for each are markedly different, as well as to know the important "palpable mistake" exception to the unilateral mistake general rule. Regarding fraud, also known as "deceit" in the old common law, first, the student must be aware that fraud is also an intentional tort as well as a contract defense and grounds to rescind a contract. The student must know that there is a difference among deceit, that is, intentional fraud, negligent misrepresentation, and an innocent misrepresentation (which latter situation most states treat as equivalent to a mistake). For deceit, the student must be aware of the several requirements that will turn a misstatement or misrepresentation into fraud.

These requirements, moreover, must be established by the plaintiff bringing the lawsuit by "clear and convincing" evidence, one recalls, and not merely by a "preponderance of the evidence" which is the standard burden of proof in a civil case. Fraud in the form of deceit is, in essence, legally recognized lying; and as such is difficult to prove. Particularly important for the tort of deceit are the distinctions between a person misrepresenting or concealing facts and a person merely giving his or her opinion or prediction. Moreover, the student must be aware of the old common law "scienter" requirement to deceit, that is, the evidence that the allegedly fraudulent wrongdoer intentionally and knowingly lied in order to induce the victim into entering into the contract or some type of business dealings. Furthermore, the student must know that there is a requirement that the victim of fraud must have "reasonably relied" on the misrepresentation of fact. Two other problem areas that the student needs to be aware of deal with misrepresentations of the law which are not actionable as fraud, as opposed to misrepresentations of fact which can be the basis for fraud, as well as the doctrine that silence is not fraud under the common law, though there are exceptions for both the preceding areas that the student must be aware of too. For duress, the basic point for the student is to know is the distinction between threatening criminal prosecution vs. a civil lawsuit when it comes to a finding a duress. Finally, as to undue influence, the student should be aware of the basic rule and definition, but also realize that its use is rare in contract cases but much more prevalent in contested Wills cases.

True and False Questions with Answers and Explanations

1. The legal wrong of fraud is based on a false statement of fact that is knowingly and purposefully made with an intent to deceive.
(True: Fraud in the "olden days" was known as deceit which emphasizes the knowing and intent aspects of this type, as opposed to the tort of negligent misrepresentation, based on carelessness.)

2. Fraud renders a contract null and void.
(False: Even though a legal wrong fraud makes a contract merely voidable; the wronged party must assert fraud as an affirmative defense, seek to get the contract rescinded, or sue for the tort of fraud.)

3. In a fraud case the false statement must relate to past, existing, or future facts.
(False: The misrepresentation must concern past or present facts; as such, not performing a promise made in a contract in-and-of-itself is not fraud but only a breach of contract.)

4. Undue influence that will render a contract voidable consists of undue and unfair persuasion and/or manipulation.
(True: Undue influence in essences means over-influencing another to enter into a contract, thereby rendering it voidable, but not void.)

5. Threatening a person with a civil lawsuit constitutes duress thereby rendering any contract void.
(False: The threat of a criminal prosecution will render a contract voidable.)

6. As a general rule a unilateral mistake in making a contract will not be grounds for relief.
(True: A bilateral mistake will make a contract voidable by either party; and there is an exception for unilateral mistake, called the Palpable Mistake doctrine which may provide relief for a unilateral mistake.)

7. A mistake in computation made by a subcontractor in preparing a bid to a general contractor will not nullify any resulting contract since the subcontractor is a business person who will be held liable for any negligence.
(False: The subcontractor may be protected by the Palpable Mistake doctrine if the mistake is an obvious or patent one.)

8. As a general rule the failure to disclose a material fact during contract negotiations is fraud.
(False: The general rule is that silence is not fraud, based on the old Latin maxim, Caveat Emptor, that is, let the buyer beware. However, there are exceptions, for example, under the law where silence by a fiduciary is fraud, and under federal securities law where silence in the purchase or sale of securities could rise to the level of securities fraud (and with criminal as well as civil penalties for the latter.)

9. Under the common law a requirement for the intentional tort of fraud is that the party making the misrepresentation must have done so knowingly, purposefully, and with the intent to induce the other party into a contract.
(True: This element is called Scienter. The older name for fraud is "deceit," which more accurately describes the Scienter element, the presence of an "evil mind.")

10. If there is fraud or deceit in a contractual transaction the aggrieved party can affirmatively rescind the contract, interpose fraud as an affirmative defense if sued on the contract, and/or sue for money damages for the intentional tort of fraud.
(True: Fraud can be used in a variety of ways, but in most states the plaintiff must prove all the elements of fraud by a standard of "clear and convincing evidence" as opposed to the usual civil standard of a "preponderance of the evidence.")

11. Threatening a party with criminal prosecution in order to compel them to enter into a contract is considered to be duress so as to make the contract voidable by the aggrieved party.)
(True: As opposed to threatening a party with a civil lawsuit which is not considered to be duress.)

12. A unilateral mistake as to the value of the subject matter of a contract ordinarily will provide relief and make the contract voidable since it would not be fair to the mistaken party.

(False: A unilateral mistake made by one party to the contract as a general rule will not provide relief unless the mistake is palpable, that is, obvious; whereas a mutual mistake made by both parties to the contract will provide relief to either party.)

13. The failure to disclose a material fact will amount to fraud and thus render a contract voidable by the defrauded party.
(False: The failure to disclose, that is, silence, will as a general rule not constitute fraud unless one has a duty to speak, for example, if the parties are in a fiduciary relationship, such as a lawyer or accountant and a client or between partners. This "silence" rule harkens back to the old Roman saying, Caveat Emptor, or "let the buyer beware.")

14. If a party is fraudulently deceived into entering into a contract, he or she can sue only for money damages.
(False: In addition to money damages the defrauded party can interpose fraud as an affirmative defense if sued for breach of contract and the defrauded party can also go to a court of equity and use the fraud as a means for the court to rescind, or cancel, the contract.)

15. The use of exaggeration by a seller to persuade a person to purchase a product usually will be construed as undue influence rendering the transaction voidable.
(False: Exaggeration as well as the usual "sales talk" or "sales pitch," at times called "puffing," will not in itself render the contract voidable for undue influence.)

16. Economic need by one party ordinarily will not rise to the level of duress to render a contract voidable.
(True: The exception will be if the other contract party created the need and especially if the need is dire.)

17. A covenant not to compete will not be enforced in most states if it prohibits an employee from making a "good living" for his-or-herself and family.
(False: If the covenant is reasonable as to time and place and the employer can demonstrate a business need for the covenant, such as the employee having access to customers or clients and pertinent lists, the covenant is valid and enforceable in most states regardless of economic distress to the employee and his or her family. However, a small minority of states will not enforce the covenant against the employee if a court determines it is "oppressive" or will impose an "undue burden" on the employee. Moreover, in California covenants not to compete are illegal by statute in employment contracts.)

18. Punitive damages are typically awarded for a breach of contract that is purposeful and intentional since the breaching party has exhibited bad faith conduct.
(False: Even though intentional, perhaps to secure a better deal elsewhere, a breach of contract is not considered to be sufficiently heinous or malicious to warrant punitive damages, as opposed to fraudulently inducing a person into entering into a contract which usually would warrant punitive damages.)

Multiple Choice Questions with Answers and Explanations

1. Which type of mistake will make a contract voidable at the option of the mistaken party?
    a. a mutual or bilateral mistake
    b. a unilateral mistake
    c. a unilateral palpable mistake

d. Both a. and c.
(The correct answer is d. As a general rule a mutual mistake renders the contract voidable at the option of either party, though obviously it will be the mistaken and aggrieved party who wants to set aside the contract. Note, however, in some jurisdictions there may be an exception when the value of the subject matter is in issue and the parties are aware of the uncertainly of the value. As a general rule a unilateral contract is not voidable and thus the mistaken party must "live" with his or her mistake. The exception is called the unilateral mistake exception, meaning that the mistake is so patent, obvious, and thus "palpable," for example, a contractor's bid that is clearly out of line with the other bids and architect's estimate as to construction costs. Consequently, since "two wrongs do not make a right" the non-mistaken party is not allowed to "snap up" the mistaken bid.)

2. Which of the following is a TRUE statement?
  a. Generally, a unilateral mistake does not allow either party to a contract to rescind or cancel it.
  b. Where two people contract for the sale of an old baseball card and the seller does not realize that it is a "Mickey Mantle" rookie card, and thus a very rare and extremely valuable one, then the seller, the mistaken party, can cancel the contract since it would then be unfair to him or her.
  c. In a fraud case the victimized plaintiff needs just prove that he or she relied on the false statement.
  d. Fraud typically renders a contract null and void.

(The correct answer is a There is as a general rule no relief for unilateral mistake, though there is the "palpable mistake" exception. As such, say "goodbye" to that Mickey Mantle card. Reliance on the misrepresentation must be "reasonable" by the deceived party. Fraud renders a contract voidable, not void. Fraud can also be used as an affirmative defense and as grounds to rescind and cancel the fraudulently induced contract.)

3. Which of the following is a TRUE statement?
  a. Fraud by active concealment occurs when a party to a contract fails to disclose all of the known facts about the subject matter of the contract.
  b. To be actionable for fraud, a misrepresentation must pertain to a future opinion.
  c. The threat to bring criminal charges against a person to obtain an agreement may be grounds for duress.
  d. A mutual mistake renders a contract null and void.

(The correct answer is c. To compare, threatening to bring a civil lawsuit against a person is not duress. Fraud by active concealment means that one is purposefully covering something up, for example, painting over the cracked engine block in a car. Concealment is treated as making an intentional misrepresentation. Opinions and predictions cannot as a general rule be the grounds for fraud, though there is an exception when the person making them is an "expert." A mutual mistake renders the contract voidable at the option of either party, though realistically it is the party aggrieved by the mistake who will set it aside.)

4. Which of the following is a TRUE statement?
  a. A contract that benefits one party to the contract over the other is automatic grounds for undue influence.
  b. A contact that was entered into by one party unduly influencing the other is a voidable contract.
  c. The primary purpose of the Statute of Frauds in contract law is to punish bad people who perpetuate frauds using contracts.
  d. A misrepresentation of law by a lawyer is not fraud since everyone is presumed to know the law.

(The correct answer is b. Undue influence is grounds to set aside a contract, as well as will, where one typically sees the doctrine asserted. Simply benefiting one party is not enough grounds; there must be evidence that one party was so dominated or manipulated or coerced by another to have a

viable case of undue influence. Despite the recurrent use of the word "fraud" do not confuse the Statute of Frauds, which is a state statute dealing with the types of contracts that must be evidenced by a writing, with the common law tort of fraud, also called "deceit" under the old common law. Yet note that one key rationale behind the Statute of Frauds is to prevent people from using fraud and deceit in supposedly oral agreements. Misrepresentation of the law by a lawyer is clearly fraudulent activity.)

5. Under which of the following can a party collect damages?
   a. Unilateral mistake
   b. Mutual mistake
   c. Palpable mistake
   d. Fraud in the inducement.

   (The correct answer is d. Mutual mistake as well as a palpable unilateral mistake will allow a party to avoid a contract but fraud in the form of deceit in inducting a victim to enter into a contract is an intentional tort, meaning that a full range of tort damages can be recovered, including punitive damages to punish the wrongdoer and to act as a deterrent to other possibly deceitful and unscrupulous people.)

6. A plaintiff in a fraudulent misrepresentation case must prove all of the following elements EXCEPT:
   a. Reasonable and justifiable reliance
   b. False statement of material fact
   c. Intent to deceive
   d. Physical injury

   (The correct answer is d. Physical injury is not required, though naturally if present will compound the damages. Fraud in the form of deceit is an intentional tort meaning that recovery of emotional distress and punitive damages are likely. Moreover, if there is neither physical nor economic harm in most states even a recovery of nominal damages for the fraud will support an award of punitive damages.)

7. Under the common law:
   a. Fraud is an intentional tort
   b. Fraud is a defense to a breach of contract lawsuit
   c. Fraud can be used affirmatively to rescind a contract induced by fraud
   d. All of the above

   (The correct answer is d. Fraud as an intentional tort is often called by its older name, "deceit," to indicate its purposefulness and wrongfulness. Note that fraud is an "affirmative" defense to a breach of contract, which means it must be interposed by the defendant when sued for breach of contract or else lost.)

8. Under the common law:
   a. A unilateral mistake generally will not provide relief to the mistaken contract party.
   b. A mutual mistake generally will provide relief to the aggrieved party.
   c. A unilateral palpable mistake can provide relief to the mistaken contract party.
   d. All of the above.

   (The correct answer is d. Unless there is fraud, a court will not provide relief as a general rule to the one mistaken party, which can be a very big problem if the mistake pertains to the value of the subject matter, for example, a "junk car" vs. a "classic car" or an "old painting" vs. a "famous work-of-art." So, let the buyer or seller beware! Either party can avoid a contract based on mutual mistake, for example, as to the existence, character, nature of the subject matter or the means of delivery. A unilateral mistake to be "palpable" must be patent and obvious. The rationale for the

palpable mistake doctrine is that "two wrongs do not make a right"; that is, one party made a mistake, the unilateral mistake, but it is so obvious to a reasonable person that the other contract party should not be able to "snap up" the mistaken contract.)

9. What is FALSE about fraud?
   a. Fraud is based on a false statement or misrepresentation of a material fact.
   b. There must be evidence of "scienter," that is, evidence of a "bad intent" to purposefully defraud a victim and induce the victim into entering into a contract.
   c. Erroneous opinions and incorrect predictions generally will give rise to a lawsuit for fraud.
   d. Silence as a general rule is not fraud.

   (The correct answer is c. Opinions and predictions even if erroneous are not fraud, unless given by a person deemed to be an "expert." The misrepresentation of fact must be of a "material" fact, that is, one not trivial, but one that influenced the decision to contract. Evidence of bad intent, that is, that the perpetrator had an "evil mind," which is called the "scienter" requirement under the common law, is notoriously difficult to prove and consequently which makes fraud in the form of deceit a very difficult lawsuit to sustain legally. Silence is not fraud as a general rule but a major exception under the common law arises when there is a fiduciary relationship among the parties, for example, between a attorney and his or her client, between partners, or between a principal and his or her agent.)

10. The reliance element of fraud requires as a general rule reliance on:
    a. an incorrect prediction
    b. a misstatement of fact
    c. a false opinion
    d. "puffery" or sales talk

    (The correct answer is b. Reliance, moreover, must be "reasonable," and as such a party cannot have reasonably relied on a lie if he or she knew the truth or a reasonable person SHOULD have known of the truth, for example, regarding patent defects to goods, such as when the seller of a car claims the tires are new but on inspection one can clearly see that they are worn.)

11. The common law tort of fraud (deceit) requires all the following elements EXCEPT:
    a. a misrepresentation of material fact
    b. "scienter" (knowledge of the falsity of the statement and an intent to deceive)
    c. violation of a moral duty to act in an ethical and honest manner
    d. reasonable reliance by the deceived party on the misrepresentation

    (The correct answer is c. It may be immoral to lie and to commit fraud but violating an ethical duty of honesty is not a required legal element to fraud.)

12. As a general rule under the common law when can a deceived party NOT rescind a contract based on fraud?
    a. When there is silence regarding material facts.
    b. When there is a misrepresentation of law.
    c. When there is active concealment of material facts.
    d. A and B.

    (The correct answer is d. Silence and misrepresentation of the law are not fraud as a general rule but there are exceptions.)

13. To be actionable for fraud or deceit a misrepresentation under the common law must be based on:
    a. Statements of material and objective facts.
    b. Statements regarding the law and legal interpretations
    c. Statements of opinion and prediction
    d. Statements of sales talk or "puffing.

(The correct answer is a. As a general rule statements regarding the law are not actionable as fraud if incorrect since "every is supposed to know the law" since "ignorance of the law is no excuse." However, exceptions arise if the misstatement is made by an attorney or another professional in his or her area of legal expertise, for example, a real estate agent misstating local zoning laws. Opinions and predictions are not actionable as fraud if incorrect but an exception arises if the person giving the incorrect opinion or prediction is deemed to be an "expert" by virtue of his or her occupations, avocation, training, education, knowledge or expertise, for example a stock broker making a stock prediction or a Coast Guard ensign selling his or her boat.

15 - Statute of Frauds

Introduction

Oral contracts are enforceable as a general rule, though certainly not advisable for obvious reasons. However, as per the Statute of Frauds, which is state-based statutory law, certain contracts must be evidenced by a "writing." The student must note first that if a writing is required but it is not present the contract is neither void nor voidable but merely "unenforceable," meaning that certain circumstances can occur to bring the contract "back to life" and enforceable. The student next must note that this required "writing" does not have to be a formal contract prepared by an attorney (though in most cases advisable) but rather some memo, sales slip, invoice, piece of paper, or pieces if inter-related, with the "essential terms" and the signature of the "party to be charged" (that is, the person against whom enforcement is sought). So, what type of contracts must be evidenced by a writing to be enforceable? The student must know the following major types: contacts for the sale of land, real estate, interests in land, such as easements, and fixtures; guaranty contracts, that is, an agreement whereby one party promises to pay the debts of another; long-term contracts, typically over one year; contracts in consideration of marriage, that is, pre-nuptial agreements; and promises by an executor or administrator of an estate to pay estate obligations out of his or her own funds. Regarding land and real estate contracts, the student must be sure not to confuse the real estate contract with the deed (which latter instrument passes title to the realty); and the student also must be aware of the "part performance" exception to the Statute of Frauds regarding land and real estate.

Regarding guaranty contracts, it is essential for the student to differentiate a guaranty agreement from a suretyship agreement since the latter can be oral as well as the fact that there are materially different rights and obligations of the parties to these agreements. Also, the student must be aware of the "benefit to the promisor" exception to the guaranty rule requiring a writing. Regarding long-term contracts, the student must know that this rule requiring a writing applies to bilateral executory contracts which by their own terms are incapable of being performed within a year. Moreover, the student must know the exception, that is, if there is any possibility of a contract being performed in a year, even if that performance is remote, the contract can be oral, even if actual performance takes longer than a year, the prime example being a contract for a care-taker to take care of a person "for life" since the person could die within a year even if that is remote. At this time the student should be aware that the Uniform Commercial Code also has a Statute of Frauds provision requiring a writing for contracts for the sale of goods $500 or more. Finally, the student should be cognizant of the Parole Evidence Rule, which is not only a contract rule but also an evidentiary principle, and which limits changes to final contracts by prior or contemporaneous oral or written "side" agreements, though as usual there are some exceptions.

True and False Questions with Answers and Explanations

1. Oral contracts are never enforceable since peoples' memories fade with time.
(False: There are exceptions where oral contracts are enforceable, though they are certainly not advisable)

2. A contract with a collateral promise involves at least three parties and at least two promises to pay the debt or obligation of a party.

(True: Collateral promises are often called secondary promises; first promise is made by a promisor to pay the debt or obligation; and then there is a secondary or collateral promise by another promisor to pay if the first promisor does not.)

3. In a collateral or secondary promise type of contract the primary promise to pay the debt or obligation can generally be oral.
(True: Oral is permissible unless the Statute of Fraud applies; but the secondary or collateral promise must be evidenced by a writing.)

4. In order to comply with the Statute of Frauds a memorandum with the required contract terms need only be signed by one party – the "party to be charged."
(True: The other party need not sign since he or she is trying to enforce the contract; rather, it is the signature of the potential defendant that is critical).

5. As a general rule the Parole Evidence rule will prohibit the use of prior or contemporaneous statements or agreements that add to, detract from, alter, or contradict the terms of a contract.
(True: If the additional material was important it should have been in the ultimate contract; however, parole evidence can be used to explain the terms of a contract or to show fraud, mistake, or duress.)

6. The Statute of Frauds provides for the criminal prosecution of people violating its provisions since fraud is a very unethical act.
(False: The Statute of Frauds just deals with the types of contracts that must be evidenced by a writing; it has civil implications only.)

7. Pursuant to the UCC the partial delivery of goods is an exception to the Statute of Frauds to the extent of the goods delivered under an oral contract that should have been written.
(True: This is a UCC Statute of Frauds exception; but note that the whole contract is not enforceable.)

8. The "benefit to the promisor" principle under the Statute of Frauds make oral promises unenforceable since it is difficult to get clear evidence of what was said during contract negotiations.
(False: The "benefit to the promisor" exception makes oral secondary or collateral promises to pay the debt or obligations of party enforceable if there is evidence that the promisor making the secondary promise will be benefit from the transaction.)

9. The Statute of Frauds requires that all contracts must be in a formal writing prepared by an attorney since a court will not deal with memos, invoices, receipts, and scraps of paper.
(False: Contracts as a general rule can be oral unless the Statute of Frauds applies. Moreover, if memos, etc. have the necessary contract terms and can be sufficiently integrated and the have the requite signature (of the "party to be charged," that is, the one saying there is no contract) the memos can form a contract.)

10. In order to satisfy the requirements of the Statute of Frauds a contract must be in writing and just needs one signature, the signature of the party against whom enforcement is sought.
(True: This party is called the "party to be charged." The other party's signature is not needed as he or she is seeking enforcement of the contract.)

11. Pursuant to the Uniform Electronic Transactions Act (UETA) an electronic signature is equal to a written signature on a paper contract.
(True: Also, the electronic record satisfies the requirement of the Statute of Frauds for a writing.)

12. The Statute of Frauds requires all contracts to be evidenced by a writing in order to prevent fraud in contractual dealings.
(False: Oral contracts as a general rule are permissible, though inadvisable for obvious reasons; whereas the Statute of Frauds requires only certain types of contracts to be evidenced by a writing, for example, contracts for the purchase/sale of real estate.)

13. Pursuant to the Statute of Frauds a contract for the purchase of real estate must be in a signed writing prepared by an attorney which is witnessed and notarized.
(False: A simple writing with the essential terms and the signature of the "party to be charged" (that is, the one denying the validity of the contract) is all that is required, for example, an invoice, sales slip, or memo could suffice, though naturally with real estate having an attorney prepare the contract is certainly advisable.)

14. An exception to the Parole Evidence Rule will arise if the parties subsequently modify a written contract.
(True: However, a writing will be required if the original contract and/or the modification are under the Statute of Frauds and new consideration may be necessary if the contract is governed by the common law (though not pursuant to the Uniform Commercial Code for goods.)

15. Oral contracts as a general rule are valid and enforceable.
(True: Yet oral contracts are not advisable as memories fade and witnesses if any leave the jurisdiction and such contracts are obviously susceptible to fraud and perjury. There are several exceptions, however, as dictated by the Statute of Frauds, that require certain types of contracts, for example, for the purchase and sale of real estate, long-term contracts more than a year in length, or guaranty contracts (where one party is promising to pay the debt of another) which must be in writing.)

16. Electronic signatures are not legal in the United States.
(False: The Uniform Electronic Transactions Act now treats electronic signatures the same as written ones for contracting purposes.)

Multiple Choice Questions with Answers and Explanations

1. Which of the following contracts must be in writing to satisfy the Statute of Frauds?

   a. An employment contract for a five-year term.
   b. A contract to sell two acres of land.
   c. A contract for the purchase of large, flat-screen TV for a price of $2500.
   d. All of the above.

   (The correct answer is d. The first answer is an example of long-term contracts, that is, contracts for more than one year, which must as a general rule be evidenced by a writing. Yet note that a lifetime contract, for example, a contract to take care of someone for his or her life is not governed by the Statute of Frauds since there is a possibility, even if remote, that the person could die in less than a year. Answer b is an example of the rule that all contracts for the purchase or sale of real estate, land, structures firmly attached to land, and interests in land, such as easements, must be evidenced by a writing, typically the standard real estate contract but actually a memo, etc. with the essential terms could suffice. Answer c is an example of the UCC principle that a contract for the purchase and sale of goods over $500 must be evidences by a writing as a general rule. An exception to the preceding principle would be a contract for "specially manufactured goods," that is, goods not suitable for resale in the normal course of the seller's business.)

2. Which of the following is a TRUE statement?
    a. As a general rule, if the Statute of Frauds requires a contract to be evidenced by a writing an oral contract will be unenforceable.
    b. The "part performance" exception to the Statute of Frauds may permit an oral contract for the sale of land to be enforced if part of the purchase price is paid.
    c. A mortgage represents an interest in personal property and thus can be oral.
    d. A contract for lifetime employment must be in writing to be enforceable since usually the performance will be for a long time.

    (The correct answer is a. As emphasized, a contract in violation of the Statute of Frauds is only unenforceable, not void or voidable, meaning that it can be enforced if certain events occur, for example, a party admitting in his or her pleadings, deposition, or interrogatories, or in open court that a contract existed. In most states the part performance exception to the Statute of Frauds regarding oral contracts to buy land has three requirements, to wit, payment of part of the purchase price, the buyer physically coming on the land, and making valuable improvements to the land. A mortgage is an interest in real property and thus, must be in writing. Recall the "remote possibility" test dealing with long-term contracts that holds that if performance is possible within a year, for example, the employee or employer could die in less than a year under the lifetime contract, the contract can be oral even if the employee lives longer than one year.)

3. Which of the following is a FALSE statement?
    a. As a general rule, collateral or secondary promises must be in writing to be enforceable.
    b. A guaranty contract situation involves three parties.
    c. To comply with the Statute of Frauds the contract must be signed only by the party who is bringing the lawsuit to enforce the contract.
    d. Oral contracts are never enforceable since parties and witnesses die or move out of the jurisdiction as well as the known fact that people lie.

    (The correct answer is c. Oral contracts are not advisable due to the preceding reasons, but they are valid contracts unless the Statue of Frauds requires a writing. A guarantee contract does involve three parties – the two original contract parties, one of whom is promising to pay a creditor or seller some debt or obligation, and a third-party, the guarantor, who makes a secondary or collateral promise to pay the debt or obligation if the initial promisor does not pay. To compare, in a suretyship agreement, which can be oral, the two parties promising to pay are "co-signers" who are both making primary promises to pay the seller or creditor. Only one signature is technically required to satisfy the Statute of Frauds, and that is the signature of the "party to be charged," that is, the party who is denying the contract or refusing to perform and who likely will be the defendant in a breach of contract lawsuit. The other party is not only admitting the existence of the contract but he or she is suing to try to enforce it.)

4. Which of the following is FALSE about the writing requirement for contracts?
    a. Contracts for the sale of land must be evidenced by a writing.
    b. Guaranty contracts as a general rule must be evidenced by a writing.
    c. If a writing is required for a contract, it must be evidenced by a formal written contract prepared by an attorney.
    d. The Parole Evidence Rule may disallow any modification or contradiction of a written contract by oral testimony.

    (The correct answer is c. Formal written contracts prepared by an attorney or otherwise are not required; rather, just some type of writing, such as a memo, with the essential terms and the signature of the "party to be charged," that is, the one whom enforcement is sought, is required. The rationale behind the rule requiring guarantee contracts to be in

writing is that it is very unusual for people to go around and to promise to pay the debts and obligations of other people if they cannot fulfill their promises to pay. The Parole Evidence Rule can also exclude prior or contemporaneous written agreements that modify or contract the contract, assuming that the contract is the final and complete expression of the agreement between the parties.)

5. In order to comply with the Statute of Frauds a writing can be:
   a. a formal, written, and sealed document prepared by an attorney
   b. a written memorandum containing the essential terms of the parties' agreement
   c. signed by the "party to be charged," that is, the party against whom enforcement is sought.
   d. B and C

   (The correct answer is d. A written contract prepared by an attorney is very likely most advisable in the business realm, but it certainly does not have to be "under seal," which is an Old English requirement.)

6. An oral contract for the sale of land as a general rule is:
   a. Void
   b. Voidable
   c. Unenforceable
   d. Valid if the land is under $75,000 in appraised value

   (The correct answer is c. The key word is "unenforceable," meaning the contract can come "back to life" as an enforceable contract if the parties are not careful about what they say and do.)

7. Once there is a final and complete written contract, the Parole Evidence rule would as a general rule prohibit evidence of the following:
   a. Prior or contemporaneous oral statements that explain ambiguities in the contract
   b. Subsequent oral statements that would modify the contract
   c. Prior or contemporaneous oral statements that define trade terms in the contract
   d. Prior or contemporaneous oral statements that alter, modify, contradict, or add to the terms of the contract.

   (The correct answer is d. Note too that the Parole Evidence Rules bars prior as well as contemporaneous agreements, usually called "side-agreements," that alter or modify a complete and final written contract. Note too that many contracts have Integration clauses which state that the contract is the final and complete agreement between the parties and thus incorporates all prior or contemporaneous oral or written agreements. Note that subsequent oral statements do not violate the Parole Evidence rule but if they modify a contract, they may have to be supported by consideration to be enforceable.)

8. An oral contract whereby one party agrees to take care of another party for that person's life is:
   a. Not enforceable under the Statute of Frauds since it is very likely that it will be longer than a year and thus need a writing.
   b. a guarantee contract
   c. void for vagueness since there is not a certain time period
   d. enforceable under the Statute of Frauds even if performance is for more than a year.

   (The correct answer is d. As noted, the correct answer is an example of the "remote possibility" test and thus an exception to the rule that long-term contracts for more than a year must be in writing. Note that if actual performance was actually more than a year the oral contract is still enforceable since there was the possibility that performance could be less than a year.)

9. Generally, what type of contract is NOT required to be in writing to satisfy the Statute of Frauds?
   a. A contract that can be performed in less than a year.
   b. A contract for the purchase of real estate.
   c. A guarantee contract to pay another party's debts or obligations.
   d. An agreement by an executor or personal representative of an estate to pay the estate obligations out of his or her own personal funds.

   (The correct answer is a. These are all basic legal principles, but as noted there are exceptions to the real estate and guaranty rules).

16 – Third-party Rights and Responsibilities

Introduction

Generally, only the parties to the original contract have rights and duties therein. However, there are three major exceptions in the law whereby third-parties can acquire rights and duties under the original contract. Consequently, it is essential to know the definitions and rules pertaining to the assignment of contract rights, the delegation of contract duties, and third-party beneficiary contracts. Regarding assignment, the student first must know who the key "players" are, to wit: the assignor, the party who is transferring his or her contract rights; the assignee, the transferee of those rights; and the obligor, the other original contract party who generally is obligated to perform for the new third-party, the assignee. Next, the student must know of the effect of an assignment when it comes to the rights of the assignee to enforce the contract against the obligor as well as the defenses the obligor can assert against the assignee. As a general rule, all contract rights can be assigned, though there are some important exceptions the student must be aware of, for example, the non-assignability of what the law deems to be the right to receive "personal" services as well as a situation where the assignment would materially increase the duties of the obligor. The student must be cognizant of the fact that consideration is not required for an assignment, but also what can happen to the assigned contract rights when there is a gratuitous assignment to the assignee. Similarly, the student must be cognizant of the fact that notice of the assignment by the assignee or assignor to the obligor is not technically required, but also what can happen to the assigned contract rights of the assignee when there is no notice to the obligor.

Regarding delegation, initially, the student must know that delegation is the transfer of contract duties, as opposed to the assignment of contract rights (though in the "real-world" the two concepts get combined). As with assignment, in delegation the student must know the "key" players – the delegator, the original contract party who is transferring his or her contract duties; the delegatee, the third-party to whom the duties are transferred; and the other original contract party, called the obligee, who is entitled to receive the performance of the contract duties. The student must know the general rule that all contract duties can be delegated, but also the exceptions thereto, for example, the performance of a personal duty. Most importantly, the student must know that a mere delegation does not relieve the duty of the delegator to perform; rather, the delegatee is primarily liable to perform but the delegator is still secondarily liable to perform the contract duties. Finally, the student should be aware of the legal doctrine of Novation, which incorporates aspects of assignment and delegation.

Regarding third-party beneficiary contracts the student first must be able to distinguish a beneficiary situation from an assignment since both involve third-parties who are acquiring rights. The difference is that in a third-party beneficiary situation the third-party is obtaining rights in the original contract, whereas in an assignment there is the original contract and then later there is the assignment of the rights by the assignor to the assignee. The student must know the three types of third-parties, to wit: third-party beneficiaries who are creditor beneficiaries and who can enforce the contract in their own names; third-party beneficiaries who are donee beneficiaries who though receiving a gift can still enforce the contract in their own names; and third-party incidental beneficiaries who are only indirectly affected by the contract and who consequently cannot sue to enforce the contract.

True and False Questions with Answers and Explanations

1. Generally, the law favors the free assignability of contracts.
(True: Because to do so is thought to be good for business, but there are exceptions.)

2. Pursuant to an assignment the assignee possesses all the rights that his or her assignor had under the contract.
(True: But the assignee is also subject to defenses that could be asserted against the assignor by the obligor, as opposed to a Holder in Due Course situation under commercial paper law.)

3. An obligor who has been given notice of the assignment must perform for the assignee and thus if the obligor performs for the assignor the obligor may have to perform again.
(True: Consequently, it is essential that the assignee give notice to the obligor of the assignment even if the assignor does not.)

4. The assignor impliedly warrants to the assignee that the obligor is solvent and can fulfill the contract.
(False: The assignor warrants that he or she has good title to the assigned right and not that the obligor can fulfill any promises made in the contract.)

5. The delegation of contract duties completely extinguishes any duty on the delegator to perform under the contract.
(False: The delegator is still secondarily liable under the contract. To be relieved there must be a novation.)

6. A duty is not delegable if there is a personal aspect to the performance.
(True: An example would be portrait-painting or serving as an executive's administrative assistant; only routine duties are delegable, such as in a general contractor and sub-contractor situation.)

7. Third-party beneficiaries who can sue on the original contract can be either creditor or donee beneficiaries.
(True: Only incidental beneficiaries not directly affected by the contract cannot sue.)

8. A gratuitous assignment is automatically revoked by the subsequent assignment of the same contract right by the assignor to another assignee.
(True: Consideration is required from the assignee to the assignor to avoid a revocation.)

9. As a general rule all contract rights are assignable.
(True: But there are exceptions, for example, for rights that are uniquely personal to the assignor, such as having one's picture painted.)

10. A delegation of duties under a contract frees the delegator from any liability under the contract as the delegatee now is liable.
(False: The delegator for example, a general contractor, is still secondarily liable with the delegate, for example a plumbing sub-contractor, being primarily liable. For the delegator to be completely relieved of liability a three-party Novation must be entered into by the parties.)

11. In a Novation situation three contract parties are involved; and the two original contract parties agree that one party will drop out of the contract and the other party will be the substitute performer.
(True: This is quite legal and is to be differentiated from a delegation situation where the delegator of contract duties is still secondarily liable to perform the duties.)

12. An incidental third-party beneficiary can sue on the contract since he or she is at least indirectly benefitted.
(False: Only third-party beneficiaries who are creditor and donee beneficiaries can sue to enforce the contract; a beneficiary whose benefit is indirect or incidental cannot sue.)

13. A donee third-party beneficiary cannot sue to enforce the contract since the donee was in essence the beneficiary of a gift.
(False: A donee third-party beneficiary can sue to enforce the contract made for his or her benefit; that is, a contract party can intend to use the performance of the contract as a means to make a gift to a third-party.)

14. Generally, a contract for personal services is assignable in most circumstances.
(False: Just the opposite, personal services contracts are not assignable as a general rule unless the services are very routine and ordinary.)

15. A contract that has a clause that forbids the assignment of any rights under the contract will always be enforceable since the law disfavors assignment.
(False: The public policy is to favor assignment of contract rights as being good for business and the economy; but a clause forbidding assignment will be upheld as a general rule, but it will not be operative if the assignment involves the transfer of the contract right to receive money.)

16. A contract duty cannot be delegated when the performance depends on the personal knowledge and skills of the obligor.
(True: Whereas routine performance, such as in a general contractor and subcontractor construction situation, can be delegated and without the consent of the obligee.)

17. When an assignor assigns his or her right to receive payment on a loan to a third-party that third-party becomes an incidental beneficiary of the contract.
(False: The third-party becomes an assignee. An incidental beneficiary is a party who is only indirectly and minimally affected by a contract, for example, when the parties in a construction contract anticipate buying supplies from a local retailer.)

18. A donee beneficiary typically gives some type of consideration to the original contract parties in return for receiving some benefits under the contract.
(False: A donee is the recipient of a gift. In a third-party donee contract situation the original contract parties make a contract with the performance to benefit a third-party, the donee beneficiary, who is not required to provide consideration. The best example is a life insurance contract.)

19. A creditor beneficiary can sue on the original contract to enforce a promise to pay made for his or her benefit.
(True: Donee beneficiaries can sue on the original contract but just the party who has promised to perform for the donee. However, the donee cannot sue the other original contract party since he or she is considered as a donor of a gift which can be revoked.)

20. A creditor beneficiary can only be incidentally related to the original contract and nonetheless still sue to enforce the contract.
(False: Creditor beneficiaries typically can sue to enforce the original contract made for their benefit, but not if that benefit is indirect, remote, or incidental. An example would be when a contractor who is under contract with a homeowner to build an addition to a home, and the contractor gets supplies on credit from a hardware store, and the owner breaches the contract. In such a case the contractor

certainly could sue but not the hardware store since its benefit from the contract was merely incidental.)

Multiple Choice Questions with Answers and Explanations

1. What third-party CANNOT sue to enforce rights in the original contract?
   a. a third-party creditor beneficiary
   b. a third-party donee beneficiary
   c. a third-party incidental beneficiary
   d. an assignee
   (The correct answer is c. A third-party who is only incidentally or indirectly affected by a contract cannot sue to enforce the original contract. Creditor and donee beneficiaries can; however, the donee beneficiary can only sue the party who is supposed to perform the contract and not the other party, the donor, since the latter is merely making a gift to the third-party. An assignee is in a different category since his or her rights are not created in the original contract but come into existence later when the original contract party, the assignor, transfers those rights to the third-party assignee.)

2. Which of the following is a TRUE statement?
   a. Third parties cannot acquire enforceable rights under a contract.
   b. The beneficiary of a life insurance policy is an intended third-party beneficiary.
   c. An assignment is the transfer of contract duties.
   d. A non-assignment clause in a contract will always prohibit the right to receive money.
   (The correct answer is b. Third parties, as noted, certainly can acquire rights under a contract by virtues of an assignment as well as duties by virtue of a delegation. The beneficiary of a life insurance policy would be an intended beneficiary, called a "donee" beneficiary. Courts will usually uphold non-assignment clauses in contracts, for example, clauses in rental contracts prohibiting "sub-leasing" of the premises, but a major exception is the right to receive money which is always assignable despite a non-assignment clause in a contract.)

3. What is/are examples of third-party contract rights and obligations?
   a. Third-party beneficiary contracts
   b. Assignment
   c. Delegation
   d. All of the Above.
   (The correct answer is d. These are very basic legal principles.)

4. Which is FALSE about assignment and delegation?
   a. An assignment arises when on contract party transfers his or her duties and obligations to a third-party.
   b. As a general rule all contract rights are assignable.
   c. The assignee is the person to whom contract rights are transferred.
   d. A delegation does not extinguish the duty of the original contract party, the delegator, to perform.
   (The correct answer is a. The transfer of duties is a "delegation": and the other responses are true and fundamental legal principles.)

5. Which of the following is a TRUE statement?
   a. A creditor beneficiary cannot sue directly to enforce a promisor's promise made in an original contract.
   b. Statutes of Limitation are not enforceable in third-party situations since they may deprive the third-party of his/her "day in court."
   c. Most creditor beneficiaries are only incidentally related to the original contract.
   d. In a delegation of contract duties, the delegatee is primarily liable to perform the contract duties and the delegator is secondarily liable.

   (The correct answer is d. Creditor beneficiaries are intended third-party beneficiaries who can not only sue to enforce the contract made for their benefit, but they can sue either or both of the other contract promises, one on the contract promise and the other on the original debt obligation)

6. Duties under a contract:
   a. Are freely transferable under all circumstances so as to promote business and industry.
   b. Can be delegated only if there is a signed and notarized writing.
   c. May be delegated without assigning rights under the contract.
   d. May be delegated only if the delegate/transferee is paid for assuming the duties.

   (The correct answer is c. One can be delegated duties without having assigned rights, yet if a delegatee is not paid for assuming the duties, for example, in a general contractor and sub-contractor situation, one would think that the delegatee would also want the complementary assignment rights. A writing is not required, notarized or otherwise, for a delegation, though naturally advisable, and neither is a notarized document required. However, as always, the Statute of Frauds may require a writing for a delegation or an assignment. Only routine and standard duties can be delegated, not personal or professional duties.)

7. Pursuant to the assignment of contract rights, which of the following is/are TRUE?
   a. The party who transfers his or her contract rights is called the assignor.
   b. The party to whom the contract rights are transferred is called the assignee.
   c. The other original contract party who owes the duty of performance is called the obligor.
   d. All of the above.

   (The correct answer is d. These are basic definitions. Pursuant to the assignment the assignee now has the contract rights and thus the other original contract party, the obligor, must perform for the assignee, who can sue the obligor in the assignee's own name to enforce the rights, though, as usual, there are some exceptions.)

8. Which of the following third-party beneficiaries acquire rights under the original contract?
   a. Creditor, donee, and incidental
   b. Creditor only
   c. Delegatee only
   d. Creditor and donee.

   (The correct answer is d. Delegatees get duties; and incidental beneficiaries get nothing since they are only indirectly affected by the contract).

17 - Performance, Discharge, and Termination of Contracts

Introduction

Performance and discharge are major areas of contract law, which deal with how contracts come to an end. Now, initially, the student should be aware that most contracts come to an end normally and naturally, that is, by the performance of the contract promises and acts therein. There are some performance problem areas that the student must be aware of, to wit: time of performance, substantial performance, and satisfactory performance. Regarding the time of performance, the student must be aware of the important common law rules regarding the time of performance, including when there is no set date for performance in the contract, and where there is a set date. In addition, the student must know the important effect a "time-is-of-the-essence" clause will have on the date of performance as well as when timeliness can be implied from the subject matter of the contract. Regarding substantial performance, the student must be aware that a common law contract need not be completely or perfectly performed; rather, it needs to be only "substantially" performed. As such, the student must be aware of the doctrine of substantial performance and what its legal requirements are and the effect it has on a contract. Regarding satisfactory performance, the student must know how a "satisfaction" clause in a contract is measured and the difference between routine performance and matters of "personal taste and fancy" when it comes to meeting a party's satisfaction pursuant to a satisfaction clause in the contract. The next area the student must comprehend is conditions to performance in a contract. It is critical for the student to know the distinction between express conditions, implied conditions, concurrent conditions, as well as the critical distinction between a "condition precedent" and a "condition subsequent" as well as the effect of the latter two on a contract.

In the area of discharge of contracts the students must understand the main ways that contract duties can be discharged (aside from performance, of course), to wit: death or injury to a party in a personal service type contract, supervening illegality of the subject matter or means of performance, impossibility of performance due to the destruction of the subject matter of the contract or the means of performance or the source of supply, and the "frustration of purpose" doctrine. Finally, the student must know how contracts and the duties therein can be discharged by the agreement of the parties, principally by the doctrines of Accord and Satisfaction as well as by a Novation.

True and False Questions with Answers and Explanations

1. If there is a satisfaction clause in a contract the court will always apply the usual, objective, "reasonable person" standard to determine if satisfaction of a party is present.
(False: If the subject matter is a personal one, such as having one's portrait painted, the satisfaction must be personally and subjectively of the person for whom the satisfaction clause benefits.)

2. Under the common law the substantial but not complete performance of a contract will not cause a contract breach if the missing or incorrect part was not caused intentionally or by bad faith.
(True: The Substantial Performance doctrine is the careless contractor's "best friend," though the missing or incorrect part will have to be rectified monetarily or otherwise.)

3. A contract can always be discharged by mutual agreement.
(True: The doctrine is called Mutual Rescission.)

4. The death of a party to a contract automatically discharges any and all contract duties to perform.
(False: Discharge will occur in personal services types of contracts; but in all others the estate of the contract party will be responsible for the performance of the contract.)

5. If the purpose of a contract becomes worthless or valueless the Frustration of Purpose doctrine will automatically discharge the contract and all duties therein.
(False: The majority rule is that for the Frustration of Purpose to discharge a contract the purpose of the contract must be known by both parties and specified in the contract.)

6. The Frustration of Purpose doctrine may act to discharge a contract if its purpose becomes valueless although performance is still technically possible.
(True: However, in most states the purpose must be stated in the contract or in some states at least known to the other contract party.)

7. The occurrence of a condition subsequent will cause the contract to come to an end and discharge all contract duties.
(True: A condition subsequent must be distinguished from a condition precedent. In the former there is some contract performance but then the condition, as specified in the condition subsequent clause in the contract, occurs and the contract comes to an end. Whereas with a condition precedent certain conditions must occur for the contract to come into being, and if the condition, for example, obtaining a mortgage, does not occur the contract, for example to purchase real property, comes to an end. There is no contract performance with a condition precedent since there is no contract.)

8. The legal effect of an accord-and-satisfaction will be to discharge duties in the original contract.
(True: The Accord is the agreement to provide a different type of performance in lieu of the performance in the original contract. The Satisfaction is the performance of the Accord which discharges the Accord as well as the Satisfaction.)

9. A failure of a condition as set forth in a condition precedent clause in a contract means that the contract never comes into existence and the parties are discharged of any duties.
(True: Look for condition precedent language, such as "provided that," "on condition that," or "however, if." Whereas in a condition subsequent situation there is a valid contract and some performance but when the condition occurs the contract comes to an end. Look for language that the contract becomes "null-and-void" when the specified condition occurs.)

10. Full and complete performance of a construction contract is required under the common law or else there will be a breach of contract situation.
(False: Under the common law for construction contracts as well as other contracts the standard is the Substantial Performance test, meaning that a party need only perform the substantial or major portions of the contract, but the missing party must not have been caused by fraud or bad faith. In such a case the substantially performing party gets the contract price minus the amount necessary to correct the missing and/or defective performance.)

11. An accord is an executory agreement to perform an act that will satisfy an existing contract duty.
(True: And when the accord is performed there is a "satisfaction" and thus an "accord-and-satisfaction" and the original contract and the duties therein are discharged.)

12. A party's duty to perform a contract may be discharged by the occurrence of a condition subsequent.

(True: A condition subsequent typically occurs after some contract performance, that is, the party begins to perform, the stipulated condition occurs, and the contract is rendered null-and-void. Whereas with a condition precedent if the condition does not occur, for example, the condition of obtaining a mortgage in a real estate contract, the contract never comes into being due to the failure of the condition and the parties are discharged from any performance.)

13. A contract which is executed is one in which each party has fully performed his or her contractual promises and obligations.
(True: Whereas an executory contract is one in which either one party or both parties to the contract owe some performance.)

Multiple Choice Questions with Answers and Explanations

1. Which of the following are TRUE about the performance of a contract?

a. Under the common law, a clause in a contract that contract performance must be "satisfactory" is measured by the "reasonable person" standard.
b. Under the common law, the performance of a contract must meet the "substantial performance" standard.
c. Under the common law, a contract with a time for performance must be performed as a general rule on the contract date or a reasonable time thereafter.
d. All of the above are true.

(The correct answer is d. These are all basic and accurate principles of the common law. Note, however, that for satisfaction if the subject matter is one the common law deems to be one of "personal taste and fancy," such as having one's portrait painted, the party who has the benefit of the satisfaction clause must be personally and subjectively satisfied, assuming good faith in being dissatisfied, of course. The substantial performance doctrine is known as the contractor's "best friend" since performance, unlike the UCC, need not be perfect but "merely" substantial. However, as per the title to the doctrine, the performance must be of a major part of the contract, that is, the missing and/or defective part must be minor, as well as caused "merely" by negligence or mistake and not by bad faith, fraud, or deceit. Finally, as to time of performance if the time is regarded explicitly in the contract as "time is of the essence" or implied from the subject matter, such as putting on a fire-works display for the 4th of July, then the performance must be on the exact date specified or else there will be a breach of contract.)

2. Which of the following is a TRUE statement?

a. A promise that contains a condition that must be met before the promise is binding is known as a covenant-not-to-compete.
b. In a condition subsequent, the duty of performance is discharged upon the failure to meet a condition after the duty to perform has already arisen.
c. An accord and satisfaction cannot discharge a contract.
d. The destruction of the source of supply or means of performance of a contract will always discharge contract duties and end the contract.

(The correct answer is b. It is critical to know the difference between a condition precedent, wherein if the condition never occurs, for example, obtaining a mortgage, the contract, the real estate contract, never comes to life due to failure of the condition precedent. Whereas in a condition subsequent situation the contract is a good one and there is some performance, but then the condition occurs, and the contract becomes null-and-void. An accord is an agreement by the contract parties to do and accept some other type of performance; and when the substitute performance is done and satisfied, the accord agreement as well as the original contract comes to an end. This arrangement must be

distinguished from a novation, which is a three-party agreement by which a new party comes in to perform, an original contract party drops out, and the other original contract party agrees to this arrangement. Note that regarding the source of supply and/or means of performance being destroyed, some states will require that they be specified in the contract for the impossibility doctrine to discharge duties therein.)

3. Which of the following is a TRUE statement?
   a. Substantial performance alone entitles the performing party to full and immediate payment of the purchase price.
   b. A breach of contract under the common law cannot occur until the exact time for performance of the duty in question.
   c. A supervening illegality makes a contract voidable.
   d. If a contract to paint one's portrait has a "satisfaction" clause in it the party being painted typically must be personally and subjectively satisfied with the work.

   (The correct answer is d. Satisfaction clauses regarding routine type of performances are measured by the "reasonable person" standard, but contracts involving "personal taste and fancy," like portrait-painting, that have a satisfaction clause mean that a party must be personally satisfied, even if not reasonable, though he or she must express the dissatisfaction in good faith and honestly. The substantial performance doctrine required not only substantial performance, that is, a major part of the contract being done and done correctly, but also that the missing or defective part was not caused by fraud or bad faith, though negligence is permissible; and if so, the substantially performing party gets the contract price minus the amount necessary to complete performance or repair the defects. Under the common law even if there is a set date for performance in a contract performance is not due until that date AND a reasonable time thereafter. If a party wants to avoid the "reasonable" time rule, he or she can try to insert in the contract a "time-is-of-the-essence" clause whereby performance will be due on the exact contract date for performance or else there will be a breach of contract. Illegality, initially or subsequently, will render a contract void.)

4. Which of the following is FALSE about the performance and discharge of contracts?
   a. If a contract does not specify a time for performance, each party has a reasonable time to perform.
   b. A satisfaction clause in a contract always requires that the personal and subjective satisfaction of the contract party be satisfied.
   c. The substantial performance doctrine holds that a substantially performing party can recover the contract price minus any amount to correct the defect or deviation in performance.
   d. Pursuant to the impossibility doctrine, a party's performance will be discharged if without the fault of the party, performance is impossible to perform.

   (The correct answer is b. If the contract performance is routine, for example, in a construction contract, the satisfaction that must be met is that of a "reasonable person"; whereas if the subject matters involves "personal taste or fancy" then the satisfaction that must be met is that of the individual contract party personally. If a contract does not have a time for performance the parties have a reasonable amount of time to perform, depending on the subject matter of the contract, the market for the subject matter, and the means of communication used to form the contract. Note again that for substantial performance to work the performance must be major, and not minor, and the missing or defective part was caused only by negligence or carelessness and not fraud or bad faith.)

5. The agreement to release one party from a contract and to substitute another party to perform is called:
   a. Novation
   b. Accord-and-Satisfaction
   c. Impossibility of Performance
   d. Substantial Performance.
   (The correct answer is a. Note that the novation is a three-party agreement in which all three parties must agree to the substitution and the release of one of the original contract parties. An accord-and-satisfaction is a two-party agreement whereby one contract party agrees in an "accord" to acceptance a different performance to fulfill the contract, and when the "accord" is satisfied by its performance, the original contract and the accord agreement come to an end.)

6. Under the common law a minor and good faith omission or deviation from otherwise complete contract performance is governed by what legal rule?
   a. The Perfect Tender rule
   b. The Substantial Performance rule
   c. The Palpable Mistake rule
   d. The Frustration of Purpose rule
   (The correct answer is b. This is an important common law principle, known as the "contractor's best friend" since 100% performance is not required. The Perfect Tender rule is, as will be seen, a Uniform Commercial Code rule, and one which is quite different from the common law.)

7. Which of the following circumstances would MOST LIKELY excuse performance of a contract because of the "commercial impracticality" doctrine?
   a. A severe shortage of goods due to a war and trade embargo
   b. The destruction of the subject matter of the contract
   c. An increase in the cost of the goods due to inflation
   d. Death of the performing party under a personal services contract.
   (The correct answer is a. Commercial impracticality means that performance is still technically possible, but very, very difficult and expensive, for example, hindered by a natural disaster, major crop failure, as well as a war or embargo; and as such inflationary increases to the subject matter of the contract will be insufficient to trigger the doctrine. Death and destruction come under the heading of the "impossibility" doctrine.)

8. Pursuant to the common law Substantial Performance doctrine, where one party has in good faith substantially but not completely performed the contract duties.
   a. The unfinished duties cannot be delegated to another.
   b. There is a breach of contract and the other party can bring a lawsuit.
   c. There is no breach of contract and the other party is entitled to the contract price minus the amount necessary to correct any defects and/or finish performance.
   d. The court first will create a Quasi-Contract.
   (The correct answer is c. Note that if either one or both requirements are lacking there will not be any application of the Substantial Performance doctrine; rather, there will be a breach of contract, though perhaps a court may then grant some relief pursuant to quasi-contract. Duties, if routine, can be delegated to complete the contract or repair the defective parts.)

9. A clause in a contract in which a party's duty to perform does not arise until a specified event occurs is called a:
   a. Condition subsequent
   b. Condition precedent
   c. Implied covenant of good faith and fair dealing

d. Covenant of satisfaction

(The correct answer is b. As noted, a contract does not come to life and a party's duty to perform does not arrive until the condition occurs; whereas in a condition subsequent there is a good contract and some performance, but then the condition occurs and the contract is thus rendered null-and-void.)

10. A novation can most accurately be described as:
    a. A combination of an assignment and delegation.
    b. A combination of a third-party creditor and donee beneficiary.
    c. Drafting a brand-new contract to replace an old one.
    d. An accord-and-satisfaction.

    (The correct answer is a. Drafting a new contract is usually done by mutual rescission of the first contract and the drafting of the new one. As noted, under a novation a new party is substituted to perform the duties and receive the benefits of the contract with the original performing party dropping out, and with the agreement of the other original contract party.)

11. A person may be discharged from his or her contractual duties pursuant to what common law doctrine(s)?
    a. Substantial performance
    b. Complete performance
    c. Impossibility of performance.
    d. All of the above.

    (The correct answer is d. These are very basic principles.)

12. The legal doctrine under the common law that may apply when a party can technically perform a contract, but the performance is now worthless and valueless is MOST ACCURATELY called:
    a. Frustration of purpose
    b. Supervening illegality
    c. Impossibility of performance
    d. Commercial impracticality

    (The correct answer is a. Again, these are very basic principles. Note that for the "frustration of purpose doctrine to apply most courts would require that the purpose of the contract be known to the other party.)

18 - Damages and Remedies

Introduction

What happens when there is a breach of contract? The student must know the types of remedies and redress available to the aggrieved party. Remedies based on the old common law are divided into "legal" remedies and "equitable" remedies. A judge today can mandate either type, though money damages must be inadequate to "right a wrong" before an equitable remedy can be ordered. The main legal remedy is money damages. Accordingly, the student must know the basic types of money damages and when they are available, to wit: nominal damages, compensatory damages, consequential damages, incidental damages, emotional distress damages, and punitive damages. The latter two the student should note are very rare in breach of contract cases. The student also should know what "liquidated damages" are and the limitations on these types of damages. Regarding consequential damages, the student must be aware of the "foreseeability" requirement as well as the "no speculation" limitation. Moreover, the student must understand that an aggrieved contract party who has suffered a breach must still make a good faith attempt to lessen his or her damages and not let the mount up pursuant to the Mitigation Rule. Regarding equitable remedies, the student must know the main types, to wit: the injunction, a decree of specific performance, and a decree of rescission, and when they are available. Also, very important for the student to know is that specific performance can only be used for a contract whose subject matter is rare and/or unique or for contracts to sell land or real estate, which the law considers to be automatically unique.

True and False Questions with Answers and Explanations

1. The aggrieved party in a breach of contract situation nonetheless has a duty to attempt to mitigate or lessen his or her damages.
(True: "Two wrongs do not make a right"! Thus, the aggrieved party must try in a good faith and honest manner to lessen his or her damages and not let them mount up.)

2. Speculative damages are never recoverable.
(True: Damages must be proved with mathematical certainty. An example would be asking for lost profits from a business that has not even commenced.)

3. A condition subsequent is a clause in a contract that says that if a certain condition occurs the contract is null-and-void and the parties contractual duties are discharged.
(True: Whereas with a condition precedent if the condition occurs the contract and the parties contract duties never come to life, such as a condition of obtaining a mortgage in a real estate contract.)

4. If the subject matter of a contract is destroyed the contract comes to an end and the parties' duties of performance are discharged.
(True: Whereas under the Frustration of Purpose doctrine performance is still possible but the value of the performance has become meaningless.)

5. If the means of performance of a contract is destroyed the contract always comes to an end and the parties' duties of performance are discharged.

(False: Not necessarily, as many courts will require that the means of performance be specified in the contract.)

6. A remedy is a legal means granted to an aggrieved party to compensate for the violation of some right or duty.
(True: Remedies can be "legal" in nature, that is, in the form of money damages, or equitable, such as an injunction.)

7. A legal action to cancel a contract and to return the parties to the *status quo* before the contract was formed is called specific performance.
(False: The remedy is called rescission; specific performance is an order by a court commanding a party to perform a contract.)

8. A decree of Specific Performance is available as a remedy to compel the performance of personal services in a contract.
(False: Specific performance is available to compel performance of real estate contracts as well as for contracts for goods which are very rare or unique. The remedy is not available for personal services contracts due to the difficulty of monitoring performance as well as for the 13th Amendment to the Constitution which prohibits "involuntary servitude.")

9. In a breach of contract situation compensatory damages are typically assessed to place the aggrieved party in the position he or she would have been in if there was not a breach of the contract.
(True: This principle can also be stated as the need to compensate the non-breaching party for the loss-of-the-bargain caused by the breach.)

10. As a general rule punitive damages can be assessed against a party intentionally breaching a contract in order to secure a better deal elsewhere since the breach was purposeful and motivated by greed.
(False: Punitive damages are very, very rare in contract breach situations even if the breach is intentional and for monetary motives, as opposed to intentional torts committed in an outrageous manner, such as invasion of privacy or infliction of emotional distress.)

11. A party will not be awarded Nominal damages in a contract breach situation if there is no loss because to do so would be a waste of time and effort for the judge, jury, and parties involved.
(False: Nominal damages can be awarded in a breach of contract situation even if there is no real loss. The amount would be a token amount of $100, for example. The aggrieved party may want to pursue the lawsuit and obtain nominal damages to act as a deterrent to the other party and other people in the business community that the aggrieved party will not tolerate a breach of contract and will assert his or her rights under the contract to the fullest extent.)

12. A liquidated damage clause in a contract will be enforced to the amount of damages the parties have agreed to in the liquidated damage clause.
(False: Even though specified and agreed to in the contract the amount of liquidated damages must be reasonable and not be a penalty.)

13. An injunction is a remedy by which a court will order a party to stop performing a certain act.
(True: Examples are trespass and nuisance situations as well as competing in violation of proper covenant-not-to-compete clause in a contract. However, most courts will require a showing of irreparable harm before issuing an injunction.)

14. Specific performance is generally the appropriate remedy when a buyer breaches a contract for the sale of bananas since the fruit is known to be perishable.
(False: For goods, for specific performance to be available as a remedy the goods must be very unique, rare, or in short supply.)

15. A decree of specific performance must come from an appellate court since the essence of the remedy is to force a person to perform a specific action.
(False: The remedy is issued by courts of original jurisdiction, such as state trial courts; but the remedy is limited to goods that are rare or in very short supply or to real estate contracts since real estate is considered to be unique under old English law, as per "The Englishman's home is his (or her) castle").

16. Compensatory damages are assessed against the breaching party in order to punish him or her for breaching the contract.
(False: The purpose of compensatory damages is to make the aggrieved party "whole," that is, to put him or her in the position he or she would have been in if there were no breach of contract.)

17. Typically, punitive damages are awarded in breach of contract situations when the breaching party intentionally breaches the contract in order to get a better deal with a third-party.
(False: Even if intentional a breach of contract is not thought to be such a serious wrong to impose punitive damages above-and-beyond compensatory and consequential damages. However, if there is fraud which induces a party to enter into a contract the victim can sue for the intentional tort of fraud, which usually contains a punitive damage element.)

18. Liquidated damages in a breach of contract situation can be greater than the actual damages sustained by the non-breaching party.
(True: So long as the amount of liquidated damages pursuant to a liquidated damage clause in a contract is not deemed to be excessive or a "penalty," the non-breaching party gets the liquidated amount of damages even if his or her actual damages are less.)

19. Fraud will provide the basis for the equitable relief of rescission or cancellation of the contract.
(True: The victim of fraud can also interpose fraud as an affirmative defense if sued on the contract. Moreover, the victim can sue the fraudulent party for the intentional tort of fraud.)

20. Specific performance cannot be used in a real estate situation to compel a seller to fulfill the contract if the property is not a unique piece of property as opposed to just being a standard house in subdivision of uniform structures.
(False: Once again, "An Englishman's home is his (or her) castle," meaning that all real property regardless of how modest or standard is considered "unique" under the common law.)

21. When a party attempts to recover in quasi-contract that party must demonstrate that the other party's conduct indicated acceptance of the contract.
(False: There is no contract when quasi-contract relief is sought. Quasi-contract is a legal fiction, a "pretend" contract created by a judge pursuant to the old common law, to prevent the unjust enrichment of one party by another.)

22. Specific performance is always a remedy for a buyer when the seller of goods refuses to perform.
(False: Specific performance under the Uniform Commercial Code is applicable only if the goods are rare, unique, or in very short supply. The standard remedy is for the aggrieved buyer to sue the breaching seller for breach of contract.)

23. When the employer breaches a contract with the employee the employee is under no further obligation and can take his or her time to sue the former employer for breach of contract.
(False: The employee, as well as any aggrieved party in a contract breach situation, is held to a legal duty pursuant to the Mitigation Rule to attempt to lessen his or her damages, for example, in the employment context by the employee making a good faith effort to find suitable and comparable work so as to lessen his or her damages. The aggrieved party is not allowed to do nothing and let the damages mount. "Two wrongs do not make a right.")

24. Consequential damages will be awarded in breach of contract cases for all damages that are caused by the breach regardless of how remote and indirect.
(False: Consequential damages, that is, additional damages above-and-beyond compensatory damages, are only available if they were reasonably foreseeable by the parties, for example, when the seller's breach by not supplying a known critical part to the buyer temporarily shuts down the buyer's manufacturing line until the buyer gets the part from another supplier, resulting in lost sales and lost profits.)

Multiple Choice Questions with Answers and Explanation

1. Which of the following is FALSE about damages for breach of contract?

   a. Money damages can consist of compensatory and consequential damages.
   b. Consequential damages must be reasonably foreseeable by the parties as likely occurring as damages stemming from the breach of contract.
   c. Liquidated damages fixed in a contract must be a reasonable amount and not an excessive penalty.
   d. The Mitigation Damage rule does not apply when an employer breaches an employment contract with an employee and thus the wrongfully fired employee does not have to look for work.

   (The correct answer is d. Responses a, b, and c are all fundamental, accurate, and true contract damage principles. The Mitigation Rule requires all aggrieved parties who suffered a breach of contract, including employees, to make a good faith and reasonable attempt to lessen their own damages and not let them unnecessarily mount up. Accordingly, an employee must make an honest and adequate attempt to find other comparable work. Another example, a non-employment situation, would be when a buyer breaches a contract with the seller of perishable goods; and as such the seller must make an attempt to sell the goods to another buyer; yet if at a lesser price the seller can recover compensatory and incidental damages.)

2. Which of the following is a FALSE statement?
   a. Only those consequential damages that are known or that are likely or reasonably foreseeable are recoverable.
   b. Liquidated damages will be invalid if they are deemed to be excessive and thus a penalty.
   c. The mitigation of damages rule requires the non-breaching party to a contract to make a good faith effort to minimize his or her damages.
   d. Specific performance is the main remedy used to compel a party perform his or her duties under a personal services contract.

   (The correct answer is d. The 13th Amendment to the Constitution which prohibits slavery and involuntary servitude negates the use of specific performance for the breach of a contract for personal services; rather, the redress will be by means of a lawsuit for money damages. The other responses are all accurate and fundamental legal principles.)

3. Damages awarded to punish a defendant and to deter future wrongdoers are called:
   a. Punitive damages
   b. Retribution damages
   c. Consequential damages
   d. Nominal damages
   (The correct answer is d. As noted, punitive damages are very rare in breach of contract situations unless there is some type of fraud or deceit or duress involved.)

4. Which of the following is NOT an equitable remedy?
   a. Injunction
   b. Specific Performance
   c. Money Damages
   d. Equitable Rescission
   (The correct answer is c. Money damages are known under the common law as a "legal" remedy.)

5. What is a FALSE statement regarding contract damages?
   a. The Mitigation Rule requires an aggrieved breach of contract party to make a good faith and reasonable effort to lessen his or her damages.
   b. Consequential damages cannot be speculative.
   c. Emotional distress damages are never recoverable for breach of contract.
   d. Liquidated damages are permissible if they are not deemed to be a "penalty."
   (The correct answer is c. Emotional distress damages are rare, but may be recoverable, for example, in a breach of contract by a funeral home or a hotel for the honey-moon suite. Speculative damages, which are damages that cannot be calculated with mathematical certainly, are not recoverable, for example, damages for lost profits by a business that has not commenced business yet. If liquidated damages are determined by the judge to be excessive, they will be deemed a penalty and consequently not recoverable.)

6. Which of the following is a FALSE statement?
   a. Liquidated damages must be a reasonable amount.
   b. Specific performance is the remedy customarily used when one party has breached a contract for the sale of unique goods or goods in very short supply.
   c. When an employer breaches an employment contract, the aggrieved employee is under no legal obligation to find another job but can sit back and plan his or her legal strategy.
   d. Consequential damages are awarded in breach of contract cases to cover all the damages sustained, even if only reasonably foreseeable, that resulted from the original wrongful breach of contract.
   (The correct answer is c. The Mitigation rule of damages says "two wrongs do not make a right," so even if there is a breach of an employment contract the aggrieved employee can just sit around but he or she must make a good faith and honest effort to find a comparable position, but if not then the damages for the breach will accrue.)

7. A decree of rescission is:
   a. an equitable action to cancel a contract and return the parties to the positions they held before the contract's formation.
   b. an award of damages.
   c. an order to do or refrain from doing a particular act.
   d. an order to perform what was promised.
   (The correct answer is a. Rescission usually occurs when a contract is produced by fraud or deceit. An order to stop doing a certain action is an injunction.)

8. Consequential damages for breach of contract are:
   a. Awarded to make the aggrieved party "whole," that is, in the position he or she would have been in if there was no contract breach.
   b. Non-speculative in nature, that is, they must be capable of mathematical calculation.
   c. Additional damages that arise from the reasonably foreseeable consequences that occur from a breach of contract.
   d. B and C

   (The correct answer is d. Damages to make a party "whole," that is, to place him or her in the position he or she would have been in absent the breach, are called "compensatory" damages.)

19 - Sales Law and the Uniform Commercial Code

Introduction

The Uniform Commercial Code (UCC) is a state-based *corpus* of statutory law governing the sale of goods. Though the UCC is more-or-less uniform among the several states it is not identical; and as such reference must be made to the particular state's version of the UCC when resolving a commercial law dispute in that state. First and foremost, the student must know that the UCC does not supersede the entire body of common law contract law; rather, the UCC makes changes, including some very significant ones, when the subject matter of a contract is/are "goods." Consequently, the student must know the definition of "goods" and that mainly "goods" are tangible personal property. Thus, the common law of contracts still applies to real estate, service, construction, and employment contracts. Moreover, the student must understand that the UCC applies to any contract for the sale of goods, and not just to the sale of goods by merchants. However, there are many UCC provisions that just apply to merchants, and these provisions make it easier for merchants to enter into contracts for the sale of goods. Consequently, the student must know exactly who a "merchant" is. Actually, a philosophy behind the UCC is to make it easier generally for people to make contracts for the sale of goods, and, as noted, especially by merchants, since as per the UCC rationale, contracts are good for business, and business is good for the economy.

The student must be aware of how a sales contract is formed, especially the changes the UCC makes in the common law of contracts, particularly regarding the price provision, firm offers, additional terms in the acceptance, and the consideration requirement for modifying UCC contracts. The student also must know the UCC's Statute of Frauds, which requires a writing for goods that are priced at $500 or more, as well as the exceptions to the Statute of Frauds. Regarding risk of loss rules when the goods are damaged or destroyed during shipment, the student must comprehend that the UCC has abandoned the old common law concept of title to the goods as being dispositive of who bears the risk of loss; rather, the UCC has specific and detailed risk of loss rules no longer dependent on who has title to the goods. Another important feature of the UCC is the area of warranty law. First, the student must be able to distinguish a breach of warranty lawsuit under the UCC from a common law negligence as well as strict liability for products lawsuit. Next, the student must be able to differentiate express vs. implied warranties under the UCC, warranties of title from warranties of quality, and the three types of implied warranties: merchantability (and note the merchantability warranty is made only by merchants), fitness for a particular purpose, and wholesomeness (for food and beverages). Moreover, regarding warranties the student must know the problems that can arise by means of the notice and privity requirements as well as the key fact that implied warranties can be disclaimed and thus excluded from the sales contract. Pertaining to the performance of the sales contract, the student must be cognizant of the seller's and buyer's obligations under the sales contract, as well as the remedies of the seller and buyer when there is a breach of the sales contract. Particularly important is the "perfect tender" rule obligating the seller and the "cure" exception thereto. Note that the "perfect tender" rule is a major change the UCC makes in the common law of contract's "substantial performance" doctrine. Note, finally, that though the UCC is a lengthy and detailed commercial law code, if the UCC is silent as to a contract issue regarding goods then perforce the common law body of contract law will be applicable.

True and False Questions with Answers and Explanations

1. A firm offer must be made by a merchant in a signed writing and contain a promise to hold the offer to sell real estate open for a period of time.
(False: Firm offers by merchants only apply to the UCC and the sale of goods, not real estate).

2. The shipment of non-conforming goods by a seller to a buyer on a "rush order" will form a contract if the goods are more-or-less comparable in quantity and quality.
(False: The Perfect Tender rule of the UCC requires that goods be perfect, that is, strictly in conformity to contract specifications.)

3. The Uniform Commercial Code applies to the sale of goods only by merchants.
(False: The UCC applies to anyone who sells goods, though certain provisions apply only to parties designated as "merchants.")

4. A UCC contract without a price term is null-and-void.
(False: The contract is still valid; and then certain rules apply to supply the price term, for example, for a missing price term the designation of a "reasonable" price at the time and place of delivery of the goods.)

5. The Uniform Commercial Code governs the sale of real property that has personal property attached to the land or structures on the land.
(False: The UCC applies to the sale of goods – tangible, personal property – and not real estate, which is governed by the common law. Note that if a piece of personal property is so firmly affixed to real estate that it cannot be removed without damaging the real property, the personal property is considered to be a "fixture" and thus is governed by the common law like real property.)

6. A merchant pursuant to the UCC must be an entity on the marketing chain, that is, a manufacturer, wholesaler, distributor, or retailer.
(False: A "merchant" under the UCC can also be any person who because of his or her knowledge, training, or occupation possesses expertise regarding certain goods. Moreover, a person can be deemed a merchant by means of agency law, that is, by hiring a merchant to represent him or her in a transaction.)

7. Pursuant to the UCC if a contract lacks a place of delivery the place will be the buyer's place of business.
(False: The place of delivery as per the UCC will be the seller's place of business.)

8. A merchant's firm offer under the UCC can only be made by a merchant to another merchant.
(False: A merchant's firm offer can be made to anyone. Of course, the requirements for a firm offer must be satisfied, such as a writing signed by the merchant stating that the offer is "firm" and will be held open for a time-period.)

9. The Mirror Image rule applies to offers and acceptances between merchants.
(False: Unless an exception applies additional terms in an acceptance by a merchant automatically become part of the contract between the merchants.)

10. A take-it-or-leave-it clause in an offer by a merchant will preclude any additional terms in the acceptance being imposed on the offeror merchant.
(True: The additional terms can be avoided if the merchant objects or if the additional terms are a material alteration to the contract. Yet the safest way to avoid additional terms is to use the take-it-or-leave-it clause in the contract.)

11. Under the UCC a buyer of goods must have title to the goods before he or she can obtain insurance on the goods.
(False: The goods need only be identified to the contract; having legal title is not necessary for insurance purposes.)

12. A contract that obligates a seller of goods to deliver the goods to the buyer's place of business is called a shipment contract.
(False: It is called a destination contract.)

13. A seller of goods has voidable title to goods that were stolen if the seller did not know that the goods were originally stolen.
(False: Stolen goods render any subsequent title void, regardless if the seller was an innocent and ignorant good faith purchaser of the stolen goods.)

14. In a UCC destination contract if the goods are lost or damaged in transit to the buyer the buyer bears the risk of loss.
(False: The seller bears the risk of loss in a destination contract as opposed to a shipment contract.)

15. Under the UCC's Perfect Tender rule a buyer can reject an entire shipment of goods if part of the goods do not conform to the contract.
(True: Such is the nature of the Perfect Tender rule which allows a buyer to reject the goods if they are non-conforming in even a minor degree. An exception would be the UCC's Cure Doctrine, where a seller who performs early may be allowed to ship conforming goods before or on the contract date.)

16. When goods are shipped and are destroyed in transit the risk of loss will always fall on the party who is a merchant since a merchant typically will have insurance to cover the loss.
(False: The UCC risk of loss rules would apply; and the first determination is whether the goods were shipped pursuant to a shipment or destination contact and not whether a party is a merchant.)

17. Under the UCC whoever has legal title to the goods bears the risk of loss for damage or destruction of the goods during transit.
(False: UCC risk of loss rules will supersede who has legal title to the goods.)

18. If a UCC contract does not specify the place where the goods are to be picked up and the seller is a merchant, the place for pick-up is the buyer's place of business.
(False: The place is the seller's place of business, assuming that there is neither a destination nor shipment clause in the contract.)

19. The right of a buyer of goods to reject the goods if they do not conform to the terms of the contract is called the "Substantial Performance" doctrine.
(False: The right is called the "Perfect Tender" rule; substantial performance is a common law doctrine which states that performance of a contract must be substantial, not total or perfect, and the missing or incorrect part was not caused by any bad faith or fraud.)

20. In an installment contract under the UCC if one installment is partially defective the buyer can reject the entire installment contract pursuant to the UCC Perfect Tender rule.
(False: Installment contracts are an exception to the Perfect Tender rule; as such, only the defective installment can be rejected and not the whole contract. However, there is an exception to the installment contract rule if the installments form an integrated whole of goods, for example, a matching suite of furniture to be delivered in installments.)

21. As a general rule under the UCC a buyer has the right to inspect goods before deciding whether to accept or reject them.
(True: An exception would be when the goods are delivered COD, cash-on-delivery.)

22. When goods are shipped from a seller to a buyer if the buyer says or does nothing within 10 business days the UCC deems the buyer's silence and inaction to be an acceptance of the goods.
(False: The UCC time-period is a "reasonable" amount of time. Note, too, that an acceptance can be implied, for example, by the buyer using or reselling the goods.)

23. When a buyer breaches a UCC contract the seller can resell the goods and receive damages for any loss in the resale.
(True: The seller has other remedies too, but resale is the main one; and the seller can also recover incidental damages on the resale.)

24. An agreement for specially manufactured goods over $500 can be oral and enforceable under the UCC.
(True: This an exception to the Statute of Frauds for specially manufactured goods, that is, goods which are not suitable for resale in the ordinary course of the seller's business.)

25. When a buyer breaches a contract with a seller of goods the seller can keep the goods and receive as damages the difference between the contract price and the market price.
(True: This is a principal remedy afforded to the aggrieved seller, along with resale and recovery of damages, as well as incidental damages.)

26. Any buyer who rightfully rejects goods is allowed as a remedy the right to resell them and receive a commission from the seller.
(False: The buyer as well as the seller must be merchants as defined by the UCC; and also the buyer must attempt to receive instructions from the seller merchant what to do with the goods.)

27. Once a buyer accepts goods the buyer is still allowed to revoke his or her acceptance under certain circumstances.
(True: This is a UCC remedy for a buyer, for example, when a latent defect in the goods is later discovered.)

28. Only a merchant can make the implied warranty of fitness for a particular purpose of goods.
(False: Anyone can make this warranty, as opposed to the implied warranty of merchantability which can only be made by a merchant. However, for the fitness warranty to arise the seller of goods must possess special knowledge and skills pertaining to the goods and the buyer must have relied on the seller's expertise to select suitable goods.)

29. A statement by a seller of boats to a prospective buyer that the buyer and his family will have "years of happy sailing" on this boat will typically be construed as an express warranty.
(False: Such language usually will be construed as a mere opinion, "sales talk," and "puffing," which as a general rule are not actionable as express warranties.)

30. In determining whether food with an object in it is unwholesome and unmerchantable under the UCC a key factor is whether the object in the food is "foreign" or "natural" to the food.
(True: This is the traditional "foreign" v. "natural" test under UCC implied warranty law. An example would be a can of tuna with a nail in it as opposed to a tuna bone. In the former case the warranty would be breached, but in a majority of states the latter would not cause liability. However, even if an object in the food is deemed natural or incident to the food, a minority of states use the "reasonable expectation" test, that is, would a reasonable person expect a tuna bone in a can of tuna.)

31. Today, the majority rule is that the Privity of Contract doctrine means that only the buyer of goods who purchased the goods from a seller can sue for a breach of warranty.
(False: The old doctrine of Privity of Contract has been abolished by the UCC when it comes to suing for breach of warranties in most states. Accordingly, a member of the buyer's family or household can sue even though not in a contractual relationship with the seller.)

32. Only merchants can make implied warranties under the UCC; non-merchants need only worry about making express warranties.
(False: Merchants only can make the implied warranty of merchantability; but any party can make the implied warranty for fitness for a particular purpose.)

33. The Uniform Commercial Code is a federal law that preempts state contract law regarding the sale of goods.
(False: The UCC is state-based statutory law which attempts to make the law regarding the sale of goods more consistent and uniform, but there are differences in the states' UCC statutes.)

34. Pursuant to the UCC an agreement modifying a contract will always need new consideration.
(False: The agreement itself will be sufficient; no new consideration is required, which is the opposite of the common law; but note that the UCC modification agreement may have to be in writing if the Statute of Frauds governs the contract and/or the agreement.)

35. Pursuant to the UCC specially manufactured goods made for a buyer are considered to be "goods" governed by UCC law.
(True: Specially manufactured goods are thus "goods" governed by the UCC and not services governed by the common law.)

36. When a buyer comes upon a seller's land to remove for purchase raw materials the transaction is governed by the UCC.
(False: The entry into the land combined with the buyer removing the raw materials renders the contract a real estate one governed by the common law and not the UCC.)

37. A UCC contract that does not specify the time and place of payment is void for ambiguity.
(False: The contract is valid and the UCC holds that payment will be due at the time and place where the buyer is to receive the goods.)

38. If a UCC contract lacks a price term it will be void for vagueness.
(False: A UCC contract can be valid even without a price term as opposed to the common law; and then the UCC will deem the price to be a "reasonable" price at the time and place of delivery of the goods.)

39. The "mirror image" rule regarding offers and acceptances applies to merchants under the UCC.

(False: The "mirror image" rule (requiring the acceptance to be identical to the offer) is a common law rule and is not fully applicable to UCC contracts. The major terms in a UCC contract must be the same. Yet under the UCC an acceptance can contain additional terms; and, moreover, if both parties are merchants the additional terms are automatically part of the contract unless the offeror merchant said "take-it-or-leave-it" in the offer, or the offeror merchant objects to the additional terms in a reasonable amount of time, or if the additional terms will be a material alteration of the contract.)

40. In a contract for the sale of goods between merchants the contract will satisfy the Statute of Frauds if one merchant timely files a notice of the oral contract in the public records of the county will the goods are located.
(False: The UCC requires contracts for the sale of goods over $500 to be in writing as per the Statute of Frauds, regardless of merchant status of the parties. Filing of a public notice will not obviate the Statute of Frauds. Of course, there are exceptions to the UCC Statute of Frauds, for example, for specially manufactured goods not suitable for resale in the ordinary course of the seller's business.)

41. Who has the legal title to goods controls on the question as to who bears the risk of loss if the goods are damaged, destroyed, or lost during transit from the seller to the buyer.
(False: Title was the controlling factor before the UCC. Now, the UCC has specific risk of loss rules to determine who bears the risk of loss, depending on the type of contract involved – shipment v. destination or of the parties are merchants.)

42. If a person buys stolen property and is ignorant and innocent of the original theft the buyer will be considered a *bona fide* purchaser for value and have good title and be allowed to keep the property.
(False: The theft renders any subsequent title void title regardless of lack of knowledge and/or complicity in the theft. Void title is no title and the original owner and victim of the thievery can reclaim the property. The purchaser can sue his or her seller for breaching the implied warranty, of good title, assuming, of course, the purchaser can find the seller.)

43. When a person who gives goods to a merchant for repair and the merchant innocently sells the goods in the ordinary course of the merchant's business a buyer in good faith can keep the goods and the owner cannot recover them.
(True: This UCC rule is called the Entrustment to a Merchant doctrine. The owner of the goods, however, will have a breach of contract lawsuit, and perhaps negligence if there are additional facts and damages, against the merchant.)

44. When the parties are not merchants and the goods are to be picked up the risk of loss transfers from the seller to the buyer when the buyer picks up the goods.
(True: This UCC rule means that if the good are damaged or destroyed or lost or stolen while at the seller's place of residence ready to be picked up the loss falls on the buyer.)

45. The UCC's requirement that the parties act in good faith may be disclaimed by the parties if in a writing, in conspicuous print, and supported by adequate consideration.
(False: The good faith requirement in the UCC that the parties always conduct themselves in good faith cannot be disclaimed or excluded from the UCC contract, as opposed to warranties which can be disclaimed under certain circumstances.)

46. If a seller delivers goods that are incomplete or defective but there is still time left for performance of the contract the UCC allows the seller to cure the imperfect ship of goods by giving timely notice and then tendering perfect goods before or on the contract performance date.
(True: This is the Cure doctrine which is an exception to the UCC's Perfect Tender rule, which requires the tender of the goods as well as the goods themselves to be perfect in all respects. Compare

and contrast the UCC rule to the common law Substantial Performance doctrines which only requires the substantial performance of a contract.)

47. One party to a UCC contract can demand an adequate assurance of performance of the contract if that party has reasonable grounds to feel insecure about the other contract party performing.
(True: The best example would be the insolvency of the other contract party.)

48. If a contract party has reasonable grounds to believe that the other party will not perform he or she is entitled to ask for adequate assurances of performance.
(True: And if not given the contract party can suspend his or her performance.)

49. In a shipment contract under the UCC the seller of goods is obligated to ship the goods to the buyer's destination and if the goods are damaged during shipment the seller is responsible.
(False: The seller merely has to put the goods in the hands of the carrier and the risk of lass passes to the buyer upon delivery of goods to the carrier.)

50. The buyer of goods has the right to reject the goods if they fail to conform to the contract in any respect.
(True: This is the Perfect Tender rule of the UCC, though there is an exception, the Cure doctrine.)

51. Commercial impracticality may excuse a seller's duty to deliver goods to the buyer even though performance is still technically possible if the seller promptly notifies the buyer.
(True: The standard for "commercial impracticality" is a high one, however. For example, a mere increase in price caused by inflation or changing market conditions is insufficient; rather, a drastic increase in price or severe and unforeseen shortages caused by war, embargos, or crop failures will suffice.)

52. Once a buyer accepts the goods it is too late to reject them; however, the buyer may be able to revoke his or her acceptance.
(True: For the acceptance to be revoked there must be a defect in the goods that substantially impairs the value of the goods and the revocation must occur within a reasonable time after the buyer discovers the defect.)

53. As a general rule a buyer is entitled to inspect any goods he or she receives from the seller.
(True: The exception is a shipment of goods COD – Cash-on-Delivery – in which payment must be made before inspection, but payment is not construed as an acceptance of the goods meaning that the buyer can still reject the goods.)

54. An anticipatory breach of contract can occur when one party clearly announces his or her intention not to perform.
(True: The result is the other contract party can treat the anticipatory breach as a breach of contract and seek legal redress. Moreover, anticipatory breach can be implied from conduct, for example, the seller selling the contracted goods to a third-party.)

55. A seller can cancel a contract if the buyer wrongfully rejects the goods.
(True: The seller can also sue for money damages as well as obtain other breach of contract remedies.)

56. When a buyer is forced to "cover," that is, buy other goods in the marketplace, the buyer can recover from the breaching seller as damages the cover price minus the contract price of the goods.
(True: The buyer also may be able to recover consequential and incidental damages.)

57. Consequential damages under the UCC can include additional monetary damages above-and-beyond compensatory damages suffered by the buyer as a result of the breach that the seller could have reasonably foreseen at the time of contracting.
(For example, if the seller knows that a certain mechanical part is critical to the buyer's production line the seller may be liable for any losses caused by the disruption to the buyer's business until the buyer can "cover" and obtain the part elsewhere.)

58. An express warranty under the UCC can result by the seller providing the buyer with a sample of the goods.
(True: A model of the goods will also create an express warranty.)

59. Statements of opinion or prediction typically can form the basis of an express warranty.
(False: They are not considered to be sufficiently factual to be express warranties; however, there is an exception if an opinion or prediction is made by a person deemed to be an "expert.")

60. In order to meet the UCC's standard for "merchantable" goods the goods delivered by the seller to the buyer must be of the highest-grade, best, and finest quality.
(False: The goods merely must be of average, fair, or medium-grade quality.)

61, Only a seller deemed to be a "merchant" can make the implied warranty of merchantability.
(True: Whereas any seller can make the implied warranty of fitness for a particular purpose if the buyer relies on the seller's knowledge and expertise to select suitable goods.)

62. A buyer of goods has a duty to carefully inspect the goods to discover latent defects.
(False: The buyer has the right to inspect the goods for patent defects and non-conformities, but there is no duty to do so. The buyer can inspect before accepting or paying for the goods. The inspection must occur in a reasonable time, place, or manner.)

63. If a buyer of goods fails to make an inspection and nonetheless accepts the goods, the buyer is precluded from any remedies if the goods later on turn out to be defective.
(False: The buyer may be able to revoke his or her acceptance if the defect was a latent one, that is, hidden and difficult to ascertain or if the seller assured the buyer that there were no defects to the goods.)

64. For something to be classified as a "good" under the UCC the item must be intangible.
(False: Goods must be tangible, physical, personal property, like a piece of furniture, and not intangibles such as copyrights or good will.)

65. Under the UCC the modification of a contract need not be supported by consideration.
(True: This rule is a major change from the common law. However, an agreement between the parties to modify is of course needed and the agreement may have to be in writing if the original contract is governed by the Statute of Frauds or the modification brings the contract into the Statute of Frauds or the original contract requires any modification to be in writing.)

66. Statements or affirmations of fact made by a seller about a product during the bargaining process that become part of the basis of the bargain become express warranties.
(True: This is a basic UCC warranty principle. Express warranties can also be made by using a picture, model, or sample of the goods.)

67. In a shipment contract the risk of loss passes to the buyer when the seller places the goods in the hands of a carrier.
(True: As opposed to a destination contract, where the risk of loss passes to the buyer when the goods arrive at the specified location and the buyer is given notice that the goods are available to be picked up.)

68. A seller who ships nonconforming goods has the right under the UCC to "cure" the ship by notifying the buyer and then shipping conforming goods within the time set for performance.
(True: However, this "cure" exception to the Perfect Tender rule only helps sellers who perform early and thus have time to cure the defect and/or omission in the goods delivered to the buyer.)

69. The implied warranty of merchantability usually can be disclaimed by the use of a catch-all expression such as buyer takes the goods "AS IS."
(True; Such catch-all words will exclude the merchantability warranty if the words are bold and conspicuous in the agreement and not "fine-print." Other similar exclusionary expressions are buyer takes the goods "AS THEY STAND" or "IN THEIR PRESENT CONDITION.")

70. An increased cost to goods resulting from inflation usually will not excuse a supplier from performing the contract and delivering goods on grounds of "commercial impracticality."
(True: The cost increase must be severe or drastic, perhaps caused by natural disasters, embargoes, or war for a supplier to not perform a UCC contract on grounds of commercial impracticality.)

71. A buyer of goods is generally obligated by the UCC to immediately inspect goods that the buyer receives.
(False: Though prudent and advisable, immediate inspection is not required. The problem arises when the buyer does not inspect yet accepts the goods and later inspects and discovers that the goods are non-conforming, and then the buyer seeks to revoke his or her acceptance.)

72. When a party to a UCC contract clearly announces that he or she will not be able to fulfill the contract when performance is due that party has unilaterally rescinded the contract.
(False: This is an example of Anticipatory Breach which the other contract party can treat as a breach of contract when the announcement was made without waiting for the performance date to arrive.)

73. To be deemed to be a "merchant" under the UCC a party can only be a person or entity on the marketing chain, that is, a retailer, wholesaler, distributor, or manufacturer.
(False: A party can also be a merchant due to his or her knowledge, expertise, and skills regarding a certain type of product, for example, an Ensign in the Coast Guard who sells his or her used boat in a private transaction. A person can also be a merchant by hiring a merchant as his or her agent.)

74. The Uniform Commercial Code applies only to merchants of goods.
(*False: The UCC applies to anyone who sells goods, though there are certain provisions that just apply to sellers who are deemed to be "merchants."*)

75. Under the UCC an opinion even if given by an expert will be considered as mere "puffing," that is, typical sales talk, and thus not be actionable as a warranty.
(False: An opinion given by an expert is treated as "fact" and thus can become the foundation for a warranty.)

76. The implied warranty of merchantability can usually be disclaimed by the expression sold "AS IS."
(True: Otherwise, to disclaim the merchantability warranty the exact word "merchantability" must be used. "AS IS" language as well as sold "IN PRESENT CONDITION," sold "AS THE GOODS

STAND," are regarded as general "catch-all" disclaimers and will exclude the merchantability warranty as well as the other implied warranties from the sale of goods transaction. Note, though, that a "catch-all" disclaimer must be bold and conspicuous and not in "fine print.")

77. The mere expression of an opinion cannot as a general rule be treated as creating a warranty.
(True: The exception is if the person making the warranty is deemed to be an "expert." So, if your basically land-lubber neighbor sells you his used boat and says it is a "fine" boat and a "great" boat, which promptly sinks, there is no liability for the opinion' but if your neighbor is an Ensign in the Coast Guard there likely would be warranty liability since opinions made by experts are treated under UCC law as "facts.")

78. Express warranties can arise by the selling of goods using a sample or model of the goods.
(True: This is basic UCC express warranty law. Pictures as well as statements or affirmation of fact about the goods will also create express warranties.)

79. To disclaim the implied warranty of merchantability, a merchant typically must use the exact word "merchantability."
(True: The use of catch-all expressions such as "AS IS" will also exclude the warranty.)

80. The implied warranty of fitness for a particular purpose can be disclaimed orally but the exact word "fitness" must be used.
(False: A disclaimer of the fitness warranty must be in writing; however, as opposed to a disclaimer of the merchantability warranty the exact word "fitness" does not have to be used, though, obviously for evidentiary purposes it should.)

81. Under the UCC the performance of a contract must meet the "perfect tender" rule.
(True: This is a basic UCC performance principle, markedly different from the common law's substantial performance doctrine. There is an important UCC exception to the perfect tender rule, called the Cure Doctrine, whereby if a seller delivers defective or incomplete goods to a buyer, but before the contract due date, the seller is allowed to "cure" the shipment by promptly notifying the buyer of the seller's intent to cure and then by delivering conforming goods on or before the contract due date.)

82. In every UCC contract there is an implied warranty of good faith and fair dealing.
(True: This is a seminal UCC principle, which cannot be eliminated contractually or disclaimed.)

Multiple Choice Questions with Answers and Explanations

1. The implied warranty of merchantability:
   a. is imposed by the UCC on every sale of goods by any type of seller, including merchants and non-merchants.
   b. can be disclaimed and excluded by a statement to the effect that the "Seller disclaims any and all warranties.
   c. applies to both goods and services.
   d. None of the above.

   (The correct answer is d. The merchantability warrant just applies to the sale of goods by merchants. It can only be disclaimed by the explicit and conspicuous use of the word "merchantability" as well as by catch-all disclaimers, such as buyer buys the goods "AS-IS.")

2. Pursuant to the Uniform Commercial Code:
   a. the merchant seller of a product impliedly warrants that it is fit for its ordinary purposes.
   b. implied warranties can be disclaimed.
   c. the plaintiff does not have to prove negligence in order to recover under warranty.
   d. All of the above.
   (The correct answer is d. Fitness for a good's ordinary purposes is part of the implied warranty of merchantability made by a merchant seller. Implied warranties can be disclaimed, though particular requirements may have to be met, for example, the exact word "merchantability" being used to disclaim the implied warranty of merchantability. Negligence is not an issue in warranty law; rather, the gravamen of the lawsuit is whether a warranty was made and breached. A plaintiff injured by a product can always sue the seller and/or manufacturer on a separate count for negligence.)

3. Which of the following is FALSE about contracts pursuant to the Uniform Commercial Code?
   a. A UCC contract must have a clear and precise price term initially in the contract to be valid.
   b. A merchant's firm offer can be valid and enforceable even without payment of consideration.
   c. Additional terms in an acceptance will as a general rule not render the acceptance invalid.
   d. The UCC as a general rule requires a writing for contracts for the sale of goods $500 or more.
   (The correct answer is a. The UCC does not require an initial price term as opposed to the common law of contracts. The price term can be left blank and the price will be deemed to be a "reasonable" price at the time and place of delivery of the goods. Moreover, the parties can in the contract agree to agree on the price later or one party can be given the right to set the price though that party is obligated to act in good faith. The merchant's firm offer, as opposed to an option under the common law, does not require consideration, but does require a writing signed by the merchant and a maximum duration of 30 days. Again, as opposed to the common law "Mirror Image" rule, additional terms in an acceptance will not as a general rule negate a contract. If the parties are not merchants, the additional terms in essence "drop out" of the contract and are left for future negotiations between the parties; but there is a contract. Yet if both parties are merchants the additional terms become part of the contract unless 1) the offeror merchant said "take-it-or-leave it" to his or her terms; 2) the offeree merchant objects to the terms within a reasonable time; and 3) the additional terms are a material alteration of the contract, for example, using arbitration as opposed to a court trial for litigating disputes.)

4. Which of the following is TRUE about warranties under the Uniform Commercial Code?
   a. A disclaimer of the implied warranty of merchantability generally must use the word "merchantability" in the disclaimer.
   b. The implies warranty of merchantability is made by any person who sells goods.
   c. The implied warranty of merchantability is made by a merchant can never be disclaimed since it would not be fair to the non-merchant consumer.
   d. Express warranties can never be made by pictures, samples, or models since written words are required.
   (The correct answer is a. The implied warranty of merchantability can only be made by a merchant; but it can be disclaimed, yet the exact word "merchantability" must be used or a catch-all disclaimer, such as "buyer buys the goods AS IS," can be used too. Express warranties can be made by pictures, samples, models, as well as oral and written words.)

5. Which of the following is a TRUE statement?
   a. Goods are defined as only intangible personal property, such as trade secrets, stocks, bonds, commercial paper, and patents.
   b. The Uniform Commercial Code does not have any Statute of Frauds provisions.

c. A" fixture" is personal property affixed to real property, but which can be readily removed.
d. The Uniform Commercial Code's implied warranty of merchantability is only imposed on merchants.

(The correct answer is d. A good is a fixture if it can only be removed from the real property by damaging the real property. The UCC does have a Statute of Frauds requiring a writing for a contract for goods of $500 or more, but there are exceptions. The UCC's definition of goods does not include intangible property, only personal property that has a physical existence.)

6. Which of the following is a TRUE statement?
   a. The Uniform Commercial Code governs contracts involving real property and personal property leases.
   b. The adoption of the Uniform Commercial Code has completely eliminated the need for the common law in the area of contracts.
   c. The Uniform Commercial Code only applies to a contract if the parties explicitly state so in their contract.
   d. The Uniform Commercial Code takes precedence over the common law of contracts regarding contracts for the sale of goods.

   (The correct answer is d. The UCC is statutory law which takes precedence over the common law of contracts which is based on judge-made law. The parties do not have to expressly state that the UCC applies to a contract, because if the subject matter is/are "goods" the UCC governs the transaction. If the UCC is silent on a contract law issue a court will apply a common law contract principle.)

7. Which of the following is a TRUE statement?
   a. The Uniform Commercial Code is an example of federal Congressional law in the United States.
   b. The Uniform Commercial Code's implied warranty of fitness for a particular purpose applies only to merchants.
   c. To disclaim the implied warranty of merchantability the exact word "merchantability" must be used.
   d. A Uniform Commercial Code contract must have a definite price-term or it will be invalidated for vagueness.

   (The correct answer is c. The UCC is a state statutory law. A UCC contract does not have to have a price term, which is a major change in the common law of contracts. Anyone can make the fitness warranty if the required elements of knowledge, reliance, skill, and judgment of the seller in selecting suitable or "fit" goods for the buyer are present.)

8. Which of the following is a TRUE statement?
   a. For an express warranty to be created, the exact words "warrant" or "guarantee" must be used.
   b. A retailer is not bound by a warranty made by a manufacturer.
   c. In order to be the "basis of the bargain" in a sale of goods transaction, a warranty must have been the sole reason for the purchase of the product.
   d. The implied warranty of merchantability includes a warranty that if goods are sold in bulk or in lots they must be in the medium range of quality.

   (The correct answer is d. The warranty just needs to have an influence on the buyer to purchase the goods and does not have to be the sole reason. The express words "warranty" or "guaranty" need not be used; any statement or affirmation of fact about the goods will create an express warranty. A retailer is bound by the manufacturer's warranties; of course, a retailer who must pay a judgment based on the breach of warranty can always sue "up-the-chain" to get the manufacturer to reimburse the retailer, assuming jurisdiction, of course.)

9. Which of the following is a TRUE statement?
    a. The UCC holds that an opinion or prediction given by an expert may rise to the level of an express warranty.
    b. The law assumes that a seller who makes a statement about goods is just giving his or her opinion unless the seller clearly says that he or she is making a statement of fact.
    c. The UCC requires merchants to make express warranties about the quality of the products they sell.
    d. The implied warranty of merchantability applies only to the quality of the goods themselves, but not to the manner in which the goods are packaged or labeled.

    (The correct answer is a. Opinions and predictions are generally not regarded as facts and thus cannot be the basis for an express warranty; however, a major exception is when the opinion or prediction is given by someone whom the law regards as an "expert." The UCC does not require any express warranties from anyone. The implied warranty of merchantability has several components, including that the goods be adequately packaged and labeled.)

10. Which of the following is a TRUE statement?
    a. Pursuant to the implied warranty of merchantability, fungible goods must be of very high quality.
    b. A foreign object in a food or beverage will violate the implied warranty of wholesomeness or fitness.
    c. The implied warranty of fitness for a particular purpose automatically arises any time a seller is a merchant.
    d. In mixed transactions involving both services and goods, the contract price of the services and goods determines whether the Uniform Commercial Code applies.

    (The correct answer is b. A foreign object like a piece of metal in the food will clearly violate the wholesomeness warranty. The problem arises when there is a "natural" object in the food, for example, a nut shell in a jar of peanut butter. Some states will not impose liability since the object is natural to the food, but others use a "reasonable expectations" test, that is, should a reasonable consumer expect a nut shell in a jar of peanut butter. In a mixed transaction of goods and services the courts will use the "predominant feature" test to see what prevails and then apply the pertinent body of law. The implied fitness warranty is not automatic; rather, it arises when a buyer relies on a seller's knowledge, skill, and judgment to select goods suitable for the buyer's known intended use.)

11. Which express warranties are sellers of goods legally required to make by the UCC?
    a. Warranties regarding the title to the goods.
    b. Warranties regarding the length of time that the product can be returned.
    c. Warranties regarding the length of time that the seller will repair or replace the product.
    d. None of the above.

    (The correct answer is d. Note, however, that there is an implied warranty of good title to the goods.)

12. Which of the following is NOT required in order for the implied warranty of fitness for a particular purpose to apply to a sale of goods transaction?
    a. The seller knows or has reason to know of the buyer's intended use of the goods.
    b. The seller is an entity on the marketing chain.
    c. The seller states that the goods will serve the purpose of the buyer's intended use.
    d. The buyer purchases the goods in reliance on the seller's knowledge, skill, and judgment.

    (The correct answer is b. Any seller can make this warranty if the requirements are met.)

13. For which of the following warranties must the seller be a merchant?
    a. Express warranties.
    b. Implied warranty of merchantability.
    c. Implied warranty of fitness for a particular purpose.
    d. None of the above.
    (The correct answer is b. This is a basic UCC proposition.)

14. Which of the following is TRUE about the difference between express and implied warranties?
    a. Express warranties can be readily disclaimed.
    b. Express warranties apply to merchants and implied warranties apply to nonmerchants.
    c. Express warranties arise from the conduct of the parties and implied warranties arise automatically by operation of the law.
    d. Implied warranties cannot be disclaimed and excluded from the sales contract.
    (The correct answer is c. It is virtually impossible for a seller to exclude an express warranty once it has been made. The cases allowing such exclusion are exceedingly rare. One example concerns express warranties made concerning seeds.)

15. Which of the following is NOT one of the components of the implied warranty of merchantability?
    a. The goods are suitable for the ordinary purposes for which they are used.
    b. The goods are adequately contained, packaged, and labeled.
    c. The goods are priced justly, ethically, and fairly.
    d. The goods will do their ordinary job safely.
    (The correct answer is c. Price is not an issue under the UCC merchantability warranty. However, the UCC does have a doctrine of "unconscionability" whereby a court will rescind a contract if someone, usually a poor, uneducated, non-English-speaking, and/or elderly person has been so wrongfully and grossly taken advantage of so that there is such a very unfair and unjust price for the goods that the contract "shocks the conscience of the court.")

16. Pursuant to the implied warranty of merchantability:
    a. Both merchants and non-merchants generally are liable.
    b. The warranty includes a requirement that the goods do their ordinary job safely.
    c. The warranty applies even if a product is misused and instructions are disregarded.
    d. The warranty is based on a "reasonable expectation" test as to what a "good" quality good should be according to a reasonable consumer
    (The correct answer is b. Misuse and abuse of a product as well as disregarding instructions are all valid defenses to a breach of warranty lawsuit as well as a lawsuit for strict liability. The "reasonable expectations" test applies to the implied warranty of wholesomeness and asks what a reasonable consumer would expect if there is an object in the food that is natural to the food.)

17. Which of the following statements is TRUE?
    a. An agreement under the UCC usually consists of an offer and a counteroffer.
    b. In most states in the U.S., the revocation of a UCC contract is not legally effective until it is actually received by the merchant seller.
    c. For something to be classified as a good pursuant to the UCC, it must be intangible.
    d. Pursuant to the UCC, an agreement modifying a contract needs no new consideration to be binding.
    (The correct answer is d. The fact that no new consideration is required for a modification of a UCC contract is a major change from the common law. The UCC just applies to tangible goods.)

18. Which of the following statements is FALSE?
    a. Statements of fact regarding a product that are made during the bargaining process that become part of the basis of the bargain are not express warranties if they are not designated expressly as a "warranty" or "guarantee."
    b. Pursuant to a shipment contract, the risk of loss passes to the buyer when the seller places conforming goods in the possession of the carrier.
    c. A seller who ships nonconforming goods has the right to cure the shipment within the contract time for performance if proper notice is given.
    d. The implied warranty of merchantability typically can be disclaimed by such "catch-all" expressions, for example, sold "AS IS."

    (The correct answer is a. Any affirmation of fact or statement of fact regarding the goods can be the basis for an express warranty; the exact words "warranty" or "guaranty" are not required.)

19. Which of the following is a TRUE statement?
    a. Increased cost resulting from inflation probably will not excuse a supplier from performing a contract on the grounds of "commercial impracticality."
    b. A buyer of goods generally is required to inspect any goods he or she receives.
    c. A party to a sales contract clearly announcing that he or she will not be able to perform the contract as agreed prior to the date of performance is called the "lack of substantial performance" doctrine.
    d. A person is a "merchant" under the UCC if he or she holds himself or herself out by occupation or training as having knowledge and skill unique to certain types of goods.

    (The correct answer is d. One does not necessarily have to be a retailer, wholesaler, distributor, or manufacturer to be deemed a "merchant" under the UCC. Clearly announcing that one will not perform a contract is called "anticipatory repudiation," which means the aggrieved party can immediately sue for breach of contract. "Substantial performance" is a common law doctrine. For commercial impracticality to be a valid defense to performing a UCC contract the increase costs must be drastic not merely inflationary increases.)

20. Pursuant to the UCC, a sales contract typically is enforceable even if one of the following terms is omitted:
    a. Price.
    b. Quantity.
    c. Price or quantity.
    d. Neither price nor quantity may be omitted.

    (The correct answer is a. The price term in the contract for the sale of goods can be completely eliminated, and as such the UCC will imply a "reasonable price" at the time and place of delivery of the goods. The quantity term, however, must be present and must be specific or the contract will be void for vagueness. The omission of the price term is a major change the UCC makes in the common law of contracts.)

21. Which of the following is TRUE relating to a "firm offer" under the UCC?
    a. It can be made only by a merchant.
    b. It must be in writing and signed by the merchant.
    c. It may provide that the offer will remain open for any time period up to four months.
    d. a and b only.

    (The correct answer is d. The maximum time period is one month. The other responses are basic requirements to the merchant's firm offer under the UCC. Note, most importantly, that the common law element of consideration, as in an option, is not required here.)

22. Pursuant to the UCC, if a purported acceptance to an offer contains additional terms:
    a. It is treated as a rejection and counteroffer.
    b. If both parties are merchants, there is a contract and the additional terms may or may not become part of the contract.
    c. If neither party is a merchant, there is no contract.
    d. It is treated as a counteroffer, but it does not reject the original offer.

    (The correct answer is b. Under the common law, of course, as per the Mirror Image rule, any additional changes in the purported acceptance would be viewed as a counteroffer and a rejection of the offer. However, the rule is different in the UCC. First, if the parties are not merchants there is a contract on the original terms and the additional terms sort of "fall out" of the contract and become "proposals" for negotiation between the parties. However, if both parties are merchants the additional terms may become part of the contract unless 1) the offeror merchant has said "take-it-or-leave-it" to the terms of the offer, 2) the offeree merchant has notified the offeror merchant that he or she objects to the additional terms within a reasonable amount of time, and 3) the additional terms are a material alteration of the contract, for example, disclaiming warranties or waiving the right to a jury trial for arbitration.)

23. Which of the following is TRUE regarding the modification of a sales contract under the UCC?
    a. A contract modification needs new consideration to be enforceable, which is the same as the common law rule.
    b. A contract modification needs no new consideration.
    c. Modifications of UCC contracts must always be in writing to be enforceable.
    d. a and c only.

    (The correct answer is b. The fact that a contract modification of a UCC contract does not need any new consideration is a major change in the common law. However, agreement to the modification by both parties is, of course, necessary. A writing is not required unless the modification comes within the UCC Statute of Frauds or brings the original contract into the Statute of Frauds.)

24. A destination contract requires that the seller:
    a. Deliver the goods to a common carrier.
    b. Deliver the goods to the buyer.
    c. Provide proper and adequate notice to the buyer.
    d. b and c.

    (The correct answer is d. A destination contract, as opposed to a shipment contract where the goods are just delivered to a common carrier, requires that the goods be delivered to the specified destination and that the buyer be notified to pickup the goods.)

25. If a buyer delivers nonconforming goods prior to the date that delivery is due, the seller can make the shipment conform and avoid breaching the sales contract pursuant to which UCC doctrine:
    a. Time-is-of-the-essence
    b. Right to make perfect.
    c. Substantial performance
    d. Right to cure.

    (The correct answer is d. The doctrine is the cure doctrine, which means that though the initial early delivery is not perfect, the seller can cure it by delivering conforming goods on or before the contract due date. Responses a and c are common law contract doctrines.)

26. If a seller breaches a contract for the sale of goods and the buyer then acquires similar goods from another seller, this is known as the right of:
    a. Rescission
    b. Specific performance.
    c. Cover.
    d. Contract cancellation.
    (The correct answer is c. Cover is a basic right of an aggrieved buyer under the UCC. The buyer is entitled to any difference in price as damages as well as incidental damages. Rescission is the cancellation of a contract mutually by the parties or by a court as an equitable remedy for fraud, mistake, duress, or undue influence. Specific performance is another right an aggrieved buyer has under the UCC. It is an equitable remedy by which a judge will order a party to perform a contract if goods are unique or rare or in very short supply.)

27. The seller can recover the purchase price for the goods only under certain circumstances when:
    a. The buyer accepts the goods, but the buyer fails to pay for the goods.
    b. The goods are destroyed after the risk of loss passes to the buyer.
    c. The buyer rejects specially manufactured goods that cannot be resold.
    d. All of the above.
    (The correct answer is d. These are all basic UCC principles. Note that for specially manufactured they must not be able to be resold in the ordinary course of the seller's business. Also note that the UCC construes specially manufactured as "goods" and not a service.)

28. Which of the following is TRUE about the distinction between express and implied warranties?
    a. Express warranties apply to merchants and implied warranties apply to all sellers of goods.
    b. Express warranties apply to merchants and implied warranties apply to non-merchants.
    c. Express warranties arise from conduct of the parties and implied warranties arise automatically by operation of law.
    d. Implied warranties cannot be disclaimed, but express warranties can be disclaimed.
    (The correct answer is c. Implied warranties come from the UCC and are imposed regardless of the wishes of the seller, though implied warranties can be disclaimed. Warranties can be made by anyone though with the important exception that the implied warranty of merchantability is imposed only on merchants. It is extremely rare for an express warranty to be disclaimed.)

29. Which of the following is TRUE about the UCC and the common law of contracts?
    a. The common law generally takes precedence over the UCC since the common law existed a long time before the UCC/.
    b. A primary purpose of the UCC is to eliminate the differences from state to state which existed under the common law of contracts.
    c. The UCC applies to a contract only if the parties explicitly state so in their contract.
    d. The adoption of the UCC has eliminated the need for common law in the field of contract law.
    (The correct answer is b. The UCC as state statutory law takes precedence over the common law, that is, judge-made, law of contracts. However, the UCC is not an exhaustive commercial code, so if the UCC is silent on a matter the old common law of contracts will provide the legal precept. A goal of the UCC is uniformity and another objective is to make it easier for parties, especially merchants, to enter into contract, which are good for business and thus the economy. If the subject matter of a contract is or are "goods" the UCC applies.)

30. Article 2 of the UCC covers which types of transactions:
    a. Sales of goods and sales of real property.
    b. Sales of goods and leases of goods or real property.
    c. Sales of goods and contracts for the providing of services.

d. Sales of goods and leases of goods.
(The correct answer is d. Service and real estate contracts are governed by the common law of contracts.)

31. The sales provisions of Article 2 of the UCC apply to:
 a. Neither merchants nor nonmerchants.
 b. Nonmerchants, but not to merchants.
 c. Merchants, but not nonmerchants.
 d. Both merchants and nonmerchants.
 (The correct answer is d. Any seller of goods is governed by the UCC, though there are special provisions that just apply to "merchant" sellers; and note that these provisions make it very easy for a merchant, and perhaps an unwitting one, to find himself or herself in a contract.)

32. Regarding differences under the UCC in the treatment of merchants and nonmerchants, which is TRUE?
 a. The UCC applies to merchants, but not to nonmerchants.
 b. The UCC requires merchants' contracts to be in writing, but not those of nonmerchants.
 c. The requirements for a merchant to form a contract are less stringent than those for nonmerchants, and merchants receive fewer protections than nonmerchants.
 d. The consideration requirement has been eliminated for contracts between merchants, but it is still present in contracts involving at least one nonmerchant.
 (The correct answer is c. The UCC applies to both merchants and non-merchants. A sales contract must be in writing if governed by the UCC Statute of Frauds, though there are exceptions; and consideration is also required for a valid sales contract, though there are exceptions, for example, the merchant's firm offer as well as modification of contracts.)

33. If the time, place, and manner of delivery of goods is not expressly stated in a UCC contract:
 a. The place of delivery is the buyer's place of business.
 b. The contract is void for lack of definiteness.
 c. The place of delivery is the seller's place of business.
 d. The seller is obligated to pay for shipping to the buyer's place of business.
 (The correct answer is c. The contract is still a valid contract since one recalls the philosophy behind the UCC to make it easier to enter into contracts, as opposed to the stricter requirements of the common law.)

34. A provision in the UCC which affects merchants differently from nonmerchants is:
 a. The effect of additional terms in an acceptance.
 b. The firm offer rule.
 c. The written confirmation doctrine.
 d. All of the above.
 (The correct answer is d. These are all major changes the UCC makes in the common law, again with the purpose of making it easier to enter into a sales contract.)

35. Under the UCC, firm offers can be made:
 a. Orally or in writing by merchants.
 b. Orally or in writing by merchants, but only in writing by nonmerchants.
 c. In writing by either merchants or nonmerchants.
 d. In writing by merchants.
 (The correct answer is d. Only merchants make the firm offer, which is why it is called the "merchant's firm offer. Consideration is not required but a signed writing by the merchant is;

however, the common law requirement of consideration which would turn a firm offer into an option is not required. Note too that there is a one-month limit for the firm offer to be open.)

36. Under the UCC, between merchants, if a purported acceptance contains additional terms, there is an acceptance, and
    a. The additional terms are not part of the contract.
    b. The additional terms are part of the contract.
    c. The additional terms do not become part of the contract if they materially alter the contract.
    d. There is no contract since the Mirror Image rule is violated.
    (The correct answer is c. This is a major change in the common law as the old "Mirror Image" doctrine has been abrogated by the UCC. So if both parties are merchants the additional terms automatically become part of the contract, though there are exceptions, one being when the additional terms are a material alteration of the contact, such as waiving a jury trial in favor of arbitration.)

37. Risk of loss passes to the buyer in a contract for the sale of goods which does not involve a common carrier:
    a. Upon tender of delivery for both merchant sellers and nonmerchant sellers.
    b. Upon tender of delivery for merchant sellers and when goods are received by the buyer in the case of nonmerchant sellers.
    c. Upon tender of delivery for nonmerchant sellers and when goods are actually received by the buyer in the case of merchant sellers.
    d. When goods are received by the buyer for both merchant sellers and nonmerchant sellers.
    (The correct answer is c. If the contract is silent as to when the risk of losses passes from the seller to the buyer the UCC risk of loss rules apply. If there is no specific provision in the contact and a common carrier is not involved the rule is as per answer c. Note that "tender of delivery" means the goods are put at the disposal of the buyer and the buyer is notified to pick them up.)

38. The requirement that goods tendered to a buyer must conform in all ways to the terms of the contract is called the:
    a. Complete Performance rule.
    b. Perfect tender rule.
    c. No right to cure rule.
    d. Substantial performance rule.
    (The correct answer is b. This is another major change the UCC makes in the common law, that is, the distinction between common law "substantial performance" and UCC "perfect tender.")

39. Which of the following would constitute a valid acceptance?
    a. The buyer tells the seller that the nonconforming goods which were shipped will be kept and paid for.
    b. The buyer waits for four months before notifying the seller that the goods are nonconforming.
    c. The buyer immediately resells the nonconforming goods.
    d. A, B and C.
    (The correct answer is d. Responses b and c would be implied acceptances; and in b the time period is clearly unreasonable.)

40. If the buyer breaches the contract before the goods are completed, the seller can:
    a. Complete the goods and resell them.
    b. Stop work on the goods and resell them as scrap.
    c. Recover damages from the buyer.
    d. A, B and C.

(The correct answer is d. These are all options for the seller under the UCC.)

41. Which of the following statements is FALSE regarding the buyer's right to cover?
    a. The buyer must cover.
    b. The measure of damages in a cover is cover price less contract price.
    c. Cover must be done in a commercially reasonable manner and without undue delay.
    d. Consequential damages can be recovered in addition to the cover damages.
    (The correct answer is a. The buyer has to option to cover, or perhaps the buyer will avail himself or herself of another remedy, that is, to sue for breach of contract and recover the difference between the market price of the goods and the contract price.)

42. For which of the following warranties must the seller be a merchant?
    a. Express warranties.
    b. Implied warranty of merchantability.
    c. Implied warranty of fitness for a particular purpose.
    d. Implied warranty of title.
    (The correct answer is b. Anyone can make an express warranty as well as be held by the UCC to the title and fitness implied warranties.)

43. Which of the following elements is the MOST IMPORTANT in determining whether personal property has become a fixture?
    a. Whether the personal property has been attached to the land or a structure on the land.
    b. Whether the personal property is used in the same manner as the structure on the land.
    c. Whether the personal property can be removed without damaging the land or a structure on the land.
    d. The intent of the parties.
    (The correct answer is c. Damage is the key factor, though the other criteria are also factors.)

44. The Uniform Commercial Code is:
    a. A state law governing commercial transactions
    b. A federal law governing commerce
    c. An international law governing commerce
    d. A proposed model commercial act.
    (The correct answer is a. The UCC is state-based statutory law, based on the "model" prepared by commercial law experts. The UCC is more-or-less uniform among the several states, meaning that if a UCC dispute arises in a state reference perforce must be made to the UCC version as promulgated by the legislature of that state and not the "model" act.)

45. The UCC is:
    a. Concerned with the sale of goods
    b. Concerned with employment contracts
    c. Concerned with service contracts
    d. Concerned with real estate contracts.
    (The correct answer is a. Real estate, service, and employment contracts are still governed by the old common law.)

46. Under the UCC a merchant is MOST ACCURATELY described as a
    a. A salesperson of goods
    b. A retailer of goods
    c. An inventor of goods
    d. A Venetian who trades goods

(The correct answer is b. Anyone on the marketing chain will be deemed to be a merchant under the UCC, thereby including manufacturers, wholesalers, distributors. Moreover, one even if not on the marketing chain can become a "merchant" by virtue of his or her specialized knowledge and expertise regarding certain goods, such as a non-merchant SCUBA instructor selling SCUBA gear to a neighbor.)

47. Under Article II of the UCC a seller may NOT:
    a. Withhold delivery
    b. Seize the goods back on his or her own
    c. Stop delivery in transit
    d. Sell the goods
    (The correct answer is b. Self-help, which borders on "lawlessness," is not an option!)

48. Which of the following is a FALSE statement?
    a. Pursuant to the UCC, an agreement modifying a contract generally needs no new consideration to be binding.
    b. An oral contract for goods that are specially manufactured for a particular buyer may be enforceable under the UCC even without a writing.
    c. The Convention on Contracts for the International Sale of Goods is closely patterned after the Uniform Commercial Code of U.S. law.
    d. Pursuant to the Uniform Commercial Code, a merchant who sells one type of good will be considered a merchant for any other type of good that he or she sells since a merchant is a merchant.
    (The correct answer is d. A merchant is just a merchant for the type of goods the merchant regularly sells and not for every type of commercial transaction. The UCC is the basis for the international treaty. The other responses are exceptions to common law rules for sales contracts.)

49. Which of the following is a FALSE statement?
    a. If a contract for the sale of goods does not include a price term, it nonetheless may still be enforceable pursuant to the Uniform Commercial Code.
    b. If a contract for the sales of goods does not include the exact terms for payment, it normally will be unenforceable since it is impermissibly vague.
    c. When an offer for the sale of goods does not specify a means of acceptance, the offer usually can be accepted by any manner reasonable under the circumstances.
    d. A warranty is an assurance by the buyer to the seller that he or she will pay valid and good consideration for a product.
    (The correct answer is d. A warranty is a guarantee by a seller that goods will meet a certain standard of quality of operate in a certain way; buyers do not make warranties. The other responses are again major changes the UCC makes in the common law of contracts, again based on the rationale of making it easier to enter into sales contracts.)

50. Which of the following is a TRUE statement?
    a. Statements of fact regarding a product that are made during the bargaining process can never be express warranties since facts can be "checked out."
    b. A seller must use the specific words "warrant" or "warranty" or "guaranty" in order to create an express warranty under the UCC.
    c. An implied warranty of merchantability arises in every sale of goods by a merchant who deals in the kind of goods sold unless otherwise disclaimed.
    d. A seller must provide a written warranty for every sale of consumer goods based on federal consumer law.

(The correct answer is c. A fundamental concept in the UCC is the merchant's implied warrant of merchantability which is imposed on merchants who deal in the kind of goods. However, what the UCC "giveth" the UCC "taketh away" by allowing merchants to disclaim the warranty. Statements of fact pertaining to the goods form the basis for express warranties, though the exact words "warranty" or "guaranty" or equivalent need not be used. Federal law does not require the seller to make any warranty, but if one is made there are some requirements, for example, being clear and conspicuous and not "fine-print.")

51. Which of the following is a FALSE statement?
    a. A merchant can disclaim the implied warranty of merchantability.
    b. If the seller is not a merchant, and the goods are not to be moved, then the risk of loss passes to the buyer on tender of delivery of the goods plus notification.
    c. If the seller is not a merchant, and the seller holds the goods, and the buyer is to pick them up, then the risk of loss passes to the buyer when the buyer acquires good title to the goods.
    d. If a seller is a merchant, and the goods are not to be moved, the risk of loss passes to a buyer when the buyer takes physical possession of the goods.

    (The correct answer is c. Prior to the UCC the issue of who had the risk of loss for damage or destruction of goods was based on which party had good title to the goods. Under the UCC now title is not dispositive on risk of loss; rather, the UCC specific risk of loss rules, as noted above, apply.)

52. Which of the following is a FALSE statement?
    a. Pursuant to a destination contract, the risk of loss typically passes to the buyer when the goods are duly delivered to the carrier.
    b. Pursuant to a shipment contract, the risk of loss typically passes to the buyer when the seller places conforming goods in the possession of the carrier.
    c. The UCC implies a duty of good faith and fair dealing in all sales contracts.
    d. A philosophy behind the UCC is to make it easier for people to enter into contracts.

    (The correct answer is a. Under a destination contract the risk of loss passes to the buyer when the goods arrive at the destination and the buyer picks them up. Note that the good faith duty in the UCC cannot be disclaimed or excluded.)

53. Which of the following is a TRUE statement?
    a. Goods are defined as only intangible personal property such as stocks, bonds, money, and patents.
    b. The Uniform Commercial Code does not have any Statute of Frauds provisions.
    c. A fixture is personal property affixed to real property, but which can be readily removed.
    d. The Uniform Commercial Code's implied warranty of merchantability is only imposed on merchants.

    (The correct answer is d. "Goods" mean tangible property, that is, with a physical existence, and thus the UCC does not deal with intangibles. If something can be readily removed from the land or a structure on the land then it is not a "fixture," that is, part of the real estate, and thus governed by common law; rather, it is a good subject to the UCC.)

54. Which of the following is a TRUE statement?
    a. The Uniform Commercial Code governs contracts involving real property and personal property leases.
    b. The adoption of the Uniform Commercial Code has completely eliminated the need for the common law in the area of contracts.
    c. The Uniform Commercial Code only applies to a contract if the parties explicitly state so in their contract.

d. The Uniform Commercial Code takes precedence over the common law of contracts regarding contracts for the sale of goods.

(The correct answer is d. The UCC takes precedence over the common law for a contract wherein the subject matter is a "good"; however, if the UCC is silent on a contract law issue the old common law of contracts will apply.)

55. Which of the following is a TRUE statement?
    a. The Uniform Commercial Code is an example of federal Congressional law in the United States.
    b. The Uniform Commercial Code's implied warranty of fitness for a particular purpose applies only to merchants.
    c. To disclaim the implied warranty of merchantability the exact word "merchantability" must be used as a general rule.
    d. A Uniform Commercial Code contract must have a definite price-term or else it will be invalidated for vagueness.

    (The correct answer is c. Note, however, that though the word "merchantability" must be used to have an effective disclaimer, a "catch-all" disclaimer, such as "buyer buys the goods AS-IS, will also eliminate the merchantability warranty. The UCC is state statutory law, which is more-or-less uniform. A major change that the UCC makes in the common law is that a UCC contract does not need a price-term, and as such the contract is still good and the UCC will imply a reasonable price at the time and place of delivery.)

56. Which of the following is a TRUE statement?
    a. For an express warranty to be created the exact words "warrant" or "guarantee" must be used.
    b. A statement that a truck has a carrying-capacity of 2000 pounds would likely be treated as a mere opinion and thus could not become a warranty.
    c. In order to be the "basis of the bargain" in a sale of goods transaction, a warranty must have been the sole reason for the purchase of the product.
    d. The implied warranty of merchantability includes a warranty that if goods are sold in bulk or in groups they must be in the medium range of quality.

    (The correct answer is d. The trailer statement clearly seems factual and thus would form the basis for an express warranty. To meet the "basis of the bargain" warranty requirement the warranty must just be one of the reasons that influenced the buyer to purchase the goods.)

57. Which of the following is a TRUE statement?
    a. The doctrine of *Caveat Emptor* means: "Let the buyer beware."
    b. The law presumes that a seller who makes a statement about goods is just giving his or her opinion unless the seller clearly says that he or she is making a statement of fact.
    c. Implied warranties do not apply to the sale of goods.
    d. The implied warranty of merchantability applies only to the goods themselves, and not the way the goods are packaged or labeled.

    (The correct answer is a. Any affirmation or statement of fact about the goods will suffice to form the basis for an express warranty without the need to any specific factual reference. The UCC imposes three types of implied warranties on the seller of goods, the implied warranty of merchantability made only by merchants, which includes adequate packaging and labeling of the goods, the implied warranty of fitness for a particular purpose, and the implied warranty of wholesomeness regarding food and beverages. Caveat Emptor is important under the common law due to the old maxim that as a general rule "silence is not fraud.")

58. Which of the following is a TRUE statement?
   a. Pursuant to the implied warranty of merchantability, fungible goods must be of very high quality.
   b. A consumer who is injured by a piece of bone in a cheeseburger may be able to recover under the implied warranty of wholesomeness.
   c. The implied warranty of fitness for a particular purpose automatically arises any time a seller is a merchant.
   d. In mixed transactions involving both services and goods, the contract price of the services and goods determines whether the Uniform Commercial Code applies.

   (The correct answer is b. Wholesomeness means that food and beverages are not contaminated and that no foreign objects are in the food. It is likely that a bone in a cheeseburger would be considered a foreign object. But if not, some states would use the "reasonable expectations" test, that is, would a reasonable consumer expect a bone in a cheeseburger, as opposed to a fish bone in a fresh grouper sandwich in the Florida Keys. Anyone can make the fitness warranty, but it is not automatic, but rather based on the buyer relying on the seller's knowledge and skill to select goods that are "fit" for the buyer's intended purpose. In mixed transactions that have a combination of goods and services, the courts use the predominant feature test to determine if the UCC or the common law prevails. So, a construction contract would be construed under the common law as a service even though wood, nails, etc., are sold along with the construction service.)

59. Which express warranties are sellers of goods legally REQUIRED to make under the UCC?
   a. Warranties regarding the quality of goods.
   b. Warranties regarding the length of time that the goods can be returned.
   c. Warranties regarding the length of time that the seller will repair or replace the goods.
   d. None of the above.

   (The correct answer is d. None of these warranties are required by the UCC; rather, they are optional on the part of the seller. Note that a disclaimer of a warranty might say in part that "The seller is only responsible for the repair or replacement of defective goods.")

60. Which of the following is NOT necessary in order for the implied warranty of fitness for a particular purpose to apply?
   a. The seller knows or has reason to know of the buyer's intended use of the goods.
   b. The seller is a merchant.
   c. The seller states that the goods will serve the purpose of the buyer's intended use.
   d. The buyer buys in reliance on the seller's knowledge, skill, and judgment to select suitable goods.

   (The correct answer is b. Anyone can make the implied warranty of fitness for a particular purpose if the requirements of purpose, fitness, knowledge, and reliance are present. To compare, only merchants make the implied warranty of merchantability.)

61. For which of the following warranties MUST the seller be a merchant?
   a. Express warranties.
   b. Implied warranty of merchantability.
   c. Implied warranty of fitness for a particular purpose.
   d. Implied warranty of merchantability and express warranties.

   (The correct answer is b. Only merchants have the implied warranty of merchantability imposed on them by the UCC. Any person can make the fitness warranty or an express warranty.)

62. Which of the following is TRUE about the difference between express and implied warranties?
    a. Express warranties apply to merchants and implied warranties apply to all sellers of goods.
    b. Express warranties apply to merchants and implied warranties apply to nonmerchants.
    c. Express warranties arise from the conduct of the parties and implied warranties automatically by operation of the law.
    d. Implied warranties cannot be disclaimed.

    (The correct answer is c. Anyone can make an express warranty; anyone can make the implied fitness and wholesomeness warranties; but only merchants make the implied warranty of merchantability, which can be disclaimed.)

63. Which of the following is NOT one of the aspects of the implied warranty of merchantability?
    a. The goods are suitable for the ordinary purposes for which they are used.
    b. The goods are adequately contained, packaged, and labeled.
    c. The goods are priced justly, ethically, and fairly.
    d. The goods within each unit or part are of an even quality.

    (The correct answer is c. Pricing of the goods, just, ethical, fair or otherwise, is not part of the merchantability warranty.)

64. Pursuant to the implied warranty of merchantability:
    a. Both merchants and nonmerchants generally are liable.
    b. The warranty includes a requirement that the goods be adequately packaged and labeled.
    c. The warranty applies even if a product is misused and instructions are disregarded.
    d. The warranty is based on a "reasonable expectations" test as to what a consumer thinks the high quality of a good should be.

    (The correct answer is b. The "reasonable expectations" test deals with the implied warranty of wholesomeness of food and beverages. The problem arises where there is an object in the food that is not foreign to the food, like a nail, but is considered to be "natural" to the food, such as a tuna bone in a can of tuna. In some states if the object is natural like the bone the food is not unwholesome or unfit and the warranty is not breached. Yet in most states the courts use the reasonable expectations test and thus a jury would decide if a reasonable consumer would expect a fish bone in a can of tuna, as opposed to a bowl of fish soup.)

65. Which of the following is FALSE about the Uniform Commercial Code?
    a. It applies only to the sale of goods by merchants.
    b. A covenant of good faith and fair dealing is implied in all UCC contracts.
    c. There are special UCC provisions that just apply to "merchants."
    d. The UCC makes several major changes to the common law of contracts.

    (The correct answer is a. The UCC applies to the sale of goods by anyone! The other responses are all fundamental UCC precepts.)

66. Regarding the formation of a sales contract under the UCC, which is a FALSE statement?
    a. A merchant's "firm offer" can be held open even without consideration.
    b. If the quantity term is missing in a UCC contract the courts will deem the contract to be nevertheless valid and the courts will then imply a "reasonable" quantity.
    c. The price term can be left open in a UCC contract.
    d. When the price of goods is $500 or more the UCC will require a writing to have a valid contract.

    (The correct answer is b. One area of the law that has remained constant between the old common law and the UCC is the need in both types of contracts for a precise quantity term; the courts will not under the UCC imply a "reasonable" quantity of the goods, as they would for the price of the goods.)

67. Under UCC warranty law, which of the following is a FALSE statement?
    a. An express warranty can be based on a statement of fact or affirmation of fact relating to the goods which becomes part of the "basis of the bargain."
    b. Implied warranties of quality cannot be disclaimed by such "catch-all" language, such as buyer takes the goods "AS IS," because to do so would be very unfair.
    c. To disclaim the implied warranty of merchantability the exact word "merchantability" must be used in the disclaimer.
    d. The law will require that any disclaimer of a warranty be conspicuous.

    (The correct answer is b. A "catch-all" disclaimer if clear, conspicuous, and bold will disclaim all implied warranties, including merchantability.)

68. What is FALSE about the performance and remedies of the sales contract under the UCC?
    a. The "perfect tender" rule requires that the goods and delivery of the goods by the seller be perfect and must conform exactly to the terms of the contract.
    b. A seller who tenders defective goods is never allowed to "cure" the defective delivery since it was not perfect.
    c. Before accepting the goods, the buyer is allowed to inspect the goods at a reasonable time and manner.
    d. If the seller fails to deliver the goods, the buyer is allowed to "cover" by buying the goods elsewhere in a commercially reasonable manner and receiving money damages.

    (The correct answer is b. The "cure" doctrine is a major exception the UCC makes to the "perfect tender" rule.)

20 - Agency Law

Introduction

Agency is a very important area of the law for businesspeople and thus for business students. A great deal of business is conducted by agents, especially by corporations which are not "real" people and thus who have to act through human beings, including of course agents. First and foremost, the student must be aware of three critical sets of definitions and differentiations that the law makes: employer and employee, principal and agent, and employer and independent contractors. The principal/agency relationship is an elevated one under the law as it is considered to be a fiduciary relationship, that is, one of trust and confidence. As such, the student must know the fundamental hallmarks of a fiduciary relationship. The essence of agency is that the agent is representing his or her principal for the main purpose of effectuating contractual relations for the principal. Next the student must know how an agency relationship can be created, to wit: expressly, impliedly, by the apparent agency doctrine, and by ratification. Regarding express agency agreements the student must be aware of the applicability of the Statute of Frauds as well as the Equal Dignity Rule. Regarding ratification, the student must know what ratification by the principal is as well as the limitations on the principal's power to ratify an unauthorized contract or transaction by his or her agent. Regarding the apparent authority doctrine, the student must be aware of what it is and how it can create authority in an agent, and it is absolutely critical for the student to comprehend that an agent can never create his or her own apparent authority. Then the student must know of the ways that an agency relationship can come to an end, including by the operation of the law as well as by the acts of the parties, particularly for the latter by means of the doctrines of revocation and renunciation.

The liability of the parties in the agency relationship, including naturally the third-party, is another important area for the student to understand. Accordingly, the student must comprehend how an agent's authority can be created expressly, impliedly, incidentally, apparently, and by ratification. One problem area that the student needs to be aware of deals with the liability of the agent when the agent acts for non-existent principals, undisclosed principals, and partially disclosed principals.

Though most of agency law is based on contract law principles, tort law does affect the principal/agent relationship as well as the employer/employee and employer/independent contractor relationship. As such, the student must know the principles regarding the tort liability of the principal for the acts of his or her agent, the tort liability of the employer for the torts of his or her employees, and the tort liability of the employer for the torts of his or her independent contractors. Regarding tort liability in the employer/employee context it is critical for the student to know of the doctrine of *Respondeat Superior* and the vicarious or imputed tort liability of the employer pursuant to the doctrine. Moreover, critical to vicarious liability is the fact that the employee must be acting with the "course and scope" of the employee's employment. Accordingly, knowledge of what situations are within the scope and which, such as, "frolic and detour," are not is of great importance to the student. Finally, the student must know what the traditional employment at-will doctrine is, that it is the initial core legal principle regarding the employment relationship, particularly how it can result in a legal but immoral discharge, as well as the many statutory and common law exceptions to employment at-will, especially for the latter the "public policy" exception.

True and False Questions with Answers and Explanations

1. An agent can create his or her own apparent or ostensible authority by words or conduct made to a third-party.
(False: Only a principal can create an agency relationship or empower an agent beyond the scope of his or her actual authority by means of the apparent or ostensible authority doctrine.)

2. An employer can convert an employee into the employer's agent by means of the Apparent Authority doctrine.
(True: Even though technically an employee the employer by holding out the employee to a third-party as his or her agent creates the apparent authority in the "employee" to act as the employer's "agent.")

3. A person can hold himself or herself as an agent of another to a third-party and thus by means of the Apparent Authority create an agency relationship.
(False: One cannot create his or her own agency status by means of the Apparent Authority doctrine; only a purported principal by holding a person out to a third-party can create an agency relationship by means of the Apparent Authority doctrine.)

4. If one employs another person and controls the physical manner by which that person does his or her job typically the relationship is one of employer and independent contractor.
(False: The relationship is one of employer and employee, wherein the employer has the right and power to direct and control the physical manner by which the employee performs his or her work.)

5. One who employs an independent contractor is usually liable for the torts committed by the independent contract while he or she is doing a job for the employer.
(False: Pursuant to the doctrine of Respondeat Superior or imputed liability a employer is vicariously liable for the torts of his or her employees, and not as a general rule for the torts of independent contractor. Of course, the employer may be liable directly in either case for the employer's own negligence in selecting incompetent employees as well as independent contractors.)

6. An employer is legally obligated to pay for unemployment compensation and workers compensation insurance of any independent contractors it retains.
(False: The employer must provide these for its employees, not its independent contractors.)

7. A key factor in determining if a person hired by another is an employee or an independent contractor will be if the person is paid or a regular basis, for example, bi-weekly, or by the completed job.
(True: Other factors indicating the independent contractor relationship are whether the person provides his or tools, equipment, and vehicles and the fact that the person has the discretion as to how to perform the physical manner of performing the work.)

8. It is not necessary to have an agent's authority to buy or sell real estate to be in writing so long as the agent's real estate contract between the principal and a third-party is in writing.
(False: Two writings are required as per a rule called the Equal Dignity rule. That is, if the subject matter of the contract is governed by the Statute of Frauds, such as real estate, the agency relationship must be evidenced by a writing as well as the ultimate contract negotiated by the agent.)

9. In a agency relationship notice and knowledge to the agent regarding matters within the scope of the agency relationship are imputed to the principal.
(True: This rule is a hallmark of the agency relationship.)

10. A principal can be vicariously liable for the intentional tort of fraud committed by the agent in representing the principal.
(True: The majority rule is that principals are not liable for the torts of their agents as opposed to employees; however, an exception is fraud since the essence of an agency relationship is for the agent to represent the principal in business dealings and to negotiate and enter into contracts on behalf of and for his or her principal.)

11. Absent a violation of a covenant not to compete, a non-disclosure agreement, or intellectual property law, the education, knowledge, and skills that an agent learns while performing his or her duties for the principal can be used by the agent for his or her personal gain upon the termination of the agency relationship.
(True: Such is the nature of our capitalistic system, assuming as noted in the question there is no superseding legal principle prohibiting the use of info learned while an agent.)

12. When there is a written agency agreement that spells out the rights and duties of the parties the agent is said to have Ostensible Employment authority.
(False: The authority created by a written agreement is called express. Apparent authority is authority created by the principal by misleading a third-party as to a person's authority as an agent. Ostensible employment is related to apparent authority but is found in the employer-employee context.)

13. The Equal Dignity rule requires a contract made by an agent with a third-party for the purchase of real estate to be in writing; however, the agency agreement between the principal and the agent can be oral.
(False: The "equal" in Equal Dignity means that both the agent's contract with the third-party and the agency agreement with the principal must be in writing.)

14. An agency agreement that authorizes an agent to perform narrow specialized tasks for a principal is usually called a Special Power of Attorney.
(True: As opposed to a general power of attorney which authorizes the agent to perform all tasks for a principal.)

15. An agent can ratify an unauthorized contract with a third-party if the agent has the implied authority to do so.
(False: Only principals can ratify unauthorized contracts made by an agent, though the principal can do so impliedly, for example, by using the subject matter of the contract.)

16. For Apparent Authority to exist the third-party must reasonably believe the "principal's" assertion that a person is his or her agent.
(True: Reasonableness on the part of the third-party is a requirement of Apparent Authority.)

17. An unauthorized contract made by an agent with a third-party on behalf of the principal that is not ratified is binding on the agent only even if the agent signs the contract as an agent in a representational capacity.
(True: The agent alone is liable to the third-party due to lack of authority regardless of any indication of agency status.)

18. A contract made by an agent for an undisclosed principal is never enforceable against a third-party as it would not be fair to do so.
(False: The contract generally is valid and enforceable against the third-party assuming no fraud or misrepresentation by the agent.)

19. A principal may create apparent agency authority in an agent by giving the agent possession and apparent ownership of the principal's property.
(True: This is an example of the Apparent Agency doctrine created impliedly by possession and ownership of the principal's property.)

20. A principal is liable in tort for the fraudulent misrepresentations made by his or her agent within the course and scope of the agent's duties.
(True: As a general rule, principals are not liable for the torts of their agents, as opposed to employers and employees; but fraud is an exception since the essence of the agency relationship is to negotiate and enter into contracts on behalf of a principal.)

21. An employer is liable in tort for the negligent conduct committed by his or her employee acting within the scope of his or her duties even if the employer was careful in selecting and supervising the employee.
(True: This an example of liability without fault in the employment relationship based on the old common law principle of Vicarious Liability, also called the doctrine of Respondeat Superior.)

22. An employer is liable for the negligence of its independent contractor who carelessly performs an ultrahazardous activity.
(True: Generally, employers are not liable for the torts of its independent contractors, but ultrahazardous activities, such as aerial spraying with toxic chemicals or transporting volatile and dangerous chemicals, are an exception.)

23. Assuming no deception an undisclosed agent can make a binding contract with a third-party on behalf of his or her principal.
(True: And the third-party must perform for the now disclosed principal, though there could be an exception if there is a personal element such as personal services involved in the contract. The best example of the general rule occurred when the Walt Disney Company used undisclosed agents to purchase land in the Orlando area for Disney World and later Epcot.)

24. In order to determine if a person is an independent contractor or an employee a key factor is the control of the person by the employer.
(True: The employer's right and power to control is critical; and as such if the employer can control a person as to the physical manner by which he or she does a job that person is an "employee"; whereas independent contractors are typically professional or skilled tradespersons hired to do a job and who have the discretion on how to do the work.)

25. As a general rule an agency relationship can be created orally.
(True: This is not advisable, of course, but generally permitted, but the exceptions would be if the Statute of Frauds is implicated, for example, the agent's job is to buy or sell real estate, or if the agent's contract with the principal is longer than a year.)

26. Anyone can be an agent.
(True: Even minors can be agents since they are "merely" representing and standing-in-the-shoes of another party, a principal, who should be an adult (otherwise if a minor one enters into the voidable contract situation).

27. Agents can create their own agency authority by claiming to a third-party that the agent is in fact an agent of a principal.

(False: Apparent agent authority can only be created by a principal who makes an assertion to a third-party that another person is the principal's agent and the third-party reasonably relies on that assertion.)

28. The agent owes to his or her principal duties of good faith and loyalty.
(True: And similarly, the principal owes such duties to the agent as the principal-agent relationship is deemed to be a fiduciary one of trust and fair-dealing.)

29. An agent who owns property can sell the property to his or her principal without letting the principal know of the agent's ownership but only if the sale is a good and fair deal.
(False: The agency relationship as a fiduciary one means that the agent must make full disclosure to the principal prior to any sale of the agent's ownership interest.)

30. If the principal gives an agent an exclusive sales territory the principal cannot retain any other sales agents in that territory but the principal himself or herself can make sales in the territory.
(False: The fiduciary nature of the agency relationship would prohibit the principal from "invading" the agent's exclusive territory and competing with the agent.)

31. If a contract executed by an agent must be in writing to satisfy the Statute of Frauds the agent's authority to act for his or her principal also must be in writing.
(True: This is called the Equal Dignity rule.)

32. An example of implied authority in an agency relationship would be when a part-time employee tells a person that he or she has the power and authority to hire employees.
(False: This type of conduct is beyond the scope of what would be implied for a part-time position as opposed to a full-time manager. Moreover, there is no apparent authority since the part-time employee made the assertions and one cannot create one's own apparent authority as an agent, as such authority must come from a principal's statements or conduct.)

33. The fact that an employer forbids an employee for doing a certain act means that the act is outside of the scope of the employee's employment.
(False: Lack of authority is evidence that an act is outside the scope of employment, but the prohibition of the act is not dispositive of the case. For example, the owner of a gun store can tell the sales employee never to show the gun when it is loaded, but the issue remains even with the prohibition whether it is within the employee's course and scope of employment to show loaded guns to prospective customers.)

34. Employers are strictly liable for the torts of their independent contractors who engage in ultra-hazardous activities for the employer.
(True: This is an exception to the rule that employers are not liable for the wrongs o their independent contractors. An example would be a farmer who hires a crop-dusting service to spray poisonous weed and bug killer.)

35. An agency "coupled with an interest" is not revocable by the principal.
(True: Such an agency is created for the benefit of the principal and not the agent, for example, when the principal owes a debt to the agent and the principal gives the agent authority to sell some of the principal's property to pay the debt to the agent.)

36. The principal-agent relationship will be terminated when the agent fulfills the purpose of the agency agreement.
(True: This is a basic proposition of agency law.)

37. To avoid liability on a contract signed on behalf of his or her principal an agent must possess proper authority, name the principal, and sign in a representative capacity.
(True: For example, assuming proper authority, the agent should sign "Alberto, Agent, for Paul, Principal," and thus Paul will be liable but not Alberto.)

38. Under the employment at-will doctrine one can be discharged for an immoral or unethical reason but not an illegal reason.
(True: The employment at-will doctrine means that an employee at-will, that is, one without a contract that limits the circumstances under which he or she can be discharged, can be terminated for any reason, even if immoral, such as nepotism, but not an illegal reason, for example, due to the employee's race or religion under civil rights laws.)

39. Discharging an employee who refuses to do an illegal act will likely be a violation of the "public policy" doctrine and thus an exception to the employment at-will doctrine.
(True: "Public policy" is a major exception to employment at-will and thus public policy protects employees who act to protect the health, welfare, and safety of members of the community.)

40. Apparent agency authority will arise when the principal causes a third-party to reasonably believe that a person is the principal's agent.
(True: Such apparent authority can only arise from the principal's words and/or conduct, whether intentional or negligent, when the third-party has a reasonable belief that a person is the principal's agent. Note that apparent authority can never rise from a purported agent's words or conduct to the third-party indicating he or she is an agent.)

41. The principal/agent relationship is a fiduciary one.
(True: This is a basic proposition of agency law, meaning that the parties have to act in an honest, ethical, good faith, and confidential manner avoiding any conflicts-of-interest.)

42. An employer will be held vicariously liable pursuant to the doctrine of *Respondeat Superior* for the negligent harms caused by the employer's employee who acts in the course and scope of employment.
(True: Moreover, this liability is "vicarious," that is, the negligent conduct is imputed to the employer even if the employer was not negligent. Of course, if the employer was negligent, perhaps in the hiring or supervision of the employee, the aggrieved party has a direct lawsuit for negligence against the employer.)

43. A critical factor in determining whether an employer will be held vicariously liable is if the person causing the harm was the employer's employee or independent contractor.
(True: Vicarious liability applies as a general rule just to employees, not to independent contractors unless there is some type of non-delegable duty of the employer in the latter case, such as a landlord's duty to keep the premises safe for the tenants.)

44. When an employee leaves the course or scope of employment the employer is no longer vicariously liable if the employee negligently causes harm.
(False: Under the old common law when the employee leaves the scope of employment, called a "detour and frolic," the employer was no longer vicariously liable. However, when the employee ends the "frolic" and returns reasonably close to the point of departure and now has the intent to do the employer's business, the employer is now vicariously liable.)

Multiple Choice Questions with Answers and Explanations

1. An independent contractor:
    a. is a type of principal.
    b. who commits a tort during the scope of his or her employment as a general rule incurs the tort liability of the employer.
    c. is not controlled by his or her employer as to the manner of performing the job.
    d. None of the above.

    (The correct answer is c. As opposed to an employee who the employer can control as the manner of doing the work, the independent contractor has discretion as to how to perform the job; the employer is just contracting for results. The general rule is that independent contractors do not incur tort liability for their employers, though there are exceptions for non-delegable duties, such as a landlord's duty to provide safe premises for a tenant, and for ultra-hazardous activities, such as crop-dusting with chemicals. There is nothing to prevent an independent contractor to be empowered as an agent to make contracts on the behalf of his or her employer/principal, but the independent contractor is certainly not a species of principal.)

2. An example of an employee-at will is:
    a. An employee who is covered by a collective bargaining agreement.
    b. An employee who has a written five-year employment contract with a "just cause" termination clause.
    c. An employee covered by Civil Service.
    d. None of the above.

    (The correct answer is d. In the typical collective bargaining agreement there will be a clause taking the members of the bargaining unit out the employment at-will category, usually by saying a termination must be for a legitimate or just or good reason. The employee can also take himself or herself out of employment at-will status by securing a contract with the employer that limits the circumstances under which the employee can be terminated. Finally, most employees that work for the government are covered by Civil Service statutes which state that except for very high-level government officials, employees of government – federal, state, and local – cannot be discharged except after a hearing and a showing of good cause.)

3. The doctrine of employment at-will:
    a. Can result in a legal but immoral and unethical discharge.
    b. Prohibits employers from firing employees for union activities.
    c. Has been abolished in most states in the United States.
    d. Does not apply to minority employees.

    (The correct answer is a. Employment at-will is the majority rule in the U.S., and as such to be an employee at-will is to be in a very legally exposed position for an employee, who can be fired for any reason, no reason, or no good reason, or even a morally bad reason, but not for an illegal reason. An example of a legal but perhaps immoral discharge would be to fire an employee who is supporting a sports team contrary to the owner's team. If an employee is protected by the National Labor Relations Act, he or she cannot be terminated for union activities. Minority employees, even if employees at-will, may be protected from a discriminatory discharge but by Title VII of the Civil Rights Act.)

4. Agents can bind principals if they have:
    a. Actual authority.
    b. Implied authority
    c. Apparent authority
    d. All of the above.

(The correct answer is d. Actual authority can be express in the form of words or a writing, including a formal Power of Attorney (In-Fact), the latter of which may be required by the Statute of Frauds. Implied authority is the authority that normally and reasonably would be concomitant with the agent's position and function, for example, when a principal hires an agent to sell his or her boat it would be implied that the agent could get the boat serviced, cleaned, and advertised without needing the express authority to do those tasks. Finally, apparent authority is authority the principal creates in an agent by manifesting by words and/or conduct that a person is the principal's agent or that the agent has authority beyond that actually granted.)

5. Which of the following is FALSE about agency relationships?
   a. The agent owes a duty of obedience to the principal.
   b. The agent owes a duty of due care to the principal.
   c. The agent owes a duty of accounting to the principal.
   d. The agent does not owe a fiduciary duty to the principal as the agent is merely an employee with some more discretion in performing his or her tasks.

   (The correct answer is d. A hallmark of the principal-agent relationship is that it is a fiduciary relationship, meaning the parties owe to one another duties of confidence, loyalty, honesty, good faith, and fair dealing. The other answers reflect fundamental and accurate characteristics of the agent's duties to his or her principal.)

6. Which of the following is/are TRUE about the principal-agent relationship?
   a. In a non-disclosed principal situation, the third-party is liable on the contract made by the principal's agent.
   b. Under the ratification doctrine, a principal can ratify and thus authorize an agent's contract with a third-party what was not originally authorized by the principal.
   c. Under the imputed knowledge and notice doctrine, a principal can be charged with the knowledge of facts that have been disclosed to the principal's agent.
   d. All of the above.

   (The correct answer is d. In the non-disclosed principal situation, the third-party is liable unless the principal's agent was deceitful with the third-party as to the existence of the principal. The principal has broad authority to ratify unauthorized contracts; however, there are exceptions, for example, if it would be unfair to the third-party to do so, such as when the subject matter of the contract is damaged or destroyed to the detriment of the third-party. Imputed knowledge and notice are hallmarks of the principal-agent relationship.)

7. When is an employer liable for the negligent torts of its employees?
   a. When there is vicarious liability and the doctrine of *Respondeat Superior* applies.
   b. When the torts are committed by the employee acting in the "course and scope" of employment.
   c. When an employer is directly negligent for selecting and supervising an incompetent and careless employee who commits the tort.
   d. All of the above.

   (The correct answer is d. These are all fundamental and accurate principles of negligence law as applied to the employer-employee relationship. Note, moreover, that in some circumstances the employer may be liable for the intentional torts of an employee, for example, when the employee commits the intentional tort during the course and scope of employment AND with the intent of furthering the employer's business, such as a "bouncer" in a bar using excessive force to eject a patron and thereby committing a battery.)

8. Which of the following is a FALSE statement?
    a. Agency law consists of contract law as well as some tort and employment law.
    b. An agency relationship typically exists when one person is authorized to act on behalf of another and represent another in business transactions.
    c. Corporations are usually set up so that they can conduct business without the use of any agents.
    d. An employee can also be an agent of the employer.

    (The correct answer is c. Corporations are artificial legal entities created by state law; and thus, the corporation can act only through human beings, to wit: directors, officers, employees, and agents, for example for the latter, a sales force. A corporate employee can also be an agent, for example, a salesperson who is an employee but who is authorized to negotiate and form contracts for purchase and sale. Agency is a very broad area of the law with contract liability, tort liability, and employment law ramifications.)

9. Which of the following is a TRUE statement?
    a. Contractual capacity is not needed for the principal in a principal-agent relationship.
    b. One characteristic of independent contractors is that they can never also be agents and thus enter into contracts on behalf of a principal.
    c. Even when an employee is an employee at-will, statements made in the employer's policy and procedure manual may give employees implied-in-fact contracts right that limit the circumstances under which the employer can discharge the employee.
    d. A power of attorney requires that the agent with the power be an attorney licensed by at least one state bar association as well as the federal bar association.

    (The correct answer is c. The implied-in-fact contract theory is theoretically true and possible but to avoid its consequences most companies have express statements in their personnel manuals that state that the employee is an at-will employee and only a writing signed by a company executive can alter that status. The principal must have contractual capacity but not necessarily the agent who "stands in the shoes" of the principal. An independent contractor can become an agent, expressly or by the apparent agency doctrine, for example, an architect who is empowered to contract for surveys, contractors, supplies, etc. Any person can be granted a power of attorney, typically being called an "attorney-in-fact," as opposed to a practicing and licensed "attorney-at-law.")

10. Which of the following is a TRUE statement?
    a. In order to create an agency relationship there must always be a written agreement prepared by a licensed attorney.
    b. An agency that is created due to the acts or conduct of the parties is called an express agency.
    c. Agency by ratification can occur in a situation where there was no authority for the agent's actions when the agent originally undertook them.
    d. An apparent agency can only be created by the actions of the agent.

    (The correct answer is c. A principal can ratify contracts and transactions made in the principal's behalf, either expressly or impliedly, even though the agent exceeded his or her authority, though there are certain limitations on the principal's power to ratify. An agency relationship can be oral as a general rule unless the Statute of Frauds applies to the subject matter of the agency and/or the contracts that the agent is making with a third-party. Agencies based on conduct are called either "implied" agencies or "apparent" or "ostensible" agencies. Only the principal can create an apparent or ostensible agency by manifesting words or conduct to a third-party indicating that a person is the principal's "agent," though the third-party must have reasonably relied on these representations. Express agencies are created by words, written or oral.)

11. Which of the following is a FALSE statement?
    a. An agent who has held himself or herself out as having greater than usual knowledge and skills will be held to that higher standard when doing the principal's business.
    b. The "reasonable person" standard typically applies to the degree of care required of an agent when conducting the principal's business.
    c. Most information that comes to the attention of an agent is assumed to be known by her principal.
    d. Duties of loyalty and accountability are not duties that the agent owes to his or her principal since the agent is not a fiduciary like a partner.

    (The correct answer is d. The principal/agent relationship is a fiduciary one, just like partners or an attorney and client, and as such duties of loyalty, accountability, good faith, honesty, notice, and avoiding conflicts-of-interest are all essential aspects of the principal/agent relationship. Imputed notice and knowledge by the agent to the principal are important aspects of the principal/agency relationship.)

12. Which of the following is a FALSE statement?
    a. The principal always has a duty to compensate the agent since who would work for free.
    b. An agent is generally not liable on contracts made in connection with a fully disclosed agency.
    c. The principal has a duty to cooperate with his or her agent.
    d. A partially disclosed agency exists where the third-party is aware that the party he or she is dealing with is an agent, but he or she does not know the identity of the principal.

    (The correct answer is a. There is no implied duty of compensation and consequently the agent's compensation, if any, must be spelled out in the agency agreement. A gratuitous agency is certainly permissible. An agent is generally not liable on a contract made on behalf of his or her principal if the agent indicates that he or she is an agent, names the principal, and signs in a representative capacity, that is, indicating "agent" after his or her name. The duty of cooperation is a basic feature of the agency relationship; as such, the principal cannot usurp the agent's functions, particularly regarding sales and commissions. There is no problem with a partially disclosed agency, assuming no fraud, and both the principal and the third-party are liable on the contract too, as would be the agent if he or she signed in his or her own name without indicating agency status.)

13. Which of the following is a FALSE statement?
    a. An agent has no duty to disclose her agency status to third parties with whom the agent deals.
    b. An agent who enters into a contract with another party on behalf of the principal impliedly warrants that he has the authority to do so.
    c. A principal may be liable for the tort of fraud committed by the agent if the agent makes misrepresentations to a third-party in the course of negotiating a contract for the principal.
    d. The basic rule for whether an employer is liable for the tort of negligence committed by his or her employee is whether the employer knew of the employee's commission of the tort

    (The correct answer is d. Tort liability of an employer for the negligent wrongs of its employees is premised on the employer directing the wrong, being careless in hiring or supervising employees, that is, being directly negligent, and being vicariously liable for the negligent wrongs of its employees by virtue of the doctrine of Respondeat Superior, which is imputed liability on the employer, regardless of knowledge. As a general rule a principal is not liable for the intentional torts of his or her agents, but a major exception is the tort of fraud or deceit since a major purpose of any agency relationships is to produce contracts with third parties. If an agent enters into a contract with a third-party and the agent lacks the authority to do so the agent is liable on the contract unless the principal ratifies. "Silence is not fraud," says the common law rule, so an

agent need not disclose the agency relationship to a third-party. In such a situation, assuming no fraud, the principal and third-party are liable on the contract and the agent is too.)

14. Which of the following is a FALSE statement?
    a. The negligent act of driving in a careless manner could be construed as being within the scope of a delivery employee's employment.
    b. When determining whether or not the employee's intentional tort was committed while the employee was operating within the scope of his or her employment, the courts will examine the employee's motivation and whether the conduct was related to his or her work.
    c. The legal doctrine that holds that an employer is liable for the negligence of an employee who is acting within the scope of his or her employment is called *Respondeat Superior*.
    d. Under the "coming and going" (that is, commuting) to work rule, an employer usually is liable for injuries caused by its employees while they are on their way to and from work.

    (The correct answer is d. As a general rule the employer is not liable for negligence by employees who are merely commuting to-and-from work, but an exception would arise if the employee is also doing some type of chore for the employer. The key test of imputed or vicarious liability under the doctrine of Respondeat Superior, which means "let the master answer for the wrongs of the servant," is was the employee acting within the course or scope of employment when the negligent act occurred. Regarding intentional torts, the general rule is that the employer is not liable for the intentional torts of his or her employees, only the negligent wrongs, but an exception arises if the employee's mind-set in committing the tort was to further his or her employer's business and the conduct was related to the employee's job, for example, a club "bouncer" using too much force to eject a customer and thereby committing a battery for which the employer would be liable; but not the bouncer battering a customer who is flirting with the bouncer's girlfriend.)

15. Which of the following is a FALSE statement?
    a. In general, the bankruptcy of the principal, but not necessarily the bankruptcy of the agent, will terminate an agency relationship.
    b. In all circumstances where an agency is terminated, notification must be given to third parties.
    c. An agency can be terminated by the acts of the parties or by operation of the law.
    d. An agency-coupled-with-an-interest is typically not revocable by the principal.

    (The correct answer is b. The fact that the agent goes bankrupt will not legally affect the principal/agent relationship, though practically one would think it would, especially from the principal's perspective. Notice is not required to terminate the agency relationship, though it would be a good practice on the part of the principal so as to avoid any apparent agency lawsuits. An agency-coupled-with-an-interest usually exists to benefit the agent, who typically is a creditor of the principal, who has impowered the agent to sell some property of the principal to then pay himself or herself to satisfy the obligation.)

16. Which of the following is a TRUE statement?
    a. Death of an agent or the principal terminates an agency only after notification of death is received by the living party.
    b. An agency-coupled-with-an-interest usually terminates on the death of the principal.
    c. An agency-coupled-with-an-interest is usually revocable by the principal.
    d. Revocation of the agency relationship is done by the principal whereas renunciation of the agency relationship is done by the agent.

    (The correct answer is d. Death of either party usually will be an automatic termination of the relationship regardless of notice to the other party or for that matter a third-party. However, an exception is the agency-coupled-with-an-interest which exists, as noted, to benefit the agent, and which is also not revocable by the principal. Note that either party to the relationship has the

power to end it since it is a consensual one, but a party may not have the right to do so, for example, if there is an express agency agreement, which means that the relationship is ended but the aggrieved party can sue the breaching party for breach of the agency agreement.)

17. Which of the following is a FALSE statement?
    a. An agency relationship can be created by mutual agreement.
    b. An agency relationship can be created by ratification.
    c. An agency relationship can be created under the apparent agency doctrine by the acts of the "agent."
    d. An agency relationship can be created under the apparent agency doctrine by the acts of the "principal."

    (The correct answer is c. A basic and important rule of agency authority is that an agent can never create his or her own apparent authority, which must come from words or conduct by the principal directed to the third-party indicating in a reasonable manner that someone is the principal's agent. The other responses are also basic agency rules.)

18. Which of the following is a FALSE statement?
    a. There are several common and statutory exceptions to the employment at-will doctrine.
    b. Terminating an employee who refuses to commit an illegal act most likely will violate the "public policy" doctrine.
    c. Apparent authority exists if a principal causes a third-party to reasonably believe that the principal's agent has the authority to act.
    d. Since an agent is a fiduciary who represents his or her principal, an agent can create his or her own apparent authority.

    (The correct answer is d. Actually, there are many exceptions to the employment at-will doctrine, most notably the Civil Rights Act, which of course is statutory, as well as the common law "public policy" doctrine which says that an at-will employee cannot be fired if the discharge would violate the fundamental public policy of a state. Public policy is determined by legislative and judicial pronouncements and is premised on protecting and advancing the health, safety, welfare, and morals of the people in that state. Accordingly, firing the employee who refuses to commit an illegal act, for example, lying under oath about the employer's business, would very likely be a violation of public policy; and also note that in some states a public policy violation is construed as an intentional tort, meaning the discharged employee can sue for emotional distress and punitive damages along with compensatory damages. An agent is a fiduciary, of course, which is an elevated position of trust and confidence in the law, but nevertheless the agent cannot create his or her own apparent authority.)

19. Which of the following is a FALSE statement?
    a. An employer can be held vicariously liable for harm to third parties caused by the negligent conduct of its employees acting in the scope of employment even if the employer itself is not negligent.
    b. Historically, at-will employees in the U.S. ordinarily could be fired simply because their employers did not like the clothes they were wearing or the sports teams they were supporting.
    c. The terms of company personnel manuals have at times been construed by the courts to constitute implied employment contracts.
    d. An agent who is paid by the principal is not in a relationship of trust and confidence since the agent is getting compensated for the work.

    (The correct answer is d. An agent is a fiduciary regardless of compensation. Vicarious liability is a principle of imputed liability and as such the employer need not be directly negligent, though of course if the employer was, for example, hiring an incompetent employee, the employer can be

sued directly too. If the employee's clothes indicate a pro-union animus or are tied to the employee's national origin or religion the at-will employee may have a viable lawsuit for wrongful discharge under the National Labor Relations Act or the Civil Rights Act.)

20. Which of the following is a TRUE statement?
    a. Ratification of an agent's unauthorized contract on behalf of the principal may be done by the principal in some circumstances.
    b. Vicarious liability very likely will be imposed on an employer who hires an independent contractor to take care of the storage of poisonous gases and who does so by carelessly causing harm.
    c. A change in the value of the subject matter of the agency if substantial usually will end the agency relationship by operation of the law.
    d. All of the above.

    (The correct answer is d. There are some limitations on the principal's ability to ratify, for example, when the third-party would be harmed, such as when the subject matter of the agency is damaged or destroyed. Normally, employers are not liable for the negligent wrongs of their independent contractors, but an exception is when the independent contractor is engaging in very dangerous activities. A change in value will terminate the agency relationship if substantial and thus a reasonable person would think that the principal would want the agency cancelled, for example, when oil is discovered on the supposed "scrub land" the agent is attempting to sell.)

21. The principal/agency relationship requires as a general rule:
    a. a written agreement and consideration
    b. a written agreement only
    c. consideration only
    d. neither a written agreement nor consideration.

    (The correct answer is d. Oral agency agreements are permissible unless the Statute of Frauds applies. Moreover, consideration is not required for a principal/agency relationship, meaning that either party can terminate the relationship at-will.)

22. An agency relationship always requires:
    a. Both an agent and principal who are adults.
    b. A written contract.
    c. Consideration on the part of both the principal and the agent.
    d. An intent by both the principal and agent to be in the relationship.

    (The correct answer is d. Minors theoretically can be either principals or agents. A written contract is not required unless the Statute of Frauds applies to the subject matter of the agency relationship or if the agent is making contracts that are governed by the Statute of Frauds, in which latter case the Equal Dignity Rule would require the principal/agent agreement to be in writing. Consideration is not required; there can be a gratuitous agency.)

23. Where the principal makes representations to a third-party about the role that an agent is to play, which kind of authority USUALLY arises?
    a. Apparent authority.
    b. Ratification authority
    c. Fiduciary relationship authority.
    d. Warranty authority.

    (The correct answer is a. Note that apparent authority arises based on the principal's words and/or conduct manifested to a third-party about an employee's or any other person's purported authority to make contracts for the principal. Apparent authority will create an agency relationship even if one did not exist.)

24. Where the principal makes representations to a third-party about the contractual authority an employee has, which type of authority USUALLY arises?
    a. Apparent authority.
    b. Implied authority
    c. Inherent authority.
    d. Express authority.
    (The correct answer is a. See above.)

25. In an agency relationship involving a principal, an agent, and a third-party the fact that the agency relationship was not disclosed to the third-party would likely affect:
    a. The contract liability of the principal to the third-party on a contract made by the agent on the principal's behalf.
    b. The tort liability of the principal to the third-party for a tort of the agent.
    c. The tort liability of the agent to the third-party for the agent's tort.
    d. The contract liability of the agent to the third-party on a contract made by the agent on the principal's behalf.
    (The correct answer is d. Tort liability is separate and distinct and not affected legally by non-disclosure, though naturally practical problems of identification might ensue. Regarding contract liability the fact that the agent does not disclose the agent relationship and signs the contract in his or her own name means that the principal is liable, assuming the agent had authority, the third-party is liable assuming the agent did not fraudulent hide the identity of the principal, and the agent is liable as he or she neither named the principal nor signed in a representative capacity.)

26. A principal hires an agent to manage his or her sales business. Then the agent hires people to work as salespersons. This is an example of TYPICALLY what type of agency authority?
    a. Implied.
    b. Express.
    c. Apparent.
    d. Ratified.
    (The correct answer is a. The hiring of sales personnel would be considered a normal part of a manager's job and thus within his or her implied authority. Of course, a manager could have any other of the above agency authorities too.)

27. An agent enters into a contract with a third-party for which the agent did not have actual express authority to do. Which of the following is TRUE?
    a. The principal can never be held liable on the contract because the agent exceeded his authority.
    b. The principal can be liable on the contract only if the agent had implied authority to enter into the contract.
    c. The principal can be liable on the contract only if apparent authority was present.
    d. Either implied or apparent authority might cause the principal to be liable on the contract.
    (The correct answer is d. Either implied or apparent authority, at times called "ostensible" authority, might cause the principal to be liable; and of course the principal may be able to ratify the unauthorized contract and thus be liable on the contract. Otherwise, only the agent is liable on the contract with the third-party. Note too that the third-party can treat the contract with the unauthorized agent as a mere "offer" and thus revoke it.)

28. In the context of a principal and agent relationship, ratification refers to:
    a. Reaffirming a contract which one previously agreed to.
    b. A minor agreeing, after reaching majority, to a contract entered into as a minor.
    c. Agreeing to be bound to a contract entered into by an agent, which exceeded the agent's authority at the time the agent entered into it.
    d. The U.S. Congress ratifying by statute a rule made by an administrative agency.
    (The correct answer is c. Principals can ratify, but must ratify the whole contract, do so in a reasonable amount of time, comply with the Statute of Frauds if pertinent, and also cannot ratify to disadvantage the third-party if the subject matter of the contract is damaged, destroyed, or lost. Minors can ratify contracts too, but that is a separate area of contract law.)

29. The significance of a "frolic and detour" under the common law is that:
    a. It determines if an employee can be liable on a contract made on the employer's behalf.
    b. It can determine if someone working for a business is an employee or independent contractor.
    c. It can determine if an employer is liable for the negligence tort of an employee.
    d. It can determine if an employee is liable for torts he commits on the job.
    (The correct answer is c. "Frolic and detour" means that an employee has taken himself or herself out of the course and scope of employment in a "detour" for some purely personal reason, typically to "frolic" with a paramour. Consequently, the employer is not vicariously liable for negligent wrongs committed by the employee while on the "frolic and detour"; however, liability will be imposed on the employer when the employee commences to return to fulfilling his or her work duties and has the business intent to do so.)

30. Which of the following is FALSE statement?
    a. An employee also may act in the capacity of an agent.
    b. An independent contractor's physical manner of doing a job is controlled, or is subject to the control, by his or her employer.
    c. A principal has a duty to cooperate with his or her agent.
    d. A principal generally is required to indemnify an agent for liabilities incurred because of authorized and proper acts by the agent.
    (The correct answer is b. An independent contractor has the discretion as to how to perform a job; the employer has no control nor right to control the contractor's performance; the employer is just contracting for results, for example, by the plumber or electrician who has his or her own tools and truck and who is paid on the completion of the job. An employee can certainly be an agent, either expressly, impliedly, or by virtue of the doctrine of apparent agency. The other responses are basic legal aspects of the principal/agent relationship.)

31. Which of the following is a TRUE statement?
    a. Building contractors and sub-contractors are usually not independent contractors.
    b. An agency relationship can be formed only in a witnessed and signed writing since it is a high-level business and fiduciary relationship.
    c. There generally does not need to be a written agreement between the principal and agent in order to create an agency relationship.
    d. An agent does not owe to his or her principal a duty to act in good faith.
    (The correct answer is c. The agency relationship can be oral, but it must be written if the Statute of Frauds applies to the subject matter of the agency or, pursuant to the Equal Dignity Rule, the agents' contracts with third-parties must be in writing as per the Statute of Frauds. Building contractors and subcontractors are probably some of the best examples of independent contractors since they are professionals with specialized knowledge and skills and have an independent "calling" or business, as well as the fact that they are typically not governed as to the

manner of performance to complete the building task. Good faith is a hallmark of a fiduciary relationship, such as the principal/agent one.)

32. Which of the following is a FALSE statement?
    a. A principal owes to his or her agent a duty to act in good faith.
    b. If an agent's contract with a third-party is required to be in writing, then the agent's authority from the principal to enter into that contract generally must be in writing.
    c. An agent's authority to act on behalf of a principal derives exclusively from the agent's express actual authority.
    d. A principal may confer authority on an agent by manifesting words or conduct to a third-party.

    (The correct answer is c. Authority can be express, implied, apparent, which is caused by the principal's words and conduct towards a third-party, and by means of ratification. Good faith, as noted, is part of the principal/agent fiduciary relationship. The Equal Dignity Rules says that if the contract an agent makes with a third-party, such as a real estate contract, must be in writing, so must the agent's authority from the principal.)

33. Which of the following is a FALSE statement?
    a. Agency law consists of contract law as well as some tort law.
    b. An agency relationship typically exists when one person is authorized to act on behalf of another in business matters.
    c. Corporations are usually structured so that they can conduct business without the use of any agents.
    d. An employee can also be an agent of the employer.

    (The correct answer is c. Corporations as "artificial" legal "persons" created pursuant to state statute can only conduct business through people, including of course agents as well as employee, officers, executives, and directors. The other responses are basic agency principles.)

34. Which of the following is a TRUE statement?
    a. Contractual capacity is not needed for the principal in a principal-agent relationship.
    b. One characteristic of independent contractors is that they can never also be agents and thus enter into contracts on behalf of a principal.
    c. Even when an employee is an employee at-will, statements made in the employer's policy and procedure manual may give employees implied-in-fact contracts right that limit the circumstances under which the employer can discharge the employee.
    d. A power of attorney requires that the agent with the power be an attorney licensed by at least one state bar association as well as the federal bar association.

    (The correct answer is c. As noted, however, employers are well aware of this implied contract theory so typically one will find disclaimers in company manuals saying that the employee's at-will status cannot be changed except by a signed writing and usually by a high-level company official. Note that there is a distinction between an "attorney-at-law," that is, a licensed attorney pursuant to state law, and an "attorney-in-fact," that is, any person, including an agent, who is given the power to represent another in personal and/or business dealings.)

35. Which of the following is a TRUE statement?
    a. In order to create an agency relationship there must always be a written agreement prepared by an attorney.
    b. An agency that comes into existence due to the acts or conduct of the parties is called an express agency.
    c. Agency by ratification can occur in a situation where there was no authority for the agent's actions when the agent originally undertook them.
    d. An apparent agency can only be created by the actions of the agent.

(The correct answer is c. The principal can authorize an agent's unauthorized transaction or contract by means of the doctrine of ratification, assuming the transaction was legal when the agent entered into it and is legal at the time of the ratification. Moreover, the principal must ratify the whole transaction, not merely the "good" parts.)

36. Which of the following is a FALSE statement?
    a. An agent who has held herself out as having higher-than-customary knowledge and skills will be held to that higher standard when doing the principal's business.
    b. The "reasonable person" standard typically applies to the degree of care required of an agent when conducting the principal's business.
    c. Most information that comes to the attention of an agent is assumed to be known by her principal.
    d. Duties of loyalty and accountability are not duties that the agent owes to his or her principal since the agent is not a fiduciary like a partner.

    (The correct answer is d. Agents clearly are fiduciaries, like partners, and thus owe to their principals the duties of loyalty and accountability. A basic rule of agency law is that notice to and knowledge by the agent are imputed to the principal.)

37. Which of the following is a FALSE statement?
    a. The principal has a duty to compensate any agent, including a gratuitous one.
    b. An agent is generally not liable on contracts made in connection with a fully disclosed agency.
    c. The principal has a duty to cooperate with his or her agent.
    d. A partially disclosed agency exists where the third-party is aware that the party he or she is dealing with is an agent, but the third-party does not know the identity of the principal.

    (The correct answer is a. Consideration is not required for a valid principal/agent agreement, and thus compensation if any to the agent must be contractually based. If an agent acts within the scope of his or her authority, names the principal, and signs in a representative capacity, that is, with the word "agent" after his or her name, then the principal and the third-party are liable but the agent is not liable.)

38. Which of the following is a FALSE statement?
    a. An agent has no duty to disclose her agency status to third parties with whom the agent deals.
    b. An agent who enters into a purchasing contract with a seller on behalf of a principal must disclose to the principal any commissions and rebates received.
    c. A principal may be liable for the tort of fraud committed by the agent if the agent makes misrepresentations to a third-party in the course of negotiating a contract for the principal.
    d. The basic rule for whether an employer is liable for the tort of negligence committed by his or her employee is whether the employer knew of the employee's commission of the tort.

    (The correct answer is d. Knowledge is not necessary. Under the principle of Respondeat Superior the employer's liability is "vicarious," that is, the negligent act of the employee is imputed to the employer if the employee committed the act while acting in the course or scope of employment. Agents have no duty to disclose their agent status; they can remain silent since under the common law "silence is not fraud"; but agents cannot fraudulently misrepresent or actively conceal their agency status. Fraud, moreover, is one intentional tort that a principal will be responsible for if the agent committed the fraud in furthering his or her principal's business.)

39. Which of the following is a TRUE statement?
    a. Death of an agent or the principal terminates an agency only after notification of death is received by the living party.
    b. The insanity of the principal terminates the agency relationship when the agent is notified that his or her principal has gone insane.
    c. An agency-coupled-with-an-interest is usually revocable by the principal.
    d. Revocation of authority is done by the principal whereas renunciation of the authority is done by the agent.

    (The correct answer is d. Death of either party is an automatic termination of the agency relationship. Consequently, any transaction or contract by an agent after the principal's death is not binding on the principal's estate. The rule is the same when the principal goes insane.)

40. Which of the following is FALSE about agency law?
    a. An agent can create his or her "apparent authority."
    b. Ratification can create an agency relationship.
    c. Agents and principals are considered to be in a fiduciary relationship.
    d. The Equal Dignity rule requires that if a principal appoints an agent to sell real estate the agent's authority must be in writing.

    (The correct answer is a. As emphasized, only principals can create an agency relationship by means of the apparent authority doctrine. The other responses are basic features of the agency relationship. If the agent's contract with a third-party is governed by the Statute of Frauds the agent's authority to enter into that contract must be in writing too as per the Equal Dignity rule.)

41. Which of the following is FALSE about the liability of the parties in an agency relationship?
    a. When an agent acts without authority or exceeds his or her authority the principal is not liable to the third-party, but the agent is.
    b. As a general rule, a principal can go back and ratify a contract made by his or her agent even though the agent exceeded his or her authority at the time of contracting.
    c. If the agent does not affirmatively disclose the existence and identity of his or her principal the third-party can always get out of the contract.
    d. An important aspect of the principal-agency relationship is the doctrine of imputed knowledge.

    (The correct answer is c. Assuming no fraud the third-party is bound on the contract with the undisclosed principal; but the agent is liable on the contract too as is the principal.)

42. Which of the following is a TRUE statement regarding tort liability for acts of others?
    a. The doctrine of *Respondeat Superior* will usually impose criminal liability on an employer for the criminal acts of its employees.
    b. An employer cannot be held vicariously liable for the negligent acts of its employees if the employer was careful in selecting the employees.
    c. As a general rule, employers will not be liable for the negligent acts of their independent contractors.
    d. A principal is not usually liable for the fraudulent misrepresentations of his or her agent since the agent is an independent entity.

    (The correct answer is c. The exception would be if the employer engages the independent contractor to engage in an ultra-hazardous activity or to fulfill a non-delegable duty, for example, the duty of a landlord to keep the premises safe for a tenant. Respondeat Superior is a principle of civil liability, not criminal. Vicarious liability is a principle of imputed liability; and as such the carefulness of the employer, that is, its direct liability for negligence, is irrelevant, though it may be grounds for a separate lawsuit for the negligence of the employer in selecting or managing its employees. Usually, principals are not liable for the intentional torts of their agents, but a major exception is fraud since

the essence of the principal/agent relationship is for the agent to effectuate business dealings, including contracts, for his or her principal.)

43. What is a TRUE statement about the employment at-will doctrine?
    a. It can result in an immoral but legal discharge.
    b. It has been virtually eliminated in the United States by federal legislation.
    c. It takes precedence over the Civil Rights Act.
    d. It is not modified by the Public Policy doctrine since the latter is too vague.

    (The correct answer is a. Nepotism would be an example of an immoral but legal discharge under employment at-will, as would discharging an employee because he or she does not support the same sports team as the employer. There is no federal legislation abrogating the common law employment at-will doctrine, but a handful of states have eliminated it by statutes which require a good or just reason for a discharge. Both the Civil Rights Act and the public policy doctrine supersede the employment at-will doctrine and thus a discharge in violation of either would be a wrongful, that is, illegal discharge. Public policy is state-based policy that supports and advances the health, safety, and morals of the people of that state.)

21 - Business Organizations

Introduction

Business organizations, that is, the ways of doing business, are obviously very important legally and practically to the business student. As such, the student must know and be able to differentiate the main ways of doing business, to wit: sole proprietorship, joint venture, partnership, limited partnership, limited liability partnership, corporation, limited liability company (LLC), and franchise. Regarding partnerships, the student must be aware that a partnership is governed b the Uniform Partnership Acts (UPA), which is a *corpus* of state statutory law; but, also, that the partners in their partnership agreement can make major changes in UPA precepts, yet certainly not by changing the inherent fiduciary nature of the relationship. The student must know that a partnership is considered to be a mere association of people doing business together for some respects but also construed as an entity for other respects. The student must know how partnerships are formed, typically by an express partnership agreement, but also impliedly when the key factors of intent, management control, and sharing of profits are present. The student also must know how to distinguish partnership property from the property of the individual partners. As per the UPA, the governance of a partnership is based on the partners having an equal vote in the management of the business, with a majority vote of the partners controlling. However, the student also needs to be aware of those transactions requiring a unanimous vote of the partners. Moreover, as per the UPA, profits and losses of a partnership are shared equally between or among the partners. However, it is important for the student to know that partners' capital contributions have to be repaid before any profits can be distributed. Next, the student must comprehend the tort and contract liability of the partnership and the individual partners, especially noting that partners are considered to be agents of the partnership when conducting partnership business. Most importantly, partners are personally and unlimitedly liable for the debts and obligations of the partnership. Finally, the student must understand how partnerships come to an end, especially the distinctions among a dissolution, winding up and liquidation, and termination of the partnership. The student must realize that pursuant to dissolution law the partnership is a very "fragile" way of doing business as well as one that risks personal liability. Although there are specialized forms of doing business, the student should know the basic definitions and rules for a limited partnership as well as a limited liability partnership.

A corporation is an artificial legal entity created pursuant to state corporation law. The corporation is owned by its shareholders and governed by a board of directors elected by the shareholders. The student likely is cognizant of the major benefit of the corporate way of doing business, that is, the limited liability of the shareholders who just have their investment in the corporation at risk and not their personal liability at stake. The student first must know how a corporation is formed, principally by the filing of an Articles of Incorporation with the appropriate state official. The student must know the requirements to have a proper Articles as well as the difference between the Articles and the corporate bylaws. It is also important for the student to know the differences among a valid *de jure* corporation, a *de facto* corporation, and a corporation by estoppel. Moreover, the student must be aware of the doctrine of "piercing the corporate veil" or disregarding the corporate entity, whereby a court can disregard the corporate entity and hold the shareholders personally liable for corporate obligations. Next, the student must know the rights and responsibilities of the board of directors as well as the shareholders of the corporation. Regarding the board of directors, the students must know of the Business Judgement Rule, which protects the directors in decision-making as well as the ways that the shareholders can control the board, for example, by cumulative voting. The student must understand some of the basics of corporate finance, such as the difference between common and preferred stock, as well as the legal source of dividends for the shareholders. In addition, the student must know of the types of fundamental corporate change, such as amending the articles, mergers, and consolidations, and the basic procedural rules for approving such changes. Finally, the student must be aware of two types of specialized corporations, the "close" or "closely held" corporation as well as the Subchapter S-Corporation.

A limited liability company (LLC) is a relatively new way of doing business that propitiously combines the management aspects of a partnership with the limited liability of a corporation. As such, the business student, contemplating an entrepreneurial career, should very seriously consider the LLC as a relatively easy business entity to form and manage as well as one that affords protection to the entrepreneur's personal assets. LLCs are governed by separate state LLC statutes, which require the filing of an Articles of Organization, sometimes called a Certificate of Formation, with the appropriate state official. The students must know the formalities in creating an LLC as well as the rights and duties of the members of the LLC, which typically are governed by the LLC operating agreement, which can make certain changes in the state's LLC statute, for example, regarding the equal sharing of profits and losses. The student must know the management rights of LLC members, that an LLC can be member-managed or management-managed, as well as the duty of care of LLC members. In addition, the student must know the contract and tort liability of the members of an LLC as well as how LLCs come to an end, principally by "disassociation" (as opposed to "dissolution" for a partnership). Finally, the student should know what a franchise is and that this specialized way of doing business is not only governed by state franchise law, but also very heavily regulated on the federal level by the Federal Trade Commission.

True and False Questions with Answers and Explanations

1. In a sole proprietorship the personal liability of the owner is limited to funds designated in separate business accounts.
(False: The liability of a sole proprietor is theoretically unlimited.)

2. A court will disregard the corporate entity if the main reason for the shareholders to incorporate was to achieve limited liability.
(False: It is quite permissible to have as a main motive obtaining the limited liability that the corporate form of business provides. The corporate entity will be disregarded, also known as "piercing the corporate veil," when the purported corporation is merely a "shell" or a conduit to conduct one's personal business affairs.)

3. One-person corporations are permissible in most states.
(True: And the one person can assume the roles of sole shareholder, director, president, and other corporate officers. However, under the "piercing the corporate veil" doctrine that person must be very careful to differentiate his or her personal affairs from the corporation's business activities.)

4. A limited partnership must have a least one general partner.
(True: The general partner manages the partnership and is personally and unlimited responsible for the partnership's obligations, whereas the limited partners have no management role, though giving advice is permissible, but are only liable to the extent of their contribution to the limited partnership.)

5. The liability of a corporation's shareholders is limited to the amount they invested in the corporation.
(True: As opposed to general partners who are unlimitedly and personally liable for the partnership debts and obligations.)

6. One advantage of a limited liability company (LLC) is that the members can participate in management.
(True: In this respect the members of an LLC is like a partnership where the partners have equal rights to manage. In the LLC the members can have a member-managed entity or chose a manager and have a manager-managed LLC.)

7. The key feature in determining whether a business arrangement is a partnership is whether the parties called their arrangement a "partnership."
(False: What the parties call the arrangement is evidence as to its legal status, but merely evidence. The key feature is whether there is a sharing of net profits (or losses) from a business, which actually creates a presumption that a partnership exists.)

8. The joint owner of personal property by two people will create a presumption that a partnership exists.
(False: Such ownership is merely evidence. People can own property together as tenants-in-common, joint tenants, or by means of a tenancy of the entireties, that is, property ownership between a husband and wife).

9. Under federal law a partnership will be treated as an entity for paying taxes.
(False: A partnership files an "information return," but any profits or losses are attributed to the individual partners who pay any tax. However, for federal bankruptcy purposes a partnership is treated as a separate legal entity.)

10. A partnership is treated as a legal entity for the purpose of filing and defending lawsuits.
(True: However, the plaintiff suing the partnership should also sue the individual partners in case the partnership assets are not sufficient to pay any judgment received.)

11. If a partnership agreement has a specified duration for the partnership a partner cannot dissolve the partnership until the termination date.
(False: A partner always has the power, though not necessarily the right, to dissolve a partnership, meaning that if a dissolution occurs in violation of the agreement the partnership is dissolved but the dissolving partner can be sued for breach of the partnership agreement. However, whether the dissolving partner or any other partner can convert the dissolution to a liquidation and termination of the partnership reference must be made to the partnership agreement and if silent the Uniform Partnership Act.)

12. If a partnership is at-will, that is, there is no specified termination date, any partner can dissolve the partnership upon giving two-weeks formal notice.
(False: No notice is required. In such an at-will situation any partner at any time can dissolve the partnership and that partner and any other can compel a liquidation and termination, assuming no provisions in the partnership agreement to the contrary.)

13. A decision by partners to embark on an entirely new line of business for the partnership requires a majority vote.
(False: Such a decision would be regarded as a fundamental change in the nature of the business and thus would require a unanimous vote, as per the UPA; but the partners can change that vote to a majority in the partnership agreement.)

14. A partner's interest in the property of the partnership is considered to be personal property of the partner.
(*True: Partners hold partnership property as "tenants in partnership," meaning that they are co-owners of the property for partnership purposes, and also that they are entitled to distribution of proportional profits upon dissolution, winding-up, and termination. This interest, moreover, is deemed to be personal property, for example, for inheritance purposes.)*

15. All property purchased by a partner on account of the partnership is considered to be partnership property.
(True: And even if the partner uses his or her own funds.)

16. When the term of a partnership with a fixed term ends and the partners decide to continue to carry on the business the partnership becomes one that is terminable at-will.
(True: Each partner then has the power and right to terminate at any time and compel a winding-up and liquidation and ultimate termination.)

17. When the partners in a partnership agree to take on a new partner and carry on the business a new partnership arises.
(True: A technical dissolution is caused by the change in partnership members, but if the partners choose not to convert the dissolution to a winding-up, liquidation, and termination but to carry on the business, a new partnership is formed with the newly added partner.)

18. Once a partnership is dissolved it is automatically terminated.
(False: Dissolution merely means there is a change in the membership of the partnership, for example, when a partner dies or a new partner is admitted. However, dissolution may give the remaining partners the power and the right to compel a winding-up, liquidation, and termination of the partnership, as per the partnership agreement or if silent the UPA.)

19. When the assets of a partnership are distributed during liquidation partners' capital contributions are paid before profits to the partners.
(True: Yet note that creditors are paid first and then partners for any loans to the partnership.)

20. Absent any agreement the partners share equally in profits regardless of how much work or effort any one partner exerted in producing those profits.
(True: If the agreement is silent the partners share profits equally regardless of effort. Hence, if one partner is going to do the bulk of the work or management this fact should be addressed in the agreement.)

21. If a limited partner undertakes management responsibilities in the limited partnership, he or she will lose the limited status and thus be personally and unlimitedly liable for the limited partnership's obligations.
(True: Only the general partner in the limited partnership can manage the business, but a limited partner can give advice to the general partner and not lose his or her limited status.)

22. Corporations possess the First Amendment right to Free Speech.
(True: Corporations possess most, but not all, of constitutional rights as "natural" persons do; for example, a corporation does not have the Fifth Amendment privilege against self-incrimination.)

23. A promoter who enters into a contract for a corporation that is not yet formed is personally liable on those contracts.
(True: The situation is analogous to a purported "agent" acting for a non-existent principal, that is, the "agent" is liable on the contract. However, the corporation may ratify the contract, release the promoter from liability, or enter into a novation with the third-party getting the third-party to release the promoter from liability and to accept substitute performance by the corporation.)

24. The exact date and location of the corporation's annual meeting are usually set forth in the articles of incorporation.
(False: The articles contain the major provisions required by the state for the corporation to receive a charter from the state, for example, the nature of the business, its duration, the initial directors, and an agent for service of process. Other provisions that deal with the running of the business, such as the date and location of meetings, are usually set forth in the bylaws.)

25. If a corporation complies with all the state's requirements for incorporation the corporation is said to have *de facto* status.
(*False: The status is de jure; de facto status is achieved when there is a minor irregularity or omission in the articles of incorporation, for example, one incorporator not signing the document, and the corporation is acting as a corporation nonetheless. The de facto corporation is treated as a real corporation in its dealings with third parties, but the state can always compel the "corporation" to complete and/or correct the articles and thus achieve proper de jure status.)*

26. When a person comingles his or her personal assets and personal business dealings with those of his or her corporation to the extent that the corporation loses its own separate identity as a business entity the corporate entity can be disregarded by a court and thus the "shareholders" will be personally and unlimitedly liable.
(True: This principle is also known as "piercing the corporate veil." Consequently and especially in a one person or small corporation, the shareholder(s) must keep their personal dealings separate form the corporation's and must treat the corporation as a separate and distinct legal entity.)

27. A shareholder of common stock owns a proportionate share and interest of the corporation's control, assets, and earnings.
(True: This is a basic corporation principle. Control is exercised by means of voting for directors. Preferred stock typically is not voting but can be voting shares. Preferred stockholders get a preference on distribution of earnings and assets.)

28. In most states today members of the corporation's board of directors can vote by appointing another person to act as the director's proxy and vote for him or her at a board meeting.
(False: Directors traditionally must appear and vote in person at board meetings, though electronic presence at a meeting is now permissible. Shareholders, however, can vote by proxy.)

29. The decision to award dividends is a function and responsibility of the board of directors.
(True: Shareholders cannot vote on dividends. However, if the corporation has a very large accumulated amount of earnings and the board has no plans on what to do with the money the shareholders may be able to convince a court to order a distribution of dividends.)

30. A director of a corporation who secretly goes into business with a competing company has committed an *ultra vires* act.
(False: An ultra vires act is an act by the corporation itself that is beyond the purposes stated in its charter, for example, a company that is set up to buy and sell goods that is now investing in real estate. The director who competes is breaching the duty of loyalty to the corporation.)

31. Notice of special shareholder meetings must be in writing and contain the date, hour, location, and purpose of the meeting.
(True: And if the purpose is to elect directors the nominees must be specified.)

32. Cumulative voting is designed to allow a minority of the shareholders to take control of the corporation.
(False: Cumulative voting, which allows the shareholders to multiply their votes times the number of shares they own (when directors are chosen together from a list of nominees), is designed to give minority shareholders some representation on the board of directors but not to give them majority control.)

33. A preemptive right is a right given to a shareholder to purchase on a *pro rata* basis shares of new issue of stock by the corporation.
(True: Such a right allows a shareholder to keep his or her proportionate interest in the corporation.)

34. Dividends must be payable in cash.
(False: Dividends can also be in the form of stock, for example, a stock-split.)

35. Most state laws require that dividends must be payable at least once a year as the shareholders may be dependent on the income.
(False: The payment of dividends (time and amount) is in the discretion of the board of directors. However, shareholders can go to court to force the dividend is the corporation has a large amount of accumulated earnings and the board has no plans on what to do with the money.)

36. In most states corporate funds that are available for the payment of dividends are net profits, earnings that have been retained, but not capital surplus funds.
(False: Capital surplus is the consideration paid for par value shares in excess of par value; and such funds can be used for the payment of dividends in most states.)

37. Directors in the minority can bring a derivative suit on behalf of the corporation if the majority of the directors are unwilling to do so.
(False: The derivative lawsuit is a remedy for the shareholders when the directors refuse to bring an action and some harm is being done to the corporation. There are several requirements for the shareholders to institute a derivative suit, however.)

38. A shareholder may incur personal liability for corporate obligations if he or she purchases shares at too deep a discount.
(False: The shareholder will not be personally liable for corporate obligations but if the shares are sold to him or her for less than fair consideration the shareholder may be liable for the "water," that is, the monetary deficiency, in the shares.)

39. A consolidation is the combination of two corporations, with both ceasing to exist, and a new company emerging.
(True: Whereas a merger is the combination of two companies with one incorporating the other and with that one dominant company emerging.)

40. In a short-form merger where the parent is seeking to merge with a subsidiary company the parent must own at least 80% of the stock in the subsidiary company.
(True: And it some states the percentage is 90%).

41. In a short-form merger, the approval of the board of directors of the parent company and the subsidiary company are required to effectuate the merger.
(False: Only the approval of the board of directors of the parent company is required.)

42. The right of a shareholder to compel the corporation to buy back his or her shares after a merger is called an "appraisal right."
(True: The appraisal right is also called a "dissenting right" and exists for other types of fundamental corporate change, such as consolidation or the sale of a substantial portion of the corporation's assets.)

43. The liabilities of a partnership can include amounts of money owed to partners for their capital contributions.
(True: And note this could be a "trap" for an unwary partner since one partner contributes his or her skill, knowledge, and managerial expertise, thereby basically running the partnership; and the other partner "only" contributes money in the form of a capital contribution to the partnership; but if the partnership fails the managerial partner owes his or her partner one-half of the capital contribution.)

44. The Articles of Incorporation of a corporation are promulgated at the first organizational meeting of the entity.
(False: The Articles are first submitted to the state to form the corporation and receive a charter; the it is the bylaws, that is, the internal rules for operating the corporation, that are typically drawn up by the board of directors at the first organizational meeting of the corporation.)

45. As a general rule the promoter of a corporation is personally liable for pre-incorporation contracts made for the corporation.
(True: That is the risk being a promoter, whose situation is like an "agent" contracting for a non-existent principal since the corporation is not yet formed. Liability can be diminished if the corporation when formed adopts the promoter's contract or there is a novation, whereby the third-party agrees to release the promoter from the contract and accept the corporation as a substitute.)

46. The bylaws of a corporation set forth the classes, amounts, and values of corporate stock.
(False: That is done in the Articles of Incorporation. The bylaws are the internal rules and regulations governing the corporation, such as when and where directors and shareholder meetings will be held.)

47. When people hold themselves out as doing business as a corporation the law may deem a Corporation by Estoppel to exist.
(Ture: Estoppel basically means that out of fairness the people who engaged in deception in holding them out as a corporation will be "estopped," that is, prevented from denying corporate status.)

48. Preferred shareholders typically hold voting rights as well as the right to receive dividends each year the corporation makes a profit.
(False: Dividends are solely a function of the board of directors and shareholders, preferred as well as common, are not entitled automatically to any dividends. Moreover, it is the common shareholders that have voting rights. Preferred shareholders may have preferences to receive dividends before common shareholders when and if dividends are authorized by the board of directors.)

49. The Business Judgment rule makes members of the board of directors strictly liable when they make a wrong decision resulting in the loss of money by the corporation.
(False: The Business Judgment rule actually protects board members. That is, if the board acts in a reasonably prudent and careful manner upon proper advice and counsel they are not liable if their decisions are the wrong ones and result in losses to the company. They are not guarantors of profits.)

50. Both corporate directors and officers owe a duty of loyalty to the corporation.
(True: This is a fundamental principle based on statute and the common law and prohibits, for example, conflicts-of-interest and competing with the corporation.)

51. A franchise exists when one party called the franchisor grants to another party called the franchisee the right to do business under a certain name and in a certain territory pursuant to the terms of a franchise agreement.
(True: This is a basic principle though it should be noted that the franchise method of doing business is governed not just by state law but by federal law pursuant to Federal Trade Commission regulations.)

52. A partner does not have the power to wrongfully dissolve a partnership.
(False: A partner always has the power to dissolve the partnership but not necessarily the right to do so, and thus a wrongful dissolution, for example, in contravention of the agreement, will make the dissolving partner liable for damages to the partnership and other partners.)

53. A partner in a general partnership is personally and unlimited responsible for the debts and obligations of the partnership if the partnership lacks sufficient assets to pay all its creditors and claimants.
(True: This is the major disadvantage of a partnership as opposed to a corporation or a limited liability company (LLC) where only one's investment in the entity is at risk.)

54. A partner owes to the partnership but not directly to the other partners a duty of good faith and fair dealing.
(False: The partnership relationship is a fiduciary one and thus the partners must exhibit good faith and fair dealing to each other as well as the partnership.)

55. Promoters as well as incorporators must execute and sign the articles of incorporation of a corporation.
(False: Only incorporations need to do so, though in many cases the promoters and the incorporators are the same people.)

56. A short-form corporate merger will be available when a parent company owns at least 51% of the stock of a subsidiary company.
(False: The percentage required for this simplified merger procedure is typically 90% though some states have only an 80% requirement.)

57. Appraisal rights are usually available to shareholders who vote against a regular corporate merger and lose the vote.
(True: These rights to minority in number shareholders are also called "dissenting rights" and require that the corporation pay fair market value for the shares, for example, at the time of the merger the minority shareholders voted against and lost.)

58. A small issue of stock in an intrastate offering usually will not be governed by the registration requirements of the federal Securities Act of 1933.
(True: However, state security law, called "Blue Sky" laws, would govern the small intrastate offering; moreover, state securities laws typically follow the federal laws and thus registration at the state level typically would be required.)

59. Property purchased with partnership funds is presumed to be partnership property even if the title and possession is with an individual partner.
(True: This presumption can be rebutted, however, with contrary evidence.)

60. A partner who is the managing partner and devotes a significant amount of time to running the business is automatically entitled to a reasonable amount of compensation.
(False: Any compensation to a partner must be specifically and explicitly stated in the partnership agreement.)

61. The liabilities of a partnership can include amounts owed to partners for their capital contributions to the partnership.
(True: This principle can be a "trap for the unwary" if one partner devotes time and effort to the partnership and the other contributes capital when the partnership ends and after creditors are paid and there are no partnership funds remaining, the one partner must pay one-half of the other partner's capital contribution since such "losses" are to be shared equally absent any agreement to the contrary.)

62. When a partner assigns his or her interest in the partnership the assignee acquires the status and rights of a partner.
(False: The assignee does not become a partner; rather the assignee just acquires the right to the assigning partner's share of the profits of the partnership.)

63. A limited partnership must have at least one general partner.
(True: This is a basic proposition since the general partner will be the managing partner and be personally and unlimitedly liable for the partnership's obligations, whereas the limited partners cannot manage the firm, or else they will lose their "limited" status, and thus be personally and unlimitedly liable.)

64. The liability of a shareholder of a corporation is limited to his or her investment in the corporation.
(True: This is a basic proposition; and this limited liability is the chief advantage of the corporate form of doing business as opposed to a partnership.)

65. A close or closely-held corporation is exempt from all corporate formalities.
(False: States typically have special corporate statutes for closely-held corporations with small numbers of shareholders, usually less than 35, who can participate in management. The articles of incorporation must be filed pursuant to the state statute.)

66. A limited liability company (LLC) is exempt from all corporate formalities.
(False: There are special state statutes governing LLCs. Though the articles of incorporation of a traditional corporation need not be filed the state would require the filing of the Articles of Organization as well as the use of the words "limited" or "LLC" after the company's name.)

67. The members of an LLC can manage the business like a partnership.
(True: This feature along with the limited liability status of the members make the LLC a very attractive means to do business, especially for small start-up companies.)

68. The major disadvantage of doing business as a sole proprietorship is that one is personally and unlimitedly liable for the business' obligations and debts.
(True: As such, it would be advisable to do business as a one-person corporation or one-person LLC if permitted by the pertinent state laws.)

69. All partnership agreements must be in writing.
(False: Though certainly advisable a written partnership agreement can be oral unless the Statute of Frauds applies, for example, for partnerships to buy and sell real property or by their own terms to last longer than a year.)

70. For federal taxation purposes, a partnership is considered to be a tax-paying entity.
(False: A partnership is considered to be an entity for some purposes, such as owning real property or bringing a lawsuit, but not for federal taxation purposes since the gains (or losses) of the partnership are taxed (allocated) to the individual partners. However, the partnership still must file an "information return" with the IRS.)

71. A form of doing business that is owned by shareholders who have limited liability is a limited liability company (LLC).
(False: A corporation is owned by shareholders who have limited liability. While members of an LLC also have limited liability, they are not shareholders of the business but its members.)

72. Since the members of a limited liability company (LLC) can run and manage the business like a partnership they lose their limited liability and are liable personally and unlimitedly for the LLC's debts and obligations.
(False: The advantages of an LLC are that the members can run the business-like a partnership and still have the limited liability like the shareholders of a corporation.)

73. A joint venture is similar to a partnership with the major exception that the joint venture can issue and sell stock to outsiders to increase its capitalization.
(False: A joint venture is treated as a partnership except that it is for a more limited purpose. As such, the joint venture like a partnership does not and cannot issue stock like a corporation.)

74. A limited liability company (LLC) is like a corporation in that it can issue and sell stock to outsiders in order to increase its capitalization.
(False: The LLC is like a corporation in that its members have limited liability but a major disadvantage of the LLC way of doing business is that the LLC does not have access to capital markets by the issuance and sale of stock. The LLC can increase its capitalization by bringing in other members who bring in capital as well as securing advances from members and loans from financial institutions.)

75. When a person pays a percentage of the profits of his or her business to a creditor to pay off a debt the law deems the debtor business person and the creditor to be partners.
(False: Generally, the payment to a person of part of the profits of a business creates a presumption that the person is a partner. However, no such inference is created if the profits are used to pay off a debt to a creditor.)

76. When a creditor obtains a judgment against a partnership the judgment must be first paid out of the assets held by the partnership.
(True: And if the partnership assets are insufficient to satisfy the judgment then the judgment creditor can proceed against the assets of the individual partners who are personally and unlimited liable.)

77. Pursuant to federal bankruptcy law a partnership is treated as a separate legal entity distinct from its members.
(True: The partnership is treated as an entity for owning property – real or personal – as well as bringing legal actions and being sued. However, for most purposes, including the payment of federal taxes the partnership is merely considered an association of its members doing business.)

78. It is necessary for all partners to sign a contract to sell any partnership property.
(False: Any one partner may have the express, implied, or apparent authority by virtue of his or her status as a partner to dispose of partnership property by contract.)

79. If the partnership agreement forbids a partner from selling partnership property any contract to sell partnership property to a third person is null-and-void.
(False: If the third-party does not have knowledge of the preclusion of sale by the one partner the contract with the third-party is valid. However, the partner who sold the property in violation of the partnership agreement may be liable for damages to the other partners.)

80. If one partner fraudulently deceives a third-party to enter into a contract for the benefit of the partnership the other partners are liable to the third-party even if the other partners were ignorant and innocent of the fraud.
(True: So long as the fraud occurred to further the partnership's business the other partners as well as the partnership would be liable based on the authority – express, implied, or apparent – of the partners to enter into contracts for the partnership and the traditional principles of vicarious liability for fraud by agents and partners.)

81. A creditor of a partner can petition the court to order the partnership to take on the creditor as a partner until the partner's debt is paid.
(False: The creditor does not become a partner without the agreement of the partners. The creditor's basic remedy is to obtain from the court a "charging order" by which the court mandates that the partnership pay the debtor partner's share of the profits to the creditor.)

82. Generally, a partner who devotes more time and effort to running the partnership business and making it successful financially is entitled to a greater share of the profits as determined by a court.
(False: The partners share the profits equally regardless of time and effort expended as well as knowledge and skill brought to the business. If it is contemplated that one partner will be doing more or achieving more, then this eventuality should be addressed in the partnership agreement and the pertinent partner should be granted some type of compensation.)

83. When a new partner is admitted to a partnership that has existing debts and obligations the new partner is not liable for those debts and obligations since he was not a partner when they were incurred.
(False: The new partner's capital contribution to the partnership can be used to satisfy the debts and obligations but the new partner is not personally and unlimitedly liable for debts and obligations that arose before he or she became a partner.)

84. All property purchased for the partnership is considered to be partnership property.
(True: Yet this is a presumption which can be rebutted by a showing of countervailing evidence that a differing intent by the partners is present, for example, that the property is being held by the partnership for convenience and that the property was purchased with the individual funds of a partner.)

85. A partner always has the power, though not necessarily the right, to withdraw from the partnership.
(True: If the withdrawing partner leaves in breach of the partnership agreement he or she has the power to do so but may be liable for damages for breach of the partnership agreement. Moreover, the withdrawing partner by leaving has caused a technical "dissolution" of the partnership by changing its members; however, a wrongfully dissolving partner cannot bring about the winding up and liquidation of the partnership. He or she gets his or her share of the profits and/or assets of the partnership minus any damages caused by the wrongful dissolution.)

86. When a partner transfers or assigns his or her interest in the partnership to a creditor the creditor automatically becomes a partner as the creditor must be able to protect the expected source of funds to repay the debt.
(False: The creditor does not become a partner, unless there is agreement by the other partners; the assignee creditor "merely" receives the assigning partner's share of the profits.)

87. An act by a partner that changes fundamentally the nature of the business, for example, buying real estate as an investment, when the business of the partnership is providing business consulting services, requires a 3/4 's vote of the partnership.
(False: This type of transaction would be considered as an extraordinary one requiring the unanimous consent of all the partners.)

88. The liabilities of a partnership can include the amounts payable to partners for their capital contributions to the partnership.
(True: Partners' capital contributions must be paid before any share of the profits can go to the partners. Moreover, if there are no profits but losses the partners must share equally in the losses, which include includes paying back the capital contributions of other partners.)

89. A corporation since it is not a real person does not have the 4th Amendment protection against unreasonable search and seizure.
(False: Corporations possess most, including the 4th Amendment, constitutional rights.)

90. Since the corporation is not a real person. government agents do not need warrants to search corporate offices.
(False: Warrants are required though the law makes a distinction between police-type warrants for criminal law searches and administrative agency-type warrants for health and safety inspections with the former requiring traditional "probable cause" and the latter merely requiring "blanket" warrants that just have the rationale for the inspections based on the purpose of the agency, for example, OHSA safety inspections at plants, and the geographic areas and types of facilities to be inspected.)

91. A promoter is personally liable for contracts made for a corporation that the promoter is attempting to create but does not yet exist.
(True: The promoter situation is analogous to a person who acts as an "agent" for a non-existent principal.)

92. One of the main functions of a promoter is to determine if the corporation made sufficient profits to issue a cash or stock dividend to the shareholders.
(False: The issuance of dividends is a function of the board of directors of a corporation and not the promoter, who seeks to secure the personnel and capital to get the corporation started.)

93. The pertinent state corporate official, usually the Secretary of State of the state, must approve the bylaws of the corporation.
(False: The state official must approve the Articles of Incorporation and thus grant the corporation a charter. The establishment of bylaws is simply a function for the board of directors, typically the initial board named in the Articles.)

94. A corporation by estoppel can arise when one person deceives another person into doing business with him or her as a corporation.
(True: There is not a real, i.e., legal, corporation in such a situation; rather, the fraudulent party due to the deception is "estopped," that is, prevented, from denying the existence of the corporation.)

95. Shareholders of common stock have priority to dividends as well as corporate assets if the company becomes insolvent because they have voting shares.
(False: The preferred shareholders have priority in both situations due to their "preferred" status.)

96. Preferred shareholders do not have voting rights, but they do have the right to an annual dividend if there is any type of corporate surplus.
(False: The issuance of dividends is solely a function of the board of directors; neither preferred or common shareholders have any right to dividends – yearly or otherwise.)

97. Directors of a corporation have an automatic right to compensation since they are the chief policy-makers of the business.
(False: Compensation, if any, of directors is a function of the board of directors of the company, typically by a compensation committee of the board.)

98. The members of the board of directors of a corporation as the highest policy-making personnel in the organization must exercise the highest standard of care in making corporate decisions and thus are liable for unprofitable decisions.
(False: Directors are protected by the "business judgment rule." That is, if they attend meetings, pay attention, ask questions, follow professional advice, and exercise reasonable care in making decisions they are not personally liable if the decisions turn out to be "bad" ones financially.)

99. A voting list is a list of all the shareholders of the corporation put together by the corporation prior to a shareholders' meeting.
(True: This is a basic proposition of corporate law and practice.)

100. Shareholders are not allowed to have preemptive rights since they could use them to maintain the control of the corporation.
(False: If granted in the Articles of Incorporation shareholders are allowed to have preemptive rights, that is, the right to buy a proportionate share of new stock issuances based on their current holdings, in order to maintain their percentage of ownership in and perhaps control over the corporation.)

101. The main purpose of the preemptive rights doctrine is to allow minority shareholders to have some voting representation on the board of directors.
(False: It is the cumulative voting doctrine that allows some minority representation on the board.)

102. Usually an issuance of dividends can be mandated by a majority of the shareholders but with board of directors' approval.
(False: The issuance of dividends is a board of director function, not that of the shareholders who have some influence by electing board members. However, if the corporation has a very large financial surplus and the board of directors does not have any plans as to what to do with it the shareholders can bring a suit to convince a court to order the directors to pay a dividend.)

103. Shares are referred to as "watered stock" if they are no-par shares.
(False: Corporations are allowed to sell shares for no-par value for their value to be determined when consideration is given later for the shares.)

104. A person who subscribes to par-value stock of a company before its technical legal formation must pay the stated value of the stock or risk a lawsuit for breach of contract.

(True: Even if the corporation is not technically formed and the promoter enters into the contract with the subscriber of stock the corporation can still pursue a remedy for breach of contract when the contract is formed.)

105. When a company effectuates a merger with its subsidiary the only approvals necessary are from the board of directors and shareholders of the "parent," i.e., acquiring company.
(True: This is an example of a short-form merger.)

106. A shareholder is allowed to exercise dissenting or appraisal rights in both a regular and short-form merger.
(True: This is a basic proposition. Note too that in the short-form merger the shareholders of the company to be acquired, the subsidiary, do not even get to vote.)

107. A written demand for payment is not required for a shareholder to exercise his or her dissenting or appraisal right.
(False: The written demand is absolutely required.)

108. Termination of a partnership usually has three main stages: dissolution, winding-up, and liquidation.
(True: Remember that dissolution means the change in the relationship of the partners for any reason, such as admitting a new partner, a partner dying, or a partner being expelled. Dissolution may or may not lead to the winding-up and termination, however, depending on whether there is a rightful or wrongful dissolution.)

109. As a general rule regarding corporate mergers the boards of directors and shareholders of both firms must approve the merger.
(True: There are exceptions for "short-form" or parent-subsidiary mergers where shareholder approval is not needed.)

110. If the corporation is currently making net profits for the year the shareholders can compel the board of directors to issue a dividend.
(False: In most states dividends cannot be paid from current earnings, but rather from retained earnings. Regardless, the decision to issue dividends is a function of the board which has a great deal of discretion; and as such the shareholders cannot force the board to issue dividends unless usually there is a very large surplus and the board has no plans as to what to do with it.)

111. The *De Facto* corporation doctrine may provide legal status to the corporation even if the Articles of Incorporation were improperly filed as against everyone except the state of incorporation.
(True: The De Facto doctrine exists to confer corporate status usually when a good faith attempt was made to file the Articles but something, for example, a signature of one of the incorporators is missing and there also was a good faith attempt to organize the "corporation," for example, having an initial board meeting, as well as some use of "corporate" powers.")

112. Comingling of assets and accounts by a person individually and his or her corporation will likely result in the "piercing of the corporate veil" and thus the person will be held personally responsible for corporate obligations regardless of his or her technical status as a shareholder.
(True: Such comingling will very likely cause a court to disregard the corporate entity and hold the shareholders personally responsible for corporate debts and obligations. Moreover, not adhering to corporate formalities, such as having bylaws, directors, and meetings of directors and shareholders also can cause the corporate entity to be disregarded.)

113. The purpose of cumulative voting is to allow the minority shareholders to eventually get a majority of the board of directors and thus to control the corporation.
(False: The purpose of cumulative voting is to afford the minority of shareholders some representation on the board, and not to control it or the corporation.)

114. A notice for a special shareholder meeting must be written and must specify the date, time, and place for the meeting as well as the purpose of the meeting.
(True: This is a basic principle. Also, if the purpose of the meeting is to elect directors the names of the nominees must be provided too.)

115. In most states, today, directors can vote by proxy.
(False: Directors are supposed to act as a board and must vote personally, though teleconferencing and other communications systems can be used to replace the actual physical presence of a director.)

116. A corporation is regarded as a "person" for First Amendment protections.
(True: Yet First Amendment rights are not absolute for a corporation as well as a natural person; and the courts make a distinction between a corporation's "political speech" and "commercial speech," with the former being granted more protection under the First Amendment.)

117. One disadvantage to a Subchapter S corporation is that this type of business entity pays double taxation.
(False: There is no double taxation as this type of corporation is treated for taxation purposes like a partnership. However, disadvantages may be limits on the number of shareholders allowed as well as who can be shareholders, for example, prohibitions against non-citizens.)

118. As a general rule, creditors of a corporation cannot reach the shareholders' personal assets to satisfy a corporate debt or obligation.
(True: This is the major advantage of the corporate form of doing business. An exception would be if "piercing the corporate veil" occurs, that is, the corporate form is disregarded since the "corporation" is a mere "shell" or alter ego of the shareholders.)

119. Continuity of existence is not a problem for most partnerships since when a partner leaves the partners can continue the business after paying off the departing partner and then the remaining partners can continue the business.
(False: A partnership is a very fragile way to do business. Unless there is a well-written partnership agreement dealing specifically with partners leaving or new partners coming in, any change in the relationship of the partners is a technical "dissolution," which means absent an agreement to the contrary any partner can force a winding-up, liquidation, and termination of the partnership despite the contrary wishes of the other partners.)

120. A sole proprietorship must include the name of its owner to conduct business.
(False: A sole proprietorship can have a name unrelated to its owner by complying with the state's Fictitious Name statute.)

121. A sole proprietorship cannot have employees; all work must be done by the owner.
(False: A sole proprietorship can certainly have employees so long as employment laws are followed. Moreover, the owner can act as a principal and retain agents to represent him or her and enter into contracts on the owner/principal's behalf.)

122. Shareholders who are also directors and officers of publicly traded companies regulated by the Securities and Exchange Commission are required to report their stock trades in their company's stock.

(True: And this information becomes public information for the investing public to consider. Moreover, such information will be critical in determining if there is any potential liability for "short-swing" profits pursuant to Section 16(b).)

123. If a partner negligently causes an automobile accident while driving a partnership vehicle while doing partnership business only the careless partner and the partnership are liable for any injuries or harms caused.
(False: The other partners are also liable – personally and unlimitedly – if the wrongdoing partner and the partnership have insufficient assets to pay a judgment claimant. Typically, in addition to suing the partnership the injured plaintiff would sue all the partners since their tort liability is "joint and several," meaning any one or all can be sued, and anyone would have to pay the full judgment, and then seek indemnification from his or her co-partners.)

124. Directors are always liable to the shareholders for the poor business decisions they make that result in corporate losses since directors are the policy-making body of the company.
(False: The board of directors is the policy-making part of the corporation, but directors are protected by the Business Judgment Rule, which states that directors are not guarantors of business success. Rather, they "merely" have to act in a careful and prudent manner, seek proper advice and counsel, and be fully informed before making business decisions; and if so directors will not be liable for poor business decisions. Of course, the shareholders may want to elect a new, and perhaps better, board of directors.)

125. A director of a company has a duty to avoid competing with his or her firm.
(True: Directors are regarded as fiduciaries vis-à-vis the corporation, meaning they have a duty of loyalty and good faith toward the corporation, which would preclude the director competing against his or her firm. Moreover, pursuant to the Corporate Opportunity doctrine if a director comes across a business opportunity that the corporation might be interested in the director must give the corporation the "right of first refusal," and only if the corporation refuses the opportunity can the director then avail himself or herself of it.)

126. A "close corporation" is one where the shares are typically owned by members of a family or by a small number of persons.
(True: This type of corporation is also known as a "closely held corporation" or "family held" or "privately held" corporation. Close corporations are usually governed by special state statutes or special statutory provisions in state corporation codes. The shareholders are related to one another or know one another, and thus there is not a large market for trading shares.)

127. A close corporation characteristically must strictly follow all the provisions of a state's corporate code.
(False: There usually are provisions in close corporation statutes that allow the members of a close corporation to depart significantly from certain formalities that would be required for a traditional corporation. For example, in some states the shareholders by unanimous agreement in writing can operate without directors or bylaws or annual or special meetings of shareholders and directors, or stock certificates.)

128. A shareholder agreement is a viable method for members of a closely held corporation to maintain control and stability of the entity.
(True: A shareholder agreement typically will state that when a shareholder dies, his or her shares of stock will be divided in such a matter that the remaining members of the close corporation retain proportionate control of the entity.)

129. If a corporation is a Subchapter S corporation (S-Corporation) and the corporation has losses the shareholders can use the losses to offset other taxable income.
(True: This is a major benefit of an S-corporation. Moreover, when a shareholder's tax bracket is lower than the tax bracket for regular corporations, the S-corporation's entire income will be taxed at the shareholder's lower personal income level, regardless of whether corporate income is distributed.)

130. A Subchapter S Corporation (S-Corporation) can have no more than 100 shareholders.
(True: Moreover, the shareholders cannot be non-resident aliens; and the S-corporation can only have one class of stock.

131. One negative aspect to an S-Corporation is that it pays double taxes.
(False: It is the traditional corporation or C-Corporation that pays the double taxes; that is, first the corporate tax on profits, and second, the shareholders' being taxed on dividend distributions. With an S-Corporation the profits or losses are attributed to the shareholders personally who only pay the personal tax rate.)

132. In a Limited Partnership the limited partners manage the business and are personally liable for any losses.
(False: The advantage of a limited partnership is that the limited partners are not personally liable for losses, just the general partner who manages the business is liable. However, if a limited partner assumes a management role, he or she will lose the limited status and be personally and unlimitedly liable for business losses. A limited partner can advise or consult with the general partner on business matters, however.)

Multiple Choice Questions with Answers and Explanations

1. Which is NOT a characteristic of the traditional business corporation?
   a. Centralized management by means of a board of directors and corporate officers.
   b. Creation by the filing of an Articles of Incorporation and approval of a corporate charter by the appropriate state agency.
   c. Personal liability of the shareholders for corporate debts and obligations.
   d. Access to capital markets by the issuance of shares of stock and their sale to the investing public.

   (The correct answer is c. The major advantage of the corporate way of doing business is the limited liability of the shareholders, that is, their investment in the corporation is at-stake for corporate debts and obligations, but, as opposed to partners, they are not personally and unlimitedly liable for corporate debts and obligations. The other responses are all principal characteristics of the corporation and centralized management and access to capital markets are advantages to the corporate way of doing business)

2. "Piercing the corporate veil" typically can occur and thus personal liability imposed on the purported shareholders when:
   a. The alleged corporation is "thinly capitalized."
   b. Corporate "formalities," such as issuing shares, electing directors, promulgating bylaws, and appointing officers, are not adhered to.
   c. An important motive of the incorporators for incorporating the business was the desire to achieve limited liability.
   d. a. and b.

   (The correct answer is d. Having a desire to avoid unlimited liability is not sufficient to disregard the corporate entity. However, not adhering to the usual corporate formalities could very result in

a "piercing of the corporate veil." Similarly, having a "thinly capitalized" corporation, that is, one without sufficient assets to take care of reasonably foreseeable obligations and debts. Note that lacking proper insurance is a key factor in being deemed a "thin" corporation.)

3. Which is FALSE regarding a traditional business partnership pursuant to the Uniform Partnership Act.
   a. Absent an agreement, partnership profits are shared equally by the partners regardless of any individual partner's contributions, knowledge, skills, or efforts.
   b. Absent an agreement, partners are not entitled to any salary or remuneration for acting in the partnership business.
   c. Partners are regarded as agents of the partnership when acting in the partnership business.
   d. The dissolution of a partnership will always lead to a winding-up, liquidation, and termination of the partnership.

   (The correct answer is d. The dissolution of a partnership results when the status of the partners in the partnership is changed, for example, when a partner dies, retires, is expelled, or a new partner is admitted. Dissolution can result in termination as a partner has the right to liquidate the business. However, the partnership agreement can specify the circumstances when a dissolution does not result in termination, but rather the remaining partners continuing the business after paying off the partner who left (minus any amount for damages if the partner who dissolved was a wrongful dissolver, for example, one who left to take advantage of a business opportunity that the partnership would be interested in doing. The partnership agreement can also specify how profits are to be divided; otherwise they are shared equally as well as losses. Partners are not entitled to any remuneration unless the agreement says so, which would be the case if one partner is the "managing partner." Partners are regarded as agents of the partnership when it comes to conducting partnership business and thus can bind contractually the partnership and other partners.)

4. What is FALSE about a board of directors of the traditional business corporation?
   a. The board must act as a collective body to legally bind the corporation.
   b. The board is protected for poor business decisions by the "business judgment rule."
   c. The board is responsible for establishing of major corporate polices and exercises ultimate control of the corporation.
   d. Board members and corporate executives are automatically entitled to compensation for serving on a board based on federal corporate law, but the compensation must not be "excessive" and the shareholders must approve of the compensation "package."

   (The correct answer is d. All other responses are basic and accurate corporate law principles. Compensation must be determined and voted on by the board, usually following the recommendations of a board compensation committee. Note that pursuant to recent SEC regulations the shareholders must be given a non-binding vote on CEO compensation, called "say-on-pay.")

5. Which corporate law doctrines are designed to give the shareholders some indirect control of the corporation?
   a. Voting for the board of directors
   b. Cumulative voting
   c. Voting trusts and pooling agreements
   d. All of the above.

   (The correct answer is d. These are all methods by which the shareholders can exercise control over the corporation, though indirectly as the board of directors is the governing body of the company. Note that cumulative voting does not guarantee minority in number of shareholders a majority on the board but rather only some representation on the board. The right to vote

cumulatively must be set forth in the Articles of Incorporation as too with voting trusts and pooling agreements. Voting on fundamental corporate change, such as mergers, consolidations, and amending the articles is another way the shareholders can exercise some control.)

6. "Fundamental corporate change" consists of:
    a. Amending the articles of incorporation
    b. Merging with another corporation
    c. Dissolution and termination of the corporation
    d. All of the above.
    (The correct answer is d. These are basic and accurate "fundamental change" examples, requiring a majority vote of the shareholders in addition to board approval unless a greater percentage is required in the articles of incorporation.)

7. Which is FALSE about a Limited Liability Company (LLC)?
    a. No formalities are required by state statute in the forming of an LLC; rather, a simple LLC agreement will suffice to establish legally the LLC.
    b. An LLC can be a member-managed or a manager-managed LLC.
    c. The name of the LLC must include the term "limited liability company" or "LLC."
    d. The members of an LLC are not personally liable for the debts and obligations of the LLC (beyond their original contributions to the LLC).

    (The correct answer is a. In order to have an LLC the parties must send to the appropriate state authority and receive approval for their Articles of Organization. Less formalities are required than in a traditional corporation, but they are essential; otherwise the risk is that the parties will be treated as a partnership. An LLC agreement, though not required, is strongly recommended so the parties are clear as to their rights and responsibilities in the entity. The other responses are all basic and accurate characteristics of doing business as an LLC.)

8. Which of the following is a FALSE statement?
    a. A partner does not have the power to wrongfully dissolve and disassociate from a partnership.
    b. A general partner is personally and unlimitedly liable for partnership debts and obligations if the assets of the partnership are insufficient to pay its creditors.
    c. A partner owes to the partnership and the other partners a duty of loyalty and good faith.
    d. Incorporators must execute the articles of incorporation.

    (The correct answer is a. A partnership is a consensual business arrangement; thus, no one can be forced to be a partner. As such, a partner always has the power to dissolve a partnership, but not necessarily the right; and if the dissolution is wrongful the dissolving partner can be sued for breach of the partnership agreement, yet the partnership is nevertheless technically dissolved. One weakness of a partnership is the personal liability of the partners for partnership debts and obligations, which is why the corporation form of doing business as well as the limited liability company is the preferred way in most cases to conduct business, and especially the latter for the small entrepreneur.)

9. Which of the following is a TRUE statement?
    a. Appraisal rights are never available under state corporate law.
    b. A person who wants to offer a small issue of stock in his or her business to the residents of just one state, which is the only state where this person does business, most likely does not have to comply with the Security Act of 1933 but usually will have to comply with state security law.
    c. If a partner buys personal property for his or her exclusive use and using partnership funds the presumption is that the property belongs to the partner who actually purchased it.

d. In general, a partner who devotes a significant amount of his or her time and effort to a partnership business will automatically be entitled to any compensation if the partnership agreement is silent.

(The correct answer is b. The "small placement" or "small offering" is an exception to federal registration requirements, though state registration requirements typically would have to be complied with. Appraisal rights, also called "dissenting rights," are available under state law for certain type of fundamental corporate changes, for example, mergers, though there are exceptions. The rationale is that a shareholder who voted against the merger should not be forced to be a shareholder of the new entity; and as such the new corporation would have to purchase the shareholder's shares for a fair price pursuant to statutory procedures. Property purchased with partnership funds is presumed to be partnership property even if title is in the name of an individual partner, as the placing of title could merely be a matter of convenience. If there is no express provision in the partnership agreement regarding compensation then the partners are not entitled to any, regardless of knowledge, skill, and time and effort devoted to producing partnership profits, which the Uniform Partnership says are to be divided equally among the partners unless there is a countervailing arrangement expressly in the partnership agreement.)

10. Which of the following is a FALSE statement?
    a. The liabilities of a partnership can include amounts owed to partners for their capital contributions.
    b. Limited partners are entitled to assign their interests in the partnership.
    c. A corporation as a business entity possesses some of the 5th Amendment constitutional rights in criminal cases.
    d. A Sub-chapter S corporation can have an unlimited number of shareholders as well as any and all types of classes of stock.
    (The correct answer is d. An S-Corporation can have no more than 100 shareholders and only one class of stock. Under the 5th Amendment the corporation has the privilege against double jeopardy, though not the privilege against self-incrimination which just protects "real people." Note that partners' capital contributions have to be repaid before any profits can be distributed. Moreover, if there are losses the capital contributions have to be repaid by the other partners after creditor obligations and loans by partners are paid.)

11. Which of the following is a FALSE statement?
    a. X Corporation buys Y Corporation. It is agreed that X will absorb Y. This business combination is typically called a merger.
    b. A limited partnership consists of at least one general partner.
    c. As opposed to the members of a partnership, the liability of a corporation's shareholders is limited to the amount of their investment in the corporation.
    d. A close or closely held corporation is exempt from all corporate "legalities," such as filing the articles of incorporation.
    (The correct answer is d. In a closely-held corporation the shareholders may be able to abolish the board of directors of a traditional corporation and run the business more like a partnership; but other corporate formalities and procedures, especially filing an articles, should be done to main the corporate character and limited liability advantage of the entity. As opposed to a merger, a corporate consolidation occurs when there is a union of two or more companies and a brand-new corporate entity emerges; that is, X plus Y + Z.)

12. What is FALSE about a partnership?
    a. It is an association of two or more persons to carry on a business as co-owners for profit.
    b. The sharing of the net profits of a business by a person indicates a *prima facie* case, that is, an initial case, that the person is a partner in that business.

c. Partners are considered to be fiduciaries of one another.
d. A "silent partner" can never be a real partner.
(The correct answer is d. There is nothing inherently wrong with a silent partner who is neither publicly know nor involved in the management of the partnership. Sharing of the net profits of a business is such strong evidence that a partnership exists that an initial case of the existence of a partnership is created. Sharing of the gross proceeds from a business is merely evidence that it is a partnership.)

13. What is FALSE about a partnership?
    a. All partners have an equal right to control and manage the business.
    b. A partner who is the "managing partner" is entitled to extra compensation as per the Uniform Partnership Act (UPA).
    c. Partnership profits and losses are shared equally, regardless of who created them, unless there is a contrary provision in the UPA.
    d. Partners are construed as agents of the partnership regarding conducting partnership business.
    (The correct answer is b. As emphasized, absent an express provision in the partnership agreement there is no right of a partner for compensation, regardless if the partner is the "managing partner." The other responses are fundamental partnership principles.)

14. Which of the following is a TRUE statement about partnerships?
    a. Partners always have the power, though not necessarily the right, to dissolve a partnership.
    b. A court cannot order the dissolution of a partnership as that matter is left up to the sole discretion of the partners.
    c. A partnership cannot own real property since it is merely an association of individual partners.
    d. Dissolution will automatically terminate a partnership.
    (The correct answer is a. A wrongful dissolver, that is, one who dissolves in contravention of the partnership agreement, will still dissolve the partnership but may be liable for damages for dissolving in breach of the partnership agreement. A court can order the dissolution of a partnership under certain circumstances, for examples, the partners are deadlocked in decision-making, no business is being done, and partnership assets are being wasted. A partnership for some purposes is merely considered to be an association of people doing business together, for example, when it comes to paying taxes, but in other situations the partnership is considered to be an entity, for example, holding property in the partnership names as well as bringing lawsuits and being sued. Dissolution is not termination; rather, it is just a change in the nature of the people doing business, for example, when a partner dies or retires or when a new partner comes in. Dissolution if done rightfully pursuant to the terms of the partnership agreement can lead to a winding-up of partnership affairs and an eventual termination of the partnership.)

15. Which of the following is a FALSE statement?
    a. In a limited partnership, the liability of the limited partners is limited to their investment in the partnership.
    b. A one-person corporation is illegal in most states as it is not right for one person to hold all corporate titles and offices.
    c. In order to from a typical business corporation a document, usually called an "articles of incorporation" must be filed with state authorities.
    d. The board of directors is the governing body of the corporation which establishes corporate policy.
    (The correct answer is b. A one-person corporation as well as a one-person limited liability company is legal in most states, but the one person must be very careful in fulfilling corporate or LLC requirements, forms, and

procedures so as to not have the entity disregarded pursuant to the "piercing the corporate veil" doctrine and thus losing the limited liability protection that each entity affords. Sometimes, the Articles of Incorporation is called the "charter," but usually the term "charter" applies to an Articles that has been approved by the state. Note that a limited liability company has to files an Articles of Organization.)

16. Which of the following is a FALSE statement?
    a. The bylaws of a corporation are the same as its articles of incorporation in most states.
    b. The articles of incorporation must include the office and registered agent of the corporation.
    c. The purposes of the corporation in the articles can be broadly stated as "any and all lawful business."
    d. The doctrine of "piercing the corporate veil" or "disregarding the corporate entity" can be used to hold the purported shareholders of a corporation personally liable for corporate obligations.

    (The correct answer is a. The Articles is the document that is prepared by the incorporations, filed with the appropriate state agency, usually the Secretary of State's office, and which creates the corporation and which has the most fundamental provisions, such as the corporate purpose, which can be very general or specific. and duration as well as the initial board of directors. The bylaws are the internal governing rules and regulations of the corporations, for example, when and where directors meet, quorums for voting, compensation for directors, etc. If something is very important, such as restrictions on transfers of shares or cumulative voting for directors, it should be in the articles. The bylaws are usually drafted by the board of directors named initially in the articles of incorporation at their first board meeting. Shareholders especially in small or closely-held corporations must be very careful to separate their corporate existence from their personal lives; and as such they must adhere to all corporate formalities, such as having shares and bylaws, as well as have required officers and meetings of shareholders and the board, and also have adequate capitalization for reasonably foreseeable corporate obligations; otherwise, the corporate entity may be disregarded and they will be personally and unlimitedly liable for corporate obligations.)

17. Which of the following is a FALSE statement?
    a. If a corporation is regarded as a *de facto* one the shareholders will be treated as partners.
    b. A major factor in deciding whether the "piercing the corporate veil" doctrine will be applied to a purported corporation is whether its capitalization is "thin."
    c. The duty of selecting top corporate officers is for the board of directors.
    d. Directors of a corporation may create board committees, for example, a compensation committee.

    (The correct answer is a. A de facto corporation will be treated as real corporation and thus protect the "shareholders" as shareholders, but of course the state can require the principals to file a correct Articles of Incorporation. Typically, there must be a good faith attempt to file the articles, but something required, such as the signatures of all the incorporations, is missing; but the business as otherwise looks and acts like a corporation and does business in the corporate name. Note that not having adequate capitalization, especially a lack of insurance for certain businesses, will risk being deemed a "thinly" capitalized entity and thus risk having its corporateness disregarded under the "piercing the corporate veil" theory. The other responses are fundamental corporate law principles.)

18. Which of the following is a FALSE statement?
    a. Directors are regarded by the law as fiduciaries of the corporation.
    b. Corporate "constituency" statutes in most states prohibit the board of directors from considering any stakeholder group in corporate decision-making except the short-term interests of the shareholders.

c. Cumulative voting is a device to help minority shareholders to secure some representation on the board of directors.
d. A "pooling agreement" is a device to help the shareholders gain some degree of control of corporate policy.

(The correct answer is b. Corporate constituency statutes today say that the board of directors may, not must, consider other stakeholders beyond the shareholders, for examples, the employees, local community, the environment, and society as a whole, in making corporate decisions. Directors are fiduciaries like partners and principals/agents; and as such directors cannot compete against their corporations or take advantage of business opportunities that their corporations might have an interest in unless of course they give their corporations the "right-of-first-refusal." Note that cumulative voting and pooling agreements are ways that shareholders can indirectly gain some control over the board of directors and thus over corporate policy; but also note that in most states these methods must be specified in the Articles of Incorporation.)

19. Which of the following is a FALSE statement?
    a. Generally, shareholders cannot compel the board of directors of the corporation to issue a dividend.
    b. Common stock represents the residual ownership of the corporation.
    c. The board of directors of a corporation must approve any merger plan.
    d. Preemptive rights of shareholders are illegal in most states since they maintain the current corporate ownership structure and thus perpetuate the "good old boy" network and "glass ceiling."

    (The correct answer is d. Preemptive rights are legal and a way for the current shareholders, usually of a small or closely-held corporation, to maintain their proportionate ownership interests and thus control. The adverse effect on gender is irrelevant in this case. Only rarely can the shareholders force the board to declare a dividend, typically when the corporation has a very large surplus of funds and the board of directors have no plans whatsoever as to what to do with it. Usually the shareholders have to approve a merger too, but there are some exceptions.)

20. What is TRUE about a Limited Liability Company (LLC)?
    a. LLCs are illegal in most states since they impermissibly combine elements of the partnership and corporation ways of doing business.
    b. An Articles of Incorporation is usually required to be filed with state taxing authorities to form an LLC.
    c. The LLC generally is not treated as a separate legal entity distinct from its members.
    d. The name of a limited liability company must include the words "Limited Liability Company" or "LLC."

    (The correct answer is d. LLCs are quite legal and a preferable way of doing business especially for a small entrepreneur as they can be managed like a sole proprietorship or partnership but retain the great corporate benefit of limited liability of the members. LLCs are formed by the filing of an Articles of Organization with the appropriate state official, who usually is the state's Secretary of State, who also is in charge of processing the filing of Articles of Incorporation for corporate formation.)

21. What is FALSE about a Limited Liability Company?
    a. An Articles of Organization must be filed with the appropriate state authority in order to have an LLC.
    b. An LLC can be member-managed or manager-managed.
    c. As a general rule, a member of an LLC has an equal share to the LLC's profits (and equal responsibility for losses) unless that allocation is changed in the LLC's operating agreement.

d. LLCs are primarily governed by the franchise rules promulgated by the U.S. Federal Trade Commission.

(The correct answer is d. Franchise rules are based on federal law, primarily FTC rules, for businesses doing business as part of a franchise structure. Of course, it is permissible for the business holding the franchise to be an LLC or a corporation, though they are governed by state law. Of course, the franchisor might object to the limited liability of its franchisees being corporations of LLCs. The other responses are fundamental LLC rules.)

22 - Personal Property, Gifts, and Bailments

Introduction

This section deals with three inter-related yet distinct legal areas – personal property law, the law of gifts, and the law of bailments. For personal property law, the student must be aware of the principal methods by which a person can acquire ownership of personal property – accession (improvement) and confusion (intermingling). Similarly, the student must know the definitions and distinctions among abandoned, mislaid, and lost property as well as how a person can obtain ownership of such property. For gifts, the student must be aware of the definitions and distinction between an *inter vivos* gift and a gift *causa mortis*. Regarding an *inter vivos* gift, it is critical that the student understand the three requirements – donative intent, delivery, and acceptance. Regarding gifts *causa mortis*, the student must be aware that such a gift may be superseded by the state's statutory law on wills. For bailments, the student must be aware of the three types of bailment – for the sole benefit of the bailor, for the sole benefit of the bailee, and a mutual benefit bailment – as well as the rights and duties of the parties regarding each type of bailment. Particularly important are the negligence rules pertaining to the degree of care required by the bailee in each type of bailment. Finally, the student should be aware that if the bailment situation involves common carriers and innkeepers the common law rules will be superseded by state statutes which were mainly designed to protect common carriers and innkeepers.

True and False Questions with Answers and Explanations

1. A trespasser by accession to personal property can never acquire title to the property.
(*False: Accession is the improvement of personal property by artificial means. If a trespasser to personal property of negligible worth greatly increases the value of the property, he or she can be granted title although the trespasser will have to pay damages for the wrongful taking. This rule would apply, for example, when a thief steals a "junk car" and by a great deal of work turns it into a "classic car," assuming the car was not abandoned property.)*

2. If a person willfully, fraudulently, or otherwise wrongfully commingles his or her goods with the goods of another, and the goods of each cannot be identified, separated, and removed, the innocent party the innocent party acquires title to all the goods.
(True: Comingling of goods is called at times "confusion." If it is done purposefully and wrongfully the wrongful comingling party forfeits all ownership and title to the goods.)

3. When personal property is abandoned, the person who discovers and takes possession of it acquires title thereto.
(True: The property must be abandoned, as opposed to being mislaid or lost. Property is abandoned when the owner has discarded it with no intention of reclaiming it.)

4. If personal property is "lost" the finder of the property has the right to possession against everyone except the true owner.

(True: Personal property is lost when through carelessness, neglect, or accident one unintentionally and involuntarily leaves the property somewhere, but there was no intention on the part of the owner to leave the property, yet the owner has no knowledge of its location. In such a case, there are state statutes that have notice and posting procedures and time period requirements that if followed will allow the finder to obtain title to the property.)

5. A person who innocently adds great value to personal property not his or her own can acquire good title to the property.
(True: This is called "trespass by accession," but if innocent, though technically a trespass to chattels or goods, the innocent party can obtain title to the property but must pay money damages to the owner. An example would be when a party purposefully but mistakenly takes the owner's grapes but converts them into wine.)

6. An *inter vivos* gift is a gift between two living persons.
(True: As opposed to a gift causa mortis which is a gift motivated by impending death, and which is not favored in the law as such a gift may contravene state statutes on wills.)

7. An *inter vivos* gift requires consideration, delivery, and acceptance of the gift.
(False: The common law requirement of consideration for a valid contract is not required for a gift. However, a donative intent is; that is, the donor of the gift must intend to make an effective present gift of the property., meaning the owner intends to transfer ownership of the property but not mere possession or the right to use the property.)

8. The expression of an intent in the future to make a gift can be the basis for an *inter vivos* gift if the subject matter of the gift is presently existing.
(False: To be effective as a gift the intent must be a present intent. For example, if a father says to a daughter that she can have the father's sports car when he dies there is no gift since there is no present intent.)

9. In order to have a valid delivery of a gift the property always must be physically delivered by the donor to the donee.
(False: A delivery can occur if the donee is already in possession of the property and as such the law dispenses with a formal delivery requirement. Moreover, a "constructive" delivery can occur when the subject matter of the gift is too large or too far away for a physical delivery, such as car or building; and as such a delivery will occur if the donor gives the donee something, for example, a key, that gives the donee control over the subject matter of the gift. Another example would be giving to the donee a safe deposit box key which would be construed as the delivery of the contents of box as the gift.)

10. A donor is allowed to revoke his or her gift to the donee if the donor has a "change of heart."
(False: When there is an inter vivos gift complete ownership is vested in the donee; and consequently the donor cannot revoke his or her gift; however, there are exceptions for fraud/deceit and mistake.)

11. When a person makes a gift intending it to be effective on his or her death there usually will be a legal gift since there is an intent to make a gift.
(False: The intent must be a present intent to make a gift. Moreover, such a purported gift may contravene the state statute for wills.)

12. A bailment is the delivery of personal property by one person to another pursuant to an agreement that the identical property is to be returned.
(True: This is the fundamental bailment definition. The person transferring the property is called the "bailor" and the person to whom it is delivered is called the "bailee.")

13. A bailment can arise only regarding personal property.
(True: There cannot be a bailment of land. However, there may be a bailment of intangible personal property, such as by means of a delivery of a stock certificate.)

14. In order to have a valid bailment, the delivery of the goods to the bailee must be a knowing delivery and acceptance.
(True: For example, when a patron goes to a restaurant and leaves his or her coat on a coat rack there is no bailment because the restaurant owner is not in knowing possession. However, if the customer checks his or her coat with an attendant in a coat room there is a bailment. Similarly, if the owner of a car parks his or her car in a parking lot and keeps the keys there is no bailment since there is no substantial control of the goods, as opposed to the car lot keeping the owner's keys.)

15. In order for there to be a valid bailment the bailor must be the owner of the property.
(False: The law only requires that the bailor have a superior interest in the property over the bailee. For example, when a person loans his or her car to a friend for the summer, and the friend takes the car to a dealership for service before returning it to the owner, a bailment has occurred.)

16. The law regards a bailee who is compensated as an insurer or guarantor of the property
(False: The bailee is only liable if there is some fault on the part of the bailee, such as negligent conduct which damages or destroys the bailed goods. However, there is a presumption of negligence when the bailed goods are damaged or destroyed while in the bailee's possession. This presumption can be rebutted by the bailee.)

17. In a sole benefit for the bailee bailment, the bailor is only legally required to disclose defects in the property which the bailor actually knows of.
(True: However, in a bailment for the sole benefit of the bailor or a mutual benefit bailment the bailor must also disclose defects that the bailor should know of.)

18. A bailment can end automatically by operation of the law if the bailee acts improperly or violates the terms of the bailment agreement.
(True: A bailment if at-will can end by the choice of either party; and a bailment for a term or for a purpose can end when the term ends or the purpose is achieved.)

19. Under the common law, common carriers and innkeepers were absolutely liable for the damage of destruction of their passengers' and guests' property.
(True: Yet note that these old common law rules have been changed today by state statutes which typically require passengers and guests to prove negligence on the part of common carriers and innkeepers as well as limit the damages that can be recovered.)

20. If there is a mis-delivery of the property by the bailee to a person who is not the bailor, the bailee is absolutely liable for any damage or loss.
(True: Even if merely mistaken, the bailee is liable; and this liability is premised on the breach of the bailment agreement.)

Multiple Choice Questions with Answers and Explanations

1. When personal property is intentionally and voluntarily left in some place by the owner and then forgot by the owner, this property is:
   a. abandoned
   b. mislaid
   c. lost
   d. a fixture
   (The correct answer is b. Calling property "mislaid" means that the owner could recollect its location and thus obtain his or her property. However, if the owner cannot be found or does not claim the property in a certain time as determined by statute, the owner of the "locus in quo," that is, the place where the property was mislaid, can obtain title to it.)

2. When the goods of different owners are intermixed or intermingled so that the property of each cannot be distinguished, this is legally called:
   a. Confusion of goods
   b. Accession of goods
   c. Mislaid goods
   d. Frustration of purpose of goods
   (The correct answer is a. This situation is known as "confusion" in the law as well as "intermingling." If the confusion, for example, of cattle or wheat, is done purposefully the wrongful intermingle loses all right and title to the goods, the innocent party acquires the goods, and is under no obligation to compensate the wrongdoer; However, there is an exception to the general confusion rule if the intermingle can prove clearly and exactly which goods are his or hers. If the confusion is done inadvertently or by mistake the parties become tenants-in-common of the intermingled goods in proportion to their interests. However, if it is impossible to tell the respective proportionate interests, the loss is placed on the party that caused the intermixture, even if innocently.

3. An *inter vivos* gift requires the following:
   a. donative intent
   b. delivery
   c. acceptance
   d. All of the above.
   (The correct answer is d. These are the basic requirements for a valid gift between two living persons. Note that the donative intent must be a present intent to make a gift and not a future one and that the common law contract of consideration is not required.)

4. To have a valid gift *causa mortis*:
   a. there must be a fear of imminent death
   b. actual physical delivery of the item or a written conveyance is necessary
   c. the subject matter is limited to personal property
   d. All of the above.
   (The correct answer is d. These are all requirements of a gift causa mortis. Constructive delivery is insufficient for this type of gift.)

5. A gift *causa mortis* is:
   a. not revocable by the donor like an *inter vivos* gift.
   b. revocable automatically when the donor recovers from the illness or escapes the peril which motivated the gift.
   c. revocable automatically if the donee dies before the donor.

d. Answers a. and b.
(The correct answer is d. A gift causa mortis is always revocable by the donor as well as revocable automatically as per the other answers.)

6. The delivery requirement for a legal bailment can be satisfied by:
   a. physical delivery and transfer of possession of the goods.
   b. the recipient being given a substantial measure of control of the goods.
   c. the delivery was knowingly accepted by the recipient.
   d. All of the above.
   (The correct answer is d. Note that there also can be a "constructive" or implied delivery, for example, when the owner of the goods, for example, a car, gives the bailee the keys as well as a copy of the title in order to obtain the car from a third-party.)

7. A bailment can be:
   a. for the sole benefit of the bailee.
   b. for the sole benefit of the bailor.
   c. for the mutual benefit of the bailor and bailee.
   d. All of the above.
   (The correct answer is d. An example of a would be when one loans a car or a tool to a friend. An example of b would be when a home owner allows a neighbor to park his or her car in the owner's garage. An example of c would be when one rents a tool from a tool renting business.)

8. Once property is delivered to the bailee the bailee has the right to:
   a. exclusive use of the property
   b. exclusive possession of the property
   c. compensation for the bailment
   d. Answers a. and b.
   (The correct answer is d. Generally, there is no right to compensation for the bailee unless specified in the bailment agreement. Moreover, there is no right to be reimbursed for minor repairs or incidental expenses unless specified in the agreement. However, regardless of any agreement there is an exception for expenses that were reasonably necessary to protect and preserve the goods, for example, veterinarian's expenses for caring for a horse that got very sick.)

9. How much care must be exercised by the bailee?
   a. In a mutual benefit bailment, the bailee must exercise reasonable and ordinary care.
   b. In a bailment for the sole benefit of the bailor the bailor must exercise slight care.
   c. In a bailment for the sole benefit of the bailee the bailee must exercise great care.
   d. All of the above.
   (The correct answer is d. Note that these "care" determinations will likely have to be made by a jury. Note too that if a bailee substantially deviates from the terms of the bailment agreement and a loss results from the bailee using the property in an unauthorized manner, the bailee is absolutely liable even without a showing of negligence.)

10. The rights of a bailor are:
    a. the return of the property at the end of the bailment period.
    b. the exercise of reasonable care under the circumstances.
    c. the use of the property in conformity with the terms of the bailment agreement.
    d. All of the above.
    (The correct answer is d. Also, the bailment agreement may give the bailor the right to compensation.)

23 - Real Property and Landlord-Tenant Relations

Introduction

Real property law is a very large and important area of the law. Critically important are knowing the major categories by which real property can be owned, that is, fee simple, life estates (including distinguishing between remainder and reversion interests), and concurrent ownership, that is, joint tenancy, tenancy by the entirety, and tenancy in common. The student also must be aware of non-possessory interests in land and thus should know the definitions of and distinctions among an easement, license, and a profit. Pertaining to the transfer of ownership of real estate the student must know the distinction between the real estate contract and the deed, what a closing is, and the seller's implied warranty of habitability. Furthermore, the student must be able to define and differentiate among a general warranty deed, a special warranty deed, and a quitclaim deed. Good title, marketable title, title insurance, abstracts of title, and recording statutes are also aspects of real property law that the student should be cognizant of. Finally, the student must be aware of the doctrines of adverse possession as well as eminent domain, though the latter subject will also arise in constitutional law.

Landlord-tenant law is a body of law that is heavily dependent on state and local statutes, particularly with regard to evicting tenants. Nevertheless, the student must be aware of fundamental common law definitions and principles, such as knowing the parties, the landlord/lessor and the tenant/lessee, as well as knowing that the lease agreement is a contract as well as the basic nature of that contract. The student also must able to differentiate among a fixed tenancy, a periodic tenancy, and a tenancy at-will. Moreover, the student must know the basic principles regarding the possession, use, and enjoyment, and maintenance of the leased premised, called the leasehold, and the obligation to pay rent. The landlord's implied warranty of habitability, imposed by common law or statute, is an important feature of landlord-tenant law. Another important aspect of this body of law deals with the tenant's attempted transfer of the lease, called an assignment of the lease, or the tenant's attempted transfer of a part of the lease, called sub-leasing (which the authors believe is also of very practical importance to college students).

True and False Questions with Answers and Explanations

1. Fee simple ownership of real property is the highest form of ownership recognized by the common law.
(True: "An Englishman's home is his (or her) castle.")

2. The landlord-tenant relationship is established by contract.
(True: The contract is a lease contract, where the landlord, the lessor, agrees to lease to the tenant, the lessee, the exclusive right to rent and possess the property, the leasehold, typically for a specified period of time and for a specified price.)

3. A lease contract must be in writing as per the Statute of Frauds since it is an interest in land.
(False: In most states lease contracts can be oral if they are less than one year, though, obviously, written contracts are preferable in all cases.)

4. The landlord owes to the tenant a covenant of "quiet enjoyment."
(True: Pursuant to this covenant, which is implied in the landlord-tenant relationship, the landlord promises that the landlord will not disturb the tenant's use and enjoyment of the property.)

5. A "constructive eviction" is when the landlord acts or fails to act and consequently hinders or prevents the tenant from using and enjoying the leased premises.
(True: The "classic" example is when the landlord turns off the heat in the premises located in New Jersey during the winter, or the AC in Florida in the summer.)

6. Pursuant to some state statutes as well as the common law a landlord is deemed to make an implied warranty of habitability regarding the leased premises.
(True: In essence, this warranty simply means that the premises are fit for human beings to live in. However, this warranty is limited to major and substantial defects, such as a hole in the roof, that the landlord knows or should know of, and not merely a condition that is minor and insubstantial, such as a crack in the wall or an old water spot on the ceiling.)

7. As a general rule, a tenant is still obligated to pay rent even if the tenant does not occupy the premises or moves out.
(True: This rule assumes that the tenant was not justified in not moving in or moving out and the lease contract is still in effect.)

8. A sublease does not release the original tenant from his or her responsibilities in paying the rent.
(True: A sublease occurs when the tenant seeks to transfer part of the premises for a period that is shorter than the original lease term. Whereas an assignment of a lease occurs when the tenant seeks to assign or transfer his or her entire interest in the lease to the assignee/transferee. Note that most lease contracts have clauses either prohibiting assignment or subleasing or requiring the landlord's approval.)

9. A periodic tenancy will renew automatically unless either the landlord or tenant gives timely notice of non-renewal.
(True: An example would be a lease without a fixed term or a fixed-term lease that ends but the tenant remains and pays rent on a month-to-month basis. As such, a periodic tenancy is created and one month's notice by either party is required to terminate the tenancy.)

10. When a tenant breaches the lease agreement and leaves the property the landlord does not have to rent the premises but can sue the tenant for all the remaining rent as *per* the lease.
(False: The landlord must adhere to the traditional contract rule of Mitigation of Damages and thus make a reasonable and good faith effort to rent the premises to suitable tenants; but if that effort was unsuccessful the tenant is liable for the rent.)

11. The ownership of real property includes the rights to the surface of the property as well as the subsurface.
(True: Subsurface rights include the rights to find, remove, and sell oil, gas, and minerals, which is called a profit right.)

12. A tenancy by the entirely is a joint tenancy between a husband and a wife.
(True: However, one key difference in most states is that neither husband nor wife may transfer his or her interest in the property during his or her lifetime unless the other spouse consents.)

13. Community property refers to property acquired by a husband and wife during their marriage wherein they own an undivided one-half interest in the property.
(True: However, property acquired prior to marriage or property acquired during marriage by gift or inheritance is not community property.)

14. A fixture is a piece of personal property that becomes permanently fixed to real property and thus becomes part of the real property.
(True: This is because a fixture cannot be removed without damaging the real property. An example would be floor tiles that are affixed to the floor.)

15. The "closing" is the real estate transaction where the buyer and seller sign the real estate contract.
(False: The closing is where the previously signed real estate contract is effectuated and the deed to the property is transferred from the seller to the buyer.)

16. Pursuant to the implied warranty of habitability the seller of a home impliedly warrants that the home is fit for habitation by human beings.
(True: Today this warranty is based primarily on state statutes; and a "reasonableness" test is used to measure "fitness.")

17. In a quitclaim deed the grantor/seller of real property transfers whatever interests he or she has in the property and the grantor/seller also makes a warranty that he or she has good title to that interest.
(False: No warranties are made with a quitclaim deed; the grantor only conveys the interest he or she had in the property, nothing more.)

18. In a special warranty deed the grantor warrants that he or she has the right to sell the property, but the grantor does not warrant the genuineness of any prior grantor's title.
(True: This type of deed is mainly used by executors and administrators of estates, trustees, and sheriffs at foreclosure sales; and as such they only warrant that they have the right to sell whatever interest the owner had in the property.)

19. Delivery of the deed is an essential requirement to the transfer of real property.
(True: Delivery means the grantor/seller must give up possession and control of the deed to the grantee/buyer. A deed is not effective to transfer real property until it is delivered.)

20. The recording of a deed is essential to its validity and the transfer of real property.
(False: A deed need not be recorded to transfer ownership of real property; however, the deed most certainly should be recorded pursuant to state recording statutes to provide clarity and certainly as to ownership and to prevent fraud.)

21. Obtaining title insurance is a requirement to the transfer of real property.
(False: Title insurance, purchased from a title insurance company, is not required but certainly is advisable. Consequently, if there is any loss to the insured grantee due to undiscovered title defects to the property, the grantee will be reimbursed by the title insurance company. Note that an Abstract of Title is usually a component to the purchase of title insurance; the Abstract shows the complete history of the property – deeds, mortgages, taxes, judgments, liens, paid and unpaid.)

22. A life estate with a remainder means that once the life tenant dies the property remains with the original owner.
(False: When the property goes back to the original owner when the life tenant dies the real property interest is called a reversion; a remainder occurs when the property remains away from the owner and goes to a third-party.)

23. Accretion of property occurs when the boundary to property is a river, stream, lake, or ocean, and the land is increased by the shifting flow of the water or the depositing of soil, silt, or sand on the bank.
(True: Accretion must not be confused with accession, which is an increase in property by substantially improving it or the increase in property already owned, such as the products of the land or offspring of animals.)

24. Adverse possession is a means of acquiring title to real property by occupying it for a period of time set by statute, usually 21 years, if the occupation is continuous, open, visible, exclusive, interrupted, and hostile.
(True: "Hostile" does not imply any violence! Hostile occupation merely means that one is asserting an ownership interest in the property against the legal interests of the title holder.)

25. In a condominium and a cooperative the owners have fee simple ownership to their units.
(False: In a condominium the owners own their units in fee simple, but the condominium association owns the common elements, e.g., grounds, driveways, pool, clubhouse, etc.; whereas in a cooperative a corporation owns the buildings, land, and improvements, and the individual unit owners own stock in the corporation which enables them to enter into long-term leases for their respective units.)

26. A mortgage is a lien on real property to secure a debt.
(True: Note that the mortgage is not the debt itself, but only security for the debt. A mortgagor is the person who gives the mortgage for the loan of money and as security for the debt; and the mortgagee, typically a bank, is the entity that holds the mortgage for security; and if the debt is not paid the mortgagee takes possession of the property or sells it.)

27. When a buyer buys mortgaged property "subject to the mortgage" the buyer becomes primarily liable on the property as fully as the original mortgagor.
(False: Buying "subject to the mortgage" means the buyer is not personally responsible on the mortgage debt; Whereas buying and "assuming the mortgage" means the buyer is primarily liable on the mortgage as fully as the original owner. This is a very important distinction in mortgage law.)

28. A variance is an exemption to a local zoning law.
(True: Zoning laws specify permissible uses of property, for example, residential neighborhoods, business and commercial, industrial, mixed, etc. An exemption for a different use is accomplished by seeking a variance. This exemption is usually granted by the local zoning board. The party requesting the variance must show hardship if the variance is not granted, and also must show that the character of the neighborhood will not be materially changed by the variance.)

29. Marketable title means that the grantor/seller owns the property free from any encumbrances, liens, prior interests, and defects (except those disclosed to the grantee/buyer).
(True: Marketable title is good title! If the buyer discovers after signing the real estate contract that the seller does not have good title the buyer can withdraw from the contract without penalty. The buyer and/or lender usually performs a title search, that is, an examination of public records, in order to ascertain if the seller's title is marketable.)

30. Eminent domain is the power and right the government has to take private land for public use.
(True: This is also called the "condemnation power." An example would be local government taking private homes to extend an airport runway. However, pursuant to the 5th Amendment to the U.S. Constitution the government must pay the property owners just compensation for the "taking.")

Multiple Choice Questions with Answers and Explanations

1. When Joseph transfers his house by means of a deed to his mother for her lifetime and with a remainder to his sister, Joseph:
   a. Created a life-estate in his sister.
   b. Reserved a remainder to himself.
   c. Created a remainder in favor of his sister.
   d. Did nothing since all future interests in properties are illegal.
   (The correct answer is c. Joseph's mother is granted a life-estate. When she dies the property "remains away" from Joseph and goes to his sister in the form of a remainder. If the property when back to Joseph after the death of his mother, he would have a reversion. Future interests in property are permissible but one must be aware of the Rule Against Perpetuities which places constraints on the long-term passing of title.)

2. Which of the following is TRUE about real property?
   a. In a joint tenancy with a right of survivorship, when one joint tenant dies his or her interest in the property passes automatically to the surviving joint tenant.
   b. The real estate contract is the legal instrument that transfers title to property.
   c. "Quitclaim deeds" are illegal since no warranties of title are made by the grantor.
   d. Real property cannot be owned concurrently in the U.S. since the government will not know exactly who is going to pay the taxes on the property.
   (The correct answer is a. If the joint tenants are spouses, the tenancy is called a "tenancy by the entireties." The legal instrument that transfers the title to the property is called the "deed." The real estate contract is "merely" the legal agreement of purchase/sale which designates a time for a "closing" and the transfer of the property by means of the deed, which must be recorded in the county where the property is located. Quitclaim deeds are permissible, but the grantor is merely transferring whatever interest he or she has in the property without making any warranties as to title. Real property can be owned concurrently in the U.S. by means of the afore mentioned joint tenancy, tenancy by the entirety, as well as by means of a tenancy in common, though in the later there is no right of survivorship.)

3. In a landlord-tenant relationship, the tenant:
   a. is responsible for damages caused to the leasehold intentionally or through carelessness.
   b. cannot create a nuisance by engaging in conduct which prevents other tenants or people from enjoying the possession and use of their property.
   c. generally, is not responsible for ordinary wear-and-tear to the leasehold
   d. All of the above.
   (The correct answer is d. These are all fundamental principles of landlord-tenant law. Note too that the tenant is not responsible for the ordinary depreciation of the leasehold as it ages.)

4. The following are all examples of concurrent ownership of real property EXCEPT:
   a. tenancy in common
   b. joint tenancy
   c. life estate
   d. tenancy by the entirety
   (The correct answer is c. A life estate is an estate in property that exists only for the life of a specific named individual, called the life-tenant, who has the exclusive ownership and use of the property until he or she dies.)

5. What is FALSE about a tenancy in common?
   a. It is a form of co-ownership of real property by two or more people who own an undivided interest in the property.
   b. Each tenant has the right to the whole property.
   c. When a co-tenant dies his or her interest passes to the co-tenants.
   d. A co-tenant can transfer his or her interest in the property without the permission of the other co-tenants.

   (The correct answer is c. When a tenant in common dies, his or her interest in the property goes to his or her heirs pursuant to the will or the state's laws of intestacy if there is no will. Note that the agreement creating the tenancy in common may require the consent of the other co-tenants for a transfer by a co-tenant.)

6. What is FALSE about a joint tenancy?
   a. Each of two or more people own an undivided interest in real property.
   b. When a joint tenant dies his or her ownership interest in the property automatically passes on to the surviving joint tenant(s).
   c. A joint tenant can transfer his or her interest in the property with the consent of the other joint tenant(s).
   d. When a joint tenant transfers the property, the transferee becomes a joint tenant along with the other joint tenant(s).

   (The correct answer is d. When a joint tenant transfers his or her ownership interest in the property by sale of gift, the joint tenancy terminates, and the transferee and the remaining joint tenants become tenants in common of the property.)

7. What is TRUE about a periodic tenancy?
   a. It is created when a lease does not specify a length but does provide for a date by which rent is to be paid at certain intervals, such as month-to-month.
   b. It can arise when a landlord allows a tenant to hold-over, that is, to retain possession and pay rent after a lease-term ends.
   c. Generally, notice equivalent to the rental period must be given to terminate a periodic tenancy, for example, a one month's notice for a month-to-month tenancy.
   d. All of the above are true.

   (The correct answer is d. These are all characteristics of a periodic tenancy; but note that there may be state statutes dealing with the notice time periods required for termination.)

8. Non-possessory interests in land include:
   a. Easements
   b. Licenses
   c. Profits
   d. All of the above.

   (The correct answer is d. An easement is the right to make use of another person's land without taking anything from the land, for example, an easement across the land to provide walking access to the beach. A profit is an easement but also includes the right to take away part of the land or something from the land, for example, soil, gravel, or sand. A license is merely a right given by the owner of the land, which is a revocable right, to allow someone to come on the land, for example, the right to park a car on someone's property; it is not a conveyance of an interest in the property.)

9. Pursuant to a general warranty deed:
   a. The grantor/seller warrants that he or she has good title to the property and all prior grantors had good title.
   b. The grantor/seller warrants that there are no defects in the grantor/seller's title.
   c. The grantor/seller warrants that there are no defects in any prior grantor/seller's title.
   d. All of the above.

   (The correct answer is d. This is the type of deed typically required in real estate contracts. Note that the grantor/seller also warrants that he or she will defend the grantee/buyer against any claims against the property.)

10. A deed must contain the following elements:
    a. The names of the grantor and the grantee and the signature of the grantor.
    b. Words indicating an intent to convey the property.
    a. A legally sufficient description of the land.
    b. All of the above.

    (The correct answer is d. Note that the signature of the grantor's spouse is usually required too. Examples of words that convey the intent to convey are "sell," "grant," "give," and, of course, "convey." Note also that the description of the property must be sufficiently detailed to distinguish the conveyed property from every other piece of land, which is usually accomplished by using official recorded land and plat surveys and boundary maps, as well as measuring distances between points and physical features of the land and surrounding land.)

24 - Commercial Paper and Banking Transactions

Introduction

Commercial paper law consists of the law of commercial paper as *per* the Uniform Commercial Code as well as the law of banking transactions, which is also premised on the UCC though modified by federal banking regulations. The student should be aware of the rationales behind commercial paper law, especially the intent that such paper flow freely in commerce and be a substitute for money. The student must first know the types of commercial paper as well as the parties thereto, especially who is primarily liable on a negotiable instrument and who is secondarily liable. The student then must know what makes an instrument a "negotiable" instrument and thus governed by the UCC. Next, the student must know how negotiable instruments are issued and transferred, which is the area of commercial paper law dealing with the "negotiation" of negotiable instruments. Particularly important to the negotiation process are the types of endorsements on negotiable instruments. Next, the student must know who can become a "holder" of a negotiable instrument, and then, most importantly, who can become a holder-in-due-course (HDC) of a negotiable instrument, which is a very elevated position under commercial law. However, there are some defenses that will preclude even an HDC from recovering on an instrument; and thus the student must know the distinction between as well as the types of personal defenses as opposed to real, also called "universal," defenses. Regarding the liability on negotiable instruments the student must be cognizant of the distinction between contract liability, called liability "on the instrument," including the parties who are primarily and secondarily contractually liable on negotiable instruments. Moreover, the student must know the conditions or requirements that a holder of a negotiable instrument must fulfill when a primary party dishonors an instrument in order to hold a secondary party liable. Moreover, in addition to contract liability, the student must know the essential aspects of implied warranty liability. This type of liability, at times called liability "off the instrument," is based on the transfer of an instrument as well as based on the presentment of a negotiable instrument for payment. Regarding banking transactions, the student must know the basic rules dealing with the bank's relationship with its customers as well as basic bank collection procedures, especially the federal regulations and the protections afforded to customers in this era of electronic and online banking. Finally, to go back to commercial paper law the student should understand that just because an instrument is not a "negotiable" one it is not worthless; rather, it is evidence of contract rights and duties and thus governed by the common law of contracts and not the UCC, particularly the contract rules dealing with assignment of contract rights.

True and False Questions with Answers and Explanations

1. For a negotiable instrument to be used as a credit device it must be payable only a demand.
(False: A negotiable instrument can be payable on a future date, for example, a promissory note with a promise to pay at a future specified date.)

2. The person who writes a check is called a drawer.
(True: A check is a form of a draft, a three-party negotiable instrument. The drawer by writing the check orders the drawee, typically a bank, to pay a sum of money to a payee.)

3. A trade acceptance is a promise by a buyer to purchase goods from a seller.
(False: A trade acceptance is a special form of a draft used in the sale of goods.)

4. A promissory note can be made payable at a definite time in the future.
(True: A note can also be payable on demand. In either case it acts as a credit device as well as a negotiable instrument.)

5. A clause in a promissory note that states that payment is contingent on a fund that may or may not materialize renders the note non-negotiable.
(True: An example would be payment is to be made "from the proceeds of the sale of my business." The rationale is that negotiable instruments are supposed to be a substitute for money and thus should "flow freely" in commerce and not be impeded by contingencies, such as restricted payment sources.)

6. A promissory note can refer to an agreement on which the note is based and still be a negotiable instrument.
(True: Mere reference to other agreements or contracts is permissible; however, making an instrument contingent on another agreement or incorporating its terms will render the instrument non-negotiable. For example, a note that is "subject" to a contract is not negotiable.)

7. A promissory note with a clause stating that the payee or any holder can demand payment in full, including interest, if the maker fails to make one payment is not negotiable.
(False: This is an example of a valid acceleration clause in a note, which makes the note more valuable and transferable in commerce.)

8. A promissory note with a set date for payment but also including a clause saying that the payee or any holder of the note can extend the time of payment indefinitely if so desired renders the note non-negotiable.
(False: The clause when operational will convert the instrument into a demand instrument. The payee or any holder will know when he or she will be paid, that is, on demand, and thus the time-period as per the clause is not uncertain.)

9. If a person loses an instrument made "payable to bearer" a finder of the instrument cannot collect on it since he or she did not pay for the instrument or do anything for it.
(False: The finder is a holder and can collect, which demonstrates the risk of making instruments payable to bearer as opposed to the order of a specific person, who must endorse the instrument to transfer it legally to a holder.)

10. A special endorsement occurs when the payee of an instrument endorses it over to another specific person.
(True: For example, the payee endorses the instrument "pay to the order of X" and then the payee signs his or her name.)

11. A holder may give "value" for an instrument if the holder takes the instrument as payment for an antecedent debt.
(True: Value will also be present if the holder takes the instrument as security for an antecedent debt.)

12. A forgery of a name in the chain of title of an instrument will prevent any subsequent person from becoming a legal "holder" of the instrument.
(True: Such a forgery will destroy the chain of title and prevent any subsequent transferee from being a holder and thus not a holder-in-due-course either.)

13. A check that is returned with an "insufficient funds" notice on it will prevent any subsequent holder from being a holder-in-due course.
(True: The reason is that the holder is deemed to have notice of a problem with the instrument, thus precluding holder-in-due-course status.)

14. A transferee of a negotiable instrument cannot achieve holder-in-due-course status pursuant to the Shelter Doctrine if he or she knows of a problem with or a claim or defense to the instrument.
(False: The transferee can obtain the rights of a prior holder-in-due-course who lacked knowledge of the problem pursuant to the Shelter Doctrine. However, the transferee must not be connected to any problems with the instrument and the transferee cannot be a prior holder with knowledge of a problem (and thus attempt to "wash" the instrument through a holder-in-due-course.)

15. Personal defenses can be used by holders of instruments as well as holders-in-due-course to prevent payment on the instrument.
(False: A holder-in-due-course (HDC) can cut through personal defenses and recover on the instrument as HDC status is an elevated one in the law and designed to promote the use of negotiable instruments as a substitute for money.)

16. The unauthorized completion of an incomplete instrument is a real or universal defense that will preclude a holder-in-due course from recovering on the instrument.
(False: Unauthorized completion is only a personal defense which an HDC can cut through, and which thus illustrates the risk of signing incomplete instruments.)

17. Fraud-in-the-inducement is only a personal defense that will not stop a holder-in-due-course from recovering on the instrument.
(True: This type of fraud must be distinguished from fraud-in-the-factum where a person signs a negotiable instrument not knowing that he or she is even signing one because of the deceit. For example, a person is told to sign a form to open a bank account, but the "form" is really a negotiable instrument. Fraud-in-the-factum is a real defense that will stop and HDC. With fraud-in-the-inducement a person knows that he or she is signing a negotiable instrument, but the victim was fraudulently deceived as to the reason or signing the instrument.)

18. Breach of contract is a real or universal defense.
(False: It is merely a personal one which an HDC can cut through.)

19. A drawer is primarily liable on a negotiable instrument because the drawer was the party who originally created the instrument.
(False: The drawee, once it accepts the draft, becomes primarily liable, and the drawer is only secondarily liable.)

20. When a dishonest employee deceives his or her employer into signing a negotiable instrument payable to a payee who has no rightful claim to the instrument a transferee who takes the instrument in good faith can acquire legal title.
(True: This is called the Fictitious Payee doctrine.)

21. When a person presents an instrument for payment he or she impliedly warrants that he or she has good title to it.
(True: That is, the presenter warrants that he or she has "holder" status, that is, there were no forgeries in the chain-of-title of the instrument and the endorsements over to the holder were genuine.)

22. As a general rule, when a bank learns of a customer's death it can pay or certify checks for 10 days after death.
(True: The exception is when any person who claims an interest in the account can order the bank to stop payment or no longer certify checks regardless of the validity of that person's claim.)

23. A draft is a conditional promise to pay money to a person.
(False: A draft is an instrument whereby a person, the drawer, orders another, the drawee, which is typically a bank, to pay money to a third-party payee. Conditions in an instrument, whether draft or promissory note, render it non-negotiable.)

24. A draft payable at a definite time in the future is a sight draft.
(False: Such a draft is a time draft, whereas a sight draft is a demand instrument, that is, one that is payable "on sight" or whenever the payee presents it to the drawee for payment.)

25. If there are only two parties to a negotiable instrument it is very likely a promissory note.
(True: A note would have as parties the Maker and a Payee, whereas a draft is a three-party instrument consisting of a drawer, a drawee, and a payee.)

26. For a promissory note to be negotiable it need not state the consideration given in exchange for the maker's promise to pay.
(True: The note could be given in the form of a gift or as security; and thus consideration need not necessarily be stated let alone be given. However, consideration given may later be a factor in determining whether the holder of the note has given value for it and thus may qualify as a holder-in-due-course.)

27. A written and signed "IOU" can be construed as a negotiable instrument if one can logically infer a promise to pay by the person signing.
(False: A negotiable instrument requires a promise or order to pay. As such, the mere acknowledgment of a debt, as in the form of an "IOU," is not adequate for the instrument to become a negotiable instrument, but it may be evidence of the debt to sustain a lawsuit.)

28. The maker stating in a promissory note that source of funds that the maker plans to make payment of the note renders the note not negotiable.
(False: Merely mentioning the source of the expected or planned payment, for example, from the sale of some property, does not ruin negotiability. However, conditioning the note on a specific source of expected funds will destroy negotiability since the payee or subsequent holder will not know if the source of funds is available.)

29. If the amount of money fixed in an instrument is to be paid with interest, in installments, or with a discount for early payment, the instrument is not negotiable since the amount is not specific and definite.
(False: Such provisions do not impair negotiability because one can determine mathematically at some point what the exact amount to be paid will be.)

30. An instrument is payable if the interest rate stated is the "legal rate."
(True: The legal rate would be the highest amount allowed by state law. The interest could also be paid at the "judgment rate," which is the amount of interest the state provides for legal judgments which are not immediately collectable. Such interest rates can be readily determined and thus do not impair negotiability.)

31. An extension clause in an instrument by which the holder can extend the time for payment at his or her option will render the instrument not negotiable due to its uncertain time of payment.
(False: The time period is certain since the holder is the one extending the time period and thus he or she knows exactly when the instrument is payable.)

32. An acceleration clause in a promissory note that allows the payee or holder to demand payment of the entire amount due on the note, with interest, if the maker fails to make a payment will render the note not negotiable.
(False: The parties know when they will be paid and how much and thus the note is negotiable; moreover, the acceleration clause makes the note even more valuable and marketable)

33. When a promissory note is payable "at or before" a specified date the time-period is deemed to be certain for negotiability.
(True: The time-period is certain because the holder or any subsequent holders know that they will be paid on that set date or whenever before that date they present the instrument to the maker. Such an instrument is in essence a "demand" one.)

34. The omission of a date on an instrument (other than a definite time for payment) adversely affects the negotiability of the instrument.
(False: A date is not necessary on an instrument except as noted above unless the date is critical to the time when the instrument is to be paid. For example, if the instrument states it is payable a year from the date on the instrument, then there obviously must be a date on the instrument to toll the one-year period, or else the time-period is not definite and the instrument is not negotiable.)

35. Indorsements are required to negotiate both bearer and order instruments.
(False: Indorsements are just required to negotiate order instruments, that is, an instrument payable to the order of a named person who must endorse it to effect a negotiation; whereas bearer instruments, that is, payable to bearer or to cash, can merely be negotiated by transfer to a person who becomes a holder without any indorsing.)

36. The indorsement of an order instrument on the back by the payee without naming another payee converts the instrument to a bearer one.
(True: Such an indorsement is called a "blank indorsement." The payee should indorse and then state "pay to the order of" a named payee in order to maintain the order nature of the instrument. This latter type of indorsement is called a "special indorsement.")

37. A qualified indorsement where the indorsing party signs on the back of the instrument but adds the phrase "without recourse" on the back of the instrument will prevent the further negotiation of the instrument.
(False: This type of indorsement is permissible; a negotiation thus can be made; title to the instrument can be passed; but the indorsing party does not incur any contract liability on the instrument.)

38. Payment of value is not a requirement for a holder of an instrument to become a holder-in-due course (HDC).
(False: Value is a requirement. Value is the consideration given for the instrument which consideration has been performed. In addition to value, the holder must take the instrument in good faith and without notice of any claims to it or defenses against the instrument.)

39. In order to be a holder-in-due course (HDC) of an instrument a person must be the original payee.
(False: The original payee can indorse the instrument and negotiate it to a transferee who can qualify as a holder and then become an HDC if the HDC requirements are met.)

40. When a person purchases a time instrument one week after its expressed due date the negotiability of the instrument is ruined.
(False: The instrument is still negotiable, but the holder of the instrument is going to have a very difficult time qualifying as an HDC because he or she is now on notice that there may be a problem with the instrument.)

41. Conditioning the payment of an instrument on an expected future source of funds will ruin the negotiability of the instrument.
(True: Making a mere reference to an expected source of funds, such as stating a bank account number on the instrument, is permissible; but conditioning the payment on an expected source of funds in the future, such as the sale of one's stock, will destroy negotiability since any transferee of the instrument would have to wait and check to see if the funds are present; and thus such a condition would impermissibly impede the free flow and transferability of the instrument.)

42. To achieve holder-in-due course (HDC) status a holder of an instrument can take the instrument as payment for a prior debt.
(True: Taking the instrument as payment for the antecedent debt will fulfill the "value" requirement of being an HDC.)

43. If an instrument is discounted for early payment of the instrument the instrument is not negotiable since the selling price can vary and consequently the amount is not definite.
(False: The amount is definite since at any one time the discounts if any can be factored into the amount due.)

44. A holder can be a partial holder-in-due course (HDC) of an instrument if the consideration given by the holder to the instrument is only partially performed.
(True: When the consideration is fully performed then the holder has given value for the whole instrument.)

45. A maker of a negotiable promissory note can raise "universal" or "real" defenses to stop a holder from recovering on the instrument but not a holder-in-due course.
(False: Universal or real defenses, such as fraud-in-the-factum, bankruptcy, or duress will preclude even an HDC from recovering on the instrument. Fraud-in-the-factum is also known as fraud-in-the-execution. It occurs when a victim is deceived into signing a negotiable instrument not knowing due to the misrepresentations that he or she is signing the instrument.)

46. Fraud in the inducement is a real or universal defense.
(False: Fraud-in-the- inducement is merely a personal defense that will not stop an HDC. Fraud-in-the-inducement occurs when one defrauds a person into signing a negotiable instrument by misrepresentations of certain facts, but the victim knows that he or she is signing a negotiable instrument.)

47. Prior payment of an instrument is a universal or real defense that will preclude a holder-in-due course (HDC) from recovering on the instrument.
(False: Prior payment is merely a personal defense which the HDC can "cut through" to recover. However, obviously, in order to be a HDC in the first place the holder cannot be on notice of the prior payment of the instrument.)

48. Breach of contract is a personal defense.
(True: This is a basic proposition meaning an HDC can recover on the instrument even if there was a breach of contract in the original transaction between the maker and payee.)

49. Changing the amount of an instrument by only a penny is considered to be a material alteration of the instrument.
(True: The change, even if slight in monetary terms, is nonetheless considered to be "material" because the original obligation of the parties has been changed.)

50. If a holder presents a promissory note for payment to the maker late the maker is discharged from liability.
(False: Makers are primarily liable on their promissory notes even if they are presented beyond the due date for payment. Actually, the presentment for payment can be months, even years, late, and the maker is still liable subject to the "running" of any applicable Statute of Limitations. Note, however, that any endorsers on the note who are only secondarily liable parties are discharged if the note is presented late for payment.)

51. A drawee who accepts a draft becomes primarily liable thereon.
(True: By typically signing on the face of the instrument the drawee becomes an "acceptor" and thus a primarily liable party like the maker of a promissory note.)

52. When a party indorses an instrument with the words "without recourse" the indorsing party has eliminated all his or her liability on the instrument.
(False: Such a restrictive indorsement will eliminate the endorser's contract liability on the instrument, but not his or her implied warranty liability based on the transfer of the instrument, for example, that the endorser in fact had good title to the instrument, that all signatures are genuine and authorized, and that there has been no material alteration. Implied warranty liability lawsuits based on the transfer of an instrument are called "liability-off-the-instrument" as opposed to contract liability lawsuits by signing instruments called liability-on-the-instrument.)

53. When a bank accepts a check that has been presented for payment the bank has become secondarily liable on the check.
(False: The bank as a drawee who accepts a check becomes an "acceptor" and thus primarily liable on the instrument.)

54. The presenter of a negotiable instrument for payment impliedly warrants that she or he has good title to it.
(True: The presenter is in effect warranting that he or she is a "holder" of the instrument and thus that neither the payee's name nor any prior special endorsees' names were forged. The presenter also impliedly warrants that there has been no material alteration to the instrument.)

55. For an agent to avoid liability on a negotiable instrument he or she must just sign the principal's name and not the agent's name at all.
(False: The agent can sign his or her name but must name the principal and sign as an agent in a representative capacity, for example, "Paul, Principal, by Alice, Agent," or "X Corporation, by Theresa, Treasurer.)

56. When the president of a company carelessly leaves payroll checks in the open, and then a dishonest employee inserts his or her name as payee and next forges the president's signature neither the president nor the company are obligated to pay any party who later acquires the check due to the forgery.

(False: Although the forgery of a drawer's or maker's signature is a defense to payment if known by the transferee there is an exception called the "fictitious payee" rule, which is applicable here and which is based on negligent conduct. Note that there is no forgery in the chain-of-title here as the dishonest employee is not forging the payee's name, which is his or her own name, but rather the drawer's, and thus the transferee of the instrument can become a holder and an HDC.)

57. A holder-in-due course (HDC) who presents a promissory note to the maker with knowledge acquired after becoming an HDC violates the presentment warranty that the presenter lacks knowledge that the maker (or drawer's signature) is forged.
(False: If the HDC acts in "good faith," that is, has no knowledge of the forgery when taking the note but then afterwards acquires knowledge the HDC does not violate the presentment warranty because the knowledge is after-acquired and the maker of a note or the drawer of a draft is expected to know his or her own signature.)

58. When a bank refuses to certify a check for the payee there is a dishonor of the check.
(False: The bank has no legal obligation to the payee to certify a check. The bank may be in breach of contract with its customer, the drawer of the check, for refusing to certify, however. As to the payee, after the bank refuses to certify the check, the payee can then simply present it for payment, and if the bank then does not pay there is a dishonor.)

59. When a bank refuses to pay a check to the payee even though the bank's customer, the drawer of the check, has sufficient funds in his or her account to pay it, the payee has a successful lawsuit against the bank.
(False: The bank may have liability to is customer, but not to the payee who presents the check as the bank is only the drawee and not an acceptor on the check. However, the payee can treat the bank refusal to pay as a dishonor and then sue the drawer and any other secondarily liable parties.)

60. A "stale check" is one that is presented to the bank for payment more than six months after its issue.
(True: The bank has the option to pay such a check but is not legally obligated to do so.)

61. When a bank certifies a check, the bank becomes an "acceptor" of the check.
(True: The drawee bank by certifying the check is now an acceptor and thus primarily liable on the check like the maker of a promissory note.)

62. A bank usually will not be liable for paying a check with a forged drawer's signature if the customer was negligent in detecting and/or reporting the forgery.
(True: The bank's customer has a duty to examine bank statements to discover forgeries and alterations and to not do so in timely manner will preclude the bank's liability.)

63. Under the Electronic Funds Transfer Act a customer whose debit card is stolen and used without his or her permission may be financially liable if the customer does not report the theft in a timely manner to the bank or financial institution.
(True: This is a basic proposition of the statute; and the customer's liability depends on the number of days and months the customer delays in reporting the theft.)

64. In order to be a holder-in-due-course of a negotiable instrument one must first be a holder.
(True: This is a basic commercial paper principle. As such, to have "holder" status one must have the instrument properly negotiated either by proper indorsement and transfer or by being in rightful possession of a bearer instrument.)

65. Pursuant to the federal Expedited Funds Availability Act a "local" check deposited by a customer must be available for withdrawal by cash or check within one business day from the day of deposit. *(True: This federal statute supersedes the old UCC rules on "float" time for availability. Note that a "check" is deemed to be a "local" one if the depositary bank and the payor bank are in the same banking region as designated by the Federal Reserve. For a non-local check, the funds must be available within five business days. Cash deposits and funds for government checks the funds must be available the next business day.)*

Multiple Choice Questions with Answers and Explanations

1. Commercial paper consists of which of the following:
 a. Promissory notes
 b. Drafts
 c. Checks
 d. All of the above.
 (The correct answer is d. These are all types of commercial paper. Another example would be certificates of deposit (CD). A promissory note is a two-party instrument whereby the creator, the maker makes a promise to pay a sum of money to a payee. A draft, also called a bill-of-exchange, is a three-party instrument, whereby the creator, called the drawer, orders another party, called the drawee, to pay money to a third-party, called the payee. A check is simply a draft where the bank is the payee and where the instrument is payable on demand. A Certificate of Deposit (CD) is a variant of a note, where the bank, the maker, acknowledges a sum of money and promises to pay it at a certain later time or on demand.)

2. What is FALSE about commercial paper?
 a. A demand instrument is payable whenever the holder of the instrument choses to present it to the maker if a note, or to the drawee if a draft.
 b. A time instrument is payable at a specific future date.
 c. Notes and drafts can be either time or demand instruments.
 d. Since a check must be a demand instrument it cannot be post-dated.
 (The correct answer is d. A check can be post-dated and can still be negotiated prior to the date shown, but it is not payable on demand until the date stated. Note that demand instruments are also called sight instruments.)

3. What is FALSE about the parties to commercial instruments?
 a. A drawee who accepts a draft thereby incurs secondary liability on it.
 b. A "bearer" is any person in possession of an instrument made payable to bearer or to cash.
 c. A holder is a person in possession of a bearer instrument or an order instrument that has been properly endorsed and transferred to the person.
 d. A blank endorsement will convert order paper into bearer paper.
 (The correct answer is a. A drawee who accepts a draft by signing his or her name to the face of the instrument becomes primarily liable on the instrument, just like the maker of a note. An order instrument is an instrument made payable to the order of a named party. When that party endorses on the back of the instrument that party can then state that the instrument will be payable to the order of a new named payee. Conversely, the initial payee can endorse "in blank" by merely signing his or her name, thereby converting the order paper to bearer paper. If one is a "holder" of a negotiable instrument one can become a holder-in-due course, which is a very elevated position in commercial paper law.)

4. In order to be a negotiable instrument under commercial paper law the instrument must be:

a. In writing and signed by the maker or drawer.

b. Contain an unconditional order or promise to pay a sum certain in money, on demand or at a definite future time.

c. Contain the "words of negotiability"

d. All of the above.

(The correct answer is d. These are the fundamental requirements of negotiability. Also, to be negotiable an instrument as a general rule must be free from other promises. The "magic" words of negotiability are that the instrument must be payable "to the order of" a named payee or to "bearer." If an instrument lacks one of these afore mentioned requirements it is not a negotiable instrument and thus not governed by the Uniform Commercial Code; however, it is not a "worthless" piece of paper and still can form the basis of an obligation to pay but the instrument is governed by contract law, particularly assignment law, whereby, one recalls, an obligor can assert against the third-party assignee any defense that the obligor had against the assignor-transferor.)

5. What is FALSE about negotiable instruments?

a. An IOU can form the basis of a negotiable note if the party owing the money signs the instrument.

b. The reference to a separate agreement in an instrument will not impair its negotiability.

c. The sum is "certain" in an instrument if it is payable with different rates of interest before or after default or a specific date.

d. An instrument payable on the happening of an event will render it non-negotiable even if the event is very likely to occur or in fact has occurred.

(The correct answer is a. An IOU is merely the acknowledgment of a debt, and without the requisite promise to pay it cannot be a negotiable promissory note. Yet it is still evidence of a debt which can be sued on pursuant to contract law and creditor-debtor principles. Referring to separate agreements is permissible; however, incorporating the terms of a separate agreement into an instrument, for example, a separate contract is made "part hereof of this note," will destroy its negotiability. The rationale is that a negotiable instrument is supposed to be, as the old maxim says, a "courier without baggage," and thus flow in commerce as a substitute for money; and as such forcing a potential buyer of the instrument to track down the separate incorporated agreement will impede this "free flow," and consequently render the instrument non-negotiable. Exact mathematical certainty at the time the instrument is made is not necessary for the "sum certain" requirement; rather, just at any particular time it must be able to be determined what the exact sum is, so, for example, an instrument can be payable in installments and with different rates of interest. Conditioning payment of an instrument on an event, for example, "when I sell my stock," will render it non-negotiable since any buyer/transferee would have to check to see if the condition occurred. Similarly, even if the event is very likely to occur, for example, "payable when my rich uncle dies," or has occurred, since the uncle is already dead, the instrument is still not negotiable since any buyer/transferee would still have to check to see if the condition occurred, thereby once again hindering the "free flow" of the instrument like money.)

6. What is FALSE about the effect of acceleration and extension clauses in negotiable instruments?

a. An acceleration clause will not impair negotiability.

b. An extension clause makes an instrument payable later than its maturity date.

c. If an extension is at the option of the holder the instrument is not negotiable since the time for payment is not certain.

d. An extension based on the happening of an event is permissible if a definite time period is stated for the extension.

(The correct answer is c. An acceleration clause makes an instrument payable earlier than its maturity date, for example, "Maker promised to pay on or before March 15." Acceleration

clauses can be granted to the maker or holder unconditionally; they do not impair negotiability. An extension clause may impair negotiability. However, an extension granted to the holder of an instrument is permissible, but unless specified in the instrument the time period of the extension cannot be any longer than the time period originally in the instrument. The rationale is that the holder can always delay seeking payment, but the holder cannot exercise that option if the maker or acceptor tenders full payment when the instrument is due. Otherwise, the holder could "keep the clock ticking" and thus keep the interest running. Also, an extension can be for the benefit of the maker or drawee/acceptor but only if a definite time period is stated in the instrument; otherwise it is not negotiable. Finally, an extension based on an event is permissible but only if a definite time period is stated.)

7. What promises in a note will render it non-negotiable?
   a. A promise to pay $500 and goods
   b. A promise to pay joint payees
   c. A promise to confess judgment
   d. A promise to pay attorneys' fees upon default.

(The correct answer is a. A negotiable instrument must be based on a promise or order to pay money and not goods. Joint payees are permissible, but both must endorse the instrument to transfer it. Promises to confess judgment, that is, authorizing the holder to enter judgment if the note is not paid, as well as to pay attorneys' fees and collection costs on default, are permissible. In fact, the two latter promises make the note more valuable.)

8. What is FALSE about the negotiation requirement to commercial paper?
   a. Anyone in possession of bearer paper has good title to it.
   b. If an instrument is order paper the named payee has good title by acquiring possession of the instrument.
   c. A non-negotiable instrument cannot be transferred by means of a negotiation.
   d. Good title to an order instrument does not pass unless the payee's endorsement is valid and authorized

(The correct answer is a. Anyone in possession of bearer paper is a "holder," but the possessor of bearer paper may lack good title unless there was a rightful delivery. However, since a thief of bearer paper is a "holder," the thief can transfer good title to a subsequent transferee. A payee in possession of order paper has good title but before a subsequent transferee can acquire title the payee must endorse the instrument, that is, sign his or her name on the back, over to the subsequent transferee and surrender possession of it to the transferee, which is a "delivery." Non-negotiable instruments can be transferred but only pursuant to assignment of contract rules, and not by a UCC negotiation, meaning that no one can become a "holder" of the instrument and consequently not the elevated position of a "holder-in-due-course." A "holder" is a person in possession of a negotiable instrument that has been issued to him or her or endorsed to him or her, or to "bearer" or "in blank" (that is, the payee just endorsing without naming a new payee.)

9. What is FALSE about endorsements of negotiable instruments?
   a. A qualified endorsement, that is, with the words "without recourse," means that the endorser does not incur any contract liability on the instrument.
   b. A restrictive endorsement prevents the further transfer or negotiation of an instrument.
   c. A special endorsement arises when a payee of order paper names a new payee by writing in the name of the new payee above his or her endorsement.
   d. A blank endorsement occurs when the payee of order paper signs his or her name on the back of the paper without naming a new payee.

(The correct answer is b. A restrictive endorsement does not prevent further transfer or negotiation, and an endorsee or subsequent transferee can still qualify as a holder; however, the restrictive

endorsement may require the endorsee or subsequent transferees to see that the funds for the instrument are applied in accordance with the endorsement. Examples of restrictive endorsements would be an endorsement with "for deposit only" or one with a condition attached to it, that is, pay to the order of X if X fulfills a condition, for example, delivering goods. An endorser who endorses "without recourse" makes a qualified endorsement, meaning that he or she can still pass good title to the instrument, but that he or she will not incur contract liability on the instrument, which is based on signing instruments. Note, however, that the qualified endorser still may be liable for "implied warranty" liability on the instrument. Regarding special endorsements it is important to note that the payee does not have to use the "magic words" of negotiability in making the special endorsement. So, for example, a endorsement with "pay x" is permissible as opposed to "pay to the order of X," which words must be used on the face of the instrument to make it a negotiable one. Note that endorsing "in blank" is a risky thing to do since the order paper is now converted to bearer paper, which can be negotiated without further endorsement.)

10. In order to be a "holder-in-due-course," a holder must take a negotiable instrument?
    a. for value.
    b. in good faith.
    c. without notice that the instrument is overdue or dishonored or that any defenses exist against it or claims to it on the part of any person.
    d. All of the above.

    (The correct answer is d. These are the fundamental requirements of becoming a holder-in-due course (HDC), which is a very elevated position in UCC commercial paper law since an HDC can cut through most defenses to payment on the instrument, as opposed to an assignee of a contract right pursuant to assignment law. Note that to be an HDC one first must be a holder and the instrument, of course, must be a negotiable one.)

11. What is FALSE about a holder-in-due-course (HDC)?
    a. Paying for an instrument or delivering goods for it meets the "value" requirement for HDC status.
    b. An executory promise to pay money or deliver goods for an instrument is "value" since such an executory promise is "consideration" to support a contract.
    c. Under the "good faith" requirement to HDC status a holder is not required to exercise ordinary prudence or reasonable diligence.
    d. The "notice" requirement to HDC status is measured by an objective "reasonable person" test.

    (The correct answer is b. An executory promise is not value needed to support HDC status since the promise may be breached. However, there is an exception where the executory promise is embodied in a negotiable instrument, such as a promissory note. "Good faith" is a subjective test, which simply means that the holder is acting honestly, not necessarily carefully. As such, there is no duty to investigate what would appear to be a reasonable person's suspicions about an instrument. As per the old maxim, one can have a "good heart" and "empty head" and still act in "good faith." The requirement that the holder take the instrument without notice that it is overdue or dishonored or that there are any claims to it or defenses against it is measured by the reasonableness standard. For example, acquiring an instrument after its fixed maturity date, or with knowledge that it has been defaulted, or with knowledge that installment payments have been missed, or that the instrument is irregular or incomplete would very likely preclude HDC status.)

12. What is FALSE about the Shelter Doctrine and HDC status?
    a. A party who was involved with any fraud or illegality affecting the instrument cannot acquire HDC rights pursuant to the Shelter Doctrine.
    b. As a general rule, a transferee who acquires an instrument from an HDC can obtain the rights of an HDC pursuant to the Shelter Doctrine.
    c. If a person acquires a negotiable instrument knowing there is a problem with it that person can still obtain HDC rights under the Shelter Doctrine if he or she later re-acquires the instrument from an HDC.
    d. Once a person qualifies as an HDC as a general rule the Shelter Doctrine will grant HDC rights to all subsequent transferees of the instrument, regardless of how far "down the chain" of succession they are.

(The correct answer is c. Transferees of instruments from HDCs do not have to be HDCs themselves, for example, receiving a negotiable instrument as a gift and thus not paying "value" for it; yet nonetheless under the Shelter Doctrine the transferee obtains the rights of an HDC. Recall that the purpose of the HDC rule and the Shelter Doctrine is to help commercial paper "flow" in commerce like money. However, a prior holder with knowledge of a problem in an instrument cannot take advantage of the Shelter Rule since he or she will not be allowed to "wash" the instrument through an HDC. However, a transferee can have knowledge of a problem when taking the instrument from an HDC, unless, he or she was part of the problem.)

13. Which is the following is NOT a Real Defense that will prevent an HDC from recovering on a negotiable instrument?
    a. Forgery
    b. Minor Status
    c. Fraud in the Inducement
    d. Discharge in bankruptcy

(The correct answer is c. Fraud in the inducement must be distinguished from fraud in the execution, also called fraud in the factum, which is a real defense. In the latter a person is deceived as to the character of what he or she is signing, that is, the victim honestly and reasonably does not know that he or she is signing a negotiable instrument, believing it to be something else. Whereas with fraud in the inducement, which is only a personal defense, a person knows that he or she is signing a negotiable instrument but was deceived as to the reasons for signing it. Forgery first depends on whose signature was forged. If it was the signature of the payee or an endorser, then the "chain of title" to the instrument is broken and no one can become a holder let alone an HDC. However, if the signature that is forged is that of the maker, drawer, or acceptor, which are outside of the chain of title, then the forgery does not affect title and thus one can become a holder and an HDC, BUT the forgery outside the chain emerges as a real defense. As to minor status or infancy, if state law makes the contract of a minor, typically a person under 18 years of age, void or voidable, usually the latter, then the minor can assert infancy as a real defense against an HDC. A discharge in any insolvency proceeding as well as bankruptcy are real defenses.)

14. Which of the following is NOT a personal defense?
    a. Breach of contract
    b. Breach of warranty
    c. Illegality
    d. Prior payment of the instrument.

(The correct answer is c. If state law renders the underlying transaction illegal and void illegality is a real defense. Yet if state law renders the underlying transaction merely voidable then that type of illegality is only a personal defense. The HDC can cut through the typical personal defenses of breach of contract and warranty as well as failure of consideration. Prior payment on the instrument is merely a personal defense, meaning that unless there is some notation on the instrument or

knowledge that it has been paid, even if paid, the party primarily liable will have to pay the HDC again.)

15. What is FALSE about contract liability for negotiable instruments?
    a. A qualified endorsement will not prevent further negotiation of the instrument.
    b. Primary parties are makers of notes and drawees of drafts.
    c. Endorsers are secondarily liable.
    d. In order to hold a secondary party contractually liable on an instrument the holder must first properly present the instrument for acceptance or payment if a draft or for payment if a note.

    (The correct answer is b. Contract liability for negotiable instruments is at times called liability "on the instrument. Makers of notes and acceptors of drafts as well as checks are parties primarily liable on negotiable instruments. The drawer of a draft is only secondarily liable, as well as are endorsers of any instrument. The drawee has not signed the draft and thus is not liable at all. However, when the drawee signs the draft on its face the drawee thus becomes an acceptor and he or she is now a party primarily liable. The holder of an instrument must proceed first against a party primarily liable, that is, the maker or acceptor, or if a drawee against the drawee. Once an instrument is properly presented for payment and/or in the case of a draft for acceptance, and payment or acceptance by the drawee is refused, then there is a dishonor and the holder can proceed against the secondary parties – the drawer or an endorser of the instrument. However, the holder must give proper notice of the dishonor to the secondary party. Note that if an endorser signs "without recourse" he or she thereby eliminates his or her contract liability on the instrument, though there still may be warranty liability.)

16. What is/are types of implied warranty liability based on the transfer of a negotiable instrument?
    a. The transferor warrants that he or she has good title to the instrument and that the signatures thereon are genuine and authorized.
    b. The transferor warrants that there is no material alteration on the instrument.
    c. The transferor warrants that there is no defense good against the transferor.
    d. All of the above.

    (The correct answer is d. These are the types of implied warranty liability based on transferring negotiable instruments. This type of liability is called at times liability "off the instrument" and is not based on signing the instrument but on transferring it and/or presenting it for acceptance or payment. Note that the forgery of a party in the chain of title, that is, the payee or any subsequent endorser will cause the transfer warranty to be breached as the party transferring it does not possess good title. However, a forgery of the drawer's signature or the forgery of a signature on bearer paper will violate the warranty since those signatures are not genuine. Regarding material alteration we are presuming that the alteration occurred before transfer. Note that regarding the "defense good against the transferor" warranty that if the transferee is an HDC, who may be able to cut through a defense if merely "personal," the warranty is still breached and the HDC can enforce the instrument based on the implied warranty being breached or in the alternative cut through the personal defense, which, however, would entail the HDC proving that he or she is an HDC. Also, note that there is one more implied transfer warranty, that is, the transferor has no knowledge of any insolvency proceedings against a party from whom payment is expected.)

17. What is FALSE about the implied warranties that arise from the presentment of a negotiable instrument?
    a. The presenter warrants that he or she has good title to the instrument.
    b. The presenter warrants that the signature of the maker or drawer is neither forged nor unauthorized.

c. An HDC with knowledge that the signature of the maker or drawer is forged will not violate the presentment warranty if the HDC was not aware of the forgery when the HDC took the instrument.
d. The presenter warrants that there is no material alteration to the instrument.

(The correct answer is b. The presenter warrants that he or she has no knowledge that the signatures of the maker or drawer are forged or unauthorized. Good title means that the presenter is warranting that he or she is a "holder" and that there are no forgeries in the chain-of-title. Regarding the HDC with knowledge it is critical that the HDC had no knowledge of the forgery when the holder became the HDC. Also, another rationale is that the maker or drawer, when presented with the forged instrument by the HDC, is supposed to know his or her own signature. Regarding material alteration note that this is an absolute warranty which does not depend on knowledge of the alteration.)

18. What is FALSE about a bank's relationship with its customers?
    a. A "wrongful dishonor" occurs when a check is properly payable from a customer's account and the bank refuses to honor the check.
    b. Once a bank learns of its customer's death it must stop paying or certifying checks.
    c. A bank can charge its customer's account for a check only if the check is properly payable.
    d. If a bank customer signs checks with blanks, that is, an incomplete check, the bank can assume that what was filled in and completed was proper and thus charge the customer for the full completed amount.

    (The correct answer is b. Once a bank learns of its customer's death or incompetency it can still pay or certify checks for 10 days; however, if a person asserts an interest in the account, regardless of validity, he or she can then stop the bank from paying or certifying checks for the ten-day period. If there is a wrongful dishonor the bank customer has a breach of contract action against the bank. "Properly payable" means that the signature of the drawer, that is, the bank's customer, is not forged; otherwise the bank has to recredit the customer's account. Regarding "blank checks," that is the risk one takes by signing a check with the amount blank, unless of course the bank knows or should know that the completion was improper.)

25 - Creditor and Debtor Law and Secured Transactions

Introduction

Laws assisting creditors that the student must be aware of encompass the common law doctrine of suretyship (which the student must be able to distinguish from guaranty contracts), secured transactions (premised on the UCC), as well as artisan's liens, mechanic's liens, writs of execution on a judgment, garnishment, and receivership. For laws assisting debtors, the main one for the student to be cognizant is bankruptcy, particularly the changes in federal law pursuant to the Bankruptcy Reform Act of 2005, as well as the Homestead exemption based on state statutory law. Regarding bankruptcy, it is also essential for the student to know the types of bankruptcies, especially the main provisions of Chapters 7, 11, and 13, the role of the bankruptcy trustee, the components of the debtor's estate, the list of exemptions, and, most importantly, the definition of and distinction between a voidable transfer and a voidable preference, what causes a debtor to be discharged, how a debtor's estate is distributed upon discharge, and, finally, those claims against the debtor which are not dischargeable in bankruptcy.

True and False Questions with Answers and Explanations

1. The best way for a secured party to achieve perfection of the security interest is by the filing of a financing statement.
(True: Another method is perfection by possession, also called a pledge, where the secured party, typically a creditor, keeps possession of the collateral.)

2. In order to create a valid security interest, there usually is a written security agreement regarding the security interest in the collateral.
(True: Another less common method is when the person acquiring the security interest, usually the creditor, plans to keep possession of the property.)

3. A security interest is enforceable when attachment occurs.
(True: Attachment occurs when there is an agreement that the security interest attaches, that is, the security agreement, the secured party gives "value," that is, consideration) to the debtor, and the debtor has "rights" in, that is, ownership interests, as well as possession of the collateral.)

4. A financing statement is usually filed with the federal district court in the district where the collateral is located.
(False: The UCC says that the states can chose "local" filing at the county level, which most do, or at the state level at the state Secretary of State's office.)

5. Among preferred creditors the first secured creditor to file a financing statement has priority.
(False: The UCC rule is the "first to file or perfect" which means that the secured party who first files or perfects the security interest has priority.)

6. In order to collect a debt a loan company can use as a pre-judgment remedy execution on the goods.
(False: Attachment is the proper remedy in a pre-judgment situation if the creditor can demonstrate to the court insecurity, for example, an affidavit stating that the debtor is trying to hide property or remove property. Execution, that is, seizure and sale of property, only occurs after a successful lawsuit by the creditor and the obtaining a judgment by the court and a court order.)

7. The remedy of garnishment cannot be used to seize a debtor's wages, just bank accounts.
(False: Garnishment can be used for both, though there are federal and state statutory limits on the types and amounts of property and money that can be garnished.)

8. The primary purpose of bankruptcy law is to give creditors the legal means to seize and sell debtors' property to fully settle debt obligations.
(False: A principal purpose of bankruptcy law is to relieve "honest" debtors from the weight of oppressive debt and to give them a "fresh start" in life free from former obligations. Another purpose is to allow an equitable distribution to the debtor's creditors, meaning that in most cases creditors will not be fully repaid but rather will only receive a percentage portion of the debt obligation.)

9. A voluntary petition for bankruptcy will automatically subject the debtor and his or her property to the jurisdiction and supervision of the bankruptcy court.
(True: The petition must contain specific items as well as sufficient information so as to guide a judge on how to proceed, that is, for the judge to decide to continue with a Chapter 7 or not, or encourage a Chapter 11 or 13, or order a Chapter 11 or 13.)

10. When a petition for a discharge in bankruptcy is filed, property received by the debtor 180 days after filing the petition is subject to the claims of creditors, but not property in the form of inheritances as that would be unfair to the debtor's heirs.
(False: After-acquired property also includes inheritances pursuant to the 180 days rule.)

11. The objective of a Chapter 7 bankruptcy proceeding is to obtain and sell the debtor's assets, pay off the debtor's creditors as much as possible, and then pursuant to court order to legally discharge the debtor from further responsibility to pay.
(True: Whereas a Chapter 11 proceeding is the adjustment of a person's debts whose has regular income; and a Chapter 13 is a specialized proceeding for small farmers and people in the family fishing business.)

12. When a debtor makes a preference to a creditor, that is, preferring a creditor and paying a debt in full, the preferential transfer is voidable and can be set aside by the bankruptcy trustee if it occurred 90 days prior to the filing of the bankruptcy petition.
(True: And note that if the transfer is to a person deemed to be an "insider," for example, a family member or close friend or business associate, such as a partner, the time-period is one year.)

13. The filing of a financing statement is the best way to achieve perfection of a security interest.
(True: Filing is also the most common way. Other methods are perfection by attachment and perfection by possession of the collateral, also called a "pledge.")

14. A purchase money security interest (PMSI) is created when a lender agrees to lend money or credit for the purchase price of consumer goods.
(True: Note that a security agreement is still required; but filing a financing statement to achieve perfection of the PMSI is not required.)

15. The most prevalent way to perfect a security interest is for a creditor to retain possession of the collateral.
(False: Filing a financing statement is the most common way to perfect a security interest. The creditor retaining possession of the collateral is not the most practicable way to do business as the debtor typically needs the collateral.)

16. Pursuant to Article 9 of the UCC whichever secured party is either the first to file a financing statement or perfect the security interest has priority.
(True: This is the fundament "first to file or perfect" rule, which means that the first secured party to file a financing statement has priority even though a later creditor perfected first, for example, by taking possession of the collateral.)

17. Priority among competing security interests is determined by whoever was the first to obtain a signed security agreement.
(False: Priority is determined by the UCC's "first to file or perfect" rule.)

18. A "mechanics lien" is a lien acquired by an auto technician or car dealership for work and materials provided to the owner of a car or truck.
(False: A mechanic's lien is a lien against real property for labor, services, and materials used to improve the real estate. If the lien is not paid the lien-holder can foreclose on the property. Moreover, the lien is considered an encumbrance on the title to the property precluding any sale until the lien is satisfied.)

19. The primary function of bankruptcy courts is to put people who cannot pay their debts into prison.
(False: Debtors' prisons are long historical now. The primary purpose of bankruptcy courts is to effectuate a marshalling of the debtor's assets, pay off the debtor's creditors to the extent possible, and discharge the remainder of the debtor's obligations, thereby giving the debtor a "fresh start in life.")

20. Bankruptcy proceedings under Chapter 7 of the bankruptcy act must be initiated by the debtor's creditors.
(False: The creditors of the debtor can file an involuntary petition for bankruptcy; but the debtor can also file a voluntary petition for bankruptcy, which automatically subjects the debtor and his or her property to the jurisdiction and supervision of the bankruptcy court.)

21. When a person files for bankruptcy the bankruptcy trustee can reclaim for the debtor's estate the payment of last month's usual bill for phone and Internet service as a voidable transfer.
(False: This is an exception to the voidable transfer doctrine because the payment was made recently and in the ordinary course of the debtor's business or personal affairs.)

22. A debtor in bankruptcy proceedings is allowed to give preferences in payment so family members, close friends, and business associates since they are in pre-existing relationships.
(False: Such payments would very likely be deemed voidable preferential transfers, which can be set aside by the bankruptcy trustee because the result would be unfair to other ordinary creditors, as the afore mentioned preferred creditors would be receiving more money than they ordinarily receive.)

23. The Bankruptcy Reform Act of 2005 established a new form of "means testing" based on the debtor's income to determine if there is a presumption of "substantial abuse" of a Chapter 7 bankruptcy proceeding.
(True: As per the Act, if a debtor makes more than the state's median household income, the debtor will be compelled to use a Chapter 13 proceeding and go into a five-year repayment plan.)

Multiple Choice Questions with Answers and Explanations

1. What is FALSE about the law of suretyship vs. the law of guaranty?
   a. In a suretyship relationship the surety is primarily liable for the debt or obligation of another party.
   b. A guarantee promise to pay the debts of another can be oral if the guarantor and the guarantee are in a close family relationship.
   c. When the surety pays the debt of the principal debtor the surety can sue the principal debtor for reimbursement.
   d. Payment by the principal debtor of the debt will not only release the principal debtor but also the surety on the debt.

(The correct answer is b. Suretyship is a primary promise to pay the debts of another, which can be oral. Since a surety is primarily liable the surety can be sued immediately on the obligation, without the creditor needing to sue the principal debtor first, though the surety is entitled to reimbursement from the principal debtor. A guarantee is also a promise to pay for the debtors or obligations of another, but it is a secondary or collateral promise, an example of which would be the following promise to a creditor: "If X, debtor does not pay for the goods, then I, guarantor, promise to pay." A guarantee promise as per the Statute of Frauds must be in writing to be enforceable, though there is an exception called the "benefit to the promisor exception, whereby in making the secondary promise the promisor/guarantor seeks to benefit from the guarantee promise.)

2. How is a security interest in goods created?
   a. When the goods are placed in the possession of the secured party.
   b. When there is a written security agreement signed by the debtor which describes the goods.
   c. When a creditor seizes a debtor's goods pursuant to a writ of execution on a judgment.
   d. Both a and b.

(The correct answer is d. Placing the goods in the possession of the secured party is called a "pledge," but it is a rare way to create a security interest since the debtor likely needs the goods. Note that the security agreement also contains other terms, for example, the amount of the debt, the terms of payment, and the debtor's responsibilities with respect to the goods. A writ of execution is a separate remedy for creditors, based on a successful lawsuit and an order from a judge authorizing the sheriff to seize the debtor's goods to pay off a judgment.)

3. When does a security interest "attach" to the goods?
   a. When there is a security agreement stating the agreement will attach.
   b. When the secured party gives value to the debtor.
   c. The debtor has rights to the collateral.
   d. All of the above.

(The correct answer is d. It is very important to note that a security agreement is not enforceable until it "attaches" as per the preceding methods, all of which are required by the UCC. Note that "value" can be any consideration that would support a simple contract, such as delivering goods or loaning money. The debtor having rights to the collateral means the debtor has ownership of the goods or the right to obtain possession. Note, finally, that the three afore mentioned requirements can occur in any order.)

4. How is a security interest "perfected"?
   a. When the creditor keeps possession of the collateral, called a "pledge."
   b. Automatically by means of a "purchase money security interest" (PMSI).
   c. When the secured party files a financing statement regarding the collateral.
   d. All of the above.

(The correct answer is d. Perfection can be obtained by any of the three preceding methods. Perfection is a critical UCC concept because perfection, though not required, will give the holder of the security interest a priority over other persons who claim an interest in the collateral. Note that with a pledge there is no requirement that there even be a written security interest. With a PMSI situation, typically a merchant is advancing a consumer money to purchase and the resulting security agreement is automatically perfected. Filing a financing statement is the most common way to perfect a security interest. The financing statement states the security agreement, states the parties, describes the collateral, and provides contact information. Where to file depends on the jurisdiction, but usually it is at the county level where the goods are located or at the state's Secretary of State's office. Note, finally, if there are more than one creditor with a perfected security agreement who has priority is determined by the "first to file or perfect" rule, which means that a secured party who files first has priority even though another creditor perfected the security interest first.)

5. What is FALSE about other laws assisting creditors?
   a. An artisan's lien protects laborers who add to the value of real property.
   b. A writ of execution on a judgment is a court order that will authorize a sheriff to levy, that is, to seize the non-exempt property in the jurisdiction, sell it, and pay off the judgment.
   c. A writ of garnishment is an order by a court to people who own property or money of the debtor to turn it over to the court to pay a judgment against a party.
   d. A creditor may be able to attach, that is, seize, a debtor's property even before the creditor obtains a judgment against the debtor.

   (The correct answer is a. An artisan's lien protects laborers who add value to personal property by their labor or services. A mechanic's lien is the lien against real estate for labor, services, and/or material used in improving the real estate. Note that the remedy of garnishment is typically used to seize wages, but there are both federal and state limitations as to the types of property that can be garnished as well as the amounts. Attachment of property before a judgment is obtained can occur when the creditor can demonstrate to a court that the creditor has a reasonable belief that the debtor may conceal or remove property from the jurisdiction before a judgment can be obtained.)

6. What are the major type(s) of bankruptcy proceedings pursuant to the Bankruptcy Act of 1978?
   a. Chapter 7 liquidation
   b. Chapter 11 reorganization and continuation of a business
   c. Chapter 13 readjustment of the debtor with regular income
   d. All of the above.

   (The correct answer is d. These three are the fundamental legal proceedings authorized by the bankruptcy act. Note that a Chapter 7 liquidation is most common form of bankruptcy and it is also called a "straight" bankruptcy. Note that a bankruptcy court judge can order a Chapter 7 to be converted to a Chapter 13.)

7. What is FALSE about a Chapter 7 bankruptcy proceeding?
   a. It can be either voluntary initiated by the debtor or involuntary by the creditors.
   b. The debtor must be insolvent.
   c. If the debtor has less than 12 creditors one or more may file, the involuntary petition.
   d. If a debtor contests an involuntary petition by creditors, the creditors must demonstrate at a hearing before the bankruptcy judge that the debtor has not been paying his or her debts when they become due.

   (The correct answer is b. The debtor need not be technically insolvent, that is, the debts exceeding the fair market value of assets of non-exempt property. A voluntary Chapter 7 commences with the debtor filing a detailed petition of bankruptcy, which automatically subjects the debtor to the

jurisdiction of the bankruptcy court. The petition includes a detailed list of financial affairs, creditors, both secured and unsecured, assets, assets the debtor claims are exempt, liabilities, and current expenses. If the debtor has more 12 creditors, at least three must file the petition. The creditors can also show at a contested hearing that the debtor's property was placed in a receivership or an assignment for the benefit of creditors 120 days before the voluntary petition was filed.)

8. What property is considered as part of the debtor's estate and thus subject to the bankruptcy proceeding?
   a. Real and personal property
   b. Tangible and intangible property
   c. Property of the debtor which is in possession of another person
   d. All of the above
   (The correct answer is d. Broadly speaking these are the types of property which is subject to the jurisdiction of the bankruptcy court. Note that property in the possession of another person must be returned to the trustee in bankruptcy appointed by the judge in the bankruptcy court.)

9. What property is NOT considered part of the debtor's estate?
   a. Income from the debtor's personal services and labor earned after the petition in bankruptcy was filed.
   b. Property acquired by the debtor more than 180 days after the petition was filed.
   c. The debtor's homestead
   d. All of the above.
   (The correct answer is d. Property acquired more than 180 days can include an inheritance, being the beneficiary of a life insurance policy, and/or property or money received as a result of a divorce. Note that under federal law there is a monetary limit on the amount of the homestead exemption. There are several other exemptions, to wit: household furnishings, appliances, and clothes for personal and family use; a motor vehicle; jewelry; implements, tools, and books used in one's trade or profession; unmatured life insurance policies, all of which have monetary limits; health aides which are professionally prescribed; the right to receive government benefits, such as social security and welfare; alimony, child support and certain pensions and education savings accounts; and the right to receive personal injury awards up to a monetary limit.)

10. What is TRUE regarding voidable transfers?
    a. The bankruptcy trustee can cancel as a voidable transfer a transfer by the debtor of estate assets that was made after the debtor becomes subject to the bankruptcy proceeding but the trustee must do so within a two-year period after the transfer was made.
    b. The trustee can cancel as a fraudulent transfer made by the debtor one year prior to the filing of the bankruptcy petition.
    c. The trustee has the power to cancel a transfer on any grounds the debtor could have used.
    d. All of the above.
    (The correct answer is d. These are all fundamental powers of the bankruptcy trustee appointed by the bankruptcy judge. Note that fraud can be actual fraud or deceit against the creditors by the debtor, or any acts that fraudulently hinder, delay, or impede creditors, when an insolvent debtor sells assets for less than fair consideration. Note too that the grounds can be those that the debtor could have used, for example, ordinary contract defenses.)

11. What is FALSE regarding voidable preferences?
    a. The bankruptcy trustee has the power any transfer made by a debtor to a creditor which is deemed to be a "preference."
    b. A preferential transfer to a creditor can be cancelled by the trustee and the money or property returned to the estate if the transfer occurred within 90 days of the filing of the bankruptcy petition and the debtor was insolvent.
    c. The trustee cannot cancel transfers to family members, close friends, and business associates of the debtors as voidable preferences.
    d. Payments by the debtor within the ordinary-course-of-business.

    (The correct answer is c. Payments to so-called "insiders," such as family members, close friends, and business associates can not only be cancelled as voidable preferences by the trustee if the debtor is insolvent, but the time-period is one year prior to the filing of the petition. Note that payments in the ordinary-course-of-business have time limits and that the payment must be made according to normal business terms, for example, the payment by the debtor of the previous months utility bill.)

12. What type of claims by creditors and other claimants have *top* priority regarding the distribution of the bankrupt debtor's estate.
    a. Claims by people for wages, salaries, and commissions earned before the filing of the petition or the cessation of the debtor's business, whichever comes first.
    b. The costs and expenses involved in the administration of the debtor's estate.
    c. If the proceeding is involuntary, any expenses incurred in the ordinary course of the debtors or financial affairs after the commencement of the case but before the appointment of the trustee.
    d. Claims for government units for taxes.

    (The correct answer is b. The costs and expenses are usually always first in any type of legal proceeding. They typically include the trustee's, attorneys, and accountants' fees. Ordinary expenses in an involuntary case are the number two on the claimant list. Note that for wages, salaries, and commissions, which is the third priority, there are time and monetary limits. Surprisingly, taxes are the sixth priority, though some back taxes are not even dischargeable. Fourth are claims for employee benefit plans for services performed, again with time and monetary limits. Fifth are claims by individuals for deposits made on consumer goods and services not received but with monetary limits.)

13. What claims are NOT dischargeable in bankruptcy?
    a. Claims for back taxes that accrued within two years prior to the bankruptcy.
    b. Claims arising out of the debtor's fraud, larceny, embezzlement, or breach of fiduciary duty.
    c. Claims arising out of willful and malicious torts.
    d. All of the above.

    (The correct answer is d. Other non-dischargeable claims are for alimony and child support, unscheduled claims caused by the debtor failing to file a complete list of creditors, student loans with exceptions for hardship, and consumer debts and cash advances with monetary and time limits.)

14. What is FALSE about federal bankruptcy statutes.
    a. A Chapter 13 proceeding for adjustment of debts can be used by individuals and corporations.
    b. A Chapter 13 adjustment plan can provide for less than full payment of claims.
    c. A bankruptcy judge can convert a Chapter 7 proceeding into a Chapter 13 if there is evidence of substantial abuse of the Chapter 7 proceeding by the debtor.
    d. A Chapter 11 proceeding allows for the reorganization and continuation of a business, if feasible and preferable to liquidation.

(The correct answer is a. Chapter 13 only applies to individuals who have regular income and who can pay off debts from future income over a period-of-time. A Chapter 13 plan will include how creditors are to be paid, and how much, including perhaps less than full payment, the time period for payment, usually between three to five years, and with a maximum time period of five years. In a Chapter 11 proceeding, in addition to a trustee there must be created a creditors' committee, which will make the reorganization plan for the continuation of the business, which will be approved by the judge if it is approved by each class of creditors, including shareholders, and is fair to each class of creditors.)

26 - Wills and Trusts

Introduction

Wills and Trusts are areas of the law that are heavily dependent on state statutes, particularly regarding the administration of estates. Nonetheless, the student must know the basic rules of intestate descent and distribution, particularly the distinction between taking *per capita* v. *per stirpes*. Execution of wills is another important aspect of the law of wills and thus the student must know the basic requirements for a valid will, including testamentary intent, will formalities, and publication. The student must know the ways that wills can be revoked – revocation by written instrument, revocation by physical act, and revocation by operation of the law – and especially that in most states merely crossing-out or interlining parts of a will is not considered to be a revocation. The student must know what a codicil to a will is and how a codicil can either revoke or "save" a will. Moreover, the student must know the major restrictions on the power of testation – testamentary capacity, that is, having a "sound mind," undue influence, and fraud and mistake. Although the probate process is set forth in each state's law, the student nevertheless must know some of the basics of the probate process, such as the naming of the personal representative and his or her duties in administrating the estate, as well as the publication requirement for probate, called either a filing of the Notice of Administration or Letters of Administration, depending on the state. Also, the status of the personal representative as a fiduciary is another important aspect of the law of wills. Finally, the student must know the order of payment of claims before the estate assets can be distributed to beneficiaries.

Regarding Trusts, the student must know the elements and formalities of creating a private express trust, how such a trust is created, particularly the critical intent factor, and some of the basics of trust administration, particularly the duties of a trustee as well as the key fact that the law regards a trustee as a fiduciary. The student also must know what charitable and honorary trusts are, especially how the Cy Pres doctrine can affect the former, as well as the distinctions among a discretionary trust, spendthrift trust, and support trust. Moreover, the student must be able to define and differentiate between a resulting trust and a constructive trust. Finally, the student must be aware of the "changed circumstances" doctrine for trusts.

True and False Questions with Answers and Explanations

1. An executor, also in some states called a personal representative, is the party who drafts a will.
(False: The party who creates a will is usually called the Testator. Executors and personal representatives are the parties named in a will by the Testator to probate the will.)

2. The process by which a will is established as valid is call intestacy.
(False: The process is called probate. Intestacy refers to a person dying without a will.)

3. A lapsed devise occurs when the devisee dies prior to the death of the testator or before the devise occurs.
(True: This principle also applies to lapsed legacies.)

4. The residuary of an estate consists of the assets of a testator's estate that are subject to inheritance taxes.
(False: The residuary of an estate is that portion of the estate that is not specifically granted or devised in a will, which part the residuary beneficiaries will inherit.)

5. If a child is born to the testator after the testator makes a will the will is automatically revoked since it would not be fair to the child to let his or her siblings solely benefit from the will.
(False: The will is valid and it most states the child born after the will receives his or her per capita share of the estate.)

6. Pursuant to intestacy laws if there is no surviving spouse or children as a general rule the decedent's estate will pass to his or her lineal ascendants.
(False: The estate will pass to the lineal descendants.)

7. A trust created by a will to take effect after the testator's death is called a resulting trust.
(False: The trust is called a testamentary trust.)

8. A trust that protects a beneficiary from his or her foolish use of trust funds is called a constructive trust.
(False: This type of trust is called a Spendthrift Trust.)

9. When estate assets are insufficient to pay all the specific bequests in a will after any taxes and/or debts and expenses of administration, the probate court will seize the remaining assets and distribute them to heirs based on need.
(False: In such a situation, typically, first, property if any will be sold to raise the money for the specific bequests; second, if there is still not enough money in the estate the remedy is Abatement, that is, the probate judge will reduce the specific bequests accordingly; and finally if there is no money for any specific bequests there will be complete Abatement, that is, they will be gone.)

10. A holographic will is one that is a video-taped presentation by the testator.
(False: A holographic will in one entirely in the writing of the testator and signed by the testator, but because the will is not witnessed it is invalid in most states.)

11. The publication of a will is the formal reading of a will by an attorney before the heirs and other interested parties after the death of the testator.
(False: Publication is when the testator declares to witnesses that the instrument is his or her will.)

12. A separate written agreement that amends or revokes a will is called a constructive trust.
(False: Such an agreement is called a Codicil to a will and must be executed with the same formalities as a will to be legally effective. A constructive trust is a trust created by and imposed by a court for the benefit of a person when his or her assets were taken by means of fraud or breach of a fiduciary relationship.)

13. A resulting trust can arise when one person buys property but the consideration for that property is supplied by another person.
(True: A resulting trust can also arise from the failure of an express trust.)

14. Probate is the legal process wherein the validity of a will is established, and the terms of the will are carried out during an administration supervised by the probate court.

(True: The person who makes a will is called the testator; and the person named in the will to carry out its terms is called either the executor or personal representative, and if one is not named in the will, an administrator will be appointed by the court.)

15. A gift of real estate pursuant in a will is called a bequest.
(False: It is called a devise. A bequest, also called a legacy, is a gift of personal property under a will. The recipient is called a devisee or legatee.)

16. When a will provides that any assets remaining after specific devises and bequests have been made and debts have been paid that part of the estate is called a lapsed legacy.
(False: The remaining part is called the residuary estate, which goes to the residuary beneficiary as named in the will, and if none the residuary estate passes to heirs according to the state's laws of intestacy, that is, estate distribution when there is no will. A lapsed legacy arises when the legatee dies prior to the testator. In the past the legacy then lapsed or ended and the property went into the residuary estate; but today if the legatee has a child or other blood relative pursuant to most state laws the heirs of the legatee will inherit the gift.)

17. Publication of a will, that is, the testator declaring that this will about to be signed is his or her final will and testament, is a requirement to a valid will.
(False: In the most states today the formal requirement of publication is no longer necessary.)

18. The distribution of the assets of a decedent' estate is first given to the government for taxes.
(False: The expenses of probating the will, that is, the administration of the estate, are paid first, followed by funeral expenses (usually to a maximum amount), and then taxes and debts, followed by medical and hospital expenses (for a time-period prescribed before the decedent's death), family allowances as determined by statute, business debts for a business continued after death, and finally all other claims against the estate. Then, after all the foregoing have been satisfied, the estate can be distributed.)

19. The law regards the personal representative or executor of a will as a fiduciary.
(True: This is a fundamental principle of the law of wills. The personal representative who administers the estate is in a relationship or trust, confidence, loyalty, good faith, disclosure, and fair-dealing with the beneficiaries of the estate. The breach of a fiduciary duty is equivalent to fraud.)

20. A private express trust does not necessarily need a beneficiary since a charitable organization can always be named by a judge as the beneficiary.
(False: A private express trust fails for a lack of a beneficiary or beneficiaries since at least one ascertained beneficiary is needed to enforce the terms of the trust. In such a case a resulting trust is formed for the benefit of the creator of the trust, called the "settlor." However, if the trust is a charitable one, a beneficiary is not a prerequisite since if one is lacking or no longer in existence a judge can name another charitable entity as the beneficiary.)

21. A Resulting Trust can arise when one obtains title to property fraudulently or through theft of embezzlement.
(False: This would be a Constructive Trust, which would be imposed by a court which would order the trustee to convey title to the property to the proper beneficiaries or recipients. Whereas a Resulting Trust arises upon the failure of an express trust, which becomes void or unenforceable for any reason, for example, the lack of a beneficiary; and as such the trustee's only duty is to convey the property back to the settlor.)

22. A Discretionary Trust affords the trustee the discretion to apply of withhold payments of income and/or principal to beneficiaries at his or her discretion.
(True: And until such payments are made the creditors of the beneficiaries cannot reach the beneficiaries' interests. Note that this type of trust should not be confused with a Support Trust that allows the trustee only to pay to the beneficiaries so much income and/or principal necessary for their support.)

Multiple Choice Questions with Answers and Explanations

1. The requirements for a valid will are:
   a. Legal age and testamentary capacity
   b. The intent to transfer and distribute property on death
   c. A signed writing witnessed by typically two witnesses
   d. All of the above.

(The correct answer is d. These are the basic requirements for a valid will. Legal age is typically 18 years of age, Testamentary capacity means that one has a "sound mind" and thus knows what his or her will is, what one's property consists of, to whom it is to be given, particularly family members, good friends, and other natural objects of his or her bounty, as well as the creation of an orderly scheme of distribution. The writing can be in the testator's own hand, called a holographic will. Note that today oral wills regardless of witnesses are not permissible. Finally, note that in some states three witnesses are required, particularly if the testator is devising land in the will.)

2. Which of the following is a FALSE statement?
   a. The laws of intestate descent and distribution govern the disposition of property when a person dies without having a will.
   b. Lineal heirs are people who stem from one another in a line which includes the intestate decedent, for example, one's mother or father or grandmother or grandfather.
   c. *Per Stirpes* distribution means that when all members of a class of "takers" are the same they all take an equal share of the estate.
   d. Collateral heirs stem not from one another but from a common ancestor, for example, one's brother or sister of cousins.

(The correct answer is c. Per stirpes distribution means that when a relationship between "takers" is unequal, then each person takes by representation, that is, he or she takes his deceased ancestor's share. For example, if a decedent leaves one son and two grandchildren from a previously deceased daughter, the son takes one-half of the estate and the grandchildren split their mother's share. Per capital distribution means that when all members of a class of "takers" is the same, for example, all are children of the decedent, then they all take the same equal share.)

3. A testator can revoke his or her will prior to death by the following means:
   a. Revocation by written instrument.
   b. Revocation by a physical act performed on the will.
   c. Revocation by operation of the law.
   d. All of the above.

(The correct answer is d. These are all valid methods to revoke a will. A written instrument can expressly revoke a prior will or do so impliedly, for example, by having subsequent inconsistent provisions with the prior will. To be effective, physical revocation must involve destroying or defacing the whole will and not merely part of it. Revocation by operation of the law would include a situation where the testator subsequent to the will gets married or has children – natural or adopted.

The will is not revoked in such a situation, but the surviving spouse and the subsequent children get their intestate share.)

4. To have a valid physical revocation of a will:
    a. the will can be burnt, obliterated, torn up, defaced, or destroyed.
    b. the testator must have the simultaneous intent to presently revoke his or her will.
    c. the will can have sections crossed-out or interlined.
    d. a and b.

    (The correct answer is d. Crossing-out or interlining a portion of a will is legally ineffective; and accordingly, the part attempted to be revoked can be admitted into probate if it can be recreated.)

5. Which of the following is a FALSE statement?
    a. A will can be revoked in part by a subsequent will.
    b. A codicil is a testamentary instrument executed with the same formalities as a will, which usually modifies, alters, expands or changes the will.
    c. A codicil can "save" a will if the will was not legally sufficient
    d. A will cannot be revoked in part by a subsequent codicil.

    (The correct answer is d. So long as the codicil is executed with the same formalities as the will and refers to the will, the two instruments will be read together as one based on the date of the codicil.)

6. Restrictions on the power of testation include:
    a. Testamentary capacity
    b. Undue influence
    c. Fraud
    d. All of the above.

    (The correct answer is d. Testamentary capacity has been referred to, but it also should be noted that the testator must have this capacity at the time of the making of his or her will and not necessarily at death. Undue influence regarding the validity of wills as well as contracts is a difficult area of the law – legally and practically. In essence, undue influence means a person has over-influenced, excessively persuaded, manipulated, or "brain-washed" the testator into making or changing his or her will. However, if there is a confidential relationship between the parties, for example, attorney and client, or a close personal relationship, such as caretaker and ward, and the testator's distribution is not "natural," for example, disinheriting his or her children and favoring the "stranger," a presumption of undue influence can arise, especially if the beneficiary was involved with procuring, drafting, or keeping the will. Fraud, that is, deceit, can render a will invalid as it can to a contract.)

7. Which are necessary parts to the estate administration and probate process?
    a. Appointing a personal representative
    b. Securing "proof of will"
    c. Publishing a Notice of Administration
    d. All of the above.

    (The correct answer is d. The personal representative, also called an "executor" in some states, is the person named in the will by the testator to administer his or her will; but if one is not named the probate judge will appoint one. Proof of will is the proceeding to determine if the will submitted for probate is in fact the will of the testator. However, note that if a will is "self-proving," that is, signed by the testator and witnesses before a notary in conformity with state law, such a will can be admitted to probate without further proof. Notice of Administration, also called in some states Letters of Administration, is a publication by the personal representative of notice of probate in a paper of local circulation in conformity with state law giving notice to any

interested parties in case they have an interest in or claims to the estate of the deceased testator so they can file their claims against the estate in a timely manner.)

8. The Ademption rule means that:
   a. A specific devise will be revoked if it is not in the testator's estate at the time of his or her death.
   b. all the decedent's medical and hospital expenses prior to death are revoked.
   c. if a beneficiary is dead any and all gifts to the beneficiary are revoked.
   d. when a beneficiary in a class of beneficiaries dies his or her gift(s) is/are revoked.
   (The correct answer is a. A specific devise is a gift of a particular object that is distinct from other objects, for example, a certain diamond ring. If the gift is no longer in the testator's estate at the time of his or her death it is "adeemed," that is, revoked, regardless of the testator's intent. Whereas a general devise is a gift of general economic benefit payable out of the assets of the estate, for example, a gift of $10,000. If the money is not there the gift is not revoked and the personal representative will have to sell estate assets to come up with the cash. Abatement is the process of reducing gifts because the assets of the estate are insufficient to pay the obligations of the estate as well as the gifts to the beneficiaries. If a beneficiary of a gift is a lineal descendant of the testator and fails to survive the testator the gift, pursuant to state Anti-Lapse statutes, does not lapse but goes to the descendants of the deceased beneficiary, who take per stirpes, that is, they take their deceased ancestor's share. Anti-Lapse statutes also apply when one in a class of beneficiaries dies, and as such the gift does not lapse but the descendants of the deceased class member get his or her share per stirpes.)

9. In order to have a valid express private trust all the following elements are necessary EXCEPT:
   a. an intention on the part of the creator of the trust, called the "settlor," to create the trust.
   b. consideration.
   c. a trustee
   d. trust property, called the trust "*res*."
   (The correct answer is b. Consideration is not necessary to form a trust; a trust can be created gratuitously. Note that a valid trust purpose as well as a beneficiary or beneficiaries are also required to have a valid trust.)

10. Which of the following is a FALSE statement about a private express trust?
    a. If the subject matter of a trust is real property, the intent to create a trust must be evidenced by written words.
    b. The intention to create a trust must be manifested by the settlor at the time that he or she owned the property.
    c. A trust will fail due to the lack of a trustee.
    d. In order to have a valid trust there must be a trust *res* or *corpus*, that is, trust property.
    (The correct answer is c. A trust will not fail due to the lack of a trustee, for example, if the trustee dies or becomes incapacitated, since a successor trustee can be appointed by the court. Note that if the subject matter of a trust is personal, as opposed to real, property, the intent to create a trust can be demonstrated through oral words, though obviously oral trusts are not advisable. A trust must have a res or corpus, but the subject matter of the property can be intangible as well as intangible property but not property which the creator of the trust expects to own in the future.)

11. Which of the following is FALSE about trusts?
    a. A charitable trust can be created for particular named persons but only if they are very poor and destitute.
    b. An *inter vivos* trust can be created by a Declaration of Trust.

c. A testamentary trust is created by a person in his or her will.
d. The *cy pres* doctrine allows a judge to substitute a charitable beneficiary in a charitable trust.

(The correct answer is a. A charitable trust must have as a beneficiary that is indefinite, unnamed, and in a changing class, such as the "needy," and not definite identifiable persons, regardless of whether they are very needy. A Declaration of Trust is simply a statement by the owner of property that he or she holds the property in trust for a beneficiary, thereby creating an inter vivos trust. A testamentary trust is permissible, but it must be created in conformity to the state statute regarding the validity of wills and trusts in wills. Cy pres will allow substitution for beneficiaries in a charitable trust, but only if a judge can ascertain that the settlor had a general intent to aid charity of a particular type of charity; otherwise, the judge will create a resulting trust in favor of the settlor.)

12. Which of the following is FALSE about trusts?
    a. An Honorary Trust is to take care of graves or animals is recognized in some states even though technically there is no beneficiary to enforce the trust.
    b. The law holds a trustee to be a guarantor that the trust's financial investments are profitable ones.
    c. A Spendthrift Trust is one created by the settlor with restraints on the beneficiaries transferring trust property.
    a. d. The doctrine of "changed circumstances" can give a court the power to direct a trustee to deviate from the terms of the trust.

(The correct answer is b. A trustee is not a guarantor of financial success of trust assets. The trustee is held to the "prudent investor" standard and thus act in a reasonable and prudent matter in making investment decisions for the trust, for example, by diversifying trust assets and using financial, accounting, and legal experts. Note that not all states recognize the Honorary Trust. In a Spendthrift Trust the beneficiaries cannot transfer their interests in the trust, but creditors also cannot reach those interests until income is distributed to the beneficiaries. In a Spendthrift Trust the settlor typically has serious reservations about the beneficiaries' capability of managing their own affairs. The doctrine of "changed circumstances" will give a court the afore mentioned power, but only if compliance with the terms of the trust would impair or defeat trust purposes and the settlor did not anticipate the changed circumstances. However, note that the doctrine cannot be used to change the rights of the beneficiaries, that is, by "invading" trust principal to favor income beneficiaries to the detriment of the remainder beneficiaries.)

27 - Intellectual Property

Introduction

Intellectual property law is premised on several important bodies of law, to wit: federal patent law, federal copyright law, federal trademark law, state trade secret law, and international treaty. Though intellectual property is a very specialized area of the law, the student must know some of the basic provisions of the federal laws, which are primarily statutory, including what can be protected, duration of the protections, and the sanctions for infringement. Particularly important are exceptions in the laws, that is, the "reverse engineering" exception to patent law as well as the "fair use" exception to copyright law. The student also must be aware that state law, either statutory based on the Uniform Trade Secret Act (UTSA) or state common law, can provide an alterative and easier method to protect intellectual property. As such, the student must know the requirements that can turn information into a legally protected trade secret as well as the fact that there are criminal as well as civil sanctions for misappropriating trade secrets. The student must be cognizant of the critical fact that a confidentiality or non-disclosure agreement is a very important factor in determining whether information rises to the level of a legally protected trade secret. Moreover, particularly important to the business student is the fact that a business plan can be converted into a legally protected trade secret. Also, although covered in the "legality" section to contract law, the student should be aware that covenants-not-to-compete as well as non-solicitation and non-piracy agreements are other methods to protect at least indirectly intellectual property. Finally, some basic knowledge as to the existence and principal provisions of the major international treaties that protect intellectual property should be required.

True and False Questions with Answers and Explanations

1. Patents, trademarks, and copyrights are all examples of government-granted monopolies to the holders of such intellectual property.
(True: This is a basic proposition. However, there are limits as to the duration of these exclusive ownership rights.)

2. The Fair Use Doctrine would prohibit the use of copyrighted material in the classroom unless permission is obtained from the copyright holder.
(False: Permission need not be obtained so long as the use is limited, non-commercial, and does not harm the value and potential market for the copyrighted work. So, for example, copyrighted works could be used for case studies, discussion, comments, criticisms, research, and scholarship.)

3. A key factor in determining whether information rises to the level of a legally protected trade secret is the degree and extent of the employer's effort to maintain the secrecy of the information.
(True: For a trade secret, such as a customer list, to arise there must be 1) information (broadly construed), 2) possessing economic value to a competitor, and 3) subject to reasonable efforts to maintain its secrecy, for example, non-disclosure and confidentiality agreements in contracts, having information password protected, under lock-and-key, with access limited to those who have a need-to-know and who have been informed that they are dealing with confidential, non-public, proprietary information.)

4. A business plan can never be a trade secret since it is too non-scientific to be considered as "information" and the plan only has potential value.
(False: "Information" under the Uniform Trade Secret Act (UTSA) as well as under the common law is very broadly construed to encompass plans, strategies, and concepts in addition to the more scientific devices, formulas, patterns, techniques, and methods. Moreover, the value to a competitor requirement is satisfied if the value is real or potential as in a business plan with prospective value.)

5. Copyright infringement does not occur if a computer program's structure, sequence, and organization are copied since computer programs are not protected by copyright law.
(False: Computer programs are specifically covered by and protected by the Computer Software Copyright Act.)

6. In order to obtain a valid copyright, one must apply to and obtain the official copyright and registration thereof from the Patent and Copyright Office.
(False: Copyright protection is now automatic and extends to original works of authorship in a fixed, tangible medium. Registration with the Copyright Office is not required, though certainly advisable for maximum protection of the copyrighted work.)

7. Protection of trade secrets extends only to scientific and manufacturing devices, formulas, and processes, and to "softer" information so as business strategies and marketing plans.
(False: The foundational requirement for trade secret protection is "information," which term is very broadly construed to include "hard" scientific info as well as "soft" info, such as ideas, concepts, plans, and strategies.)

8. Trade secret protection of intellectual property is theoretically perpetual so long as one acts in a reasonable manner under the circumstances to maintain the secrecy of the information.
(True: This is a benefit of trade secret protection as opposed to patents and copyrights which have time limits.)

9. Covenants-not-to-compete are never enforceable in employment situations because there is the potential that an employee who is "down-sized" for economic reasons will be precluded from finding another comparable job in his or her chosen field and locality.
(False: Except in California where covenants-not-to-compete are illegal in employment contracts due to legislative fiat, in most states they are legal if certain requirements are met, for example, being reasonable in time and area as well as the employer having a legitimate reason for the covenant; and in the vast majority of the states the harm or burden on the employee is not a factor.)

10. Harm to the employee is never taken into consideration if a covenant-not-to-compete is reasonable as to time and place and the employer has a legitimate business reason for the covenant.
(False: This is the general rule; however, some states have additional requirements to protect the employee, for example, New Jersey which says that the covenant cannot be an "undue burden" on the employee; and Pennsylvania which says that the covenant cannot be "oppressive" on the employee.)

11. An agreement providing for the International Protection of Copyrights is the Berne Convention.
(True: The Berne Convention is an 1886 international treaty. Note that under the treaty copyright notice on the work itself is not required, though strongly recommended to avoid situations of "innocent" copyright infringement.)

12. Misappropriation of a trade secret can result in criminal as well as civil sanctions.
(True: Civil sanctions encompass lawsuits for money damages and an injunction; and criminal sanctions, which are typically under the theft category under state criminal law, can result in fines

and/or imprisonment depending on whether the misappropriation is a misdemeanor or a felony. And not that misappropriating a trade secret on the behalf of a foreign government or an entity controlled or dominated by a foreign government is a violation of the federal Economic Espionage Act which has very severe criminal penalties including imprisonment for up to 20 years.)

13. Trademark protection extends to the registering of names as domain names on the Internet.
(True: This protection also extends to famous names, and if registering is improperly done by usurping a famous name or using a deceptively similar one the illegal practice is called "cyber-squatting.")

14. Trademark law protects the holder of the trademark from people who might use the same trademark on their products and services.
(True: The law also precludes using similar trademarks, such as in the classic "Coke" v. "Koke" dispute, since such actions might be misleading and confusing to the public.)

15. The Paris Convention is an important international treaty protecting intellectual property.
(True: The Paris Convention of 1883, which over 90 countries adhere to, allows a party in one signatory country to sue for patent and trademark protection in the other member countries.)

Multiple Choice Questions with Answers and Explanations

1. With respect to patents:
   a. the holder has a monopoly over the use of a patented invention for his or her lifetime.
   b. to be patented the invention must be novel, useful, and non-obvious.
   c. the patent holder can seek remedies of an injunction and damages against the patent infringer.
   d. All of the above.

   (The correct answer is d. These are basic propositions but note that the usefulness of an invention is not always measured at the time it is patented; rather, it may become useful in the future due to other scientific and technological advancements.)

2. The "fair use" doctrine applies to:
   a. Patent law
   b. The employment at-will doctrine
   c. Copyright law
   d. The National Labor Relations Act

   (The correct answer is c. Fair use allows limited, non-commercial use of copyrighted work for purposes of education, criticism, analysis, and commentary if such use does not harm the market for the copyrighted work.)

3. How can intellectual property be protected in the United States?
   a. By patent law
   b. By copyright law
   c. By trade secret law
   d. All of the above.

   (The correct answer is d. These are the main ways to protect intellectual property in the U.S. Patent law and copyright law are based on federal law. But note that trade secret law is based on state law, typically the Uniform Trade Secret Act, and that trade secret protection can theoretically be perpetual as opposed to patent and copyright protections which have limited duration as per federal statutes.)

4. When can a customer list of an employer rise to the level of a legally protected trade secret?
   a. When the list has information in it which possesses value and which the employer has made reasonable efforts to keep the list secret.
   b. When the employer obtains a federal copyright or trademark on it.
   c. When there is concrete evidence that all the employer's customers on the list would be willing to continue doing business with the employer.
   d. When the people on the customer list are readily obtainable from public sources.

   (The correct answer is a. Answer a includes the three required components of a legally protected trade – information, which is broadly construed, value to a competitor, which can be real or potential, and evidence of reasonable measures to maintain the secrecy of the information. Patent, copyright, and trademark law are separate ways to protect intellectual property; and they are based on federal law as opposed to trade secret law which is primarily state-based law, particularly the Uniform Trade Secret Act. If information is publicly available, it does not possess the requisite "value"; and customer preferences are irrelevant in finding that a trade secret has been misappropriated.)

5. What is FALSE about a trade secret?
   a. The "information" predicate is broadly construed by the courts.
   b. Business plans cannot be trade secrets is any value they have is merely potential future value.
   c. Misappropriation of trade secrets can result in criminal as well as civil sanctions.
   d. A non-disclosure or confidentiality clause in an agreement is evidence that one is taking reasonable measures to maintain the secrecy of the information.

   (The correct answer is b. The value to a competitor of the information sought to be protected can be actual value as well as potential future value, such as a business plan or a company business strategy. "Information" is very broadly construed by the courts to encompass "hard" information, such as scientific formulas, as well as "soft" information, such as ideas, concepts, and plans.)

6. Which of the following is a FALSE statement?
   a. The Fair Use doctrine is an exception to copyright law.
   b. Computer software can be copyrighted.
   c. Registration of a copyright by the U.S. Copyright Office is mandatory in all cases in order to have a valid, legally protected, and enforceable copyright.
   d. The Digital Millennium Copyright Act holds that an Internet service provider is not liable for copyright infringement by its customers unless it was aware of the customers' violations.

   (The correct answer is c. Registration is no longer required as copyright protection extends now automatically to original works of authorship in a tangible medium. However, registration is strongly advised for evidentiary purposes of proving the existence of the copyright as well as the time when it was obtained.)

7. What bodies of law can be used to protect intellectual property?
   a. Patent law
   b. Copyright law
   c. Trade Secret law
   d. All of the above

   (The correct answer is d. Patent and copyright law are based on federal statutes. Trade secret law is either based on state statutes, generally following the Uniform Trade Secrets Act, or state common law. Trade secret law provides a relatively simple, straightforward, and inexpensive way to protect intellectual property; and, moreover, the protection can be potentially perpetual.)

8. What is FALSE about U.S. patent law?
   a. To be patentable an invention must be novel, useful, and non-obvious.
   b. Mathematical formulas can be patentable but only if they are complex.
   c. Once a patent is approved the patent holder must put the words "patent" or "pat" on the product or device.
   d. "Reverse engineering" is an exception to patent law.

(The correct answer is b. Mathematical formulas cannot be patented, regardless of complexity, since they are just mimicking mental processes as well as being considered part of the "laws of nature," and thus not new or "novel." "Reverse engineering" occurs when a person takes the basic idea and function of an invention and accomplishes the same result through a different series of steps, thereafter, being legally able to sell the "new" device.)

9. What is FALSE about U.S. copyright law?
   a. Computer programs cannot be copyrighted since they are not the equivalent of books, plays, movies, and songs and other works of authorship.
   b. The duration of a copyright is the life of the author plus 70 years.
   c. The "fair use" doctrine is an exception to copyright law.
   d. Copyright law protects the "expression" of an idea but not the idea itself.

(The correct answer is a. Computer programs and software can be protected by Copyright law by virtue of the Copyright Reform Act of 1976 which treats them the same as literary works. "Fair use" allows limited use of copyrighted materials, principally for educational use as well as criticism and commentary, without the need to pay royalties to the copyright holder. A person legally can take the basic idea of a copyrighted work, and then by means of different expressions recreate it as an independent work, and then resell it. Note that for duration for publishers the time period is 95 years from the date of publication.)

10. What factors are applicable in determining whether the use of a copyrighted work is "fair use" and thus an exception to copyright law?
    a. The nature of the copyrighted work and character of the use, particularly if it is commercial or not
    b. The amount and substance of the copyrighted work used
    c. The effect of the use on the value and potential market of the copyrighted work
    d. All of the above.

    (The correct answer is d. These are all key factors. However, if the use amounts to a substantial revision or is transformational, for example, by adding new information, interpretations, and/or understanding of the copyrighted work, the use is more likely to be deemed a "fair" one. Conversely, the more commercial is the use is and the more it diminishes the value of the copyrighted work, the less likely that the use will be construed as "fair.")

11. What are the elements of a legally protected trade secret?
    a. Information
    b. Value of the information
    c. Reasonable steps to maintain the secrecy of the information
    d. All of the above.

    (The correct answer is d. These are the three main requirements; and note that trade secret protection is based on state law, and thus no federal registration is required as with patent and copyright law.)

12. What is TRUE about trade secret law?
   a. It only protects "hard," scientific information like devices and formulas.
   b. The value requirement must be present value to a competitor.
   c. A non-disclosure or confidentiality agreement is very strong evidence that one has engaged in reasonable steps to maintain the secrecy of the information.
   d. Trade secret protection lasts for the life of the owner plus 95 years.

(The correct answer is c. A confidentiality or non-disclosure is probably the best way to gain trade secret protection for information that has value. Trade secret law in addition to protecting "hard" information also protects "soft" information, such as ideas, concepts, strategies, plans, including, and most importantly, business plans. The value to competitor of the information can of course be present value but it can also be potential value, such as in a strategy, plan, and business plan. Trade secret protection theoretically can be perpetual, so long as reasonable steps are taken under the circumstances, for example, comparing the "reasonable" efforts of a small retail firm vs. a huge defense contractor, to maintain and secure the secrecy of the information.)

28 - Internet Regulation

Introduction

The old maxim is: "The law takes time to catch up to technology." Nevertheless, today there are certain important statutes dealing with Internet regulation, especially online contracting. These statutes are as follows: the Uniform Electronic Transaction Act (UETA), the Uniform Computer Information Transaction Act (UCITA), and the Electronic Signature in Global and National Commerce Act (E-Sign). Critically important for the student to know is the fact that these statutes have validated electronic signatures and records to legal and enforceable contracts. Moreover, the student must be aware of some of the significant changes these statutes have made to the common law of contracts, especially regarding offers and acceptances. Also important for the student to be aware of are the following statutes: the anti-spam law, called the U.S Safe Web Act, the Electronic Communications Privacy Act (ECPA), and the Anti-cybersquatting Consumer Protection Act.

True and False Questions with Answers and Explanations

1. It is illegal in the U.S. for websites to collect personal information from people.
(False: Such information can be collected but for children under the age of 13 the consent of a parent must be obtained.)

2. The Electronic Communications Privacy Act (ECPA) makes it illegal for an employer to intercept and read the emails of its employees.
(False: A major exception in the statute is for a party who provided the service, typically an employer to its employees. Moreover, the employer can access stored email communications too.)

3. The Internet Corporation for Assigned Names and Numbers is authorized to arbitrate and settle Internet domain name disputes.
(True: This is a private entity under contract with the U.S. government. All people who register domain names agree to this dispute resolution procedure as part of the registration process.)

4. Since "spam" is usually regarded as a form of electronic "junk mail" it can be totally prohibited by the federal government.
(False: Certain types of spam could be regarded as forms of political and commercial speech and thus be protected by the First Amendment. However, voluminous spamming which causes serious economic harm may be actionable under a trespass to chattels theory. Moreover, the federal CAN-SPAM Act prohibits certain types of spamming practices, such as having no return address on an email or a false return address on an email.)

5. As a general rule courts will hold that state Website content restrictions violate the First Amendment.
(True: However, if the censorship is done by the Website owner or the Internet Service Provider the restrictions would be legal as these are private entities and not government, and then the issue

becomes an ethical as well as likely a "political" one. The situation is naturally different in Communist China were Websites cannot use or have searches using certain words, such as "human rights" and "democracy.")

6. "Cybersquatting" results when a person or business registers a domain name which is the same, or confusingly similar to, another's domain name.
(True: The "squatter" then often attempts to sell the domain back to the original owner. This practice is illegal under federal law, specifically by means of the Anti-cybersquatting Consumer Protection Act, if there is evidence of bad faith intent, for example diverting customers or clients, harming good will, or even "merely" offering to sell the domain name back to the original owner.)

7. The Federal Communications Commission is primarily responsible for regulating the issuance of domain names on the Internet.
(False: The entity is called the Internet Corporation for Assigned Names and Numbers. ICANN is a private entity under contract with the U.S. government; it has established an arbitration process, called the Uniform Dispute Resolution Policy, to resolve domain name disputes (which all users of the ICANN registration process are held to agree to use.)

8. According to the Uniform Computer Information Transaction Act (UCITA) if an offer to form a contract is in electronic form, thereby evoking an electronic response in order to accept the offer, the electronic acceptance is effective when received by the offeror.
(True: This is a major change in the common law of contracts for e-contracts since under the common law if the same medium is used to transmit the acceptance as was used in the offer the acceptance is effective on dispatch, not receipt.)

9. The Uniform Electronic Transaction Act (UETA) which makes electronic signatures equal to written signatures for contract purposes applies to all contracting situations.
(False: UETA applies only to transactions between parties or entities that have agreed to conduct their businesses by electronic means, such as by using the Internet.)

10. Under the Uniform Computer Information Transaction Act counteroffers are invalid in electronic contracting.
(True: This is another major change UCITA makes in the common law of contracts where a counteroffer is construed as a rejection of the original offer. That is, a counteroffer by an offeree is under UCITA not effective against an electronic offeror since most electronic entities do not have the ability to evaluate, accept, or even make counteroffers.)

11. A court will not enforce a "shrink-wrap" agreement if the buyer and user of the goods did not read the terms of the agreement.
(False: A shrink-wrap, which is typically used in the sale of computer software, is an agreement in which the provisions are expressed inside a box in which the goods are packaged, and when the buyer opens the box he or she is informed that by retaining the goods in the box, he or she thereby agrees to the terms of the agreement; and it is immaterial that the buyer did not read the terms therein. A shrink-wrap agreement must be distinguished from a "click-on" agreement whereby a buyer, usually of computer software, is asked to click-on an "Agree" button to agree to the offer, and when he or she does that click-on signifies an acceptance.)

12. Under the Electronic Signature in Global and National Commerce Act (E-Sign Act) a valid signature on a contract can be any mark or process intended to be the signature on an electronic contract.

(True: The best example would be the name typed at the bottom of an e-mail message. Another example would be when a buyer clicks on the "I Agree" or "Agree" button on a webpage.)

13. Cybersquatting is now illegal pursuant to the Anti-cybersquatting Consumer Protection Act.
(True: Cybersquatting arises when a person registers a domain name that is the same or very similar to another's name, including a "famous" person's name. The "squatter" then attempts to sell the domain name back to the original owner. This is illegal if the name is the same or confusingly similar and there is evidence of bad faith, for example, diverting customers, harming good will, and "merely" attempting to sell the name back.)

14. An employer can access the stored electronic e-mail communications of its employees who utilized the employer's email system.
(True: This is a major exception to the Electronic Communications Privacy Act, which makes it a crime to intercept electronic communications at the point of transmission, in transit, when stored by a server, or after receipt by the intended recipient.)

Multiple Choice Questions with Answers and Explanations

1. What is/are very important statutes governing "e-contracts"?
   a. The Uniform Electronic Transaction Act (UETA)
   b. The Uniform Computer Information Transaction Act (UCITA)
   c. The Electronic Signature in Global and National Commerce Act
   d. All of the above.

   (The correct answer is d. These are the three main statutes that govern entering into contracts on-line and which have validated e-contracts and electronic signatures.)

2. What is FALSE about online contracting on the Internet?
   a. The Uniform Electronic Transfer Act (UETA) places electronic records and signatures on the same level as paper contracts and written signatures.
   b. Under the Uniform Computer Information Transaction Act (UCITA), if an offer is in electronic form, and the offer is accepted electronically, a contract is formed when the electronic acceptance is received.
   c. Under UCITA, a purported electronic acceptance is ineffective and treated as a counteroffer if it adds to changes or qualifies the terms of the acceptance.
   d. Regarding mistakes in contracting, under UCITA a consumer is not liable for unilateral mistakes if there is prompt notification of the mistake and the consumer has not benefited from the information.

   (The correct answer is c. The UETA statute will now have electronic records and signatures as satisfying the Statute of Frauds and signature requirements of common law contracts. UCITA makes some major changes in the common law. Counteroffers are not recognized under UCITA, and thus a contract is formed even if it changes the terms of the offer, which of course would be invalid under the old common law "mirror image" rule. Moreover, under the common law an acceptance is effective on dispatch if the means of acceptance is reasonable, but this fundamental common law principle has been changed by UCITA. So too had the unilateral mistake common law rule, whereby as a general rule there is no relief to a unilateral mistake. However, in addition to notice and not receiving a benefit, the consumer must also deliver or destroy the information received at the request of the other party as well as pay the costs for shipping, reshipping, and reprocessing.)

29 - Securities Regulation

Introduction

Securities regulation is another major area of government regulation of business law. Securities regulation is primarily based on three main federal statutes – the Securities Act of 1933, the Securities and Exchange Act of 1934, and the Sarbanes-Oxley Act (SOX) of 2002. However, the student should be aware of the existence of state law, which is primarily statutory, called "Blue Sky" law, which also regulates the issuance and sale of securities, especially since if an issuance of stock or other securities matter is too small or inconsequential for the federal government to get involved there nonetheless will be a parallel body of state law regulating the subject matter. The student first must know that the term "security" is very broadly construed by the courts to encompass not merely traditional stocks and bonds, but also "investment contracts." As *per* the 1933 Act the student must know that it is basically a disclosure type of statute, requiring sufficient information being given to the Securities and Exchange Commission and the investing public by means of a registration statement and prospectus. As *per* the 1934 Act the student must know that this statute is a very broad anti-fraud statute, which makes illegal civilly and criminally false and misleading statements regarding buying and selling securities. The Act also makes manipulation of the stock markets and stock trading illegal. Most importantly, the student must know of a major change the federal law makes to the common law, since in the latter "silence" is not fraud, but regarding buying and selling securities silence, that is, omitting material facts, can be construed as securities fraud. The student must also be aware of the main rule governing insider trading, Rule 10b-5, which makes trading on material, inside information by misappropriators, insiders, and tippees of insiders a civil and criminal wrong. Moreover, the student must know the two exceptions by which one can legally trade on inside information, to wit: trading by the "lucky," who by chance oversee or overhear or stumble on insider information, and the "smart," who by means of their own intelligence and deductive ability and using legitimate sources of information "ferret out" or deduce the existence of inside information. As such, the student must be cognizant of the critical distinction made today in U.S. securities laws, that is, insider trading is illegal, BUT trading on inside information MAY be legal. Finally, as *per* the fairly recent SOX statute the student must be aware of the key certification requirements, the protections afforded whistleblowers, and the very draconian criminal penalties that can be imposed for securities fraud.

True and False Questions with Answers and Explanations

1. The courts have interpreted SEC Rule 10b-5 as making a distinction between insider trading and trading on inside information.
(True: Insider trading is clearly illegal, whereas trading on inside information may be legal, for example, if one propitiously overhears company personnel discussing material, non-public information, such as a merger plan.)

2. Federal securities laws require that a Registration Statement be filed for public offerings of stock unless the offering can qualify for an exemption.
(True: The Registration Statement must contain sufficient information for a member of the investing public to know the nature of the business, the principals behind the business, the purpose and plans for the business, and the financial condition of the business. An example of an exemption would be a Private Placement, that is, a company offering stock to its employees who presumably know sufficient information about the business of the firm.)

3. A securities stock offering that involves a small amount of money usually would be exempt from federal securities registration requirements.
(True: The federal Securities and Exchange Commission which regulates the "publicly traded" stock market has "jurisdictional yardsticks" in terms of dollar amounts and thus will not deal with "small" stock offerings. However, the states have securities laws and regulatory agencies that parallel the federal laws and the SEC so a small stock offering may still have to comply with federal law.)

4. Pursuant to Securities and Exchange Commission Rule 10b-5 corporate "insiders" only include directors, officers, and high-level executives and managerial employees.
(False: The SEC and the courts give an expansive meaning to the term "insiders" to include all employees of the corporation as well as majority shareholders and even "outsiders," such as lawyers, accountants, independent sales personnel, and financial printers, who regularly deal with the corporation and thus have access to material confidential information.)

5. Anyone who knowingly receives material inside information as a result of an insider's breach of a fiduciary duty can be liable under SEC Rule 10b-5 for insider trading.
(True: Insiders are liable for insider trading but so are their tippees, even "remote" tippees, with the requisite knowledge who are in conspiracy with insiders.)

6. The principal purpose of the Securities Act of 1933 is to prevent manipulation of the stock market by "pump-and-dump" misconduct.
(False: The primary purpose of the 1933 Act is disclosure, that is, by mandating disclosure to the investing public of the company, its business, principals, and plans by means of the filing of a registration statement with the SEC and the providing of a Prospectus to investors. The primary purpose of the Securities and Exchange Act of 1934 is to prevent fraud and deceit in the marketplace for stocks, which would encompass stock manipulation by means of "pump-and-dump" practices.)

7. Even if information is deemed to be "public information" the corporate insider still must disclose it to a potential purchaser of the company's stock since that person may not have read about the information in the *Wall Street Journal* or other business publication.
(False: Once information is "public" it can be traded on regardless of any lack of actual knowledge by a buyer or seller.)

8. To be liable for "short-swing" profits under Section 16(b) of the Securities and Exchange Act of 1934 the corporate insider must possess inside information.
(False: Liability is based on the corporate insider buying and selling, or selling and buying back, of the company's stock within a six-month period, even without any inside information.)

9. The Securities and Exchange Act of 1933 regulates the payment of dividends by corporate boards of directors.
(False: The payment of dividends is a responsibility of the board of directors and is governed by state corporate law. The 1934 Act is a disclosure statute mandating a registration statement being filed with the SEC and a prospectus being given to investors.)

10. Federal securities laws apply just to the buying and selling of shares of stocks and bonds.
(False: The laws apply to what the Supreme Court defines as "investment contracts," that is, business arrangements, such as a limited partnership, where one invests in a business and expects to make a profit based on the work and management of third parties, such as the general partner of a limited partnership.)

11. State laws that were promulgated to regulate the intrastate offering of securities are known as "blue sky" laws.
(True: The purpose of which is to protect the citizens and residents of the state from buying stock as worthless as the "deep blue sky.")

12. Generally, securities offerings that involve a small amount of money will be exempt from the registration requirements of federal securities law.
(True: However, the transactions will usually be governed by state securities laws and regulations which parallel the federal laws.)

13. Federal securities laws regarding the purchase and sale of stock follow the common law rule that generally "silence is not fraud."
(False: Material omissions in the purchase and sale of securities if knowingly done are considered to be securities fraud pursuant to the 1934 Act. This is a major change in the old common law rule that just applies to securities.)

14. Pursuant to Rule 10b-5 corporate "insiders" are narrowly construed to include only directors, officers, high-level executives, and majority shareholders.
(False: Any employee of a firm can be an "insider" for insider trading purposes, though typically it is the higher-level employees who have access to confidential material inside information. Moreover, the Securities and Exchange Commission takes a broad view of "insiders" to include actually "outsiders" who are not technically employees of the firm but rather independent contractors and/or agents, such as lawyers, accountants, sales personnel, and even financial printers.)

15. Anyone who knowingly trades on inside information commits the legal wrong of insider trading.
(False: Only those people who misappropriate (e.g., steal or bribe for) inside information, or who are insiders, or who are tippees in conspiracy with insiders are liable. Consequently, people who by luck or happenstance come across inside information can trade (and who are called "inadvertent tippees"). Moreover, market professionals as well as others who ferret out and deduce information, which is not yet public, using public sources and their own knowledge, intelligence, and skill, can legally trade on the information.)

16. The Securities and Exchange Commission requires that all publicly traded companies have a Code of Ethics.
(False: The Sarbanes-Oxley Act of 2002 merely says that if companies do not have a Code of Ethics that omission must be made public. The result, of course, is that most companies do have a Code of Ethics though a code is not legally required.)

17. A person who knowingly receives confidential information from a corporate insider who has breached his or her fiduciary duty can be liable for insider trading pursuant to SEC Rule 10b-5.
(True: This would be the classic case of a tipper and tippee.)

18. The Securities Act of 1933 requires that securities that are not exempt must be registered with the Securities and Exchange Commission (SEC) and that the SEC approve the issuance of the securities before they can be sold to the public.
(False: The 1933 Act does not require government approval. Rather, the Act is a disclosure-type statute requiring the filing of a registration statement with the SEC and the providing a prospectus to potential purchasers so as to give a member of the public enough information so that he or she can make an informed decision as to whether to purchase the stock.)

19. A shareholder can authorize another person to vote for him or her at a shareholders' meeting by means of a proxy, but this proxy must be given to another shareholder of the company unless the Articles of Incorporation permit "outsiders" to have proxies.
(False: A proxy can be given to any person, not only to shareholders. Moreover, the Articles can neither deny nor unreasonably restrict the shareholders' rights to grant proxies.)

20. A "tender offer" is usually not involved in a company's offering its initial sale of stock to the public.
(True: A tender offer is an invitation to the present shareholders of a public traded company to sell their shares. Tender offers are regulated by the Securities Act of 1934.)

21. If a person obtains confidential corporate information by means of wiretapping or "hacking" and trades thereon he or she would be considered to be a "misappropriator" and subject to civil and criminal liability for insider trading.
(True: Misappropriators also include thieves of confidential info as well as people who bribe insiders to obtain the information.)

22. Section 16(b) of the Securities Exchange Act of 1934 governs the making of "short-swing" profits by anyone trading on a public exchange.
(False: Section 16(b) only applies to "short-swing" profits gained by "insiders.")

23. The liability of tippees is governed by Section 16(b) of the Securities Act of 1934.
(False: Tippees are governed by SEC Rule 10b-5.)

24. In order to find an insider liable for making "short-swing" profits under Section 16(b) of the Securities Act of 1934 the government must prove that the insider used confidential inside information to make the trade.
(False: The use of inside information is not required under Section 16(b); rather, liability is premised on an insider trading his or her own company's stock (either purchasing and selling or selling and repurchasing) with a six-month time-period. Actually, the use of inside information is conclusively presumed due to the insider's "inside" status and short time period for the trading.)

25. Anyone who trades on inside information regardless of how acquired commits a legal wrong since the goal of securities law is to create a "level-playing-field" for investors.
(False: The level-playing-field theory is not the prevailing legal theory of securities law; rather, it is the insider theory whereby misappropriators, insiders, and tippees in conspiracy with insiders will be liable for insider trading.)

26. A primary objective of the Securities and Exchange Act of 1934 is to empower the Securities and Exchange Commission to protect members of the public who are not sophisticated regarding finance from making unwise stock investments by requiring prior approval of stock offerings.
(False: The federal government does not give prior approval to stock offerings – initial or subsequent; rather, the government just requires that by means of the filing of a registration statement and the

providing of a prospectus to potential investors a member of the public is given adequate, truthful, and accurate information in order to make a decision to invest.)

27. Corporate managers and supervisors would be considered to be "insiders" with potential liability for insider trading under Rule 10b-5.
(True: The key term "insider" has been broadly construed by the courts and it most certainly includes managers and supervisors who as employees typically would have access to confidential, non-public, material "inside" information.)

28. Pursuant to the federal courts' interpretation of securities laws the definition of a "security" is broadly construed to include other investments in addition to the traditional stocks and bonds.
(True: The Supreme Court has determined that securities laws apply to "investment contracts"; that is, business arrangement and investments where one party seeks to make profits primarily by the efforts of a third-party.)

29. Every initial sale or subsequent issuance of securities in the U.S. is subject to federal registration with the Securities and Exchange Commission.
(False: There are exemptions, for example, for "small" in dollar offerings, private placements to a company's management, and offerings to "sophisticated" investors. However, regarding "small" offerings, even if the SEC does not take jurisdiction the issuing company may still have to register the stock pursuant to state securities laws.)

30. The prospectus is the primary source of information regarding a company that is issuing securities to potential investors.
(True: And there is civil and criminal liability for misstatements, misrepresentations, and material knowing omissions in the prospectus. Information can also be found in the registration statement filed by the company with the SEC.)

31. The Securities and Exchange Commission can impose civil and criminal penalties, including imprisonment, for violations of securities laws.
(False: Like other agencies the SEC can impose civil penalties after an administrative hearing before an Administrative Law Judge, but criminal sanctions can only be imposed by a court after a traditional federal court prosecution with typically a jury.)

32. If a member of an outside CPA firm working on the corporation's "books" becomes aware of confidential information that the corporation is going to make a major acquisition of another company the CPA can buy stock in the "target" corporation since the CPA is not an employee but acts as an independent contractor.
(False: Insider trading laws as interpreted by the courts and the SEC have been construed broadly to consider as an "insider" not only employees but "outsiders," like CPAs, lawyers, brokers, sales personnel, who as independent contractors perform work for the corporation.)

33. A major function of the Securities and Exchange Commission is to require prior approval of stock offerings in order to ensure that an investment is relatively safe and offers at least some financial return to the investor.
(False: The SEC just requires that by means of the filing of a registration statement with the agency and the giving of a prospectus to the investing public that a person has the information needed to make a decision as to whether to purchase certain stock.)

34. If a person has a corporation in just one state that does business in only that one state if that person wants to issue securities, he or she nonetheless must comply with the registration requirements of the federal Securities Act of 1933.
(False: The Act exempts purely intra-state offerings; however, state registration procedures would have to be followed.)

35. Corporate managers very likely will be considered "insiders" with liability for insider trading.
(True: The SEC and the courts construe the term "insiders" very broadly and corporate managers, who have access to confidential inside information, would certainly be viewed as "insiders" with potential for insider trading liability.)

36. A corporate officer can avoid liability for insider trading merely by "tipping off" his or her spouse or "significant other" and having him or her make the stock trades.
(False: Liability for insider trading extends to insiders and tippees in conspiracy with insiders, assuming, of course, the government can obtain adequate evidence.)

37. In order to hold a tipper liable for providing confidential inside information to a tippee the government must demonstrate that the tipper as well as the tippee received a tangible monetary reward for the insider trading.
(False: Monetary benefit to the tipper is not required; a family, friendship, or social relationship between the parties will be sufficient to base liability for the tipper.)

38. The current U.S. legal position on insider trading is that the mere possession of material, non-public information and trading thereon constitutes a violation of the law.
(False: This is the broad theory or "level-playing-field" theory of insider trading, which is merely historical now. Today, liability is premised on the narrow theory or "insider" theory under which misappropriators, insiders, and tippees of insiders are only liable. Consequently, one can trade on material, non-public information if one obtains it fortuitously by luck or chance or one deduces it from using legitimate sources of public information. As such, the narrow theory allows trading on inside information by the "lucky" and the "smart.")

39. An investment in a limited partnership that develops oil wells very likely would be considered a "security" under federal securities law.
(True: The term "security" has been broadly construed by the Supreme Court to encompass not just traditional stocks and bonds, but "investment contracts," that is investments in a business that is managed and run solely by the efforts of another with the expectation of making a profit, with the limited partnership being the best example.)

40. A material omission regarding the purchase and sale of stock may be grounds for a securities fraud violation if the necessary elements of materiality, intent, and reliance are present.
(True: This type of omission regarding the purchase and sale of a security is considered fraudulent type behavior under federal securities law, specifically the Securities and Exchange Act, and thus this rule is a major change from the old common law rule that "silence is not fraud," which of course is still in effect, though with exceptions, for non-securities transactions.)

41. The Securities and Exchange Act of 1934 is concerned primarily with the disclosure of information about securities offered for sale.
(False: That is the 1933 Act; the 1934 Act is a very broad anti-fraud statute, which makes any fraud, deceit, misrepresentations, knowing omissions, and manipulation regarding the purchase and sale of securities a civil as well as criminal wrong.)

42. Even if a corporate officer does not use inside information in the purchase or sale of his or her company's stock, the officer still may be liable for "short swing" profits pursuant to Section 16(b) of the Securities and Exchange Act.
(True: The use of inside info is presumed; and thus if a purchase and then sale, or sale and then re-purchase occurs within a six-month period the officer must disgorge the profits.)

43. The Sarbanes-Oxley Act of 2002 requires that all publicly traded ethics must have a Code of Ethics.
(False: Codes of Ethics are not required; however, if a company does not have a Code of Ethics this omission must be reported to the SEC and made public.)

44. The Sarbanes-Oxley Act of 2002 is primarily a certification type statute.
(True: CEOs and CFOs of publicly traded companies regulated by the SEC must certify that the financial statements provided to the SEC are true and accurate and that there are no material omissions. Moreover, there are civil as well as criminal penalties for misrepresentations, misstatements, and omissions.)

45. The Sarbanes-Oxley Act (SOX) includes protections for company "whistleblowers" who disclose financial wrongdoing of their company to the SEC.
(True: Whistleblowers will be reinstated with back-pay, seniority, and benefits restored. Moreover, there is in SOX a very harsh penalty of up to 10 years in prison for managers, officers, and executives who retaliate against whistleblowers by firing or otherwise sanctioning them.)

46. No money can be made in the U.S. through an offering of stock without first registering the shares with the federal Securities and Exchange Commission.
(False: Although the SEC may have jurisdiction, the agency, like most federal agencies, has "jurisdictional yardsticks," meaning that if a case is too small for the agency in dollars the agency will not assume jurisdiction. However, in the case of securities registration the securities would likely have to be registered under the pertinent state's securities laws.)

47. Any issue of stock that is exempt from federal registration rules is automatically exempt from state laws too.
(False: Although the federal government, specifically the SEC, may have jurisdiction, there are exceptions where an issuing company does not have to comply with SEC rules, for example, "small" offerings, "private placement," and offerings to "sophisticated investors," as well as purely intra-state offerings. However, the issuing company very likely will have to comply with state security laws, including registration. These state security laws are often called "Blue Sky Laws," meaning the state's objective is to protect investors from buying securities as worthless as the "deep blue sky.")

48. Shareholders who are directors and officers of a publicly traded company are required to report their trading of their company's stock to the Securities and Exchange Commission.
(True: This rule is to support the enforcement of the Section 16b prohibition on Short Swing Profits as well as to guard against insider trading.)

49. Limited Liability companies (LLCs) combine the tax and operating advantages of a partnership with the limited liability protection of a corporation.
(True: And as such, the LLC way of doing business is very desirable for a small entrepreneurial venture, particularly in those states which allow one-person LLCs. However, it must be emphasized to maintain whatever LLC formalities required by the state, such as the filing of an Articles of Organization and the words "limited liability company" or "LLC" after the name of the company, as well as to establish and maintain other business formalities, such as having an operating agreement, a

separate LLC account, and signing any contracts or documents as a member of the LLC or as the managing member of the LLC. All the afore mentioned formalities will prevent the LLC form from being disregarded and consequently the members being held personally and unlimited responsible for LLC debts and obligations.)

50. An LLC must be managed by its members either as a group, or by means of a management committee of members, or by one member who is the managing member.
(False: All-of-the-above are permissible, but the members of the LLC are also allowed to select a professional manager as the manager of the entity.)

51. The law makes a distinction between insider trading and trading on inside information.
(True: Insider trading is legal; but trading on inside information may be legal if the information, though not yet public, was deduced from legal sources of information by a smart person using his or her intellectual powers as well as skills and knowledge of a sector of the economy. Also, if one is "lucky" and stumbles across or overhears inside information in a fortuitous and propitious way then one may trade on it legally.)

52. It is permissible to trade shares of stock based on immaterial inside information.
(True: Liability is premised on having information which is non-public and which is "material," that is, info which if made to public would be likely to affect the price of a share of stock up-or-down. An example would be a change in a minor HR matter, such sick day or vacation policy change, as opposed to the company getting a new CEO.)

Multiple Choice Questions with Answers and Explanations

1. Which of the following is FALSE about SEC Rule 10b-5:
   a. A tippee is a person who receives confidential inside information from an insider.
   b. Tippees in conspiracy with insiders violate the law by trading on inside information.
   c. The violation of this rule is a civil as well as a criminal violation.
   d. For the tipper to be held liable he or she must have received a tangible monetary benefit from the tip to the tippee

   (The correct answer is d. The tipper can be held liable for making the tip due to family, friendship, or social reasons; there is no requirement that the tipper benefit in a tangible monetary way. The other response are true basic principles.)

2. Who is NOT potentially liable for insider trading?
   a. Corporate insiders.
   b. Tippees of insiders.
   c. Misappropriators of insider information.
   d. An inadvertent tippee not in a fiduciary relationship.

   (The correct answer is d. An inadvertent tippee not in a fiduciary relationship can trade as he or she obtained the information by luck or chance, perhaps inadvertently hearing it while corporate insiders were speaking in an elevator. The rest of the answers reflect people who are potentially liable for insider trading; and note that misappropriators are usually thieves, bribers, or "hackers" of inside information.)

3. SEC Rule 10b-5 makes in unlawful regarding the purchase and sale of security to:
   a. employ any manipulative scheme to defraud.
   b. engage in any negligent action which would operate to deceive another person.

c. make an immaterial untrue statement.
d. for an insider to trade on non-public information.

(The correct answer is d. Rule 10b-5 deals with insider trading. Stock manipulation, which is illegal, is covered separately by the 1934 Securities and Exchange Act. Negligence is a separate wrong from intentionally engaging in deception and fraud. For any liability to occur under securities law the deception must involve material facts.)

4. A stock offering will be more likely to be treated as an exempt private offering under federal law if:
   a. the number of offerees is few.
   b. the offerees are "sophisticated" investors.
   c. the offering is small.
   d. All of the above.

(The correct answer is d. The SEC has jurisdictional "yardsticks" to determine if the number of investors or monetary size of the offering is too insignificant for the SEC to take jurisdiction. However, it is important to note that a state regulatory agency then likely will have jurisdiction over the offering. Offerings to "sophisticated" investors are exempt, that is, offerings to people who by virtue of their education, training, knowledge, and/or experience, can judge the value and risk to a stock offering.)

5. Which of the following is FALSE about U.S. securities laws?
   a. The definition of a "security" is broadly construed by the courts.
   b. Insider trading by an insider and by a tipee in conspiracy with an insider is illegal.
   c. Trading on inside information by the "lucky" or the "smart" is always illegal since it is not fair to the other party who does not have the inside information.
   d. Silence, that is, the failure to disclose material facts regarding the purchase or sale of a security is illegal.

(The correct answer is c. Under the prevailing "narrow" theory of U.S. security law not all trading on inside information is illegal. If one is "lucky" and overhears or "stumbles" into inside information, or if one using public sources of information in an intelligent and deductive way "ferrets" out inside info, one is acting legally. A "security is broadly construed by the courts as encompassing traditional securities as well as "investment contracts," for example, including an interest in a limited partnership. Trading by means of a tipper and tippee conspiracy is clearly illegal. Pursuant to federal security law, as opposed to the common law of fraud, silence is legally actionable.)

6. Who can be deemed liable for trading on material inside information based on U.S. securities laws?
   a. Misappropriators of inside information
   b. Insiders and tippees in conspiracy with insiders
   c. Inadvertent tippees who are in a fiduciary relationship with the disclosing party
   d. All of the above.

(The correct answer is d. These are the three categories of people that can be liable under the prevailing "narrow" theory of U.S. security law.A "misappropriator can be a thief, briber, or "hacker," for example, who trades. There must be evidence of a conspiracy between the tipper and the tippee, that is, they acted in a knowing wrongful manner; but there is no requirement that the tipper received anything of monetary value for the tip; rather, a family, friendship, or social arrangement will suffice. Note that an inadvertent tippee not in a fiduciary relationship can legally trade if he or she receives the inside info in a fortuitous and propitious manner.)

7. What is FALSE about the Sarbanes-Oxley Act (SOX)?
   a. SOX provided certain legal protections for whistleblowers of SOX regulated companies.
   b. SOX required all corporations, partnerships, and limited liability companies in the United States to have enforceable Codes of Ethics.
   c. SOX created a new federal agency – the Public Accounting Oversight Board (PAOB) – which oversees and regulates public accounting firms.
   d. SOX mandated certification requirements and statements (for financial statements and reports) for CEOs and CFOs of SOX regulated companies.

   (The correct answer is b. SOX does not require business entities and companies to have Codes of Ethics; however, if a company is a publicly traded one and thus regulated by the SEC the company must inform the SEC and make public the fact that it does not have a Code of Ethics. SOX has provisions to protect whistleblowers who disclose to the SEC and other pertinent government entities suspected violations of federal securities laws. Moreover, there are very harsh provision, including up to 10 years in prison, for managers and other corporate personnel who retaliate against whistleblowers. Certification statements are the "heart" of SOX as well as enhanced regulation by the PAOB.)

8. What is FALSE about the Securities Act of 1933?
   a. Unless a security qualifies for an exemption it must be registered before it is offered to the public by the issuing company filing a registration statement with the Securities and Exchange Commission (SEC).
   b. Investors must be provided with a prospectus which is a document that describes the securities sold, the issuing corporation and the principal parties behind the sale, as well as important facts about the financial operations of the company, as well as the nature and risk of the investment.
   c. Once registered, the SEC must approve or disapprove the issuance of the securities and if the approved the SEC must certify the risk of the investment.
   d. A detailed financial statement certified by a Certified Public Accountant must be included with the registration statement.

   (The correct answer is c. It is not the role of the SEC to formally approve or disapprove stock offerings or officially certify the level of risk; rather, the agency by means of the registration, financial statement, and prospectus requirements just seeks to insure that the investing public as sufficient accurate information to determine if they want to purchase a particular company's stock with the attendant risk thereto.)

9. Which of the following is/are exemptions to the registration filing requirement of the Securities Act of 1933?
   a. "Small offerings" for the sale of securities below a specified dollar amount and/or to a specified small number of investors.
   b. Offerings to "sophisticated investors," who have enough knowledge and experience in business and financial matters, and who are capable of evaluating the merits and risks of a particular investment.
   c. "Private offerings" to a limited number of people who would have the necessary knowledge to make an informed decision about investing.
   d. All of the above.

   (The correct answer is d. Note that if an offering is too small for the SEC there nevertheless will be a comparable state registration process. An example of a "private offering" would be an offering by a corporation to its own management personnel. Who exactly is financially "sophisticated" enough to be a "sophisticated" investor is a most interesting question, though one beyond the purview of this basic exam review book?)

10. The Securities and Exchange Act of 1934 makes the following practices illegal?
    a. Making false and misleading statements regarding the purchase or sale of securities.
    b. Engaging in manipulation regarding the purchase and sale of securities.
    c. Omitting material information regarding the purchase and sale of securities.
    d. All of the above.

    (The correct answer is d. The 1934 Act is a very broad anti-fraud statute that encompasses all the above legal wrongs. An example of manipulation would be the classic "pump-and-dump" scheme whereby a person goes into Internet stock trading sites, utilizing dozens of aliases, artificially "pumps" up the price of the stock until it reaches a certain point, and then "dumps," that is, sells it. As opposed to the common law general rule that "silence" is not fraud, pursuant to the 1934 Act, "silence," that is, knowing material omissions pertaining to the purchase and sale of stock, is illegal if the omissions are done knowingly).

11. What is FALSE about U.S. securities laws?
    a. Section 16(b) of the 1934 Act which prohibits "short-swing" profits requires evidence that corporate directors and/or officers used inside information in buying or selling their companies' shares of stock.
    b. The term "insider" under Rule 10b-5 can encompass not only employees of a firm but independent contractors, such as outside sales personnel, lawyers, and accountants.
    c. An "inadvertent tippee" who is in a fiduciary relationship with the tipper can be held liable for insider trading.
    d. Opinions and predictions since they are not "facts" cannot as a general rule form the basis for illegal stock trading if they are incorrect.

    (The correct answer is a. For short-swing profits, that is, profits obtained by a corporate director or officer by selling and buying or buying and selling his or her own company's stock, inside information is presumed and the use thereof does not have to be demonstrated. The term "insider" is very broadly construed by the courts and the SEC to encompass not only traditional insiders like directors, officers, and employees, but also "outsiders" who have a relationship with the company. An "inadvertent tippee" is a "lucky" person who fortuitously and propitiously overhears or sees inside information. The general rule is that the lucky "inadvertent tippee" can legally trade on the information. However, the major exception deals with an "inadvertent tippee" who is in a fiduciary relationship with the insider, for example, a lawyer, doctor, or accountant, who cannot trade regardless of not being in any conspiracy with the insider. The foundation requisite for legal liability for securities fraud and insider trading is possessing and trading on "information" (which must be confidential and material). "Information" means factual, objective, historical, and/or scientific type information, and not rumors, speculation, opinions or predictions. However, a major problem in the law deals with opinions and predictions that are based on some facts, and thus the thorny legal question arises as to how much fact one needs behind an opinion or prediction to turn it into a "fact" and thus "information." That difficult question, however, is also beyond the purposes of this basic exam review book.)

12. What is FALSE about the Sarbanes-Oxley Act (SOX) of 2002?
    a. It requires CEOs and CFOs of companies whose stock is publicly traded to certify that their companies' financial statements contain no untrue facts or material omissions.
    b. It provides legal protections for "whistleblowers."
    c. It requires companies to have a Code of Ethics that is certified by a business ethics professor.
    d. It prohibits companies from making most personal loans to directors and officers.

    (The correct answer is c. Companies are not required to have a code of ethics, let alone one certified by a business ethics professor, though that would be "nice"; rather, if a company does not have a code of ethics it has to notify the SEC of that fact and make that omission public. Of

course, there is no guarantee that if a company does have a code of ethics that it will act ethically, like Enron. The certification requirements are the most important part to SOX; and there is civil as well as criminal liability for misrepresentations and knowing material omissions. Job protection is afforded to "whistleblowing" employees who disclose suspected financial wrongdoing and violations of securities laws to the SEC, Congress, and other pertinent law enforcement agencies. Note that the "whistleblower" need only have a reasonable belief as to the wrongdoing, even though later it is determined to be unfounded. Also note that there are very severe provisions, including up to 10 years in prison, for managers who retaliate against "whistleblowers." Finally, note that some personal loans may be permitted, for example, for housing and consumer loans.)

30 - Anti-Trust

Introduction

Anti-Trust law in the U.S. is designed to protect and promote competition (and not necessarily competitors) and thus is designed to ultimately benefit the consumer. This body of law is based primarily on statutory law – federal and state. State law and state regulators come into play when an anti-trust case is too "small" for the federal government to get involved. There are civil as well as criminal penalties for anti-trust violations. At the federal level the three main statutes are the Sherman Anti-Trust Act, the Clayton Act, and the Robinson-Patman Act.

The Sherman Act has two very important sections: Section 1 which makes restraint of trade illegal; and Section 2 which makes monopolizing commerce illegal. Most important for the student to know is the distinction made under Section 1 between horizontal restraints of trade, which are *Per Se*, that is, automatically, illegal, and vertical restraints of trade, which MAY be legal if they pass the critical Rule of Reason test. Equally important for the student to understand is that in order to be guilty of monopolizing commerce under Section 2 a company first must have a monopoly AND secondly it must engage in intentional wrongful conduct to maintain or expand that monopoly. Critically important is the fact that "wrongful" conduct includes not only, obviously, illegal conduct, but also conduct which is legal but which the law regards as predatory, abusive, and unethical (consequently bringing in the fields of ethics and morality into legal anti-trust analysis). Pertaining to the Clayton Act, the student must be aware of the merger test in Section 7 as that is the test that the Justice Department and the Federal Trade Commission use to judge the legality of corporate mergers (as these agencies have overlapping jurisdiction). Finally, the student must be aware of the Robinson-Patman Act's prohibitions against price discrimination, tying arrangements, and exclusive dealing contracts.

True and False Questions with Answers and Explanations

1. Pursuant to the Sherman Anti-Trust Act all monopolies are illegal.
(False: A monopoly is not illegal in-and-of-itself, as one can gain a monopoly by being very successful by virtue of one's intelligence, hard-work, perseverance, and vision, at times called a "thrust-on monopoly," or perhaps by being the sole business, such as a gas station in a small town, at times called a "natural monopoly." Most importantly, the legal wrong is not necessarily having a monopoly but rather monopolization or monopolizing commerce (by first having the monopoly and then engaging in wrongful conduct to maintain or expand the monopoly).

2. All price-fixing is illegal pursuant to the Sherman Anti-Trust Act.
(False: Horizontal price-fixing, that is, a price fix by competitors at the same level in the marketing chain is per se or automatically illegal. However, vertical price-fixing as to the minimum and maximum of prices may be legal if the price fix passes the Rule of Reason test, that is, the price fix is ultimately good for the consumer).

3. Private parties cannot bring lawsuits for wrongful anti-competitive conduct under anti-trust laws, only the government can.
(False: Private parties can not only sue but if they prevail they are entitled to treble damages as well as an award for attorneys' fees. This concept of allowing private parties to sue based on certain U.S. regulatory law is called the "private attorney general" concept.)

4. U.S. anti-trust laws cannot be applied to foreign companies or business people.
(False: As opposed to health and safety laws as enforced by OHSA, anti-trust laws have "extra-territorial effect" and thus are applicable to foreigners, whether businesses or people, assuming, of course, that jurisdiction can be obtained.)

5. In order to be liable for the legal wrong of monopolization there must be a showing of wrongful intent.
(True: Liability is premised on first, having the monopoly, and thus doing intentional wrongful acts to maintain or expand the monopoly.)

6. The purposeful, intentional, and wrongful conduct necessary to a finding of monopolizing commerce must be illegal conduct.
(False: Illegal conduct will suffice, of course, but unethical, predatory, and abusive conduct will also be deemed wrongful even though not technically illegal, for example, when a company gives away goods and services to harm an "upstart" competitor's business.)

7. A 51% share of a defined market will usually be sufficient to constitute a monopoly.
(False: The percentage is typically in the 70-90% range to be a monopoly. However, there are other factors that may negate even a very high market share, for example, a showing that the competitors now in the market or those that have plans to enter the market are big and powerful ones, and thus the monopoly company despite its high market share does not have the power to raise or lower prices at will.)

8. The Justice Department in the U.S. is most interested in prohibiting horizontal mergers.
(True: In a merger between direct competitors on the same level on the marketing, for example, two manufacturers, there is the greater likelihood that the merger would fail the merger test in the Clayton Act of 1914, where a merger would be illegal if there would be a reasonable possibility of a substantially lessening of competition in a relevant market. Whereas there would be less possibility if the merger was a vertical one, that is, between entities at different levels in the marketing chain, as when a manufacturer merges with a retailer.)

9. An otherwise illegal merger can be saved by the "failing company" defense.
(True: If the only other option is bankruptcy of the company the law may allow its takeover by another company in the same industry.)

10. Some of the benefits of a merger are the elimination of unnecessary duplication and the economies of scale achieved.
(True: This is basic merger economic analysis. Of course, one would hope that the shareholders would see some of the financial benefits resulting from the afore mentioned benefits.)

11. The Rule of Reason holds that all restraints of trade are automatically illegal.
(False: It is the Per Se doctrine that holds that some restraints of trade, such as horizontal price-fixing and horizontal geographic market divisions, are automatically illegal. The Rule of Reason will legalize certain restraints of trade, such as vertical price-fixing and territorial divisions, if the benefits of these restraints ultimately inure to the consumer.)

12. Group boycotts that are designed to harm a competitor are *per se* illegal.
(True: Group boycotts are also called horizontal refusals to deal; they are automatically illegal as they are viewed as inherently anti-competitive. Note, however, that the motivation is economic, that is, to harm a competitor. A group boycott that is motivated by political or public policy reasons, such as the grape boycott years ago to protest working conditions, is protected by the First Amendment to the Constitution.)

13. A manufacturer can legally suggest a price at which its products are to be sold and then unilaterally refuse to deal with a retailer who undercuts that "suggested" price.
(True: This is not a group boycott of the retailer, nor is it a price-fix with the retailer; rather, this is "merely" a "suggestion" followed by a unilateral refusal to deal if the manufacturer's suggested retail price (MSRP) is not complied with. The situation then becomes not a legal issue but an economic one as to who has more economic clout – the manufacturer or the retailer.)

14. Generally, price discrimination in violation of the Robinson-Patman Act would involve selling basically the same goods during the same period to different buyers at different prices.
(True: This would be an anti-trust violation as a general rule; however, there are exceptions, for example, if one buyer buys in bulk and thereby gets a discount, or a seller lowers prices to meet the prices of a competitor.)

15. The doctrine of Conscious Parallelism is not a violation of anti-trust law.
(True: A competitor is allowed to track by legal means the pricing policies of its competitors, for example, when winter season rates begin in the Florida Keys, and then independently arrive at the same pricing level.)

16. Horizontal territorial, geographic, and customer divisions and allocations may be deemed legal if they pass the Rule of Reason test.
(False: These are examples of Per Se restraints of trade and thus are automatically illegal.)

17. A defense to a horizontal territorial or geographic division is that the companies involved would now be stronger to compete against others in their respective territories and thus the consumer would ultimately benefit.
(False: Such territorial and geographic divisions if done horizontally are automatic Per Se violations of anti-trust law; and as such there are no defenses, including any asserted benefits to the consumer.)

18. Under the Sherman Anti-trust Act all monopolies are unlawful.
(False: There is nothing inherently wrong with a monopoly, as it may have been achieved by "natural" conditions, such as one's vision, knowledge, skill, entrepreneurship, innovation, and hard work. It is monopolizing commerce or monopolization that is the legal wrong. Of course, one first must have a monopoly to be a monopolizing company.)

19. Monopolization requires a monopoly as well as evidence of abusive or predatory conduct in achieving or maintaining the monopoly.
(True: Under the Sherman Act, Section 2, there is the two-part test for the legal wrong of monopolization, to wit: first, the monopoly; and second, the wrongful conduct. Moreover, the requisite wrongful conduct can be either illegal conduct, such as theft of a competitor's intellectual property, or legal but unethical conduct, such as lowering prices unrealistically low or giving away goods or services, to drive an "upstart" competitor from the marketplace.)

20. Sherman Act *per se* violations are federal criminal law felonies.
(True: Imprisonment is a potential sanction too. Of course, they are civil law violations too. Examples of per se violations are horizontal price-fixing, horizontal territorial division, and horizontal refusals-to-deal, also called "group boycotts." Note that "per se" means there is no defense; there is automatic liability if the government has adequate evidence.)

21. Conglomerate mergers are the type of mergers that will draw the greatest scrutiny from the Federal Trade Commission.
(False: Horizontal mergers, that is, mergers by competitors on the same level on the marketing chain, for example, Staples and Office Depot, which was disapproved by the government, will draw the greatest attention since the possibility of failing the merger test in the Clayton Act (which test is: a reasonable possibility of a substantial lessening of competition or the tendency to create a monopoly in a relevant market). Whereas a conglomerate merger, that is, a merger of companies who deal in unrelated products and services, for example, the CVS and Aetna Insurance merger, which passed government muster, even though both are in the health-care field but offer difference products and services.)

22. Individual states are allowed to pass their own anti-trust laws.
(True: The U.S. system of government is a federal one, composed of a national government as well as constituent government entities called "states." So long as a state law is not in direct conflict with a federal law or Congress has not totally preempted the field, such as with airline safety, states can pass laws based on their inherent "police power," that is, the power of a state legislature to pass laws to benefit and to protect the health, welfare, and safety of the citizens and residents of the state. As such, states can pass anti-trust laws, and if an anti-trust case is too small for the Federal Trade Commission or the Justice Department to get involved, the state can assume jurisdiction.)

23. An otherwise unacceptable merger under the Clayton Act can be "saved" by certain defenses.
(True: The best example is the "failing company" defense where a company is allowed to purchase another company to save it from probable bankruptcy.)

24. Members of a business trade association who jointly agree to hire a lobbyist to represent them in Congress in an attempt to influence proposed legislation are likely committing a Sherman Act, Section 1, restraint of trade violation.
(False: Trade association activities, though joint, are permissible, for example, educational and training efforts as well as lobbying. However, since a trade association is likely composed of companies who are competitors at the same level of the marketing chain, company representatives have to be very careful not to engage in talk or action that could be construed as illegal under Section 1, for example, agreeing to set prices or divide up territories.)

25. It is an important aspect of monopolization analysis to ascertain market share.
(True: One cannot be a monopolizing company unless one has a monopoly and one cannot have a monopoly unless one has a very large share of a defined market, with a percentage for the share usually construed as 70% or more. However, even if a company has such a percentage share it is not necessarily a monopoly as it still has to have market power, that is, the power to raise or lower prices in the market at will. If there are competitors in the market who are big and powerful, though now with small shares, or even potential competitors, there may not be the requisite market power. The best example goes back to when Gator Aide had a 80% plus share of the "sports beverage" market, but it did not have a monopoly since two other competitors in the market were Coke and Pepsi.)

26. Labor unions are exempt from anti-trust law.
(True: Because technically and at one point historically they were considered to be in restraint of trade and commerce and illegal, but not today; however, labor unions are regulated by federal statutes, principally the National Labor Relations Act and the Labor Management Relations Act.)

27. The government is most interested in preventing horizontal mergers.
(True: A horizontal merger would be the type of merger that most likely would fail the merger test in the Clayton Act, though many have been approved, most notably the Exxon-Mobil merger, because the relevant market was construed as a global market for oil and gas exploration, service, and sales.)

28. One possible benefit to a business merger is that it may produce "economies of scale."
(True: Yet one "price to be paid" by the merger may be the elimination of unnecessary duplication, especially of employees.)

29. The Rule of Reason refers to a Supreme Court doctrine that all restraints of trade are automatically illegal.
(False: The Per Se doctrine holds that certain types of horizontal restraints of trade, such as price-fixing, are automatically illegal. Whereas the Rule of Reason holds that vertical restraints of trade, that is, agreements by parties on different levels of the marketing chain, such as an agreement to fix prices by a manufacturer and a retailer, may be legal if they benefit the consumer in the long-run.)

30. A policy of "conscious parallelism" is not a violation of the Sherman Anti-Trust Act.
(True: A competitor is allowed pursuant to this doctrine to track by legal means the pricing and other policies of its competitors and to decide by independent means whether to follow them or not. For example, a motel owner in the Florida Keys can see when his or her competitors begin "winter season" and thus charge higher rates and then decide whether he wants to commence the higher winter season rates at that date too. Similarly, if one airline can "get away with" charging for luggage then another airline may decide to do this too. These examples are much different from a conspiracy by competitors to agree to set the price and date for winter season or to charge for luggage, both of which would be Sherman Act, Section 1, restraint of trade violations.)

31. Group boycotts by competitors at the same level designed to remove a business from the marketplace are *per se* illegal under the Sherman Act.
(True: They are also known as group refusals to deal and are viewed as so inherently anti-competitive that they are automatically illegal. A good example would be when manufacturers of "high-end" goods agree to stop supplying goods to a "low-cost" retailer who is selling the goods below what the manufacturers want.)

32. The legal wrong of price discrimination under the Robinson-Patman Act is premised on selling basically identical goods during the same time-period to different buyers at different prices.
(True: Yet there are exceptions, for example, when one buyer is a buyer in bulk of the goods and as such gets a lower unit price.)

33. Manufacturers are allowed under anti-trust law to suggest a price by which their products are to be sold and then unilaterally refuse to deal with anyone who substantially undercuts that price.
(True: This is a legal unilateral refusal to deal, as opposed, as a group boycott. An example would be when a manufacturer of "high-end" purses or shoes "suggests" a price at which the goods are to be sold or states that certain goods can never be put on sale. If the retailer refuses to abide by these suggestions the manufacturer can stop as an individual entity supplying goods to the recalcitrant retailer. However, in such a case the manufacturer will lose an outlet for the sale of its goods.

Consequently, these situations are more economic disputes, that is, who-needs-whom-more, rather than legal controversies.)

34. Horizontal customer and territorial allocations are resolved under the Rule of Reason of anti-trust law.
(False: These allocations because they are horizontal are per se illegal. Vertical allocations, for example, when a manufacturer sets up a system of exclusive distributorships and retail outlets for its goods, may be legal if they benefit the consumer in the long-run, for example, by being a more efficient way to distribute and sell goods as well as having "approved" distributors and retailers who are knowledgeable about the goods and who will provide good customer service to the consumer.)

35. Horizontal price-fixing can be defended legally by showing that the prices set are in fact reasonable and lower than they were before, and thus the price-fix benefits the consumer.
(False: Horizontal price-fixing is viewed as so inherently anti-competitive that it is deemed to be per se, that is, automatically illegal – civilly and criminally; there are no defenses, though for liability the government must have sufficient evidence, of course.)

36. Horizontal price-fixing is permissible if it allows smaller companies to compete more effectively against bigger ones and thereby benefit the consumer.
(False: Horizontal price-fixing is per se illegal; it is viewed as inherently anti-competitive; there is no defense to this legal wrong, regardless of any perceived consumer benefit.)

37. Pursuant to the Clayton Act, the Federal Trade Commission will invalidate a merger if the merger is likely to result in material employee terminations.
(False: The merger test in the Clayton Act is whether the merger will result in a reasonable probability of a substantial lessening of commerce in a relevant market or create a tendency toward a monopoly; employee layoffs are not a legal factor under the Clayton Act.)

38. Meeting the price of a competitor may constitute a valid defense to a charge of price discrimination pursuant to the Robinson-Patman Act.
(True: Granting lower prices to a buyer who buys in bulk is also a valid defense.)

39. Vertical territorial allocations are ordinarily resolved under the Rule of Reason.
(True: And as such, and opposed to horizontal allocations, vertical territorial geographic allocations or division of territories usually will be held since they benefit the consumer in the long-run by a manufacturer having an efficient distribution and retail network and with the retailers providing good and knowledgeable customer service since they are "approved" retailers.)

40. Vertical price-fixing as to the minimum price of goods is legal pursuant to the Rule of Reason if consumers ultimately benefit from the price-setting.
(True: Vertical price-fixing as to the maximum price of goods has long been permissible; but only until fairly recently has the Supreme Court ruled that vertical price-fixing as to the minimum price of goods is governed by the Rule of Reason. One possible benefit to consumers would be for a manufacturer to keep the brand status of "high-end" goods by getting the retailer to agree not to sell them below a certain price and not to put them on sale.)

41. A horizontal restraint results from an agreement between firms at different levels in the manufacturing, distribution, and retail process.
(False: This would be a vertical restraint. The distinction is critical as vertical restraints are governed under anti-trust law by the Rule of Reason whereas horizontal restraints are governed by the Per Se doctrine.)

42. Illegal price discrimination under the Robinson-Patman Act may occur if a seller charges competitive buyers different prices for identical goods.
(True: Yet there are exceptions, for example, due to seasonal or other price fluctuations, or when buyers buy in bulk.)

43. A joint venture by two firms to research, develop, and produce new goods for a particular manufacturing line would be subject to anti-trust analysis under the Rule of Reason.
(True: This is an exceptional situation since even if the two firms in the joint venture are horizontal, that is, on the same level in the marketing chain, joint ventures are governed by the Rule of Reason. Note that a joint venture, though governed predominantly by partnership law, has a much narrower focus, typically the performance of one undertaking, such as when two big competing oil companies agree to form a venture to drill for oil in Siberia.)

44. If a merger in all probability will result in a substantial lessening of competition in a relevant market or the tendency to create a monopoly the merger will be deemed illegal pursuant to the Clayton Act of 1914.
(True: This is the main merger test in anti-trust law, though there are additional tests for communications and bank mergers under different laws. A key factor is the definition of the relevant "market," for example, office supply super-stores or all stores that sell office supplies, since the broader the market is the more likely the merger will pass the Clayton Act, and the obverse, for example, the Staples-Office Depot merger, which the FTC said was in narrow office supply super-store market, and consequently failed the Clayton Act test.)

45. A policy of Conscious Parallelism is not a violation of U.S. anti-trust laws.
(True: A business is allowed to track by lawful methods the policies and practices of its competitors and then so long as by independent determination to follow them. For example, an airline can decide independently to charge for baggage or the second bag if it sees its competitors are charging for bags and the charges are not dissuading customers from flying with that airline. The airlines jointly agreeing to do so would be a horizontal price-fix and a Per Se illegal restraint under anti-trust law.)

46. Private parties instituting anti-trust lawsuits may be able to recover treble damages under the Sherman Act.
(True: Not only the government but private parties adversely affected by anti-trust violations can not only bring a lawsuit but if victorious collect triple damages and be awarded attorneys fees. This concept is known as the "private Attorney General" doctrine.)

47. Anti-trust laws of the U.S. cannot be applied to foreign corporations.
(False: Anti-trust laws, like Civil Rights laws, of the U.S. have extra-territorial effect. However, acquiring jurisdiction and obtaining evidence may present large legal and practical problems. Moreover, the Act of State and Sovereign Immunity doctrines may preclude application, for example, suing OPEC, which consists of foreign government oil companies, for price-fixing, or suing Chinese vitamin companies, which are controlled and dominated by the government, for price-fixing.)

48. A primary concern with a vertical merger is market foreclosure.
(True: The threat is that the merged companies, even though not direct competitors, may combine in such a large and powerful entity that no one will want to enter those markets. An example, would be the CVS-Aetna health-care merger of the Comcast-Universal-NBC communications merger.)

49. Monopolization requires a monopoly and evidence of intentional bad conduct in acquiring, maintaining, and expanding the monopoly.
(True: And note, most importantly, that the "bad" conduct can consist of illegal conduct as well as conduct that the law regards as abusive, predatory, and/or unethical, such as a company giving away goods for free or at very low prices to destroy an "upstart" competitor who dares to enter the market. An example would be the airlines' use of "bracketing," that is, offering flights right before and after a competitor's flight to the same locale and at very reduced prices. Of course, in order for an airline to be liable for monopolization, it first must be determined if it has a monopoly in a relevant market, for example, perhaps a major "hub.")

50. A primary consideration in determining a relevant product market for monopoly purposes is the cross-elasticity of demand.
(True: That is, are certain products substitutable for others? For example, is the market coffee, gourmet coffee, or coffee and tea? Is the market beer or micro-brewery beer or beer and wine?)

51, A seller is allowed to "suggest" a price for which it products are to be sold and then unilaterally refuse to deal with anyone who does not adhere to the price.
(True: This is known as a resale-price-maintenance-agreement; and is usually seen by the initials MSRP. This is quite legal so long as it is done unilaterally, because if it is done by a group of manufacturers to freeze out a retailer who is selling their products too cheaply this agreement is a horizontal refusal to deal and a Per Se violation of the Sherman Act. An example would be the large music companies who were accused of refusing to provide CDs to Wal-Mart and Target because the latter two were selling them too inexpensively.)

52. Vertical price-fixing is always illegal under the Sherman Act since it is so inherently anti-competitive.
(False: Vertical restraints, including price-fixing and territorial allocations, are governed by the Rule of Reason which means they may be legal if "reasonable," that is, if the consumer ultimately benefits from the price-fix. Note that the Rule of Reason by Supreme Court ruling applies both to price-fixing as to the maximum as well as the minimum price of goods.)

53. Trade associations are illegal under Section 1 of the Sherman Anti-Trust Act since they typically are composed of competitors in the same field and thus there is a likelihood that they will engage in restraint of trade.
(False: There is nothing inherently wrong with trade associations as they can combine for legitimate activities, such as information sharing, education, joint advertising and lobbying, which eventually will benefit the consumer. However, the members of a trade association must be very careful that their joint discussions, activity, and agreements do not appear to be, or are, impermissible restraints of trade under Section 1, such as price-fixing.)

54. Tying arrangements are illegal anti-trust violations pursuant to the Clayton Anti-Trust Act.
(True: A tying arrangement is an agreement that a customer can buy a desired product, the "tying" product, but only if the customer buys another product (the "tied" product. The purpose of the law is to prevent a company, which presumably has market power in one market, from extending that market power into another product line.)

55. "Exclusive dealing contracts" are *Per Se* illegal under the Clayton Act?
(False: An exclusive dealing contract is an agreement between a buyer and a seller in which the buyer agrees to deal contractually only with a specific seller. This type of contract is not necessarily illegal; rather, it is governed by the "substantial lessening of competition" standard.)

56. U.S. anti-trust law just applies to U.S. citizens who do business in the U.S.
(False: U.S. anti-trust law has extraterritorial effect. That is, first, it applies to U.S. nationals doing business abroad that restrain trade or monopolize commerce in the United States; and second, it applies to foreigners and foreign companies that conduct activities that restrain trade or monopolize commerce in the United States.)

Multiple Choice Questions with Answers and Explanations

1. What are key analytical factors in determining whether a business is a monopoly.
   a. Defining the relevant product or service market
   b. Defining the relevant geographic market
   c. Ascertaining the business' market share
   d. Ascertaining the business' "market power"
   e. All of the above.

   (The correct answer is e. Initially determining the market is critical, as the broader the market is defined, whether product, service, or area, the less likely one will have a monopoly. Then once the market is defined the company's market share needs to be determined, with a share of 70% or more typically being a monopoly-like percentage. However, even if a company has a very large market share the company may not have the requisite "market power," which is the power to raise or lower prices pretty much at will. This lack of power in the market despite the large percentage share could be due to other strong competitors in the market who have the capability to rachet up their market share by advertising, marketing, etc., or due to other potential strong competitors who have the capability to enter the market.)

2. Which is NOT a violation of U.S. anti-trust law?
   a. Horizontal price-fixing by competitors
   b. Vertical price-fixing that is *not* supported by the Rule of Reason
   c. A group boycott of manufacturers against retailers motivated by economic reasons
   d. A unilateral refusal to deal by a manufacturer against a retailer who disregards the manufacturer's MSRP (manufacturer's suggested retail price).

   (The correct answer is d. Horizontal price-fixing and group boycotts, also known as refusals-to-deal, are Per Se automatic violations of anti-trust law; there is no defense. Vertical price-fixing as to the maximum as well as minimum price of goods MAY be legal if the price-fix passes the Rule of Reason test, that is, it is ultimately beneficial to the consumer. A unilateral refusal to deal, as opposed to a group refusal to deal, is legal, assuming of course there are no other forms of discrimination. Consequently, in such a unilateral situation the "contest" is an economic one; that is, who needs whom more – the retailer who needs the manufacturer's goods or the manufacturer who needs the retailer as a sales outlet.)

3. Which statement is TRUE regarding U.S. anti-trust law?
   a. All monopolies are illegal pursuant to Section 2 of the Sherman Anti-trust Act.
   b. All horizontal mergers are illegal pursuant to Section 7 of the Clayton Act.
   c. Vertical territorial division is a restraint of trade that is governed by the Rule of Reason of anti-trust law.
   d. Evidence of predatory, abusive, and unethical conduct by a monopoly is insufficient to show intentional wrongful conduct for monopolization purposes.

   (The correct answer is c. There is nothing inherently wrong with a monopoly so long as one achieved it properly, for example, in an inventive, innovative, entrepreneurial manner. A merger, even if horizontal, may be legal under the Clayton Act. The test is: Does the merger create a

reasonable probability of a substantial lessening of competition in the relevant market? The definition of the market is the critical factor. The broader the wider the more likely the merger will pass muster, even if horizontal; whereas the more narrow the market the more likely the merger will fail the Clayton Act test. For example, the Exxon-Mobil merger passed because the market was defined very broadly as the world oil market; whereas the Staples-Office Depot merger failed because the market was defined narrowly as only including office supply "super-stores," which there were just the two. Vertical territorial divisions are governed by the Rule of Reason, which means they may be legal is there are more pro-consumer benefits, for example, when a manufacturer sets up exclusive wholesale, distribution, and retail networks consisting of business entities that are "approved" by the manufacturer and who thus have knowledge of its products as well as providing good customer service. Evidence of illegal conduct will support a showing of monopolization by a company that has a monopoly. Moreover, even if the conduct is legal if the law regards it as predatory, abusive, and/or unethical a company may be deemed to be an illegal monopolizing company.)

4. What is a FALSE statement regarding monopolization analysis pursuant to Section 2 of the Sherman Act?
   a. One generally cannot be guilty of or liable for monopolization without having a monopoly first.
   b. One can have a monopoly but not have monopoly power and thus not be a monopolizing company.
   c. All monopolies are illegal since they are inherently unfair to consumers.
   d. Wrongful conduct by a monopoly to establish the legal wrong of monopolization includes illegal AND unethical, predatory, or abusive conduct (which is not necessarily illegal).

   (The correct answer is c. One must have a monopoly to be liable for the legal wrong of monopolization pursuant to Section 2 of the Sherman Act. However, there is nothing inherently wrong with having a monopoly if one achieved it by proper means, that is, by being a very smart and very good business person. Even if one has a monopoly one may not have monopoly power, that is, the power to raise and lower prices at will and being so powerful in the market that competitors are fearful from entering the market. Wrongful conduct to support a finding of monopolization can consist of illegal conduct and legal conduct which is regarded as predatory, abusive, and/or unethical, for example, substantially reducing the price of goods to drive the competitor out of business, giving away goods near a competitor's business, or leasing at very favorable terms business locations where the competitor wants to expand.)

5. What fields and entities are exempt from federal anti-trust law?
   a. Labor unions
   b. Insurance
   c. Utilities
   d. All of the above.

   (The correct answer is d. Labor unions are regulated by the National Labor Relations Act and other federal and state labor laws. Insurance is heavily regulated at the state level, primarily by state insurance commissions. Utilities are also heavily regulated at the state level, primarily by state utility commissions which grant quasi-monopolies to utilities. Note that banking, again heavily regulated by at the federal as well as state level is exempt from anti-trust law. Finally, note that through an odd historical happenstance professional baseball is also exempt, though other professional sports are covered by anti-trust laws.)

6. What is FALSE about the Sherman Anti-Trust Act?
    a. An agreement by two or more parties to restrain trade or commerce can be a Section 1 restraint of trade violation.
    b. Engaging in "conscious parallelism" is legal.
    c. Monopolies are *per se* illegal under Section 2.
    d. Anti-trust violations can result in criminal as well as civil penalties.
    (The correct answer is c. There is nothing inherently wrong with attaining a monopoly if one achieves it by "natural" means, for example, intelligence, vision, hard-work, innovation, etc. However, when one does have a monopoly one has to be careful if one uses monopoly power to wrongfully maintain or expand the monopoly, which is the legal wrong of monopolization. For a Section 1 violation you need, as the old saying goes, "two to tango," as it is critical that there be some type of agreement, contract, conspiracy, or combination to restrain trade or commerce. "Conscious parallelism" means that a company can track the pricing and other policies and practices of its competitors by lawful means, and then, as a result of independent determination, decide whether to meet them or not. Civil penalties can include treble damages as well as attorneys' fees; and criminal sanctions include imprisonment for felony.)

7. What is FALSE about restraints of trade under Section 1 of the Sherman Anti-Trust Act?
    a. Horizontal territorial divisions are lawful if they enable the companies to compete more effectively in their respective territories and thus ultimately benefit the consumer.
    b. Group boycotts or joint refusals to deal are illegal.
    c. Horizontal price-fixing as to the minimum price of goods is illegal even if the consumer ultimately benefits.
    d. Vertical price-fixing as to the maximum price of goods may be legal if it passes the Rule of Reason test.
    (The correct answer is a. Horizontal restraints, including territorial divisions, group boycotts, and price-fixing are Per Se, that is, automatically illegal; there is no defense. However, note that a unilateral refusal to deal, typically by a manufacturer boycotting a retailer which does not adhere to the manufacturer's "suggested" retail price for the goods, does not violate anti-trust law, though other bodies of law may be triggered. Vertical restraints, whether price-fixing as to the maximum as well as the minimum price of goods as well as territorial divisions are legal if they pass the Rule of Reason test. This test holds that if there are more pro-competition and pro-consumer consequences than negative effects the vertical restraints may be legal. Regarding a vertical fix as to the maximum price of goods protecting the consumer from being gouged in times or shortage is given as a rationale; and regarding the minimum price of goods the rationale given is to protect the brand, especially high-end brands, and thus the consumer who buys the brand and wants to keep the status thereto. Finally, regarding vertical territorial allocations efficiency in setting up manufacturer/wholesaler/distributor/retailor networks is the reason given as well as the consumer benefitting from retailers "approved" by the manufacturer who should be knowledgeable about its products as well as provide good service to the consumer.)

8. What is FALSE about monopolization law under Section 2 of the Sherman Act?
    a. In order to be an illegal monopolizing company, one must first have a monopoly with market power.
    b. Determining the applicable "market" for goods and services is an indispensable feature of Section 2 analysis.
    c. In order to be a monopolizing company, one must have a monopoly with market power and then engage in illegal actions to preserve or expand the monopoly.
    d. An "oligopoly" is a shared monopoly where a few companies share monopoly power.

(The correct answer is c. The legal wrong of monopolization arises when in a given market, which is initial critical determination, a company, and it can just be one company, has approximately 70% or more of market share, which is a monopoly, but this company also must have "market power" (that is, being so strong in dominant in the market as to be able to raise or lower prices at-will and intimidate competitors from even entering the market. Next, assuming market/monopoly/market-power, the issue then arises as to whether the company did any wrongful to maintain or expand the monopoly, and, most importantly these wrongful actions can of course be illegal actions, such as stealing trade secrets, AND also actions which are not illegal, but the law regards as predatory, abusive, and unethical, such as giving away free goods near an upstart competitor until it goes out-of-business. Finally, there is nothing inherently wrong with an oligopoly though those few companies controlling the market better be very careful not to engage in Section 1 restraint of trade violations.)

9. What is FALSE about the Clayton Anti-Trust Act?
   a. The narrower the market is the more likely the merger of two companies will be approved pursuant to the merger test in the Clayton Act.
   b. A merger will fail the merger test in the Clayton Act if there is a reasonable probability of a substantial lessening of competition in a given market.
   c. Horizontal mergers are more likely to be challenged by the government.
   d. The Justice Department (DOT) and the Federal Trade Commission (FTC) have over-lapping jurisdiction when it comes to approving mergers.

   (The correct answer is a. The broader the market is defined the more likely the merger will pass the Clayton Act test; conversely, the narrower the market is defined, the more likely it is that the merger will fail the Clayton Act merger test. The goal of the merging companies, therefore, will be to convince the government regulators that the market is broad, as Exxon-Mobil did in their successful merger, arguing that the oil market was global, as opposed to Office Depot and Staples, which could not convince the government that the market for office supplies was broader than "office supply superstores," of which there were only two, and thus the merger failed. Note that the afore mentioned mergers were horizontal ones, which are the types of mergers most likely to be challenged by either the DOJ or the FCT.)

10. When is it legal for a seller to discriminate in price when selling the same goods to different buyers pursuant to the Robinson-Patman Act?
    a. The price differences were due to sales discounts for buying goods in volume.
    b. The goods were not substantially the same type of goods.
    c. The price differences were caused by meeting the lower prices of competitors.
    d. All of the above.

    (The correct answer is d. Other defenses are that the goods were not sold to the different buyers at contemporaneous times as well as the fact that changing market conditions affected the price of the goods.)

31 - Employment and Civil Rights Law

Introduction

Although also covered in the Agency section of this book, the employment at-will doctrine is again the starting-off point for an examination of civil rights laws as well as labor laws (which will be covered in the next chapter). One recalls that under the employment at-will doctrine an employee can be discharged for any reason, regardless of morality and ethics, but not an illegal reason. Consequently, a major illegal reason for a discharge of an at-will employee, or for that matter any employee, would be when the discharge is in violation of civil rights laws. Of course, the student must be aware that the civil rights laws apply not "merely" to discharge but to all the "terms and conditions" of employment, such as hiring, transfers, promotion, etc. Most importantly for the business student, of course, is Title VII of the Civil Rights Act which applies to the employment sector. Critical to Title VII are the "protected" characteristics, that is, race, color, national origin, religion, and gender. Also, equally important is the fact that the prohibition against discrimination based on sex now includes sexual harassment, and sexual orientation. Furthermore, the student must know that the Supreme Court has enunciated a principle of absolute liability, which is very rare in the law, when the harassment is by a manager or supervisor against a subordinate employee. Procedurally, the student must be aware of the two main ways of proving discrimination: the disparate treatment lawsuit and disparate or adverse impact lawsuit, and how they differ. Pertaining to national origin discrimination, the student must be cognizant of the fact that the courts construe language discrimination as a form of national origin discrimination, as well as the fact that legal problems ensue when the employer adopts English-only policies. Regarding religious discrimination, the student must be aware of the double-duty of the employer, that is, not to discriminate, but also to make a reasonable accommodation to the religious beliefs, practices, and observances of its employees unless it would be an undue hardship to do so. The student also must be aware of the two main exceptions to the civil rights acts: appearance discrimination (that is, preferring the "attractive") and the *bona fide* occupational qualification exception (BFOQ), as well as always remembering for the latter that race and color can never be BFOQs. The student also must be aware of two other important civil rights acts: the Age Discrimination in Employment Act (ADEA) and the Americans with Disabilities Act, and again remembering as with religious discrimination, the employer has a double-duty here too, that is, not only not to discriminate against older or disabled workers but also to make a reasonable accommodation to their needs unless it would be an undue burden to do so.

True and False Questions with Answers and Explanations

1. As a general rule pursuant to the traditional employment at-will doctrine the employer as well as the employee can terminate the employment relationship at any time for any reason with no notice, warning, or explanation.
(True: Yet the employer cannot terminate for an illegal reason, such as discrimination in violation of civil rights laws, which would turn the legal discharge into a "wrongful discharge," that is, an illegal one.)

2. An employer's "English-only" policy will be presumed to be illegal national origin discrimination if it applies to all times and all places in the workplace.
(True: The policy must be limited to work areas and work times; and moreover, the employer must be able to demonstrate a legitimate business reason for the policy, such as safety or security.)

3. Even if an employee's carelessness contributed to his or her injury at work the employee still will be compensated by the typical state Workers Compensation law.
(True: Negligence will not preclude recovery as opposed to an employee's recklessness or intentional self-harm conduct.)

4. Customer preference is a valid reason for an employer to justify legally a limited English-only policy.
(True: Usually, customer as well as employee preferences cannot be used to justify discriminatory policies, but in the case of language policies there is an exception if the employer believes that the employees speaking another language other than English would be intimidating to, and thus "scaring off" customers.)

5. Private sector employers can violate the federal constitution's Fourth Amendment prohibition of unreasonable search and seizure if they monitor their employees and engage in surveillance in too intrusive a manner.
(False: Constitutional rights under the federal, as well as most states, constitution, can only be asserted against public sector entities, that is, government, including government employers, but not against private parties (with the exception of the 13th Amendment).
However, a private sector employer could be liable for the intentional tort of intentional invasion of privacy if the employers' actions in monitoring and engaging in surveillance are deemed to intrude on a private sphere of the employee and are also outrageous.)

6. Title VII of the U.S. Civil Rights Act protects employees, as well as applicants and union members, from discrimination based on race, color, religion, national origin, gender, and political affiliation and views.
(False: At the federal level one's political affiliations and views are not protected by the Act, but there may be state or local laws that prohibit such discrimination.)

7. The disparate treatment theory of civil rights law requires that the aggrieved party produce evidence that the employer had a discriminatory motive and thus intentionally discriminated against the employee.
(True: The evidence, though, can be direct (e.g., discriminatory statements by a manager) or indirect or circumstantial (such as a qualified minority candidate being passed up for a job but with the position still be held open until filled by a non-minority). Note too that the disparate or adverse impact theory of discrimination does not require evidence of intentional discrimination.)

8. *Quid-pro-quo* sex discrimination occurs when a job is offered contingent of the performance of sexual favors.
(True: The other type of sexual discrimination is sexual harassment based on a finding of an abusive, offensive, or hostile sexual environment at work.)

9. An employer will be absolutely liable for sexual harassment committed by a manager against a subordinate employee who suffers some type of tangible job loss regardless of the employer's actions to prevent sexual harassment in the workplace.
(True: Principles of absolute liability are rare in the law, but this is one of them, affording the employer no defense, which is why many employers now have sexual harassment insurance policies.)

10. In order to be actionable as illegal age discrimination the discrimination must be intentional according to the Age Discrimination in Employment Act.
(False: The disparate impact or adverse impact theory of discrimination applies to age discrimination cases, and as such a neutral employment practice, such as down-sizing after a merger, may have an adverse and disproportionate impact on older workers and thus could violate the ADEA.)

11. The *bona fide* occupational qualification exception in the Civil Rights Act will allow an employer to discriminate on the grounds of race or color if that characteristic is a necessary and essential aspect of a particular job.
(False: Race and color can never be BFOQs, so, for example, an ad for an actor to play Hamlet that says must be "white" would be illegal discrimination.)

12. The employment at-will doctrine generally allows an employer to terminate an employee at any time without notice or explanation and for any reason or no reason.
(True: But not for an illegal reason, such as discrimination under civil rights acts. The result is that an employee can be discharged immorally and unethically but legally, for example, nepotism in a small company. There are several exceptions to the employment at-will doctrine, for example, to protect "whistle-blowing" employees who disclose wrongdoing at or by a firm.)

13. In a disparate or adverse impact discrimination case the aggrieved employees must demonstrate that the employer had a discriminatory motive or animus against them.
(False: Discriminatory motive is required for a disparate treatment case, that is, one of intentional discrimination. In an adverse or disparate impact case there is no intent to discriminate required; rather, an employer policy which is neutral on-its-fact has a disproportionate adverse impact on a protected group of employees.)

14. Discharging an employee to hire a relative is presumed to be illegal discrimination under Title VII of the Civil Rights Act.
(False: Absent any discriminatory motive such a discharge would be illegal, assuming the employee is at employee at-will; yet whether it is moral is another question.)

15. "Code words" can form the basis for an inference of discriminatory intent under civil rights laws.
(True: For example, calling an African-American employee a "boy" or a Muslim employee a "terrorist" should give rise to an inference of discriminatory motive.)

16. The federal Constitution prohibits the drug testing of employees of both public and private companies.
(False: The federal Constitution only protects government employees, not employees in the private sector. Moreover, regarding government employees, drug testing may be permissible if there are no 4th Amendment or right to privacy violations.)

17. Whistleblowing statutes will protect employees who report wrongdoing at or by their companies to the media.
(False: The reporting of wrongdoing typically must be made to an "appropriate government agency." However, once the government agency is notified the whistleblowing employee can then go to the media.)

18. Once a discharged employee has made out his or her initial case of employment discrimination to the Equal Employment Opportunity Commission (EEOC) the employee will not prevail in his or her civil rights lawsuit.

(False: If the employee demonstrates a prima facie or initial case of discrimination in discharge the employee does not automatically prevail; rather, the burden of proof and persuasion is now shifted to the employer to show a legitimate, bona fide, and justifiable reason for the discharge.)

19. To sustain a case of disparate treatment discrimination the employee must show that he or she was intentionally treated differently based on a protected category, such as race or gender.
(True: The employee can use direct evidence or indirect or circumstantial evidence, that is, for the latter, evidence in which a jury could draw an inference of discriminatory animus or intent. Note that a case of disparate or adverse impact does not require evidence of an intent to discriminate.)

20. Title VII of the Civil Rights Act specifically includes homosexuality as a protected category.
(False: The statute just deems "sex" as a protected category; but the Supreme Court has interpreted the prohibition against sex discrimination to encompass protections for gays, lesbians, transgenders, and sexually transitioned people (that is, "gender identity").

21. The Americans with Disabilities Act requires employers to make a reasonable accommodation to the needs of their disabled employees.
(True: However, the employer need not do so if the accommodation would cause an undue burden or hardship on the employer.)

22. It is always illegal for an employer to have "English only" policies in the workplace since language is tied to one's national origin which is protected by Title VII of the Civil Rights Act from discrimination.
(False: Employers may have valid and enforceable "English only" policies if they are limited to working times and areas and can be justified by some type of business necessity, such as ensuring the free and understandable flow of communications for safety, health, security, and supervisory reasons.)

23. Race and color can rise to the level of a bona fide occupational qualification (BFOQ) if these characteristics are reasonably necessary for successful job performance.
(False: Race and color can never be BFOQs. For example, for a producer to advertise for an actor to play Hamlet and say he must be "white" would be illegal. However, it is an open question whether the producer could say must be "male" since it is possible that gender could be a BFOQ.)

24. Employers are allowed to discriminate on the basis of attractiveness of appearance.
(True: Appearance discrimination does not violate the Civil Rights Act per se; and thus employers are allowed to "prefer the pretty"; however, appearance and attractiveness standards (e.g. "cute") must be applied to all employees and not just women employees or else there will be disparate treatment discrimination.)

25. Title VII of the Civil Rights Act only affects companies that do business within the U.S. and its territories and thus the statute cannot be used to reach discriminatory actions by U.S. companies doing business overseas.
(False: The U.S. Civil Rights Act has "extra-territorial" effect and thus as a general rule will reach such activities. Some U.S. statutes, such as the Occupational Health and Safety Act do not have extra-territorial effect.)

26. U.S. anti-discrimination laws make it virtually impossible to fire a minority employee who is not performing well.
(False: Only discrimination against minorities as well as other members of the protected classes is impermissible. A poorly performing minority employee most certainly can be fired but the employer

should have justifiable, non-discriminatory, work-related reasons to do so and the employer should have the so-called "paper trail" to support the reasons.)

27. Discriminating against an applicant for employment based on gender may be permissible if gender is reasonably necessary for normal and successful job performance.
(True: This is legal discrimination pursuant to the BFOQ doctrine (bona fide occupational qualification), which the courts do not like, but will uphold, for example, when a company is hiring a model for women's clothes it can specify that "only females need apply.")

28. In order to prevail in a sexual harassment case, the aggrieved employee must be able to demonstrate some type of physical harm from the harassment.
(False: A showing of physical harm is not required; the fact of the harassment is the gravamen of the wrong. Of course, any physical harm as well as emotional distress would factor in determining damages. Moreover, the physical harm could constitute a battery, which is an independent civil wrong, an intentional tort, as well as a crime.)

29. When a company refuses to hire a 25-year-old applicant because the president of the company does not feel that anyone under 30 is mature enough for serious work the company is violating the Age Discrimination in Employment Act (ADEA).
(False: Applicants and employees must be 40 years of age or older to be protected by the ADEA.)

30. To prevail in a disparate treatment case under Title VII the aggrieved applicant or employee must produce evidence of the employer's intent to discriminate.
(True: This is a basic proposition as this type of discrimination is intentional. However, evidence can be in the form of "direct evidence," for example, the plaintiff or witnesses hearing discriminatory statements, or "indirect evidence," also called "circumstantial" or "inferential" evidence, for example, when a manager calls a rejected applicant a "terrorist," "Taliban," or "towel-head," which statements or "code words" would give rise to an inference to discriminate. Another example would be when a minority applicant applies for a position, is qualified, but is rejected, and the position continues to remain open until it is filled by a non-minority applicant.)

31. Undue hardship or burden would be the employer's main defense in a lawsuit for disability discrimination pursuant to the Americans with Disabilities Act (ADA).
(True: The ADA requires that an employer make a "reasonable accommodation" to the needs of its disabled employees, but the employer need not do so if the accommodation would be an undue hardship or burden on the employer.)

32. A company's rejection of job applicants because they have foreign accents would likely be illegal discrimination under Title VII.
(True: Since language is considered to be part of one's cultural identity and thus national origin to reject applicants with accents would typically be a form of national origin discrimination, unless perhaps the accents are so "heavy" that the speaker could not be understood in a position where accurate communication is critical.)

33. A bi-lingual employee who speaks English in addition to another language can never complain about his or her employer's "English-only" policy since the employee can readily switch to English.
(False: If the employer's language policy mandates the speaking of English at all times and at all places in the workplace it is presumed to be illegal since such policies must be limited to work times and work places as well as be justified by a legitimate business reason. As such, the bi-lingual employee while on break in a rest area can speak any language he or she so chooses.)

34. The Supreme Court has enunciated a principle of absolute liability for employers whose managers or supervisors sexually harass a subordinate employee who suffers some type of tangible job loss.
(True: Absolute liability principles are rare but according to recent Supreme Court cases one now exists as noted above, and consequently even if the employer has acted carefully in selecting managers and supervisors and even if the employer has policies and programs to combat sexual harassment in the workplace. As a side-note, these rulings and this principle of absolute liability have engendered a whole new field of insurance – sexual harassment insurance.)

35. When the Equal Employment Opportunity Commission (EEOC) determines that the employer has not committed a violation of Title VII and dismisses discrimination charges, the allegedly aggrieved employee is forever precluded from bringing a lawsuit.
(False: The purportedly aggrieved employee can still bring a lawsuit for money damages on his or her own; however, it would certainly be advantageous for the employee to have the EEOC bringing suit (and shouldering the legal expenses) for the employee. Moreover, the EEOC's not taking the case may call into question the legal or factual validity of the employee's charge of discrimination.)

36. Rejecting a job applicant because he or she is known as a "political activist" is a violation of Title VII of the Civil Rights Acts.
(False: Neither political beliefs, party affiliation, nor political activism are "protected categories" under Title VII, assuming no other discrimination. However, note that some states, counties, and/or municipalities may have statutes or ordinances that prohibit discrimination based on political beliefs, etc.)

37. A refusal by a majority of the employees to work with a prospective employee because of his or her national origin and/or religious beliefs is a defense under Title VII to a discrimination charge when the employer does not hire the applicant.
(False: Employee preferences are not a defense to or an excuse for discrimination under Title VII.)

38. The determination as to whether a work environment is a sexually offensive one contains an objective as well as a subjective test.
(True: This is a confusing area of the law. Ordinarily, whether a work environment is offensive, abusive, or hostile is determined by a "reasonable person" standard. However, the EEOC has stated that "reasonableness" should be also considered from the perspective of the aggrieved party, who might be on the sensitive-side, and thus a personal and subjective element has come into sexual harassment law.)

39. The *bona fide* occupational qualification (BFOQ) doctrine may rise to the level of a viable defense to a claim under Title VII that an employer has engaged in discrimination based on sex.
(True: Race and color may never be BFOQs, but gender certainly can be, for example, an employer stating that only females can be locker room and bathroom attendants at a women's health club.)

40. The federal courts current interpretation of the adverse or disparate impact theory of discrimination is that the aggrieved employees have to show that the employment policy or practice under question was a purposeful subterfuge for discrimination.
(False: In an adverse impact case no showing of discriminatory intent, subterfuge, or pretext is necessary; rather, a neutral employment policy or practice when applied to all the employees has an adverse and disparate, that is, disproportionate, effect on employees in a protected class under Title VII.)

41. If a plaintiff employee can show that the employers' purportedly legitimate reason for the employee's discharge was merely a "pretext" the employee will prevail in a Title VII discrimination lawsuit.
(True: A "pretextual" reason is no good reason; rather, it is a subterfuge to hide or mask a discriminatory intent. Pretext can be determined by the lack of weight behind the asserted reason, whether other employees similarly situated were treated the same, and especially the timing of the reason, that is, the purportedly legitimate reason was devised shortly after the employee alleged discrimination.)

42. The federal Constitution provides a right to privacy that protects virtually all U.S. employees from employer surveillance and monitoring absent a showing of probable cause.
(False: Government employees have a Constitutional right to privacy, though of course not absolute. However, employees in the private sector are not protected by the federal Constitution as it just protects against government interference and abridgement of certain rights, such as privacy. Yet a few state constitutions, for example, California, do provide some rights, including a right to privacy, to private parties, including private sector employees.)

43. As a general rule, pre-employment drug-testing has been deemed to be lawful by the courts.
(True: And in both the public and private employment sectors; the practice has not been construed to violate the 4th Amendment prohibition against unreasonable searches and seizures or the constitutional right to privacy as well as not to violate the common law tort of invasion of privacy.)

44. As a general rule in the U.S., employees who are employees at-will can be discharged simply because their employers did not like the clothes they are wearing.
(True: An employee at-will can be fired for any reason, no reason, no good reason, or even an arbitrary and capricious reason, like clothes style. However, an employee at-will cannot be fired for an illegal reason, so perhaps if the clothes style has race, religious, or national origin implications, thereby bringing in the Civil Rights Act, the discharged employee may have a wrongful discharge claim by means of a Title VII discrimination lawsuit.)

45. The terms of company personnel manuals could be construed by a court as constituting an employment contract.
(True: The legal means would be the Implied Contract theory, whereby past practice, employment manuals, codes of conduct, and statements by management might provide sufficient conduct to form an implied contract from all the facts and circumstances. However, realizing this possibility, many employers have disclaimers in their manuals and codes stating clearly and conspicuously that nothing therein should be construed as creating a binding contract.)

46. The Public Policy doctrine is an important exception to the employment at-will general rule.
(True: Even an employee at-will cannot be discharged for a reason that violates the fundamental public policy of the state as determined by the high court of the state guided by legislative pronouncements. Public policy protects activities that benefit the health, welfare, safety, and morals of citizens and residents of the state. Prime examples would be a discharge for performing jury duty or testifying truthfully before a government body investigating the employer or "blowing the whistle" on the employer's or fellow employees' legal wrongdoing.)

47. Seniority clauses in collective bargaining agreements are unlawful under Title VII of the Civil Rights Act.
(False: This is an important exception to the Act's coverage, even though seniority clauses could perpetuate past discrimination and stereotyping.)

48. Employees who seek protection under the Age Discrimination and Employment Act (ADEA) must be 55 years of age or older.
(False: The ADEA age limit is 40 years of age.)

49. The Reasonable Factor Other Than Age (RFOA) doctrine is an important exception to the ADEA.
(True: If the discharge of older workers is motivated by "reasonable factors other than age," for example, economic reasons caused by older workers causing higher health care costs, then there is no age discrimination lawsuit pursuant to the ADEA.)

50. Success in a disparate treatment discrimination case under Title VII of the Civil Rights Act requires a showing of intent.
(True: Yet the intent can be demonstrated by direct evidence as well as inferred from indirect or circumstantial evidence. One example of an inference of intent would be when a minority applicant who is qualified for a position is not hired, the position remains open, and a non-minority with lesser qualifications is hired. Another example would be the use of Code Words, such as calling a black candidate a "boy" or a woman a "bitch.")

51. Undue hardship is the employer's primary defense under the Americans with Disabilities Act (ADA).
(True: This is a basic proposition of the ADA; and at times the phrase "undue burden" is used; however, note that the mere increased cost of accommodating the needs of a disabled worker is neither an undue burden nor hardship to the employer.)

52. Undue hardship or undue burden is the employer's primary defense against an assertion of failure to accommodate the religious beliefs and practices of its employees.
(True: The employer need not make a religious accommodation to an employee if it would be an undue hardship or burden to the employer. For example, overturning a seniority system to accommodate employees who worship on Fridays or Saturdays, which would be too burdensome, as opposed to releasing an employee early for Friday prayers or providing an office or space for daily prayers, which though inconvenient and involving some expense would likely not be construed as an undue burden to the employer.)

53 Punitive damages were added as a potential remedy under Title VII discrimination claims by the Civil Rights Act of 1991.
(True: However, the traditional standards for imposing punitive damages, such as evidence of hate, malice, and spite, still must be demonstrated.)

54. Court decisions indicate that a fair arbitration system can be used to avoid litigation by employees of discrimination and harassment claims.
(True: Arbitration has always been favored by the courts, though at times criticized by employees, especially when coupled with mandatory confidentiality agreements. However, even though the employee is bound by the arbitration clause in the contract with the employer, the EEOC is not and thus can still proceed against the employer for Title VII violations.)

55. Title VII of the Civil Rights Act allows for the Bona Fide Occupational Qualification (BFOQ) defense in race and color discrimination claims.
(False: Race and color can never be BFOQs; however, gender, religion, and national origin may be if a certain characteristic is reasonably necessary for normal and successful job performance, such as hiring only females to model women's clothes or to serve at bathroom/locker attendants at an all-women's health-club.)

56. A legitimate business justification can rise to the level of a valid defense in a disparate impact case.
(True: In a disparate impact case there is no evidence of intentional discrimination but rather the employer's policy or practice, though applied to all employees and applicants, for example, not having a felony conviction, or passing a strength test, or height or weight requirements, causes an adverse and disproportionate impact on minority or women employees. In such a situation the burden shifts to the employer to produce a legitimate business reason to justify the policy or practice.)

57. A business organization must develop and institute a fixed quota system to remedy the effects of past social stereotyping of women.
(False: A fixed quota system is certainly not a legal obligation of the employer. Moreover, if done, the quota would likely be viewed as intentional discrimination of male employees so as to violate Title VII. Of course, an employer surely can institute affirmative action efforts to search for, recruit, train, and mentor women applicants and employees to remedy past societal stereotyping and discrimination.)

58. It is very difficult for an employee to establish his or her initial case before the EEOC in a disparate treatment case.
(False: Just the opposite, as inferential, indirect, or circumstantial evidence of an intent to discriminate will be sufficient for the agency, at least initially.)

59. Whistleblowing legal protection for employees pursuant to state statutes is more likely to be available when an employee informs on employer immoral as opposed to illegal conduct.
(False: Whistleblowing statutes are consistent in stating that the employee must report on illegal conduct by the employer or fellow employees; reporting immoral or socially irresponsible conduct that is not also a legal violation is insufficient.)

60. Whistleblowing legal protection for employees pursuant to state statutes is available to protect employees who report legal violations by their employers to the media.
(False: State whistleblowing statutes are consistent in stating that the employee must first report to an appropriate government agency to obtain the protection of a whistleblower protection act.)

61. An employer would likely be held liable for the tort of negligent hiring for hiring an applicant as a driver without inquiring and checking into the applicant's driver license status and driving record.
(True: This is a basic application of the negligence principle that one must act as a reasonable and prudent person in the employment hiring context.)

62. Generally, the U.S. offers less legal protection against unfair or unjust dismissal of employees than is the case in most industrialized countries.
(True: The majority rule in the U.S., with the exception of a couple of states, is the traditional employment at-will doctrine, which holds that an employee can be discharged for any reason, no reason, no good reason, and even a morally bad reason, but not an illegal reason, such as illegal discrimination in violation of the Civil Rights Act. Whereas in most countries, such as France or Germany, an employee must be discharged for a good or just cause; otherwise, the employer must pay the employee severance as determined by government statutes. Another example is in Italy where an employee can challenge his or her discharge if the employee believes it is not "fair.")

63. An employer may be held legally liable for the torts committed by its employees acting within the scope and course of employment pursuant to the doctrine of *Respondeat Superior*.
(True: This principle is one of vicarious or imputed liability, and thus is applicable even if the employer itself was not negligent. This principle, moreover, applies not only to negligent torts but also intentional torts but only in the latter case if the employee's intent was to further the business of his or her employer.)

64. The Public Policy exception to the employment at-will doctrine may protect an employee from an unjust discharge.
(True: All states adhere to the Public Policy doctrine, though to varying degrees depending on state court interpretation. In essence, the doctrine holds that an employee, even an at-will one, cannot be discharged for a reason that violates the fundamental public policy of the state, that is, policies designed to protect and better the health, safety, and welfare of the people of the state. An example would be an employee "blowing the whistle," that is, disclosing legal wrongdoing or testifying as to same, even in a state that does not have a Whistleblower Protection Act. Note, too, that in most states a public policy violation by the employer will also give rise to tort liability.)

65. A successful defense to a sexual harassment claim will always be that the employer lacked knowledge of the harassment.
(False: Mere ignorance is insufficient because under traditional negligence principles the employer has a duty to engage in reasonable management and supervision of the employees and thus perhaps should have known of the harassment.)

66. A prudent employer will promulgate policies to combat sexual harassment and communicate them to the employees, have communication channels and "hot-lines," and conduct appropriate education and training to prevent sexual harassment in the workplace.
(True: It is certainly in the legal, ethical, and practical self-interest to do so too. Pursuant to Supreme Court rulings if sexual harassment is committed by an employee's co-workers the employer may have a defense if the employer institutes such practices and policies and the victimized employee does not take advantage of them. However, if the sexual harassment is committed by a manager or supervisor of the employee, who suffers a tangible job loss, even if just losing a few hours of work, the employer is absolutely liable for the harassment regardless of such policies and regardless of any fault itself. This principle of absolute liability, which is rare in the law, is the main reason for the development and growth of the sexual harassment insurance field.)

67. Sex discrimination in the form of culturally-biased consumer preference for a particular sex can be the basis for a legitimate Bona Fide Occupational Qualification (BFOQ).
(False: Cultural preferences, whether gender- or national origin-based, are not grounds for a BFOQ. The afore mentioned characteristics, however, can form the basis for a legal BFOQ if they are reasonably necessary for normal and successful job functions. Race can never be a BFOQ and race-based consumer preferences cannot be grounds to discriminate.)

68. Since achieving the goal of a diverse workforce is a positive and laudable one in today's heterogeneous society race and color can rise to the level of a BFOQ.
(False: Race and color can never be BFOQs, regardless of any beneficent intent.)

69. *Quid pro quo* sexual harassment is a form of discrimination and a violation of the Civil Rights Act.
(True: Quid pro quo means "something for something," that is, an offer to have sex for a job or a promotion; and this is a form of sexual harassment prohibited by Title VII of the Civil Rights Act.)

70. Under the disparate or adverse impact theory of discrimination the challenged employment policy or practice is neutral on-its-face.
(True: It is the effect of the policy when applied to all employees that is the gravamen of the legal wrong, that is, the policy, though neutral, has an adverse, disproportionate effect on protected classes under the Civil Rights Act, for example, a strength or agility test for firefighters and paramedics that has a disparate impact on female candidates.)

71. Granting employment preferences to people who are "socially and/or economically disadvantaged" or who are "strivers" (that is, with a record of success despite social and economic hardships) may be legal if no applicants are automatically excluded because of their race, color, gender, or national origin.
(True: These are neutral categories on which an employer can legally base an affirmative action plan since white men are not automatically excluded and preferences are not given based on immutable characteristics, such as race or color.)

72. Firing an employee because he is dating the boss's daughter against the wishes of the boss would very likely be legal under the traditional employment at-will doctrine in the United States.
(True: An employee at-will can be fired for any reason, even an arbitrary, capricious, or spiteful reason, but not an illegal reason, say perhaps if the discharged employee was a minority.)

73. A business employer's rule that English must be spoken at all times and all places in the workplace is presumed to be legally valid if the employer has a large number of customers and clients that only speak English.
(False: A rule that English must be spoken at all times and all places in the workplace is presumed to be invalid by the EEOC and only very strong countervailing evidence as to the need for such a broad rule will sustain it, for example, a rule that all cadets at the police academy whether in class, training, athletics, meals, or on "breaks" speak English in order to ensure effective communication among police officers. The fact that a large number of customers and clients only speak English may justify, however, a limited English-only policy.)

74. In a sexual harassment case, an employer cannot be held legally liable if one of its employees committed the harassment without the knowledge of the employer.
(False: Under traditional negligence principles the employer perhaps should have had knowledge based on a duty to manage and supervise its workforce in a reasonable manner. Also, pursuant to Supreme Court decisions an employer regardless of knowledge can be absolutely liable when a manager or supervisor harasses a subordinate employee who suffers some sort of tangible job loss.)

75. Disparate treatment discrimination under Title VII occurs when an employer intentionally discriminates against an employee due to a protected category, such as race or color.
(True: Some evidence, direct or indirect, of a discriminatory animus on the part of the employer is critical.)

76. An employer need not provide an "interpreter" to a hearing-impaired employee if it would cost the employer extra-money.
(False: Usually, mere increased cost or expense is insufficient to rise to the level of an undue burden or hardship to the employer. If it is thus deemed to be a "reasonable accommodation" to provide an interpreter than the employer is legally obligated by the ADA to do so.)

77. The common law "public policy" exception to the employment at-will doctrine may protect a whistle-blowing employee from an unjust discharge even though the employees lacks any statutory whistleblower protection.

(True: The Public Policy doctrine is created by state common law to protect employees who disclose employer conduct that violates the fundamental public policy of the state, as determined by the high court in the state, and usually defined as activities that protect the health, welfare, safety, and morals of the people in that state. Note that in some states a discharge in violation of public policy is construed as an intentional tort, thereby affording the discharged employee much better legal relief, particularly in the form of damages, than the typical state Whistleblower Protection Act.)

78. If the employer adopts reasonable policies and procedures against sexual harassment, communicates them to the employees, provides appropriate training to combat sexual harassment, and designates appropriate contact persons and channels for complaints, the employer will not be absolutely liable for sexual harassment committed by an employee's non-managerial and non-supervisory co-workers.
(True: This is the affirmative defense provided by the Supreme Court, and which naturally indicates that it is in the prudent employer's self-interest to act accordingly. However, if the sexual harassment is committed by a manager or supervisor against a subordinate employee, who suffers some sort of tangible job loss, the employer is absolutely liable and this affirmative defense of polices, procedures, training, etc., is irrelevant.)

79. If an employer has to undergo undue hardship or burden in accommodating the religious needs or practices of its employees, the employer need not do so and cannot be sued for religious discrimination under Title VII.
(True: There is a duty to accommodate the religious beliefs, needs, and practices of the employees but not if it would be an undue burden or hardship to do so. For example, materially changing the seniority system for scheduling due to employees who cannot work on Saturdays or Friday afternoons for prayers would be an undue burden, whereas releasing an employee early from work on Friday for prayers or providing a place to pray at work might entail some inconvenience or cost but not be an undue hardship for the employer.)

80. If an employee is discharged when an employer finds out the employee's political beliefs, which are contrary to the employer's, the discharged employee can institute a successful discrimination lawsuit under Title VII of the Civil Rights Act.
(False: Political beliefs and political party affiliation are not "protected" categories under Title VII and thus the employee would have no relief under federal law. However, some states, counties, and/or municipalities might have protection against discharge for "political" beliefs or party membership or political activities.)

81. Title VII of the Civil Rights Act only affects companies doing business in the U.S., and thus cannot be used to restrain the business activities of U.S. companies doing business abroad.
(False: Title VII like some other U.S. statutes has "extra-territorial effect," that is, the statute can be used to reach activities by U.S. firms overseas. However, only U.S. employee working overseas for U.S. firms (or firms controlled by U.S. firms) are protected. Accordingly, foreign nationals employed by U.S. firms in their own country are not protected due to international law considerations. Moreover, even if an employee is a U.S. citizen, if the employment discrimination is mandated by the law of the host country, for example, Saudi Arabia requiring any person visiting or doing business in Mecca during certain important religious times must be a Muslim, the discrimination is not unlawful due to notions of Sovereign Immunity.)

82. The Family Medical Leave Act (FMLA) provides up to 12 weeks of paid leave for the birth or adoption of a child or a serious illness of the employee, his or her spouse, child, or family members.
(False: The leave provision in the FMLA is for unpaid leave. At the end of the leave the employee is entitled to the same or an equivalent position back but with no accrual of seniority.)

83. Federal law requires that all firms of 100 or more employees must provide a 60-day notice to workers and the local community of an impending plant closing or major layoff.
(True: This is the major provision of the Worker Readjustment and Training Act of 1988, called the WARN Act. There are exceptions to the notice, however, for example, when the closing or layoff is caused by unforeseen circumstances beyond the control of the employer.)

84. An employer may be held liable under Title VII if it asks employees questions about a disability that are not clearly related to the job.
(True: The employer would be advised to ask only if the employee can perform the job with or without an accommodation to his or her disability.)

85. Title VII of the Civil Rights Act makes it impossible to discharge an employee who is not performing well on the job if that employee is a member of a protected class.
(False: Title VII is not a guarantor of incompetent work performance. However, the employer must have, and be able to demonstrate sufficiently, a legitimate business-related reason for any discharge of any employee, that is, the "paper trail," but especially so for one covered by Title VII.)

86.. Disparate impact lawsuits are based on a statistically significant deficiency in the percentage of minority employees in the employer's workforce compared with the percentage of minorities available in the employer's labor pool.
(True: Also called adverse impact lawsuits, an employment policy or practice, such as requiring no criminal record, though neutral and applied to all applicants, creates the disproportionate adverse impact on minority employees. Note that the EEOC has percentage formulas for ascertaining if the deficiency creates the requisite disparate impact.)

87. Setting aside a specific and fixed percentage of a state or local government's contracts for women or minority contractors is legally permissible to achieve diversity.
(False: While diversity may be a very laudable goal, using a specific and fixed percentage would be deemed to be a "quota," which the courts have ruled violates the 14th Amendment Equal Protection clause and is thus unconstitutional and illegal. However, an affirmative action plan that uses gender or race as one factor in awarding contracts along with other "neutral" factors such as socio-economic status likely would be legal.)

88. A *prima facie* case of discrimination under Title VII means that there is initial evidence of discrimination for the case to proceed.
(True: An example would be when a minority applicant applies for a job, the applicant is qualified, the applicant is rejected, the job position stays open, and a non-minority is chosen for the position. However, this initial finding of discrimination can be rebutted by an employer providing evidence of a job-related reason for not hiring the minority applicant.)

89. The Equal Pay Act of 1963 requires that men and women be paid identical pay for the same job.
(False: "Equal" in the Act means "substantially" equal and not necessarily identical.)

90. Customer preference can never be the basis for an English-only language policy since customers might be bigoted.
(False: The courts have upheld customer preferences as a legitimate business reason for an English-only policy regardless of any subjective beliefs of the customers. The leading case dealt with a retail store by the Mexican border in which the owner required employees who were working and at the sales counted to speak English, even in casual conversations, unless the customers approached the sales personnel speaking Spanish, and then it would be permissible for the employees, who were bi-

lingual, to speak Spanish. The court's reasoning was that English-only speaking customers might be too intimidated or embarrassed to approach sales personnel speaking in Spanish, thereby causing the store owner to lose sales.)

91. Title VII of the U.S. Civil Rights Act protects all employees of U.S. companies doing business overseas.
(False: Title VII does have some extra-territorial effect as it protects U.S. citizens who are employed overseas by U.S. companies or firms controlled by U.S. companies; however, Title VII does not apply to foreign employees when they are employed by U.S. firms in a foreign country. Foreign employees are protected, though, when they work in the United States.)

Multiple Choice Questions with Answers and Explanations

1. Pursuant to Title VII of the Civil Rights Act:
    a. Discrimination in employment is legal if it results unintentionally from a valid seniority system.
    b. Discrimination in employment is legal if it is based on the *bona fide* occupational qualification (BFOQ) exception.
    c. Discrimination in employment is legal if the employer is engaging in "lookism," that is preferring "good looking" applicants for positions.
    d. All of the above.

    (The correct answer is d. Seniority systems assuming they are legitimate are an explicit exception to Title VII. The BFOQ exception is based on a certain characteristic, but never race or color, being reasonably necessary for normal and successful job functions. Appearance discrimination, also at times called "preferring the pretty," is legal unless one's appearance can be tied to a protected category under Title VII or another civil rights statute.)

2. The Pregnancy Discrimination Act:
    a. requires employers with health plans to cover pregnancy in the same manner that other health conditions are covered.
    b. allows the employer to specify how long a leave of absence must be taken after childbirth so long as the time period is reasonable.
    c. requires any leave of absence to be paid-leave.
    d. Allows the employer to compel a pregnant employee to stop working until the child is born.

    (The correct answer is a. Pregnancy is treated under the Act has "merely" another health disability which must be covered by health and/or disability plans. The employer can neither specify the length of absence nor force the employee to stop working, assuming in the latter case that the pregnant employee is still capable of performing her job duties satisfactorily. For paid-leave to occur it must be covered in the employee's contract with the employer. Otherwise, one can move to Sweden, and for paternal paid-leave too)!

3. The Age Discrimination in Employment Act (ADEA):
    a. protects persons between 45-60 years of age.
    b. protects persons between 45-60 years of age.
    c. does not have an upper-age limit to the statute's protection.
    d. prohibits the termination of older workers.

    (The correct answer is c. To be protected the employee must be at least 40 years of age but there is no upper-age limit to the statute's coverage. The ADEA protects against the discrimination of older workers, not their termination.)

4. A minimum height and weight requirement for a certain job:
   a. Would be illegal under Title VII if not legitimately related to job performance since Asian applicants might be discriminated against.
   b. Would trigger the adverse or disparate impact theory of discrimination if the result was that a disproportionate number of women were excluded from employment.
   c. Both a and b.
   d. Neither a nor b.
   (The correct answer is c. If there is a disparate impact on women the burden would shift to the employer to justify the height and weight requirements, for example, for efficiency and safety reasons for flight attendants. The same result would occur for Asian applicants too.)

5. Which of the following job requirements is MOST LIKELY to be legal under Title VII of the Civil Rights Act?
   a. A janitor cleaning a men's locker-room at a health club must be male.
   b. A delivery person serving in a predominantly Hispanic neighbor must be Hispanic.
   c. A "contact" prison guard who has to search male prisoners must be male.
   d. A salesperson selling women's cosmetics must be female.
   (The correct answer is c. This question deals with the bona fide occupational qualification exception (BFOQ) to Title VII where discrimination may be legal, but never for race or color, if it is necessary for normal and successful job functions. The strongest example of the BFOQ would be answer c for safety, security, and personal reasons. A janitor could always temporarily close a bathroom for cleaning or clean off-hours. A delivery person might have to learn some Spanish if that is a legitimate prerequisite for the position. And a man certainly could sell women's cosmetics successfully.)

6. Regarding employer English-only policies under Title VII, which of the following are TRUE:
   a. They must be limited to working times and places.
   b. They must be based on legitimate business reasons.
   c. The employer must give the employees time to adapt to the policy.
   d. All of the above.
   (The correct answer is d. These are all fundamental requirements for a legal English-only policy. If the policy applies to all aspects of the workplace, for example, to employees on-break at the cafeteria, the EEOC will presume that the policy is invalid. Note that the courts accept several rationales by the employer to substantiate an English-only policy, for example, safety and security, ease of communication and supervisory function, perceived customer preference, and avoiding or elimination a language-based "rumor" or "back-stabbing" environment at work.)

7. When must a private sector employer accommodate an employee's religious beliefs and practices under Title VII of the Civil Rights Act?
   a. Never, as the employer's sole duty is not to discriminate against employees based on religion.
   b. Always, since freedom of religion is protected by the First Amendment in the Bill of Rights.
   c. When the accommodation can be arranged and managed with only minimal cost and inconvenience to the employer.
   d. When the accommodation can be arranged and managed with no undue burden or hardship on the employer.
   (The correct answer is d. The employer has a double-duty regarding religion under Title VII – not to discriminate and to make a reasonable accommodation to the employee's religious beliefs and practices. Cost or expense or inconvenience for the employer if only minimal is not an issue; rather, the burden on the employer must be "undue" or cause a serious hardship, for example,

over-turning a seniority system for Saturday over-time to try to accommodate religious practices occurring on Saturday. The first Amendment right to free exercise of religion is inapplicable in private sector employment, only in the public sector, since constitutional rights at the federal level can only be asserted against government.)

8. Which of the following MOST LIKELY is illegal discrimination pursuant to Title VII of the *federal* Civil Rights Act?
   a. Not considering applicants for manufacturing sales positions because of their political beliefs in socialism.
   b. Not hiring applicants for sales positions who are smokers of tobacco products.
   c. Not hiring based on "gender identity," that is, gay, lesbian, bisexual, sexually transitioning, or transgender employees.
   d. Not hiring candidates whether male or female who are parents when extensive travel is involved with the position.

   (The correct answer is C. Political beliefs are not a protected category. Discrimination against smokers is permissible under Title VII as smokers are not a protected category. Travel requirements so long as they are legitimate job requirements are permissible so long as they are applied equally to male and female applicants.)

9. Which of the following is TRUE regarding Title VII of the federal Civil Rights Act in the workplace?
   a. The plaintiff employee must always prove a malicious and spiteful intent to discriminate on the part of the defendant employer against the employee to prevail in a Title VII civil rights lawsuit.
   b. Only "big" employers with 2000 or more employees are covered by the federal Title VII Civil Rights Act due to the voluminous record-keeping requirements.
   c. The employer must make an accommodation to an employee's religious beliefs, observances, and practices regardless of the expense, cost, or burden since freedom of religion is a very important civil right in the United States.
   d. As a general rule, an employer can discriminate on the basis of appearance by selecting only "good-looking" and attractive male and female applicants for its sales force.

   (The correct answer is d. Malice and spite are not requirements to a successful Title VII law disparate treatment lawsuit, only evidence that the discrimination based on a protected category was intentional. The Act applies to employers who only have 15 employees. The employer need not accommodate an employee's religious beliefs if it would be an undue hardship or burden to do so. Appearance discrimination, also called "preferring the pretty" and "lookism," is legal if the appearance standards are applied equally to men and women and0 no other aspects of Title VII of violated.)

10. Which of the following constitutes illegal discrimination under Title VII of the Civil Rights Act?
    a. A retail store refuses to hire Hispanics as employees.
    b. A sporting goods store refuses to hire anyone over the age of 40.
    c. A large retail store refuses to hire anyone in a wheelchair.
    d. All of the above.

    (The correct answer is d. Refusing to hire Hispanics is national origin discrimination. Refusing to hire "older" workers is age discrimination under the ADEA. And not hiring the handicapped is disability discrimination under the ADA. Note, too, that in the latter case the employer also has a duty to make a reasonable accommodation to the needs of its handicapped employees.)

11. Regarding sexual harassment claims filed by an employer against his or her employer:
    a. Companies are absolutely liable for all sexual harassment claims since sexual harassment is a serious legal and moral wrong.
    b. Companies are absolutely liable for sexual harassment inflicted by a manager or supervisor against a subordinate employee who suffers a tangible job loss or harm.
    c. Companies are not liable for sexual harassment claims unless they actually knew of the sexual harassment and condoned it.
    d. Companies are never liable for sexual harassment claims since the meaning of a "hostile" or "offensive" sexual work environment is too vague and subjective to impose legal liability.

    (The correct answer is b. The Supreme Court has enunciated a principle of absolute liability for certain types of sexual harassment as per answer b. However, the Supreme Court also has ruled that if the harassment is done by co-workers at the same level the employer has a defense if it has policies and practices, education and training, as well as channels of communication, to prohibit, prevent, and redress sexual harassment. A company is liable, nevertheless, if it knew of the harassment or should have known of it and did nothing. Finally, the definitions for sexual harassment may be a bit vague, as offensiveness, hostility, and abusiveness are premised on a "reasonable person" standard, but that is just the nature of this area of the law. All of the foregoing are very good reasons for a company to obtain sexual harassment insurance.)

12. The Americans with Disabilities Act (ADA) requires that:
    a. Employers make an all-out effort to accommodate disabled employees regardless of cost or expense.
    b. Employers must make a "reasonable" accommodation to disabled employees.
    c. Only large employers with over 1500 employees must make a reasonable accommodation to disabled employees due to the burdens involved.
    d. None of the above.

    (The correct answer is b. The ADA Covers employers who have 15 or more employees. The employer must not only not discriminate against handicapped employees but must make a reasonable effort to accommodate the employee's disability. However, the employer need not make the accommodation if it would be an undue burden or hardship to do so.)

13. Which is a FALSE statement about U.S. civil rights laws?
    a. The Age Discrimination in Employment Act protects against age discrimination in the workplace.
    b. Language discrimination in the form of "English-only" policies can be a form of national origin discrimination.
    c. Even an employee at-will can sue for wrongful discharge if she was terminated because of her gender.
    d. An employer is allowed to have an Affirmative Action plan that has rigid and fixed quotas for hiring based solely on race due to the history of discrimination in the United States.

    (The correct answer is d. Quotas, unless imposed by a court as a remedial measure violate Title VII as well as the 14th Amendment Equal Protection clause. An employer can have an affirmative plan based on neutral factors, such as socio-economic status or a candidate being a "striver," that is, a high-achiever under challenging circumstances. All the other responses are basic and true applications of Title VII.)

14. Which is TRUE regarding the employment at-will doctrine in the United States?
    a. If can result in a legal but immoral discharge of an employee.
    b. It cannot be changed by a contract between the employer and the employee.
    c. It is operable in the U.S. and can result in a discharge without notice or cause or good cause, but the employer based on federal law has to pay severance to the discharged employee based on the number of years he or she has worked for the firm.
    d. It supersedes and prevails over Title VII of the Civil Rights Act.

    (The correct answer is a. Employment at-will, which is a common law rule, can result in legal but immoral discharge of an employee, for example, for rooting for the "wrong" sports team than the boss, but not a wrongful, that is, illegal, discharge, for example, a discharge that violates Title VII of the Civil Rights Act, which as a statute supersedes the common law. An employee can always attempt to obviate his or her employment at-will status by seeking a contract that states that he or she will be discharged only for good, just, or reasonable cause. Severance pay is not mandated by federal law; it may be part of the employee's contract with the employer, however.)

15. Even an employee at-will can sue for wrongful discharge when he or she:
    a. Is discharged in violation of Title VII of the Civil Rights Act.
    b. Is discharged in violation of the Public Policy doctrine.
    c. Is negligently discharged by the employer.
    d. All of the above.

    (The correct answer is d. All are exceptions to employment at-will. Title VII of the Civil Rights Act supersedes the common law employment at-will doctrine and thus a discharge of an employee at-will based on discrimination by race, color, gender, religion, or national origin would be illegal. A discharge in violation of Public Policy would be a discharge that violates the fundamental public policy of a state, that is, policies, programs, and activities designed to protect the health, welfare, safety, and morals of the people of that state, as determined by the high court in the state. An example would be a discharge of an employee for "blowing the whistle" on employer wrongdoing to an appropriate government agency. Employees, even employees at-will, have to be discharged in a careful, reasonable, and prudent manner, and if the employer fails to do so the discharged employee may have a lawsuit for the common law tort of negligence.)

16. Which of the following is FALSE regarding lawsuits pursuant to Title VII of the Civil Rights Act?
    a. An employer can be liable for discrimination pursuant to Title VII based on the "disparate impact" theory even if there is no evidence of intentional discrimination.
    b. Language discrimination based on an English-only policy can be grounds for a national origin discrimination lawsuit if the employer does not have a legitimate business reason for requiring its employees to speak English.
    c. Discriminating against applicants for employment based on their appearance because they are not sufficiently attractive, pretty, or handsome is as a general rule a Title VII violation since the non-attractive are discriminated against.
    d. Sexual stereotyping of women based on stereotypical notions of appropriate female behavior by male managers is a violation of Title VII.

    (The correct answer is c. Being not sufficiently attractive is not a protected category under Title VII so long as the appearance standard is applies equally to men and women. Disparate impact discrimination, also called "adverse impact," does not require evidence of intentional discrimination; rather, the employer's neutral policy, such as a height or weight requirement or a strength or agility test, has a disproportionate adverse impact on a group protected under Title VII, such as female candidates. In order to have a valid English-only policy the employer must have a legitimate business reason for the policy, such as facilitating effective communication for safety and security reasons, for examples, the nurses all speaking English while they are on-duty

at the hospital. Sexual stereotyping can form the basis for a discrimination lawsuit under Title VII, for example, an attitude of not hiring women as truck drivers since that is a "rough" and "tough" job fit only for males while women should be at home taking care of the family.)

17. Which of the following is/are TRUE about U.S. civil rights laws?
    a. An employer can defend a lawsuit pursuant to the Age Discrimination and Employment Act (ADEA) by interposing a BFOQ (bona fide occupational qualification) defense.
    b. The "disparate impact" theory of Title VII of the Civil Rights Act now applies to discrimination lawsuits based on the ADEA due to a Supreme Court decision.
    c. The Americans with Disabilities Act requires that an employer not only not discriminate against disabled people but also that the employer makes a "reasonable" accommodation to the needs of its disabled employees.
    d. All of the above.

    (The correct answer is d. These are all fundamental and true legal principles. The BFOQ defense, which courts disfavor since it is legal discrimination, means that a certain characteristic, but never race or color, is reasonably necessary for normal and successful job functions, such as hiring only females to model women's clothes.)

18. The following are limitations on the employment at-will doctrine EXCEPT:
    a. The employee is discharged in violation of Title VII of the Civil Rights Act.
    b. The employee is discharged for "whistleblowing," that is, disclosing to the appropriate government agency serious legal wrongdoing by the employer
    c. The employee is discharged for nepotism, that is, the employer fires the employee to hire a relative.
    d. The employee is discharged for filing a truthful safety report to the pertinent state regulatory agency.

    (The correct answer is d. It may be immoral and unethical to engage in nepotism, but in the private sector at least it is permissible unless prohibited by a company's internal rules. Whistleblowing can be a protected activity pursuant to the common law "public policy" doctrine as well as pursuant to state or federal Whistleblower Protection Acts. Title VII as well as other civil rights statutes are the major exception to the common law employment at-will doctrine.)

19. What is FALSE about the *Supreme Court's* interpretation of Title VII of the Civil Rights Act regarding sexual discrimination and sexual harassment?
    a. Sexual harassment is a form of sex discrimination and as such is prohibited by Title VII.
    b. There is a principle of absolute liability for employers if a managerial or supervisory employee harasses a subordinate employee who suffers a tangible job loss.
    c. The prohibition in Title VII against discriminating on the basis of sex encompasses discrimination based on political beliefs.
    d. *"Quid pro quo"* behavior is a form of sexual harassment.

    (The correct answer is c. The Supreme Court some time ago ruled in the famous Meritor *case that the prohibition against discrimination based on "sex" includes sexual harassment. Moreover, though principles of absolute liability are rare in the law, the Supreme Court has enunciated one as described above. "Quid pro quo," that is, something-for-something, that is, a job for sex, is the "classic" form of sexual harassment.)*

20. What is NOT illegal pursuant to Title VII of the Civil Rights Act?
    a. Disparate treatment discrimination
    b. Adverse or disparate impact discrimination
    c. Seniority systems which have the result of perpetuating past discrimination
    d. Affirmative action quotas which have a fixed quota for minority employees.
    (The correct answer is c. Seniority systems, regardless of the present discriminatory effect, are legal and a major exception to Title VII. Disparate treatment, that is, intentional discrimination based on a protected category, as well as disparate impact, that is, a neutral employment policy or practice that has a disproportionate adverse effect on protected categories and which cannot be justified, are illegal. Fixed rigid quotas are illegal "reverse discrimination." However, an employer perhaps be able to consider race as one factor in an otherwise "holistic" approach to hiring (though the authors would advise to stay away from the "race" factor and rather use neutral, socio-economic factors.)

21. What would typically be an UNDUE BURDEN for the employer regarding accommodating the religious beliefs of its employees?
    a. Lateral transfers and change of job assignments
    b. Changing its seniority system to guarantee that the employee does not work on certain days.
    c. Voluntary substitutes and "job swaps"
    d. Unpaid leave for religious holidays.
    (The correct answer is b. changing a company's seniority system to accommodate an employee's religious beliefs, practices, and observances normally would be construed as an undue burden or hardship for the employer. Otherwise, the other options usually would be considered as reasonable alternatives and even if there is some inconvenience and expense to the employer.)

22. What is NOT illegal job discrimination pursuant to Title VII of the Civil Rights Act?
    a. Preferring applicants who are "attractive" and "sexy"
    b. Sexual stereotyping of applicants
    c. Having educational or testing requirements for applicants that are not significantly related to or predictive of important elements of work behavior and work success
    d. Having a *bona fide* occupational qualification (BFOQ) based on race or color.
    (The correct answer is a. Appearance discrimination, that is, hiring certain applicants based on "good looks," also called "lookism" or "preferring the pretty," is generally legal so long as the appearance standards are applied equally to men and women as well as other protected categories. Sexual stereotyping, that is, not hiring a female candidate based on stereotypical notions of appropriate female behavior or roles is illegal as are educational and testing requirements that cannot be justified. Race and color can never be BFOQs!)

23. Which of the following would MOST LIKELY be a valid *bona fide* occupational qualification?
    a. A hospital not hiring male nurses for the maternity ward since some female patients might find it uncomfortable being taken care of by a man
    b. A "high-end" restaurant not hiring women for wait-staff positions since the restaurant wants to achieve an "old-world, European" atmosphere
    c. A cruise ship not hiring a woman as an engineer since she might have to have a private cabin
    d. A maximum-security male prison not hiring a woman as a "contact" prison guard.
    (The correct answer is d. Due to safety and security issues and based on precedent the woman could be discriminated against for "contact" guard positions, though one would assume there would be other employment opportunities available at the prison or in the prison system generally. The other examples would likely not be valid BFOQs, even though there may be some attendant expense, inconvenience, or discomfort, as these gender characteristics are not reasonably necessary for normal job functions.)

24. What is FALSE about English-only language policies pursuant to Title VII of the Civil Rights Act?
    a. If not properly formulated and implemented they can be the basis for a national origin discrimination lawsuit under Title VII.
    b. They can restrict the speaking of English in all places and at all times in the workplace.
    c. They must be justified by legitimate business reasons.
    d. The employer must give the employees a reasonable amount of time to adopt to the English-only policy.

    (The correct answer is b. First, the courts have ruled that language discrimination can be the basis for a national origin discrimination lawsuit. Second, an overbroad policy where English is forbidden in all places and times in the workplace is presumed to be invalid, and it will be very difficult for a private sector employer to rebut that presumption. Third, if there are legitimate reasons for the policy, such as safety, security, enhancing supervision, efficient, or dispelling rumors, an English-only policy may be valid if it is limited to work times and work places, and not "break" or lunch times and lunch places, lounges, lockers, etc. Not only must the employer give the employees a reasonable amount of time to adopt to the policy, but if some employees do not know English the employer must teach them English!)

25. What is FALSE about sexual harassment under Title VII?
    a. The Equal Employment Opportunity Commission (EEOC) uses a strictly objective "reasonable person" test to determine if the conduct is offensive sexually.
    b. If sexual harassment is committed by an employee's co-workers the employer may have a defense if it did not know, or should not have known, of the harassment and had in place programs, policies, and reporting channels to prevent or stop sexual harassment.
    c. The more frequent and severe the sexual conduct is the more likely the courts will regard it as offensive and hostile.
    d. Occasional sexual language and jokes ordinarily will not be considered sufficiently offensive or hostile to be sexual harassment.

    (The correct answer is a. In a rather confusing aspect of sexual harassment law the EEOC maintains that the "reasonable" of the allegedly sexually offensive conduct should be measured by not the mythical and typical "reasonable person" but a reasonable person "standing in the shoes" of the aggrieved party, thereby bringing a subjective element into what was thought of to be a strictly objective "reasonable person" test. In addition to frequency and severity other important factors are whether the conduct is threatening, ridiculing, or humiliating, as well as the effect of the conduct on the employee's work performance. Note that if the sexual harassment is committed by a manager or supervisor against a subordinate employee who suffers a tangible job loss the employer is absolutely liable; the fact that there are programs and policies to combat sexual harassment is no defense. Finally, though typically stated as legal "trials and tribulations" of the workplace, the authors would advise against any sexual jokes, language, teasing, etc., no matter how "innocent" the language or conduct may be perceived to be, particularly since the EEOC has introduced a subjective element into the supposed objective reasonable person test.)

26. What is FALSE about the Age Discrimination in Employment Act (ADEA)?
    a. The ADEA bars the termination of older workers.
    b. The "reasonable-factor-other-than-age" (RFOA) test is a valid defense for an employer.
    c. The *bona fide* occupational qualification (BFOQ) test is a valid defense for an employer.
    d. In order to be protected by the ADEA an employee must be at least 40 years of age.

    (The correct answer is a. The ADEA does not prohibit the termination of older workers; rather, it just forbids discrimination against older workers. The RFOA means that an employer can point to other permissible factors in terminating older workers, for example, increased health costs. BFOQ is a valid defense if age is reasonably related to the essential aspects of the employer's business, for

example, airline pilots. Forty years of age is the minimum age for legal protection under the ADEA; yet note that there is no upper limit.)

27. What is TRUE about U.S. civil rights laws?
   a. The Pregnancy Discrimination Act does not protect unmarried women in the workplace.
   b. The Americans with Disabilities Act (ADA) does not require employers to make an accommodation to the needs of its disabled employees, just not to discriminate against them.
   c. Third-party retaliation is an illegal civil rights violation.
   d. The Family Medical Leave Act (FMLA) requires employers to provide 12 weeks of paid leave to employees who have serious medical problems.

   (The correct answer is c. Third-party retaliation is retaliation against a spouse, relative, or good friend of the employee who brings a civil rights lawsuit; it is illegal retaliation and is the basis for a lawsuit even if the underlying discrimination charge by the employee is found to be wanting. The Pregnancy Discrimination Act protects married and unmarried women. The ADA, like the ADEA, imposes a double-duty on employers: first, not to discriminate against disabled or older workers; and second, to make a reasonable accommodation to them unless to do so would be an undue hardship of burden for the employer. The leave in the federal FLMA is unpaid; however, today, some states are mandating by state statute certain periods of paid leave by employer depending on the employer's size.)

32 - Labor Law and Relations

Introduction

Labor law is another very large subject matter, and one which is principally dependent on federal labor law statutes. Consequently, the student must be aware of the fundamental aspects of the Norris-LaGuardia Act of 1932, the National Labor Relations Act (NLRA)(Wagner Act) of 1935, the Labor Management Relations Act (LMRA)(Taft-Hartley Act) of 1947, the Fair Labor Standards Act of 1938, and the Worker Adjustment and Retraining Act (WARN) of 1988. Particularly important is the NLRA, especially its applicability only to "employees" and not managers and supervisors, the duty on both the employer and union to bargain in good faith, as well as the "unfair labor practices" (ULP) which can be committed by the employer. Also important is the fact that the NLRA protects "concerted activities" by the employees, including today on social media, to advocate or support unions and/or to improve working conditions.

True and False Questions with Answers and Explanations

1. The National Labor Relations Act (NLRA) protects all employees of a company.
(False: Managers and supervisors are not protected by the NLRA.)

2. The National Labor Relations Board does not have jurisdiction over labor matters and disputes that arise on social media.
(False: If activities on social media are construed as "concerted" activities, that is, communications between or among employee, for the purpose of improving conditions at work the NLRB does have jurisdiction, as such concerted activities on social media are protected by the National Labor Relations Act, which the NLRB enforces.)

3. The Omnibus Budget and Consolidation Act (COBRA) of 1985 requires employers to provide paid maternity leave of up to one year for mothers and six months for fathers.
(False: Maternity/paternity plans are optional for a company and not mandated by COBRA, as opposed to the laws of Scandinavian as well as more socialist-minded countries.)

4. Discrimination against employees because of their advocacy, supporting, and/or joining of unions is an unfair labor practice under the NLRA.
(True: This is a fundamental right of employees under the NLRA. However, managers and supervisors are not considered to be "employees" under the law.)

5. Unemployment compensation for employees comes from a federal fund that is based on taxes imposed on working employees.
(False: The tax is on employers not employees.)

6. Pursuant to the Fair Labor Standard Act (FLSA) employers are not allowed to demand that employees work beyond the typical 40 hour per week duration.
(False: There is no law that prevents employers from demanding long hours. However, if an employee works more than 40 hours the employer must pay time-and-one-half as per the FLSA.)

7. Pre-employment drug testing is an unlawful invasion of an employee's privacy.
(False: The courts have upheld pre-employment drug testing in both the private and public employment sectors.)

8. A showing of probable cause is required for an employer to test current employees for drugs without violating the employees' right to privacy.
(False: A showing of probable cause, such as appearing under-the-influence or causing an accident, would certainly justify drug testing; but the courts have upheld mandatory, random drug testing too for "sensitive" or "high-risk" positions.)

9. It is an illegal invasion of privacy for an employer to monitor an employee's computer use at work even if the employer has notified the employees of such monitoring since the employee may have pressing personal emails to transmit.
(False: The legal wrong of invasion of privacy arises only when one has a "reasonable expectation" of privacy. Consequently, how can an employee have such a reasonable expectation regarding computer use if he or she has been told of the monitoring?)

10. The terms of a company's personnel manual or code of conduct could be construed as an "implied contract" between the employer and employee so as to negate the employee's employee at-will status.
(True: Well, technically true, based on traditional contract principles, yet most employers state that nothing in these manuals or codes can be construed as having the legal force of a contract. Moreover, most employers also have disclaimers stating that the only way that an employee's at-will status can be changed is by a written document signed by the employee and a high-level officer or manager.)

11. COBRA requires the mandatory funding of retirement benefits for older workers if a corporation is a large one.
(False: COBRA may provide many benefits to employees, such as carrying over their employer-based health insurance when they leave the firm, but retirement benefits are not required by the statute.)

12. ERISA requires the mandatory funding of pension plans for all employees of large firms.
(False; ERISA provides many protections for pension plans, but it does not mandate them.)

13. The Immigration Reform and Control Act (IRCA) requires employers to seek the prior approval of Homeland Security before hiring employees.
(False: The statute does not require government approval; however, there are certain verification procedures that an employer must fulfill before hiring employees in order to ascertain their legal right to reside and work in the United States.)

14. Requiring "comparable pay" for "comparable work" for employees of different genders is a major feature of the Fair Labor Standards Act (FLSA).
(False: The statute requires "equal pay for equal work," for example, paying male and female nurses at the same level the same pay; but the FLSA does not require "comparable," that is, trying to determine the comparable worth of employees of different genders doing different jobs, for example, a female nurse and a male electrician working at a hospital.)

15. Child labor laws in the U.S. allow children aged 12-14 to engage in sales work for a limited number of hours but only after school hours and weekends.
(False: Labor laws totally prohibit children between 12 and 14 working.)

16. Seniority clauses in collective bargaining agreements are illegal as they have the tendency to provide greater working benefits to older, white men, to the detriment of younger, minority, and/or female employees.
(False: Seniority clauses have been held not to violate civil rights laws, though they may perpetuate past discrimination or stereotyping.)

17. During a campaign to unionize the employer's workforce it is generally permissible for the employer to offer additional benefits to the employee.
(False: Offering such benefits would be construed as an "unfair labor practice," thereby negating an employer victory in a representation election. However, there are exceptions where benefits are permissible during the campaign, for example, when they were previously established and planned for during this time-period.)

18. An employer arguing during an election campaign that the union has a reputation for making unrealistic wage and benefit demands which if the employer is forced to grant might drive the employer into bankruptcy.
(False: Such assertions if true and standing alone will usually not be enough to constitute an "unfair labor practice.")

19. A determination of "bad faith" will arise in labor negotiations when one party makes a counter-offer to the proposal of the other party.
(False: Just the opposite, as the duty established by the National Labor Relations Act to bargain in good faith not only assumes but requires that proposals be made and then counter-offers be made in response.)

20. If the union and the employer despite bargaining in good faith cannot reach a collective bargaining agreement the National Labor Relations Board (NLRB) will establish a binding agreement on the parties.
(False: The NLRB will assist with mediation of the dispute to try to help the parties reach an agreement, but the government will not mandate one.)

21. A union does not have any legal duty to represent employees in the bargaining unit who did not vote for the union and did not join the union.
(False: The union has a duty to represent all employee members of the bargaining unit regardless if they are union members or not. Of course, the question as to whether all employees in the bargaining unit must join the union and thus pay union dues depends on state law and whether a state is a "right-to-work" state or a "union shop" one, with the latter requiring all members of the bargaining unit to join the union and pay dues.)

22. Public sector employees generally have the same right to strike as private sector employees.
(Public sector employees are regulated by federal and state statutes and specifically by Public Employees Relations Commissions and not the National Labor Relations Act and the National Labor Relations Board which govern private sector employees. One big difference between the private and public sector is that public sector employees generally are precluded from striking; rather, the government will impose mandatory binding arbitration in public sector labor disputes.)

23. The National Labor Relations Act (NLRA) requires that employers and the union representing the employees must bargain over wages.
(True: The duty to bargain in good faith extends not only to wages but to all the terms and conditions in the proposed contract. However, there is no legal obligation for the parties to come to an agreement and thus have a collective bargaining agreement, assuming they bargained in good faith, though without success.)

24. After the union wins an election those employees in the bargaining unit who did not vote for the union can choose another unit as their bargaining representative.
(False: The union that prevails represents all the employees in the unit regardless of whether they supported and voted for the union. The union, however, has a duty to represent them all in good faith.)

25. During a representative election campaign, it is always an unfair labor practice (ULP) for the employer to assert that if the employees vote in the union as their bargaining representative the union will drive the employer into bankruptcy.
(False: If the employer makes such an argument and justifies it with facts about past union demands as well as the employer's own, and presumably precarious, financial condition, the assertion of possible bankruptcy is deemed to be one based "reason" and not "emotion" and thus permissible.)

26. When the employer includes in the employees' paychecks written arguments against the union the employer will usually be deemed to have committed and unfair labor practice (ULP).
(False: This type of objection by the employer is permissible and not a ULP so long as there are no threats of retaliation or promises of benefits included with the anti-union arguments.)

27. Generally, secondary picketing and secondary boycotting are illegal.
(True: One purpose of labor law is to keep any labor dispute between the employer and employees "localized" to the parties directly in dispute; and thus not to extend the labor dispute to parties only secondarily involved, such as the employer's suppliers or distributors.)

28. A key factor the National Labor Relations Board (NLRB) considers in determining what is an "appropriate bargaining unit" for a union representative election is whether the employees can afford to pay the union initiation fees and dues.
(False: This affordability factor is irrelevant. The NLRB examines whether certain groups of employees have a commonality of duties and responsibilities as well as interests and concerns at work to compose a viable unit for representation and for hopefully successful collective bargaining.)

29. During the course of negotiations with the union, if the employer refuses to make a concession to a specific union proposal the employer will be deemed to have engaged in bad faith bargaining.
(False: The duty to bargain in "good faith" does not contemplate making concessions to any specific demands. However, making proposals and counterproposals is evidence of good faith, It is conceivable as well as permissible for the parties to have bargained in good faith but nonetheless without achieving a collective bargaining agreement.)

30. When the union institutes an economic strike against the employer the employer then is allowed to hire permanent replacements for striking employees.
(True: This is a risk to the employees of an economic strike, but employers cannot hire permanent replacements, only temporary, if the employees are conducting an unfair labor practice strike, which is why when you see employees picketing they are always carrying signs that say "unfair labor practice" employer or "ULP.")

31. In those states that have passed "right-to-work" laws any person who wants to be employed will be given a job and by the government if necessary.
(False: Right-to-work laws state that one does have to join a union to work at a particular firm even if the union wins a representation election, as would be the case in those states that have "union shop" laws where one must join the union or at least pay union dues. There long has been a proposal in the U.S. Congress, called the Humphry-Hawkins Full Employment bill, which would guarantee anyone a job, but that bill has very little chance, if ever being passed into law.)

32. It is an unfair labor practice (ULP) for an employer to donate money to help create a union.,
(True: Any such support of a union is a ULP as such a union would likely be controlled, dominated, or at the least beholden to the employer and not the employees it is supposed to represent.)

33. The National Labor Relations Act requires that both unions and management have a legal duty to bargain in good faith on wages and hours and other terms and conditions of employment.
(True: The idea is that if the parties bargain in good faith a collective bargaining agreement will be achieved and labor peace will be attained for the life of the agreement; however, the duty is only to bargain in good faith and not necessarily to achieve a collective bargaining agreement; and furthermore the government will not impose one on the parties.)

34. The National Labor Relations Act requires that bargaining between management and the union must lead to a collective bargaining agreement or else one will be mandated by the National Labor Relations Board (NLRB).
(False: The only legal duty is that the parties must bargain in good faith, which hopefully will lead to an agreement. The NLRB will not impose one.)

35. After a union certification election, the employees who did not vote with the majority for the union can choose another union as their bargaining representative.
(False: One the union prevails in the election it is the sole representative of the employees in the bargaining unit; and thus the union has the duty to represent fairly all the employees in the bargaining unit, whether they voted for the union or not. All the employees, of course, must now pay union dues.)

36. The distribution by the employer of written arguments and objections to the union along with the employees' paychecks is an unfair labor practice due to the implicit threat of retaliation therein.
(False: This type of distribution is permissible, assuming of course there are no threats of retaliation or promises of benefit for not voting for the union. However, the employer must provide to the union a list of the employees in the bargaining unit, so that the union can contact the employees with arguments for voting for the union.)

37. As a general rule, secondary picketing and boycotting are illegal.
(True: Picketing and boycotting of the employer are of course permissible, assuming no violence, but not of parties connected to the employer, such as suppliers and distributors, as the objective is to keep the labor dispute focused on the two direct parties and not have the dispute expand outwards through the economy.)

38. A primary function of the National Labor Relations Board is to determine appropriate bargaining units of employees for union certification elections.
(True: Such determinations are critical to determining if the union will prevail in the election. For example, in a union campaign at a hospital, should register nurses be designated as a separate bargaining unit or grouped in with LPNs, nurses' aides, and orderlies? If a separate unit, the union may lose as the nurses may not want a union as they have enough economic power to negotiate effectively on their own. However, the union may win with a health care unit without the nurses, but

how much clout would it have in bargaining? The ideal for the union would be to prevail in a general health-care unit with the nurses included as that then would be a powerful entity for bargaining, but what if the nurses vote against the union and sway the election, and then the union has nothing!)

39. State right-to-work laws provide that employees do not have to be members of a union but must pay union dues.
(False: In those states with right-to-work laws, even if the union prevails, the employees in the bargaining unit to not have to pay dues. The union calls these employees "free-riders." Nevertheless, that is why one sees large auto manufacturing facilities being set up in Mississippi, Alabama, South Carolina, and Tennessee as they are right-to-work states, where it is much more difficult for the union to prevail in attempts to unionize the workers.)

40. An employer legally may deny reinstatement of economic strikers if permanent replacements have been hired.
(True: This is a risk of conducting a purely economic strike. However, the situation is just the opposite if the strike is to protect unfair labor conditions and practices, and consequently the union will always attempt to bring the strike within the parameters of being to protest "unfair" labor practices.)

41. Discrimination against employees who express their desire to be members of a union is an unfair labor practice.
(True: This is a basic proposition in the NLRA, and as such discrimination in assignments or promotions or pay to punish employees for pro-union activity is illegal discrimination, and if prevalent will cause the NLRB to overturn a union certification election that the union lost.)

42. An employer who fires all strikers and hires permanent replacements may be committing an unfair labor practice (ULP).
(True: An employer is allowed to discharge economic strikers and replacement them with permanent replacements but not strikers who strike to the employer's purported unfair labor practices. ULP strikers must be re-hired at the end of the strike and any temporary replacements let go.)

43. An employer's "free speech" rights under the National Labor Relations Act ordinarily will permit the employer to disclose to its employees that the leaders of the union seeking certification as the employees' bargaining representative are convicted felons.
(True: The NLRA grants employers "free speech" rights so long as there is no promise of benefit or threat of reprisal attached to the speech.)

44. Managers can take advantage of the National Labor Relations Act (NLRA) protections for union advocacy and support.
(False: Managers and supervisors are not protected by the NLRA, just "employees." Moreover, the NLRB takes a broad definition of "supervisor," that is, a person need not be explicitly designated a "supervisor" to be a supervisor or manager, just that he or she has the power to hire or fire, or adjust grievances, or recommend so doing, even if only occasionally doing supervisory type work.)

45. An employee who is fired for disclosing to the pertinent government agency health violations by his or her employer may have a "public policy" lawsuit against his or her employer.
(True: This is the Public Policy doctrine, based on state court decisions, that protects employees, even employees at-will, who disclose legal wrongdoing by their employers or fellow workers to an appropriate government agency. A public policy lawsuit is separate and distinct from protections afforded by a state's Whistleblower Protection Act, if a state has one.)

46. A U.S. company doing business overseas does not have to comply with Occupational Safety and Health Administration (OSHA) regulations regarding worker health and safety in its overseas facilities.
(True: Some U.S. law, for example, the Civil Rights Act, has certain extra-territorial effect but not OSHA rules and regulations.)

47. Right-to-work laws, such as those in Texas and Florida, provide that employees neither have to be members of the union nor do they have to pay union dues.
(True: These laws are the complete opposite of Union Shop laws, for example, in New York and New Jersey, where if the union is certified as the representative of the employer all the employees must join the union and pay union dues, though in the latter case there is a limited exception on First Amendment grounds for union dues going purely for political activities that certain employees are opposed to.

48. The employer risks violating labor law if during negotiations with the union the employer makes no meaningful proposals, counter-proposals, or concessions.
(True: The employer as well as the union are under a duty to bargain in "good faith," though there is no requirement of a collective bargaining agreement being agreed to. An impasse legitimately could occur, but there must be some evidence of "movement" during negotiations to meet the "good faith" bargaining standard.)

49. Employers can agree with unions not to handle, use, or deal in non-union produced goods.
(False: These agreements are called "hot cargo" agreements and are illegal under the National Labor Relations Act.)

50. Employment considered to be "at-will" means that employers can fire employees without having a good cause or reason.
(True: However, employers cannot fire employees for an illegal reason, such as racial, gender, or national origin discrimination under the Civil Rights Act. It should also be pointed out that the employment at-will doctrine is a symmetrical one in that at-will employees can quit at any time and for any reason.)

51. Requiring union membership as a prior condition to employment is prohibited by U.S. labor laws.
(*True: This is an illegal practice, sometimes called a "closed shop." However, in those states without "right-to-work" laws, called "union shop" states, if a union wins a certification election to represent the employees in a bargaining unit, all the employees in the unit must join the union and pay dues.)*

52. Employees have no right to engage in collective bargaining through their elected representatives since such concerted activity would be deemed an illegal restraint of trade.
(False: This was the very old historical position. Today, by virtue of the National Labor Relations Act employees can advocate, organize, support, and join unions, as well as engage in concerted activity, such as picketing and striking, without fear of anti-trust law sanctions.)

53. An employer can refuse to bargain with the union chosen as the employees' bargaining representative if the employer fears that the union will make unreasonable demands.
(False: The employer as well as the union have a duty under the National Labor Relations Act to bargain in "good faith," and as such the employer must negotiate with the union. Of course, the extent of any unreasonable demands may adversely affect whether a collective bargaining agreement results from the negotiations and bargaining.)

54. During the course of an election campaign, the employer is allowed to threaten employees with the loss of their job if the union prevails in the election.
(False: This is clearly an Unfair Labor Practice under the NLRA and would result in the election if in favor of the employer being overturned.)

55. An employer's promises of job security in its employment manuals are never legally binding because they are not in the form of a formal express contract.
(False: If the provisions in the manual or other employer document are construed as an "implied contract," based on the old common law, the provisions could be legally binding. However, many employers have disclaimers in their materials saying that nothing written therein as well as statements made by managers or officers shall be construed as contractual in nature.")

56. An employer who is asked to make a statement to a prospective employer about the reasons for the termination of a former employee could be held liable for defamation if the reasons given are very negative and false.
(True: This fact is why employers just like to provide beginning-and-end dates to employment and say nothing further. Even though truth is an absolute defense, and even though there is a qualified immunity to protect even false defamatory statements if it was in the public interest to make the statements and there was no malice in so doing, most employers are not willing to take the risk of a lawsuit, and thus say nothing beyond providing employment dates.)

57. Whistle-blowing legal protection for employees is more likely to be available for employees who "blow the whistle" and disclose employer conduct that is immoral and unethical as opposed to illegal conduct.
(False: Whistleblower protection statutes are uniform in that the employee must disclose to the appropriate government agency legal wrongdoing.)

58. Whistleblowing statutes are uniform that the whistle-blowing employee be correct when he or she discloses illegal conduct on the part of the employer to the appropriate government agency.
(False: Some conservative state statutes, like in Florida, state that the employer must report an actual legal violation, so the employee better be correct in his or her assertion of employer illegality. However, other more liberal statutes, like that in New Jersey (called appropriately the Conscientious Employee Protection Act) only requires that the employee have a good faith belief in the legal wrongdoing by his or her employer.)

59. The First Amendment right to Free Speech in the federal Constitution will protect all workers who "blow the whistle" on employer wrongdoing from retaliation by their employers.
(False: The Constitution affords rights to the citizens and residents against government abuse, interference, and infringement of rights, and thus will protect only government employees. Private sector employees who "blow the whistle" are at the mercy of their employers, especially if the employees are employees at-will, unless there is some federal or state Whistleblower Protection Act or non-retaliation provision to a statute like in OSHA and Title VII, or unless the employee can use the common law Public Policy doctrine to overturn the discharge.)

60. Union members can successfully sue their union if union officials negotiate a bad bargain in the collective bargaining agreement with the employer or union officials make a bad decision regarding settling a labor strike with the employer.
(False: Union leaders are not guarantors of union success; similarly, boards of directors are not guarantors of business success. Union leaders thus can only be sued if they acted in an unreasonable manner and consequently are negligent. Of course, in any event, the employees if unhappy can decertify the union and choose another union as their bargaining representative.)

61. Public sector employees have the same right to strike as private sector employees.
(False: Strikes typically are illegal for public sector employees pursuant to federal and state public sector labor laws. However, as opposed to the private sector, there typically is mandatory binding arbitration of public sector labor disputes.)

62. The National Labor Relations Board has the power to decide whether a bargaining unit of employees is an "appropriate" one for collective bargaining purposes.
(True: Accordingly, the NLRB will determine if there is a "community of interest" among the employees in order to bring about effective collective bargaining.)

63. It is illegal for an employer to use as a stalling tactic in negotiations the designation of employees with no authority to negotiate to act as representatives of the employer in collective bargaining negotiations.
(True: This would violate the duty set forth in the NLRA for the parties to bargain in "good faith.")

64. A "yellow dog" contract was a contract, which an employer required the employee to sign, whereby the employee promised not to join a labor union upon penalty of losing his or her job.
(True: This type of contract, which obviously was a major detriment to union organizing, was banned by the federal Norris-LaGuardia Act of 1932.)

65. The Worker Adjustment and Retraining Act (WARN) requires a 60-day notice to the employees when any plants are closed or any layoffs are contemplated.
(False: WARN just applies to large employers and large layoffs as per the statute. Moreover, there are exceptions if the plant closing or layoff is caused by factors that were not reasonably foreseeable by the employer or where the employer is seeking financing to keep the plant open and the notice might be inimical to obtaining the financing.)

66. The Electronic Communication Privacy Act forbids employers from accessing stored email communications of employees who use the employer's electronic communication system.
(False: The employer can access these stored emails. Also, the government and law enforcement agencies during an investigation or suspected criminal activity can access the emails pursuant to a valid search warrant. Moreover, as per the "business extension" exception to the Act employers can monitor employees' electronic communications made in the ordinary course of business, but not the employees' personal communications. Finally, the employee can give consent to having all of his or her electronic communications intercepted and monitored.)

67. The Fair Labor Standards Act (FLSA) requires time-and-on-half pay for independent contractors of the employer who work more than 40 hours a week.
(False: The FLSA just applies to "employees" and independent contractors, such as outside sales personnel. Moreover, the FLSA does not apply to managerial employees or professionals. However, who exactly is an "employee" as opposed to an non-exempt worker is an oft-litigated issue.)

68. The Fair Labor Standards Act (FLSA) restricts children age 16 to 17 from working more than 20 hours a week.
(False: The FLSA allows for unlimited working hours for such children, subject to over-time rules, of course; however, the work must be non-hazardous. Once a person becomes 18 years of age he or she can work in a hazardous job.)

Multiple Choice Questions with Answers and Explanations

1. An inspector from the Occupational Health and Safety Administration (OSHA) who is conducting an inspection of a workplace for health and safety violations:

   a. Must have a search warrant based on a finding of "probable cause" by a judge of violations.
   b. Can only conduct an inspection if an employee or a representative of the employee, such as a union, requests one.
   c. Can only require employers but not employees to follow OHSA safety and health standards.
   d. None of the above.

   (The correct answer is d. OHSA inspectors must have warrants, but they are administrative type warrants, called "blanket warrants," which allow them to search certain businesses in certain areas for compliance with OHSA regulations. Probable cause is not required. The inspection is not contingent on an employee contacting OHSA, though a report of a violation would prompt an inspection. Finally, the employer as well as the employees must follow OHSA regulations.)

2. An employer's written and oral statements to the employees as to the negative consequences of the employees voting to certify a union as their bargaining representative:
   a. Are protected under the "free speech" provision of the National Labor Relations Act if they contact no threats of reprisal and/or promises of benefit.
   b. Are illegal if the employer predicts severe economic consequences as a result of unionization and the employer can make its prediction come true.
   c. Are legal if the employer can demonstrate through economic and financial evidence that extreme union demands may force it into bankruptcy.
   d. All of the above.

   (The correct answer is d. All these statements are legal "free speech" under the NLRA as they are an appeal to reason and not emotion or fear.)

3. Which is TRUE regarding the legal duty of an employer pursuant to Title VII:
   a. The employer as a general rule cannot discriminate against employees based on their religious beliefs and practices.
   b. The employer has a duty to make an accommodation to the religious beliefs and practices of its employees.
   c. The employer need not make an accommodation to the religious beliefs and practices of its employees if it would be an undue burden or hardship to do so.
   d. All of the above.

   (The correct answer is d. All these are very basic principles as the employer has a double-duty under Title VII regarding religion, that is, not to discriminate and to make a reasonable accommodation unless the latter involves undue hardship or burden. For example, a court ruled that an employer must release a Muslim employee to make a religious pilgrimage to Mecca, but when the employee requested a second release for another trip the court said that this would be an undue burden for the employer, especially considering the Koran just says that a Muslim is required to make one trip only.)

4. Which of the following is an unfair labor practice (ULP) in negotiations between an employer and union representatives?
   a. Refusing to meet at a reasonable time and place.
   b. Refusing to reduce agreements to writing.
   c. Refusing to make proposals and counterproposals.
   d. All of the above.

(The correct answer is d. Any and all of these will violate the duty to bargain in good faith. However, the NLRA just requires good faith bargaining, not necessarily that the parties reach a collective bargaining agreement.)

5. If an employee who is also a union organizer is usually late for work and insults customers, may the employer discipline the employee/organizer?
   a. No, as he or she would be protected by the National Labor Relations Act.
   b. Yes, under all circumstances.
   c. Yes, but only if the insults were very rude and the tardiness was severe.
   d. Yes, if the employer's motivation was the misconduct of the employee and not his or her union activity.

   (The correct answer is d. Answer d is also the best answer. The NLRA protects union organizing efforts by employees, but the statute does not protect misconduct.)

6. Which of the following types of conduct would be LEAST LIKELY to be protected by the National Labor Relations Act (NLRA)?
   a. An employee signing a union authorization card.
   b. An employee selected by a committee of a dozen employees to present a list of grievances to the employer.
   c. An employee protests when the employer selects another employee for promotion to a supervisory position.
   d. The employees walk off the job to protest unsafe working conditions.

   (The correct answer is c. Promotion decisions are within the purview of the employer's fundamental right to manage its business. The other types of conduct are clearly protected by the NLRA.)

7. Which of the following types of social conduct would MOST LIKELY be protected by the National Labor Relations Act?
   a. An employee whining and complaining to another employee on social media about an arrogant and "jerky" boss.
   b. An employee communicating on social media with another employee about unsafe conditions at work and how to improve them.
   c. An employee communicating on social media with a family member who is not an employee about a "sexist" boss.
   d. No social media conduct is protected by the NLRA since everyone knows that nothing is private on social media.

   (The correct answer is b. Answer b is an example of "concerted" or joint activities by employees, which would be protected even if on social media. The communications, however, must be between or among co-workers. Merely whining and complaining, especially if improper language is used, is not protected as there must be evidence of an intent to improve working conditions.)

8. Which statement is FALSE about the National Labor Relations Act?
   a. Employers can commit unfair labor practices (ULPs) by using inflammatory and manipulative "scare tactics" and coercive techniques against employees to prevent unionization.
   b. Secondary boycotts of companies doing business with a company that the union is striking against are permissible as a legal means to enhance the union's power against the primary employer, which typically is a large corporate entity.
   c. Supervisors and managers are not covered by the NLRA.
   d. Both the employer and the union have a legal duty to bargain in good faith on the terms and conditions of a collective bargaining agreement.

(The correct answer is b. Secondary boycotts are illegal as a major policy of U.S. labor law is to limit the employment dispute to the primary employer and the union and not to expand it to other employers and unions. Certain language used by the employer to intimidate employees from voting for the union can rise to the level of a ULP and thus result in the overturning of an election. The NLRA protects "employees"; and supervisors and managers are not considered to be employees for the purpose of the NLRA. The theory is that they have enough bargaining "clout" based on their education, knowledge, and skills to "take care of themselves" in dealing contractually with the employer. Both parties are under a legal duty to bargain in good faith, that is, to make some proposals and counter proposals, as well as some concessions. and to avoid any "take-it-or-leave-it" stances; however, there is no legal requirement that a collective bargaining agreement be achieved so long as the parties bargained in good faith.)

9. What is FALSE about the National Labor Relations Act (NLRA)?
   a. It is a complete labor code, governing labor relations in the public as well as private sector.
   b. Section 7 of the NLRA grants fundamental rights to employees, including the rights to form, join, and assist labor organizations, the right to bargain collectively through a representative of their own choosing, and the right to engage in mutual concerted activity for the purposes of collective bargaining.
   c. Section 8 of the NLRA imposes a duty on the employer to bargain collectively and in good faith with a representative of the employees.
   d. It is an "unfair labor practice" for an employer to interfere with, restrain, or coerce employees in the exercise of their rights granted by the NLRA.

   (The correct answer is a. The NLRA is not a complete labor code; it is mainly concerned with the organizing phase of labor relations. The substantive terms of any collective bargaining agreement are left up to the parties and their private negotiations. Moreover, the NLRA just applies to private sector employees. Public sector employees are governed by separate federal and state labor laws, which are typically administered by specialized agencies called Public Employee Relations Commissions.)

10. What is NOT an employer unfair labor practice (ULP) pursuant to the NLRA?
   a. Having employee committees that facilitate communication, teamwork, and productivity.
   b. The employer having a supervisor as the main bargainer for the union.
   c. The employer sponsoring or promoting a union as well as contributing to a union.
   d. Discrimination against employees to discourage union membership.

   (The correct answer is a. So long as employee committees merely inform management and do not represent the employees or engage in labor relations such committees are permissible and not an ULP, even if the employees are allowed to meet and confer on working time, in working places, and are paid.)

11. Which is NOT an employer unfair labor practice (ULP) pursuant to the NLRA?
   a. Refusing to engage in collective bargaining with the union.
   b. Predicting, in a rational manner, adverse consequences to the employees if they vote for the union.
   c. Terminating employees who have been communicating on social media about supporting the union.
   d. Refusing to draft a written agreement if an oral one already exists

   (The correct answer is b. An employer has "free speech" rights pursuant to the NLRA as well as the Constitution, of course. As such, predicting adverse consequences is permissible if the employer is appealing to the reason of the employees and not to their fear. The employer must have a reasonable belief in adverse consequences as well as some objective facts to back up that belief. The employer as well as the union have a duty to bargain in good faith, though not

necessarily to achieve a collective bargaining agreement. Employee communications that are aimed at advocating or supporting unions as well as improving working conditions are protected by the NLRA, but they must be "concerted activities" to be protected, that is, by at least two employees and with the goal of changing working conditions or joining a union, and not merely complaining, whining, or griping about work and especially not about "bad-mouthing" or "trashing" the employer, co-workers, or the employer's customers and clients.)

12. What is FALSE about the Labor Management Relations Act (LMRA) (Taft-Hartley Act)?
    a. It banned the "secondary boycott" by unions.
    b. It established the Federal Mediation and Conciliation Service.
    c. It empowered the President to dictate to the parties the terms of a collective bargaining agreement in order to keep labor peace in key industries.
    d. It banned the "closed shop" by unions.

    (The correct answer is c. Pursuant to the LMRA the President, if there is a strike which endangers national safety or health, can seek a federal injunction against the strike for an 80 day "cooling off" period, after which the strike could continue unless banned by Congress citing a national emergency. The now outlawed secondary boycott is a boycott by the union of employers who are removed from the actual labor dispute with the employer but who typically do some sort of business with the employer. The now outlawed closed shop was a union demand that required union membership even before employees were hired by the employer. Note that in the private sector a "union shop" may still be permissible under state law; a union shop will require the employees to remain as union members while they are employed by the employer. States, however, can ban union shops; and those states are called "right-to-work" states.)

33 - Consumer Protection

Introduction

Consumer protection is a very broad area of the law encompassing state common law contract, state common law fraud (deceit), state warranty law pursuant to the Uniform Commercial Code, state consumer protection laws, and federal law, principally rules and regulations of the Federal Trade Commission (FTC), the Consumer Products Safety Commission, and the Federal Drug Administration (regarding for the latter the regulation of advertising of prescription drugs). Common law relief as well as warranty law redress have been covered in previous sections of this book. Regarding federal law, particularly important to the student is the FTC's standard for "deceptiveness" pertaining to the advertising and marketing of products and services.

True and False Questions with Answers and Explanations

1. As a general rule silence is not construed as fraud only the common law.
(True: "Let the buyer beware" is thus the old maxim. However, there is an important exception when the parties are in a fiduciary relationship.)

2. Banning a product from the market is usually the first remedy sought by the Consumer Products Safety Commission.
(False: It is the last remedy after requiring notices and recalls. Moreover, a product has to be imminently hazardous to the consumer to be banned.)

3. When a manufacturer in its advertising fails to include all the relevant facts about its product the manufacturer typically will be liable for deceptive advertising.
(False: Omissions typically do not render an ad automatically deceptive unless what is omitted would likely influence the consumer's choice to purchase a product, for example, omitting health and safety information.)

4. When a manufacturer seeks to make a claim in an advertisement about the quality of its products the Federal Trade Commission (FTC) will first require that the manufacturer get prior approval for the ad from the FTC.
(False: Prior approval is not required. However, if the quality claim is false or deceptive the FTC can fine the manufacturer, compel "corrective advertising," and seize the products if there is a danger to consumers.)

5. Suggestive advertising whereby the advertiser focuses on the positive aspects of a product and ignores the negative aspects will be deemed to be deceptive advertising.
(False: Suggestive advertising is permissible, for example, when a car manufacturer focuses in on the "positives," that is, the fuel economy of a small car and the safety of a big bar, and omits the negatives, that is, results in crash tests and low gas mileage. However, manipulative advertising, whereby the advertiser unduly and overly influences a consumer to purchase a product may be deemed to be illegal, especially if the target-audience is a very young or very old one.)

6. The Fair Debt Collection Practices Act prohibits debt collectors from calling debtors at inconvenient times.
(True: This is a basic feature of the law.)

7. For the Federal Trade Commission to deem an advertisement to be a "deceptive" one there must be evidence of intent on the advertiser to deceive.
(False: Intent to deceive is not required under FTC law and practice; rather, it just must be shown that the advertisement by words or omissions is false or is misleading that is, the ad would cause the reasonable consumer to reach an erroneous conclusion.)

8. A suggestive ad that promises "sex appeal" to the consumer would likely be regarded as illegal by the Federal Trade Commission (FTC) because the consumer's hope of becoming "sexy" may not be fulfilled by the product.
(False: The FTC bans deceptive advertisements, that is, those that are false and/or misleading to the reasonable consumer as well as manipulative ads that unduly influence the consumer (usually a very young or old or otherwise susceptible consumer). Suggestive ads which promise something good beyond and extrinsic to the product are permissible. As the old advertiser's maxim goes, "soap doesn't sell, sex sells.)

9. An advertiser who selectively emphasizes the positive aspects of its product but who fails to mention the negative aspects is very likely acting illegally pursuant to Federal Trade Commission (FTC) standards.
(False: Like suggestive ads, selective ads are generally permissible. However, if what is omitted would likely influence the reasonable consumer in decision-making about the product, for example, the omission of health and/or safety info, the ad may devolve from a legal suggestive ad to an illegal half-truth one.)

10. An advertisement that is in poor taste usually will be considered as an illegal ad by the FTC.
(False: Illegal advertisements include ads that are deceptive because they are false or misleading because they cause the reasonable consumer to reach an erroneous conclusion. As such, poor taste ads, such as ads for bug extermination during dinner hours, even though perhaps upsetting to some consumers, are legal.)

11. An advertiser who fails to include all the relevant facts in an ad about a product will automatically be held liable for a deceptive ad pursuant to Federal Trade Commission standards.
(False: Only if the omitted material, for example, health and safety information, would affect the reasonable consumer's choice to purchase the product will there be liability under the deceptive ad standard.)

12. When an advertiser makes a claim about the quality of its product the FTC requires that the advertiser provide the agency with proof of its claim prior to the advertiser disseminating the ad.
(False: Prior approval is not required. Rather, if the claim later turns out to be deceptive the FTC can impose fines and other sanctions.)

13. The Consumer Products Safety Commission has the power to recall dangerous products from the market.
(True: The products must present an imminent risk of harm to the consumer. The agency also has the power to ban products from the market.)

14. Since as a traditional common law rule, "silence is not fraud," the FTC lacks the power to punish "half-truth" ads where significant information is omitted.
(False: The FTC's deceptive standard as a regulatory rule prevails over the old common law, judge-made precept, and thus the agency can deem a half-truth ad to be deceptive and illegal.)

15. In order to find an advertiser liable for disseminating a deceptive ad the agency must produce evidence of the advertiser's intent to deceive.
(False: Bad intent is a prerequisite of common law fraud; however, pursuant to FTC standards it is the effect on the reasonable consumer, for example, by a misleading ad which causes the consumer to reach an erroneous conclusion, that makes the ad deceptive and illegal.)

16. A Federal Trade Commission (FTC) finding of deception in advertising requires proof of a representation, omission, or practice likely to deceive or mislead the reasonable consumer, but no demonstration that the advertiser actually intended to deceive.
(True: This is a basis proposition of FTC regulatory law, as opposed to the common law tort of fraud, where the aggrieved party has to demonstrate that the defendant possessed an actual "bad" intent to deceive, which is a very difficult task from an evidentiary standpoint.)

17. The FTC prohibits the disclaimer of the implied warranty of merchantability if made by a merchant in a consumer transaction.
(False: The FTC as well as the UCC allow the implied warranty of merchantability to be disclaimed. However, as per UCC law, the word "merchantability" must be used in the disclaimer. Yet the use of "catch-all" disclaimers, such as AS-IS or "WITH ALL FAULTS," if conspicuous, will exclude the warranty from the sales transaction.)

18. An advertisement can been deemed deceptive and thus illegal if the ad is misleading to the reasonable consumer who thereby makes an erroneous choice, even if the advertiser did not intend to deceive the consumer.
(True: Pursuant to FTC deceptive standards the focus is on the consequences caused to the consumer by the deceptive ad and not the advertiser's intent, as opposed to the common law tort of fraud or deceit where evidence of an intent to defraud is required but very difficult to obtain.)

19. The Magnuson-Moss Warranty Act requires express written warranties on all consumer products.
(False: This federal statute merely says that if a seller does put an express warranty on a product the warranty must be clear, conspicuous, and understandable.)

20. Federal consumer protection law provides a private cause of action with the potential of treble damages and an award of attorneys' fees to a consumer who is the victim of false or misleading advertising.
(False: The Congressional act that created the FTC did not provide for a cause of action for an aggrieved consumer. However, the FTC can sue and order restitution to an aggrieved consumer.)

Multiple Choice Questions with Answers and Explanations

1. The practice of "bait-and-switch":
   a. is considered by the Federal Trade Commission to be an illegal sales tactic.
   b. is only illegal when used in the sale of major appliances, furniture, and automobiles.
   c. is a rule designed to protect merchants from being "over-accepted."
   d. will result in criminal sanctions by the FTC if the victim is an elderly person.

(The correct answer is a. The FTC considers "bait-and-switch" to be deceptive and misleading and thus illegal. The FTC prohibition covers all types of goods, though if the dispute is too small the FTC may defer to state regulatory agencies. The FTC can impose civil fines and sanctions, not criminal.)

2. The following are types of remedies the Federal Trade Commission (FTC) can impose to redress deceptive marketing practices EXCEPT:
   a. Corrective advertising
   b. Civil fines
   c. Barring a company from doing business in interstate commerce.
   d. Refund of money or payment of damages to consumers

   (The correct answer is c. The FTC can also order the return of property to consumers, but neither the agency nor the courts can bar a company from doing business.)

3. In order to have a "full warranty" label under the Magnuson-Moss Warranty Act, the party making the warranty:
   a. Must warrant to repair or replace a defective product at no cost.
   b. May not impose any limitation or exclusion on the duration of an implied warranty on the product.
   c. May limit damages by conspicuously disclosing any limitations on the face of the warranty.
   d. All of the above.

   (The correct answer is d. These are all basic features of the statute, which, it must be noted, does not require any warranties to be made at all.)

4. Which statement is FALSE about the Federal Trade Commission's (FTC) regulation of advertising in the U.S.?
   a. The FTC can sanction a company's advertising if it is either false, that is, a lie, or deceptive, that is, misleading.
   b. The FTC's legal standard for false and deceptive advertising is the same as common law tort of fraud since "a lie is a lie."
   c. An omission of something important in a product advertisement, especially if what is missing relates to health and safety, can render the advertisement deceptive according to the FTC.
   d. "Bait and switch" advertising and marketing practices have been deemed deceptive and thus illegal by the FTC.

   (The correct answer is b. Under the common law the legal wrong of fraud or deceit requires "scienter," that is, knowledge by the wrongdoer of the falsity of his or her misrepresentations as well as evidence that the wrongdoer purposefully sought to induce the victim to enter into a contract or some business arrangement. However, under the FTC's standard, a statement can be deceptive if it is false, that is, an intentional lie, OR misleads the reasonable consumer into making a decision to purchase the product. "Scienter" is not required under the FTC standard. An omission regarding a product, especially if it is health- or safety-related, can render a product advertisement misleading. "Bait and switch" tactics, whereby a merchant "baits" a consumer to come in to buy a product which is supposedly for sale, and then "switches" the consumer to a higher-priced product, are illegal pursuant to FTC standards.)

5. Which of the following are remedies that the Federal Trade Commission possesses?
   a. Imposing civil fines and restitution
   b. Issuing "cease and desist" orders
   c. Mandating "corrective advertising"
   d. All of the above

(The correct answer is d. These are all sanctions the FTC can impose to redress violations of its rules and regulations. FTC is a very powerful agency with broad powers to prohibit and punish deceptive advertising and unfair practices in the marketplace.)

6. What is FALSE about the FTC's "deceptiveness" standard?
   a. The claims in an advertisement are false.
   b. The claims in an advertisement are misleading to a reasonable consumer.
   c. The agency must prove by "clear and convincing" evidence that an advertiser intentionally sought to deceive the consumer.
   d. A half-truth advertisement can be deceptive if the omission causes the ad to be misleading to the reasonable consumer.

   (The correct answer is c. As opposed to the intentional tort of common law fraud, the FTC's standard for deceptiveness does not require evidence that an advertiser knowingly and purposefully tried to deceive the consumer. False ads, that is, outright falsehoods are illegal, as well as misleading ads that cause the consumer to reach an erroneous conclusion. If a half-truth ad omits something that pertains to the health or safety of the consumer it very likely will be deemed to be deceptive.)

7. What is FALSE about the Consumer Products Safety Commission?
   a. It creates a private cause of action for a consumer to sue for damages due to harm from a product.
   b. It can ban the manufacture and sale of any product that the agency deems to be hazardous to the consumer.
   c. It can issue recalls of products that the agency deems to be hazardous to consumers.
   d. It requires manufacturers to notify the agency of products sold that have proven to be hazardous to the consumer.

   (The correct answer is a. No private cause of action is created by the Consumer Products Safety Commission or the Congressional law that created the agency. An injured consumer can sue the manufacturer or other entities on the marketing chain for breach of contract, negligence, strict liability, breach of warranty, and/or fraud/deceit. Of course, the injured consumer needs the requisite evidence to sustain any of these causes of action.)

34 - Environment Protection

Introduction

Environmental laws are heavily dependent on statutory law, particularly federal statutes, as well as rules and regulations from the Environmental Protection Agency (EPA) which enforces federal law. The student should be cognizant of creation of the EPA by the National Environmental Policy Act of 1970, including the jurisdiction, and power of the EPA, and the requirement of the filing of an "environmental impact statement" for proposed legislation and federal actions which significantly affect the environment. The student also should be aware of other major federal statutes protecting the environment, to wit: the Clean Air Act, the Clean Water Act, and the "Superfund Act." The student also should be aware of the very controversial pollution "credit" or permit system which can result in legal pollution.

True and False Questions with Answers and Explanations

1. Companies are allowed to buy and sell rights to pollute, called "pollution" credits.
(True: When a company pollutes less than allowed by federal environmental law it can sell the right to that gap in the form of a pollution credit to another firm which is polluting more than the law allows but is using the "credit" so as to avoid violating environmental laws.)

2. The Solid Waste Disposal Act leaves solid waste problems principally to the federal government.
(False: State and local governments have the primary responsibility to deal with solid waste problems.)

3. The federal Environmental Protection Agency (EPA) has the primary responsibility for promulgating and enforcing zoning laws for cities and towns.
(False: Local zoning regulations as well land use plans are the principal responsibility of local government, that is, counties and municipalities.)

4. The Clean Air Act requires that all motor vehicles be completely fueled by alternative fuels by 2025.
(False: There are now requirements for bio-fuel, for example, corn-based fuels, to be added to gasoline, but a total alternative fuel-based system for motor vehicles is not contemplated by the Act.)

5. Pursuant to the U.S. Clean Air Act's emission "credit" or "permit" plan, companies can sell and buy rights to pollute in excess of federal standards, consequently resulting in legalized pollution.
(True: A company that cannot meet federal pollution standards can buy "credits" from a company that pollutes less than the standards, thereby allowing the latter company to sell the difference as a "credit.").

6. Local governments can control some aspects of the local environment by promulgating zoning laws. *(True: For example, certain areas can be deemed to be only "residential," or "commercial," or "light industrial," or "heavy industrial," or "mixed.")*

7. A person or business can request an exemption to a zoning law by seeking a "variance" from the local zoning board.
(True: For example, if an area is zoned for residential use only, a semi-retired accountant who wishes to open at his or her home a limited tax practice during tax "season" can ask the zoning for a variance, which can be granted or denied, and if the latter, appealed to the traditional court system.)

8. If a U.S. citizen owns real property in a foreign country and that property is expropriated by the foreign government, the U.S. citizen cannot sue the foreign government in a U.S. court.
(True: This is based on the international law doctrine called Act of State, whereby one country has no authority to challenge the domestic acts of another country government's in their own country.)

9. The substantial and unreasonable infringement on the private use and enjoyment of another's land is called the tort of negligence.
(False: The legal wrong is called a "nuisance." Note that nuisance differs from trespass which requires some physical invasion of the land whereas a nuisance can be created by activities, such as very loud music or very bright lights, which do not physically invade another's property but diminish the property owner's enjoyment of the property.)

10. The main purpose of the Comprehensive Environmental Response, Compensation, and Liability Act of 1980 is to allow private citizens to sue for damages caused by hazardous chemicals.
(False: The main purpose is to clean up hazardous wastes. Pursuant to the law the present owner or operator of real property may be liable to clean up the hazardous even if it was placed there by a previous owner. However, the present owner may be able to avoid liability by showing it acquired the property after the waste was placed on the property and the current owner lacked knowledge or reason to know of the waste.)

11. Pursuant to the National Environmental Policy Act (NEPA) of 1970 an environmental impact statement (EIS) must be prepared for every major federal action significantly affecting the quality of the environment.
(True: This requirement includes proposed federal legislation. The EIS must have a detailed explanation of the anticipated environmental impact of the action or proposed legislation, particularly any adverse consequences thereof.)

12. The Clean Air Act of 1970 empowers the Environmental Protection Agency to promulgate national air quality standards for major pollutants from stationary sources as well as timetables for implementation of such standards.
(True: The result is that the EPA will force polluters to reduce pollution or face fines and other sanctions.)

13. The Toxic Substances Control Act of 1976 requires the clean-up of hazardous waste sites.
(False: The statute that requires the clean-up is called the Comprehensive Environmental Response, Compensation, and Liability Act, also known as the Superfund Act. The Toxic Substances Control Act requires that chemicals be tested by the manufacturer to determine if there are any harmful effects on human beings or the environment before being introduced into commerce.)

14. The states have the primary responsibility to enforce the Clean Water Act based on EPA rules and standards.
(True: But if the states do not act the EPA as well as private citizens can sue to enforce the Act.)

Multiple Choice Questions with Answers and Explanations

1. Which statement is FALSE about the Clean Air Act and the Clean Water Act?
   a. Both strictly forbid any air or water pollution in the United States.
   b. Both allow the Environmental Protection Agency (EPA) to set air and water standards and to enforce them along with the states.
   c. Both are major Congressional statutory enactments designed to protect the environment.
   d. Both require companies to use the best available technology to reduce and to curtail pollution.
   (The correct answer is a. Principal federal environment laws, including the Clean Water Act and the Clean Air Act, which were promulgated by Congress and which are administered by primarily by the EPA, do require companies to use the best available pollution technology, but also do allow some pollution to legally permissible limits set by the agency.)

2. What common law remedies can be used to protect the environment?
   a. Negligence
   b. Strict Liability
   c. Nuisance
   d. All of the above.
   (The correct answer is d. The tort of negligence would apply to any activities done in an unreasonable, careless, and imprudent manner that harm the environment. Strict liability would apply to ultra-hazardous activities, such as blasting, spraying pesticides and other chemicals, or transporting and disposing of hazardous waste. Nuisance is the intentional use of one's property in such a manner that the use constitutes an unreasonable interference with another person's use and enjoyment of his or her property. Pollution would be a legally actionable nuisance.)

3. The National Environmental Policy Act (NEPA) of 1970:
   a. created the Council of Environmental Quality.
   b. makes federal agencies take environmental protection into account when making decisions.
   c. required that an "environmental impact statement" (EIS) be prepared for every piece of proposed legislation and every major federal action significantly affecting the quality of the environment.
   d. All of the above.
   (The correct answer is d. These are all fundamental components of NEPA. The EIS must be a detailed explanation of the anticipated environmental impact, especially any adverse consequences, the commitment of resources for the proposed legislation of action, as well as any alternatives that might have a lesser environmental impact. Federal, state, and local governments as well as citizens are permitted to comment on the proposed legislation or action.)

4. Which is FALSE about the Environmental Protection Agency (EPA)?
   a. It was created in 1970 by Congress to consolidate all federal government environmental responsibilities in the United States.
   b. It has the power to promulgate rules and regulations to protect the environment.
   c. It can impose civil as well as criminal penalties for violations of environmental laws.
   d. It can conduct inspections and monitoring to make sure its rules and regulations as well as federal environmental statutes are complied with.

(The correct answer is c. The EPA can only impose civil sanctions, such as fines, as well as seeking injunctions. However, it cannot impose criminal sanctions; rather, it can only suggest criminal prosecutions to the Department of Justice. The EPA also has the powers to conduct research, issue grants, and require record-keeping for both governmental and private sector entities.)

5. What is/are TRUE about the Clean Air Act?
   a. It sets standards for auto emissions as well as emissions from other mobile transportation sources.
   b. It sets forth gas mileage requirements for different types of vehicles and regulates fuel additives.
   c. It allows polluters to purchase "pollution credits" that allows them to pollute beyond federal limits.
   d. All of the above.

   (The correct answer is d. The Clean Air Act sets forth national air quality standards for major pollutants from stationary sources, and then, in the most controversial part to the statute, if certain companies cut pollution to below the prescribed federal limits, they can sell their unused pollution rights as "credits to other companies which cannot meet the federal standards, perhaps because they cannot afford expensive anti-pollution technology and maybe avoiding a plant shutdown, yet nevertheless resulting in legalized pollution.)

6. Which is a FALSE statement about the following environmental protections statutes?
   a. The Clean Water Act sets timetables and deadlines to clean up and control water pollution from industrial sources, municipalities, and other polluters.
   b. The primary responsibility in enforcing the Clean Water Act is with the federal government
   c. The Marine Protection Act completely forbids the dumping in the ocean of radiological, chemical, and biological warfare substances.
   d. The Safe Water Drinking Act empowers the EPA to set standards for public drinking water, including the types and amounts of pollutants that can be present in drinking water.

   (The correct answer is b. Although a federal statute the states have the primary responsibility to enforce the Clean Water Act, pursuant to EPA rules, standards, and guidelines; however, if the states do not act the EPA, as well as private citizens, can sue to enforce the Act.)

7. Which is a FALSE statement about the "Superfund Act" (technically called the Comprehensive Environmental Response, Compensation, and Liability Act?
   a. The Act provides money for the cleanup of dangerous hazardous waste disposal sites by means of a fund, called the Hazardous Substance Response Trust Fund.
   b. The EPA is authorized to clean up hazardous waste sites itself and then seek the recovery of the costs from the parties responsible.
   c. The Act imposes strict liability for unauthorized dumping and requires that a violator either clean up the waste or reimburse the Superfund.
   d. If more than one party causes hazardous waste a party can only be liable for the waste it caused.

   (The correct answer is d. Liability under the Superfund Act is "joint and several," meaning that if there are multiple parties, and one party caused only a portion of the hazardous waste, that party may be liable of all the cleanup costs. However, the party that pays can seek contribution from the other polluting parties.)

35 - Liability of Accountants and Tax Law

Introduction

This section deals with the liability of the accountant pursuant to contract and tort law as well as federal securities and criminal law. The section also examines in depth federal tax law and tax procedures, particularly personal taxation and the taxation of business entities. The taxation of trusts and estates as well as the taxation of gifts are also covered. Furthermore, the relationship between federal and state taxation is addressed. Particularly important to the business student is the differentiation in taxation among traditional C-corporations, S-corporations, partnerships, and Limited Liability Companies (LLCs).

True and False Questions with Answers and Explanations

1. If an accountant breaches a contract with a client the aggrieved client can sue for monetary damages, including typically emotional distress, and punitive damages since the accountant as a professional "should know better" than to breach a contract.
(False: Emotional distress and punitive damages are very rare in breach of contract cases, even for purposeful breaches by a professional, such as an accountant. Compensatory damages are of course recoverable.)

2. Under the common law accountants may be liable to clients for breach of contract, negligence (malpractice), and strict liability of professionals.
(False: Strict liability arises for defective products and for ultra-hazardous activities. Accountants typically are sued for breach of contract, negligence (that is, malpractice), or fraud/misrepresentation under the common law.)

3. An accountant can successfully defend against a lawsuit for professional malpractice if he or she can demonstrate the absence of an "evil mind" or bad intent in that the accountant did not intend to purposefully harm the client.
(False: An evil mind or bad intent, called under the old common law, "scienter," are part of a lawsuit for fraud or deceit, not negligence, as the latter only requires evidence that the accountant did not perform in a reasonably competent and prudent professional manner.)

4. Evidence that an accountant contravened generally accepted accounting principles and/or generally accepted auditing standards will be construed as *prima facie*, that is, initial, evidence that the accountant committed professional malpractice.
(True: This is a very basic liability principle.)

5. Securities laws in the U.S. do not apply to accountants employed by corporations as employees as only the corporation as employer is liable.
(False: Securities laws apply to all accountants.)

6. Pursuant to U.S. law the aiding and assisting in the preparation of a false tax return is punishable as a criminal law felony by the person signing and submitting the return but only a civil law fine by the person aiding and assisting.
(False: Both are punishable as criminal law felonies.)

7. Working papers, such as ledgers, notes, and computations, that are created by an accountant when preparing a client's tax returns are owned by the client.
(False: They are owned by the accountant.)

8. Members of the accounting profession are governed by the laws as well as by the codes of professional conduct established by the accounting profession.
(True: This is a basic proposition.)

9. An accountant's violation of generally accepted accounting principles and/or generally accepted auditing standards will be construed as *prima facie* evidence that the accountant committed professional malpractice.
(True: Prima facie means "initial" evidence which can be rebutted; and malpractice is "simply" negligence committed by a member of a profession, like a doctor or lawyer or as here, an accountant.)

10. Accountants are subject to legal liability for malpractice only by those clients whom they are in a contractual relationship with.
(False: Liability extends to parties who are reasonably foreseeable victims of the malpractice.)

11. Section 11 of the Securities Act of 1934 requires that accountants use due diligence in the preparation of financial statements for a company's registration statement.
(True: And if so, the accountant can avoid legal liability.)

12. John purchased a warehouse building. As part of a major restoration plan to make the warehouse suitable for a frozen food company converted a section of the ware into a freezer. John can deduct the cost as a repair expense.
(False: Since the freezer are a major restoration, the cost must be capitalized [Sec. 263(a)(1)].)

13. Interest and penalties paid on an individual income tax deficiency are deductible as a business expense if the deficiency was related to income from a business.
(False: Penalties paid are not deductible [Sec. 162(f)]).

14. John gave two tickets to a music performance to a business customer. The tickets cost $50 each. John did not go with his customer to the performance. He can deduct the tickets as a gift.
(False: The taxpayer may treat the tickets as a gift, but under Sec. 274(b), the limit for deduction is $25 per person per year.)

15. Any expenses incurred in order to produce some form of income are deductible for adjusted gross income.
(False: Section 212 allows a deduction only for ordinary and necessary expenses paid or incurred for the production or collection of income.*)*

16. John contributed $1,000 to the presidential campaign in the current year. John can deduct the $1,000.
(False: Section 170(c)(2)(D) states that an organization is not qualified if it participates in any political campaign on behalf of (or in opposition to) any candidate for public office).

17. An individual may obtain an automatic 6-month extension to file his or her individual income tax return and pay any balance of tax due by filing Form 4868, Application for Automatic Extension of Time to File U.S. Individual Income Tax Return.
(False: An individual who is required to file an income tax return is allowed an automatic 6-month extension of time to file the return by filing Form 4868. However, no extension of time is allowed for payment of the tax due).

18. If a child's parents elect to include the child's income in the parents' return, the child will still be required to file a return in most cases.
(False: Under Sec. 1(g)(7), a child is treated as having no gross income and is not required to file a return if the parents elect to include the child's income in their own return.)

19. John receives tips at this job as a bartender which are substantial. His regular wages are too small for her employer to withhold the taxes due on the tips. John may pay estimated tax payments instead of giving her employer the extra money.
(True: Anyone may make estimated tax payments. The penalty for underpayment of estimated tax is based on the amount of underpayment each quarter after treating amounts withheld from wages as being paid in equal parts on each due date of estimated taxes. Therefore, either withholding or timely payment of estimated taxes will avoid the penalty.)

20. The child tax credit is a refundable credit.
(True: The credit is refundable to the extent of 15% of earned income in excess of $2,500.)

21. John worked for two employers and had income reported on his w-2's of $180,000 and $60,000 respectfully. Both of his employer withheld Social Security (FICA) tax on the entire amount. John may claim a credit against his income tax for the excess FICA tax withheld.\
(True: Excess FICA withheld when an employee works for two employers may be used as a credit against income taxes.)

22. John was a mail truck driver until he retired on disability in 2019. He has a statement from his doctor that due to an injury he will never be able to drive a truck again. He is 56 years old and now does volunteer work at a religious organization. He sets his own hours and is not paid. John is eligible for the credit for the elderly.
(False: Section 22 allows a credit for individuals who retire on disability and are permanently and totally disabled. Section 22(e)(3) defines permanently and totally disabled as being unable to engage in any substantial gainful activity by reason of any medically determinable physical or mental impairment.)

23. If a student is enrolled in full-time college graduate program after they have already received an accredited bachelor's degree, (s)he may use the American Opportunity Tax Credit for this calendar year.
(False: The American Opportunity Tax Credit is available during a student's first 4 years in college.)

24. Capital assets may be given preferential tax treatment. Some examples of capital assets are stocks and bonds held in a personal account.
(True: To determine the tax treatment of a capital asset transaction, the holding period of the asset must first be known. Capital transactions are treated as long-term if held for more than 1 year, while capital assets held for 1 year or less are considered short-term and are subject to the ordinary income rates.)

25. Nonbusiness bad debts are deductible only as short-term capital losses on Form 8949.
(True: Under Sec. 166, a nonbusiness bad debt is treated as a short-term capital loss. Under Sec. 166, when a nonbusiness bad debt becomes worthless, the resulting loss is treated as a short-term capital loss. Individual taxpayers report short-term capital losses on Form 8949.)

26. Section 1245 property includes tangible as well as intangible personal property that is or has been amortized under Sec. 197.
(True: Section 1245 property means any property that is or has been property of a character subject to the allowance for depreciation or amortization and is either personal (tangible or intangible) property or other property (not including a building or its structural components)).

27. If depreciable real property is held for 1 year or less, any depreciation that has been deducted is treated as additional depreciation for purposes of figuring the part of any gain to be reported as ordinary income.
(True: In addition to accelerated depreciation in excess of straight-line, all depreciation is subject to recapture if the Sec. 1250 property has not been held more than 1 year.)

28. A gain or loss is recognized on the exchange of an annuity contract for another annuity contract.
(True: Section 1035 allows tax-free exchanges among real property not contracts.)

29. John's egg-laying hens developed a disease that required him to sell the chickens for less than the going market rate. This is considered an involuntary conversion.
(True: Livestock that are sold or exchanged because they are diseased or have been exposed to disease and that would not otherwise have been sold or exchanged at that particular time are treated as involuntarily converted [Sec. 1033(d)]).

30. A partner's adjusted basis for an interest in a partnership cannot be less than zero.
(True: A partner's basis may not be decreased below zero [Sec. 705(a)(2)]).

31. Under the terms of a partnership agreement, John is entitled to a fixed annual payment of $15,000 without regard to the income of the partnership. John's distributive share of the partnership is 20%. The partnership has a $80,000 loss after deducting John's guaranteed payment. John must report the full amount of the guaranteed payment and separately take into account his share of the partnership loss.
(True: When computing taxable income, a partner must include his or her distributive share of partnership items for any partnership tax year ending within his or her tax year [Sec. 706(a)]. A partner must also include guaranteed payments deducted in a partnership's tax year ending within his or her tax year. Guaranteed payments are deductible by the partnership [Sec. 707(c)]).

32. All partners are required to sign a partnership return.
(False: Section 6063 provides that a partnership return may be signed by any one of the partners. The signature of a partner on the return is considered evidence that such partner is authorized to sign the return.)

33. Once a Sec. 754 election is made, a partnership can revoke the election with the consent of all partners.
(False: A Sec. 754 election may only be revoked with the approval of the district director for the Internal Revenue district in which the partnership return is required to be filed [Reg. 1.754-1(c)]).

34. If a corporation issues its own bonds at a discount, it has in effect paid additional interest that is deductible over the life of the bonds.
(True: For bonds issued prior to July 2, 1982, Reg. 1.163-4 permits the deduction of the original issue discount (as interest) over the life of the bond on a ratable basis. For bonds issued after July 1, 1982, Sec. 163(e)(1) allows the deduction of original issue discount over the life of the bond based on the "yield" method of amortizing the discount.)

35. A corporation distributes property with a fair market value of $25,000 and an adjusted basis of $30,000 to a shareholder. The property's basis in the shareholder's hands is $30,000.
(True: Under Sec. 301(d), the basis of property received by a distributee in a dividend distribution is the fair market value of such property. The distributee will have a basis in the property of $25,000, even though the corporation's basis was higher.)

36. In the current year, an S corporation distributed property to a shareholder that had a fair market value in excess of its adjusted basis to the S corporation. The shareholder must use the basis of the property in determining the amount of the distribution as opposed to the basis of the property in the hands of the S corporation.
(False: When an S corporation distributes as a non-liquidating distribution property that has a FMV in excess of basis, then the S corporation must recognize gain as if it sold the property at its FMV [Sec. 311(b)]. The FMV of the property then reduces the shareholder's basis for the stock.)

37. The tax on built-in gains generally does not apply to any corporation if an election to be an S corporation was in effect for each of its tax years and was never a C-Corporation?
(True: For a former C corporation electing S corporation status after 1986, Sec. 1374 imposes a tax on any gain accruing prior to the conversion that is recognized by the S corporation within a 5-year period beginning with the first day of the first taxable year for which the corporation was an S corporation. Section 1374(c) states that this tax is not imposed on a corporation that has always been an S corporation).

38. A trust may be a complex trust for one year and a simple trust for another year.
(True: The rules for classifying trusts are applied on a year-by-year basis. Thus, if trust income is accumulated in one year, the trust is a complex trust for that year, but if in a later year, its income is required to be distributed currently and no other amounts are distributed, the trust qualifies as a simple trust in the later year.)

39. Payments to a widow or dependent for support by estate are deductible.
(True: Payments to a widow or dependent for support by estate, whether from income or principal, are deductible by estate if paid pursuant to a court order or decree.)

40. C corporation does not have to elect to use the calendar year as its tax year.
(True: In general, in a corporation's first year, it may choose any taxable year that meets the requirement in Sec. 441 without obtaining prior approval. This is true for a C corporation).

41. A general partner does not have to include his or her distributive share of partnership income or loss in computing net earnings from self-employment.
(False: Under Sec. 1402(a), net earnings from self-employment include the distributive share (whether or not distributed) of ordinary income or loss from any trade or business carried on by a partnership of which the taxpayer is a member. Special rules apply to limited partners in a limited partnership in determining their self-employment income [Sec. 1402(a)(13)]).

42. A taxpayer cannot use private delivery services designated by the IRS to meet the "timely mailing as timely filing/paying" rule for Form 941 and payments.
(False: A taxpayer may use certain private delivery services designated by the IRS for tax returns and payments. The IRS updates the list of designated private delivery services when necessary.)

43. Gifts between spouses never generate taxable gifts.
(False: The marital deduction provided in Sec. 2523 is not available to a donor who is not a U.S. citizen. Furthermore, Sec. 2523(b) disallows the deduction in most cases if the interest passing to the spouse by gift is a terminable interest. A terminable interest is generally one that could end or terminate when some event occurs or a specified amount of time passes so that the property passes to someone else in such a way that the interest would not be included in the spouse's estate.)

44. Medical expenses, if deducted on both the estate and final income tax return, are fully deductible as administration expenses.
(False: section 2053 allows a deduction from the gross estate for claims against the estate. Medical expenses are deductible. Section 213(c) provides that medical expenses paid within 1 year of death may be deducted on either the estate tax return or the final income tax return of the decedent, but not on both returns.)

45. All compensated tax return preparers are not required to have a PTIN for any such work performed.
(False: Any individual who, for compensation, prepares, or assists in the preparation of, all or substantially all of a tax return or claim for refund after December 31, 2010, must have a PTIN. Failure to do so could result in the imposition of IRC Sec. 6695 penalties, injunction, referral for criminal investigation, or disciplinary action by the IRS Office of Professional Responsibility).

46. John employed in the accounting department of Partnership J, prepares the partnership's income tax return John is considered a return preparer.
(False: Under Sec. 7701(a)(36)(B)(ii), a person who prepares a return or claim for refund of the employer by whom (s)he is regularly and continuously employed is not considered a tax return preparer. Since Mr. P is an employee of the partnership, he is not considered a return preparer.)

47. John is a college student working his way through school. During the tax season, he is paid to prepare his friends and family members tax returns. John was paid $1,000. John is a tax preparer.
(True: Section 7701(a)(36) defines a tax return preparer as any person who prepares for compensation any return of tax or any claim for refund of tax imposed by the IRC (Title 26)).

48. Generally, in preparing a return, the preparer may in good faith rely without information furnished by the taxpayer as long as they made reasonable inquiries if the information as furnished appears incorrect or incomplete.
(True: Regulation 1.6694-1(e)(1) requires a return preparer to make reasonable inquiries if the information as furnished appears incorrect or incomplete. The preparer may not ignore the implications of information furnished.)

49. A signature stamp is not sufficient to meet the return preparer signature requirement for an original return.
(False: Regulation 1.6695-1(b)(1) requires an individual who is a tax return preparer to manually sign the return after it has been completed and before it is presented to the taxpayer. However, since 2004, three alternative methods, (1) computer software program, (2) rubber stamps, and (3) mechanical devices, have all been approved for original returns, amended returns, and extension requests.)

50. More than one preparer may be subject to the willful understatement of tax liability penalty on the same tax return.
(True:Regulation 1.6694-2(a)(1) provides that if an understatement of tax liability is due to a willful attempt by one or more income tax return preparers, each preparer who knew or reasonably should have known of the position will be subject to a separate penalty. Regulation 1.6694-1(b)(1) holds for documents prepared and advice given after December 31, 1991, that no more than one individual associated with a firm (e.g., as a partner or employee) is treated as a preparer with respect to a return or refund claim.)

51. Revenue rulings of the IRS are private rulings specific to a taxpayer's issue concerning the application of tax law to a specific set of facts.
(False: A revenue ruling (abbreviated Rev. Rul.) is substantive, pertains to a specific set of facts, and sets forth the IRS's interpretation of the tax law and its application to those facts. IRS employees must follow published rulings.)

52. If the Internal Revenue Service has selected your return for examination, you may make a video recording of the examination interview if you follow certain procedures prescribed by the IRS.
(False: Section 7521(a) allows taxpayers to make audio recordings but, not video recordings of the interview but with advance request and at the taxpayer's expense. IRS officers and employees are also permitted to make audio recordings of the interview. Advance permission of the taxpayer is required for IRS audio recordings, and a copy of the transcript or recording must be provided to the taxpayer.)

53. A tax information authorization is required of a taxpayer's representative at a conference with IRS officials which is also attended by the taxpayer.
(False: Submission of a tax information authorization to request disclosure of confidential tax information does not constitute practice before the IRS [26 CFR 601.504(b)(1)]. A tax information authorization is not required of a taxpayer's representative at a conference that is also attended by the taxpayer.)

54. A representative having a power of attorney is not permitted to endorse a refund check if the taxpayer authorizes him to receive it.
(True: 26 CFR 601.504(a)(5) provides that a taxpayer's representative may receive a refund check if the taxpayer specifically authorizes this in IRS Form 2848, Power of Attorney and Declaration of Representative. However, the representative is not authorized to endorse and collect the refund check.)

55. There are multiple levels of appeals that exists within the Internal Revenue Service. All appeals are made to the appeals office.
(False: Other than a conference with the examining agent's supervisor, there is only one level of appeal within the IRS. All appeals are made to the appeals office in the taxpayer's region [26 CFR 601.105(c), (d) and 601.106]).

Multiple Choice Questions with Answers and Explanation

1. During the year John had the follow receipts of income:
   Wages: $65,000
   Interest Income from Municipal Bonds: $500

Dividend Income: $800
Interest Income from his Bank: $20

What is the total amount that must be included in gross income on John's income tax return for this year?

a. $66,320
b. $66,300
c. $65,820
d. $65,520

(Answer (C) is correct. Sec. 103 excludes from gross income interest on most obligations of states or municipal bonds).

2. In year 1 John earned a salary of $100,000 at Lifetime Corporation. However, he elected to only take $50,000 in year 1 and have the other $50,000 paid in year 2. Lifetime corporation had the financially ability to pay John the full amount in year one. How much does John have to include in gross income in his year 1 income tax return?

a. $100,000
b. $75,000
c. $50,000
d. $25,000

(Answer (A) is correct. Section 61(a)(1) specifically provides that compensation for services is to be included in gross income. The $50,000 that was not actually received until Year 2 is considered to have been constructively received in Year 1 Sec. 451(a)).)

3. John had the following amounts paid to him during the year; how much should be included on his income tax return for the year?

Punitive Damages awarded from a Jury due to an accident: $5,000
Loan from a Bank: $3,000
Unrealized Gain on Stock he owns: $500
Compensation from the same accident for personal injury $5,000

a. $10,800
b. $10,500
c. $10,000
d. $5,000

(Answer (D) is correct. Section 104(a) includes punitive damages in gross income whether or not they relate to physical injury or physical sickness. Money borrowed from a bank is not included in gross income because there is a legal obligation to return it. Section 104(a)(2) compensation for personal injury or illness is paid to replace the personal capital destroyed is specifically excluded from income. An unrealized gain or loss is not taxable only a recognized gain or loss can be).

4. Which of the following should not be included in John's income for the current year?

a. $80 in repairs to his local baker's oven in exchange bread received from the baker
b. $5,000 in life insurance proceeds as a beneficiary as a result of the death of John's mother

c. $1,000 Bonus given to him from his employer for his good work
d. $50 of lottery ticket winnings that he was given him from his friend for his birthday

(Answer (B) is correct. Sec. 101(a) specifically excludes from gross income amounts received under a life insurance contract if such amounts are paid by reason of death of the insured.)

5. For the current year, John's employer paid the following:

$500 Premium on $40,000 of nondiscriminatory group-term life insurance of which John's wife was the sole beneficiary
$800 Premiums on $30,000 nondiscriminatory ordinary life insurance of which John's wife was the sole beneficiary
$1000 Train pass for commuting to and from work.

What amount must John include in gross income for the current year?

a. $2,300
b. $1,800
c. $1,500
d. $1,000

(Answer (B) is correct. Fringe benefits received from an employer must be included in the employee's gross income unless specifically excluded. Section 79 specifically excludes premiums paid by an employer for up to $50,000 of nondiscriminatory group-term life insurance for each employee. The others must be included in gross income.)

6. John was in an accident. As a result of his injuries, he received an insurance check for $10,000 from a self-insured plan. His medical bills relating to the accident were $6,000 and were taken as a deduction on his tax return this year. How much of this amount can John exclude from gross income?

a. $16,000
b. $10,000
c. $6,000
d. $4,000

(Answer (D) is correct. Section 104(a)(3) there is an exclusion from gross income for amounts that are received from a self-insured plan. However, the exclusion is limited to amounts that are not deducted under Sec. 213. Since the $6,000 medical expenses are deductible, the exclusion would be limited to $4,000.)

7. A Section 125 plan also known as a "cafeteria plan" maintained by an employer means that:

a. The "Participant" the employee selects their own benefits from a variety of options
b. There are provisions for deferred compensation not including a 401(k) plan
c. At least 4 years of service before an employee can participate in the plan
d. Participant employee are restricted to their spouses and dependents

(Answer (A) is correct. Section 125 defines a cafeteria plan as a written plan under which all participants are employees and the participants may choose among benefits.)

8. All of the following statements about fringe benefits for 2018 are true except:

   a. An employer can exclude transportation expenses from an employee's wages for the year if they are provided instead of actual wages
   b. Bonuses in the form of a gift card are not excluded from wages
   c. Employee wages exclude *De Minims'* fringe benefits that are so little in value it would be unreasonable to account for them
   d. An employer can treat all meals furnished to employees on the premises as furnished at the employer's convenience if half of the employees are furnished for a substantial non-pay business reason.

(Answer (D) is correct. More than one-half of all meals furnished to employees on an employer's premise must be furnished for a substantial non-pay business reason.)

9. Which of the following income items may *not* be excluded from gross income?

   a. A holiday ham or turkey given to employees worth approximately $15.
   b. A $100 bonus received in cash at year end.
   c. Coffee, tea, and water provided in the breakroom.
   d. A hat and mug with the company logo given to each employee at the year end.

(Answer (B) is correct. Benefits received from an employer as compensation for services are included in gross income under Sec. 61 unless provided otherwise. There is no provision excluding a Christmas bonus no matter how small.)

10. Which of the following income items may not be excluded from gross income?

   a. Social Security benefits in excess of MAGI (modified adjusted gross income) will be included in gross income.
   b. Social Security benefits in excess of exactly one-third of MAGI (modified adjusted gross income) will be included in gross income.
   c. 85% of Social Security benefits is the maximum amount that can be included in gross income
   d. Social Security benefits in excess of the of MAGI (modified adjusted gross income) of over $33,000 will be included in gross income.

(Answer (C) is correct. The actual taxable portion of Social Security benefits will depend upon the base amount and the adjusted base amount known as the provisional income. If provisional income exceeds the adjusted base amount, up to 85% of Social Security benefits might be taxable.)

11. CERI Inc is a business which incurred the following as its miscellaneous expenses:

Bank service charges $50
Office supplies $200
Advertising $30
Professional Fees $3,000
Interest for the entire period of a 4-year loan taken out on January 1 $2,000.

How much of the above may CERI Inc deduct for the current year?

   a. $5,280

b. $3,780
c. $3,080
d. $2,200

(Answer (B) is correct. Professional fees, offices supplies, advertising, and a bank service charges are all deductible under Sec. 162. However, the interest was prepaid for 4 years, thus only one-fourth of the interest may be deducted in the current year.)

12. The state of Florida imposes a tax based upon the property a business owned by a sole proprietor. An individual proprietor would deduct this tax on which schedule?

a. Schedule A
b. Schedule B
c. Schedule C
d. Schedule D

(Answer (C) is correct. A tax on business for their property is ordinary and necessary expense of the business and would be deducible under Sec. 162 and it is reported on Schedule C, which is used to report the income and expenses of a sole proprietorship, then carried onto page 1 of Form 1040).

13. John sustained a Net Operating Loss (NOL) for the 2019 tax year. John can apply the NOL to what years?

a. Back 1, Forward 20
b. Back 3, Forward 5
c. Back 5, Forward 20
d. Back 0, Forward Indefinitely

(Answer (D) is correct. For the 2019 tax year a NOL sustained cannot be carried back but, can be carried forward to another year without any time limit).

14. Which of the following types of entities can be entitled for a net operating loss deduction?

a. Not-For Profit Organizations
b. Partnerships
c. S-Corporations
d. C-Corporations

(Answer (D) is correct. Section 172 allows most taxpayers to deduct a NOL from trade or business income. Exceptions to the general availability of the deduction include regulated investment companies, life insurance companies, partnerships (not partners), and S corporations (not investors)).

15. What is the tax treatment of losses resulting from a passive activity? Assuming the taxpayer only has one passive activity and they do not materially participate in anyway.

a. Any losses are carried forward till next year
b. Losses are deducted from their taxable income
c. Losses are carried forward indefinitely until the taxpayer has passive income
d. Losses are deducted from their taxable income first then are carried forward till next year

(Answer (C) is correct. The losses are carried forward without expiration and are deductible against income in future years from that activity.)

16. John has an adjusted gross income (AGI) of $110,000 without taking into consideration $30,000 of losses from rental real estate activities. John actively participates in the rental real estate activities. What amount of the rental losses may John deduct in determining taxable income?

    a. $0
    b. $15,000
    c. $20,000
    d. $30,000

    (Answer (C) is correct. A person who actively participates in rental real estate activity is entitled to deduct up to $25,000 in losses from the passive activity against other than passive income. However, the $25,000 limit is reduced by 50% of that person's MAGI (AGI, Social Security, and qualified retirement contributions) over $100,000. John has $10,000 of MAGI over $100,000. Accordingly, the $25,000 loss deduction must be reduced by $5,000 ($10,000 MAGI excess × 50%), resulting in $20,000 of deductible loss limitation).

17. John is a passive investor in three activities which have been profitable in previous years. The profit and losses for the current year are as follows: Gain (Loss)

    Activity A $(40,000)
    Activity B (60,000)
    Activity C 30,000
    Total $(70,000)

    What amount of suspended loss should John allocate to Activity A?

    a. $20,000
    b. $28,000
    c. $35,000
    d. $40,000

    (Answer (B) is correct. The passive activity income is allocated pro rata between the two activities with passive losses. As Activity A accounts for 40% = $40,000 ÷ $100,000 total loss of the passive losses, it is allocated $12,000 = $30,000 × 40% of the passive activity income. This results in a net $28,000 = $40,000 – $12,000 passive activity loss allocable to Activity A).

18. During the current year, John, who is single, had the following income and expenses:

    Salary $80,000
    Dividend income 3,000
    Travel expenses for employer 1,000
    Contribution to IRA 6,000
    John's travel expenses, which were then reimbursed by his employer and haven been accounted for.

    What is John's adjusted gross income?

a. $111,000
b. $110,000
c. $78,000
d. $77,000

(Answer (D) is correct. Adjusted gross income is defined in Sec. 62 as gross income minus specified deductions, which included reimbursed employee expenses and contributions to an IRA. Since the travel expenses were accounted for, the reimbursement need not be included in gross income, and are not deducted.)

19. Which of the following is deductible by a calendar-year taxpayer to arrive at adjusted gross income in the current year?

a. 100% of the medical insurance expense of a self-employed individual.
b. Medical Expenses
c. Charitable Contributions
d. One-half of a net long-term capital gain in excess of a net short-term capital loss.

(Answer (A) is correct. Sec. 162(l) allows a self-employed individual to deduct 100% of the insurance for family medical insurance expenses as business expenses.)

20. On April 15, Year 3, John filed Form 4868, Application for Automatic Extension of Time to File, extending the due date for filing his Year 2 income tax return to October 15, Year 3. By what date must he make his IRA contribution to qualify for an IRA deduction on his Year 2 return?

a. December 31, Year 2.
b. January 1, Year 3
c. April 15, Year 3.
d. October 15, Year 3.

(Answer (C) is correct. All IRA contributions for a particular year must be made no later than the due date for filing that year's tax return without regard to any filing extensions that may have been granted [Sec. 219(f)(3)]).

21. A lump-sum distribution from one retirement program may be reinvested in another retirement program. This rollover must be completed within how many days after receipt of the lump-sum distribution?

a. 30
b. 60
c. 90
d. 120

(Answer (B) is correct. Under Sec. 408(d), a lump-sum distribution from one retirement program may be treated as a tax-free rollover if the entire amount is reinvested in another retirement program no later than 60 days after the day in which the lump-sum distribution is received).

22. Which of the following qualify as deductible medical expenses?

1. Payments to medical doctor
2. Payment for an emergency room visit

3. Vitamins for general health not prescribed by a physician
4. Payments for an elective cosmetic operation
5. D Health club dues

a. 1, 3, and 5.
b. 1 and 2.
c. 1, 2, and 4.
d. 1 and 4.

(Answer (B) is correct. Payments to a medical doctor and payments for an emergency room visit are both expenditures made for the diagnosis, cure, mitigation, treatment, or prevention of disease, or for the purpose of affecting any structure or function of the body. Accordingly, they fall within the definition of medical care under Sec. 213 and are deductible expenses).

23. All of the following taxes are deductible on Schedule A (Form 1040) except:

a. Taxes that the taxpayer paid on property owned by his or her parents or children
b. State income tax.
c. State real estate tax on a personal residence.
d. Personal property taxes.

(Answer (A) is correct. Taxes paid on another person's property are not deductible because the tax liability is the liability of the other person).

24. The amount of investment interest deductible in the current year is limited to:

a. Net investment income.
b. Net investment income limited up to $10,000.
c. Net investment income in excess of 10% of adjusted gross income
d. Net investment income limited up to 3,000.

(Answer (A) is correct. Section 163(d) limits the deduction for investment interest to the net investment income.)

25. Donations to all of the following organizations are deductible as charitable contributions except:

a. Charitable community chest.
b. Civic leagues and chambers of commerce.
c. Nonprofit hospital.
d. Churches, synagogues, temples, mosques, and other religious organizations

(Answer (B) is correct. Charitable contributions are deductible only if they are made to qualified organizations. Qualified organizations can be either public charities or private foundations. A civic leagues and chambers of commerce does not meet this definition)

26. When figuring if a dependent child who is a full-time student meets the support test, all of the following items are taken into account in determining total support except:

a. Food.
b. Scholarships.
c. Entertainment.

d. Gifts.

(Answer (B) is correct. To determine whether an individual has not provided more than one-half of his or her own support, the amount of support provided by the qualifying child is compared to the entire amount of support received from all sources. However, amounts received as a scholarship are not considered).

27. John and Brenda are single and live apart for most of the year. However, on December 31, of this year they were legally married. Which of the following is the only filing status choice available to them for the current year?

   a. Married filing joint return.
   b. Married filing separate return.
   c. Head of household.
   d. Single.

   (Answer (A) is correct. In order to filing a joint return, they must be married at the end of the year. In this case John and Brenda are married at the end of the year and thus would file a joint return).

28. Which of the following are eligible expenses for the American Opportunity Tax Credit?

   I Tuition
   II Fees required for enrollment
   III Room and board
   IV Course materials

   a. I and II only.
   b. I, II, and III.
   c. I, II, and IV.
   d. I, II, III and IV.

   (Answer (C) is correct. Tuition, fees, and course materials required for enrollment are eligible expenses for the credit. The credit may not be used for room and board, activity fees, athletic fees, insurance expense, or transportation)

29. In Year 1, John purchased three blocks of ABC Company common stock as follows: March 25, 100 shares at $150 per share; June 3, 100 shares at $155; October 31, 100 shares at $160. On January 15 of Year 4, John sold 200 shares at a price of $170 per share. Under IRS regulations, which two of the following cost flow assumptions are acceptable in determining the cost basis to be used in measuring John's gain on the sale?

   a. FIFO or LIFO.
   b. Specific identification or weighted average.
   c. FIFO or weighted average.
   d. Specific identification or FIFO.

   (Answer (D) is correct. If the taxpayer can specifically identify the lots being sold, this method may be used. If they cannot be specifically identified, the taxpayer must assume that they are being sold on the first-in, first-out (FIFO) basis.)

30. Kate's father, John, gave Kate a gift of 1000 shares of Pear Corporation common stock in the current year. John's basis for the Pear stock was $8,000. At the date of this gift, the fair market value of the Pear stock was $7,000. No gift tax was paid with respect to the transfer. If Kate sold the 1000 shares of Pear stock in the current year for $10,000, her basis is:

    a. $10,000
    b. $8,000
    c. $7,000
    d. $0

    (Answer (B) is correct. The basis of property acquired by gift is generally the donor's adjusted basis, plus any gift tax attributable to appreciation (Sec. 1015). This rule applies when the donee determines any gain on a sale of the property. Since no gift tax was paid attributable to appreciation, Kate's basis is the same as her father's, or $8,000.)

31. The basis in property inherited from a decedent may be determined as follows:

    a. The fair market value at the date of death or the fair market value at an alternative valuation date.
    b. The decedent's basis plus any inheritance tax paid on the increased value.
    c. The fair market value at an alternate valuation date.
    d. The fair market value at the date of death.

    (Answer (A) is correct. The basis of property received from a decedent is generally the fair market value of the property on the date of the decedent's death [Sec. 1014(a)]. If the executor elects the alternate valuation date for the estate tax return, the basis of the assets is their fair market value 6 months after death or the date of sale or distribution, if earlier.)

32. The basis of property received in exchange for service is determined by which of the following?

    a. The value of the services rendered.
    b. The basis of the property received.
    c. The fair market value of the property received.
    d. The property has will have a basis of zero.

    (Answer (C) is correct. Section 83(a) provides that the receipt of property for services provided is a taxable transaction. Accordingly, the fair market value of the property must be included in gross income as compensation, and the basis of the property will be its fair market value.)

33. In Year 1, John bought 100 shares of ABC stock for $2,000 or $20 a share. In Year 2, she bought 100 shares of XYZ stock for $2,400, or $24 a share. In Year 3, ABC declared a 2-for-1 stock split. Which of the following is true?

    a. John now has 200 shares with a basis of $10 per share.
    b. John now has 200 shares with a basis of $12 per share.
    c. John now has 400 shares with a basis of $22 per share.
    d. John now has 200 shares with a basis of $10 per share and 200 shares with a basis of $12 per share.

    (Answer (D) is correct. A distribution of common stock as a stock split is generally a tax-free distribution. The basis of the original stock is allocated between it and the new stock based on

their relative fair market values. The 100 shares purchased in Year 1 have a basis of \$2,000 (100 shares × \$20 per share), which must be allocated to the additional 100 shares from the stock split. The basis for the Year 1 stocks will be \$10 per share (\$2,000 ÷ 200). The 100 shares purchased in Year 2 have a basis of \$2,400 (100 shares × \$24), which must be allocated to the additional 100 shares from the stock split. The basis for the Year 2 stocks will be \$12 per share (\$2,400 ÷ 200).

34. Which of the following assets are depreciable or amortizable for federal income tax purposes?

    1. Land
    2. Business Truck
    3. Rental Residence
    4. Inventory
    5. Personal Residence
    6. Business Equipment

    a. 2, 3, and 6.
    b. 1, 2, and 3.
    c. 1, 4, and 5.
    d. 3, 4, and 6.

    (Answer (A) is correct. Section 167(a) provides a depreciation deduction with respect to property used in a trade or business or held for the production of income. A rental residence and a business automobile are both used in a trade or business or for the production of income. Therefore, they are depreciable.)

35. John, a sole proprietor, purchased \$10,000 worth of office equipment and furniture for use in his business. He elected to take the maximum Sec. 179 deduction. What is John's basis for the MACRS computation?

    a. \$10,000
    b. \$5,000
    c. \$2,500
    d. \$0

    (Answer (D) is correct. The original cost of an asset must be reduced for any Sec. 179 expense up to \$1 million in 2018. Since John took the Sec. 179 expense deduction of \$12,000 in 2018, he must reduce the cost of his property. John's depreciable basis is Original cost \$10,000 Less: Sec. 179 deduction (10,000) Depreciable basis \$ 0)

36. During the current year, John, a calendar-year taxpayer, acquired and placed in service the following business assets:

    January: Delivery trucks \$ 25,000
    March: Warehouse building 75,000
    June: Computer system 15,000
    September: Automobile 15,000
    November: Office equipment 45,000

    Which convention(s) is(are) used to figure John's depreciation for the current year?

a. Mid-quarter for all assets except the warehouse building, which uses mid-month.
b. Half-year for all of the assets.
c. Mid-quarter for all of the assets.
d. Half-year for all assets except the warehouse building, which uses mid-month; half-year for the automobile and the office equipment.

(Answer (A) is correct. Under the MACRS rules, the mid-quarter convention must be used for all personal property placed in service during the year if substantial property was placed in service during the last 3 months of the year [Sec. 168(d)(3)]. Substantial property is defined as greater than 40% of the aggregate bases of property placed in service during the year. The $90,000 office equipment constitutes 45% ($45,000 ÷ $100,000) of all personal property placed in service, so the mid-quarter convention must be used. A mid-month convention is used in the year of acquisition for real property. Therefore, the mid-month convention is used for the warehouse building.)

37. John purchased a business on July 1 of the current year. Of the purchase price, $60,000 was attributable to the acquisition of existing employment contracts. The contracts are deemed to have a useful life of 12 years. What is John's allowable amortization deduction for the current year?

a. $0
b. $2,000
c. $4,000
d. $5,000

(Answer (B) is correct. Under Sec. 197, the cost of acquiring existing employment contracts is amortizable over a 15-year period beginning in the month of acquisition. Actual useful life is ignored. Joseph's deduction for the current year is $2,000 = [($60,000 ÷ 15) × 6/12 months]).

38. All of the following are Sec. 197 intangible assets except?

a. Trademarks.
b. Leasehold improvements.
c. Covenants not to compete acquired in the purchase of the assets of a business.
d. Any interest in a corporation, partnership, trust, or estate.

(Answer (D) is correct. Section 197(e)(1) specifically excludes from the definition of a Sec. 197 intangible any interest in a corporation, partnership, trust, or estate.)

39. On July 1 of the current year, Mario sold 500 shares of Pear Corporation stock. Luigi had received this stock on June 1 of the same year as a bequest from the estate of his uncle, who died on April 1 of the current year. Luigi's basis was determined by reference to the stock's fair market value on April 1. Luigi's holding period for this stock was:

a. Short-term.
b. Long-term.
c. Short-term if sold at a gain; long-term if sold at a loss.
d. Long-term if sold at a gain; short-term if sold at a loss.

(Answer (B) is correct. Under Sec. 1223(11), if property acquired from a decedent is sold or otherwise disposed of by the recipient within 12 months of the decedent's death, then the property is considered to have been held for more than 12 months.)

40. John bought an asset on July 19, 2018. What is the earliest date on which John could have sold that asset and qualified for long-term capital gain or loss treatment?

    a. December 30, 2018.
    b. December 21, 2018.
    c. June 19, 2019.
    d. June 20, 2019.

    (Answer (D) is correct. For assets acquired after 1987, long-term capital gain or loss treatment is provided if the asset is held for more than 1 year. The general rule is that the date the property is acquired is excluded and the date that the property is disposed of is included in this computation of the holding period.)

41. Capital losses incurred by a married couple filing a joint return:

    a. Will be allowed only to the extent of capital gains.
    b. Will be allowed to the extent of capital gains, plus up to $3,000 of ordinary income.
    c. May be carried forward up to a maximum of 5 years.
    d. Are not allowable losses.

    (Answer (B) is correct. The amount of capital losses that can be deducted is the lesser of the excess of capital losses over capital gains or $3,000 [Sec. 1211(b)]. The maximum amount in excess of capital gains allowed as a deduction is $3,000 ($1,500 for married taxpayers filing separately).

42. Which of the following items qualifies for treatment under Section 1231 (Property Used in the Trade or Business and Involuntary Conversions)?

    a. Trademarks bought that are used in the business, held for 5 years.
    b. Building used in the business, held for 8 months.
    c. Machinery used in the business, held for 3 months.
    d. Equipment used in the business, held for 3 years.

    (Answer (D) is correct. Section 1231 property is property held for more than 1 year and includes all real or depreciable property used in a trade or business.)

43. Which of the following is not Sec. 1245 property?

    a. Livestock.
    b. Office building.
    c. Professional athletic contracts.
    d. Covenant not to compete.

    (Answer (B) is correct. Section 1245 property generally is depreciable personal property. It is tangible or intangible depreciable personal property, recovery property including specified real property, and tax benefit property. Other tangible property (excluding a building or its

structural components) includes property used as an integral part of a trade or business, e.g., manufacturing or production equipment used in a trade or business. Intangible amortizable personal Sec. 1245 property examples include Leaseholds of Sec. 1245 property, Professional athletic contracts, Goodwill acquired in connection with the acquisition of a trade or business, Livestock, Covenant not to compete.)

44. The following property is all used in a trade or business and has been held in excess of 1 year. Which property will not qualify for gains or losses from Sec. 1231 property upon its disposition by sale or exchange?

a. Property used for rental income.
b. Business property sold.
c. Depreciable property used in a trade or business.
d. Property includible in inventory.

(Answer (D) is correct. Gains and losses receive special treatment under Sec. 1231. Property that qualifies under Sec. 1231 generally must have been held for more than 1 year and either have been used in a trade or business or be an involuntarily converted nonpersonal capital asset. Inventory is specifically excluded.)

45. The deferral of taxation on unrecognized gains from a nontaxable property transaction:

a. Generally, is an adjustment to the basis of the new or acquired property.
b. Becomes a permanent tax savings.
c. Generally, has no effect on the basis of the property.
d. Results in a reduction of the basis of the acquired property by the amount of tax paid in a subsequent transfer of the property.

(Answer (A) is correct. A nontaxable property transaction generally results in the deferral of gain rather than a permanent tax savings. This is usually accomplished by transferring the basis of the old property to the new or by determining the basis of the new or acquired property at its cost less the unrecognized gain. One major exception is the exclusion of gain on the sale of a personal residence for which there is a permanent tax savings.)

46. If the taxpayer owns an apartment building that (s)he does not personally manage and the apartment building is involuntarily converted, which of the following will qualify as replacement property with nonrecognition of gain?

a. A retail store that the taxpayer will personally manage.
b. An interest in a coal mine.
c. An office building which the taxpayer will not personally manage.
d. 50% interest in a retail partnership.

(Answer (C) is correct. Section 1033(a) provides for the nonrecognition of gain if property is involuntarily converted and replaced with property similar or related in service or use. "Similar or related in service or use" has been interpreted to mean, for an investor, that the property must have a similar service or use with respect to the taxpayer-owner. Since both the office building and the apartment building are operated as passive leasing investments, they will qualify as replacement property.)

47. Which of the following statements is true regarding exclusion of the gain on the sale of a principal residence?

    a. An individual may exclude $500,000 of gain on the sale of a residence (s)he purchased 10 years ago.
    b. A married couple may exclude $500,000 of gain on the sale of a residence they purchased jointly 5 years ago.
    c. An individual may exclude $250,000 of gain on the sale of a residence (s)he purchased 1 year ago.
    d. A married couple may exclude $500,000 of gain on the sale of a residence they purchased jointly 1 year ago.

    (Answer (B) is correct. An individual may exclude $250,000 ($500,000 for married individuals filing jointly) on the sale of a principal residence provided (s)he lived there for at least 2 years. Additionally, a pro rata exclusion is available if the sale occurred prior to 2 years if the sale was as a result of a change in job locations or other unforeseen circumstances.)

48. For federal income tax purposes, a partnership other than a publicly traded partnership is:

    a. Required to pay a tax upon its profits, which in reduced individual taxes by its partners.
    b. Considered to be a nontaxable entity but must file an information return.
    c. A taxable entity similar to a corporation.
    d. Treated the same as a trust for tax purposes.

    (Answer (B) is correct. Section 701 states that the partners, not the partnership, are subject to federal income tax. The partnership is required to file an information return (Form 1065) under Sec. 6031.)

49. Which of the following can be an advantage of a limited liability company over an S-corporation?

    a. Double taxation of profits is avoided.
    b. Owners have limited liability.
    c. Appreciated property can be distributed tax-free to an owner.
    d. Stock in the company is easily transferable.

    (Answer (C) is correct. Unlike an S-corporation, an LLC can distribute appreciated property without incurring a taxable gain.)

50. The CPA was preparing the financial statement for a limited liability company. To which of the following would the CPA's report be addressed?

    a. Member.
    b. Shareholder.
    c. Managing partner.
    d. Owner.

    (Answer (A) is correct. The report would be addressed to the owners of the LLC. The owners are known as members.)

51. On June 1 of the current year, John received a 10% interest in HLM Co., a partnership, for services contributed to the partnership. HLM's net assets at that date had a basis of $60,000 and a fair market value of $110,000. In John's current-year income tax return, what amount must John include as income from the transfer of the partnership interest?

   a. $6,000 ordinary income.
   b. $6,000 capital gain.
   c. $11,000 ordinary income.
   d. $11,000 capital gain.

   (Answer (C) is correct. An individual must recognize compensation income when a partnership interest is received in exchange for services (whether current or past) rendered [Reg. 1.721-1(b)(1)]. The receipt of a capital interest in a partnership for services must be included in the year of receipt under Sec. 83. The income that should be recognized is the $11,000 ($110,000 × 10%) fair market value of the partnership interest received unless the interest is nontransferable or subject to a substantial risk of forfeiture. The income is ordinary because it is compensation for services.)

52. The following information pertains to land contributed by John for a 50% interest in a new partnership: Adjusted basis to John $200,000 Fair market value 600,000 Mortgage assumed by partnership 60,000 The partnership has no other liabilities. The basis for John's partnership interest is:

   a. $140,000
   b. $170,000
   c. $200,000
   d. $600,000

   (Answer (B) is correct. Under Sec. 722, the basis of a partner's interest in a partnership is the partner's adjusted basis in the contributed property. When the partnership assumes a mortgage or takes the property subject to a mortgage, the contributing partner is deemed to have received a distribution of cash to the extent of the relieved liability [Sec. 752(b)]. This deemed distribution reduces the partner's basis. Adjusted basis of land contributed $200,000 Less: Share of mortgage assumed by the other partners ($60,000 × 50%) (30,000) Basis $170,000.)

53. Dan and John form Rose Partnership with a cash contribution of $120,000 from Dan and a property contribution of land from John. The land has a fair market value of $120,000 and an adjusted basis of $70,000 at the date of the contribution. Dan and John are equal partners. What is John's basis immediately after formation?

   a. $0
   b. $50,000
   c. $70,000
   d. $120,000

   (Answer (C) is correct. A partner's basis in contributed items is exchanged for basis in the partnership interest received, adjusted for gain recognized and liabilities. John' basis is equal to his adjusted basis in the contributed land of $70,000. No other property was contributed, nor did he recognize gain on the contributed property, receive liability relief or assume any liability from the partnership.)

54. Partner J's basis in partnership XYZ is $10,000 at the beginning of the year. During the year, Partner J received a non-liquidating distribution of $6,000 cash and property with an adjusted basis of $5,000 and fair market value of $6,000. What was Partner J's basis in the property received?

   a. $4,000
   b. $5,000
   c. $6,000
   d. $10,000

   (Answer (A) is correct. A partner's basis in the distributed property is the partnership's adjusted basis in the property immediately before the distribution. However, this amount is limited to the distributee's adjusted basis in his or her partnership interest minus any money received in the distribution. Although the adjusted basis of the property distributed is $5,000 in the hands of the partnership, the partner's basis in the property is only $4,000 ($10,000 interest in partnership – $6,000 cash distributed)).

55. In February of Year 1, Dan contributed cash of $100,000 and John contributed land with an adjusted basis of $140,000 and a fair market value of $100,000 to form a partnership. In Year 3, the land was sold for $72,000. John's share of the loss from the sale of land is:

   a. $68,000
   b. $54,000
   c. $34,000
   d. $14,000

   (Answer (B) is correct. Gain or loss with respect to property contributed to the partnership must be allocated to take into account the variation between the basis of the property to the partnership and its fair market value at the time of contribution. Dan and John did this by allocating the $40,000 ($100,000 FMV – $140,000 basis) of pre-contribution decline in value. Upon the sale for $72,000, John's share of the loss is: Pre-contribution loss is $40,000; Post-contribution loss [($100,000 – $72,000) × 50%] + 14,000: Total share of the loss = $54,000)

56. The adjusted basis of John's partnership interest is $5,000. He receives a distribution of cash of $4,000 and property with an adjusted basis to the partnership of $11,000. (This was not a distribution in liquidation.) What is the basis of the distributed property in Stan's hands?

   a. $1,000
   b. $4,000
   c. $5,000
   d. $11,000

   (Answer (A) is correct. Section 732(a) provides that the basis of property distributed to a partner is the property's adjusted basis to the partnership immediately before such distribution. This basis, however, cannot exceed the adjusted basis of the partner's interest in the partnership less any money received in the same distribution [Sec. 732(a)(2)].)

   John's basis in the property distributed is:
   Basis of partnership interest $5,000

Less: Cash received	*(4,000)*
Basis in distributed property	*$1,000).*

57. The adjusted basis of John's partnership interest in VIR Associates was $190,000 immediately before receiving the following distribution in complete liquidation of Lex:

	Basis to Lex	Fair Market Value
Cash	$100,000	$100,000
Real Estate	$75,000	$125,000

What is Vance's basis in the real estate?

a. $125,000
b. $100,000
c. $90,000
d. $75,000

(Answer (C) is correct. In a liquidating distribution, a partner's basis for his or her partnership interest is reduced by the amount of money received [Sec. 732(b)]. Any remaining basis is then allocated to other property received. John's partnership interest basis of $190,000 is reduced by the $100,000 cash distributed. Accordingly, John's basis in the real estate distributed is the remaining $90,000).

58. Chris, Dan, and John each owned a one-third interest in the capital and profits of their calendar-year partnership. On September 31, Year 1, Chris and Dan sold their partnership interests to Mike and immediately withdrew from all participation in the partnership. On March 15, Year 2, Chris and Dan received full payment from Frank for the sale of their partnership interests. For tax purposes, the partnership:

a. Terminated on September 18, Year 1.
b. Terminated on December 31, Year 1.
c. Terminated on March 15, Year 2.
d. Did not terminate.

(Answer (D) is correct. A partnership terminates when no part of the business, financial operation, or venture of the partnership continues to be carried on by any of its partners. There are two partners.)

59. On December 31 of the current year, the basis of John's interest in Rose Partnership was $60,000, which included his $40,000 share of partnership liabilities. There were no unrealized receivables or inventory items. John sold his interest in Rose for $40,000 cash, and the purchaser assumed John's partnership liabilities. John's basis had already been adjusted for his share of Rose's income for the year. What is the amount of John's gain or (loss)?

a. $20,000
b. $10,000
c. $(10,000)
d. $(20,000)

(Answer (A) is correct. Because there were no unrealized receivables or inventory, the sale of the interest in the partnership results in capital gain or loss (Sec. 741). The relief from partnership liabilities is treated as an amount realized on the sale [Sec. 752(d)].

Partner John's gain is
Proceeds ($40,000 cash + $40,000 liabilities assumed by purchaser) $80,000
Less: Adjusted basis (60,000)
Capital gain $20,000.)

60. JAY incorporated a sole proprietorship by exchanging all the proprietorship's assets for the stock of Rose Co., a new corporation. To qualify for tax-free incorporation, JAY must be in control of Rose immediately after the exchange. What percentage of Rose's stock must JAY own to qualify as "control" for this purpose?

a. 50%
b. 67%
c. 75%
d. 80%

(Answer (D) is correct. Section 351 provides the rules for a tax-free incorporation. It refers to Sec. 368(c) for the definition of "control." Section 368(c) defines "control" as the ownership of stock possessing at least 80% of the total combined voting power of all classes of stock entitled to vote and at least 80% of the total number of shares of all other classes of stock of the corporation.)

61. You transfer property with an adjusted basis of $20,000 and a fair market value of $41,000 in exchange for 100% of the stock in a new corporation. You receive 100 shares of stock having a fair market value of $16,000 and $8,000 in cash. The corporation also assumes a $5,000 mortgage on the property. Which of the following is true?

a. $19,000 gain realized; $0 recognized.
b. $21,000 gain realized; $8,000 recognized.
c. $19,000 gain realized; $8,000 recognized.
d. $21,000 gain realized; $15,000 recognized.

(Answer (C) is correct. The gain realized on this transaction is $19,000 [($16,000 FMV of stock + $8,000 cash + $5,000 assumption of liability) – $20,000 adjusted basis of transferred property]. However, the transaction qualifies under Sec. 351 for nonrecognition. Transfer of mortgaged property to a controlled corporation does not require the recognition of gain unless the liabilities transferred or assumed are greater than the basis of all the property transferred. Accordingly, the only gain that must be recognized is the gain attributable to the amount of boot property received. The $8,000 cash received is boot property.)

62. Which of the following are organizational costs?

a. Expenses of temporary directors; a survey of potential markets.
b. Advertisements for the opening of business; state incorporation fees.
c. Deductible research and experimental costs; set-up accounting services.
d. Legal services for drafting the charter; Fees paid to the state of incorporation.

(Answer (D) is correct. Organizational expenditures include those that are incidental to the creation of a corporation, chargeable to a capital account, and amortizable over a limited life if they are expended incident to the creation of a corporation with such a life. Examples of organizational expenditures include expenses to obtain the corporate charter, fees paid to the state of incorporation, and expenses of temporary directors. Organizational costs must be distinguished from start-up and investigation costs.)

63. Rose Corporation is a publicly traded corporation whose top executives are subject to the $1 million limitation on their compensation. Johnny Rose, the corporation's chief executive officer, receives $1.75 million of salary for the current year. How do the executive and the corporation report the compensation that is paid?

  a. Johnny Rose reports $1 million of earned income and $750,000 of dividend income, and the corporation deducts $1 million.
  b. Johnny Rose reports $1.75 million of earned income, and the corporation deducts $1 million of compensation.
  c. Johnny Rose reports $1 million of earned income, and the corporation deducts $1 million of compensation.
  d. Johnny Rose reports $1.75 million of earned income, and the corporation deducts $1.75 million of compensation.

(Answer (B) is correct. Section 162(m) disallows a deduction to a publicly held corporation for compensation in excess of $1 million paid to the chief executive officer in any tax year. The $1 million is deductible by the corporation as compensation expense under Sec. 162 and is included by the CEO as ordinary income under Sec. 61(a). The disallowance of the compensation deduction under Sec. 162(m) does not automatically require reporting of the nondeductible portion of the payment as a dividend. Therefore, one could suspect that the payment would be called compensation provided that it is reasonable in amount under Sec. 162(a) even though it is not deductible under Sec. 162(m).)

64. The dividends-received deduction for a corporation allows a(n)

  a. 80% deduction for all dividends received from nonaffiliated corporations.
  b. 65% deduction for all dividends received from nonaffiliated corporations.
  c. 50% deduction for all dividends received from nonaffiliated corporations.
  d. 50% deduction for dividends received from a corporation when ownership is less than 20%, a 65% deduction for dividends received from nonaffiliated corporations when ownership is 20% or more (but less than 80%), and a 100% deduction for dividends received from affiliated corporations when ownership is 80% or more.

(Answer (C) is correct. Section 243 permits a corporation to deduct 50% of dividends received from a domestic taxable corporation of which it owns less than 20% of the stock, 65% of dividends received if the stock is 20% or more (but less than 80%) owned, and 100% of dividends received if the stock is 80% or more owned.)

65. Dice, a C corporation, owns 20% of Owen Corporation. Owen paid a $3,000 cash dividend to Dice. What is the amount of Dice's dividend-received deduction?

  a. $3,000
  b. $1,950

c. $1,500
d. $0

(Answer (B) is correct. The DRD is available only to corporations. The deduction is based on the distributee corporation's percentage ownership of the distributing corporation, and it may be limited to taxable income. The deduction percentage is 65% for corporations with a 20% ownership in the distributing corporation. Dice's deduction is $1,950 ($3,000 dividend x 65%)).

66. During the current year, a corporation contributed three computers (that were for sale as inventory) to the New Roses Elementary School. The computers had a fair market value of $900 each and a basis of $700 each. What is the corporation's charitable contribution with regards to the computers?

a. $2,700
b. $2,100
c. $1,800
d. $1,400

(Answer (C) is correct. A corporation may deduct the AB of ordinary income property contributed.)

67. Rose Corporation had a net operating loss in the current year. The net operating loss:

a. Can only be carried back to each of the 3 years before the current year and not carried forward.
b. May be carried back to each of the 3 years before the current year and then carried forward to each of the 5 years after the current year.
c. Must be carried back to each of the 3 years before the current year and then carried forward to each of the 7 years after the current year.
d. May not be carried back though it may be carried forward indefinitely.

(Answer (D) is correct. For tax years beginning after 2017, a net operating loss may not be carried back though it may be carried forward indefinitely. However, the 3-year carryback period is retained for the portion of the NOL that relates to casualty and theft losses of individual taxpayers and to NOLs that are attributable to federally declared disaster areas and are incurred by taxpayers engaged in farming or a small business.)

68. Rose Corporation, a C corporation, ends its tax year on November 30. When must ABC's income tax return be filed for the year ending November 30, Year 1?

a. February 15, Year 2.
b. April 15, Year 2.
c. January 15, Year 2.
d. March 15, Year 2.

(Answer (D) is correct. Section 6072(b) provides that a C corporation must file its return on or before the 15th day of the fourth month following the close of the tax year. For a fiscal-year corporation with a year-end of 11/30/Yr 1, the return must be filed by 3/15/Yr 2.)

69. John has owned all 100 outstanding shares of Rose Corporation's stock for the past 10 years. John's basis for the stock is $50,000. Rose have earnings and profits of $100,000. The

corporation redeemed 25 shares of John's stock for $85,000 in the current year. How will John report this?

a. $85,000 gain.
b. $85,000 dividend.
c. $50,000 gain.
d. None of the answers are correct.

(Answer (B) is correct. Because John owns 100% of the stock before and after the redemption, the transaction is a dividend to the extent that Rose Corporation has E&P. Because the distribution ($85,000) is less than earnings and profits ($100,000), the entire amount is taxable as a dividend.)

70. Corporation J, with earnings and profits of $80,000, distributed cash of $40,000 and property with a fair market value of $45,000 and an adjusted basis of $60,000 to its corporate shareholders. What is the amount of the distribution received by the shareholders?

a. $40,000
b. $60,000
c. $85,000
d. $100,000

(Answer (C) is correct. Section 301(b) provides that the amount distributed to a shareholder (corporate or noncorporate) is equal to the amount of money received, plus the fair market value of other property received. Corporation J distributed cash of $40,000 plus property with a fair market value of $45,000. Hence, the corporate shareholders will recognize a distribution of $85,000.)

71. A corporation had $20,000 of earnings and profits (E&P) for the current year and accumulated negative E&P of $100,000. It paid a cash distribution of $40,000. What amount represents the taxable dividend to the shareholder for that year?

a. $100,000
b. $40,000
c. $20,000
d. $0

(Answer (C) is correct. A distribution is taxable as a dividend to the extent of earnings and profits. In this case, the corporation has $20,000 of current E&P to use in characterizing a distribution as a dividend. The remaining $20,000 is treated as a return of basis to the extent that the shareholder has stock basis remaining. Any excess over the shareholder's stock basis is treated as a capital gain).

72. In the consolidated income tax return of a corporation and its wholly owned subsidiary, what percentage of cash dividends paid by the subsidiary to the parent is tax-free?

a. 20%
b. 65%
c. 80%
d. 100%

(Answer (D) is correct. Dividends received by group members are treated differently depending on whether they come from corporations inside or outside the affiliated group. A dividend paid from one group member to another group member is an intercompany transaction [Reg. 1.1502-13(f)(7), Ex. (1)]).

73. What is the maximum number of shareholders allowable for eligibility as an S corporation in the current year?

a. 15
b. 25
c. 75
d. 100

(Answer (D) is correct. Under Sec. 1361(b), one of the requirements of an S corporation is that it have no more than 100 shareholders. Note: All members of a family (up to six generations from the common ancestors of lineal descendants) are counted as a single shareholder for purposes of Sec. 1361(b) so, in effect, 1,000 individuals composing 100 families constitutes 100 shareholders).

74. Which of the following items is not a separately stated item for Form 1120S shareholders?

a. Charitable contributions made by the corporation.
b. Section 179 deduction.
c. Rental Expense
d. Tax-exempt interest.

(Answer (C) is correct. An S corporation passes a pro rata share of its total income (loss) through to the individual shareholders, except for items that require separate treatment by the shareholder. Charitable contributions made by the corporation, Sec. 179 deduction, and tax-exempt interest must be separately stated. Rental Expense, however, is combined with other non-separately stated income or loss).

75. What is the non-separately stated income amount of an accrual-basis, calendar-year S corporation with the following items?

Gross receipts $200,000
Interest income 12,000
Rental income 25,000
Cost of goods sold and commissions 125,000
Net long-term capital gain 17,000
Compensation paid to shareholder 10,000.

a. $65,000
b. $75,000
c. $119,000
d. $129,000

(Answer (A) is correct. Items of income, gain, expense, loss, and credit must be separately stated if those items are specially treated for tax purposes at the shareholder level. These items include interest income, rental income, and net long-term capital gains).

76. John owns 50% of Rose, Inc., an S corporation, filing returns on a calendar year basis. For the Year 1 tax year, the corporation has an operating loss of $26,000 and separately stated tax-exempt income of $20,000. John's basis on January 1, Year 1, is $4,000. What is his basis at the end of the Year 1 tax year?

a. $0
b. $(1,000)
c. $500
d. $1,000

(Answer (C) is correct. Section 1367 provides guidelines for adjustments to the basis of a shareholder's S corporation stock. The increases include items of income (including tax-exempt income) that are passed through to the shareholder, non-separately stated (ordinary) income, and the excess of deductions for depletion over the basis of the property subject to depletion. The basis of John's stock is decreased by the amount of loss allocable to him; however, it cannot reduce his basis below zero.)

Basis at January 1 $4,000
Tax-exempt income ($20,000 × 50%) 10,000
Ordinary loss of S corporation ($26,000 × 50%) (13,000)
Basis at December 31 $1,000)

77. The two equal shareholders of a C corporation are thinking of filing an election to have the company treated as an S corporation. Which of the following consequences is an advantage of this election?

a. The corporation's net operating loss carryovers from prior years are immediately deductible by the shareholders.
b. The corporation's tax-free fringe benefits for the shareholders will be deductible by the corporation and the shareholders.
c. The shareholders of the S corporation will be taxed on all distributions from the corporation.
d. The corporation's capital losses can be claimed on the tax returns of the shareholders.

(Answer (D) is correct. Capital losses of the corporation will flow-through to the shareholders, who may use them to offset any of their own capital gains.)

78. Rose Corporation (an S corporation) is owned entirely by John. At the beginning of Year 1, John's adjusted basis in his Rose Corporation stock was $20,000. Rose reported ordinary income of $10,000 and a capital loss of $10,000. John received a cash distribution of $35,000 in November Year 1. What is John's gain from the distribution?

a. $5,000
b. $10,000
c. $20,000
d. $35,000

(Answer (A) is correct. The basis is increased by the ordinary income to $30,000. The $35,000 distribution is taken next and since it exceeds the basis, there is a $5,000 gain. The capital loss is nondeductible because there is no basis and is carried over.)

79. J, an S corporation, is liable for the tax on its excess net passive income for the current year of $100,000. What is the amount of the tax?

a. $15,000
b. $20,000
c. $21,000
d. $40,000

(Answer (C) is correct. Section 1375(a) provides that the tax on the excess net passive income of an S corporation is the excess net passive income times the highest corporate tax rate (21%). Thus, the tax is $21,000 ($100,000 × 21%)).

80. What is the tax rate for an S corporation that pays tax on built-in gains?

a. The highest trust tax rate.
b. The highest partnership income tax rate.
c. The highest individual income tax rate.
d. The highest corporate income tax rate.

(Answer (D) is correct. The tax rate for the built-in gains tax is defined by statute to be the highest corporate income tax rate.)

81. The charitable contribution deduction on an estate's fiduciary income tax return is allowable:

a. If the decedent died.
b. To the extent of the same adjusted gross income limitation as that on an individual income tax return.
c. Only if the decedent's will specifically provides for the contribution.
d. Subject to the 2% threshold on miscellaneous itemized deductions.

(Answer (C) is correct. An unlimited estate income tax deduction is allowed for transfers to charitable organizations [Sec. 642(c)]. Although the taxable income of an estate is generally computed in the same manner as in the case of an individual, Sec. 642(c) provides that a deduction for a charitable contribution is only available if paid pursuant to the terms of the will of the decedent.)

82. Which of the following statements is true regarding estate income tax returns filed on Form 1041?

a. Form 1041 has its own tax rate schedule.
b. Estates are never liable for the alternative minimum tax.
c. All estates are subject to the same estimated tax rules that apply to Form 1040.
d. They have the same charitable contribution limitations that individual taxpayers have.

(Answer (A) is correct. Form 1041 is subject to its own tax rate schedule.)

83. An estate has $9,000 of dividends from domestic corporations and $6,000 of tax-exempt interest. Its only expense is $1,500 of interest incurred to carry the tax-exempt bonds. What is the estate's distributable net income?

   a. $8,400
   b. $9,000
   c. $13,400
   d. $13,500

   (Answer (D) is correct. Under Sec. 643(a), distributable net income includes dividends and tax-exempt interest less expenses allocable to it. The personal exemption is not allowed. Here, the estate's taxable income is $7,400 ($9,000 dividends – $600 personal exemption.)

   The estate's distributable net income is:
   Taxable income $8,400
   Add back: Personal exemption 600
   Add: Tax-exempt interest (net $1,500 of nondeductible interest) 4,500
   Distributable net income $13,000.)

84. Trust C, a complex trust, is not required to distribute any income currently to its two beneficiaries. It has $12,000 of taxable interest and $12,000 of tax-exempt interest for the year. Trust C distributes $10,000 of income to Beneficiary A and $4,000 of corpus to Beneficiary B. What is Trust C's distribution deduction?

   a. $4,000
   b. $6,000
   c. $7,000
   d. $10,000

   (Answer (C) is correct. The distribution deduction for complex trusts and estates is determined under Sec. 661. The deduction is the sum of the fiduciary income required to be distributed and any other amounts properly distributed but limited to distributable net income (DNI). This amount eligible for the deduction is treated as consisting of the same proportion of each type of income included in the DNI. Furthermore, no deduction is allowed for any portion treated as distributed which is not included in gross income of the trust or estate.
   Trust C has both fiduciary income and DNI of $24,000. The amount of each portion of DNI that is treated as distributed will be 50% (since half of the DNI is tax-exempt). A total of $14,000 of DNI is distributed, of which $7,000 is treated as tax-exempt income. Thus, the distribution deduction is $7,000. This portion of distributable income flows out of the trust with any distribution including that of corpus.)

85. Which of the following organizations, exempt from federal income tax under Sec. 501(a), must file an annual information return on Form 990 or Form 990-PF?

   a. An organization, other than a private foundation, having gross receipts in each year that normally are not more than $50,000.
   b. Any K-12 school, affiliated with a church or operated by a religious order, that is not an integrated auxiliary of a church.
   c. A private foundation exempt under Sec. 501(c)(3) of the Internal Revenue Code.
   d. A pension, or profit-sharing trust that qualifies under Sec. 401 of the Internal Revenue Code.

(Answer (C) is correct. A private foundation must use Form 990-PF as its annual information return.)

86. A cash-basis taxpayer should report gross income:

   a. Only for the year in which income is actually received in cash.
   b. Only for the year in which income is actually received whether in cash or in property.
   c. For the year in which income is either actually or constructively received in cash only.
   d. For the year in which income is either actually or constructively received, whether in cash or in property.

   (Answer (D) is correct. A cash-method taxpayer accounts for an item of income when the first of the following occurs: (1) cash is actually received; (2) an equivalent of cash is actually received; (3) constructive receipt of cash or its equivalent occurs. Notice that each answer is better than the previous answer.)

87. Which of the following entities may not use the cash method of accounting?

   a. A partnership with average annual gross receipts in excess of $26 million.
   b. A C corporation whose average annual gross receipts for the preceding 3 taxable years do not exceed $26 million.
   c. A C corporation with annual gross receipts in excess of $26 million for the preceding 3 taxable year.
   d. An S corporation.

   (Answer (C) is correct. Certain entities are required by Sec. 448 to use the accrual method of accounting. A C corporation is one such entity unless it is a qualified personal service corporation or its annual gross receipts are small enough. To qualify as a personal service corporation, substantially all of the corporation's activities must involve the performance of services in health, law, engineering, architecture, accounting, actuarial science, performing arts, or consulting. A C corporation's average gross receipts must be $26 million or less for the prior 3 years to qualify for the cash method based on gross receipts.)

88. Upon completion of a long-term contract, interest is computed under the look-back method by applying the Sec. 6621 general overpayment rate to the over- or underpayment of tax for each year. The over- or underpayment is determined by allocating contract income among taxable years prior to the year of contract completion on the basis of:

   a. The actual contract and estimated costs.
   b. The estimated price and actual costs.
   c. The estimated costs and actual costs of construction.
   d. The actual contract price and actual costs.

   (Answer (D) is correct. Interest is computed under the look-back method by (1) allocating income under the contract among taxable years before the year in which the contract is completed, on the basis of the actual contract price and actual costs; (2) determining the over- or underpayment of tax for each year (solely for purposes of computing such interest); and (3) applying the Sec. 6621 general overpayment rate to the over- or underpayment [Sec. 460(b)(2)]).

89. Which of the following is the most important principle in valuing inventories?

   a. Generally accepted accounting principles.
   b. Clear reflection of income.
   c. Lower of cost or market.
   d. Frist-in, first-out.

   (Answer (B) is correct. Regulation 1.471-2(a) provides that the method of valuing inventory must conform as nearly as possible to the best accounting practice in the trade or business, and it must clearly reflect income. Courts have held that the overriding concern is the clear reflection of income. Conformity to the best accounting practice is considered only a method of achieving a clear reflection of income. The inventory practice should also be consistent from year to year to clearly reflect income).

90. Which of the following items is not included in inventory?

   a. Raw material.
   b. Goods you received on consignment.
   c. Work in process.
   d. Finished goods.

   (Answer (B) is correct. Regulation 1.471-1 provides that inventory should include all finished goods, work in process, and raw materials and supplies that will physically become a part of merchandise intended for sale. Merchandise should be included in inventory only if title thereto is vested in the taxpayer. In the case of goods received by the taxpayer on consignment, the title remains with the consignor and the goods are not included in inventory.)

91. Which of the following accounting changes do not require the filing of Form 3115 to request a change in accounting method?

   a. Correction of a math error.
   b. Change from accrual method to cash method.
   c. Change in the method inventory is valued.
   d. Change from cash method to accrual method.

   (Answer (A) is correct. Section 446(e) requires the taxpayer to obtain permission from the IRS to change a method of accounting. A change from the accrual method to the cash method of accounting, or vice-versa, and the change in the method of inventory valuation are changes in the method of accounting that would require the filing of Form 3115. However, a correction of an error in calculating tax is not a change in accounting method [Reg. 1.446-1(e)(2)(ii)(b)]).

92. The Social Security Act provides for the imposition of taxes and the disbursement of benefits. Which of the following is a true statement regarding these taxes and disbursements in the current year?

   a. Only those who have contributed to Social Security are eligible for benefits.
   b. As between an employer and its employee, the tax rates are the same.
   c. A credit for federal income tax purposes is allowed the employee for Social Security taxes paid.
   d. Social Security benefits are fully includible in gross income for federal income tax.

(Answer (B) is correct. Under the Federal Insurance Contributions Act (FICA), the tax rate for employers and employees is the same (7.65% for 2019). This requirement of shared responsibility has been followed since the Social Security Act was enacted in 1935).

93. The federal Social Security Act:

a. Does not apply to self-employed persons.
b. Excludes professional services such as accountants, lawyers, and doctors.
c. Does not apply to compensation in the form of tips.
d. Provides that bonuses and commissions paid as compensation are included as wages in the calculation of employer-employee contributions.

(Answer (D) is correct. The definition of wages on which contributions are based includes all remuneration for employment [Sec. 3121(a)]. Bonuses and commissions are wages and are used in the calculation of the employer-employee contributions).

94. During the current year, John paid $500 a week to a 16-year-old child (who is not John's child) to baby-sit and perform domestic services in John's home after school and on weekends while John was working. John files a Form 1040 to report her federal income taxes. Which of the following applies?

a. Form 941 must be filed.
b. Form 943 must be filed.
c. Form 943 must be filed.
d. Schedule H must be filed.

(Answer (C) is correct. A domestic worker in a private home is subject to tax if his or her wages are at least $2,100 in any calendar year. When the domestic worker is subject to taxation, the employer must withhold FICA taxes and file the appropriate forms. Schedule H is a simplified form that may be used by employers of domestic workers in private homes.)

95. The penalty for willful failure to collect or pay over to the government the amounts required to be withheld from employees is what percentage of the tax?

a. 25%
b. 50%
c. 75%
d. 100%

(Answer (D) is correct. Under Sec. 6672, any person who is required to collect, account for, and pay over any Internal Revenue tax and who willfully fails to do so may be liable for a penalty equal to the total amount of the tax not collected and paid over. For not withholding income tax, the employer may, therefore, suffer a 100% penalty. In addition, the employer is liable for the payment of the tax required to be deducted and withheld from employees' wages (Sec. 3403). As a result, the employer who fails to withhold can be required to pay, not just withhold, the tax and still be subject to a 100% penalty.)

96. In which of the following circumstances would a gift tax return be due?

a. Check for $30,000 to son.
b. Transfer of stock valued at $50,000 to spouse.

c. Payment of a friend's $20,000 tuition expense.
d. Payment of a family member's $13,000 medical expense.

(Answer (A) is correct. A donor is required to file a gift tax return, Form 709, for any gift(s), unless all gifts are excluded under the annual $15,000 exclusion, the exclusion for medical or tuition payments, and the deduction for qualified transfers to the donor's spouse. These exclusions apply for gifts of present interests only. Any gift of a future interest requires the filing of Form 709. Gift-splitting does not excuse the donor from the requirement to file. A check for $30,000 exceeds the amount of the exclusion.)

97. Which of the following payments would require the donor to file a gift tax return?

a. $42,000 to a university for a spouse's tuition.
b. $30,000 to a university for a cousin's room and board.
c. $56,000 to a hospital for a parent's medical expenses.
d. $40,000 to a physician for a friend's surgery.

(Answer (B) is correct. Although tuition is an amount excluded as a taxable gift, room and board does not qualify. It must be reported on the gift tax return.)

98. Under the unified rate schedule:

a. Lifetime taxable gifts are taxed on a noncumulative and cumulative basis.
b. Transfers at death are taxed on a noncumulative cumulative basis.
c. Lifetime taxable gifts and transfers at death are taxed on a cumulative basis.
d. The gift tax rates are equal to or higher than the estate tax rates.

(Answer (C) is correct. The same (unified transfer) tax rates of Sec. 2001 are applied to both the gift tax and estate tax bases. Any taxable gifts (other than gifts included in the estate tax base) made after 1976 are called adjusted taxable gifts, and such gifts are included in the donor's estate tax base. The addition of such taxable gifts to the estate tax base at their fair market value on the date of the gift results in the donor-decedent's estate being taxed at a higher marginal tax rate. These gifts are not taxed a second time when the donor dies because the gift taxes paid on the gifts reduce the amount of the estate tax that is owed.)

99. On March 3, Year 1, John made a gift in an amount sufficient to require the filing of a federal gift tax return. On October 31, Year 1, John died. No estate tax return will need to be filed for Mr. Smith. Assuming extensions have not been obtained, the gift tax return (Form 709) must be filed by (assuming none of the dates are Saturdays, Sundays, or holidays):

a. April 15, Year 1.
b. March 15, Year 2.
c. April 15, Year 2.
d. May 15, Year 2.

(Answer (C) is correct. Under Sec. 6075, gift tax returns are due on or before the 15th day of April following the close of the calendar year in which a gift was made. Since John made a gift in Year 1, Form 709 is generally due by April 15, Year 2. If the date falls on a weekend or holiday, the return is due the next business day.)

100. If the executor of a decedent's estate elects the alternate valuation date and none of the property included in the gross estate has been sold or distributed, the estate assets must be valued as of how many months after the decedent's death?

   a. 1
   b. 6
   c. 8
   d. 12

   (Answer (B) is correct. Under Sec. 2032, if the executor of an estate elects the alternate valuation date, and the property in the gross estate has not been sold or distributed, the estate assets are valued as of the date 6 months after the decedent's death. If property is sold or distributed within the 6-month period, it is valued as of the date of sale or distribution.)

101. Which of the following bodies has the authority to suspend or revoke a CPA's license for acts discreditable to the profession?

   a. The state society of certified public accountants.
   b. The state board of accountancy.
   c. The Public Company Accounting Oversight Board.
   d. The American Institute of Certified Public Accountants.

   (Answer (B) is correct. State boards can suspend or revoke licensure through administrative processes, such as board hearings.)

102. CPA assists a taxpayer in tax planning regarding a transaction that meets the definition of a tax shelter as defined in the Internal Revenue Code. Under the AICPA Statements on Standards for Tax Services, the CPA should inform the taxpayer of the penalty risks unless the transaction, at the minimum, meets which of the following standards for being sustained if challenged?

   a. More likely than not.
   b. Not frivolous.
   c. Realistic possibility.
   d. Substantial authority.

   (Answer (C) is correct. A member of the AICPA may not recommend a tax return position or prepare or sign a tax return absent a good faith belief that the position "has a realistic possibility of being sustained administratively or judicially on its merits if challenged." But a member may, in appropriate cases, (1) recommend a position or (2) prepare or sign the return if this standard is not met. These exceptions apply if (1) the position is reasonable and (2) the member advises disclosure [when (s)he has recommended a position], or the position is properly disclosed [when (s)he has prepared or signed the return]. Disclosure requirements include informing the taxpayer of penalty risks (TS 100). NOTE: According to the Small Business and Work Opportunity Act of 2007 (as amended), an undisclosed, non-abusive position must be supported by substantial authority. But for tax shelters and reportable transactions, the preparer must have a reasonable belief that the position is more likely than not to be sustained on its merits. If the position is disclosed, its tax treatment must have a reasonable basis.)

103. Under Treasury Circular 230, the IRS requires that certain records be returned to a client by the tax practitioner even though no payment for services has been received. Records of the client for this purpose do not include:

a. Documents that were prepared by a client's financial bank and provided to the practitioner with respect to tax preparation.
b. Work papers prepared by the practitioner that provides mathematical details of a particular amount included in a client's tax return.
c. Electronic materials provided to the practitioner that existed before the client retained the practitioner.
d. Government records given to the practitioner at the beginning of the engagement.

(Answer (B) is correct. The practitioner must return client records on request, regardless of any fee dispute. However, the practitioner may retain copies of client records. Records deemed returnable for purposes of this requirement are those records necessary for a client to comply with his or her federal tax obligations. However, documents prepared by the practitioner, with mathematical details of a particular amount included in a client's tax return, may be withheld pending payment of a fee (provided state law permits retention of records in a fee dispute)).

104. In which of the following circumstances would a tax return preparer be prohibited from disclosing a client's tax return information?

a. The information will be needed for a peer review.
b. The information will be provided in response to a court order.
c. The information will be provided to the client's bank.
d. The information will be used to prepare state or local tax returns.

(Answer (C) is correct. There is no exception to the penalty for disclosure if the disclosure was made to a bank even if it's already the client's bank without the taxpayer's consent.)

105. When or where are public hearings held on a revenue bill?

a. On the floor of the House and the Senate.
b. In the House Ways and Means Committee and the Senate Finance Committee.
c. The President of the United States.
d. The Supreme Court.

(Answer (B) is correct. In both the House Ways and Means Committee and the Senate Finance Committee, public hearings are usually held on a revenue bill to allow the administration, taxpayers, and other groups to express their views.)

106. What is the statute of limitations on a return that was filed and found to be fraudulent?

a. Indefinite.
b. 3 years.
c. 6 years.
d. 7 years.

(Answer (A) is correct. Attempting to evade taxes results in an unlimited assessment period. Fraud cannot be cured by filing a correct amended return.)

107. The initial action required in the collection process is:

a. The filing of a Notice of Levy.
b. An assessment.
c. An appeal conference with the IRS.
d. A docketed case in Tax Court.

(Answer (B) is correct. Section 6201(a) authorizes the IRS to make a determination of all taxes. If the IRS makes a determination that a tax liability exists, the IRS has the authority under Sec. 6201(a) to assess the tax. The assessment of the taxes is the initial action required in the collection process.)

108. If a taxpayer and the IRS still disagree after an appeals conference, the taxpayer can take his or her case to:

a. United States Tax Court.
b. United States Court of Federal Claims.
c. United States District Court.
d. All of the answers are correct.

(Answer (D) is correct. If a taxpayer and the IRS still disagree after an appeals conference, or the election was made to bypass the IRS appeals system, the case may be taken to the U.S. Tax Court, the U.S. Court of Federal Claims, or a U.S. District Court.)

109. The Tax Court has jurisdiction over all of the following taxes except:

a. Income.
b. Employment.
c. Estate.
d. Gift.

(Answer (B) is correct. The Tax Court is a court of limited jurisdiction. Section 7442 states that the Tax Court has such jurisdiction as is conferred on it by Title 26 of the U.S. Code; by Chapters 1, 2, 3, and 4 of the Internal Revenue Code of 1939; by Title II and Title III of the Revenue Act of 1926; or by laws enacted subsequent to February 26, 1926. The Tax Court's jurisdiction covers income, estate, gift, excise, and private foundation taxes. The Tax Court has no jurisdiction over employment taxes.)

110. One difference between the Tax Court and a district court is that:

a. The tax must be paid first to go to the Tax Court but not to a district court.
b. A trial by jury can be obtained in the Tax Court but not in a district court.
c. One can appeal an adverse decision of the Tax Court can be filed only with the U.S. Supreme Court, while an appeal from a district court can be filed to the appropriate circuit court of appeals.
d. A trial by jury can be had in a district court but not in the Tax Court.

(Answer (D) is correct. Taxpayers who choose to have their cases heard before a district court may request a trial by jury. Cases heard before the Tax Court are decided by judges.)

Summary Questions

1. The business leader today need not worry about the social responsibility or sustainability of his or her firm unless the government mandates such efforts.
(False: Today, there is a societal expectation that business conduct itself in a legal, moral, AND socially responsible and sustainable, that is, environmentally responsible manner; and consequently a business leader who neglects these values does so at the peril to his or her firm.)

2. A business leader need not be concerned with his or her firm acting immorally, since the firm cannot be sued for acting in an immoral manner, only in an illegal manner.
(False: As noted, today a business is expected to go above-and-beyond the law, which may be non-existent or weak, and to act in a moral manner too.)

3. By acting in an immoral, socially irresponsible, and unsustainable manner, business leaders risk even more government legal laws and regulations being imposed on their firms.
(True: This is a basic and logical proposition. An example would be anti-trust law which came about by business leaders engaging in monopolistic and predatory practices.)

4. One can never be an ethical business leader and a successful one too.
(False: Just the opposite as ethics is a necessary component to success as a business leader. One example, though there are many, of successful and ethical business leaders is the famous entrepreneur, H. Wayne Huizenga, who created three Fortune 500 companies, Waste Management, Blockbuster Video, and AutoNation, as well as Extended Stay America.)

5. A successful business leader will attempt to achieve a symmetry and balance among the often-competing values of the company's stakeholder group.
(True: This is a principal function of business leadership today and is in accord with stakeholder analysis in business as well as the Utilitarian ethical philosophy.)

6. Truly transformational leadership is built on a foundation of morality and ethics.
(True: One is not going to be a leader for long, let alone a transformational one, if one acts in an immoral and unethical manner.)

7. Ethical business leadership consists of:

   a. Creating, communicating, and securing acceptance of a vision.
   b. Energizing, challenging, and inspiring followers to realize the vision.
   c. Having a vision that is an inherently moral and having the moral strength of character to pursue the vision in a moral manner.
   d. All of the above.

   (The correct answer is D. These are all fundamental aspects of being a leader and most importantly a moral leader in business and otherwise.)

Conclusion

This book was intended as a practical exam review book for college students, especially business students, including accounting students, taking business law and ethics courses as well as tax courses. The objective was to provide to the students a great number of objective questions to test their knowledge of essential business law and ethics subject matters. Yet another goal of the book was to emphasize to the students that in making management and business decisions they must not only know the law, but they must go "above and beyond" the law to consider other key values. As such, the authors have included material on business ethics, social responsibility, and sustainability. Therefore, ultimately, the student when he or she becomes a manager, business owner, or member of a profession must always ask when contemplating a decision or action the following questions: Is it legal? Is it moral? And what should a socially responsible and sustainable firm or organization be doing? To ask and to properly answer these questions, the authors submit, will bring the students ultimate success, and sustainable success, and not only academically but also when they venture into the "real world." The authors sincerely hope that you have enjoyed the book and most importantly that you have found their exam review book to be a helpful exam preparation and learning tool.

Finally, the authors sincerely wish you all the very best of success academically, in business, whether manager or entrepreneur, as members of a profession, and in all respects. Because it is your success that brings us great satisfaction and happiness!

Bibliography

1. Cavico, F. J. and Mujtaba, B. G. (2021). *Common Law Torts in Business and How to Avoid Them: A Handbook for Managers*. ILEAD Academy. Florida. ISBN: 978-1-936237-18-0. Link: https://www.amazon.com/Common-Torts-Business-Avoid-Them/dp/1936237180

2. Cavico, F. J. and Mujtaba, B. G. (2020). *Business Law for the Entrepreneur and Manager (4th edition)*. ILEAD Academy. Florida. ISBN: 978-1-936237-17-3.

3. Cavico, Frank J. and Mujtaba, Bahaudin G. (2016). Developing a Legal, Ethical, and Socially Responsible Mindset for Sustainable Leadership. Davie, Florida: ILEAD Academy.

4. Cavico, Frank J. (2014). *Corporate Social Responsibility and Leadership*. Davie, Florida: ILEAD Academy, LLC.

5. Cavico, Frank J. and Mujtaba, Bahaudin G. (2014). *Legal Challenges for the Global Manager and Entrepreneur* (Second Edition). Dubuque, Iowa: Kendall Hunt Publishing Company.

6. Cavico, Frank J. and Mujtaba, Bahaudin G. (2009). *Business Ethics: The Moral Foundation for Effective Leadership, Management, and Entrepreneurship* (Second Edition). New York: Pearson Custom Publishing.

Author Biographies

Frank J. Cavico is a Professor of Law, Business Law, and Business Ethics. He has taught for over 40 years at the law school, university, and college level, most recently in the undergraduate business and MBA programs at the H. Wayne Huizenga College of Business and Entrepreneurship of Nova Southeastern University of in Ft. Lauderdale, Florida, where he recently retired as a Professor Emeritus after 30 years of service, though he is still teaching at Nova Southeastern as an adjunct professor. He came to Nova Southeastern to develop a graduate law and ethics course for the Huizenga College's MBA program. He holds a B.A. degree in political science from Gettysburg College, a M.A. in political science from Drew University in Madison, N.J., a J.D. from St. Mary's University School of Law in San Antonio, Texas, as well as an LL.M in Torts and Product Liability from the University of San Diego School of Law. He is the recipient of several teaching honors and awards; and he is the author of several books and numerous law review and management journal articles. He resides in Lauderdale by the Sea, Florida, with his wife, Nancy, a registered nurse.

Bahaudin G. Mujtaba is Professor of Human Resources Management at Nova Southeastern University in Ft. Lauderdale, Florida. Bahaudin is the author and co-author of several professional and academic books dealing with diversity, ethics, and management, as well as numerous academic journal articles. During the past twenty-five years he has had the pleasure of working with human resource professionals in the United States, Canada, Brazil, Bahamas, Afghanistan, Pakistan, St. Lucia, Grenada, Malaysia, Japan, Vietnam, China, India, Thailand, and Jamaica. This diverse exposure has provided him many insights in ethics, culture, and management from the perspectives of different firms, people groups, and countries. Bahaudin can be reached at: mujtaba@nova.edu

Nicholas-Michel Polito is currently a student at Fairleigh Dickinson University's MS in Taxation program. In addition, he holds an MS in Accounting from Fairleigh Dickinson University, an MBA in Finance from the H. Wayne Huizenga College of Business and Entrepreneurship of Nova Southeastern University in Ft. Lauderdale, Florida, a Bachelor's degree from Rutgers University, and also a degree from the Culinary Institute of America in Hyde Park, New York. Nicolas recently completed and passed all four parts of the CPA exam and presently is working at Bederson LLP, a local accounting firm. Nicolas began teaching accounting as an adjunct professor at Fairleigh Dickinson University's in 2019. Nicolas provided research assistance for many professors for their peer-reviewed articles, as well as for the school's AACSB accreditation review. Over his academic career, Nicolas has been recognized by several academic honor societies and has co-authored two peer-reviewed journal publications.

www.ingramcontent.com/pod-product-compliance
Lightning Source LLC
LaVergne TN
LVHW080011210926
848481LV00011B/2987
9781936237197